The Global Marketplace

Milton Moskowitz is the coauthor
(with Michael Katz and Robert Levering) of:

Everybody's Business: An Almanac
Everybody's Business Scoreboard
The 100 Best Companies to Work for in America
The Computer Entrepreneurs

THE GLOBAL MARKETPLACE

102 of the Most Influential Companies Outside America

Milton Moskowitz

MACMILLAN PUBLISHING COMPANY
New York

Illustrator   *Research Director*
Bob Johnson Harry Strharsky

Aide-de-camp Extraordinaire
Carol Townsend

Macmillan Publishing Company
866 Third Avenue, New York, N.Y. 10022
Collier Macmillan Canada, Inc.

Library of Congress Cataloging-in-Publication Data

Moskowitz, Milton.
 The global marketplace.

 Includes index.
 1. International business enterprises—Case studies.
I. Title.
HD2755.5.M675 1987   338.8'8   87-15897
ISBN 0-02-587590-6

Macmillan books are available at special discounts for bulk purchases for sales promotions, premiums, fund-raising, or educational use. For details, contact:

> Special Sales Director
> Macmillan Publishing Company
> 866 Third Avenue
> New York, N.Y. 10022

10 9 8 7 6 5 4 3 2 1

PRINTED IN THE UNITED STATES OF AMERICA

For Eben, a multinational-minded son

Salvation does not come through simplicities. The gray, grainy complex of existence and the ragged edges of our lives as we actually lead them defy hunger for a neat, bordered existence and for spirits unsullied by doubt or despair.

—Andrew Young, Mayor of Atlanta,
at Yale University, May 25, 1986

Contents

The Global Marketplace

Introduction

MOST OF OUR LIVES are touched today by companies whose home base is in another country. At no previous time have goods, money, and people crossed national borders so rapidly and in such high volume. The global marketplace is far from being a reality, but most companies of any size think and act today in international terms, which means 1) they are looking to sell and/or make their products in markets outside their own country and 2) they worry about the competition they face from companies based in other countries.

As a result people around the world are linked today by brand names as much as by anything else. American brands—Coca-Cola, Gillette, IBM, McDonald's, Colgate, Marlboro, Smirnoff—are known the world over, as are non-American brands: Seiko, Bic, Panasonic, Lux, Honda, Johnnie Walker, Nestlē, Shell, Mercedes-Benz.

Investors, reformers, and the plain curious have a plethora of information about United States companies at their fingertips. But that same kind of information has not been generally available for companies in other countries. It's this gap that *The Global Marketplace* addresses. It's a road map to 102 companies headquartered outside the United States.

Most of them—Shell, Unilever, British Petroleum, Bayer, Fiat, Daimler-Benz, Matsushita—are giants of the business world, with assets in the billions and employees in the tens of thousands. Others—Beretta, Club Med, the Hard Rock Cafe—are not so huge but have an international character deserving of attention.

The 102 companies hail from twenty countries. Two thirds are based in five countries: Japan (19), Britain (19), France (13), West Germany (10), and Italy (7). Two—Unilever and Shell—have dual nationalities (British and Dutch). Five are government-owned entities. Another eight are privately owned companies, meaning no stock is in the hands of the public. Virtually all of them have global reaches and are therefore likely to be found anywhere.

This is a journalist's, not a statistician's book. To be sure, there are numbers. They are there to give some sense of how big a company is and where it ranks in its industry, its country, and the world. But the more interesting and challenging task for me has been to penetrate these corporate behemoths to tell their stories from a social standpoint. How did they come to be what they are today?

I have tried to explore these companies through the people who founded and built them. And I have tried to place the companies against geographical and historical backdrops. The story of an industrial enterprise is often the story of a country or a region or a particular stage in history. I have tried also to get at the personalities peculiar to these companies.

This book is not a polemic on the tired old subject of multinationals subverting national sovereignties. The world, to my way of thinking, is more complicated than that. The stories of these companies will disclose, I think, that they are neither as powerful as their detractors make them out to be, nor as weak as they sometimes portray themselves. Their missions more often than not were harnessed to selfish national goals. These companies are creatures of their times, subject to the same mindless passions that have wreaked such havoc and destruction during this century.

A further word needs to said about numbers in an international context. They are very slippery. Let's take one example: Hitachi, a Japanese goliath. In its 1985 fiscal year, the twelve months ended March 31, 1985, Hitachi registered total sales of 5 trillion yen. Since the yen was then trading at 250 to the dollar, that translated into sales of $20 billion. A year later, in the fiscal year ended March 31, 1986, Hitachi's sales were roughly the same—5 trillion yen. However, by that time the yen had escalated in value to 175 to the dollar, which translated into sales of $28.5 billion. A year later, March 31, 1987, Hitachi reported a sales decline of 3 percent to 4.8 trillion yen. However, with the yen then worth 150 to the dollar, Hitachi's sales translated to $32 billion.

Ergo, in this treacherous world, a company's sales can go up even though they went down. The problem of sizing up these companies is further aggravated by the absence of standard measuring rods. They vary from company to company and from country to country. Some companies, for example, translate the local currency into dollars at the average rate of exchange existing during the year. Others simply take the exchange rate prevailing at the end of the year. When and how these calculations are done can make an enormous difference in the figures finally reported. And discrepancies are common. In 1986 *Fortune* reported Hitachi's sales at $22.6 billion, *Forbes* put them at $20.7 billion, and *BusinessWeek* pegged them at $13.8 billion.

One needs to keep this context in mind when looking at the figures in this book. I have generally translated local currencies into dollars at the exchange rates prevailing in early 1987. They are indicators rather than absolutes carved into granite (surreal indicators at that).

In the end this is a book about the people behind these companies. It's about Torakusu Yamaha, who together with a friend carried a reed organ on a pole 150 miles to Tokyo to have it evaluated. It's about Charles Forte, who came to Scotland from Italy when he was a little boy and built one of the world's largest hotel chains on the base of a string of milk bars. It's about Gottlieb Daimler and Karl Benz, who made the world's first automobiles, working sixty miles apart, but who never met. It's about Ivar Kreuger, the match king of the 1920s who conned governments and investment bankers. It's about the Benetton clan in Italy and the Kashio brothers in Japan. It's about William Jardine and James Matheson, two Scotsmen who established the biggest trading company in the Far East by selling opium to the Chinese.

Now that these international corporate giants are becoming ubiquitous, it's appropriate that we know more about them.

—Milton Moskowitz
Mill Valley, California
July 4, 1987

Some Thoughts on Multinational Corporations

ON MARCH 1, 1985, the Parliament of Singapore convened for its opening session. Lee Kuan Yew, the prime minister, spoke to the newly elected members and warned them not to lose sight of their values—their cultural values. He cited the example of Japan. The Japanese were smart, he said, because while they had opted for the trappings of a modern industrial society, they did not lose sight of who they are. Mr. Lee stated his prescription as follows: "We adopt enough of the West in order to hoist in their science, their technology, their competitiveness. Like the Japanese, we should try to remain as much ourselves as we can. . . . Our job is to constantly remind the people how different we are, and how important it is that we should stay different in order that we can survive."

Speaking particularly to the younger generation, Mr. Lee warned them not to ape the ways of the West. "If we go with the West," he said, "then we will have all the maladies, the malignancies of Western society." The prime minister used the oral contraceptive to illustrate how Japan rejected the West and held to its own ways.

"When the pill was discovered, it was supposed to be a blessing for mankind, and we just took the pill in, and family planning dispensed the pill. It has led to promiscuity in the West, the total breakdown of all family control over children, a new kind of society where you shack up with people and have one-parent families. It may interest members to know that the Japanese forbade the pill and it is still forbidden. If you want birth control, you buy the old-fashioned condom. They have it in multi colors. It has taken me nearly fifteen years to realize the wisdom of that move. . . . They [the Japanese] have maintained their values—chastity, high level of fidelity, maybe old-fashioned double standards for men and women, but the integrity of the family is preserved."

Those were unusual words for a head of state to deliver to a parliamentary body—not the least of its atypicality being an admission of possible error in judgment. But not everyone in Japan would agree. The

1

Japanese may have rejected the pill, but not for the reasons cited by Lee Kuan Yew, and signs of Western contamination abound in Tokyo. Many traditionalists there argue that Japan *is* sacrificing its culture on the altar of commerce and industrial progress.

This cry was strident during the debate over the ending of commercial whaling. In early 1985 employees of the Japanese whaling industry were picketing government ministries in Tokyo. They carried placards that read "SAVE OUR NATIONAL DIET." Hardly anyone eats whale meat in Japan; it accounts for only a fraction of protein consumption. And whaling does not employ huge numbers of people, only some thirteen hundred make a living from it. But it is part of the national culture that is being abandoned in the face of pressure from Green Peacers and other environmentalists who fear the extinction of whales. If the Japanese had not agreed to give up whaling, they would eventually have been barred from fishing in U.S. waters, a move that would have jeopardized $500 million in annual revenues. But the Japanese surrender left a lot of people bitter. An employee of the Joint Whaling Company in Tokyo said, "We are just like a person who has been diagnosed as having terminal cancer."

What is true in both of these countries—Japan and Singapore—is that McDonald's, an artifact of modern American culture, is accepted as apparently not posing a threat to the national culture, at least not a threat that people respond to with enough fervor to throw it out of the country. There have been more protests about the invasion of McDonald's hamburger stands in San Francisco than in either Singapore or Japan. Japan, at the end of 1986, had 573 McDonald's stores, more than any other country except the United States. And Singapore, for a while, boasted the two biggest grossing McDonald's stores in the entire system worldwide.

In his remarks to the parliament, Prime Minister Lee Kuan Yew may have been reacting to an acid comment made by *The Economist* in the summer of 1984. The London-based magazine had this to say about Singapore:

> The English language has become the main cultural unifier, much to the chagrin of Chinese traditionalists. English schools are now so popular that classes where the teaching is done in Chinese will be phased out by 1987. Singapore has become so open to foreign, and thus Western, ideas that it is in danger of being submerged by them. It is creating a Western-style economy but does not want the decadence that usually goes with it.
>
> Chinatown and almost all the rest of the old fabric of Singapore is rapidly disappearing to be replaced by square, high-rise blocks. The more squalid slums are being demolished, and with it much of Singapore's char-

acter. For all his forward thinking, Mr. Lee has not found anything to replace it with.

So here is *The Economist* deploring the razing of "squalid slums" because it takes away some of Singapore's "character." How elitist can you get? The Kentucky novelist Bobbie Ann Mason took a solid whack at this kind of elitism when she was interviewed in late 1985 by Patricia Holt, book editor of the *San Francisco Chronicle*. Mason objected to critics who put down television, junk food, and other aspects of pop culture. "My characters," she said, "are not in a world that's paved over—yet.

"In their town of Hopewell, Kentucky, they're just beginning to feel the effects of shopping malls and junk food, and they like it. To them it's the outside world they've been isolated from for so long coming into their lives at last. When I grew up, a Coca-Cola was a great treat, and going out for a hamburger was just bliss. So I think I can understand the sources of that dream, even though it has resulted in what some people call junk culture. It's ironic and self-destructive in the long run, but on a certain level, to the people who are just beginning to be affected by it, the entrance of shopping malls and fast-food chains is a positive expression of aspiration."

The same might be said for people in the developing countries of the world. Many of them welcome *I Love Lucy* and Marlboro cigarettes as amenities of a modern industrial society.

At the heart of this conflict between national values and economic progress as we know it is the multinational corporation, almost by definition a stateless entity. It's an agent of change, coming in with disposable diapers, ready-to-eat cereals, television, toothpaste, deodorants, oral contraceptives, laxatives, and dentures—incursions that do herald a revolution. They are both desired and hated. Hasegawa Michiko, a Japanese scholar who teaches at Saitama University, speaks of the "tyranny of internationalization," by which he means the imposition of Western standards on Japan (and other countries). "Internationalization," he asserts, "is a word redolent of the ruthless coercive power to which all non-Western nations are perforce subject." It's a complaint heard around the world today as local customs come under attack.

On the one hand we have worldwide poverty; on the other we have the demonic drive of businesses to expand their markets. It could be a natural marriage, but for reasons apparent to all of us, it doesn't work out so idyllically. Commercial interests are usually very narrow. Companies do not move into countries to improve the lot of mankind but to make money with new investments. And national interests can be equally narrow. History is not comforting for those who advance the liberating role of economic development. Gerald Meier, the holder of the first Konosuke Matsushita chair in international economics at the Stanford Business School and the author of *Emerging from Poverty: The Economics That Really Matters,* summed up the record succinctly: "Two centuries after the Industrial Revolution only a relatively few nations have grown rich, while there are at least one hundred that are poor."

The economic interests of one country often bump against those of another. In the latter half of 1985, Lee Kuan Yew paid an official visit to the United States. He was scheduled to deliver an address to the United States Congress on October 9, the very day that the House was to vote on a bill calling for stiff quotas on textile and apparel imports from Singapore and eleven other nations. In deference to the prime minister, Speaker "Tip" O'Neill tabled for a day a vote on the bill. Mr. Lee then told the U.S. Congress not to succumb to such protectionist measures. He pointed out that "the success of countries in East and Southeast Asia has caused much of the Third World to rethink their policies. Once infatuated with Socialist economic policies . . . Third World nations have now come to see that stagnation and decay have followed. Putting up barriers to America's markets would halt the economic advancement of the free market–oriented developing countries. It would send a signal that the model provided by the countries of East and Southeast Asia is no longer an available option. . . . Is America willing to write off the peaceful and constructive developments of the last forty years that she has made possible? Does America wish to abandon the contest between democracy and the free market on the one hand versus communism and the controlled economy on the other, when she has nearly won this contest for the hearts and minds of the Third World?"

The next day the House passed the bill, 262 to 159. Butler Derrick, congressman from South Carolina, explained his vote: "I don't have any Singapore people who vote for me. But I do have dedicated American taxpayers whose jobs are being stolen. Stolen!"

The congressman's reaction underlies the volatility of the arena in which multinational corporations operate. It's an arena where nationalism dies hard, not just in the United States but everywhere. In Korea, to keep out foreign cigarettes the government enacted a law that made it a criminal act to smoke a foreign cigarette. The reason Fiat holds 54 percent of the Italian automobile market has as much to do with effective bars against foreign-made vehicles as it does with any preference for Italian-made products. West Germany kept foreign brews from its market by banning beer containing any additives. And so it goes, around the world.

One condition has changed. As Prime Minister Lee noted in his remarks to Congress, capitalism is making a strong comeback. France's Socialist experiment failed. So did China's. So did Britain's. Socialism as a mode of economic development was in full retreat everywhere, largely because there are no successful models. On the face of it that trend would appear to bode well for the multinational corporation. But life is never that simple. Business people may be the apostles of capitalism, but that does not mean that they enjoy blanket approval and warm-hearted respect. They don't. They are not loved anywhere in the world; instead, more often than not, they are regarded as necessary evils. In the mythology developed by Richard J. Barnet and Ronald E. Müller in *Global Reach,* an influential book of the 1970s, the global corporation is both "the most dynamic agent of change in a new stage of world capitalism" and a socially irresponsible force that exacerbates all the major problems in the world—"mass starvation, mass unemployment, and gross inequality." It's a view still widely held, even though the welcome sign is now out for investments by multinationals.

One trap that's easy to fall into, especially for people unfamiliar with the world beyond their national boundaries, is the failure to see and appreciate differences. In one of his essays in *An Unfinished Journey,* Shiva Naipaul said, "To blandly subsume, say, Ethiopia, India, and Brazil under the one banner of Third Worldhood is as absurd and denigrating as the old assertion that all Chinese look alike. People only look alike when you can't be bothered to look at them too closely."

That's also true of corporations. To blandly subsume Nestlē, Toyota, Perrier, and RTZ under the one banner of "multinational corporation" is also absurd. Companies not only differ from country to country but within countries. Robert Bosch and Daimler-Benz have Swabian qualities of diligence connected with their home base in Stuttgart that are absent in Thyssen and Krupp, two industrial giants of the Ruhr. And while both may be stalwarts of the Japanese auto industry, Honda and Nissan are quite different characters. Nestlē's outlook differs from Ciba-Geigy's. And one wouldn't want to confuse the Hongkong & Shanghai Bank with Crédit Suisse.

The last word is not yet in on the multinational companies. Before we denounce or eulogize them, however, it might be useful to examine more carefully the objects of our scorn and admiration.

Who Owns America?

NO ONE WOULD DESCRIBE the United States as a colonial nation, but it may yet come to pass. In the ten years ending in 1986 foreign holdings of American assets quintupled. At that rate it will not be long before foreign investments in the United States surpass American investments overseas. The Department of Commerce reported that at the end of 1984 direct investment in the United States by foreigners had reached $159 billion, a healthy jump of 16 percent over the previous year's figure. Meanwhile U.S. investment abroad went up only 3 percent, to reach $233 billion. In 1985, as more than two hundred American companies were scooped up by outsiders, foreign investment soared to $183 billion.

The United States became an independent country because colonists chafed at being economically dependent on England. Two hundred years later dependence on foreign suppliers was becoming a fact of American life. The United States Treasury was banking on the Japanese to buy government debt—that is, be willing to lend money to America. American teenagers were growing up with emotional needs for a videocassette recorder supplied by Japanese companies and for sneakers supplied by plants in South Korea. And more and more Americans were depending on foreign companies—British, West German, Japanese, French, and Dutch—for their jobs in America.

It's ironic, in view of these developments, to return to J.-J. Servan-Schreiber's book *Le Défi Américain,* published in France in 1967 and in the United States a year later as *The American Challenge.* It caused a sensation when it appeared, warning Europeans that they would be taken over by American multinationals if they didn't bestir themselves. The book began by sounding this alarm: "Fifteen years from now it is quite possible that the world's third greatest industrial power, just after the United States and Russia, will not be Europe but *American industry in Europe.*"

That scenario has not been enacted. Not only have American companies failed to become the dominant economic force in Europe, but a number of U.S. firms cited by Servan-Schreiber as embodying that threat

(Union Carbide, Chrysler, Celanese, Remington Rand) have beat a retreat from Europe. Meanwhile European companies have mounted an unprecedented invasion of the United States. And Japanese companies, which were barely mentioned by Servan-Schreiber, have moved massively into the U.S. and European marketplaces, both by exports of goods and establishment of local manufacturing units. *Foreign investment in the United States* now constitutes one of the world's great industrial powers.

History's pendulum has a way of swinging in this manner. Former colonies become the colonizers. The world is also driven today by an economic interdependence that has ballooned world trade. The travels of Marco Polo in the thirteenth century excited people's imaginations for centuries afterward. Marco Polo, his father, and his uncle took three and a half years to get from Venice to China, where they remained for sixteen years. They then spent three years returning to Venice, arriving in 1295, with no one recognizing them because they were dressed as Tartars. After they gained readmission to their house they amazed the Venetians by displaying some of the riches of the Orient with which they had returned: rubies, sapphires, diamonds, emeralds. Today this kind of international transfer is commonplace; it goes on all the time and with unbelievable speed. Currency transactions can be executed in a flash on a computer screen. It takes Heineken only two weeks to ship its beer to the United States. In 1967, the year Servan-Schreiber's book was published, Japanese automakers sold fewer than eighty thousand cars in the United States; by 1990 six Japanese automakers will be operating U.S. plants with an annual capacity of two million cars.

It surprises many Americans to learn that Baskin-Robbins is foreign-owned; it belongs to the British beverage and food giant Allied-Lyons. Baskin-Robbins ice cream is only one of hundreds of products and services that Americans buy every day from foreign-controlled companies. "Built like a Mack truck" is a colloquial American saying, but Mack Trucks today is 42 percent–owned by Renault, the French automaker, which in turn is owned by the French government. (Renault's 46 percent stake in American Motors was in the process of being sold to Chrysler in 1987.) The French's mustard Americans smear on their hot dogs comes from an English company, Reckitt & Colman.

Chateau St. Jean is one of the finest wineries in California. Located in Sonoma County north of San Francisco, Chateau St. Jean, with its white cavelike walls and formal gardens, looks like a French winery. But there's nothing French about it. Chateau St. Jean was started in 1974 by three grape growers from the San Joaquin Valley. And the "Jean" in the name is pronounced in the American way; it stands for Jean Merzoian, the wife of one of the three founders. In 1984 Japan's largest alcoholic beverage company, Suntory, bought Chateau St. Jean for $40 million. It followed by five years Suntory's purchase of an old, prestigious winery in France's Burgundy province. Suntory is also a part owner of a Santa Barbara winery, Firestone (the name standing for the tire company heirs who are the majority owners).

The Beringer winery in California's Napa Valley is controlled by Switzerland's Nestlé, one of the world's largest food companies. Other American wineries in foreign hands include Concannon (Guinness), Domaine Chandon and Simi (Moët-Hennessey), Deutz (Deutz & Geldermann, France), Torres (Torres, Spain), Buena Vista (Moller-Racke, West Germany), and Conn Creek (Dewavrins, France, and Roppers, Britain).

It's not just boutique wineries that interest overseas investors. Some of the biggest companies in America are now, unbeknownst to most Americans, foreign-owned. Marshall Field, longtime anchor of Chicago's Loop, is British-owned. Two of the largest oil companies operating in the United States, Standard Oil of Cleveland and Shell Oil of Houston, are both foreign-owned. Mounds and Almond Joy candy bars belong to the British amalgam Cadbury Schweppes. The Lean Cuisine frozen dinners are supplied by Stouffer, a Nestlé unit. Other familiar American names that are part of a foreign entourage include:

Imperial margarine	Peoples Drug Stores
Valium and Librium	Alka-Seltzer
One-A-Day vitamins	A & P supermarkets
Marine Midland Bank	Ball Park Franks
Vaseline	Q-tips
Aquafresh toothpaste	Airwick
Alpo	Spiegel
Quasar	Bic
Chase & Sanborn coffee	Grand Union supermarkets
Glidden paints	Chunky
O Henry	Mighty Dog
Wish-Bone	Calistoga mineral water
TraveLodge	Keebler
Dannon yogurt	Shedd's margarine
Saks Fifth Avenue	Carnation
Smirnoff vodka	Viceroy
New American Library	S.O.S. soap pads

Of the one hundred largest advertisers in the United States, sixteen are companies owned or controlled by foreign investors.

The pace of foreign investment in the United States accelerated in the mid-1980s. Sweden's Electrolux became the world's largest home appliance maker by acquiring Cleveland's White Consolidated Industries (Frigidaire, Westinghouse, Kelvinator, Gibson). British Petroleum became the world's largest producer of animal feeds by acquiring Purina Mills from Ralston Purina. Hoechst became the world's largest chemical producer by acquiring Celanese. Bertelsmann became the world's largest publishing company by acquiring Doubleday. Saatchi & Saatchi became the world's largest advertising agency complex by acquiring a clutch of American shops (Compton, Ted Bates, Backer & Spielvogel). Unilever, frustrated by being beaten out by Procter & Gamble for Vicks, latched onto Chesebrough-Ponds. Nestlé bought Carnation.

Helped by the declining value of the dollar, Japanese money was coming into the United States at the rate of $4 billion a month in 1987. And the Japanese were having a ball buying various American trinkets: 12.5 percent of investment banker Goldman, Sachs (Sumitomo Bank); 13 percent of Shearson Lehman (Nippon Life Insurance); 100 percent of preppy clothes maker J. Press (Kashiyama); and all kinds of real estate, including Arco Plaza in downtown Los Angeles, the Tishman Building on New York's Fifth Avenue, One Washington Mall in Boston, and a couple of New York hotels, the Essex House and the Algonquin.

In 1984 and 1985 Nippon Kokan, Japan's second-largest steelmaker, made some giant moves in the U.S. market. It bought 50 percent of National Steel, one of the largest steelmakers in America, 40 percent of Martin Marietta's aluminum and titanium alloy fabricating plant in Torrance, California, and a silicon manufacturing plant in Arizona from General Electric. Japan's largest steel producer, Nippon Steel, then moved to strike up a joint venture with Inland Steel, the fourth-largest steel maker in the United States.

Every major Japanese auto producer was preparing to follow the lead of Honda and establish manufacturing and assembly plants in the American market. Do Americans object to this invasion? Some, yes. But it's difficult to argue with investments that create jobs. Ted Anders is the mayor of Flat Rock, Michigan, where Mazda is building a new plant. He said, "Unemployment is like a cancer; it eats away at family unity, it brings hunger and despair and sometimes leads to crime. I'm not saying that Mazda is a cure-all, but it's certainly a step in the right direction. Between ten thousand and twenty thousand people will be able to latch onto that brass ring and grab a piece of their American dream."

Courtesy of Mazda.

For Sale: The Public Sector

BANGLADESH, WHICH BROKE AWAY from Pakistan in 1971 to become an independent state, is the most densely populated country in the world. Ninety million people occupy an area one-third the size of California. With a gross national product of $140 per person, Bangladesh vies with Ethiopia, Chad, and Mali for "the poorest country in the world" title. For comparison's sake, Colombia, not exactly a prosperous place, has a gross national product of $1,400 per person. And how is poverty-lashed Bangladesh seeking to improve its economy? By selling to private investors enterprises that were once publicly owned.

In 1982 a new military government that took power in a bloodless coup announced plans to return many state-owned companies to private hands. More than one thousand companies were then denationalized, including thirty-five jute mills and thirty-seven textile mills which reverted to their previous owners. These mills represented 40 percent of Bangladesh's jute and textile capacity. (Bangladesh supplies more than one-half of the world's jute, a fiber used to make sacks and ropes.) In 1986 the government began to sell off its interests in three of the four state-owned banks, and President Hussein Mohammed Ershad said that fertilizer plants, paper mills, and engineering companies would be the next to be privatized.

In addition, Bangladesh started to reduce its holdings in the subsidiaries of foreign companies. The government had acquired ownership stakes of 35 percent to 40 percent in the local units of such companies as Philips, Pfizer, General Electric Company of Britain, and British-American Tobacco; these stakes were being shaved to 10 percent to 20 percent, with the government shares sold to private investors.

Result: In 1972, when independence dawned, the government owned 85 percent of the nation's industrial plant; by 1986, its share was down to 45 percent.

Bangladesh's revolt against Pakistan was engineered by the left-wing Awami League. But this opposition political party did not raise objections to the sale of these government entities. Indeed, Kamal Hossain, one of the leaders of Awami, was busy in 1986 setting up a Bangladesh branch of the Al Baraqa Bank of Saudi Arabia. This branch was to be 70 percent–owned by Al Baraqa, one of ten foreign banks active in Bangladesh.

The spectacle of an impoverished land such as Bangladesh dipping into the beanbag of capitalism is emblematic of a movement sweeping the world during the closing years of the twentieth century. Privatization is all the rage, both in the advanced industrial nations and in the backward developing countries. While the Reagan administration was moving to transfer the Conrail assets to the private sector, countries around the world were dismantling state-owned portfolios of companies—and this wave of divestment was occurring even in nations strongly committed to socialism. In his book *To Get Rich Is Glorious,* Orville Schell told how the Communist leaders of the People's Republic of China were allowing Western-style commerce to return to the world's most populous country. Schell delivered a talk in which he captured the trend by noting that there's a new answer to the old question, "Who won the Chinese revolution, Mao Tse-tung or Chiang Kai-shek?" The answer now is: "Neither. The winner is Hong Kong."

Nations, rich and poor, have been putting what they own on the auction block. More than fifty countries have sold off pieces of nationalized businesses since the start of the 1980s. The leader in this sell-off is clearly Britain's Thatcher government. It sold more than $15 billion in assets, including its holdings in British Aerospace, British Airways, Cable & Wireless, Britoil, British Railway Hotels, Jaguar, Rolls-Royce, and British Gas. By far the biggest transaction was the sale of Her Majesty's Government's 50.2 percent stake in British Telecom, the supplier of telephone service in the United Kingdom. It fetched $3.9 billion and was the largest offering of shares ever made anywhere in the world.

Looking around the globe, one can see these garage sales going on everywhere. Highways have been privatized in India and Malaysia. The government of Singapore sold off 16 percent of Singapore Airlines and was planning to sell more. Japan is pruning its 35 percent holding in Japan Air Lines. It may be called KLM Royal Dutch Airlines, but the government of the Netherlands cut its holding to 39 percent of the voting shares. West Germany's stake in Lufthansa is down to 74 percent. IRI, the state holding company in Italy, raised nearly $1 billion in 1985 through the sale of shares in companies it owns, including Alitalia, where the government's ownership was reduced from 98.7 percent to 76.6 percent. VIAG, the giant energy, aluminum, and chemicals concern of West Germany, sold 40 percent of its shares to the public in 1986; previously, the West German government owned 87 percent. In Japan the government tobacco monopoly has been reorganized as a private company, and Nippon Telegraph & Telephone, operator of the Japanese phone system, was partially privatized in early 1987 in an offering that created the most valuable company in the world with a market value in excess of $160 billion, double IBM's. In Turkey the government sold the bridge over the Bosphorus to private investors. The Central African republic of Cameroon announced in 1986 that over the next five years it would sell its shareholdings in sixty-two companies.

Spain's state holding company, the Instituto Nacional de Industria, under the leadership of a Socialist party economist, Carlos Croissier, has sold off a number of companies, including a hotel chain, a ball bearing manufacturer, a carpet maker, and—the biggest one of all—Seat, the Spanish automobile producer, which was acquired by Volkswagen in 1986. A chain of hotels, an auto manufacturer, and minority stakes in the nation's largest banks were sold by the Mexican government. Nacional Hotelera was sold to private investors, and Renault de Mexico went to Renault of France. Brazil has sold off a piece of the national oil company, Petrobas, and plans to sell, merge, or close more than one hundred state-owned enterprises.

Other countries treading the free enterprise path were Peru, Nigeria, Indonesia, Vietnam, Iraq, Israel, Trinidad, and Argentina. The favorite properties for the auction block are the state-owned airlines. Air New Zealand, Iberia, Royal Jordanian, Air Canada, and Air Lanka were among the carriers ticketed for privatization in 1987, joining British Airways, Lufthansa, Japan Air Lines, Alitalia, and Singapore Airlines. After Hong Kong's Cathay Pacific went public in 1986, the Communist-led People's Republic of China decided to become an investor, taking a 12.5 percent stake in the airline.

Helping to grease the sales of the state properties were low share prices. This was a deliberate policy in France and Britain, where the governments sought to curry favor with the voters by giving preference to small investors. As a result, when these companies were brought public, there was a stampede for shares—and in subsequent trading, the prices soared, giving the initial investors an instant profit if they chose to sell. In the United Kingdom privatization ballooned the number of individual shareholders from 3 million in 1979 to 8.5 million in 1986. In France the demand by small investors was so great that institutions could not get many shares at the initial offering by the government. Paribas, the leading French investment bank, drew applications from 3.8 million individuals.

The shares had to be rationed—four to a person at $65 a share—and this one offering doubled the number of personal shareholders in France.

Even more spectacular was the Japanese government's sale of 12.5 percent of Nippon Telegraph & Telephone. The price of each share doubled to $16,000 in the first four months of trading. And so popular was the issue that NTT now has seven hundred thousand shareholders, more than any other Japanese company. Being a public company also meant that NTT had to contend with the *Sokaiya,* organized gangs of harrassers who disrupt annual meetings unless they are paid off. In June 1987, at the first annual meeting of the world's most valuable company, the Sokaiya showed up in force at the Otani Hotel in Tokyo. One of them rose to shout at a director, "It is said you pinched your secretary on the Joban railway line." Hishashi Shinto, NTT chairman, replied, "Your question is inappropriate and will be struck from the minutes of this meeting."

When François Mitterrand was elected president of France in 1981, the Bourse (the stock market in Paris) suffered one of the largest one-day declines in its history. Mitterrand, a Socialist, did not disappoint his supporters. In early 1982 he nationalized the main banks and most of the top industrial groups: Saint-Gobain, Rhône-Poulenc, Bull, Pechiney, Thomson, Compagnie Générale d'Électricité (CGE). The government thus became the owner of France's three largest retail banks—Crédit Lyonnaise, Société Générale, and Banque National de Paris—which hold 70 percent of all French deposits. As a result the French government found itself employing seven million people, or one third of the total labor force. It was the largest state-held business empire in the Western world.

When a coalition of rightist parties wrested control of the French government from the Socialists in March 1986, the Bourse raced to a ten-day spree of rising prices, anticipating the return of these nationalized companies to the private sector. And the stockbrokers were correct in their assumption. The French government was planning to raise more than $20 billion by denationalizing companies that the previous government had acquired.

Ironically, these companies are worth much more now than when they were absorbed by the government in 1982. Prices on the Bourse tripled under the Socialist leadership. And everyone conceded that the nationalized companies fared well. They restructured their operations, reduced their payrolls, and made more money under a Socialist-led government than they did under private ownership, which is the point the Socialists made when they took over. They promised to help the companies perform the way entrepreneurial firms are supposed to perform: Be efficient, be profitable, be alert to opportunities, reinvest in the company (and the country) instead of hiding profits under a mattress or in a Swiss bank account. Socialism *à la française* had less to do with sharing the wealth than with revitalizing French business. In this case, as in so many others, labels mean little.

A corollary to the worldwide drift to privatization is a softer climate for multinational corporations. From one end of the world to the other, the welcome mat is out for foreign investors, whether it's the state of Tennessee trying to cajole Japanese automakers, or the People's Republic of China welcoming a baby food plant from H. J. Heinz and a cigarette plant from R. J. Reynolds. Not too many years ago "multinational corporation" was almost a pejorative term. Western corporations were viewed as imperialist exploiters, extractors of national wealth, traducers of local culture. Countries such as Mexico and India served notice on foreign companies that they could no longer have 100 percent–owned subsidiaries in their territories.

Those restrictions are being lifted—and there is fierce competition now to attract foreign investment. So there is far less fulmination today against the wicked multinational corporation. Big companies—the ones profiled in this book—are not hated the way they were ten and fifteen years ago. Sven Rydenfelt, professor of economics at the University of Lund in Sweden, has detected this change of attitude in his country, one of the pillars of the social democratic welfare state. He wrote in *The Wall Street Journal* in 1984 "Perhaps the most important optimistic sign is the dramatic change in attitude toward private enterprise. Businessmen used to be looked upon as half-criminals with dirty jobs and dirty profits; today, however, successful businessmen are hailed as providers of wealth and much-needed jobs. One might almost say they are now regarded as national heroes."

One might almost say that Professor Rydenfelt is engaging in a little hyperbole. To keep matters in perspective, we need to recall the reasons business was so disliked in the past, and is still regarded with suspicion by people in all parts of the world. When World War II ended in 1945, businessmen, far from being hailed as heroes, were blamed for greed and narrowness that had plunged the world into the Great Depression of the 1930s and led to the armed conflict that broke out in 1939. The Allied victory did not bring forth yearnings for the life before the war. On the contrary, there were cries for a new way of life, one where people would be guaranteed jobs and health insurance and social security for their old age.

It was this tide of feeling that led the British to depose their wartime leader Winston Churchill and elect a Labour government committed to socialism. In the underdeveloped areas of the world—in Africa and Asia—there was certainly no mandate for the old business establishment to return to power. Countries were determined to break their colonial ties—and in breaking with their pasts they identified the free enterprise, capitalist system as the instrument of their previous oppression. So when new countries were established, the model was not British or American capitalism, it was socialism, which served as a rebuke to the colonial masters of the past, including the corporations that had established out-posts in those countries. Nations everywhere wanted their independence, political and economic, and they wanted to do it under a socialist system.

The resurgence of capitalism results from the simple fact that econo-mies have not been productive under socialist governments. However, before business leaders rejoice, they should not assume that the tide of feeling that was running at the end of World War II has disappeared. The proposition that people should have the right to a job, good health ser-vices, and decent housing remains a driving force. Corporations that forget that proposition are likely to reap a bitter harvest. Capitalism is winning today because of default by the socialists. The *idea* of socialism is far from dead.

It's also easy to see that the move to privatization has a nonideologi-cal bent to it. The government bureaucrats who are privatizing national-ized companies do not see this action as part of a contest between capital-ism and socialism. The world today is full of hybrids: profit-making companies which are 100 percent–owned by government; companies that are owned fifty-fifty by governmental bodies and private investors; compa-nies that are largely controlled by private investors with government holding a minority stake; companies that are two-thirds owned by states and one-third by individuals. Pittsburgh ketchup maker H. J. Heinz, for example, has joint operating ventures with the governments of Zimbabwe and China. Again, labels mean little.

In 1983 Ferdinando Ventriglia, director-general of the Banco di Napoli, the seventh-largest bank in Italy and a government-owned entity, set in motion a campaign to recapitalize the bank, hoping eventually to sell shares to the public and gain a listing on the Milan Stock Exchange. Ventriglia chose to raise all his money privately, not from the government, which owned his bank. As he told Alan Friedman of the *Financial Times:* "I don't like to ask money from the state. The state is a lousy share-holder." So much for socialism Italian-style. At the same time, Babacar N'Diaye, president of the African Development Bank, said in 1986, "Africa in the 1980s is not taking account, as far as economics is concerned, of ideology. We are pragmatists. Countries that are on the moderate left or even left-left have recognized that too much centralization is a burden on the economy."

In short, whatever works, works. In many parts of the world—India, Mexico, Zimbabwe, China—virulent Marxist ideology is still spouted at political rallies, while in practice business is conducted with the giant megacorporations of the world. Corporations are savaged as imperialistic in speeches and welcomed as partners in economic development. A striking example of this incongruity was discovered by Matt Miller, a *Wall Street Journal* reporter who visited Calcutta in West Bengal, where India's Communist party has been in power for many years. Calcutta is a place where hammer-and-sickle pendants fly over the doorway of the state-owned Bank of Baroda. However, the government now is trying to get business to invest in Calcutta. One minister, Commerce Secretary Nirmal Bose, said, "We are ready to work with private entrepreneurs, ready to welcome multinationals." Another minister, Labor Secretary Shanti Ranjan Ghatak, said, "We haven't given up the struggle against multinationals." When Miller pointed out the apparent contradiction, Ghatak replied, "That's life."

So the good news for internationally minded companies is that the welcome sign is out for them—all over the world. But the welcome does not mean that they have carte blanche to do what they used to do, maximizing their profits at the expense of people. Flora Lewis of *The New York Times* reported that at a recent meeting in Zimbabwe, after Education Minister Zingai Mutumbuka stressed the need for private investment, a young woman asked, "Does this mean that socialism is over?" Mutumbuka responded, "There is nothing in socialism against profits. The difference is that under socialism, nobody gets exploited."

The Global Marketplace

Akzo	**Sales** $7.8 billion
	Profits $412 million
	U.S. Sales $850 million
	Rank 4th largest company in the Netherlands
	World's 12th-largest chemical producer
	World's 6th-largest paint maker
	World's largest maker of organic peroxides
	World's 2d-largest paper chemicals producer
	58th-largest company in Europe
	Founded 1969
	Employees 65,000 (9,000 in the United States)
	Headquarters Arnhem, the Netherlands

This Dutch chemical combine may be the biggest company you've never heard of. It may also be the only foreign company that left its stamp on America by having a town—Enka, North Carolina—named after one of its major divisions. Based on its 1985 sales volume, Akzo would have placed fifty-ninth on the *Fortune* 500 roster, sandwiched between Hewlett-Packard and Johnson & Johnson. It makes fibers, salt, drugs, plastics, detergents, coatings. And while it has 225 units in fifty countries, its main operations are in the Netherlands and West Germany, where 60 percent of its employees are based. In the United States Akzo operates one of the world's largest fatty amines plants at Morris, Illinois (amines are organic chemicals used as feedstocks for finished products such as laundry softeners) and runs an oil refinery at Bayport, Texas. It has paint plants in the Netherlands, West Germany, Austria, Belgium, France, Argentina, Brazil, Thailand, and Troy, Michigan.

Akzo also makes consumer products, but you are not likely to be familiar with them unless you have lived in Europe, where it markets vinegars (Heidelberg), soups (California), nuts (Duyvis and Benenuts), insecticides (Temana), detergents (Dobbelman), and rose hip syrup (Roosvicee).

How did Akzo come about? By a series of mergers, acquisitions, and disintegrations that go back to the early part of the twentieth century. Here's a truncated version of the family tree:

1899: Vereinigte Glanzstoff-Fabriken was founded in Germany. It developed into a large rayon and coatings producer.

1911: Nederlandsche Kunstzijdebariek (NK or Enka) was formed in Holland to make rayon.

1929: NK merges with Vereinigte Glanzstoff-Fabriken to form Algemene Kunstzijde-Unie (AKU).

19

1967: Kon. Zout-Ketjen, Dutch producer of minerals and inorganic chemicals, merges with Kon. Zwanenberg Organon, a Dutch producer of basic and organic chemicals, drugs, detergents, and cosmetics, to form Koninkijke Zout-Organon (KZO).

1969: KZO gains control of International Salt in the United States. KZO merges with AKU to form Akzo.

It's a convoluted history which can be traced back even further into Dutch history. One of the coatings units, Sikkens, was founded in 1792. A food company, Duyvis, goes back to 1806. And the company's chemical operations in the United States, carried out under the banner of Chicago-based Akzo Chemie, were once part of the big meatpacker Armour & Company, with roots going back to the 1860s in Chicago. And the confusion continues today.

Not a year goes by that Akzo is not involved in absorbing or shedding companies in various parts of the world. A standpatter it's not. Akzo did a major aboutface in 1985 when it sold its largest business in the United States, American Enka, a producer of man-made fibers, to the giant German chemical company BASF. Competition in synthetic textile fibers has been fierce, and Akzo was delighted to make its exit. It has followed a similar course in Europe, where its Enka fiber operations are based in the North Rhine-Westphalian city of Wuppertal, near Dusseldorf. Fibers represented 47 percent of Akzo's sales in 1973, and 23 percent at the end of 1985. In the process of restructuring, eleven thousand jobs were eliminated. It no longer makes nylon, but it's still big in polyester and industrial fibers in general. Josef Hutter, head of the fibers division in 1986, explained the strategy to the *Financial Times*. "We have reshaped ourselves around a smaller number of fibers so that we can be number one or, at the very least, number two in the special areas we have chosen. Being number three or four is of no interest to us at all." As an example, Hutter noted that Akzo fibers are now used in 70 percent of high-performance tires made in Europe and in 80 percent of the conveyor belts.

The sale of American Enka lopped off $450 million in sales. It also transferred to BASF forty-five hundred people who had been employees of American Enka. It brought other changes too. The plant that the Dutch put up in 1928 in the mountains west of Asheville, North Carolina, now belongs to BASF, even though the name of the town remains Enka. (It's unlikely the Germans will change it to BASF, North Carolina.) With the sale to BASF, there was also no longer any reason for Akzo to maintain its U.S. headquarters in North Carolina. So Akzo America, the principal holding company in North America, sold its headquarters building in Asheville and relocated to New York City.

One fiber that Akzo is not giving up on is aramid, a chemical relative of nylon that has five times the strength of steel but only one sixth the weight, and has applications in a wide variety of products, from bullet-proof vests to clutch and brake pads, where it replaces asbestos. In fact, the Dutch company has been embroiled in a fierce ten-year battle with Du Pont over the rights to aramid. Du Pont markets the fiber as Kevlar, Akzo as Twaron. Both companies began developing the fiber at about the same time in the late 1960s, but Du Pont marketed it more quickly than Akzo. Du Pont accused Akzo of infringing on its patent; Akzo alleged a similar violation on Du Pont's part. Du Pont succeeded in getting the Dutch product banned from the United States, and Akzo was trying to get Europe to slam the door on Kevlar. "I don't see why Du Pont has acted like this," Hutter said to *Financial Times* reporter Anthony Moreton. "We are only seeking 5 percent of the [American] market; they would have the rest."

This farflung chemical enterprise is managed from the Rhine River city of Arnhem in the eastern part of the Netherlands, just twelve miles from the German border. The Dutch have a long history of operating businesses across the world. Unilever, Royal Dutch Shell, and Philips are three multinational behemoths that come out of the Netherlands and, of course, are far more well known than Akzo because of their consumer products. The sophistication of Akzo's management is reflected in Hutter, who presided over the restructuring of the Enka fibers business. Hutter, fifty-eight years old in 1987, was born in Yugoslavia, holds Austrian citizenship, lives in West Germany (where Enka is headquartered), speaks fluent English, and can also manage in Spanish and Portuguese, thanks to Enka tours of duty in Colombia and Brazil.

Sitting at the apex of the Akzo pyramid is a very young, cool, and articulate manager, A. A. Loudon, a Hague-born lawyer who became chief executive in 1982 when he was only forty-six years old. Loudon rose through the financial side of the company and has worked in Brazil and France. His official title is president of the board of management. The board underwent a significant restructuring when he took the helm; it was reduced in size from eleven to four members. It's this quartet (the other three are all older than Loudon) that runs Akzo. Previously, the six divisional presidents sat on the board, but as Loudon explained to Harold Stieglitz, who interviewed him for a Conference Board study, it proved impossible to manage product groups centrally. Akzo therefore told the division presidents, "You remain responsible for your particular operations. But while, as a board member, you used to share overall corporate responsibilities, you are now one step lower in the hierarchy." So there.

Loudon is not a fuzzy manager. Having come up from finance, he has a proper appreciation for a tidy balance sheet. In an address he delivered in 1986 to fellow directors at other Dutch companies, he reminded his audience that "the quality of the balance sheet" is just as important to the success of the company as such attributes as product quality and responsible managers. "A business can quite as easily fail through a lack of liquid resources as through a lack of human and technical quality," he said. Loudon is also a tiger on the subject of clear goals. He believes that one of the first rules of management must be to "act naturally," but he quickly adds, "We should never lose sight of the fact that the ultimate aim of quality stimulation is the advancement of the business objective that is being pursued—*not* the optimization of human happiness." First things first.

Loudon is also very conscious of Akzo's lack of homogeneity, since it's a collection of companies with their own histories. Decentralization, he has pointed out, "is not regarded as an end in itself," rather it's an "effective means of controlling the business of the Group," and he added, "We have no intention of suppressing any of the individual cultures encountered in the divisions. Rather, we propose to superadd a shared Akzo culture. To inculcate a vivid consciousness of the identity of the Group and of the potential benefits inherent in cooperation, we will have to work at changing tendencies toward isolationism."

James Fuller, president of Akzo's Chicago-based specialty chemicals division, is an undisguised enthusiast about being part of this multinational force. "We are very different from the usual colonial enterprise," he said. "We run on a worldwide basis, but we operate as partners. The Dutch have a long international history. Being a small country, they have developed the facility of picking up other cultures while retaining their own. They are not as parochial as the English or the Germans. And Akzo has its own distinctive features. For a company of its size, it is remarkably informal, relatively free of bureaucracy, and its employees are not afraid of humor."

Akzo's stock is listed on twelve stock exchanges in Europe. Its American subsidiary used to have 34 percent of its stock traded on the New York Stock Exchange, but one of Loudon's first moves after taking the reins in 1982 was to buy up all the minority shares. In 1985 Akzo bought two diagnostics operations in the United States—the Bionetics division of Litton Industries and the diagnostic units of Warner-Lambert. It also acquired Levis, the largest paint company in Belgium. In 1986 it acquired the paper chemicals business of Monsanto and an engineering plastics company, Wilson-Fiberfil, based in New Jersey with operations in

Indiana and California. Loudon has made it clear that Akzo will use its cash to buy up other American companies to replace the business lost by the sale of American Enka.

Access 76 Velperweg
P.O. Box 186
6800 LS Arnhem, the Netherlands
(31) 085-66-46-03

Akzo America
111 W. 40th St.
New York, N.Y. 10018
(212) 382-5500

Anglo American Corporation of South Africa	Assets $13 billion
	Profits $400 million
	Rank World's largest producer of gold
	World's largest producer of diamonds
	World's largest producer of platinum
	South Africa's biggest company
	World's largest private employer of black labor
	Founded 1917
	Employees 268,000
	Headquarters Johannesburg, South Africa

Sir Ernest Oppenheimer used to stride into the Johannesburg offices of Anglo American Corporation and greet young employees with the salutation, "What shall we do to make some money today, my boy?" He didn't need to ask. Never on the South African business scene was there a man with a more unerring sense of what to do to make money.

As a youth who in 1902 followed his brothers from Germany to the South African diamond fields, he conquered and consolidated the fragmented mining industry established by Cecil Rhodes and other mining magnates of the late nineteenth century. Oppenheimer spent the rest of his life enlarging his domain to encompass not only the glittering gems and metals beneath the veldt but scores of other South African businesses and dozens of enterprises worldwide.

A latter-day dynast, he passed this conglomerate to his son, Harry Frederick Oppenheimer, making him one of the ten richest men in the world. And one day his grandson Nicholas may inherit—if the Oppenheimer companies survive whatever fate awaits big business in the aftermath of the intensifying confrontation between South Africa's white supremacist government and the long-suppressed black majority.

South Africa has been a battleground for hundreds of years, reflecting the avarice, divisions, and prejudices Europeans brought with them. The Dutch and the Huguenots were the first to arrive in the seventeenth century, and from the start they had black slaves, importing them from East and West Africa. In 1707 there were 1,780 European settlers, and they had eleven hundred slaves. The British arrived toward the end of the eighteenth century, and in 1814 the Europeans, sitting thousands of miles away in the Congress of Vienna, decided that the territory belonged to

Britain. To get away from the British settlements around the Cape, the Boers (descendants of the Dutch colonists) moved inland, fighting a series of wars with the native black tribes. The Boers were primarily farmers; the British developed the cities.

Modern South Africa dates from the latter part of the nineteenth century when first diamonds (1867) and then gold (1886) were discovered there. These discoveries set off a wild rush. In 1870 three hundred thousand whites lived in South Africa. By the end of the century, there were one million. By the end of the century there was also the Boer War, pitting the British against the Afrikaners. The British won the war, and the Union of South Africa under Jan Smuts was formed in 1910. It was a war many critics in Britain felt had been waged on behalf of the mine owners.

The original developers of the South African gold and diamond fields are wonderfully depicted—with all their scrubbiness and grandeur—in *The Randlords,* a book by British journalist Geoffrey Wheatcroft, published in 1985. He captured the rough-and-tumble days of mining, which are reminiscent of the Wild West days of the United States. In 1895, Wheatcroft tells us, the city of Johannesburg, sitting atop the gold reef of South Africa, had "fourteen thousand women, of whom at least one thousand were prostitutes. The town had ninety-seven brothels of various nationalities: thirty-six French, twenty German, five Russian, and so on. . . . When they were not drinking or whoring, many miners spent their time gambling. The men of Johannesburg bet on anything: horses, prize fights, rat-killing dogs, cars, billiards, how many flies would land on a lump of sugar—and of course gold shares."

British adventurers and Jewish immigrants from England and Germany were prominent in the early development of the mines. Anti-Semitism was rampant. Among the pet names applied to Johannesburg were "Judasberg" and "Jewhannesburg." Wheatcroft said, "The Zulus do better: they call it simply Igoli, the city of gold."

Ernest Oppenheimer, the fifth son of a Jewish cigar merchant of Friedbourg, near Frankfurt, came to South Africa as the representative of a Jewish diamond merchant in London. He set up his own diamond business in 1906, using his wife's dowry as capital, and quickly became a leading player as a result of his insight into the diamond business (he knew both the producing and the selling ends) and a certain ruthlessness that marked him as someone determined to advance into the higher circles of the industry. In blatantly anti-Semitic cartoons of the day, he was transformed into "Hoggenheimer," a hook-nosed, cigar-smoking wheeler-dealer (Oppenheimer became an Anglican in 1930).

Oppenheimer arrived on the scene when a confluence of events favored someone who could make sense out of change. The period before World War I was one of great upheavals—and the political and economic conflicts of Europe had a way of washing down to South Africa. It was also a period when the first generation of Randlords, having made their fortunes, no longer wanted to be active in the business.

"By now," said Wheatcroft, "a good two dozen of these fabulously rich men had installed themselves in England, living in London and the country in stupefying luxury. Percy FitzPatrick's address book lists them, a golden panorama of Edwardian plutocracy: Alfred Beit at 26 Park Lane and Twin Water; his brother Otto at 49 Belgrave Square; Frederich Eckstein at 15 Park Lane; George Farrar at 54 Old Bond Street and Chicheley Hall in Buckinghamshire; S. C. Goldmann, the financier and author of books on mining, at 24 Queen's Gate; 'Mikki' Michaelis at Tandridge Court in Surrey as well as Ben Alder in Scotland; J. B. Taylor at Sherfield Manor in Hampshire as well as his sporting estate in Scotland."

The most powerful of the first generation of Randlords were financiers linked to a group called the Corner House, which took its name from the location of H. Eckstein & Company at the corner of Simmonds and Commissioner streets in Johannesburg. It was always a London-controlled operation. It was Ernest Oppenheimer's perspicacity to see that this group was passing from the scene, and that the time was ripe for a new company that would be based in South Africa. The Anglo American Corporation of South Africa was launched on September 25, 1917.

"American" was part of the name because J. P. Morgan & Company and other U.S. investors supplied half of the initial capital of $1 million— thanks in part to a middleman named Herbert Hoover. "Anglo" was in the name not to honor Oppenheimer's adopted country (he was to be knighted in 1920), but as a last-minute substitution for "African," which had been Oppenheimer's first choice. The U.S. investors insisted that Oppenheimer yank the word "African." In a cable they pointed out that "African American would suggest on this side our dark-skinned fellow countrymen and possibly result in ridicule."

On Sir Ernest's side, no one was so squeamish about the connection with blacks or what people thought about it. If a company mined for gold and diamonds in South Africa, it also exploited the country's greatest raw material, cheap black labor. On the financial side, Sir Ernest turned out to be a wizard. His formula for growth was: Absorb company after company by means of stock swaps. He would raise money by selling shares to others—but he always retained control.

The result is a trio of intricately intertwined, family-dominated companies: Anglo, De Beers Consolidated Mines Ltd., and Minerals and

Resources Corporation (Minorco). In 1985 Anglo produced 254 tons of gold, 22 percent of the West's supply and 37 percent of South Africa's. It also has holdings in more than 250 mining operations in twenty-two other countries. True to Sir Ernest's penchant for buying into rival companies to control or influence their operations, Anglo owns shares in South Africa's six other mining houses. Likewise, they have cross-holdings in each other so that together they constitute the nation's most formidable economic bloc.

Through various subsidiaries Anglo American controls South Africa's largest coal producer and private steel maker, holds a majority stake in one of the country's top automakers, and owns the nation's biggest brick maker, travel agency, discount house, automobile distributor, and computer software firm. Other holdings include companies that deal in sugar, paper, beer, chemicals, farming, banking, insurance, food, and publishing. In 1986, when Anglo bought the biggest bank in South Africa from Barclays (which pulled out because of the escalating violence over apartheid), local wags quipped that if a black party such as the African National Congress ever came to power and carried out promises to nationalize the banking and mining industries, its task would be easy—only one company would have to be nationalized.

De Beers, the second company in the Anglo constellation, is renowned as the world's largest producer of diamonds. Cecil Rhodes started it in 1880, the year Ernest Oppenheimer was born. Oppenheimer wrested control of it from Rhodes's successors in 1929. Operating as a cartel with other producers, dealers, and cutters, De Beers controls the supply, price, and marketing of 80 percent of the world's diamonds, even gems from the Soviet Union, an avowed enemy of South Africa. One place De Beers does not have an office is the United States, where it could be prosecuted for antitrust violations. That does not prevent it, of course, from mounting a hefty advertising campaign in the United States to maintain the image of diamonds as "a girl's best friend." De Beers has a worldwide advertising budget of $100 million to sell that illusion.

The relationship between De Beers and Anglo is bewilderingly complex. In a sense, they own each other. De Beers is Anglo's largest corporate holding and is itself a major shareholder in Anglo. Through direct ownership and shares held by satellites, Anglo owns 34 percent of De Beers, which, in turn, owns 38 percent of Anglo. Together they have interests in companies that account for more than half of the stock traded on the Johannesburg Exchange. The Oppenheimers maintain overall control via an 8.3 percent stake in Anglo American held by the family's private company, E. Oppenheimer & Son.

Outside of South Africa, Bermuda-based Minorco pumps Anglo and De Beers money into a myriad of enterprises, from zinc mines in the Yukon (Hudson Bay Mining) to natural gas deposits in Texas (Adobe Resources) to investment banking on Wall Street (Salomon Brothers). Some studies have identified Anglo American as the largest foreign investor in the United States; but given the incestuous nature of the mining business, where many of the investments lie, the trail is not easy to follow. For example, Minorco owns 29 percent of London-based Consolidated Gold Fields, which in turn owns 26 percent of New York–based Newmont Mining, which in turn owns 30.7 percent of Peabody Holding, the largest coal producer in the United States. Minorco's biggest direct stakes in the United States are its 14.5 percent holding in Salomon Inc. (Salomon Brothers, Phillip Brothers, and Phibro Energy), its 29.5 percent holding in Engelhard (catalysts, precious metals, kaolin clays), and its 59 percent holding in Inspiration Resources (miner of copper, zinc, gold, silver, nickel, and coal). Minorco's stock is publicly traded on exchanges in London, Johannesburg, Antwerp (where 39 percent of the world's diamonds are cut), Brussels, and Paris, but Anglo American owns 39 percent of the shares, and De Beers has another 21 percent.

Anglo American began transferring assets to Minorco in the 1970s, resulting in a buying binge that netted more than one hundred companies. The ostensible reason was geographical diversification, but some political observers suggested that it was "insurance" against the possible nationalization of its South African companies should blacks—and socialism—come to power. However, with 80 percent of Anglo's assets still in South Africa, Harry Oppenheimer dismissed this idea, telling *The Economist,* "If the ship sinks, and I don't think it will, I will go down with it."

Although he is heir to a corporate colossus built upon exploitation of black labor, Harry Oppenheimer has long opposed apartheid, the system of rigid segregation of the races imposed by the Afrikaners. He spoke out against apartheid when he was a member of the South African Parliament from 1948 to 1957. Anglo, under his leadership, was the first company to advocate the legalization of black trade unions. It also reduced the gap between the wages of white and black miners from twenty-to-one to five-to-one. "If you go into business here," he once told the *Financial Times,* "you are heir, for good or evil, of what has happened before. You say to yourself, 'in so far as I can, I am going to have black people doing better work and earning better money.' "

Each year Anglo supports a group of black students to attend a university and then trains them for management roles. "Apartheid is incompatible with a sophisticated company," Oppenheimer told the *Man-*

chester Guardian in 1984. In 1985 he publicly called for reforms that would open commercial districts to business people of any race, allow blacks to own land, end the forcible removal of blacks from their tribal lands, and abolish the pass laws. At the same time, he does not favor "one man, one vote" democracy. He has told interviewers that he would give voting rights to people who had reached a certain level of education or who owned their own homes. He owns three in South Africa, one in New York, one in London, and a ranch in Zimbabwe. His idea of relaxation is to read an 1882 edition of Charles Dickens, using a snapshot of one of his racing horses as a bookmark.

Oppenheimer's criticism of apartheid made him acceptable to neighboring black nations. It helped, for example, to preserve Anglo's copper holdings in Zambia. It also won him the enmity of white workers who belong to the Mine Workers' Union. They still rail at "Hoggenheimer," and the union's paper, *Die Mynwerker,* refers to Anglo American Corporation as the "Advancement of Africans Corporation."

When Oppenheimer stepped down as chairman at the end of 1982, at age seventy-four, he installed as his successor former Rhodes scholar G.W.H. Relly, who shared his desire for reform. In 1984 Relly led a delegation of white businessmen to Zambia to meet with leaders of the African National Congress, the outlawed political party committed to the overthrow of apartheid. Prime Minister P. W. Botha denounced the trip as "treasonable." At the 1986 annual meeting of Anglo American, Relly asserted that "the piecemeal approach to reform" in South Africa "has reached the limit of its usefulness." He urged that the "residual elements of apartheid [be] expunged from the statute book." Whether such moves will endear Anglo American Corporation to blacks is dubious. "Average black youngsters," Anglo executive Zacharias J. De Beer disconsolately told *BusinessWeek* in 1985, "don't differentiate between the political system and the economic system. They see P. W. Botha and Harry Oppenheimer as part of the same system." Indeed, the liberal political stance of Anglo American contrasts sharply with its economic policy of running its mines with low-paid, migrant black labor. The Anglo American mines are the most unionized in South Africa, but they have been the scene of fierce factional fights pitting one tribe against another. More than 130 black miners died in such fights during 1986. At the start of 1987, the black National Union of Mineworkers put forth demands for a 55 percent pay hike.

Meanwhile, another Oppenheimer waits in the wings. Harry's bearded son Nicholas is the heir apparent. He was forty-two years old in 1987 and serving as one of the company's two deputy chairmen. A more reticent character than his father, Nicholas was educated at English boarding schools and went to work immediately for the family company, first as a diamond sorter at the Kimberley mines and then at Anglo and De Beers offices in Johannesburg and London. He has struck reporters who have interviewed him as quiet and self-deprecating. A *BusinessWeek* reporter noted in 1983 that instead of a chauffered limousine, Nicholas drove around Johannesburg in a modest Renault with a "Jesus Saves" bumper sticker, and described him as "private, reclusive, almost secretive." George Milling-Stanley, a *Financial Times* reporter who caught up with Nicholas the next year in London, described him as "diffident and courteous to a degree."

Milling-Stanley also asked him, *People* magazine–style, what he would like to be remembered for. Nicky, as he is known to friends, replied, "Oh, not for any particular thing. Perhaps for having lived a worthwhile life, for not being boring. It would be nice to be remembered for having been polite to people all one's life."

Access   44 Main St.
P. O. Box 61587, Marshalltown 2107
Johannesburg 2001, Republic of South Africa
(27) 11-638-9111

BASF	**Sales** $21 billion **Profits** $500 million **U.S. Sales** $3.6 billion **Rank** World's 2d-largest chemical producer World's 29th-largest industrial company Germany's 6th-largest company 8th-largest chemical producer in the United States World's 3d-largest paint maker World's largest maker of printing inks **Founded** 1861 **Employees** 131,400 (20,700 in the United States) **Headquarters** Ludwigshafen, West Germany

BASF is one of the three companies—the other two are Bayer and Hoechst—that make up the holy trinity of the West German chemical industry. All three combined in 1925, along with five smaller chemical companies, to form the I. G. Farben cartel, which later became an indispensable part of the Nazi war machine, using concentration camp labor to build a synthetic rubber plant at Auschwitz. In 1948, at the end of the Nuremberg trial of war criminals, twelve I. G. Farben executives were found guilty of such crimes as slavery, mass murder, and plunder; they received jail sentences ranging from one and one-half to eight years. Four years later BASF, Bayer, and Hoechst were all back in business as independent entities. Thirty years later they were at the top of the world chemical heap, each having passed the American giant Du Pont.

Of the three, BASF is probably the least known, although it is now the second largest (which is number one depends on the last acquisition). Originally its name was Badische Anilin & Soda-Fabrik, and it did its early work in coal tar dyes. It was the first company, in 1870, to discover a way to make the red dye alizarin; it was also the first, in 1897, to make a laboratory version of indigo, "the king of dyestuffs." The acronym BASF became its official corporate name in 1973. BASF is a chemical company's chemical company. It makes basic chemicals, the raw materials needed to make plastics and other finished products. Much of its work therefore ends up in the products of other companies. Its paints, for example, glisten on BMWs, Mercedes-Benzes, and Volkswagens (BASF is the largest supplier of paints to those German auto companies). It's also a powerhouse in dyestuffs, plastics, vitamins, and fertilizers. American audiophiles and videophiles know the company for its tapes. BASF is the company that first made magnetic tape, in 1934, and it is one of the world's largest producers of videotape. In the European market it's a major maker of videocassette recorders and floppy discs for computers.

Political controversy has long dogged BASF. Early in this century, in an effort to escape dependence on Chilean nitrate as a fertilizer and gunpowder component (saltpeter), BASF backed the research efforts of a young German-Jewish scientist, Fritz Haber, who succeeded in 1909 in combining the nitrogen of the atmosphere with the hydrogen of water to form ammonia. During World War I Haber turned his talents to the development of poison gases, which the German army used against the Allied forces. Haber was later named as a war criminal, but not before he won the Nobel prize in 1919 for his synthesis of ammonia, an award that was protested by French and British scientists. Haber converted to Christianity, but it was a conversion that didn't impress the Nazis. He fled to Switzerland where he died alone in 1934.

Carl Bosch, a brilliant metallurgical engineer, was named chief executive of BASF after World War I. He was the architect and first chairman of the I. G. Farben cartel. In 1931 Bosch became the first engineer to receive the Nobel prize for the feat, twenty years earlier, of designing a high-pressure chemical process that made possible the mass production of Haber's invention, synthetic ammonia, which in turn led to nitrogen-based fertilizers. During World War I Bosch became a hero in Germany for converting ammonia to synthetic nitrate, thereby assuring the Wehrmacht of a dependable supply of gunpowder and explosives.

In assuming the chief executive's post at I. G. Farben in 1925, Bosch headed the largest company in Europe and the largest chemical producer in the world. He was a scientist who was intent on conquering the world by breakthroughs in the research laboratories. One of his first moves was to form a partnership with the world's largest oil company, John D. Rockefeller's Standard Oil of New Jersey (Exxon today), whose leaders were bowled over by the technical sophistication of Farben's research. Bosch trooped them through the laboratories at Ludwigshafen, a Rhine River port opposite to Mannheim, and showed them how Farben was working on a hydrogenation process that would extract oil from coal. Who needed oil wells?

The terrified Americans were quick to sign a sort of nonaggression pact with Bosch under which Farben agreed to stay out of the oil business, while Standard Oil promised to stay out of the chemical business. They set up a joint company in the United States, owned 80 percent by Standard Oil, 20 percent by Farben—and Standard transferred to Farben 2 percent of its entire common stock. The Farben-Standard agreement was then expanded to include an exchange of research information on synthetic rubber, which both companies were working on. It was later alleged that the Germans held back on reporting their progress, thus hurting the American effort to develop synthetic rubber.

The cooperation between Farben and Standard Oil continued after World War II broke out in Europe in 1939, and in 1942 it resulted in an antitrust suit brought by the Justice Department. Senate hearings presided over by Senator Harry S. Truman of Missouri depicted Standard Oil in such an unfavorable light that its two top executives, Walter Teagle and William Farish, left the company shortly afterward in disgrace. Coming out of a hearing, Truman was asked by a reporter whether he saw Standard's pact with Farben as treasonable. He replied, "Why, yes, what else is it?" Thurman Arnold, the antitrust chief in the Justice Department, put it this way: "What these people were trying to do was to look at the war as a transitory phenomenon and at business as a kind of permanent thing."

Carl Bosch, however, was one of the few German industrial leaders to stand up to the Nazis during the 1930s. He met with Adolf Hitler in 1933, seeking support for a synthetic rubber plant, which he got, and he warned the Fuhrer that if Jewish scientists were forced to leave the country, physics and chemistry would be set back one hundred years in Germany. According to a biographer of Bosch, Hitler roared, "Then we'll work one hundred years without physics and chemistry." The Nazis did not have to do without physics and chemistry even after they purged the Jews—the I. G. Farben companies were harnessed to the state, providing everything the Nazis needed in their rampage through Europe.

Bosch stepped down in 1935, turning over the reins at I. G. Farben to Hermann Schmitz, who had joined BASF after World War I as head of finance. Bosch died in 1940. Schmitz was in the dock at Nuremberg and after being found guilty of plunder and spoilation was sentenced to a three-year jail term.

BASF regrouped at Ludwigshafen after World War II, rebuilding and expanding a chemical complex that was devastated by Allied bombers. It pushed forward into plastics and joined with Shell in a polyethylene venture before building its own petrochemical works at Antwerp. Then, in 1969, it began its backward integration by acquiring Wintershall, an oil and gas producer. The Ludwigshafen compound, where the company is headquartered, covers sixteen hundred acres and holds fifteen hundred factory buildings and laboratories which line fifty-six miles of streets. Above and under these streets are 1,150 miles of pipes through which move gases and liquids on their way to the refineries. More than fifty thousand people work in this complex.

While Ludwigshafen remains the most important production center,

BASF's expansion, begun in the late 1950s, has made it a global player in the worldwide chemical industry, a contender in a league whose teams include Du Pont, Dow, ICI, Akzo, Union Carbide, Montedison, Bayer, and Hoechst. Only giants suit up here. BASF tries, more than most companies in the chemical industry, to be as self-sufficient as possible. Its approach was characterized by *The Economist* as follows: "It wants to find and develop its own sources of oil and gas, which will supply its own refineries, which will churn out the naphtha to feed its own crackers, which will produce ethylene, the basic petrochemical building block for the house that BASF hopes to build."

This explains why BASF is drilling for oil and gas in the United States and why it also operates refineries here to produce the feedstocks it needs for plants making end products. BASF wants to do the whole job. In this worldwide putsch (BASF now does more than half its business outside Germany), the United States has assumed central importance. In a series of deals starting in 1958, BASF has built up a commanding U.S. presence, demonstrating that it was willing to take over operations that others were ready to abandon. Its initial foray was a joint venture with Dow Chemical—Dow Badische at Williamsburg, Virginia—but it later bought out Dow's interest. No more joint ventures. In 1985 and 1986 it plunked down something like $2 billion to acquire businesses in the United States. In this basket were the Enka man-made fibers facilities that the Dutch company Akzo was happy to unload; the Inmont printing ink and auto finish operations that United Technologies was delighted to sell for $1 billion; the high-tech plastics (composite materials) arm of Celanese; and the Zerex antifreeze business of Du Pont. (If you have a chemical business for sale, call up BASF.)

As a result BASF marched into 1987 with seventy production facilities in the United States doing an annual sales volume of $3.6 billion, which ranked the company among the ten largest chemical producers in North America.

A former BASF chairman, Matthias Seefelder, once explained at a press conference in New York's St. Regis Hotel why the company looks to America: "The United States is the largest, most competitive chemical market in the world. It has one currency. It has no language barriers. Its successful free enterprise system permits rapid adjustments to technological changes. Profit is not a dirty word here, but an incentive to do better."

It hasn't been all frictionless progress. BASF was placed on the AFL-CIO boycott list in 1984 because of a labor dispute at its chemical plant on the Mississippi River at Geismar, Louisiana, twenty miles south of Baton Rouge. The dispute erupted into one of the most bitter labor-management confrontations of the 1980s after negotiations for a new contract broke down, and BASF locked out 370 workers from the plant on the grounds that it feared sabotage by the employees. Management had been asking for a new agreement calling for wage and benefit concessions by the workers, who were making an average of $14.50 an hour. The workers, represented by the Oil, Chemical, and Atomic Workers Union (OCAW), offered to take wage cuts but balked at a change in work rules that would have weakened job security. The lockout set the stage for all-out warfare between the union and BASF.

OCAW accused BASF of polluting the Mississippi River and running an unsafe chemical plant. The Geismar facility produces highly toxic chemicals, and the union, citing the use of untrained workers, raised the spectre of "a Bhopal on the Bayou"—a reference to the 1984 gas leak at the Union Carbide plant in Bhopal, India, where more than two thousand people were killed. "BASF is gambling with human lives," declared a union press release, "If they lose, everyone loses." BASF scoffed at this charge. On June 11, 1986, Dr. Leslie J. Story, the plant manager, delivered

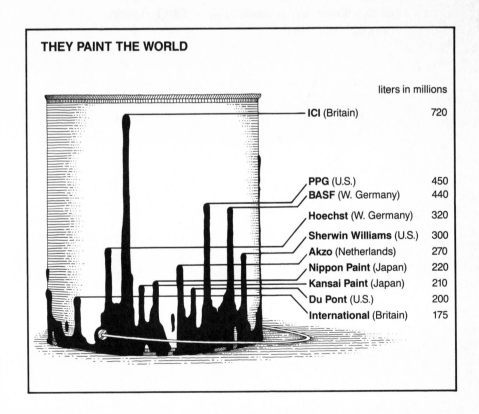

THEY PAINT THE WORLD

liters in millions

ICI (Britain)	720
PPG (U.S.)	450
BASF (W. Germany)	440
Hoechst (W. Germany)	320
Sherwin Williams (U.S.)	300
Akzo (Netherlands)	270
Nippon Paint (Japan)	220
Kansai Paint (Japan)	210
Du Pont (U.S.)	200
International (Britain)	175

an impressive stack of documents affirming the safety of the plant to a congressional subcommittee investigating OCAW's charges. Story refuted OCAW's charges, point by point, asserting in the end that the "Geismar works is one of the safest chemical plants in the nation." And he added, "No chemical company has ever been so open."

OCAW took its fight to West Germany to rally support from the trade unions that deal with BASF on its home ground. At first I. G. Chemie, the union of West German chemical workers, contributed $10,000 to the American union, but its enthusiasm for this cause flagged noticeably after BASF produced pictures of an American march in which a protestor carried a sign linking BASF with a swastika. The dispute entered 1987 unresolved. OCAW was still picketing, and BASF was still running the plant with a nonunion force.

Meanwhile, BASF moved into China, where it is helping the Chinese build two new plants, one for the production of polyurethane foam, the other for floppy discs.

Access   Carl Bosch Strasse, 38
6700 Ludwigshafen am Rhein, West Germany
(49) 621-60-99141

BASF Corp.
200 Park Ave.
New York, N.Y. 10166
(212) 682-1784

B.A.T Industries

Sales $28.7 billion
Profits $1.1 million
U.S. Sales $6 billion
Rank World's largest cigarette company
3d-largest cigarette seller in the United States
Britain's 3d-largest company
32th on the *Fortune* International 500
World's largest exporter of leaf tobacco
World's largest maker of carbonless paper
Britain's 3d-largest paper producer
4th in life insurance in Britain
7th in casualty insurance in Britain
Founded 1902
Employees 305,000 (50,000 in the United States)
Headquarters London, England

Cigarettes can lead to many things. According to some very reputable scientists, smoking cigarettes leads to lung cancer, heart attacks, emphysema, and other rather unpleasant diseases. For B.A.T Industries, making and selling them led to the creation of one of the few truly globe-girdling businesses of the twentieth century. In 1985 B.A.T (it perversely refuses to put a period after the T) ranked, by the measure of sales, as the thirty-sixth-largest industrial enterprise based outside the United States. By the measure of profits, it ranked even higher (fourteenth). And by the measure of the number of people to whom it gives employment, its rank was still higher (fifth).

From its command post on the upper floors of a nondescript slab not far from Victoria Station in London, B.A.T oversees an empire stretching into ninety countries. Excluding government tobacco monopolies, such as the ones operating in the Soviet Union and China, B.A.T is the world's largest manufacturer of cigarettes. In 1985 the company sold 570 billion cigarettes around the world. That nearly equaled the number of cigarettes sold in the United States. And it represented about 20 percent of the estimated 2.8 trillion cigarettes that were sold in the so-called free world. In 1986 B.A.T was operating 116 tobacco plants in more than fifty countries, and it was selling the output of these factories—cigarettes, cigars, cigarillos, pipe tobacco—under more than seven hundred different brand names. It had the number-one seller in thirty-five countries.

Brazil is a B.A.T power center. There its 75 percent–owned subsidiary, Souza Cruz, holds 81 percent of a huge cigarette market (well over 100 billion units a year). Souza Cruz brands—among them Hollywood, Belmont, Plaza, Arizona, Continental, and Minister—hold nine of the top ten slots in the best-selling standings. Brazil's third-largest company, Souza Cruz also processes raw tobacco, and it's the leading seller of tobacco leaf on world markets.

Another strong market for B.A.T is West Germany, where the company's subsidiary has 25 percent of the cigarette market and the national brand leader, HB. Other B.A.T brands in Germany include Kim, Krone, Kumar, Prince Denmark, Benson & Hedges, Pall Mall, and Kent.

In the United States B.A.T owns the third-largest cigarette company, Louisville-based Brown & Williamson, the purveyor of the Kool, Viceroy, Raleigh, Belair, Barclay, and Richland brands. It held close to 12 percent of the U.S. cigarette market in 1986.

While coughing up denials that cigarettes cause all those deadly diseases, tobacco companies everywhere have been using the not inconsiderable profits generated by smoking to buy their way into other businesses that, whatever else may be said about them, cannot be accused of selling products that kill people. B.A.T, addicted as it is to cigarettes (especially the money that flows therefrom), knows how to follow a trend. It has puffed its way into retailing, paper, and financial services.

B.A.T has become one of the world's great store operators. Its portfolio includes Saks Fifth Avenue and Marshall Field in the United States; 50 percent of Horten, the fourth-largest department store chain in West Germany; and Argos catalog stores (166 branches) and the Jewellers Guild shops (twenty-five units) in its home country, Britain.

In financial services B.A.T—just beginning to get warmed up here— has become one of Britain's ten largest insurance companies; this after the 1984 and 1985 acquisitions of Eagle Star and Hambro Life (since renamed Allied Dunbar). They were the largest takeovers in the history of the British insurance industry. Allied Dunbar manages $6 billion of other people's money.

In the paper industry B.A.T owns Wiggins Teape, a major British manufacturer of specialty papers. (Guess whose paper is used to print the annual report.) Wiggins Teape operates nine mills and factories in Britain as well as manufacturing facilities in Belgium, France, West Germany, Ireland, India, Zambia, and Zimbabwe. In the United States the paper holding is Appleton Papers of Wisconsin, maker of the NCR carbonless copying paper.

B.A.T developed a nervous smoker's habit of buying stuff that it discovered later it didn't really want or didn't know what to do with. In the 1960s, for example, its first diversification moves brought in a purse-full of cosmetics and fragrance houses: Yardley, Lentheric, Morny, Germaine Monteil, Cyclax, Juvena, Tuvache. They were all stubbed out in 1984. Another early acquisition was Mardon Packaging, a British carton manufacturer whose history goes back to the nineteenth century. It went into the ashtray in 1985. B.A.T entered the supermarket business in 1972 by bagging the 440-store International chain in Britain. It was snuffed out in 1984. In the United States B.A.T bought—and later sold—Kohl's supermarkets and Kohl's department stores in Wisconsin and Illinois; the Frederick & Nelson and Crescent department stores in Washington and Oregon (baggage in the Marshall Field acquisition); and the thirty-eight-unit Gimbels department store chain whose main outlets were in New York, Philadelphia, Pittsburgh, and Milwaukee. B.A.T was never really too keen on Gimbels, which was started by Adam Gimbel, an immigrant from Bavaria, in 1842. It was a store with a declassé image, the wrong place to be in the "era of the Yuppies." However, Gimbel Bros. also happened to own the classy Saks Fifth Avenue stores—and it was Saks that B.A.T wanted. The British were told, "No Gimbels, no Saks." In 1973 they bought the entire pack for $200 million. In 1986 they jettisoned Gimbels.

There are other bits and pieces around the globe that tobacco profits have collected. In West Germany B.A.T owns Pegulan, the largest floor covering manufacturer in the country. In Canada it holds 44 percent of Imasco which controls—through its Imperial Tobacco unit—more than half of the Canadian cigarette market; operates Canada's largest drugstore chain, Shoppers Drug Mart; owns the 830-store Peoples Drug chain in the United States; and also operates Hardee's, a U.S. fast-food chain with twenty-five hundred outlets in forty states. B.A.T's 40 percent–owned Australian affiliate, Amatil, is a major poultry producer and the main bottler of Coca-Cola in that country. Hotels in India, furniture manufac-turers in Denmark, and fruit juices and forestlands in Brazil are other B.A.T interests. And if you live in Florida or North Carolina or California or New York, you're shopping in B.A.T satellites when you visit Ivey's, Breuners, and Thimbles.

By 1986 B.A.T had reduced its tobacco dependency to the point where it represented only 49 percent of total sales (but 57 percent of the profits). Its cigarette business was still growing, especially in the develop-ing countries where health warnings are muted, but because of acquisi-tions the nontobacco part was expanding at a much faster pace. B.A.T's next moves in the United States appear to be predictable. It has obviously been captivated by financial services—essentially, managing other people's money—and so if you see a British-accented crew descend on a bank or insurance company in a cloud of smoke, you'll know what's up. Bring out the ashtrays.

B.A.T provides a textbook example of how to run a worldwide business empire. It's done mostly by pushing responsibility down to the national and sector levels, what the company likes to call "devolution of management." Keith Richardson, public affairs chief at the austere London headquarters office, explains, "We are not running a worldwide integrated business." The head office has only one hundred staff members to rule an employee population of 305,000. "That," said Richardson, "must be the most dramatic ratio in the world." Those one hundred people have five functions: finance, legal, personnel, planning, and public affairs. But they are not line operators. The subsidiary companies run their own shows—and are indeed headquartered elsewhere. The tobacco company, for instance, is based one-half mile down the road from B.A.T headquarters. The top people keep in touch by traveling a lot. Patrick Sheehy, who became chairman in 1982 when he was fifty-two years old, spends half his time traveling to B.A.T outposts—he has served with units in Africa and Europe. Three B.A.T directors have had long experience in Brazil. Coming out of World War II, B.A.T had two thousand British expatriates serving overseas. Today only two hundred expatriates work in the overseas companies.

B.A.T has more than 80 percent of its assets outside its home country. The United States and Canada account for 37 percent of the company's turnover, followed by Continental Europe, 29 percent; Britain, 13 percent; Latin America, 12 percent; Asia, 6 percent; and Africa, 3 percent. While B.A.T. has diversified, it's tobacco that's mostly responsible for this worldwide reach.

B.A.T takes a very low-key stance on the health questions related to smoking. It's clearly moving into other areas, but the parent company stands apart almost as a bemused outsider on the issue of smoking and health, leaving the individual companies to grapple with the problem. You'd never know, from reading a B.A.T annual report, that a controversy even existed. Richardson was asked whether the company didn't feel some obligation to put on their cigarette packs sold in the Third World the kind of health warnings that they are required to carry in Britain, the United States, and other countries. His reply: "These are sovereign countries, and they are unenthusiastic about being told what to do by pressure groups in the UK and the United States. We fit in with what the government wants in each country. We let the marketplace decide. We do not try to impose."

It's a far cry from the early days of this company. B.A.T was born a multinational, chartered to do business in every part of the world except Britain and the United States, but it was also born as a missionary for the joys of cigarette smoking. Impose this habit it did, right across the world.

When B.A.T was organized in 1902, it was called British-American Tobacco Company—the prime mover in its affairs was the rapacious James Buchanan Duke, the son of a North Carolina dirt farmer and the creator of the American Tobacco trust. By the turn of the century he had obliterated or absorbed his competition in the United States (he was selling nine out of every ten cigarettes bought), and he was ready to invade Britain to do the same there. Duke's reputation as a bulldozer who captured market share by slashing prices had preceded him. To defend themselves, the Willis brothers, the Player brothers, and the other family-owned British tobacco producers banded together to form the Imperial Tobacco Company. Duke arrived, precipitating a vicious price war whose

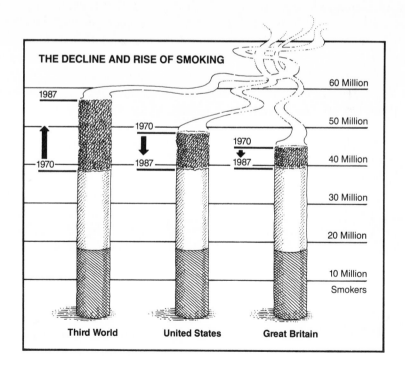

THE DECLINE AND RISE OF SMOKING

main beneficiary was the cigarette smoker. The battle went on for almost a year, and the British then served notice that they would go on the offensive by invading the American market with their cigarette brands.

Duke, whose only interest was conquering the world on behalf of cigarettes, made a deal with his British opponents. They called off their war and sat down to carve up the world cigarette market among themselves. Duke was allowed to keep the United States. Imperial was allowed to keep Britain. And they formed British-American Tobacco to make and sell cigarettes in the rest of the world. Not only that, American Tobacco and Imperial Tobacco assigned to BAT (this is how the acronym looked then) the rights to all their brands. It was stipulated that BAT would never try to enter the British or American markets. BAT made its headquarters in London, but Duke and other American investors took two-thirds of the stock; Imperial held the other third.

The worldwide cigarette cartel lasted nearly a decade. It reached the end of the line on November 16, 1911, when a U.S. Supreme Court decree breaking up the American Tobacco trust went into effect. In addition to restoring competition in the U.S. market, the decree ended American participation in British-American Tobacco. Duke and other American investors sold their stock, and BAT soon became a listed company on the London Stock Exchange. However, BAT never took the "American" out of its name, and Duke continued to serve as chairman until 1923. Moreover, B.A.T retained the brand names of its founding companies, which is why even today one will come across the confusing situation of B.A.T companies in various parts of the world selling cigarettes under the names Lucky Strike, Player, Kent, Pall Mall, and Benson & Hedges. That's a right going back to the founding of the company.

Duke's staying on as chairman of British-American Tobacco even after the breakup reflected his messianic devotion to hooking the world on cigarettes, a mission he imparted to B.A.T. It was not until the twentieth century that cigarette smoking became a popular habit, and technology had a lot to do with making that possible. In 1881 a North Carolinian named James Bonsack invented a machine that could roll tobacco into paper and make cigarettes. Duke was quick to latch onto it, indeed his alertness enabled him to quash his competitors. With that mass production capability, Duke was quick to see that the whole world could be attacked. And it was during the first decade of the century, when the cartel was functioning, that B.A.T began to put down its cigarette outposts in countries around the world, establishing the base for the corporate giant it is today. British-American Tobacco is a company that can legitimately lay claim to have inculcated a habit—cigarette smoking—on a world scale. Indeed, it was chartered precisely to do so.

The most successful of B.A.T's early moves was unquestionably its China adventure, an episode meticulously detailed by historian Sherman Cochran in his 1980 Harvard University Press book *Big Business in China: Sino-Foreign Rivalry in the Cigarette Industry, 1890–1930.* Cochran recounts that after Duke heard about Bonsack's cigarette-making machine his first words were: "Bring me an atlas." The tobacco tycoon thumbed through the atlas, checking not maps but population figures. When he came to China and saw the legend "Pop.: 430,000,000," he reportedly said, "That is where we are going to sell cigarettes." Duke began exporting cigarettes to China in 1890, but it wasn't until the formation of B.A.T that the invasion picked up the force of a steamroller.

Duke was not the first to introduce tobacco in China. It was distributed there as early as the seventeenth century, along with opium, with which it was often mixed for pipe smoking. But Duke and his B.A.T cohorts pioneered the tobacco cigarette in China. It was an auspicious time to spread this addiction because it coincided with vigorous anti-opium campaigns. The Chinese, by the millions, turned in their opium and pipes for cigarettes—and it was B.A.T that orchestrated this switch.

The cigarette's conquest of China was accomplished by Duke through much the same methods he used in the United States. He built plants in China—in Shanghai and Hankow in 1906 and 1907, in Mukden and Harbin in 1909 and 1914—and stocked them with the Bonsack cigarette-making machines. The Hankow plant could turn out ten million cigarettes a day. By 1916, according to Cochran, B.A.T employed thirteen thousand workers in these factories.

B.A.T's invasion of China was no hit-or-miss affair. On the contrary, it was extremely well thought out and executed with thoroughness. B.A.T built up an indigenous Chinese tobacco industry around cigarettes, using Chinese compradors rather than Westerners to open agencies all over the country. Duke was not interested in getting cigarettes into just the easily accessible coastal cities. His missionaries penetrated the Chinese hinterlands, preaching the gospel of cigarette smoking. It was a grand success. Between 1902 and 1920 Chinese consumption of cigarettes went from 1.2 billion a year to 25 billion.

B.A.T used trains, camels, mules, carts, wheelbarrows, and men's backs to reach every corner of China. The advertising techniques that had worked so well in America and Britain were put to use here. Here's Sherman Cochran describing B.A.T's promotion machine:

The B.A.T advertising system left no region of China untouched. In 1905 in Manchuria, for example, B.A.T put up two thousand large paper placards and two hundred large wooden or iron signboards in the city of Ying-kvou—creating an effect that reminded an American journalist of the sensational billing that the Barnum and Bailey circus arranged in advance of its arrival in American cities. In North China a newspaper correspondent in Kaifeng reported in 1907 that the "whole city has been placarded with thousands of staring advertisements," and another correspondent in Sian writing in 1911 described "huge posters on the city gates, city walls, on every vacant piece of wall or board on the street, on the brick strands supporting the masts in front of the yamens, in fact anywhere and everywhere." . . . In the Southeast, according to a report from the British consul in Foochow in 1909, B.A.T agents drummed up business by "preaching the cult of the cigarette and distributing millions gratis so as to introduce a taste for tobacco . . . into regions where it was as yet unknown." . . . Along the Lower, Middle and Upper Yangtze, B.A.T inundated every city from Shanghai to Chungking with advertising, crowning its campaigns with a large billboard placed prominently in the river gorge. . . . By 1915 B.A.T's advertising had so impressed Julean Arnold, U.S. commercial attaché in China, that he urged all American companies interested in advertising to contact and learn from B.A.T.

The Chinese turned out to be such avid smokers that by 1920 B.A.T was earning $7.6 million in China. That accounted for about one-third of its total profits, worldwide. And the habit that B.A.T introduced in China stuck. With a current annual consumption estimated at 760 billion cigarettes a year, China is the world's largest cigarette market. The product that James Duke brought to China, Cochran notes, "is now routinely served to guests (along with tea) as part of Chinese etiquette and is consumed by people throughout Chinese society." It was rare to see Chinese leader Deng Xiaoping without a cigarette in his hand.

World War II ended B.A.T's operations in China but it has high hopes of making a comeback. B.A.T has a cigarette plant in Hong Kong, and in 1986 the company told its shareholders that exports to China doubled during 1985. B.A.T tried to help it along with some hoopla reminiscent of James Duke. In September 1985 it sponsored the first automobile rally seen in China since the Paris-to-Peking race of 1906. Thirty-eight cars participated in the "555 Rally" (555 standing for State Express 555, the B.A.T brand that was the first cigarette smoked by many Chinese). The rally started from Hong Kong on September 15 and ended in Beijing's Square of Heavenly Peace on September 19. The route went through six provinces, some of which had previously been closed to foreigners, and the roadways were lined by crowds estimated by B.A.T publicists to total nine million, which would make it a candidate for a Guinness listing as the largest live audience for any spectator sport. B.A.T didn't say how many of the spectators were smoking but said it was clear that the event "had achieved top level approval," meaning that "our standing with the People's Republic would be enhanced."

B.A.T may have invented the Chinese cigarette market but it won't be so easy to reenter it. The Chinese have their own cigarette industry, and both Philip Morris and R. J. Reynolds have plans to capture the market for their brands.

After the 1911 breakup of the American Tobacco trust, British-American Tobacco was free to enter the American market—and it did so in 1927 by acquiring Brown & Williamson, then a small factor in the industry. However, its agreement with Imperial Tobacco about staying out of the British market remained in force until the 1970s when rules of the new European Economic Community barred such cozy arrangements. Imperial's holdings in B.A.T were sold—and in 1978 the world's largest cigarette maker, a British company, began selling cigarettes in

the British market for the first time in its seventy-six-year history. It had always made them there but just for export. B.A.T, with a huge advertising budget, launched three brands: State Express 555, Du Maurier, and Ardath. It was nothing like the Chinese experience in the early part of the century. Cigarette sales in Britain were declining while their prices, augmented by ever-increasing government taxes, were going up. As a result, after five years of intensive promotion and use of Duke-like tactics of price reductions, B.A.T was able to capture only 5 percent of the British market. In 1984, after losses which may have run as high as $100 million, B.A.T threw in the towel, disbanding its entire sales and distribution force in Britain and halting all advertising for its cigarette brands. It was a defeat that certainly proved Thomas Wolfe's point, "You can't go home again." B.A.T has nicotinized the entire world, but that didn't carry any weight with British smokers, already addicted to other brands.

As befitting its status as an international peddler of cigarettes, B.A.T has its shares listed on ten stock exchanges in Europe as well as on the Montreal Exchange and the American Stock Exchange in New York, where it is one of the most heavily traded issues. It's an institutional favorite. While there are 135,000 shareholders, 71 percent of the stock is held by 520 holders (banks, insurance companies, pension funds, mutual funds), each with at least 250,000 shares.

In mid-1986 B.A.T's market value was $9 billion, which ranked sixteenth among all companies in Europe.

Access   50 Victoria St.
London SW 1H ONL, England
(44) 1-222-7979

BATUS Inc.
2000 Citizens Plaza
Louisville, Ky. 40202
(502) 581-8000

Bayer	**Sales** $21.2 billion
	Profits $830 million
	U.S. Sales $4.1 billion
	Rank World's largest chemical company
	World's largest maker of pesticides and
	herbicides
	Germany's 5th-largest company
	World's 5th-largest drug producer
	World's largest maker of painkillers
	Europe's largest producer of photographic
	equipment
	Founded 1863
	Employees 173,000 (24,400 in the United States)
	Headquarters Leverkusen, West Germany

Germany in all its faces—war maker, bastion of scientific expertise, exterminator of Jews and dissidents, home to intellectual and cultural giants—is mirrored in the history of Bayer, a seemingly indestructible pillar of the German industrial establishment and the worldwide chemical industry. Bayer survived four wars, two of which Germany lost, and numerous mergers, acquisitions, dismemberments, bombings, and other calamities, to emerge in the 1980s as the world's largest maker of chemical products. It is institutional resilience of a high order, similar to the properties of synthetic rubber (which Bayer was the first to make), and it may have required many tablets of headache-relieving aspirin, which became the most widely used drug in the history of medicine after Bayer invented it in 1899.

Perhaps Bayer's darkest day was July 29, 1948, when Curtis Grover Shake, former judge of the Indiana Supreme Court, imposed sentence on the twelve I. G. Farben executives found guilty at Nuremberg of war crimes. I. G. Farben was the cartel formed in 1925 by the consolidation of the major German chemical companies, the most prominent of which were BASF, Bayer, and Hoechst. During World War II Farben operated synthetic rubber and oil plants adjacent to the Auschwitz concentration camp, thereby cinching a cheap supply of labor; when the inmates were no longer able to work, they were returned to the camp for execution by a lethal gas manufactured by another Farben unit. One of those sentenced on that day was Dr. Fritz ter Meer, the highest-ranking scientist on the I. G. Farben managing board. Found guilty of slavery and mass murder, he was sentenced to jail for seven years.

Three years later, contrary to Dwight D. Eisenhower's original plan to dismantle I. G. Farben and chop it into tiny pieces, the pre-1925 order

47

was restored with the reestablishment of BASF, Bayer, and Hoechst as independent companies. The Big Three were back in business. In 1963, on the first day of August, fifteen years and three days after the Nuremberg sentencing, Bayer celebrated its one hundredth birthday at the Cologne fairgrounds on the banks of the Rhine River. Guests from five continents attended the gala ceremonies, which opened with the Bayer Philharmonic Orchestra playing Handel's "Music for Fireworks" and ended with the playing of Wagner's "Meistersinger" overture. The opening address, reflecting on the early years of Bayer, was delivered by Dr. ter Meer, rehabilitated now as chairman of the supervisory board of Bayer. "One hundred years of company history have been shaped by outstanding men," he told the gathering.

The first of these men were Friedrich Bayer and his friend, Johann Friedrich Weskott, who formed Friedrich Bayer & Company in 1863 to make aniline dyestuffs at Barmen-Rittershausen on the Wupper River in the Upper Ruhr Valley. Otto von Bismarck had just come to power in Prussia, unifying the German states for successful wars against Denmark, Austria, and France. Meanwhile, the modern chemical industry was being born in Germany, hatched by synthetic dyestuffs. Most of the companies that entered the field (and there were many) died, but Bayer turned out to be a survivor. Few men were more responsible for that survival than Dr. Karl Duisberg, a brilliant chemist and inventor who became head of research at Bayer in 1884 when he was only twenty-two years old. Duisberg created the research laboratories and research discipline that enabled Bayer to make one breakthrough after another. Prior to his arrival chemists practiced a lonely individualism in which secrets were never divulged, not even to colleagues.

BASF and Hoechst are formidable companies, but neither has discovered as many notable products as Bayer. From the Bayer labs, in addition to aspirin, have come phenacetin, the antipyretic; Atebrin, the most effective anti-malarial agent; Germanin, the first drug to safely combat the sleeping sickness infection transmitted in tropical areas by the tsetse fly; Prontosil, the first sulfa drug, for which Bayer scientist Gerhard Domagk won the Nobel prize in 1939. Bayer introduced heroin as a cure for morphine addiction and as a cough suppressant. And just before World War II Bayer developed methadone as a morphine substitute, brand naming it Dolophine in honor of Adolf Hitler. Bayer was the first company to make synthetic rubber, it pioneered in insecticides and mothproofing agents, and it developed the AGFA photographic business.

According to Joseph Borkin, author of *The Crime and Punishment of I. G. Farben,* the first poison gas to be used by the German army in World War I came from a Bayer laboratory. Borkin said that Duisberg, by that time chairman of Bayer, "not only committed Bayer to the poison gas project but also involved himself personally in the experiments." Borkin, who was chief of the patent and cartel section of the U.S. Department of Justice from 1938 to 1946, characterized Duisberg as a "superb opportunist, never permitting devotion to principle to interfere with expediency. Whether under the Kaiser, the Weimar Republic, or the Nazis, he always made the required adjustments, and he never failed to prosper."

One unfortunate consequence to Bayer of Germany's loss in World War I was that the company lost the right to the Bayer name in the United States. Its American properties were seized after the United States entered the war, and on December 12, 1918, just a month and a day after the armistice, they were sold for $5.3 million to a small American company, Sterling Drug, marketer of a candied laxative, Cascarets. As a result, the Bayer aspirin sold in the United States belongs to Sterling, while the German Bayer company continues to sell Bayer aspirin in the rest of the world.

Bayer lost another chunk of American business as a result of Germany's defeat in World War II. Its half interest in the prescription drug manufacturer Winthrop Laboratories was bought for $9.5 million by the same Sterling Drug, which already owned the other half. In 1946 Sterling also bought out Bayer's 50 percent interest in Bayer of Canada.

Bayer's growth after its rebirth in 1951 was astounding. By 1985 its sales were nearly double Dow Chemical's, near triple 3M's, and nearly six times Merck's. It divides its business into six sectors: polymers; organic chemicals, dyes, and pigments; inorganic chemicals, polyurethanes, coating raw materials; health care; agrochemicals; and Agfa-Gevaert. Each of these sectors spans the world. In 1986 Bayer had 350 operating companies in sixty-eight countries and was deriving 80 percent of its sales outside West Germany. It's the most international of the German chemical companies. The United States alone accounts for about 20 percent of the total, and U.S. sales exceed Germany's. Bayer's two main holdings in the United States are Pittsburgh-based Mobay (which it originally started as a partnership with Monsanto, hence the name), a maker of polyurethanes, speciality plastics, and other materials for the automotive industry; and Elkhart, Indiana–based Miles Laboratories, maker of Alka-Seltzer and One-A-Day vitamins. Other Bayer holdings in the United States include Cutter Laboratories and Compugraphic.

The stories of Bayer's involvement in world wars I and II can be juxtaposed with a long record of social benefit and cultural activities inside the company. Bayer established a relief fund for workers in 1873. It started to pay for holidays in 1888. It put up an outpatient hospital at one of its factories in 1898. It has long subsidized housing for employees. It owns 24,100 apartments, which are rented out to employees, and it has given low-interest loans to 17,100 workers to enable them to buy their own homes. Bayer claims to have, among companies, the biggest twenty-five-year club in the world—one out of every ten employees. Nearly thirty-eight thousand are stockholders who can buy shares at a preferential rate and who together own 3 percent of the company.

Cultural activities go far back too. A brass band was formed in 1901; a string orchestra (today's Bayer Philharmonic) in 1904; a men's chorus, also in 1904, and a drama group in 1908. Today the company's Cultural Department supports more than seventy different clubs, including company teams in basketball, handball, water polo, rowing, sailing, and other sports. Notable too are the library facilities maintained at the Leverkusen headquarters. A technical library contains more than four hundred thousand books, fifty-five thousand doctoral dissertations, and fifty-five hundred journals; it's the largest private special library in Germany. A general library for use by employees has an inventory of more than 120,000 books, magazines, newspapers, records, cassettes, slides, and games.

Bayer's main factory at Leverkusen on the banks of the Rhine River is one of the world's largest industrial complexes, stretching over 840 acres and comprising more than six hundred buildings. Nearly forty thousand people work there. Leverkusen also houses the corporate headquarters. Towering over the complex is a 394-foot Bayer cross, weighing (including the foundation) three hundred tons and illuminated by 1,680 electric bulbs. (Leverkusen is named after Dr. Carl Leverkus, a doctor-druggist-businessman whose dyestuff factories were bought by Bayer in 1891 and 1917.)

Research is the thread that holds this company together. Forty percent of the products it sells today came out of the labs since 1971. The annual research budget, nearing $1 billion, is one of the largest in the world. Some 13,000 people (8,200 of them in Germany) work in research and development. In 1978 Bayer began putting up a huge agricultural chemical research center in Monheim just south of the Ruhr Valley; when it's completed in 1988, it will hold seventeen buildings on a 130-acre site. The cost to Bayer: $400 million.

The head of Bayer has nearly always been a chemist. But that tradition was broken in 1984 with the selection of Hermann J. Strenger as

World's Ten Largest Chemical Companies

		Sales
1.	Bayer (West Germany)	$21.2 billion
2.	BASF (West Germany)	21.0 billion
3.	Hoechst (West German)	19.7 billion
4.	Du Pont (United States)	15.8 billion
5.	ICI (Britain)	15.0 billion
6.	Dow (United States)	11.1 billion
7.	Ciba-Geigy (Switzerland)	9.9 billion
8.	Monetedison (Italy)	9.5 billion
9.	Shell (Anglo-Dutch)	8.6 billion
10.	Rhône-Poulenc (France)	8.2 billion

Note: Based on 1986 chemical sales.

chairman of the board of management. Strenger joined Bayer in 1949 as a commercial trainee and worked his way up through the chemical sales department. He has worked in Brazil and Sweden. In 1985, when he faced his first annual meeting at the fairgrounds in Cologne, Strenger was confronted with a record turnout of 5,900 shareholders and visitors, among whom were activists supporting resolutions that decried Bayer's effect on the environment. The meeting took more than eight hours to conclude, with the shareholders backing management with a 99 percent plurality. According to a postmeeting report issued by Bayer, "Herr Strenger refuted the assertions and accusations point for point and emphasized that 'the protection of man and his environment is part of our company's philosophy.' "

There's nothing like having an objective observer present.

As befitting its international scope, 39 percent of Bayer's stock is now in foreign hands. The biggest chunk, 14 percent, is held in Switzerland. U.S. holders account for 4 percent. Bayer's stock is traded only in West Germany.

In 1986 Bayer did regain the right to use its name on some products in the United States. By paying Sterling Drug $25 million, it was given permission to put the Bayer cross on industrial products and chemicals. The company then formed a new U.S. holding company, Bayer USA, which it placed in Pittsburgh (home of Mobay). Watch soon for the other shoe to drop: Bayer acquires Sterling Drug.

Access Bayer A. G.
5090 Leverkusen
Federal Republic of Germany
(49) 214-301

Bayer USA
500 Grant St.
Pittsburgh, Pa. 15219-2502
(412) 394-5554

Beecham Group

Sales	$3.9 billion
Profit	$270 million
U.S. Sales	$1.4 billion
Rank	21st-largest company in Britain
	2d-largest health-care company in Britain
	Holds 25 percent of British toothpaste market
	4th-largest seller of toothpaste in the United States
	1st in U.S. acne treatment market
	Leader of the U.S. antacid market
	Britain's leading hot chocolate maker
	Largest hair shampoo seller in Britain
	Holds 50 percent of U.S. market for musk fragrances
	Holds 50 percent of U.S. market for vaginal douches
	Leading U.S. seller of throat lozenges
	World's 7th-largest cosmetics company
	One of world's leading producers of antibiotics
Founded	1850
Employees	42,300
Headquarters	Brentford, England

In mid-1986 the Beecham Group was probably the only organization in the world whose product lineup included glue, gin, and a home-testing kit for pregnancy. If you had used them in that order, you might have also needed some Tums, which Beecham also made. The mélange did result in indigestion—for Beecham. Before long the glue and the gin were regurgitated. In the twelve months ending in June 1987 Beecham sold off thirteen different businesses.

But a lot was left.

From a single product—Beecham's Pills—this company has advanced to the point where it stocks a huge medicine chest with prescription and over-the-counter drugs, sells a wide variety of toiletries, tonics, cosmetics, and fragrances, and fields assorted food and beverage products. Ask for Brylcreem, Massengill, Macleans, Aquafresh, Geritol, Rose Milk, Femiron, Sominex, Aqua Velva, Vitabath, Sucrets, Calgon, Scott's Cod Liver Oil, Vivarin, Serutan, Lectric Shave, Jovan musk, Yardley, or Diane von Furstenberg fragrances and cosmetics—and you will have specified a Beecham product.

Most of these brands came to Beecham through acquisitions on both sides of the Atlantic. In its home country Beecham has become the supplier of quintessential British foods—Bovril meat extract to flavor stews, Marmite yeast extract to spread on toast for children at tea time, Ambrosia creamed rice pudding for dessert, and Horlick's hot chocolate before retiring at night. In the United States one of its most recent acquisitions was the Norcliff-Thayer arm of Revlon for $395 million in January 1986. It was this purchase that brought Tums and the Oxy acne medications into the Beecham column. Four years earlier Beecham paid $100 million to buy another U.S. company, J. B. Williams, which Nabisco had tired of. The Williams medicine chest included the Lectric Shave and Aqua Velva shaving lotions, Geritol vitamin supplement, Sominex sleep aid, and Vivarin stimulant tablets.

However, Beecham's biggest source of income today is its relatively unsung pharmaceutical division, whose research scientists, experimenting in a country house twenty-five miles from London, scored a breakthrough in the synthesis of penicillin in the late 1950s which led to the development of broad-spectrum antibiotics effective against a wide range of infections. In terms of new prescriptions, Beecham's Amoxil is the most widely used antibiotic in the United States, and its newer compound, Augmentin, had been prescribed more than one million times by U.S. physicians within six months of its being approved for use at the start of 1985. "People are bored with the fact that our results are so consistently good," Sir Ronald Halstead, Beecham's chairman and chief executive, was quoted as saying.

A month later, in November 1985, Sir Ronald was sacked in a boardroom coup led by Lord Keith of Castleacre, a former chairman of the Rolls-Royce aircraft engine company, who spoke bluntly of a need for "younger and more dynamic management" and hinted at a new strategy of selling off companies instead of buying them: "For the first time we are saying, 'Do we really want to be in that business?' "

That the answer to this question was frequently "no" was clear from the cathartic moves taken by the company in 1986. Purged from the Beecham lineup were Unibond adhesives and Copydex tapes (acquired in 1984 and 1985); a milk delivery business in the West of England; Batchelors canned and frozen foods in Ireland; the soft drinks Corona, Tango, Quosh, Hints, and Idris; the Diplona hair-care products marketed in Germany; and a big chunk of its Findlater wine and spirits business. And as 1987 dawned Beecham was still looking desperately for someone to buy the Germaine Monteil business in the United States that Beecham acquired in 1984 when it paid $150 million for the cosmetics operations of B.A.T Industries. It was this purchase that swung the Yardley, Lentheric, Morny, and Juvenal brands into the Beecham column. Germaine Monteil was in the red when it was acquired, and two years later it was still losing money.

The other big news at Beecham in 1986 was its hunt for a new leader. After Sir Ronald Halstead was sent on his way with a golden handshake of some $600,000 (he then became deputy chairman of British Steel), Beecham tried to find a proper replacement in Britain. After six months Lord Keith admitted in a television interview that no suitable candidate could be found. So the search widened to Continental Europe, the United States, Australia, and the Far East, with more than one hundred prospects flushed out. In August the executive search firm Russell Reynolds came up with the winner: Robert P. Bauman, fifty-five-year-old deputy chairman of Textron Inc., the American conglomerate. In moving from Providence, Rhode Island, to Beecham's art deco headquarters west of London, Bauman accepted a salary estimated at between $750,000 and $1 million a year, making him one of the highest-paid executives in European business. For finding him Russell Reynolds pocketed a fee of one third of Bauman's first-year salary.

Bauman is one of the few Americans to head up a European-based company (Richard Giordano, chairman of British Oxygen, is another), but it's not an unlikely scenario. Beecham operates twenty-three factories in the United States and derives more than one quarter of its business from the American market. And Beecham's history in the United States goes back to the last century. The company takes its name from Thomas Beecham, the eldest of seven children of a farm laborer in Oxfordshire. Beecham was born in 1820 and started working when he was eight years old. As a young boy he became interested in the medicinal properties of herbs, and when he was a teenager, he started to sell these nostrums in country markets. In 1847 he moved to the North of England, where factories were sucking people off the land, and he set himself up in Wigan as a druggist selling medicines, including the soon-to-be-celebrated Beecham's Pills, a laxative for constipated Britons. In 1859 he ran his first newspaper ads for Beecham's Pills and began manufacturing the product in the Merseyside city of St. Helens, not far from where William Hesketh Lever was to begin his grand soap business a quarter century later.

Beecham and Lever were part of the advance guard of modern advertising. They pushed their products relentlessly and not just in Britain. Beecham's Pills became one of the most well known brand names in the world on the wings of a promotional campaign that, in the last two decades of the nineteenth century, saw ads for Beecham's Pills appear regularly in fourteen thousand newspapers around the world. By the early twentieth century the factory at St. Helens was turning out one million pills a day!

Beecham formally retired from his business in 1895 but continued to be active until 1907, when he died at eighty-seven. His son, Joseph, who had joined the business in the 1860s, continued to run it until he died in 1916. It was Joseph who built up the American side of the business. Beecham's Pills was registered as a U.S. trademark in 1887, and a year later D. F. Allen of Canal Street in New York City began manufacturing them under license. According to the archives of the company, Joseph used to come to the United States twice a year to mix the secret formula of the pills. Joseph also kept the U.S. business separate form the one in Britain, and the profits from the American operation went into his private account. The profits were not inconsiderable. Between 1906 and 1911 the sales of the American company more than doubled to $100,000 a year. By 1920 the American business was throwing off a profit of $73,000 on sales of $300,000. By that time the American company was owned by Joseph's son Henry. Joseph gave the U.S. company to him in 1914. Joseph's other son Thomas had no interest in selling pills. He took his inheritance and embarked on the career that would make him a world-famous orchestral conductor.

The Beecham business on both sides of the Atlantic came under the control of a London property developer, Philip Hill, in 1924. He bought the Beecham estate primarily because it included the ground underneath London's Covent Garden Market and Opera House. Joseph had bought this property in 1914. Once Hill acquired it, however, he saw that the pill business was not something to discard. In 1928 he formed Beecham's Pills Limited, and the company soon adopted the strategy that still guides it today: expand by buying others. Veno's cough medicine and Germolene antiseptic products came aboard in 1928; Macleans toothpaste in 1938; the Lucozade glucose drink (is it a drink or a medicine?), also in 1938; Eno's 'Fruit Salt' (another laxative for constipated Britons), also in 1938; Brylcreem in 1939; the Bristow and Silvikrin hair-care businesses in 1946 and 1949, respectively.

The architect of the post–World War II transformation of Beecham was H. G. Lazell. He joined Beecham as an office boy when he was thirteen years old in 1916, became an accountant in his spare time and worked his way up until he reached the top in 1951. He retired in 1968 and died in 1982 at the age of seventy-nine. Lazell had the vision to provide (against the advice of many of his Beecham colleagues) the financial support for the research scientists who eventually synthesized penicillin. He also insisted, in a throwback to the founder, that the company build up strong brand names with blockbuster single-theme advertising. While he was in command, a Beecham ad never made more than one claim (Brylcreem's "a little dab'll do you" was one that ran for many years, and Macleans rode to the top of the British toothpaste market with its single-minded promise to deliver whiteness). Finally, Lazell recognized that to become a major player in drugs and toiletries, Beecham had to establish a strong beachhead in the American market.

In acquiring American companies, Beecham picked up various pieces of baggage. With Geritol it inherited a Federal Trade Commission cease-and-desist order barring claims that the mixture could cure "tired blood." And with Jovan musk oil it inherited ad copy hailing "the exciting scent that has stimulated passion since time began . . . it releases the animal instinct . . . your sensual power." Asked the meaning of the product's name, its developer, a Chicago adman named Bernard Mitchell, replied, "It doesn't have any. I picked it because Revlon had six letters, and Avon had four, and I didn't want to confuse people."

One of the shibboleths of consumer goods marketers is that success means coming up with new products. In recent times, however, this has not been Beecham's long suit. In 1985 it revved up a multimillion-dollar drive in the United States to introduce Delicare, a cold water fine-fabric detergent aimed at market leader Woolite. It flopped badly. In the mid-1980s then, the talk around Beecham was about pumping money into old products like Brylcreem and Lucozade, what Fiona McEwan of the *Financial Times* called "Beecham's born-again brands." It seemed to make sense to Beecham's new million-dollar-a-year chairman, Robert Bauman, who said, "Beecham has been very efficient in the past at giving old brands new life, and growing that way is much more efficient." (It's called recycling your old winners.)

Watch then for the rejuvenation of Beecham's Pills. Beecham's powders are still big sellers in Britain as cold remedies, but to most people in the world today Beecham's Pills mean nothing. Look up Beecham in the American Heritage Dictionary and there's a reference to Sir Thomas Beecham (1879–1961), who founded the London Philharmonic Orchestra in 1932. There's not a word about Beecham's Pills, a byword of the nineteenth century.

British Co-Ops Flounder

Once a powerful force in British retailing, the co-ops have fallen on lean times there. They are losing members and stores and market share. Since 1980 the number of co-op stores has dropped from nine thousand to six thousand. Customer-shareholders have declined from ten million to eight million. And their share of retail sales has fallen from 6.4 percent to 5.2 percent.

The British co-op movement, which spread to many other countries, including the United States, started in the 1840s in the Lancashire textile town of Rochdale.

Access   Beecham House
Brentford
Middlesex TW8 9BD, England
(44) 1-560-5151

Beecham Inc.
65 Industrial S.
Clifton, N.J. 07012
(201) 778-9000

Benetton	**Sales** $830 million
	Profits $87 million
	U.S. Sales $200 million
	Rank World's largest chain of sportswear stores
	World's largest manufacturer of knitwear
	World's largest consumer of virgin wool
	Founded 1965
	Employees 2,200
	Headquarters Ponzano, Italy

I f anybody has a yarn to spin about literally pulling the wool over the world's eyes, it's the Benetton bunch. Starting with a simple idea for brightly colored, dramatic sweater designs, an Italian family knitted a network of sportswear stores with a global reach—and in the mid-1980s it was still unraveling.

Luciano Benetton, fatherless by age ten and the eldest of four children, went to work when he was fifteen as a salesman in a men's clothing store in Treviso, his hometown is twenty miles northwest of Venice. His sister, Giuliana, who early on showed a flair for design (as a child she knitted colorful sweaters for friends and family members), began working when she was thirteen in one of Treviso's small knitting workshops. According to some stories he persuaded her—according to other accounts, she persuaded him. In any case, in 1955 (when Luciano was twenty years old and Giuliana eighteen) she sold his accordion and their younger brother Carlo's bicycle to buy a knitting machine on which she could try out her sweater designs. Luciano's role was to sell what she made. Her striking, moderately priced sweaters (made of wool that was softened by being beaten in water), sold well; indeed they sold so well that in 1965 the Benettons set up their own company and factory in Ponzano, a little village just outside Treviso. Joining them were the two other Benetton siblings, Carlo and the youngest brother, Gilberto.

Twenty years later Benetton was still headquartered in Ponzano. The three Benetton brothers and their sister were still leaders of the company. But their command post had been relocated to the seventeenth-century Villa Minelli, named for nobles of Venice who used to trade the summertime languors of the urban lagoon for the quiet, sweet-smelling, grape growing greenery of Ponzano. The villa has been completely restored, right down to the last painted cherub on its walls and high ceilings. Now the halls resound to the clicking of typewriters and the whir of computers. No Faustian spinning wheels spin here.

Benetton is, in fact, a child of the computer age. People who sell clothing usually have to live with the uncertain tyranny of fashion. If the garments they make suddenly go out of style, they can get stuck with a lot of merchandise. That's why security analysts who specialize in the apparel industry pay very close attention to the line on the balance sheet called "inventory." The Benettons have figured out a way to beat this system; or at least they think they have. They start with neutral, unbleached fibers and then dye a percentage of the finished garments according to daily field reports on which styles and colors customers are buying. We hear often enough about living in an age where information can be transmitted instantly from one end of the world to the other. The Benettons have harnessed that transmission system to its business. If young girls in Brazil start to buy green V-neck sweaters, Benetton in Ponzano knows about it right away, just as it learns quickly if Yuppies in San Francisco are opting for pastel pullovers. It is therefore able to react instantly to sales trends. Instead of trying to set those trends, Benetton follows them.

While Benetton has become one of the most widely distributed lines of apparel in the world, you can't buy any of its garments in a department store. You must go to a Benetton store to find Benetton garments. (And if there's not one near you now, there will be soon.) However, with the exception of a handful, Benetton doesn't own the stores. They are locally owned by licensees who put up their own money to open them. They don't pay a royalty on sales to Benetton. They simply have to order from Benetton and no one else. And they have to lay out their stores in a pattern stitched in Ponzano. It's a scheme that has enabled Benetton to expand with the speed of an automatic sewing machine (and with little risk).

The first shop was opened in 1968 in the nearby Alpine town of Belluno. The next ones followed in the ski resort of Cortina d'Ampezzo, the university city of Padua, and the southern Italian resort of Bari. By 1975 Benetton had two hundred shops in Italy. The company went international in 1969 with the opening of a Paris store. In 1983, 1984, and 1985 it opened one new store a day, on the average, bringing its worldwide total to thirty-two hundred in fifty-seven countries, including shops in Prague, Belgrade, and Budapest. It was the first Western company to penetrate the Iron Curtain on the retail level. In 1986 Benettons were opening at the rate of two a day, bringing the store count at the end of the year to more than four thousand. The company's goal for 1990 is seven thousand stores. The United States, which had more than six hundred stores at the end of 1986, is ticketed for four thousand sometime in the 1990s.

A Benetton in Tokyo's Ginza will resemble a Benetton on New York's Fifth Avenue. They won't be identical, but the decor and ambiance will be similar. A Benetton is a small shop with a flagrant green-and-white front. Sweaters are placed in open shelves that climb from floor to ceiling. Benetton clothes are nearly always made of natural fibers and meant to be handled. Instead of a spacious, gracious look, Benetton strives for a crowded, noisy environment. Music blares. You could go from a Hard Rock Cafe to a Benetton and never have to adjust your eardrums. Italian designer Tobia Scarpia designed the Benetton store look. Licensees have a dozen different store schemes from which to choose. Benetton is also not afraid of having stores chock-a-block. Fifth Avenue between 34th and 53rd streets has six Benettons. They are not identical. They even carry different merchandise. But it all comes from Benetton.

Benetton sold forty-five million garments in 1986—sweaters, jeans, shirts, caps, slacks, skirts, jumpers, jackets, tunics, tights, vests. It's predominantly casual clothing, described by some as "trendy classic," by others as "traditional chic." They feature vivid colors but are never intended to make a far-out fashion statement. And the customers, whether they be in Peru or Japan or the United States, tend to be the same: young and female. The clothes come from a host of Italian subcontractors and nine Benetton factories: five in Italy, and one each in Spain, France, Scotland, and the United States (Rocky Mount, North Carolina). According to one story in *The Wall Street Journal*, Benetton makes no more than 20 percent of its garments, farming out production to some three hundred small companies. Another story, in the *Financial Times*, said the subcontractors include thirteen clothing companies that are owned by the Benettons.

The complex of Benetton facilities around Treviso is a marvel of automation. Sweaters are designed on computers which drive giant knitting machines. In the village of Castrette the company put up, at a cost of $25 million, a cavernous warehouse where robots do all the work: twelve thousand packages are processed in an eight-hour shift. The staff numbers five. Benetton's system of subcontracting and its heavy commitment to automation may explain why there are so few employees for a company whose sales in a labor-intensive industry are approaching $1 billion. But it's still somewhat of a mystery that no reporter has managed to penetrate. It's not clear where the Benetton factories are located and who the workers are. The Benetton annual report is of no help. While it has striking photographs of multicolored children wearing the multicolored Benetton clothes, there are no pictures of any employees, nor is there any mention of employees, not even the number on the payroll.

The philosophy behind this spectacular growth has never been set down by the Benettons themselves, but it has eked out in bits and pieces during interviews with Luciano Benetton, whose round face framed in a mop of curly hair falling to his shoulders is by now a familiar sight in Italian newspapers and magazines. The fullest exposition came in a profile of Luciano by Andrea Lee in the November 10, 1986, issue of *The New Yorker.* He explained that in selecting store operators, Benetton looks for people with "the right spirit." They do not need previous merchandising experience. Luciano once told another interviewer, "The classic shop-keeper had to be killed, and we killed him." Benetton also doesn't believe in written contracts and lawyers. "It is really a rapport made of hand-shakes, of understanding, and knowledge on a human level, and also of extreme faith, total faith," he told Lee, adding, "Let's say that we work only with people whom we like on a human level. This has never been said before, but we're not interested in being represented in a city, in being represented at all, if the partner isn't to our liking."

Like Coca-Cola and Pepsi-Cola, Benetton makes a fashion or cultu-ral statement in its advertising, which shows Benetton-clad children of different races and nationalities. The original campaign was called, "Ben-etton—All the Colors in the World." The ads are done by the Italian photographer and graphic designer Oliviero Toscani, and if they resemble the graphics of the San Francisco apparel house Esprit, that's not surpris-ing. Toscani does those too. Andrea Lee, *The New Yorker* writer, believes the Toscani ads "strike the exact note of the young mood in Europe in

THE BENETTON BUNCH

the mid-eighties, in which a kind of survivalist pragmatism—born of the new conservatism, nuclear worries, and ever-increasing unemployment figures—is balanced with a cautious altruism. They reflect as well the eclectic feel of a Europe flooded with non-European races and cultures. The open stress that the company lays on its techniques of mass production—'It's industrial fashion,' Luciano Benetton remarks in interview after interview—comes over as a wry, stylish, 'in' joke to a generation raised with high technology."

Lee also placed the rise of Benetton in the context of a phenomenon that Italians call the "Third Italy" (signifying the regions around Ancona, Bologna, Florence, and Venice) as distinguished from the "First Italy" in the South, and the "Second Italy" centered in the industrial strongholds of Milan, Turin, and Genoa. In recent years the Third Italy has enjoyed the fastest economic growth in the nation. It's characterized by a maze of small companies, nearly all nonunion, popping up in areas that were previously agricultural.

For all its pretensions of modernity, Benetton is beginning to take on all the trappings of an old-fashioned wheeler-dealer. It owns a Scottish cashmere company, Hogg of Hawick, and an Italian shoe maker, Varese; it has an international holding company whose base was moved in 1985 from Luxembourg to the Netherlands; it's planning to license its name for use on a whole range of non-apparel items (toys, cosmetics, watches, household linen). It has branched out into factoring, leasing, banking, and insurance; and in June 1986 it sold 20 percent of its shares to the public in a flotation that gave it a listing on the Milan Stock Exchange and an instant market value of more than $1 billion.

While Benetton went public in 1986, the Benetton siblings continued to run the show. Luciano, who turned fifty-two in May 1987, was at the helm. Giuliana, fifty, was in charge of design. Carlo, forty-eight, headed production. And Gilberto, forty-six, directed finance and sponsorship of sporting events such as the Formula One auto racing team and their semi-pro basketball team. The Benettons are avid sports fans, especially when it comes to basketball. They built Treviso's sports stadium where they can be frequently seen as spectators. There should be plenty of Benettons on future teams. Luciano and Giuliana each have four children; Carlo, five; Gilberto, two.

They will inherit the most global of all Italian businesses. At the start of 1987 Benetton was selling in sixty countries, and exports accounted for 61 percent of total revenues. The world breakdown of sales was: Europe, 70.5 percent; North America, 26.4 percent; the rest of the world, 3.1 percent.

Access Via Chiesa
Ponzano 24,
Italy
(39) 422-6961

767 Fifth Ave.
New York, N.Y. 10153
(212) 593-0290

Beretta	**Sales** $120 million
	Profits $1 million
	U.S. Sales $30 million
	Rank Italy's largest small-arms maker
	World's 4th-largest handgun maker
	Founded 1526
	Employees 2,500 (500 in the United States)
	Headquarters Gardone Valtrompia, Italy

The Beretta family has been making guns in the Brescia province of northern Italy for nearly five hundred years, and they have won a worldwide following, on both sides of the law. Beretta makes every kind of light gun—rifles, pistols, submachine guns—in all kinds of shapes and calibers, and its weapons have been pressed into service by armies, police forces, and criminal gangs. James Bond's favorite weapon was the snub-nosed 6.35-mm Beretta 950. Shotguns made by Beretta are traditional winners of the trap and skeet shooting competition at the Olympic Games. In 1986 Berettas were being supplied to the police forces of India, Ecuador, Nigeria, Indonesia, Iraq, and, naturally, Italy, as well as to the state police departments of Connecticut and Wyoming.

In one of the signal triumphs of its long history, the company (whose formal name is Fabrica d'Armi Pietro Beretta S.p.A.) was selected in 1985 to supply the standard sidearm for all branches of the U.S. military. The Pentagon placed an order for 315,000 of Beretta's 9-mm, sixteen-shot pistols. At $75 million (including spare parts), it was said to be the contract of the century, as much for the prestige as the dollar revenues. Beretta's 9-mm pistol sells for $500. The Pentagon is getting a special price of $179.

The contract called for the first fifty thousand weapons to be made at Beretta's home plant in Gardone Valtrompia, the rest to be assembled (from parts made in Italy) at Beretta's U.S. plant in Accokeek, Maryland, near Washington, D.C.

Beretta won the Pentagon contract in a shootout with seven other companies: two from Germany; two from the United States; and one each from Austria, Switzerland, and Belgium. The Belgian bidder was Fabrique Nationale of Liege, reputed to be the largest gun maker in the world, a major supplier of the NATO forces in Europe and, incidentally, a 36 percent owner of Beretta. One of the German entrants was Karl Walther, maker of the gun Adolf Hitler used to kill himself. In the end the competition, which stretched over five years, came down to the Beretta and the

SIG-Sauer handgun jointly made by Saco Defense of Saco, Maine, and a Swiss company, SIG (Schweizwerische Industrie Gesellschaft). Beretta's pistol won out for these reasons:

- Interchangeability: having a 9-mm barrel, it could use the same ammunition used by the armed forces of the other members of the North Atlantic Treaty Organization (previously, the U.S. military was the only member not to use a 9-mm pistol as the standard sidearm).
- Safety: it has a double security device.
- Lightness: it weighs only a little over two pounds.
- Easy handling: lefthanders and righthanders found it easy to use, as did female officers, because of its reduced recoil.
- Durability: NATO specifies that a small firearm should be good for roughly seven thousand shots. The U.S. Marine Corps found the Beretta working well after thirty thousand shots.

The .38 caliber Beretta replaces the famous Colt .45, the pistol used by the American military forces since 1911. Its maker, Colt Industries, was not even in the final running, but its passing was certainly lamented. Columnist James Brady said, "First they got rid of the saber, then the cavalry, and now the .45. After seventy-four years as the standard sidearm for soldiers, sailors and marines, the .45 is being tossed aside in favor of the sort of weapon traditionally carried by card sharks and painted women."

Although the Beretta was the winner on the firing range, it still had a political fight on its hands. Smith & Wesson, a division of Bangor Punta and the handgun supplier to forty-six state police departments in the United States, complained about the test procedures and rallied support in Congress from politicians who thought it impolitic to equip the armed forces with a foreign make. In August 1986 the House Appropriations Committee voted, twenty-four to twelve, to stop payments on the Beretta contract until Smith & Wesson had another shot at the business. The resolution was opposed by the Pentagon and needed to pass both the House and the Senate to take effect. It didn't, and the Beretta contract went forward. In Gardone Valtrompe, Pier Guiseppe Beretta, chairman of the Italian gun maker and the twelfth-generation Beretta to head the company, noted that the competition was "won fairly by the best product," adding, "Suspension would be justified only by purely political reasons."

The first Beretta to make guns was Bartolomeo Beretta, known as the master barrel maker of Gardone. He was born in 1490, shortly after gunpowder made its way to Europe from China. His twelfth-generation descendant, Guiseppe Beretta, was in his seventies when the Pentagon award was made. The chief executive officer of the company since 1980 is Guiseppe's nephew, Ugo Gassali Beretta; his mother is a Beretta and he added her name to his. Born in Brescia, Ugo Gassali started working in the Beretta factory when he was twenty-one. He was forty-nine years old in 1986.

Hunting rifles account for 70 percent of Beretta's production today. The company turns out 140,000 sporting guns a year. Its most expensive rifle sells for $5,000. In addition to two factories in Gardone, Beretta has two more in Italy—at Rome and Trentino—in addition to the U.S. factory in Maryland. The Beretta family also has interests in companies that make machine tools and design numerical control systems that automate production lines. All the Beretta enterprises are privately owned, and information about them is scarce or non-existent. Journalist Robert L. Kroon visited Beretta in 1985 and described the armed camp atmosphere in an article for the magazine *Europe:*

> Visitors arriving at the cosy little airport of Brescia are driven the sixty kilometers to the factory in an unmarked black corporate limousine whose driver reports progress to company headquarters every fifteen minutes or so by two-way telephone. The fortress-like headquarters is built against a rocky mountain slope at the end of a dead-end valley. Inside the cavernous building prospective clients pass through a gunlover's Valhalla: the Beretta Museum, a collection of hundreds of handguns from the Middle Ages up to and including the trap and skeet shotguns that won Beretta Olympic gold from Melbourne in 1956 to last year's Los Angeles Olympiad.

A Beretta official explained the reason for all this security: "After all, the Mafia prefers Berettas, too, so we must presume we are a potential target at all times."

McDonald's in Rome

The McDonald's that outsold all other McDonald's units in 1986 was the new restaurant near the Piazza d'Espagna in Rome. The first McDonald's permitted to operate in Rome, it grossed nearly $5 million even though it didn't open until March. At times the crush of young people trying to get in was so great that the doors were barred until some people left.

Access Via G. Beretta 18
25063 Gardone Valtrompia, Italy
(39) 30-837261

Beretta U.S.A.
17601 Indian Head Highway
Accokeek, Md. 20607
(301) 283-2191

Bertelsmann

Sales $5 billion
Profits $200 million
U.S. Sales $1.5 billion
Rank World's largest publishing
company
World's largest book club operator
2d-largest book publisher in the
United States
World's 3rd-largest phonograph
record producer
Founded 1835
Employees 40,000
Headquarters Gütersloh, West Germany

One of the decisive battles of World War II was fought at El Alamein on Egypt's Mediterranean coast west of Alexandria when British 8th Army forces under the command of a quirky general, Bernard Law Montgomery, held off Field Marshal Erwin Rommel's crack German unit, the Afrika Korps. The battle, in the summer of 1942, turned the tide in North Africa. Rommel was forced to retreat to Tunisia, where the Afrika Korps was pinned down by British troops from the south, American troops led by General Dwight D. Eisenhower from the west, and Free French forces from the southwest. On May 12, 1943, 250,000 German and Italian soldiers, their backs to the sea, surrendered. One of those surrendering was a twenty-two-year-old German lieutenant, Reinhard Mohn. It was the end of the war for him. He was sent to a POW camp in Concordia, Kansas, where he studied engineering with visiting instructors.

At the end of the war Mohn returned to Gütersloh, the rural Westphalian town in the north of Germany where he had been born. His two brothers did not return from the war, and the family business—religious book publishing—was decimated. In Kansas he had thought that he might pursue a career in engineering. Back in Germany his father persuaded him to try and revive the family business, which had been started in 1835 to print hymnals and prayer books. The founder was Carl Bertelsmann, the son of a Lutheran pastor. His granddaughter married a Mohn, Reinhard Mohn's grandfather.

From these unlikely roots grew what is today the world's largest publishing company. The tendency of publishers to diversify into allied fields—broadcasting, recording, film—defeats efforts to arrive at hard-and-fast definitions of categories. Bertelsmann is not a "pure" publisher, but nor are Time Inc., Rupert Murdoch, Gannett, Knight-Ridder, and other big publishers. The house that Reinhard Mohn built is a complex of book and record clubs, publishing houses (both books and magazines), record pressers, printers, and broadcasting and film companies (including a 40 percent stake in one of the largest commercial television stations in Europe, RTL plus, a German-language station operating from Luxembourg). With an annual sales volume of $5 billion, Bertelsmann ranks as the world leader in communications or media or whatever you want to call this field. For comparison's sake, Time Inc. had revenues of $3.7 billion in 1986; CBS $4.7 billion.

Bertelsmann leads in one other important respect. It's the most multinational of all the world's publishing companies, doing two thirds of its business outside Germany.

Book clubs, not hymnals, powered Mohn's initial thrust. In 1950 he started Germany's first book club, Lesering, which enrolled 2 million members by 1958. He then moved on to record clubs, and when the big recording companies balked at supplying him with product, he started to press records himself. In 1979 he bought Arista Records from Columbia Pictures, and in 1986 Bertelsmann became the third-largest record producer in the world (behind CBS and Warner) by boosting its stake in the record division of RCA from 25 percent to 100 percent.

During the 1960s Mohn went international with the record and book clubs, spreading them through Europe and Latin America. He made careful studies of how books were distributed and sold. In many countries where mail was inefficient and bookstores were scarce, he distributed his books door-to-door. By 1975 the Bertelsmann clubs had enrolled 7.5 million members in eighteen countries. In 1978, in an interview with *Forbes,* Mohn said, "Recently I was in Colombia, in villages of two thousand to three thousand five hundred people, all Indians. These are poor people, really. Still, in those small villages we have one hundred to two hundred book club members." It's not the kind of business that occurred to the Book-of-the-Month Club.

In 1986 Bertelsmann's book and record clubs had 16 million members in nineteen countries and, despite expansion into other fields, they still represented the company's largest business. In its home country, West Germany, the Bertelsmann clubs have 4.3 million members and operate retail centers in 280 cities. Its French arm, France Loisirs, operates clubs in France, Switzerland, Belgium, and Canada. It stands as the largest book club in the world, with more than 5 million members.

Mohn edged into the magazine business in 1969 by acquiring a minority stake in a Hamburg publishing house, Gruner & Jahr—a holding that has since been augmented to 75 percent. It's one of the most successful magazine publishers in Europe, beginning with its flagship weekly, *Stern*, which boasts a circulation of 1.4 million, and extending to nineteen other magazines in Germany, including the leading women's monthly, *Brigitte;* two business magazines, *Capital* and *Impulse;* and a 25 percent interest in the influential German newsmagazine *Der Spiegel.* Gruner & Jahr also publishes four magazines in France, another four in Spain, and three in the United States *(Parents, Young Miss,* and *Expecting).*

Mohn believes strongly in backward integration. Wherever he goes, he likes to buy printing plants to print his books and magazines as well as the publications of other companies. Bertelsmann owns printing plants in Germany, Spain, Portugal, Italy, Austria, Brazil, Colombia, and the United States (Offset Papers Manufacturers in Dallas, Pennsylvania; Delta Lithograph in Van Nuys, California; and Brown Printing in Waseca, Minnesota).

Reinhard Mohn has always had his eye on the United States. In 1978 he told a reporter that in the years after World War II he cribbed from American business practices but now felt capable of taking on his mentors. In 1976 Gruner & Jahr launched a new magazine in Germany, *Geo,* which carried lengthy articles punctuated by striking photography. It was a great success, as was a French edition. So, on to the United States, where *Geo,* introduced in 1979, was positioned against *National Geographic.* Subtitled "a new view of our world," *Geo* proclaimed its mission "to show with truthfulness and close observation the lives of the world's people, shorn of sentimentality and clichés." *Geo* was an upscale, slick, green-covered, glossy monthly that sold for four dollars on newsstands, thirty-six dollars a year by subscription. No expense was spared to introduce the magazine to Americans. A six-page, four-color ad ran in *BusinessWeek, Newsweek,* and *Time* in January 1979 at a cost of nearly $1 million. A postmortem showed that the ad netted ten thousand subscribers; that is, it cost one hundred dollars to sign up each subscriber. *Geo* won multiple awards but went through three publishers and three managing editors, never reached its circulation goal of 300,000 (it stuck at 250,000), and attracted very little advertising. In 1981 Bertelsmann sold *Geo* to Knapp Communications, publisher of *Architectural Digest* and *Bon Appetit,* which published it for another three years before killing it in February 1985. Estimates of Bertelsmann's losses on the U.S. launch of *Geo* ranged from $25 million up to $50 million.

Mohn had better luck in book publishing. Bertelsmann paid $36 million in 1977 to acquire 51 percent of Bantam Books from I.F.I. (the holding company of the Agnelli family, whose main holding is Fiat Motor) and in 1981 it bought the remaining 49 percent to become the owner of the largest paperback house in the United States. Bantam began publishing hardcover books in 1980 and hit with a series of back-to-back best-sellers: *Iacocca, Yeager,* and *What They Don't Teach You at Harvard Business School.* Edwin McDowell, who covers book publishing for *The New York Times,* said in 1986 that Bantam's marketplace bonanzas "have established the house . . . as one that many authors and agents speak of in reverential tones."

Bantam also has an international reach of its own. It owns the Corgi imprint in Britain, subsidiaries in Canada, Australia, and New Zealand, and it has ambitious plans under its Italian-born leader, Alberto Vitale, to market books in China, Nigeria, and other countries.

If the people on New York's Book Row talk with awe about Bantam, they speak irreverently about Doubleday & Company, the ninety-year-old publishing company that Bertelsmann scooped up in 1986 for $475 million. Once the largest American book publisher, Doubleday has slipped so much in recent years that many observers thought Mohn paid too much, especially since it did not include the most profitable part of the company, the New York Mets baseball club. However, it was a good match for Mohn in the sense that Doubleday, like Bertelsmann, is a printer of books and the operator of many book clubs, the biggest of which is the Literary Guild. For many years the joke in publishing circles was that Doubleday published books to keep its printing plants running. But the books were so poorly printed that it gave rise to many more jokes. A former employee once said you can always tell a Doubleday book because "it feels so rotten." The acquisition did make Bertelsmann the second-largest book publisher in the United States after Simon & Schuster, with imprints including Dell, Delacorte, Dial, Anchor, and Laidlaw, and it vaulted Alberto Vitale into a position described as "the most powerful man in U.S. trade publishing."

Doubleday was (and is) a privately owned company. The great bulk of its shares had been held by members of the founding Doubleday family. Bertelsmann is also privately owned, with 90 percent of its stock held by Reinhard Mohn, who is known in Germany for treating his employees so well—providing strong social benefits and sharing the profits with them, for example—that unions have never made any headway in the company. Mohn abided by one of his own rules by officially retiring as chief executive when he reached the age of sixty in 1981. He continued, however, to serve as chairman of the supervisory board. Mohn was succeeded as chief executive by silver-haired Mark Woessner, former head of the printing division, who was forty-eight years old in 1987. Bertelsmann's newly formed electronic media division is run by Manfred Lahnstein, formerly finance minister in the West German government. He was forty-nine in 1987. Three employee representatives sit on the ten-man supervisory board.

Access   Carl-Bertelsmann-Strasse, 270
Postbox 55 55
D-4830 Gütersloh, West Germany
(37) 52-41/80-1

Bantam Books
666 Fifth Ave.
New York, N.Y. 10103
(212) 765-6500

Bic	**Sales** $1 billion
	Profits $60 million
	U.S. Sales $235 million
	Rank World's largest ballpoint pen maker
	World's largest producer of cigarette lighters
	World's largest maker of disposable razors
	World's largest maker of windsurfing boards
	Founded 1948
	Employees 13,000
	Headquarters Paris, France

This French company is a creature of modern times, it has prospered by making products designed to be discarded: ballpoint pens, disposable lighters, disposable razors. The force behind the company is Baron Marcel Bich, who discarded the last letter of his name to create what is now a world megabrand.

The ballpoint pen, so ubiquitous today that kids think it has been around forever, made its first appearance in 1944. It was invented by (naturally) a Hungarian, Ladislao Biro, who, working with his brother, Georg, figured out a way to get a ball bearing to roll an instant-drying ink onto paper. While illustrious Hungarian physicists were working at Los Alamos on the atomic bomb, the Biro brothers, who fled to Argentina during World War II, were working on the ballpoint pen. Inventing a product is one thing. Building a business around it is something else. A number of promoters, including Milton Reynolds in the United States, picked up on the ballpoint pen idea after World War II ended, but it was Marcel Bich, starting out in a shed in the Paris suburb of Clichy, who was the first to realize the implications of the invention.

Bich was born in Turin a week before World War I broke out. His father, an Italian engineer, was a baron who went to work in France and became a French citizen when Marcel was seventeen years old. When it came to the ballpoint pen, Marcel Bich saw that it would create a mass, not a class, market. While Milton Reynolds was selling $12.50 ballpoints, Bich was thinking along quite different lines. He sensed that the spoils would go to the producer of a reliable, inexpensive writing instrument. *Voilà,* the 19-cent Bic. Before he could even get started, though, he became embroiled in a patent fight with the company set up by Biro to license the invention. Once that was settled, with the baron agreeing to pay a huge royalty on sales (6 percent) in return for a monopoly in France, Marcel Bich was off and writing.

First he redesigned the ballpoint to make it easier to use and to produce (he put the ink cartridge into a transparent plastic tube). Then he knocked the *h* off his name to give the ballpoint a brand name that would be easy to promote. And then he promoted the Bic with massive advertising, confident that the reliability of the pens would turn triers into permanent customers. The low price, nineteen cents, was a master stroke. Bich knew he could make the pens at well below that figure (five cents), and at nineteen cents it didn't bother people to throw the product away, especially if it worked well for a good stretch of time.

Bich was also quick to see that if it worked in France, it would work anywhere. He set his sights on selling disposable ballpoint pens to the entire world. He invaded the United States in 1958 by buying the old Waterman fountain pen company, a symbolic transfer of power if there ever was one. Today Bic ballpoints are manufactured in nineteen countries and sold in ninety. Along the way critics have wondered how long the company could keep it up. In 1969, for example, when Bic was selling one billion pens a year, *Fortune* speculated that the new felt-tip pens might stop the Bic advance. By 1976 Bic was selling 10 million pens every day. In 1986 it was selling more than twelve million ballpoints a day. Bic makes one out of every four ballpoint pens sold in the world.

Looking back it seems like a logical progression: If you can get people to buy a disposable pen, you can probably also get them to buy other disposable products. Bich moved into disposable cigarette lighters (1972) and disposable razors (1975). The strategy was basically the same. Find a way to mass produce plastic-encased products at a price low enough so that people don't mind throwing them away after their ink, flame, or edge give out. And make them well enough so that users want to rebuy. Bich also found that his truncated name could serve as a brand name for all his well-advertised disposables.

Bich always played the game on a global scale. He tested his gas lighters in Sweden, home of the world's largest match maker, Swedish Match. And he made his first disposable razors in Greece, selling them in France, Belgium, and Switzerland. These are now worldwide products. Bic was not the first to make a disposable cigarette lighter but it's now the world leader, selling more than three million a day. It's also the world leader in disposable razors and second, in the shaving market as a whole, only to Gillette.

The Gillette-Bic rivalry became one of the great feuds of modern marketing history. They crossed swords in ballpoint pens (Gillette owns Paper Mate and Write Bros.), lighters (Gillette was behind Cricket), and razors in a struggle so acrimonious that Nathaniel C. Nash, a reporter with *The New York Times,* once described them as a couple of "alley cats" who can't stop fighting. In the American market, where this struggle has been the fiercest, Paper Mate has held its own in the pen business, running a strong second to Bic; but in disposable lighters, Bic crushed Gillette so decisively that the Boston company fled the field in 1984, selling its Cricket brand to Swedish Match.

In the razor market Bic's disposable struck at Gillette's lifeblood, and the response was quick and massive. Gillette rolled out its own disposable, Good News!, and the two brands have scrapped in price wars that raised the question of whether either of them was making money in their zeal to capture customers. Bic claims worldwide leadership in disposable razors, but Good News! has generally held the upper hand in the U.S. market. For Gillette, one of those rare American companies that does more than half its business outside the United States, it could be a Pyrrhic victory. Every time it converts a shaver to a disposable razor, it erodes the higher-margin blade business that has been the company's bedrock for virtually the entire twentieth century. Marcel Bich has carved out a special place of infamy for himself in Gillette's history.

Bic's flaming success with its butane lighter was tempered in 1987 when reports surfaced in the United States of people who were injured— and, in one case, killed—by Bic lighters which exploded. After settling one personal injury case for $3.25 million, Bic found itself on the front page of *The New York Times,* accused of keeping "the cases quiet by settling them out of court, usually making secrecy one of the terms of the settlement." Bic insisted that its lighters were safe and charged that personal injury lawyers had "wildly exaggerated" the number of claims made against the company. In its annual report the French parent noted that it had not encountered such claims in any other country, despite the billions of lighters it has sold outside the United States.

A loner who doesn't have much truck with organized business groups, Bich extracted $68 million from American and French investors who wanted a piece of his action in the early 1970s. First, in 1971, he sold 39 percent of his U.S. company, Bic Corporation, to the public. In 1972 he sold 20 percent of the French parent, Société Bic, to French investors in an offering that was in such demand that the shares had to be rationed at the rate of eight for each one hundred ordered. It was, up to that time, the biggest initial offering the Paris Bourse had ever seen. Bic was one of the high fliers on the Paris stock exchange during the 1980s, more than quadrupling in price, giving the company a market value of close to $1 billion in early 1987. On the American Stock Exchange, where shares of Bic Corporation trade, there was a similar escalation, and in early 1987 the company's market value reached $337 million. Société Bic continued to hold 61 percent of the shares of its American offspring, whose sales in

1986 were $267 million (8 percent coming from Canada, 4 percent from Mexico). Bic does two thirds of its business outside France.

Marcel Bich, who was seventy-two years old in 1986, sired ten children by two wives, and three of his children—Claude, François, and Bruno—are active in the highest ranks of the company, along with Bich's original partner, Edouard Buffard. Bruno, the third son, heads up the American company and is a naturalized American citizen. He became chief executive officer of Bic Corporation in 1983, when he was thirty-six years old, replacing Robert P. Adler, an accountant who had been with Waterman when Bich acquired it in 1958. Adler is credited with establishing Bic in the United States, and his departure in 1983 (when he was only fifty years old), must have been wrenching, though soothed by the sale of his 6.2 percent interest in the company for $5.6 million.

A restless entrepreneur and sailor, Bich tried three times to capture for France the America's Cup, losing out each time. The most ignominious defeat came in 1970 when his boat lost its way in the fog off Newport, Rhode Island. These defeats did not dampen his enthusiasm for new ventures in the business arena. What the company likes to call the "Groups Bic Multinational" has become a mini-conglomerate, owning the haute couture house Guy Laroche, the French pantyhose and undergarment (Rosy bras) manufacturer DIM, and the French pencil producer Conte.

When Bic gained control of DIM in the early 1970s, tentative plans were made to invade the U.S. pantyhose market (even though Gillette didn't make this product) to give Hanes, marketer of the L'eggs brand, a run for its hosiery. The theory was that Bic's distribution outlets would be perfect for this product. But after a closer look, the French backed off. DIM stayed in Europe, where it has become the largest hosiery manufac-

turer. Still, Marcel Bich may have the last laugh. In 1987 Sara Lee Corporation, owner of Hanes, agreed to put up $84 million to acquire a 34 percent stake in DIM.

Marcel Bich's feistiness may be gauged from his remarks at the 1985 annual meeting of Bic. He told shareholders: "We have three Olympic gold medals: the ballpoint pen, the lighter, and the disposable razor. We would like to have gold medals in all our products. In effect, the largest producer in the world is in the best position to make profits; the second largest is less well-placed; the third can still hope; the fourth has a greater chance of losing than winning. . . . We envision a gold medal for each product that will yield us a profit of 20 percent on sales—of which half goes to the state. . . . *Nous sommes toujours ferocement anti-technocrates, nous luttons pour maintenir la responsabilité individuelle basee sur la confiance.*"

Marcel Bich: last of the nineteenth century's unreconstructed, laissez faire, free enterprise champions.

Access   8, Impasse des Cailloux
92111 Clichy, France
(33) 1-47-39-3225

Bic Corp.
Wiley St.
Milford, Conn. 06460
(203) 783-2000

Booker	Sales $1.9 billion
	Profits $56 million

Sales $1.9 billion
Profits $56 million
U.S. Sales $110 million
Rank World's largest poultry breeder (broilers, brown-egg layers, large white turkeys)
Largest health food company in Europe
Operator of Britain's largest commercial tree nursery
2d-largest salmon farmer in Britain
Britain's 3d-largest mushroom grower
Bestower of largest annual award for work of fiction
Founded 1834
Employees 14,000
Headquarters London, England

Here's a curious corporate hodgepodge, an eccentric English company that produces breeding stock for chicken and turkey growers, farms and smokes salmon in Scotland, sells vitamins and health foods in the United States and Britain, manages a sugar plantation in Sri Lanka, operates farms in the middle of America, and collects royalties on the sale and use of works by Agatha Christie and Ian Fleming. Every time a James Bond movie is made, it redounds to the bottom line of Booker.

The roots of this company go back to the early nineteenth century when British imperialism was in style. At the Congress of Vienna in 1815, the territories on the northeast coast of South America between Venezuela and Brazil, all part of the region known as Guiana, were divided into British, Dutch, and French colonies (they are today, respectively, Guyana, Surinam, and French Guiana). English merchants from Liverpool sailed to the British settlements (which became British Guiana in 1831) to exploit the resources, principally sugarcane fields. Prominent among them were the Booker brothers—Josias, George, and Richard. They acquired plantations and shipped sugar and rum back to Liverpool, where they had their merchant banking houses. In 1854 a new partnership was formed between Josias Booker II and John McConnell, who had joined the Bookers in 1846 as a clerk. The Bookers and McConnells greatly expanded the business during the second half of the century. They became the principal shopkeepers of the colony. They started one of the leading shipping lines linking South America with Europe (originally the Liverpool Line, it was later renamed the Booker Line). They established their own trading company in London.

The last member of the Booker family to be active in the firm was John H. Booker, a younger brother of Josias II. He sold his interests to the McConnells in 1885. At the turn of the century, the McConnells had three companies—Booker Brothers, George Booker & Company, and John McConnell & Company—with operations in Georgetown, Liverpool, and London still largely based on the Guiana trade. The three companies merged in 1900 into Booker Bros., McConnell & Company. And in 1920 this company sold stock to the public for the first time and was listed on the London Stock Exchange. In 1968 the name was shortened to Booker, McConnell; and in 1986, coming full circle, it was reduced to Booker.

No more McConnells work in Booker, although as late as 1960, the company was still largely dependent on the Guyana sugar trade. When Guyana achieved its independence in 1966, it elected a Communist government. Booker's last holdings in Guyana were sold to the government there in 1976. Institutions—insurance companies, pension funds, and investment trusts—today hold 75 percent of Booker's stock. The company itself lurches on, having used the profits from one hundred years of colonial exploitation to enter a wide variety of businesses.

In Britain Booker wholesales foods to groceries, convenience stores, and restaurants; runs a ninety-unit chain of drugstores under the Kingswood name; and operates Holland & Barrett, Britain's largest health food chain. Health food is an area the company has high hopes for even though it suffered indigestion with an American acquisition, American Dietaids, which marketed vitamins and dietary supplements under the patriotic brand name American Health. Booker ditched the company in 1986 and promptly bought into a big French health food company, La Vie Claire. In the United States Booker still owned 47.6 percent of P. Leiner Nutritional Products, Los Angeles–based supplier of private label vitamins (stores put their own names on them).

Booker has a formidable presence in the health food trade in its home country. In addition to Holland & Barrett, it owns the number-one wholesaler of health foods; markets its own line of more than one hundred vitamins under the Healthcrafts label; and supplies what it purports to be health foods under such brand names as Allinson (brown bread), Prewett's, Heath & Heather, Ladycare, and Potter's Catarrh Pastilles. It's a switch for the company that used to control the Tia Maria liqueur brand.

But agribusiness, which might be considered the original business of Booker, continues to be the mainstay, bringing in about half the profits. Today it includes poultry genetics, seed breeding, and management of farms and forests. It's also a multinational business. The poultry breeding takes place largely in the United States under the aegis of Arbor Acres Farms, a company that emerged from a failed Rockefeller enterprise, International Basic Economy Corporation (IBEC). Arbor, based in Glastonbury, Connecticut, leads the world in the breeding of broilers and brown-egg layers. It has hatcheries in Alabama, Georgia, Mississippi, and Arkansas, and it supplies breeding stock, along with technical help, to poultry farmers in sixty countries. The Nicholas division, based in Sonoma, California, is the world leader in the breeding of large white turkeys; it has breeding farms in California and Scotland. Another U.S. unit, Doane Farm Management, manages more than one thousand farms in sixteen midwestern states.

With Arbor and Nicholas part of its portfolio, Booker takes a keen interest in what it calls "the growing preference for poultry meat as healthy and relatively low-cost protein food." Thus, in 1986, it pointed out to its shareholders that annual production of chicken meat, worldwide, is now valued at $37 billion. Both Arbor and Nicholas formerly belonged to IBEC, which was formed by Nelson Rockefeller and his brothers in 1947 with a mission to improve the economies of developing countries— and make a profit at the same time. IBEC was to field nearly two hundred companies in thirty-three countries, forming partnerships with local business people and local governments. Among many other ventures, it launched supermarket chains in Venezuela, Peru, and Italy; mutual funds in Brazil and Thailand; housing projects in Puerto Rico, Iraq, and Iran; soluble coffee plants in El Salvador and Guatemala; a fresh milk company in Venezuela; and a hybrid seed corn company in Brazil. Arbor Acres, active as a producer of broiler breeder stock since before World War II, joined with IBEC in 1959 to extend its chicken breeding operations to Latin America, Europe, the Middle East, and the Far East. In 1964 Arbor became an integral part of IBEC.

IBEC was a noble mission that failed to survive the political and economic upheavals of Third World development. Although a third of its stock was sold to the public and its shares were traded on the over-the-counter market, profits proved to be elusive, and the Rockefellers had to continually shore up the company. Nelson Rockefeller served as chief executive officer of IBEC until he was elected governor of New York in 1958. His son, Rodman C. Rockefeller, became president in 1968, declaring that "the best way to make money is by meeting human needs in an efficient and businesslike way." For IBEC "efficient" and "businesslike" meant pruning the high-minded, money-losing ventures overseas and investing in more prosaic businesses (machinery for chemical plants, hydraulic equipment) in the United States. But even that strategy didn't work as sales plunged from $300 million in 1974 to $85 million in 1979. Rodman Rockefeller presided over the dissolution of IBEC, the final step being the invitation to Booker to become a junior partner (and later a senior partner) in the poultry breeding businesses. When Booker acquired its first stake in IBEC in 1980, *Fortune* chortled that the company's "purpose has finally been clarified—to make money." By 1985 the IBEC name had disappeared and Booker's interest in Arbor-Nicolas was up to 89.51 percent. The Rockefellers held the remaining 10.49 percent, and Rodman Rockefeller, still serving as chairman of Arbor Acres Farms, was elected to the board of directors of Booker.

Vestiges of its days as a colonial sugar trader remain. Booker's engineering company, Fletcher and Stewart, designs and supplies sugar-processing machinery. And it has a London-based trading company that markets sugar and rum from Guyana and St. Kitts. One of its most unusual diversifications is a division that it calls "Authors." According to *The Economist,* when Booker was hunting around for some non-sugar activities in the 1960s, it hit upon a loophole in the British tax code that "enabled it to buy an author's copyrights, pay him or her a fat fee partly at the expense of the taxpayer, and then sit back and cash the royalty cheques." That's why Booker today holds the rights to the works of such best-selling authors as Agatha Christie and Ian Fleming, and why, as *The Economist* pointed out, its Authors division earned $3.4 million in 1985 with a staff of three persons.

The company's dabbling in literature also resulted in the establishment of the Booker prize, the most coveted award in British book publishing. Awarded annually since 1969 to the best novel published in Britain by a writer from the British Commonwealth, it comes today with a cash prize of $22,500. Beyond that, it has a galvanizing effect on sales, not only for the winning novel (which in 1986 was Kingsley Amis's *The Old Devils*), but on the five others that are usually short-listed for the award. Experience shows that a Booker prize can result in additional sales ranging from thirty-five thousand to one hundred thousand copies.

Legend has it that the award came about after the company hit upon its copyright scam and the late Ian Fleming, creator of James Bond, suggested to the chairman of Booker that since it was making so much money off writers, it might have the decency to put some of it back in publishing to help writers. The first Booker prize went to P. H. Newby for *Something to Answer for.* Other winners have included David Storey *(Saville),* Iris Murdoch *(The Sea, the Sea),* William Golding *(Rites of Passage),* and J. M. Coetzee *(Life and Times of Michael K).* In 1972, when John Berger won for his novel, *G,* he lambasted Booker for its colonial

The World's Largest Casino

Harrah's, a subsidiary of Holiday Inns, teamed up with an Australian property developer, Hooker Corporation, in 1986 to win a contract to build the largest casino in the world. The deal unraveled after disclosure of Hooker's chief executive's criminal record. The state government of New South Wales then awarded the contract to Genting, a Malaysian casino operator.

The casino, expected to be open in 1988, along with a seven-hundred-room hotel, will be in Sydney's Darling Harbour. Covering 125,000 square feet, it will be the world's largest, spacious enough to accommodate four hundred gaming tables, fifteen hundred slot machines, and eleven thousand gamblers at a time.

adventures in Latin America and awarded half his prize to the Black Panthers.

Access   Kent House
Telegraph St., Moorgate
London EC2R 7LN, England
(44) 1-588-0674

Bosch

Sales $11 billion
Profits $200 million
U.S. Sales $1 billion
Rank World's largest automotive components company
11th-largest company in West Germany
45th on the *Fortune* International 500
World's largest supplier of fuel injection systems
World's largest maker of anti-skid brakes
World's 2d-largest maker of electrical tools
Europe's 2d-largest producer of household appliances
Founded 1886
Employees 147,000 (3,200 in the United States)
Headquarters Stuttgart, West Germany

Stuttgart, a city in southwest Germany near the French and Swiss borders, is home to two pioneers in the world automobile industry: Daimler-Benz, builder of the Mercedes-Benz vehicles, and Robert Bosch GmbH, inventor and developer of ignition systems that make cars go. Both companies were founded in Stuttgart in 1886, and they grew up with the automobile industry. Daimler-Benz is a prime customer of Robert Bosch, as is Volkswagen, but there's more than German solidarity at work here. Bosch sells to every car maker in the non-Communist world.

Bosch has survived for more than one hundred years and has become a huge industrial enterprise without selling any stock to the public (as Daimler-Benz has) or to governmental bodies (as Volkswagen has). It's the largest privately held company in Europe.

More than half of Bosch's business owes to wizardry in the design and manufacture of high-tech auto parts: electronic fuel injection devices, starters, alternators, generators, spark plugs, ignition parts. The remainder comes from products Bosch has added over the years to reduce dependency on the cyclical fortunes of the auto industry. These include home appliances (which it makes in a fifty-fifty partnership with Siemens), telecommunications equipment, television cameras and studio equipment, packaging machines, power tools, medical equipment, hydraulic and pneumatic valves, heat pumps, home heating systems, burglar alarms, and radio-controlled devices to open garages where you can park your Bosch-equipped car. If you're lucky, your car will have a Blaupunkt radio, which Bosch also makes.

Bosch entered its second century in 1986 under the leadership of Dr. Marcus Bierich, only the fourth man to have held the top position. The first was Robert Bosch (he died in 1942 at the age of eighty-one), a meticulous master mechanic whose legacy is evident still in Bosch's corporate "culture." In 1887, a year after he set himself up in a small workshop in Stuttgart, Bosch produced the first magneto (alternator) for stationary engines. A decade later he turned out the first hand-cranked starter for automobile engines.

After the turn of the century, Bosch earned the sobriquet "red Bosch" when he began hiring leftist refugees from the failed Russian Revolution of 1905. In 1906 he introduced an eight-hour workday for his six hundred employees (eight years before Henry Ford did it) and established May Day, the international workingman's holiday, as an official holiday for employees. Bosch made it his motto to "pay your workers as well as you can," and he gave heavily of his profits to charity. During the Nazi thrall he gave a job to the former mayor of Leipzig after that official had been thrown out of office for opposing Hitler. (Bosch's nephew, Carl Bosch, was the first engineer to receive the Nobel prize for his part in figuring out how to mass-produce ammonia. He became head of the I. G. Farben trust upon its formation in 1925. He too was never an admirer of Hitler.)

Robert Bosch succeeded in bringing out a series of automotive electrical products that made his name world-famous: spark plugs (1902), starters (1912), generators, lamps, and regulators (1913). In the 1920s he added horns and batteries. He was one of the first to make windshield wipers. In 1927 Bosch produced the first fuel injection pumps for diesel engines, which made possible their use in automobiles. And in 1937 he produced the first gasoline injection pumps for aircraft engines. The first Bosch power hand tools, with the motor in the handle, were made in 1932. Blaupunkt made the first car radio in Europe in 1933.

Bosch always kept tight control of his company. His will required that the company bearing his name be restructured so that 90 percent of its assets would be lodged in a charitable foundation. (The remainder went to the Bosch family.) The trust today awards grants of $7 million a year. Its first priority is health care.

While the foundation—called the Robert Bosch Stiftung—owns 90 percent of the shares, it doesn't run the company. The voting rights on its stock reside in a separate partnership in which the head of the company has the key voice. In effect, the chief executive can run the company with long-term interests in mind. Being under no pressure to pass out fat dividends to voracious shareholders or to please narrow-minded security analysts, he can plough back most of the profits into the business. In 1986 this arrangement allowed Bosch to allocate an astronomical 5 percent of its sales to support the nine thousand people it employed in research.

Hans Lutz Merkle, who ran Bosch from 1963 to 1984, when he retired at age eighty-one, made good use of Robert Bosch's legacy. Unlike most top German executives, Merkle did not graduate from a university. The son of a printing works owner in south Germany, he joined Bosch as an eighteen-year-old office apprentice. A writer some years ago remarked that "the Godfather," as he came to be known inside and outside of Bosch, "exudes power to an almost uncomfortable degree. The more softly he speaks, and generally he speaks very softly indeed . . . the more those present crane their necks to listen." Henry Kissinger once was asked why he showed up at a ribbon-cutting ceremony for a car parts office in Detroit. "When Hans Merkle calls," Kissinger explained, "you answer."

When Merkle took over, automotive equipment represented two thirds of Bosch's sales. When he stepped aside, it accounted for a little more than half—this despite an explosive growth in Bosch's high-tech automotive, antipollution, and fuel-saving products. (In 1967 Bosch came up with an electronic fuel injector, designed and manufactured for Volkswagen so that its Beetle could pass California's tough new clean-air standards.) Whereas in 1970 the average car built in the United States contained about $25 worth of electronic components, in 1984 it had $500 worth. More than 50 percent of Bosch's sales are rung up outside Germany; and if you count exports out of the German factories, 75 percent. Through 1986 it had installed nineteen million fuel injection systems in more than four hundred different automobile models.

Bosch would be a bigger factor in the United States if not for the inconvenience of two world wars. It opened its first branch in the United States in 1906, and its properties were confiscated during World War I. Regrouping after 1919, when the U.S. automobile industry exploded, Bosch did so well that 70 percent of its sales were coming from North America. During World War II its properties were confiscated once again—and it wasn't until 1983 that it regained the right to use the Bosch name in the United States.

In 1986 Bosch was operating nine plants in the United States, including fuel injection factories in Anderson and Charleston, South Carolina, and a product development unit at Farmington Hills, Michigan, near the automotive capital of the country. Bosch was also still hanging on to a 9.3 percent interest in Borg-Warner, the largest independent automotive components company in the United States.

When he stepped down in 1984, Merkle went outside the company for a successor, recruiting the fifty-seven-year-old Bierich from Germany's largest insurance company, Allianz Versicherung, where he was the chief financial officer. The son of a university professor, Bierich studied at Cambridge after World War II. There he formed an acquaintance with Bertrand Russell, with whom he continued to correspond until the philosopher's death in 1970. Bierich took a doctorate of philosophy and mathematics at the University of Cologne. When it became clear he would not get a faculty appointment, he joined the business world, starting his career with a private bank. Intensely shy and bookish, he has been dubbed the "philosopher prince." *Financial Times* reporter Jonathan Carr described him this way: "He speaks slowly, likes understatement . . . but prefers to talk of wider social questions like the role of capital and labour and codetermination in industry."

Those are skills he may need. While there's still a paternalistic air about Bosch, a legacy from its founder, the German metalworkers' union struck the company for seven weeks in 1984. One result was the reduction of the work week from forty to thirty-eight and a half hours. In its report for 1985 Bosch made a special point of expressing its "appreciation to employees," noting that the unions were willing "to support the interests of the company as well as those of the employees." One other item in the annual report, reflecting the Robert Bosch legacy, was the note that the Robert Bosch Siedlung, a nonprofit institution then fifty years old, was managing three thousand homes and apartments where employees live, including one thousand homes that had been sold to employees. In addition, during 1985 this foundation advanced construction loans totaling $7 million to employees—at no interest.

Access   Robert Bosch Platz 1
Gerlingen-Schillerhohe
D-7000 Stuttgart, West Germany
(49) 711-811-10

Robert Bosch Corp.
2800 S. 25th Ave.
Broadview, Ill. 60153
(312) 865-5200

Bradesco	**Assets** $13.6 billion
	Profits $262 million
	Rank Brazil's largest financial group
	Largest private (nongovernment) bank in Brazil
	Largest private employer in Brazil
	Founded 1943
	Employees 146,700
	Headquarters City of God, Brazil

Banco Brasiliero de Descontos S.A.—Bradesco for short—is about as different as a bank can get.

Like the huge nation where it's based (Brazil is larger than the continental United States and more populous than any other country in Latin America), everything about Bradesco is big. In 1986 it had 1,916 branches, 807 banking posts (or teller desks) on the premises of customers, and 12.8 million savings accounts. It opened more new branches in 1985 than there were days in the year, and added about 130 jobs a day. With 146,000 workers it is not only Brazil's largest private employer but the largest bank employer in the world. (Citicorp, the largest bank in the United States, employs 81,300.) In 1985 more than 69,000 of these employees participated in educational programs; some were new-comers getting basic training, others were acquiring specialized skills. So extensive are the professional training courses that the bank bought two hotels to use as classrooms.

With assets of $13.6 billion at the start of 1987, Bradesco was easily the largest bank in Brazil outside the government's Banco de Brasil. It's also more than just a commercial bank, with a galaxy of subsidiaries active as savings and loan associations, stockbrokers, investment bankers, insurance carriers, and travel agencies, among other activities. If the offices of all these entities were added up, Bradesco would be seen to have 3,295 service points in Brazil. Bradesco also has brought banking to the people with a fleet of "day and night" mobile units, vans equipped with automatic teller machines. They are dispatched to neighborhoods where, as the bank puts it, "there is a temporary concentration of people."

Bradesco holds 14.3 percent of the country's savings deposits, finances 13 percent of its exports and 7 percent of its imports, and claims to be the leading underwriter of securities and the number one writer of insurance. It reported that at the end of 1985 its eight savings and loans, which finance home purchases, had a portfolio of 153,566 individual loans. Bradesco also has a staggering number of shareholders: 3.6 million.

Bradesco was created by Amador Aguiar, a onetime farmer and

typesetter who turned to banking in 1943 after a printing machine lopped off part of his right index finger. From the start he was a different sort of banker. In a society where only old, landed families could get credit, Aguiar wanted to provide loans to small coffee growers and ranchers. In a culture where bankers were inaccessible and haughty, he made branch managers sit at desks in the front of the bank so that people could approach them. And in rural areas his branches opened early enough for farmers to stop in on their way to work.

Bradesco's head office in the São Paulo suburb City of God retains the flavor of those early days. The top executives, many of whom started out as office boys, do not have private desks or drawers or phones or secretaries or even offices. They all sit around two giant tables in one room, taking care of business out in the open.

Bradesco goes about its moneylending business with an evangelical fervor. The company's stationery carries biblical quotations and the declaration, "Nos confiamos em Deus" (Portuguese for "We trust in God").

Devoted to the twin precepts of "work and God," Aguiar asks for the same dedication from his employees. *Wall Street Journal* reporter Lynda Schuster, visiting in 1985, found a doorway at Bradesco's headquarters festooned with a huge banner reminding employees that "only work can produce wealth." Employees sign a declaration of principles, she reported, vowing to put the bank's interests above personal cares and "to love Brazil and work hard for the country." Every day they see slogans extolling morality and cleanliness. And they study the company's message-cum-prayerbook, which has a section called "Thoughts on Smiles."

Promotions are based on how well employees assimilate the Bradesco philosophy. "What counts here is superior moral behavior," Aguiar told *The Wall Street Journal.* Entering the managerial ranks takes three or four years. It takes ten years to become a regional director. No one gets to the Bradesco board of directors without eighteen years' tenure.

Employees devoted to Bradesco find the company is equally caring about them. After work, the City of God employees return to pastel-colored houses Aguiar built for them, exercise in the Bradesco swimming pool, or throng the company stadium for sporting events. Their children attend Bradesco schools. If they fall ill, a Bradesco hospital will take care of them. Bradesco employees throughout Brazil get their workday meals and snacks courtesy of the bank.

Bradesco's humanitarian streak extends beyond its workers. The bank supports an educational foundation that runs twenty-nine schools offering free education, medical and dental care, and career training to thirty-three thousand children throughout Brazil. This is not some quiet philanthropic activity. Bradesco's envelopes carry a quotation from the biblical Book of Proverbs: "Teach children which path they must follow, and they will not leave it even as they grow old."

Some of the Bradesco bunch are the sons and daughters of employees. But many are children of the "Other Brazil," the majority of Brazil's 135 million people who lead a rural, poverty-stricken existence. Brazil is a country of striking contrasts. It has one of the fastest growing economies in the world, a coffee-driven trade surplus, abundant natural resources, giant offshoots of giant multinationals (Shell, Texaco, Volkswagen, B.A.T Industries, Nestlē), more industry and entrepreneurial spirit than any other country in South America, and some of the continent's most breathtaking beaches and exciting cities. Those same cities are hemmed in by sprawling slums and squatter settlements. Many of the denizens are jobless. One third of the country's workers earn less than the minimum wage, and the landless, rural laborers are worse off. After Haiti, Brazil has the most severe rural poverty in the Western Hemisphere. Two out of three Brazilians eat less than a minimum subsistence diet of 2,400 calories a day.

Bradesco trains urban students for work in computers and the service professions. However, most of the students in its schools learn agricultural trades that can help them get jobs near their homes. Paying for their education, Bradesco officials say, is just the bank's way of being a good citizen. "It's because of the founder's philosophy," explained Jose Guilherme L. Faria, general manager of Bradesco's Park Avenue, New York branch. "He thinks that since the bank makes a good profit, the bank should give back to the country something."

Funding for the Bradesco Foundation comes largely from profits derived from the sale of life insurance and personal accident policies. Besides supporting schools the foundation also runs the bank's training and professional development center and operates a nutrition program that supplies meals to Bradesco employees. Another program supported by the foundation is about as unusual an operation as a bank could have: artificial insemination of cattle. It maintains two semen technology centers which provide guidance on cross-breeding, computer-planned cattle handling, and mating techniques.

To be a banker in Brazil requires flexibility—if not nerves of steel—and that quality was tested in 1986 when Jose Sarney's government adopted the Cruzado Plan, an attempt to rein in Brazil's raging inflation. The problem can be grasped easily enough by looking at Bradesco's 1985 annual report. The first page lists the exchange rates in effect at the end of the year. In 1983 there were 979 cruzeiros to the dollar, in 1984 there were 3,168 cruzeiros to the dollar, and in 1985 there were 10,440 cruzeiros to the dollar. Sarney replaced the cruzeiro with the cruzado, fixed the exchange rate at 13.84 to the dollar, and froze prices. For the banks, accustomed to an interest rate of 15 percent a month, it meant a radical change in practices. In the era of hyperinflation, the Brazilian banks had gone wild, opening scores of branches and staffing their big-city branches with hundreds of tellers to service customers who rushed in every day, at all hours, to move their rapidly depreciating funds into new, higher-yielding instruments. The Cruzado Plan tried to bring order to this scene and even standardized banking hours at 10:00 A.M. to 3:00 P.M. The result, at first, was a sharp contraction. Out of a bank work force of 750,000 people, some 80,000 lost their jobs early in 1986, and hundreds of branches were closed.

But not at Bradesco. It kept all its branches and pared down its work force by attrition, cutting back by fifteen thousand people at the end of 1986. Like other banks it began charging for such services as checkbooks and stop payment orders. And instead of sending daily statements to customers (with inflation raging, you need to keep track of what's happening), it began sending them to corporate customers only after a transaction was made; individual customers were given a rundown every two weeks.

In early 1987, however, the Cruzado Plan began to fall apart. While keeping a cap on prices, the government permitted wages to rise, an almost textbook lesson of how to stimulate inflation. Brazil informed its lenders, mainly banks in the United States, that it would not be able to meet interest payments; the cruzado weakened, and prices began to climb again. And Brazilian banks reverted to their old, inflation-driven ways.

Brazil has always had a chaotic style of banking. "Each bank is a kind of supermarket," New York branch manager Faria pointed out, "and you can do anything in the market. It's different compared to banks in the United States. In Brazil banks provide a lot more services. You pay for your utilities at a bank. For businesses it's normal to use the bank to collect invoices. It's amazing to see the number of tellers, maybe two hundred, in a São Paulo or Rio branch."

While customers can take care of many transactions at a bank branch, the varied services are provided by separate subsidiaries because Brazilian banking laws restrict the kind of business particular institutions can handle. A commercial bank, for example, can do only short-term business. To handle even a one-year instrument requires an investment bank. Nor can a commercial bank offer mortgages or brokerage services. So Bradesco has an investment bank, a consumer finance company, eight savings and housing loan societies, a leasing company, a travel agency and credit card unit, an insurance broker, a stock and foreign exchange broker, and a securities dealer. It also owns a computer company and a printing business.

As a way to attract business from multinationals with offices or subsidiaries in Brazil, Bradesco has invited foreign participation in both its investment bank and insurance company. The insurance holding company, Bradesco Seguros, has joint ventures with Prudential Insurance of the United States, Allianz Versicherung of West Germany, Skandia Insurance of Sweden, and Baloise Insurance of Switzerland. "It's easier to sell a product to IBM in Brazil if we have a link to an American insurance company," said Faria. Five foreign banks are minority shareholders in Banco Bradesco de Investimento, and executives from Japan's Sanwa Bank and West Germany's Deutsche Bank sit on its board of directors.

Bradesco's New York branch, opened in 1982, was its first foreign office. Now it also has overseas offices in London and the Cayman Islands.

Access   Cidade de Deus
Osasco, SP, Brazil
(55) 11-259-2822

450 Park Ave.
New York, N.Y. 10022
(212) 688-9855

Bridgestone

Sales $4.9 billion
Profits $130 million
Rank Largest tire maker in Japan
World's 3d-largest tire maker
Largest bicycle maker in Japan
World's 5th-largest bicycle maker
Founded 1931
Employees 32,800 (average age: 38)
Headquarters Tokyo, Japan

*N*ewsweek once said that the name Bridgestone "sounds more like a domestic cottage cheese than a Japanese tire maker, and its advertising carries little or no hint of its foreign origins." According to *The New York Times* and several other authorities, Japanese companies use Anglophonic names "to gain acceptance in foreign markets and, no doubt, to deflect protectionist impulses among American consumers." In Bridgestone's case, however, this ploy was nothing if not honestly come by. The surname of its founder, Shojiro Ishibashi, means stone *(ishi)* and bridge *(bashi)*. "I translated my name into English and reversed the word order to make Bridgestone, as I felt it would be more acceptable internationally," the founder wrote in his memoirs.

He had his reasons. In the early 1930s, when the company was founded, there were fewer than forty thousand automobiles in all of Japan, and Ishibashi must have reasoned that without an export market his company lacked any reason to exist. It's a problem Bridgestone was still grappling with fifty-five years later, even though it had risen to become the world's third-largest tire maker after Goodyear and Michelin.

Most of the Bridgestone tires seen in the United States (and Europe) roll in on Japanese cars. They weren't selected by the eventual buyers; they come as standard equipment. The Japanese sell a lot of cars in the United States (and are beginning to do the same in Europe), and since Bridgestone holds 50 percent of the Japanese market, it translates to a lot of tires. Bridgestone has been the direct beneficiary of the Japanese success in automaking. But the tire business in Japan is like the tire business in the United States: Car builders drive a hard bargain on price, acting as if they are doing the tire companies a favor by putting their rubber on the wheels of new automobiles. The tire companies make their money in the replacement market.

When Japanese motorists replace worn-out tires, Bridgestone is the number one choice, just as Goodyear is in the United States. But when American owners of Japanese cars replace their tires, their first choice is not likely to be Bridgestone. The Japanese tire maker does not have much of a presence in the United States, where its market share in 1985 was estimated at 2 percent. One reason is that it was slow to develop a line of quality radials. Another is that it was slow to move into overseas production.

The handwriting was on the wall. To maintain its position Bridgestone was going to have to follow the Japanese automakers and open production facilities outside Japan. In 1983 it started to produce truck tires at an old Firestone plant at La Vergne, Tennessee, near Nashville, and in 1987 it said it would invest $70 million in this facility to set up a line for car tires. Bridgestone also makes tires in Australia, Taiwan, Indonesia, and Thailand.

Quality is something Bridgestone is beginning to wrestle with. Stories making their way back to Japan told of Americans and Europeans buying Japanese cars and immediately replacing the Bridgestones with Michelins or Pirellis.

In 1984 Bridgestone introduced a new tire design, RCOT, which it claimed gave a more comfortable ride, better tread mileage, and improved braking. In 1985 it was trumpeting the acceptance of its tires for use on all Porsche models. "Bridgestone is the first Japanese tire manufacturer in history to be granted this approval," said the company, noting that its tires had to undergo two years of testing by Porsche to get the nod.

There is a stodgy, inward-looking quality to Bridgestone that some observers ascribe to the long autocratic rule of its founder. Shojiro Ishibashi began his business career when he was seventeen years old, and he never was anything but the boss. Born into a samurai family on Kyushu, Japan's southernmost island, Ishibashi and his elder brother, Tokujiro, Jr., took over the family clothing business in 1906. But within a year they changed it into a company that made only *tabi,* the traditional, stocking-like Japanese footwear. In 1923 they put rubber soles on their tabi, and it was this work with rubber that led to tires. The Bridgestone company was founded in 1931 and three years later began producing tires at its new factory at Kurume on Kyushu. One third of the first year's output of 89,932 tires was exported. In 1935 it produced the first Japanese-made golf balls.

Ishibashi then hitched his star to the Japanese military, opening plants in China, Manchuria, Taiwan, and Korea (following their occupation by Japanese troops). In 1937 he moved the head office of Bridgestone to Tokyo. During World War II the Anglicized name had to go, and Bridgestone became Nippon Tire. In 1942 the Japanese Army took over Goodyear's factory in Java and gave it to Nippon Tire.

Where the Japanese Eat

In 1986, for the fifth straight year, McDonald's ranked as the largest restaurant operation in Japan. With 575 units open, McDonald's-Japan racked up sales of $866 million for the year, an average of $1.5 million for each restaurant.

The company emerged from the war relatively unscathed. Its head office in Tokyo was destroyed, and it lost all its overseas facilities, but the company's Kurume factory was not hit (though it stood only sixty miles from devastated Nagasaki). A new factory fifty miles east of Tokyo at Asahi, which had been built during the war to supply wheels to the aircraft industry, started making bicycles in 1946, interrupted by a forty-six-day strike in 1947. In 1949 the Asahi plant formed the core of a new subsidiary, today's Bridgestone Cycle Company.

Nippon Tire got its Bridgestone name back in 1951 and began modernizing and expanding its tire-making plant, using know-how generously supplied by Goodyear Tire, which never dreamed then that it would one day have to confront Bridgestone as a competitor. The technical pact with Goodyear, in which the American company even took a small stake in Bridgestone, lasted until 1979, by which time the Japanese company was turning out more than fifty million tires a year and ranked sixth in the world.

The drive to the top tier of the world tire industry was led by the founder. Shojiro Ishibashi, a hands-on leader, remained chairman of the company until 1973 when he took the title of corporate advisor, continuing to keep a watchful eye on his son and successor, Kanichiro Ishibashi. Shojiro died in 1976 at age eighty-seven. The photographs we have of him show a gaunt, clear-eyed, tense man. His Western-style suit hangs loosely on a frame whose tautness suggests an iron will. All the company literature describes him as the founder of Bridgestone. There's no mention of his elder brother, who was a partner when they started out in 1906. It's almost as if he was expunged from the company history.

The people who have followed Ishibashi in leadership roles did not share his daring. As the photographs appearing in annual reports show, they were a somber bunch. Smiles were nearly always forced. The contrast was captured by a *Fortune* writer, Bernard Krisher, who profiled Bridgestone in 1982. He described Kanichiro Ishibashi, who was then sixty-two, as "detached" and so cautious that "he's the type who, as the Japanese say, would tap a stone bridge three times with a stick to make sure it's safe to cross." Krisher portrayed Bridgestone managers as indecisive, don't-rock-the-boat people. In 1981, when Bridgestone was celebrating its fiftieth birthday, the president's chair was occupied by Shigemichi Shibamoto. He was succeeded the following year by Kunio Hattori. In 1985 Ishibashi was named honorary chairman, and Hattori was appointed special advisor to the board. Teiji Eguchi and Akira Yeiri were elected chairman and president, respectively. The Ishibashi family still holds more than 20 percent of Bridgestone's stock.

One legacy of Shojiro Ishibashi is a diversification that has Bridgestone making sixty-four different products, including hoses, belts, foam rubber, tennis balls, rubber bushings, and multi-rubber bearings or "rubber feet," used to protect earthquake-prone buildings from jerky movements or vibrations. Bridgestone's tire proving ground at Kuroiso, ninety miles north of Tokyo, is one of the largest test tracks in the world, featuring nearly thirty different kinds of road surfaces, including a cobblestone street imported from Belgium.

Another legacy is one of the largest private collections of French

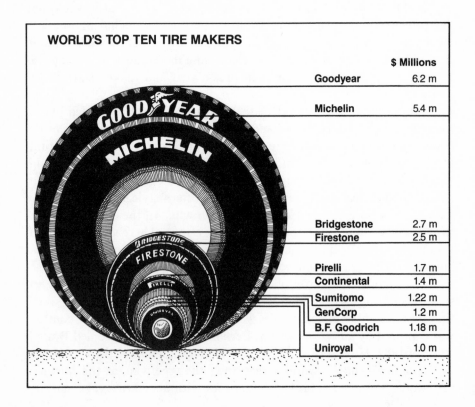

WORLD'S TOP TEN TIRE MAKERS

	$ Millions
Goodyear	6.2 m
Michelin	5.4 m
Bridgestone	2.7 m
Firestone	2.5 m
Pirelli	1.7 m
Continental	1.4 m
Sumitomo	1.22 m
GenCorp	1.2 m
B.F. Goodrich	1.18 m
Uniroyal	1.0 m

Impressionist paintings, works by Monet, Cezanne, Picasso, and Rousseau. They can be seen by the public in the Bridgestone Museum adjacent to the Bridgestone headquarters building in Tokyo.

Access   10-1, Kyobashi 1-chome, Chuo-ku
Tokyo 104, Japan
(81) 3-567-0111

Bridgestone (U.S.A.)
2000 W. 190th St.
Torrance, Cal. 90504
(213) 320-6030

British Petroleum	**Sales** $40 billion
	Profits $1.2 billion
	U.S. Sales $13 billion
	Rank World's 3d-largest oil company
	World's largest spot oil trader
	Britain's largest company
	2d on the *Fortune* International 500
	Largest shareholder in the Trans-Alaskan Pipeline
	Europe's largest producer of acetic acid
	World's largest animal feeds producer
	Founded 1909
	Employees 126,700 (47,850 in the United States)
	Headquarters London, England

British Petroleum (known the world over as BP) has been a major force on the petroleum scene for virtually the entire twentieth century, and had it exercised a little more vision and political savvy, it might easily have reigned as the largest oil company in the world—for a while, anyway. As it is, BP ranks, by most measures that can be applied, as the world's third-largest oil producer, outdistanced only by Exxon and Royal Dutch Shell. The company was originally funded by the British government, which owned varying stakes in it from 1914 to 1987. That government interest was slated to be reduced to zero by 1988. British Petroleum probably will enter the twenty-first century bearing a new name.

The figures for these oil monsters are always mind-boggling. In 1986 BP was producing oil and gas in twelve countries and exploring for new reserves in (or offshore of) twenty-nine countries. It was operating refineries in seventeen countries, and the 1.9 million barrels of oil produced *every day* by these refineries were sold in fifty countries. In 1986 BP also owned 55 percent of the eighth-largest oil company in the United States, the Cleveland-based Standard Oil Company, the original John D. Rockefeller company and the only one still using the Standard Oil name. And in 1987 BP paid $7.9 billion to buy all the Standard Oil shares it didn't already own, thereby solidifying its grip on third place in the oil business.

Aside from oil BP was running a $3.5 billion chemicals business; selling 14 million tons of coal; mining copper, zinc, silver, and gold in Brazil, Australia, Norway, Canada, and South Africa; selling $1.5 billion of animal feeds; operating thirty-one oil tankers; and selling about $250 million of detergents, household cleaners, and personal-care products mainly to European stores which sell them under their own labels.

It's amazing what drilling for oil can get you into.

BP's story all started with a British adventurer, William Knox D'Arcy, who was the first to tap into oil in the Middle East. D'Arcy had made his fortune earlier in the Australian gold rush, and at the turn of the century he had retired to lead a grand life in England. But then he became stimulated by the gusher stories from America and intrigued by the scattered but persistent reports of oil in Persia. (The reports had circulated for many years. Baron Julius de Reuter, founder of the Reuters news agency, secured a concession from the Persian government as early as 1872 but couldn't bring it in.) D'Arcy never set foot in Persia but he sent a geologist, who reported favorably on the prospects for oil, and after obtaining a concession twice the size of Texas (in exchange for £20,000, 20,000 one-pound shares, and 16 percent of the profits), he financed an exploration team headed by George B. Reynolds, a rugged, self-taught engineer who had the gritty determination to see this project to the end. The circumstances of Reynolds's efforts are well depicted in *Adventure in Oil*, a history of British Petroleum published in London in 1959. The author was Henry Longhurst, a member of Parliament at one point in his life but described on the flyleaf as "best known as the golf correspondent of the *Sunday Times.*" Longhurst tells how it was exploring for oil in Persia in the first decade of the century:

> As all the machinery and equipment had to be sent through England via Basra and Baghdad, Reynolds, traveling out through Russia and Teheran [he had been working in India], decided to make his headquarters in Baghdad. The prospect that confronted him as he rode out to survey the scene of operations may well have caused his heart to sink. A barren, inhospitable land; no roads worthy of the name; little or no water, either to drink or for the boilers when they arrived; tribesmen of uncertain temper; and all the time the sun blistering down at more than 100 degrees in the shade. In England there were long delays in assembling all the drilling gear, stores and equipment, and when it did arrive the Turks would not let the heavily loaded wagons pass over the bridge at Khanaquin, though it was manifestly strong enough, nor, they said, must they cross over into Persia by any route except the one via Khanaquin, which happened to be impassable at the time. Meanwhile, Reynolds spent much of his time haggling with the local chiefs, who made it abundantly plain that, whatever else the Shah might think he was including in his concessions, he was not conceding the use of their land without some sort of payment to them.

Exploration proved more expensive than even a gold-rush million-aire could afford, and D'Arcy had to invite in as a partner Burmah Oil, Britain's first oil company. On May 26, 1908, seven years after they started, Reynolds and his drillers struck oil at Masjid-i-Sulaiman in the southwest corner of Persia near the Mesopotamian territory ruled by the Ottoman Turks (now Iraq). The news was cabled out in code: "SEE PSALM 104 VERSE 15 THIRD SENTENCE AND PSALM 114 VERSE 8 SECOND SEN-TENCE." The translation (from the Old Testament): "That he may bring out of the earth oil to make a cheerful countenance, the flint stone into a springing well."

It was an historic find: The first oil field in the Middle East, the biggest penetrated in the world up to that time. To operate the concession, D'Arcy and Burmah Oil formed the company that was to become BP, the Anglo-Persian Oil Company. Even with Burmah's backing the company ran perilously short of money as it drilled the field and laid (with the help of six thousand mules) the first oil artery in the Middle East, a 130-mile pipeline to Abadan, an island at the head of the Persian Gulf. This time the British government came to the rescue. In a deal engineered by Win-ston Churchill, the Admiralty signed a long-term contract for fuel, and in 1914 the British government bought a 51 percent interest in the com-pany for £2 million.

Anglo-Persian's monopoly in Persia was so profitable that the com-pany wasn't too motivated to look for oil elsewhere in the world. In fact, it didn't even fight hard for concessions in neighboring countries, although its position in the Middle East was enhanced on October 14, 1927, when the Turkish Petroleum Company struck oil in neighboring Iraq. It was another huge find, and the countries that had won World War I shared in the spoils. Anglo-Persian was down for 23.75 percent of Turkish Petro-leum. The American oil companies, notably Standard Oil of California (later Chevron) and Gulf (also later Chevron), aced out the British in Saudi Arabia and Kuwait, but Persia remained the biggest oil producer in the Middle East until 1951.

Anglo-Persian never saw the revolutionary storm clouds brewing in the Middle East. In 1933 the Shah of Iran extended the company's conces-sion until 1993. So why worry? In 1935 Persia changed its name to Iran, and Anglo-Persian changed its name to Anglo-Iranian. After World War II Anglo-Iranian was under the direction of Sir William Fraser, a Scots-man who had grown up in the oil industry. When other countries (Iraq, Venezuela, Saudi Arabia) negotiated new fifty-fifty profit-sharing deals with the oil companies, Sir William was unmoved. After all, he had a better deal that ran to 1993. In 1951 the assassination of a prime minister who had said that Iran could not repudiate its agreement with Anglo-Iranian put a fiery nationalistic leader, Dr. Mohammed Mossadegh, in power. He seized the oil fields after the British showed they were not prepared to defend them with force. The Labour party, which had just nationalized a number of industries in Britain, was given this report by Kenneth Younger, one of its leaders:

> The principal reason why our advance information was inadequate was the short-sightedness and the lack of political awareness shown by the Anglo-Iranian Oil Company. They were far better placed than anybody else to make a proper estimate of the situation . . . but they never even seriously tried to do so. Sir William Fraser is no doubt a very good businessman in the narrow sense, but on every occasion when I have seen him, either at ministerial meetings or elsewhere . . . he has struck me as a thoroughly second-rate intellect and personality. He has on many occasions stated in my presence that he does not think politics concern him at all. He appears to have all the contempt of a Glasgow accountant for anything which cannot be shown on a balance sheet.

After its facilities were seized, Anglo-Iranian conceived a plan to let Iran drown in its oil. It convinced its six sister companies (Exxon, Shell, Texaco, Gulf, Mobil, and Chevron) not to buy Iran's oil. However, as Anthony Sampson pointed out in *The Seven Sisters,* the United States was not sympathetic to the British cause. In his memoirs, published twenty years later, Secretary of State Dean Acheson said Anglo-Iranian's "own folly had brought them to their present fix." In 1953 Dr. Mossadegh was toppled in a coup engineered by the Central Intelligence Agency (see Jonathan Kwitny's *Endless Enemies* for documentation) that restored the Shah to power. And after the dust had settled, a new consortium in which all Seven Sisters participated took over the oil concession in Iran. Anglo-Iranian, which previously enjoyed 100 percent of Iranian oil, was down to 40 percent. Testifying before Congress in 1974, Howard Page, the Exxon vice president who negotiated the new concession, said, "As I understand it, 40 percent for BP was the maximum that would be politically allowable within Iran." Anglo-Iranian also got $70 million in compensation.

It may have been a blessing in disguise for Anglo-Iranian, which changed its name to British Petroleum in 1954. The Americans replaced the British as the "bad guys" in the Middle East, and BP was compelled to think about the rest of the world. In 1979 the Khomeni revolution ended all Western involvement in Iran, and Nigeria nationalized BP's assets. In 1980 Kuwait slashed in half the oil supplies it had been selling through BP.

The British government's controlling share in BP escalated from 51 percent to 68 percent in 1975 when the old Burmah Oil company collapsed and had to sell its shares to the Bank of England. In 1977 the government put up $1 billion worth of BP shares for sale to the public. One investor, the Shah of Iran in Teheran, offered to buy the entire issue, even sending in a down payment of $375 million. In a rare moment of lucidity, Whitehall rejected this sentimental bid.

Forced to scramble for oil after being ejected from the Middle East, British Petroleum proved to be remarkably adept. In 1969 its exploration team made a huge strike in Alaska's Prudhoe Bay. And in 1970 it struck another huge oil field close to home, in the North Sea. BP suddenly found itself the owner of one sixth of all the oil in the North Sea and one eighth of all the oil in the United States. "People talk about gardeners having green thumbs," said Paul Frankel, president of the British consulting firm Petroleum Economics Ltd. "For my money, BP has the brownest fingers in the business." It may not be surprising that in 1983 when China issued contracts for drilling in the South China Sea, the very first award went to BP.

Despite its close ties to the British government, BP was always prone to act like other multinationals rather than an arm of the United Kingdom. In 1914, when the British government acquired its stake in British Petroleum, Winston Churchill advocated the investment because he didn't trust Shell to come through for Britain. Sixty years later it didn't seem as if BP would either. In *The Seven Sisters* Anthony Sampson disclosed that after the Middle East oil producers imposed their embargo in late 1973 to punish Israel and all states supporting Israel, British Prime Minister Edward Heath summoned the two top executives of Shell and BP—Frank McFadzean and Sir Eric Drake, respectively—to his country home to insist that the companies maintain their supplies to Britain. The oilmen said they could not make that guarantee, pointing out that if they didn't follow the allocations dictated by OPEC (the Organization of Petroleum Exporting Countries), they risked losing their concessions. Drake was not shaken when the prime minister reminded him that the British government owned 51 percent of BP. Drake said that he would have to have his instructions from the government in writing, detailing which countries would—or would not—get oil. Drake later told Sampson: "It was the first showdown with the government that BP have had." And it was clear that BP won the showdown.

In 1987 the Thatcher government decided to put its entire BP holding—32 percent of the stock—up for sale. It was expected to bring in nearly $8 billion. Although it was a Labour government that started the BP selloff in 1977, Roy Hattersley, economic spokesman for the Labour party in 1987, denounced this move, charging that the government was "selling the nation's assets to pay the Conservative party's election bills." An accountant figured out that the remaining shares held by the government were worth 2,400 times what Winston Churchill paid for the original 51 percent stake in 1914.

In 1981 fifty-year-old Peter Walters, the son of a Birmingham policeman, became the youngest chief executive in BP's history. And he injected some new excitement into the company. His prescription was to make each part of the business pay its way and not worry about chucking losers. In three years he reduced refining capacity by 35 percent, cut the payroll by 14 percent, and, because of tax reasons, sold off producing oil fields in Alaska and the North Sea. He made BP much more of a wheeler-dealer, buying the oil it needed in the spot market. In the old days oil men used to talk with awe about Texaco being able to supply all of its own needs from wellhead to gasoline station pump. Sir Peter—he was knighted in 1984—was not afraid to say, "It doesn't matter to me if one barrel of BP's production goes through the BP system." BP's strategy was made to order for a time of falling oil prices. In 1984 *BusinessWeek* reported that BP had become the world's largest trader in the spot oil market, handling more than 1 million barrels a day and filling half its needs with these purchases.

Sir Peter also demonstrated in 1986 that he was capable of being tough with any manager whose performance was found wanting. After its Alaskan oil discovery in 1969, BP traded those reserves for a minority (later expanded to a majority) stake in the Standard Oil Company of Ohio (Sohio). It was a deal that greatly expanded BP's presence in the American market. As the Alaskan oil began to flow in the 1970s, just in time to benefit from the sharp OPEC-dictated price increases, Sohio was awash in money, which it used to buy Kennecott Copper and step up exploration activities. The exploration efforts fizzled (no promising fields were found), and Kennecott was an unmitigated disaster as copper prices nosedived to all-time lows. In 1985 Standard Oil saddled London with a $1.8 billion writeoff of mining assets. In early 1986, just as Standard Oil was about to issue its annual report to shareholders, BP sacked the two top officers—Alton W. Whitehouse, Jr., and John R. Miller. To replace Whitehouse as chairman, Sir Peter sent over forty-six-year-old Robert B. Horton from London. At BP Horton had earned the nickname "Horton the Hatchetman" for closing twenty plants and laying off 60 percent of the chemical work force. *The Wall Street Journal* reported that shortly after arriving at Standard Oil's Cleveland headquarters, he was told that the city's main waterway, the Cuyahoga, means "crooked river." He reportedly said, "We'll just have to straighten it out, won't we?"

Four months after Horton's arrival, BP made another big move in America by acquiring the animal feeds business of Ralston Purina for $500 million. Added to the feed business it already had in Europe, the acquisition made BP the world's largest supplier of animal feeds with an annual output of 8 million tons. Animal feeds was Ralston's original business.

A year after Horton arrived in Cleveland, he had done such a good job straightening out Sohio's affairs that BP decided to buy up the entire company. To do the deal required some short-term bridge financing—and BP asked Morgan Guaranty in New York to syndicate a $5.5 billion loan. In five days sixty banks around the world offered to lend BP $15 billion. (It would seem that BP's credit is good.)

Despite diversification, which has given BP nonoil sales of more than $5 billion a year, finding new crude remains a top priority. In 1985 BP drilled wells in twenty-five countries, including Britain, Norway, the United States, Canada, Indonesia, Australia, and (for the first time) Ecuador and Cameroon. By the end of 1985 it had drilled fourteen wells in the South China Sea—all dry. With Sohio BP had also invested $460 million drilling in Alaska's Mukluk field only to tap into water instead of the 3 billion barrels of oil expected. *BusinessWeek* reported that the Mukluk dry holes inspired a joke in London about a Sohio executive making a transatlantic phone call to say he had some good news and bad news: "The bad news is that we didn't find any oil. The good news is that we didn't find any copper either."

Access   Britannic House
Moor Lane
London EC1Y 9BU, England
(44) 1-920-8000

Standard Oil Company
200 Public Square
Cleveland, Ohio 44114
(216) 586-4141

Britoil	**Sales** $1.4 billion
	Profits $50 million
	Rank World's largest company engaged solely in the exploration and production of oil and gas
	Biggest holder of oil reserves in the North Sea
	Founded 1976
	Employees 1,600
	Headquarters Glasgow, Scotland

The Labour party was in power in Britain when oil was discovered in the North Sea in 1969. (An American company, Phillips Petroleum, made the find—the Ekofisk field off Norway.) The next year, when the Conservatives returned to power, British Petroleum made the first find in the British part of the North Sea (the Forties field off Scotland). In granting concessions, the British government tried to favor small companies and British companies, but exploring for offshore oil calls for big bucks, and in the end it was the familiar cast of characters with rigs in the North Sea: BP, Exxon, Shell, Texaco, Chevron, Gulf, Mobil, plus some small British independents.

The North Sea discovery was great news for the British. It meant that for at least thirty years they could supply all their own oil. They didn't have to be hostages to Middle East crude. There was just one catch: The country was relying on the same companies that had made crucial mistakes in the Middle East. And, as a 1973 study commissioned by Parliament showed, no matter which party was in power, the oil companies regularly came away with very favorable terms for drilling rights in the North Sea. Britain was getting a smaller cut than were other countries in comparable circumstances. In author Anthony Sampson's words, the concessions were given "as though Britain were a gullible sheikhdom."

The results of this study were still reverberating in 1974 when the Labour party returned to power in the midst of a world oil crisis. The Organization of Petroleum Exporting Countries (OPEC) had succeeded in jacking up the price of oil to unheard of levels, good news only to someone with crude to sell. In addition, by mounting an embargo, the Middle East oil producers reinforced old fears in the West about lack of control over a vital energy resource. The Labour government moved quickly then to establish British authority over the North Sea by creating the British National Oil Corporation (BNOC). It went into business on January 1, 1976, starting with the offshore interests that had previously been assigned to the National Coal Board (it was a case of taking from one nationalized company to start another). Later in the year BNOC also picked up the North Sea interests of bankrupt Burmah Oil. And finally, to grease the path, the government agreed to award to BNOC 51 percent of all the new concessions granted in the North Sea. Nothing like having a rich (or at least a powerful) daddy to set you up in business.

To manage BNOC the government recruited Lord Kearton, a businessman who had just accomplished the startling feat of reinvigorating one of Britain's calcified corporate dinosaurs, the Courtaulds textile company. "This is a policy geared to the real world," said Lord Kearton on his appointment, emphasizing how important it was for Britain to control oil resources. It was a throwback to 1914 when Winston Churchill succeeded, for the same reasons, in getting the British government to buy a 51 percent stake in British Petroleum. The government, in 1976, went one step further: It set up its own oil company. Eric Varley, energy minister in the Labour government, said to the House of Commons in 1975, "No other government outside the United States has thought it wise to be completely dependent on the oil companies." And Anthony Sampson noted the irony of the British having protested against government participation in the oil fields of the Middle East and "having denied it to the Iraqis over the past fifty years" now insisting "on it for themselves. But it was characteristic of oil that once found in anyone's territory, it made the world look different." (It's interesting that British Petroleum was not considered an instrument of national policy even though the British government, together with the Bank of England, owned 68 percent of the shares in the mid-1970s. BP went about its business acting like a private company, treating Her Majesty's Government the way it treated other shareholders—with disdain.)

BNOC (popularly pronounced BEE-knock) started off in the oil business at the right time. With Harvard-trained Shiekh Zaki Yamani of Saudi Arabia calling the shots, the price of oil, $11 a barrel when BNOC was formed, went to $34 a barrel in six years. At that price it would have been very difficult for even an incompetent oil producer to come out on the losing side. The first oil from the BNOC fields in the continental shelf came up in 1978. In that same year a BNOC exploration team discovered a new North Sea field that was dubbed Clyde. By 1981 five-year-old BNOC was taking in more than $1 billion per year and had a staff of 3,000 directed from its Glasgow headquarters. Flush with profits from the sale of what seemed to be a dwindling commodity (from the start BNOC didn't encumber itself with any downstream activities such as refining or the operation of service stations), in 1982 the company commissioned the construction of a $50 million, "high-tech" headquarters building in Glasgow. Just because it was government-owned didn't mean it had be dowdy like the British Railways. This was, after all, the oil business.

However, BNOC was the offspring of a Labour government, and what Labour could create, the Conservatives could undo. In 1979 the Conservative party returned to power with Margaret Thatcher as prime minister and a commitment to sell government-owned entities to private investors. In 1982 they acted on this commitment by organizing a new company, Britoil, to hold the exploration and production activities of BNOC, and by putting up for sale 51 percent of Britoil. The sale raised $900 million for the government but it was not the most successful offering, as underwriters found they could sell only 27 percent of the issue at the offering price. Investors may have been frightened off by the denunciations of the Labour party, which warned that once it got back in power, it would renationalize Britoil. It must have given pause to some speculators to hear a Labour spokesman, Peter Shore, declare, "We shall take back the Britoil shares and we shall pay not a penny more than the government itself receives. Let that message be registered by all those who hope to make a killing."

The Conservatives were undeterred. In 1985 they completed the privatization of Britoil by selling the remaining 49 percent in an offering that was much more successful than the first. The price, $2.77 a share, was 15 percent lower than the 1982 price, and the offering was oversubscribed by 400 percent. Britoil thus took its place as another private operator in the oil industry, although the British government retained the so-called golden share established at the founding of BNOC, a holding that gives Whitehall veto power over any takeover bids for the company.

Measured by market value (what investors were willing to pay for the stock), Britoil ranked as the thirty-fifth-largest company in the United Kingdom in mid-1985, just before it was completely privatized. In 1985 Britoil pumped 67 million barrels of crude oil and 86 billion cubic feet of natural gas, which still makes it a small player stacked against the industry giants. (By comparison, Chevron's 1985 output was 570 million barrels of oil and more than 1 trillion cubic feet of gas.) But Britoil does have the largest oil acreage of any company in the North Sea, and it has extended its exploration activities to onshore and offshore fields around the world, including Dubai in the Persian Gulf, Indonesia, Thailand, Denmark, and Egypt. In 1986 it applied for licenses to drill in Ecuador and Angola. Britoil's track record in finding oil has not been great. Beginning in 1984, in four separate transactions, it invested $180 million of its North Sea profits in the United States, gaining exploration and drilling rights in eighteen states. Results were so poor that at the end of 1986 it put these assets up for sale—and abandoned the United States. At the same time it set for itself a goal that virtually everyone in the industry considers ambitious, if not impossible: One half of oil reserves to come from outside Britain by the year 2000.

Britoil did seem to have the perfect man at the helm in this quest for new oil reserves. Australian-born David B. Walker joined the company in March 1985 as chief executive after twenty-six years with British Petroleum. A geologist, Walker worked for BP in Britain, Gambia, Algeria, Libya, Colombia, Kuwait, and Iran, and he supervised BP's extraction of oil from the Prudhoe Bay field in Alaska with service in New York (1969 to 1974) and San Francisco (1974 to 1977).

Talk about bad timing, though. Walker entered Britoil just as the bottom was about to fall out of oil prices. In the first half of 1986, the price of crude oil was more than halved, dropping at one point to below ten dollars a barrel. As a result Britoil's profits were halved and its stock plunged so dramatically that when the *Financial Times* made its mid-year calculations, Britoil was, by market value, the eightieth-largest company in the United Kingdom, down from thirty-fifth position a year earlier.

Walker responded the way his counterparts at other oil companies have: He hacked away at the payroll. Even though a survey by the new magazine *Business* had shown that Britoil ranked fourteenth in the country in terms of profit-per-employee, the company proceeded to fire more than one thousand people, roughly one third of its staff. These moves were welcomed by outsiders, who didn't have to stand on unemployment lines. Lucky Kellaway, writing in the *Financial Times,* said that before the cuts Britoil resembled a government agency rather than a private company. "It took the shock of the fall in the oil price to force through changes that were very much needed," she added.

The gleaming new headquarters building—Britoil House—was officially opened on December 19, 1986, immediately after this drastic cutback of personnel. The times may have been bad, but Britoil now had itself the grandest office building in Scotland, a granite-and-glass structure with half a million square feet of space occupying four acres of what had been a dilapidated area of Glasgow. Features include a patio garden and an interior mall with plenty of Sicilian marble and specially commissioned works from Scottish artists.

Virtually all of Britoil's permanent employees work in Glasgow near the North Sea oil fields that made this company possible. But the company did maintain a London outpost to deal with the City (London's Wall Street) as well as some legal and insurance matters. Less than fifty Britoil staffers occupied rather fancy digs at Stornaway House, an eighteenth-century mansion next door to St. James's Palace, where the royal family lives. It became known as "the people's penthouse" after the Labour government allocated the building to its newly formed British National Oil Corporation in 1976. Sir Philip Shelbourne, the merchant banker who took BNOC into the private sector and was Britoil's first chairman, preferred London to Glasgow. *Financial Times* writer Dominic Lawson reported in 1984 that Sir Philip was kept company there by "a black dog of uncertain pedigree, by the name of Brit." When Britoil was retrenching in 1986, Lawson said that Stornaway House might be put up for sale as part of the cost-cutting. Asked about that, Ian Stewart, of the Britoil press office at Glasgow, said, "The 'people's penthouse' story was an exquisite example of journalistic licence by Dominic Lawson. The building is not up for sale. We don't even own it. We lease it." But Lawson was right—Britoil did give up Stornaway House for rooms in not-too-shabby Upper Belgrave Street. Ian Stewart called it a case of the "instilled thought" becoming "self-fulfilling."

Britoil was privatized because of the Thatcher government's free-market ideology. But in 1985 Lawson interviewed the chief executive of a small North Sea oil producer, who commented, "Brother, if they think that the oil majors believe in the free market, they aren't living in the real world."

Access   150 St. Vincent St.
Glasgow G2 5LJ, Scotland
(44) 41-204-2566

Broken Hill

Sales	$6 billion
Profits	$705 million
Rank	Australia's largest company
	84th on the *Fortune* International 500
	World's 17th-largest steel producer
	World's 7th-largest producer of iron ore
	Australia's largest oil producer
	World's 15th-largest oil producer
	World's 4th-largest black coal producer
Founded	1885
Employees	61,000
Headquarters	Melbourne, Australia

The only country to occupy an entire continent, Australia stretches over 2.9 million square miles (the size of Western Europe), most of it uninhabitable but rich in mineral resources. Broken Hill Proprietary Ltd. (or BHP, for short) owes its existence to those mineral resources. It has been the largest company in Australia for as long as anyone can remember. No one else is even close to it. Not for nothing is it known as the "Big Australian." BHP accounts for 2 percent of the nation's gross national product, 8 percent of its exports, and 10 percent of the value of all shares listed on the Aussie stock exchanges. As *New York Times* reporter Hugh Menzies once said, it's "rather like being U.S. Steel, Asarco, and Exxon rolled into one."

The company took its name from a small town, Broken Hill, in the frontier outback country of western New South Wales. There, in 1883, Charles Rasp, a German-born boundary rider working out of the Mt. Gipps sheep station, found some pieces of black rock on a low hill just south the Barrier Ranges. He thought they were unusually heavy and dense, and so he sent off samples for assay. Back came the report: The rock carried silver and lead. Rasp and his fellow workers at Mt. Gipps formed a syndicate to mine the deposits, and in 1885 the investors incorporated BHP.

Broken Hill turned out to be one of the most fabulous finds in mining history. In its first eighteen months the mine produced 1 million ounces of silver, and by 1888 the town that grew up around it had a population of ten thousand. Geologists, metallurgists, and mining engineers from all parts of the world have trekked there to examine the lodes, which are estimated to be 1.7 billion years old. The Broken Hill orebody has yielded 180 different mineral species, seven of which were previously unknown. Since mining began Broken Hill has produced more than 150 million tons of ore, from which the extractors (BHP and others) have recovered 15 million tons of lead, 12.7 million tons of zinc, and 22,000 tons of silver.

The effect on Australia was also profound. In his book *The Minerals of Broken Hill,* published in 1982, Geoffrey Blainey said, "It is unlikely that any significant mining field of the future will exert as much influence as did Broken Hill on Australian life. This can be said with some confidence, less because the finding of another Broken Hill is so improbable than because of the fact that a major mineral discovery is more influential when it is made early in the life of a nation. As a nation becomes more populous and its institutions and economic life become more settled, it is less malleable to great mineral discoveries and similar events."

The population of Australia at the time of the Broken Hill discovery was two million. It was not until 1901 that it became an independent country.

BHP grew up with Australia. It began mining South Australia's rich iron-ore deposits in 1900 (initially the company needed the iron as a flux for its Broken Hill smelters), and in 1915, using the iron ore and the profits from mining, it began making steel at Newcastle, New South Wales. To supply its steel-making operations with coking coal, BHP started to mine coal in New South Wales in 1927.

BHP, like other mining and steel companies, required colossal amounts of financing. These funds were raised in cities where bankers and stockbrokers clustered, far from the nittygritty, backbreaking, and dangerous tasks of extracting metals from the earth and forging steel ingots in blast furnaces. At the mine and mill towns the emphasis was on production at the lowest possible cost; that is, at low wage rates. Broken Hill has a long history of management-labor strife. The company had its first strike in 1889, another one in 1892, and a fierce one in 1909 that shut down the mines for two years. In 1917, toward the end of World War I, strikes erupted again at Broken Hill, continuing until 1920 when the miners gained a thirty-five-hour work week. Australian business editor Robert Gottliebsen said the strikes "produced a highly charged climate of industrial bitterness which became legendary in its intensity."

No charismatic leaders appear in BHP's history. The top executives tended to be hard-nosed engineers. First there was Guillaume Delprat, a Dutch mining engineer (his father served as minister of war in the Netherlands), who was BHP's general manager from 1899 to 1921. Then there was Essington Lewis, a former Australian football star who joined BHP in 1904, just out of the Australian School of Mines, and who was to spend nearly sixty years working for BHP, with time out during World War II to mobilize the war production effort. Ian McClennan, a Melbourne University engineer, began working at a BHP iron quarry in 1933 and worked his way up to managing director in 1966. And through all this time there were the Darlings: first John Darling, an Adelaide businessman (it was in Adelaide that the first rock from Broken Hill was assayed) who joined the BHP board in 1892 and who was succeeded on the board by his son, Harold Darling, who served as BHP chairman from 1923 until his death in 1950, when he was succeeded by his nephew, L. Gordon Darling, who was still on the board in 1986.

BHP stopped mining at Broken Hill in 1939 (two other companies, one of them a Rio Tinto-Zinc arm, still operate three underground mines there) and moved into a raft of other activities, most of them natural-resource-related. Today, by dint of acquisitions and partnerships with other companies, BHP mines coal, iron ore, manganese, bauxite, gold, nickel, copper, molybdenum, and silver. These mining operations extend to New Zealand, Brazil, Canada, Chile, Indonesia, Brazil, and Papua New Guinea.

However, BHP's most important diversification was into oil and gas. In a fifty-fifty partnership with Exxon, it found gas in 1965 and oil in 1967 in the rough waters of the Bass Strait separating mainland Australia from the island of Tasmania. By 1985 those fields, which are not too far from BHP's headquarters in Melbourne, were supplying Australia with two thirds of its oil. BHP was deriving a third of its sales and more than half of its profits from petroleum. And, bitten by the bug, BHP began exploring for oil at other Australian sites (on- and offshore), in the South China Sea, the Yellow Sea, and in the United States, where for $500 million in 1984 it acquired the Kansas-based Energy Reserves Group, which has oil and gas properties in nineteen states and Canada. Energy Reserves Group is a nondescript name, and in 1985 BHP changed it to BHP Petroleum (Americas). BHP followed up this purchase with a $745 million acquisition of Monsanto Oil, which has oil and gas interests in fourteen states, the Gulf of Mexico, and Colombia.

In 1976, as BHP was luxuriating in its flow of high-priced oil, General Electric made what was up to then the biggest acquistion in U.S. corporate history, paying $2.2 billion to absorb San Francisco–based Utah International, a mining company with operations in Australia, Brazil, Canada, New Zealand, and the United States. Six years later, with a new chief executive (Jack Welch), GE changed its mind: It didn't want to be a miner after all. Would Broken Hill like to buy Utah International? Yes, it would. In the biggest takeover in Australian corporate history, BHP paid more than $2 billion to acquire Utah International in a complicated deal that wasn't completed until 1984. With this move BHP became Australia's largest coal exporter, but the main attraction seems to have been the opportunity to become more of a multinational operator. Utah International brought BHP into copper and molybdenum mining on Vancouver Island in British Columbia; steam coal mining on the Navajo reservation in New Mexico; coal mining in Kentucky and West Virginia (with a labor history to match BHP's); pelletizing iron ore at Samarco in the Brazilian state of Minas Gerais; dredging aragonite (a calcium carbonate used in the cement and glass industries) from the seabed between Florida and the Bahamas; and sizing up Escondida ("Hidden One"), a piece of Chilean earth that is supposed to hold the largest undeveloped copper deposits in the world.

The multinationalization of BHP (nearly half of its sales came from outside Australia in 1986) represents a dramatic shift. The company had positioned itself for a century as the "Big Australian," and overseas investors looking for an stake in Australia were always pointed to BHP. The company reversed that stance in the 1980s, positioning itself now as a resource company prepared to go anywhere in the world to mine and extract the minerals, metals, and hydrocarbons buried under the earth's surface. In 1985, when it was celebrating its one-hundredth birthday, BHP produced a glossy, twenty-six-page brochure depicting itself as "Australia's International Resources Company." The publication was notable for not mentioning the name of a single human being connected with BHP.

As BHP moved into new areas in the 1980s it lessened its historic dependence on steel. In cooperation with the Australian government, which began to subsidize Australian buyers of domestic steel, BHP reduced its steel-making capacity by 25 percent, automated its plants, and chopped its payroll by 35 percent. Steelworkers struck two BHP plants in the spring of 1986. Having shaved its costs, BHP is sending steel into international markets, competing with Japanese and Korean exporters. In 1986 it recorded sales of $460 million from exports of Australian-made steel to customers in thirty-six countries; the biggest customer: the People's Republic of China.

Once a company expands the way BHP has, it picks up an assortment of baggage. The list of subsidiaries in the annual report runs to nearly three hundred names. At any one time fifty ships, some owned and the others chartered, are plying the oceans with BHP cargoes (one of them is the largest coal-carrying vessel in the world)—they carry forty million tons a year. BHP owns 55 percent of Associated Airlines, a small Australian executive air transport line, and since 1973 it has owned 67 percent of Rheem Australia, which makes water heaters, woven synthetic fabrics, steel drums, and packaging. It also happens to bottle Coca-Cola in North Queensland.

Not a hero to the workingman, BHP is also not widely admired in business circles, where it has been seen as a lethargic giant protected by an Australian monopoly. *Fortune* called the company "staid." *The Journal of Commerce* said that "boldness and dashing" were "a little out of character" for BHP. And *Business Week,* in a 1980 analysis, said that BHP "has approached business as a gambler, jumping from one industry to another even when it had no expertise." Kevin G. Figgis, a BHP manager, told *Business Week:* "Our geologists once went looking for gold and found a thirty-meter-wide seam of coal. Once we found iron ore when we were looking for water." And the company was said to have decided to explore for oil after deliberations that lasted one day. "We did it like buying a lottery ticket," said Ray Hutchinson, another BHP manager.

That record may have encouraged Australian entrepreneur Robert Holmes à Court to make a bid for BHP. Beginning in 1983 he tried five times to take over BHP through his investment company, Bell Resources. A *Wall Street Journal* headline said: "An Australian 'Ant' May Eat Broken Hill." In 1986, after his last bid had failed, Holmes à Court was left with a 28 percent holding in BHP. Throughout the fight BHP executives had repeatedly denied that Holmes à Court would ever be offered a seat on its board. In September 1986 BHP reached a truce with the raider and gave him a seat on its board.

Ian Story, an Australian stockbroker, said, "It's a temporary accommodation between the warring factions. I don't think Holmes à Court has spent $3 billion and three years of his life to stop here." On another occasion in this long-standing battle, Holmes à Court said, "The elephant is always eaten by the ant in the end."

Access   140 William St.
Melbourne 3000, Australia
(61) 3-609-3333

550 California St.
San Francisco, Cal. 94104
(415) 774-2152

BSN	**Sales** $5.8 billion
	Profits $150 million
	U.S. Sales $700 million
	Rank France's largest food company
	Europe's 3d-largest food company
	Europe's leading bottle manufacturer
	Leading yogurt seller in the United States
	Europe's 2d-largest brewer
	Europe's 2d-largest pasta maker
	France's 3d-largest champagne producer
	Europe's leading cookie and cracker maker
	World's 3d-largest cookie and cracker maker
	Europe's 2d-largest mineral water producer
	Founded 1966
	Employees 57,000
	Headquarters Paris, France

BSN originally made bottles. But Antoine Riboud, one of the three remarkable Riboud brothers from Lyon, decided that it would be better to make the products that fill bottles. Using American-style takeover tactics, he then transformed BSN into one of the largest food companies in the world. France had been longing for a French Nestlé. Riboud obliged.

The Riboud brothers—Antoine, Jean, and Marc—came from a banking family of Lyon, France's second-largest city, where eating well and making money are considered two of life's highest callings. Marc, the youngest (he was sixty-three in 1987), is a world-class photographer. Jean, who died in 1985 at age sixty-six, fought with Marc in the Resistance during World War II and spent two years in the Buchenwald concentration camp. He emerged to take command of a small oil-field services company, Schlumberger, which he catapulted into a fiercesome money-making machine, all the time keeping in the good graces of his friends in the Socialist party (see profile of Schlumberger on page 523). Antoine, the eldest (he was sixty-eight in 1987), began working when he was twenty-five at Souchon-Neuvesel, a glass bottle manufacturer that had been founded in Lyon by his maternal granduncle and was then being run by his uncle. It was not a small company, being the supplier of one-half the glass bottles sold in France. And it also owned a part of the Evian mineral water company, which had a baby food subsidiary. (Guess whose bottles they used?)

Antoine rose steadily in the ranks until he succeeded his uncle as chairman in 1965. After that it turned into a whole new ballgame. In 1966 he merged the family company with Boussois, a leading French maker of flat glass, and adopt the corporate name BSN. In 1968 he shocked a French business establishment not known for its entrepreneurial nerve by offering to buy Saint-Gobain, the three-hundred-year-old glassmaker whose mirrors can be found in the Versailles Palace. It was regarded, in the words of *Fortune* writer Robert Ball, "as an act of lese majesty almost equivalent to raiding Napoleon's tomb." Riboud's bid was rebuffed, but for him it was just a temporary setback.

He moved ahead on two fronts, shoring up the glass side by acquiring one of Europe's major flat glass makers, Glaverbel of Belgium, and integrating backward into food and beverages by taking full control of Evian and acquiring France's largest brewer, Kronenbourg. In 1973 Riboud propelled BSN into position as a European-wide food company by merging it with Gervais Danone, itself the result of a 1967 merger of a Normandy-based cheese company (Gervais) and a yogurt maker (Danone). Gervais Danone, in addition to holding substantial chunks of the French markets for fresh cheese and yogurt, had subsidiaries throughout Europe.

It didn't take Riboud long to figure out that he much preferred selling packaged, brand name foods and beverages to sheets of glass. So he began an exit from flat glass that was completed by 1981. The plants were sold off to PPG of the United States, Pilkington of Britain, and Asahi of Japan. And he put together a string of acquisitions that brought into BSN a long line of grocery products: Panzani pasta and sauces, Garbit ready-to-prepare dishes, Mac'Ani pet foods, Liebig canned meats, Amora mustards, Gallia baby foods, Diepal jams, Cracottes cracker bread, and Vandamme pastries.

BSN brands, led by the Kronenbourg label, hold 47 percent of the French beer market and 46 percent of the shandy business (BSN's brand is Force 4). The company also brews beer in Belgium (Kronenbourg), Italy (Wuhrer), and Spain (Mahou); and it sells beer under the Kronenbourg and Gold labels in Nigeria, Congo, and Gabon. BSN has two of the leading mineral waters in France, Evian (noncarbonated) and Badoit (carbonated). And it sells three brands of fruit-flavored drinks: Fruite, Eva, and Athlon.

Riboud looks increasingly to sell brand name products across many national borders. As he once told *Financial Times* reporter David Housego, "By the end of the century France will represent only one percent of the world's population, which is an insufficient market for our products." He means what he says. In 1981 he paid what some people thought was an outlandish price, $84.3 million, to recapture for France (and BSN) the Dannon yogurt business in the United States. Danone

yogurt was first produced in France by a Frenchman named Daniel Carasso, who fled to the United States during World War II. He started a
yogurt business in America, using the name Dannon. The Danone company in France became part of BSN, and the Dannon company of America became part of Beatrice Foods. When Riboud bought Dannon from
Beatrice, it had sales of $130 million; in 1985 Dannon's U.S. sales were
$213 million. It's the leading yogurt brand in the United States, with about
25 percent of the market. France, though, is where to sell yogurt. Per
capita consumption, at twenty-four pounds a year, is ten times the U.S.
level—and Danone holds better than 30 percent of this market. BSN also
sells yogurt under the Danone name in West Germany, Italy, Belgium,
the Netherlands, Mexico, Brazil, and (in a partnership with Ajinomoto)
Japan. Daniel Carasso, in 1986, was still serving as honorary chairman of
the board of BSN.

Under Antoine Riboud, a true son of Lyon, BSN has never lost its
appetite for food and drink. In 1984 two large champagne houses, Lanson
and Pommery, were quaffed. In 1985 BSN devoured 68 percent of Ponte,
Italy's fourth-largest pasta producer, and, still hungry, in early 1986 it
managed to get down a minority interest in another Italian pasta house,
Agnesi. Combined with the French pasta maker Panzani, acquired in
1974, the Italian additions make BSN one of the world's largest spaghetti
benders. Meanwhile, as insurance against indigestion, it acquired the
French pharmaceutical company Bottu, maker of the pain relievers Doli-
prane and Salipran and the artificial sweetener Pouss'Suc.

On May 22, 1986, Riboud pulled off his biggest acquisition, gaining
control of Générale Biscuit after noting that foreign food companies had
been taking an interest in the French cookie and cracker maker. "Why not
us?" was his instinctive response. In taking over Générale Biscuit, BSN
became the third-largest cookie and cracker maker in the world (behind
Nabisco and Britain's United Biscuits). Générale Biscuit resulted from a

series of mergers and acquisitions that began in 1964 and continued for the next twenty years, reaching into the United States, France, Belgium, and other European countries. During this period of furious munching, thirty-two family-owned bakeries, some with histories going back to the nineteenth century, were integrated into this corporate cake. They boasted some of the most well known brands in the European cookie constellation: LU, De Beukelaer, Brun, Guglielmone, Parein, Victoria, Heudebert, and Alsacienne. In the United States the eating binge consumed Mother's Cake & Cookie in Oakland, the Salerno cookie company in Chicago, and Burry Biscuit in New Jersey (longtime chief supplier of Girl Scout cookies). BSN now holds 15 percent of the European market for cookies and crackers and 6 percent of the U.S. market.

A heightened sense of social responsibility has been a hallmark of Riboud-managed companies. BSN likes to stress its "dual economic and social commitment." That commitment was tested in 1985 when the company closed breweries at Nantes, Melun, and Denain. To the 556 employees affected, BSN offered four options: early retirement, a job offer within or outside BSN, a retraining course, or help in starting a business. A fifth option, for immigrant workers, was help in returning to their native countries. BSN set up a European-wide personnel relations committee to exchange experiences and spur common approaches. A group of its personnel executives traveled to the United States in September 1985 to see if they could pick up any good ideas from American companies. *Bonne chance!*

Access   7, rue de Teheran
75381 Paris Cedex 08, France
(33) 1-42-99-10-10

Cadbury Schweppes

Sales $2.8 billion
Profits $133 million
U.S. Sales $600 million
Rank World's 3d-largest soft drink bottler
World's 5th-largest candy maker
Number one candy seller in Britain,
Ireland, South Africa, Australia,
New Zealand, India, and Malaysia
3d in the U.S. soft drink market
Britain's 36th-largest company
Founded 1783 (Schweppes)
1824 (Cadbury)
Employees 27,000 (2,600 in United States
and Canada)
Headquarters London, England

How sweet it is! The British sweet tooth is legendary (they have the dentures to show for it), and the Quaker chocolate firm Cadbury has been feeding it for well over one hundred years. Except now the enterprise is more than candy and it's worldwide in its scope. Cadbury, maker of Dairy Milk and a host of other candy bars and confectionery items, combined in 1969 with another venerable British company, Schweppes, maker of tonic water and other soft drinks, in a marriage that was to be blessed with many children, although some turned out to be wayward.

Cadbury Schweppes, by acquiring other companies in Britain, began distributing wines (Dubonnet, Andre Simon wines), bleaches and disinfectants (the Jeyes line), household cleansers (Scrubbs Ammonia), and fire-lighters (Wonderflame). The United States became a major target. In 1978 Cadbury Schweppes paid $59 million to acquire the third-largest candy maker in the United States, Peter Paul Inc., maker of Mounds and Almond Joy. Four years later it paid another $59 million to buy the Duffy-Mott apple juice and apple sauce business. Along the way it also acquired the Holland House cocktail mixes and majority stakes in Spain's Rioblanco (soft drinks) and Australia's Allen Confectionery.

The result was ballooning sales, half of which now come from outside Britain, but the strategy clearly failed on both sides of the Atlantic. In the United States, Cadbury has been unable to compete effectively against Mars and Hershey, which control 70 percent of the candy market between them. Cadbury, the market leader in Britain, with 26 percent of the business, holds only 8 percent of the American market. It did have high hopes for its new, textured chocolate bar, Wispa, which it spent five years

119

developing in England and launched in late 1983 with a blockbuster advertising campaign. Overnight Wispa became a $100 million product and captured third place in the British candy bar market. The achievement so overwhelmed Cadbury that the company sprang for full pages in British publications to pat itself on the back, attributing the success to "innovative and resourceful management," precisely the qualities critics had found wanting in Cadbury Schweppes. The aerated Wispa bar was tested in the United States in 1984 but failed to engender the same enthusiasm it had in Britain. *Fortune* writer Lisa Miller Mesdag interviewed the manager of a Boston store which carried Wispa. He said, "The people who buy it are business types. The kids don't go for it. They don't even steal it."

In its home market Cadbury Schweppes has been in full retreat. It sold off all its household product lines and exited the business of distributing wines and spirits. In 1986 it sold off, to managers and employees, its food and beverage division whose long line of grocery staples included Typhoo tea, Kenco coffee, Hartley jams, Chivers marmalade, Marvel powdered milk, Smash instant potatoes, Cadbury chocolate biscuits, and a product that goes back to the founding of the company, Cadbury cocoa (a goodnight toddy for many Britons).

The explanation for this retrenchment was familiar: The company wanted to concentrate on its core businesses, candy and soft drinks. One way it did that is by giving up a thirty-two-year relationship that Schweppes had with Pepsi-Cola. Schweppes was originally introduced in the United States by Pepsi; in return, Schweppes bottled Pepsi in the United Kingdom. In 1985 Cadbury Schweppes decided to cast its lot with Coca-Cola, in Britain anyway. It formed a joint company with Coca-Cola that's now responsible for the selling of all Coca-Cola and Schweppes products in the United Kingdom. In doing so it demonstrated its knack for arithmetic. Coca-Cola outsells Pepsi in Britain by four-to-one. The Coke-Schweppes combo sells one third of all the carbonated drinks downed by Britons, and it controls one quarter of the total soft drink business.

In the United States Schweppes shored up its soft drink business by two other combinations. First it acquired the Canada Dry and Sunkist brands from RJR Nabisco. And it followed that gulp by acquiring 30 percent of the Texas soft drink company Dr Pepper, which Coca-Cola wanted to acquire, only to be blocked by the Justice Department. The restructuring means that in Britain, Schweppes and Coca-Cola are partners, while in the United States they square off against each other.

Schweppes also has a secret weapon: SodaMate. This is an appliance patterned after the "Mr. Coffee" machine, enabling people to make their

own carbonated soft drinks at home with syrups they buy, presumably from Schweppes. Schweppes entered this self-destructive business in 1985 when it acquired a British outfit called Sodastream. In the United States a different corporate entity (in which Cadbury Schweppes holds the majority of shares) was formed to market a home dispenser of soft drinks. *Advertising Age* reported that in test markets salespersons were going door-to-door trying to sell $124 SodaMates to families, pointing out to them that with this device in their homes they wouldn't have to go out to the supermarket to load up on cans and bottles of Coke, Pepsi, and 7-Up, not to mention Schweppes, Canada Dry, Sunkist, and Dr Pepper.

Cadbury and Schweppes are deeply rooted British characters. Schweppes, the older of the two, qualifies for being the oldest soft drink company in the world. It has a curious history. Jacob Schweppe, a German-born Swiss, came to London in 1792 from Geneva, where he had been selling, since 1783, an artificial mineral water that had gained a reputation for its therapeutic powers. He set up a factory in London to make his mineral water and took on British partners before returning to Geneva in 1799. While he left, his name stayed on. Schweppe's mineral water was sold first through drugstores but then became popular as a mixer. It was followed in 1835 by Schweppe's lemonade, Malvern soda water (introduced at the Great Exhibition of 1851), and during the 1870s tonic water and ginger ale.

Tonic water is a quinine drink originally from colonial India. The British expatriates there took quinine to ward off malaria, and to mask the sharp taste of quinine they began mixing it with gin. They returned to England with a taste for quinine, and an enterpreneur named Erasmus Bond met that demand with a quinine tonic water in the late 1850s. However, as the historians at Cadbury Schweppes assure us, even though it was late on the scene, "it was Schweppe's tonic which soon established itself as the tonic water for the discerning adult."

Schweppes Ltd. was an early multinational. Before Coca-Cola was even born, Schweppes had bottling plants in Sydney (1884), New York (1885), and Melbourne (1885). It became a publicly owned company in 1897, and in the twentieth century it extended its reach to Europe, Africa, and Latin America; meanwhile annexing a string of other companies before the 1969 merger with Cadbury.

One of the acquisitions, L. Rose & Company (1957), has an English lineage of its own. It was the supplier, pursuant to the Merchant Shipping Act of 1867, of the lime juice that all British ships were required to carry to prevent scurvy. It was this practice that resulted in the appellation "Limey" for Britons. Lauchlan Rose, founder of this company, came from a shipbuilding family. He was the first to market a branded fruit juice. (The original product persists today as the essential ingredient of the mixed drink known as a gimlet.)

Cadbury is one of the Quaker families—Fry's, Rowntree, and Terry's are others—that came to dominate the confectionery trade in Britain. A strong strain of good works therefore runs through this history. Richard Tapper Cadbury, a draper who fought for the abolition of slavery, settled in Birmingham in 1794. John, one of his ten children, opened a tea and coffee shop next to his father's shop in 1824. Seven years later he began to make cocoa. By 1841 he was selling fifteen kinds of eating chocolate, which is made by adding massive amounts of sugar to the bitter cocoa. The Cadburys had a lot to do with cultivating the British sweet tooth. In a cold, wet climate, they supplied a product that had a warming effect.

The landmarks in Cadbury history have social and business import. The company likes to link them. A major event was the introduction of the Cadbury Dairy Milk bar in 1905. It breached the Swiss hegemony in milk chocolate and reigned as the leading candy bar in Britain for most of this century. (The leader today is the Mars bar.) Before that, in the late nineteenth century, Cadbury became the first company in Britain to give its workers Saturday afternoons off. It also closed its factory on bank holidays. In 1902 it brought on its first resident medical officer, and that was also the year it began inviting the public to tour its chocolate works. In 1905 it signed on its first full-time dentist (who probably had his work cut out for him). Cadbury's Milk Tray, "the box for the pocket," made its debut in 1915. In 1918 Cadbury merged with Fry.

One of the most famous Cadbury social experiments is Bournville, a suburb of Birmingham that John Cadbury's two sons, George and Richard, created to replace the slums which offended their Quaker sensibilities. Britain's second-largest city, Birmingham was an early industrial center of the country with deplorable housing conditions. Having outgrown their Birmingham factory in 1879, the Cadburys bought a fourteen-acre estate just outside the city to put up a new plant. They named it Bournville because it was fashionable at the time for confectionery to have a French name. They were determined, however, to build more than a factory. Beginning in 1894 they put up a model village, pleasant houses with gardens where their workers could live. In 1900 the Bournville Village Trust was established to continue this work. It's responsible today for seven thousand dwellings where twenty-three thousand people live. Many of the residents still work at the Cadbury factory, but a large number have jobs elsewhere—in the Rover auto factory and other plants that ring Birmingham. In 1900, when the Trust was established, nine of the twelve trustees were Cadbury family members. In the early 1980s nine of the twelve trustees were still Cadburys. In 1980 *Financial Times* reporter Lorne Barling visited Bournville and reported: "Even by today's standards, much of the housing in Bournville is luxurious. Some so-called workers' cottages have four bedrooms, and all houses have at least one-sixteenth of an acre, as decreed by the founder. . . . The houses are similar but different in style, setting the pattern of ordered informality, which remains the distinctive feature."

The Cadburys are not only still active in the Bournville Village Trust, they are still leaders in the company that bears their name, holding up under the sniping that has become de rigueur in today's financial discourse. Security analysts in Britain and the United States have had a field day criticizing Cadbury Schweppes for being a sleepy, family-run company, and reporters have been quick to pick up on this refrain. In 1986 *BusinessWeek* said the company had become a takeover candidate because of "stodgy management." Dominic Cadbury retorted, "We are not stodgy. We are professional and thorough." As an example he noted that right after he took over as chief executive in 1984, three hundred people left the U.S. subsidiary, by sacking or resignation.

Also in 1986 Hesh Kestin, a London-based reporter for *Forbes,* lambasted Cadbury Schweppes in an article harsh even by *Forbes* standards. Kestin depicted the company as "neo-Georgian," secretive (because they wouldn't let him visit a plant), and ruled by nepotism. He had this gratuitous warning for the Cadburys: "Big firms that can't compete can lose it all, which is essentially what happened in 1776."

There is still an old-world quaintness to Cadbury Schweppes, which markets its wares in more than one hundred countries, and that may stem from the nature of its products. Chocolate is an innocent. In its 1985 annual report the company explained how useful it was to have, unlike Hershey, an international chocolate business:

Creme Eggs and Mini Eggs, long popular in the UK, are now sold nationally in the US; and Mini Eggs are selling well in Singapore and Hong Kong. Boost was introduced in the UK from Ireland; India began manufacturing Chocolate Eclair Pops which were first developed in Africa; while Indonesia's Zip came originally from Maylasia.

Sir Adrian Cadbury, chairman of Cadbury Schweppes and Dominic's older brother, once explained to the *Harvard Business Review* the company's international philosophy: "We are a very humble kind of business: We're selling food and drink. These are commodities that any country could produce for itself. I've just been in Nigeria, where we have a sizable business. It is inconceivable to me that we could run our business successfully without a strong local content. So we have 60 percent of the business owned by the twenty-three thousand Nigerian shareholders." And Sir Adrian, who sits on the board of IBM-United Kingdom, added, "Clearly it is only a question of time before it is totally Nigerian, drawing on us for help where they require it." Those comments were made in 1982. Five years later Cadbury Schweppes was still holding its 40 percent stake in Nigeria, which happens to be the world's largest market for Cadbury's Bournvita malted chocolate milk.

The Cadburys are believed to control about 10 percent of the stock of Cadbury Schweppes, and they have expressed strong feelings about maintaining the independence of the company. Nevertheless, on January 26, 1987, they received a letter from Richard Smith, chairman of General Cinema of Chestnut Hill, Massachusetts, informing them that he had acquired 8.3 percent of Cadbury Schweppes. General Cinema operates the largest chain of movie theaters in the United States, owns the biggest independent bottler of Pepsi-Cola, and also bottles Dr Pepper and Sunkist. It was, in fact, the developer of the Sunkist brand now owned by Cadbury Schweppes. More to the point, General Cinema has never taken a position in a company (Columbia Pictures, Heublein, Carter Hawley Hale) that has *not* resulted in a major change in that company's standing as an independent entity.

Access 1-4 Connaught Place
London W2 2EX, England
(44) 1-262-1212

Cadbury USA
High Ridge Park
P.O. Box 3800
Stamford, Conn. 06905
(203) 968-7500

Canadian Pacific	**Sales** $11 billion
	Loss (1986) $60 million
	U.S. Sales $2.7 billion
	Rank Canada's largest company
	6th-largest railroad in North America
	Canada's 2d-largest producer of newsprint
	3d-largest steel producer in Canada
	Founded 1881
	Employees 93,800
	Headquarters Montreal, Canada

In 1881, when the Canadian Pacific Railway Company was organized, it had the daunting task of laying track across the top of Lake Superior through solid rock that was more than 1.5 billion years old and then through the Rocky Mountains and out to British Columbia on the West Coast. When the final spike was driven on November 7, 1885, it stood as the longest and costliest railroad ever built. One hundred years later Canadian Pacific was much more than a railroad. It towered as a hydra-headed colossus whose operations ranged from luxury hotels to grimy copper mines. It was selling newsprint in thirty-five countries and building shopping centers in Canada and the United States, and its rail receipts were outstripped four-to-one by revenues from other operations. Under the CP emblem, 110 companies now dealt not just in trains but in planes, trucks, ships, insurance, real estate, mining, chemicals, telecommunications, consulting services, steel, poultry, oil and gas, forest products, chinaware, animal feeds, pulp, and (with fingers in so many pies) even a milling company that baked pies.

In the first five years of its second century the going was not so great. Canadian Pacific went through three chief executive officers, and the peak earnings of $450 million ($580 million in Canadian dollars) in 1980 were just that, a peak never reached again. "The past year was one of unsatisfactory earnings," said the company's 1985 annual report, which may have been preparing the way for the next year, when profits vanished. A 1986 dispatch to the *Financial Times* presented this picture of CP: "The public relations department employs thirteen people in its photographic laboratory. While Mr. Stinson [William Stinson, CP's president] and his chief financial officer are based in Montreal, two group vice presidents and the vice president for administration work two thousand miles away in Calgary. The treasurer lives in Toronto."

If nothing else, this scattering of senior personnel provides a splendid testing ground for the company's techniques in teleconferencing, and indeed, CP may have been born to be scattered. At its birth it was given 25 million acres of land and $25 million of investor-subscribed money by the Canadian government. The company, many of whose directors were Scottish immigrants who had escaped poverty by means of fur trading and banking in the new land, took only fifty-three months to bond a railroad track to vast uninhabited prairie and mountain terrain.

It was an accomplishment that put the Canadian Pacific Railway (or the CPR, as it was then known) into the oceanic shipping trade, exporting goods to the Far East. It put the company into gas, oil, coal, zinc, lead, gold, and silver (the directors had thoughtfully kept the mineral rights to their 25 million acres). It opened the western Canadian prairie to settlement, with CP spearheading projects in wheat farming and irrigation. And most geopolitically of all, it helped to keep the United States from moving north. Pierre Berton wrote a history of the railway, *The Last Spike,* which captured its symbiotic relationship to Canada:

> For the next half century [1880–1930], this single corporation would be the dominant force west of Ottawa. Already its initials, CPR, had entered into the national lexicon; soon they would be as familiar to most Canadians as their own. In the decades to follow they would come to symbolize many things to many people—repression, monopoly, daring, exploitation, imagination, government subsidy, high finance, patriotism, paternalism, and even life itself. There were few Canadians who were not in some manner affected by the presence of the Canadian Pacific.

It brings to mind the story told by western settlers who resented the high-handedness of the CPR. A farmer comes home one day to find his cows with hoof-and-mouth disease, his well gone dry, his wheat flattened by hail, and his wife run off with a traveling salesman. Just then a lightning bolt strikes his barn and knocks him off his feet. As he get up, he shakes his fist at the sky and shouts, "Goddamn the CPR!"

Such was the Canadian Pacific's growth that it didn't even know how much it owned. *Moody's Industrial Manual* reported that in 1956 the company undertook a survey to determine its natural resource and real estate assets. The survey took seven years to complete.

Most of the original investors in Canadian Pacific were English, French, and American. It was not till 1965, under CP's most famous chairman, a bearlike, intimidating chainsmoker named Ian ("Big Julie") Sinclair, that the majority of shares was held by Canadians. Not content with stemming the tide of foreign investment, Sinclair was gung-ho to reverse it. "Everything in the United States is for sale," he declared. "All we have to worry about is the price."

No venture was too variegated for CP's taste. An unsuccessful attempt to take over the American manufacturer of KitchenAid appliances was balanced by the successful opening of a CP hotel in Philadelphia, another hotel in Jerusalem, and an airline catering outfit in Mexico City. In the United States CP's holdings include Syracuse China and 56 percent of the Soo Line, a large Midwestern railroad which bought out the Milwaukee Road in 1984.

Sinclair's philosophy of railroading is evidenced by the inventory of CP's railway cars in 1980, the year before he retired. The cast of characters comprised 69,000 freight cars, 1,300 locomotives, 3,600 maintenance and equipment cars, and 57 passenger cars. CPR, like railroads in the United States, had opted out of the passenger business. The mayor of a Montreal suburb once led a delegation to complain to Sinclair about the termination of commuter service to their town. "How did you get here?" Sinclair asked. "On the expressway," the mayor replied. "The meeting is ended," Sinclair said. To railroad buffs who wanted passenger trains to continue to traverse the country, Sinclair had this message: "Get on one of our planes. You'll get there faster."

The reference was to CP Air, the second-largest airline in Canada (government-owned Air Canada is the largest), which CP jettisoned in 1986 by selling it to the third-largest carrier, Pacific Western, for $215 million. For chief executive William Stinson, it was good riddance. He said that in forty-five years CP had never made any money in the airline business. While he shed the airline, Stinson held on to CP Air's string of upscale hotels, which include such posh watering places as the copper-turreted Banff Springs and the Chateau Lake Louise in the Canadian Rockies, the Chateau Frontenac in Quebec City, and the Royal York in Toronto.

Poor crop years in the early 1980s meant thousands of empty boxcars for CPR. In 1985, for example, the railroad, even with higher rates going for it, logged a revenue decline of $40 million because of reduced overseas demand for Canadian grain. And in the United States, the 7,600-mile Soo Line, serving the depressed farm belt in the Midwest, ran in the red. CP's 87 percent–owned PanCanadian Petroleum, one of Canada's largest oil and gas producers, made up for some of the shortfall in 1985, contributing three quarters of CP's profits. But when oil prices collapsed in 1986, Canada's largest company seemed to be taking a beating on all fronts. The CPR-hating farmers of yesteryear would have loved to see this day.

The one who had to face the music was William Stinson, who became chief executive in 1985. At fifty-one, he was the youngest boss in CP's history. "The probability of action being taken is increased when the person taking the action doesn't have to defend past decisions," one analyst said prophetically. Before long Stinson was hacking away at a company that because of its accretions bore only a slight resemblance to the railroad it started as. In 1986 and 1987 companies were being sloughed the way hoboes used to be thrown out of boxcars. One of the most wrenching moves was the $340 million sale of CP's 52 percent interest in Vancouver-based Cominco to a German-Australian-Canadian consortium. If Canada means anything, it's mining—and Cominco ranks as one of the world's largest miners of zinc and lead. It also mines gold, silver, and copper, and produces fertilizers and industrial chemicals. Stinson decided that CP just didn't have time to wait for metal prices to come back.

One project that was well under way by the time Stinson became president is construction of the longest railway tunnel in North America, a 9.2-mile boring through Mount Macdonald in British Columbia's Selkirk Mountains. "He doesn't care how long it is," a Toronto analyst quipped, "so long as there's light at the end of it."

Scheduled for completion at the end of 1988, the tunnel is named for Sir John Macdonald, who was prime minister of Canada from 1867 to 1873 and then again from 1878 to 1891 and who therefore had lived for quite some time with the threat of advancing American hordes. A number of American politicians viewed Canada as part of the "manifest destiny" of the United States. Macdonald seized upon the idea of a transcontinental railway to unite Canada, and in 1880 he found a trio of bearded Canadians—George Stephen, Donald A. Smith, and R. B. Angus—who were willing, with backing from French and British bankers, to organize the Canadian Pacific Railway. Associated with the company at its inception

World's Largest Paper Producers

	In tons
United States	62.4 million
Canada	14.2 million
Finland	7.3 million
West Germany	9.2 million
Sweden	6.9 million
France	5.6 million
Italy	4.7 million
Britain	3.6 million

was the legendary railway man James J. Hill, who was responsible in the 1880s for the building of the 1,500-mile Great Northern, connecting Minnesota with the state of Washington. But the man in charge of building the Canadian Pacific was William Cornelius Van Horne, recruited from the Chicago, Milwaukee & St. Paul Railroad, where he had risen from telegrapher to general manager. Van Horne was present when the final spike was driven at Eagle Pass in the Gold Range of British Columbia, where he made his famous fifteen-word speech: "All I can say is that the work has been well done in every way."

Access   P.O. Box 6042, Station A
Montreal, Quebec H3C 3E4, Canada
(514) 395-5151

Casio	**Sales** $1.5 billion
	Profits $20 million
	U.S. Sales $350 million
	Rank World's largest maker of calculators
	World's 5th-largest watchmaker
	Founded 1957
	Employees 6,800 (average age: 31)
	Headquarters Tokyo, Japan

I n 1946 *Stars & Stripes,* the American military newspaper, staged a contest in Japan that pitted a U.S.-made electric calculator against a Japanese abacus. The abacus's victory did much to ease the bruised ego of postwar Japan. Newspapers screamed: "Japan Wins!" However, at least four parties were not convinced. One was the winner himself, who realized that his victory was due to years of training. The second was a newspaper editor, who warned against over-confidence. The third was the big trading company C. Itoh, which later staged another contest that was won by the calculator. And the fourth was twenty-two-year-old Toshio Kashio, who wrote on a piece of scratch paper, "Abacus is human ability, calculator is technology." He believed that technology had no limits.

It was a prophetic statement. Eleven years later the Kashio brothers revolutionized the calculator business by introducing a ten-key relay device that didn't require separate windows for input figures, utilized a floating decimal point, making it easy for users to punch in their calculations. For example, $5 \times 3 = 15$ could be performed by pressing those keys in that order, one number disappearing as the next key is hit. This was a major advance over the unwieldy mechanism of the previous calculators, where the 5 showed in one window, the 3 in another, and the $\times$ in the third window, and *then* you hit the equal sign.

The four Kashio brothers—Tadao (born in 1916), Toshio (1923), Kazuo (1927), and Yukio (1929)—were raised in poor circumstances. Their father, Shigeru, was a failed farmer from Shikoku, Japan's smallest island, who pulled up the family's roots and went to Tokyo, where he spent four hours walking to and from work every day to save the train fare. Tadao became a skilled latheman and opened a small machine shop in 1942. It had one lathe. The family lived on the second floor. Toshio, always the tinkerer of the family, worked for the Japanese telephone company until he joined his elder brother to help him come up with new products. His first product was a ring with a cigarette holder welded to it. Wearing it enabled a worker to smoke without interrupting his labor by putting down or picking up a cigarette. In Japan, where men are heavy smokers, the ring sold well.

In 1950 the third brother, Kazuo, armed with a university degree in economics, joined his two older brothers. He took over the sales operation. It was then that Toshio, rummaging in his papers one day, came across the note he had written in 1946 about technology and was inspired to start tinkering with calculators. In 1952 the fourth brother, Yukio, joined the company. He had studied mechanical engineering.

Tadao had called his lathe company Kashio Manufacturing. But when the brothers went into the calculator business in 1957, they decided to eschew the family name and incorporate as Casio. It was a gutsy move to start a business that would go up against companies that were older, larger, and better financed and connected. The Kashio brothers flew blind, placing their bets on innovation; they believed the unique product would win. From the start Casio was not a copycat company. Toshio, the inventor, once described his creative process:

> The only thing I'm ever attracted to is creating something from zero. Knowledge often hurts. Most people, in starting something new, try to study the subject, rather than think. The knowledge they gain often limits their thinking. The world is full of people with knowledge. But knowledge alone won't produce original products. . . . Besides, it's easier to build your own hypothesis and to come up with your own solutions than try to understand someone else's theory.

It's a philosophy that helps to explain Casio's constant search for the unusual product, one with features not present in models made by other companies. And once it develops such a product, Casio prices it low, not high, and works with stores to make it a big seller. Its products are known for giving the most bang for the buck (or yen) and for their small size (Casio is a master at miniaturization).

Its assault on the hand-held calculator market was classic. In 1972, when the first electronic calculators were selling for $130 and up, Casio fielded its Casio Mini, priced at $42. It was not a puny performer, only the price was puny. Casio went on to become the leader of the calculator field. It has sold more than 300 million of them. In 1986, when it began to shift production to its Taiwanese plant because of the high value of the yen, Casio was turning out 3.6 million calculators a month—or 36 million a year!

Casio has used this same strategy in attacking other markets: digital watches, a field it entered in 1974 with timepieces that had an amazing number of functions and a low price (it has since sold 60 million digital watches), and electronic musical instruments, a field it entered in 1980 with its lightweight Casiotone keyboard powered by integrated circuits to produce various instrumental sounds.

In a Casio product the emphasis is nearly always on features you didn't think were possible in the compact machine you're looking at. In 1984 it introduced a new synthesizer that could generate the sounds of any natural phenomenon, including bird calls or the sea. It was simply a matter of storing this information in the synthesizer's electronic memory. The same technology made possible a digital watch that stores up to fifty telephone numbers. And in 1986 Casio introduced to the gadget-happy Japanese the world's thinnest pocket-sized television set. The size of a paperback, this set featured a two-inch liquid crystal display which was easy to see even in daylight and an earphone cord that doubled as an antenna. The price: $150.

Casio brings out this steady stream of new products—its 1987 item was an electronic camera—without checking first to determine consumer preferences. "New technologies never fail to open new markets," managing director Noriaki Shimura told the *Japanese Economic Journal* in 1986. "No market research is necessary for our new products." The company also doesn't have much time for theorizing. Kazuo Kashio, the economist, admitted in 1987 that Casio didn't have a plan when it started up. "Since we started out making calculators when the internationalization of this device occurred," he said, "all we did was turn out as many as we could for sale and export." Today Casio does 72 percent of its sales outside Japan.

Casio's operations in the United States, which bring in 27 percent of sales, are headed up by an American, John McDonald, whom the Kashio brothers recruited from Sperry Rand, much to his eternal gratitude. He once told Michael Schrage of *The Washington Post*, "We are a wants-gratification company. Ask me who needs one of these—and I don't know. But ask me who wants one—now, I can answer that."

Casio still doesn't rank among the super-giants of Japanese industry. It didn't make the *Fortune* International 500 roster of non-U.S. companies until 1985 when it ranked 480th (right behind Porsche). The next year it moved up to 477th place (right behind Jaguar). On the *Japan Times* 1,500, where Japanese companies are ranked by pretax profits, Casio placed

207th in 1986 (sandwiched between NGK Insulators and the Gumma Bank).

Casio has its headquarters on the thirty-eighth floor of the sixty-story Sumitomo Building in the Shinjuku section of Tokyo. It's flanked there by ten other skyscrapers, one of them a new Hyatt Hotel. You could be in Manhattan or in downtown Chicago, Houston, or San Francisco. The Casio offices are simple and spare. After being ushered into a private conference room by a couple of PR people (yes, they have those in Japan, too), you are joined by Tadao Kashio, who was seventy-one years old in 1987. He's the opposite of the usual image of the high-powered corporate executive. He has a very lean frame, almost gaunt. He replies to questions with direct, short answers. He obviously takes pride in the Casio "toys."

All the Kashio brothers were still active in the company in 1987. Their hardworking father, whom they had installed as chairman of Casio, died in July 1986 at eighty-seven. Their mother was to turn eighty-nine in 1987. In 1985 a biography of the Kashio brothers, called *The Thinking Family,* was published in Japan.

Of the sixty-eight hundred people who work for Casio, about one thousand are research and development staffers. The company allocates 4 percent of its sales to research, and each year it hires one hundred new university graduates. Tadao Kashio said Casio looks for "thinking" students who have "guts and emotional strength" to carry ideas forward. Casio gets along with so few people because it's a tiger about automation. One reporter noted, "Human beings are rarely seen engaged in the production of electronic calculators at the company's Kofu works [fifty miles west of Tokyo]."

Kazuo Kashio confirms this impression, pointing out that Casio is rapidly replacing the metal parts in its analog watches with plastic, which will make them easier to assemble (and no oil will be needed). "We are now in the process of exporting such technologies to European countries," he said. "One advantage is that there is no need to train local staffers, since machines do all the work. We already are operating some fifty such plants in China which produce calculators and electronic musical instruments on a complete knockdown basis."

The average monthly wage in Japan rose to a new high of $2,135 in 1986.

The largest-selling imported car in Japan is BMW.

Access   Shinjuku-Sumitomo Bldg.
6-1, 2-chome Nishi-Shinjuki
Tokyo 160-91, Japan
(81) 3-347-4800

Casio, Inc.
15 Gardner Rd.
Fairfield, N.J. 07006
(201) 575-7400

Ciba-Geigy

Sales $9.2 billion
Profits $472 million
U.S. Sales $3 billion
Rank World's 7th-largest chemical company
World's largest manufacturer of
dyestuffs
World's 2d-largest pesticide
manufacturer
World's 4th-largest pharmaceutical
company
World's 4th-largest vision-care
company
Switzerland's 2d-largest company
25th-largest company in Europe (by
market value)
Founded Geigy: 1758
Ciba: 1884
Employees 80,000 (13,000 in the United
States)
Headquarters Basel, Switzerland

The Swiss city of Basel, home to more major chemical companies than any other city in the world, combines old-world charms with modern angst.

Its split personality starts with geography. At the juncture of Switzerland, France, and Germany, the city is bisected by the Rhine River into two distinctive banks. The south, or left, bank holds Basel's cultural center, a warren of streets and homes, an eleventh-century cathedral (where the Dutch scholar Erasmus is buried), and twenty-seven museums. The right bank is a very different Basel; it holds the port and industrial sector, home to the factories of Basel's largest corporate citizens: Hoffmann-LaRoche, Sandoz, and Ciba-Geigy.

Proud of its intellectual heritage, the city's Old Town boasts Switzerland's oldest university, the University of Basel, founded in 1460. Erasmus taught there, and the university library houses not only his manuscripts but Martin Luther's as well. Basel was an important seat of humanism and Reformation activity. The Bernoulli mathematicians lived here, as did Friedrich Nietzsche and, in more recent times, the important Protestant theologian Karl Barth. The museums of Basel hold the world's largest collection of Holbein paintings. Basel is also home, on the south side of the river, to the shadowy Bank for International Settlements (BIS), a powerful multinational institution created in 1930 and sometimes called

135

"the central bank for central banks" or the international "lender of last resort." The banking moguls of the ten largest Western countries (the United States is represented by one of the governors of the Federal Reserve System) meet there on the second Tuesday of every month to discuss world financial problems. You never hear about the BIS—by design. The bankers who meet there are enjoined to avoid the press.

Basel does have its sentimental streak. Like Rhinelanders downstream, it cherishes the river. As a ribbon of brooding, misty beauty, banked at some points by towering rocks and at other points by vineyards and medieval towns, the Rhine evokes the romantic side of the German character. It is the stuff of myths, poetry, and operas. But its *waters* don't bear too close an inspection, not anymore. Even the most confirmed romantic would hesitate before eating a fish caught in the Rhine, an industrial water route linking big cities from the Alps to the North Sea. Coal barges ply its waters, and chemical factories, cement works, and power plants line its banks. Long before the Rhine reaches Germany's industrial Ruhr, it has collected the discharges of potassium mines, French factories, and Swiss chemical works.

Like their city and their river, the Basel chemical giants have two sides. Their products have helped people color their fabrics, treat their ailments, and protect their crops from pests. But time and again their inventions have wreaked havoc with the safety, health, and even lives of the people, animals, and plants whom they were intended to benefit. And all too often Basel's chemical makers have seemed callous about the impact of their accidents.

One of the most disastrous of these accidents occurred on November 1, 1986, when a fire at a Sandoz warehouse sent thirty tons of herbicides, fungicides, pesticides, and dyes into the river, turning a stretch of it red, killing untold numbers of fish all the way from Basel to the North Sea, and causing a shutdown of water supplies in some German and Dutch cities. Much to the embarrassment of the tidy Swiss, the Sandoz spill was followed at Basel by three other accidents in the next twenty days, including two at the Ciba-Geigy works—the leak of a weed-killer into the Rhine and the release of an acrid cloud of smoke from a phenol compound experiment that "went out of control." Ciba-Geigy apologized to the Baslers for the smoke cloud, wondering out loud about this "streak of bad luck" afflicting the Swiss chemical industry.

A report by a Swiss technical group in January 1987 found that the Sandoz spill was not as bad as first feared and that the Rhine would make a comeback as a habitat for plants and fish. So the Basel chemical makers appeared to have weathered still another crisis in a history that goes back more than two hundred years.

In 1758 Johann Rudolph Geigy, a young Basel merchant, set up a business to deal in *Materialwaren*—drugs, spices, and natural dyes. Basel was a logical place for dyes because it had a silk ribbon industry founded by Huguenot refugees from France. The Geigy family still had this business ninety-eight years later, in 1856, when the English chemist William H. Perkin found that dyes could be made synthetically, not just from natural substances like berries, bark, insects, or shellfish. He derived his coloring agent from the black sludge known as coal tar. Perkin's work was supplemented by the contemporaneous research of the German chemist, Adolf von Baeyer, who discovered the molecular structure of indigo. Perkin was knighted in 1906; von Baeyer received the Nobel prize in 1905.

The great chemical companies of Europe were founded on these laboratory breakthroughs. They began as dyestuff plants. In Germany BASF was born in 1861, Bayer and Hoechst in 1863. The Swiss actually beat the Germans to the punch. In 1859 Geigy, which had been making dyes from wood materials, started the production of fuchsine, a synthetic aniline dyestuff. In that same year Alexander Clavel, a French silk dyer from Lyons, also began to make artificial dyes in Basel. The business started by Clavel (he sold it in 1873 to Bindschedler & Busch) was converted in 1884 to a joint stock company grandiosely called Society of Chemical Industry in Basel, CIBA for short. It became so well known under its acronym that in 1945 Ciba was adopted as the official corporate name.

When Ciba and Geigy merged in 1970 in what they themselves called "the Basel marriage," each was already a potentate in the world chemical-drug complex. In 1969 Geigy registered sales of $722 million to rank as the ninety-first-largest manufacturer outside the United States, while Ciba ranked ninety-fifth with sales of $707 million. Geigy had become one of the largest insecticide manufacturers in the world after its invention, in 1940, of a white chemical compound that killed everything in its path and revolutionized pest control programs—DDT. It led to the synthesis of thousands of new organic chemicals and won the 1948 Nobel prize for its inventor, Geigy scientist Paul Muller, before provoking the "silent spring" reaction against its high toxicity (it killed "good guys" as well as "bad guys") and tendency to lodge in the food chain rather than break down. Ciba, meanwhile, had developed into a major pharmaceutical house. It pioneered in steroid hormones and for a while, after World War II, it had success making and selling a tranquilizer, Serpasil (an alkaloid derived from the roots of Rauwolfia plants). After India banned the export of Rauwolfia extracts, Ciba botanists traveled to Africa to find the stuff.

The Swiss companies have always showed a predilection for mind-altering drugs. Sandoz scientists experimented with LSD, and Hoffmann–La Roche early on developed sedatives derived from plant alkaloids (it once tried to plant opium poppies in Argentina) and later swept the tranquilizer field with Librium and Valium. The Swiss were also adept at forming cozy cartels. Geigy, Ciba, and Sandoz got together in 1918 to organize the Basel IG (for *interessengemeinschaft,* or community of interests) in which they agreed to allocate revenues according to a formula that gave Ciba 52 percent and Geigy and Sandoz 24 percent apiece. This agreement lasted until 1950 and had international ramifications. In 1929 the Swiss companies entered into a nonaggression pact with the I. G. Farben cartel of Germany. French dyestuff manufacturers then joined the cabal. And later Britain's Imperial Chemical Industries turned the group into a four-way international conspiracy.

Twenty years after dissolving the IG, Ciba and Geigy formed an association in which they could act in concert without running afoul of the antitrust laws of the United States: They merged. The Ciba-Geigy combination was dictated by a desire to eliminate duplication of research efforts. It also enabled Ciba and Geigy to forge a united front against their Basel neighbor, Hoffmann–La Roche, which was making giant strides in pharmaceuticals. The merger was completed on October 20, 1970, and nine years later it yielded one of the most unusual documents in the annals of corporate literature, a 419-page paperback book called *The Basel Marriage.* Written by a Ciba-Geigy executive, Paul Erni, the book was published in English, French, and German editions by the distinguished Swiss daily the *Neue Zurcher Zeitung. The Basel Marriage* chronicles, step by step, how the merger came about. However, unlike most business tomes, it's not a paean of platitudes. Instead, it reveals the conflicts and differences of opinion that always characterize human activity, even in a corporate setting. And—a very big bonus—the book is illustrated by the author's elder brother, Hans Erni, one of the leading Swiss artists of the twentieth century, who depicted the Ciba-Geigy mating in a series of line drawings which show a man and a woman in various stages of a romantic, sometimes sexual, encounter!

Paul Erni describes how the impetus for the merger came from two scientists with executive responsibility. In February 1969 they brought together the chairmen of both companies in a meeting where nothing seemed to happen. But Geigy chairman Louis von Planta's offer to drive his counterpart, Robert Kappeli, back to Ciba proved to be "the most decisive moment in the history of the merger." During the car ride Kappeli proposed the merger, and the two men sat in the car discussing it well after von Planta had pulled up outside the administration building. It took twenty months to complete the deal. The time was devoted to hammering out a one-to-one financial exchange, planning the amalgamation of products, marketing, and research, assuaging U.S. trust-busters, and preparing to marry two distinct working cultures. The last issue proved to be a big stumbling block. These might be two chemical-drug companies born and headquartered in Basel, but they were *different*. It seemed to employees, Erni wrote, "as if they could at once distinguish a colleague on the other side from one of their own compatriots by the way he walked, looked or talked, or even by the way he dressed."

Although it was the younger of the two companies, Ciba had an older and more staid cast to it. Ciba had achieved success early and liked to describe itself as the place "where research is the tradition." Geigy, on the other hand, had more of the underdog mentality. It was a risk-taker. It recruited under the slogan, "Future with Geigy." It believed in employee stock ownership, a concept alien to Ciba. Paul Wyss, Geigy's head of personnel, once said that researchers were burned out at forty. Ciba's research chemist, Adrian Marxer, retorted that between 70 percent and 90 percent of all drugs are discovered by persons over forty. The difference between the two organizations was brought home forcibly to Dr. Kappeli, the sixty-eight-year-old chairman of Ciba, when he had dinner one evening in the spring of 1969 at a Basel restaurant, the Schutzenhaus. A team of Geigy managers had assembled there for an annual meeting. "Dr. Kappeli looked over these younger people as they came into the restaurant and was not a little impressed by their lively demeanor," Erni reported. "They radiated a brightness which, as he himself confided, he rather missed in their counterparts at Ciba." From such chance encounters are important decisions in life made.

One of the hurdles to the merger was the Justice Department of the United States, where both Geigy and Ciba had important subsidiaries. Swiss lawyers worked for a full year with U.S. government attorneys to design a merger that would not be rejected on antitrust grounds. The final agreement called for the sale of Ciba's dyestuffs and optical brightening businesses in the United States as well as Geigy's U.S. pharmaceutical operations. The Swiss agreed to sell the Geigy drugs to USV Pharmaceutical, a division of Charles Revson's Revlon Inc., in exchange for cash and a new oral antidiabetic drug, DBI. However, a last-minute hitch developed when a medical report surfaced that questioned DBI's effectiveness in prolonging the lives of diabetics. The Swiss then decided they wanted more money. In his 1976 biography of Revson, *Fire and Ice,* Andrew Tobias described the negotiating scene in Basel:

> Charles was enormously impressed by the Ciba operation. A thousand marketing people! Scientists all over the place. It made his pride and joy in the Bronx look awfully modest. As the Revlon/USV forces were huddling on the way into the negotiations, he told them: "This is a fucking white shoe operation." Pardon? "A fucking white shoe operation," he repeated, as though that would make his meaning clear, "so I don't want any swearing or shouting in there. I don't want these guys to think we're a bunch of bums." He assigned the head of USV to be the group spokesman and asked how much the deal was worth. "Well, we've gone up to ten million dollars so far," came the reply; "I think we could go to twenty million, but I wouldn't go any higher than that." "Okay," Charles said, "let's go."
>
> In the conference room a team of Ciba professionals proceeded to assault the blackboard with numbers, relative values, best-and-worst-case growth projections, probabilities, present values, cash flows . . . they're drawing analogies with Brazilian growth rates. . . . From their point of view, a couple of hours of analysis is not unreasonable when millions of dollars are up for grabs.
>
> Charles, on the other hand, is sinking deeper and deeper into his chair. He is not used to sitting silently while someone else lectures. His hemorrhoids are bothering him. There is a draft in the room. Lyn [his wife] is back at the hotel. Basel is not the kind of city you want to stay in, if you are a jet-setter, any longer than you have to. Finally, he can no longer restrain himself. He flings out his arms, Christ-like, and says, "Fuck! How much do you guys want for this fucking deal?" The Ciba spokesman, startled, fumbled about for a few moments and said, "Twenty million dollars." "Done," says Revson, who gets up, shakes hands and walks out.

In *The Basel Marriage* Paul Erni reprinted this passage, calling it "a more pungent (if not strictly accurate in every detail) account of the bargaining."

And how has the Ciba-Geigy marriage fared? In 1986 the chief architect of the merger, Louis von Planta, then sixty-nine, was serving his last year as chairman of the enterprise, which was now much bigger, with sales of 16 billion Swiss francs versus 7 billion in 1970. The sales broke down to 30 percent pharmaceuticals, 30 percent agricultural chemicals, 21 percent plastics and additives, 14 percent dyestuffs and specialty chemicals, 5 percent electronic equipment and photographic products (Ciba owns the British-based Ilford business). When the two companies merged in 1970, Ciba had thirty-eight thousand employees, Geigy twenty-five thousand. In 1986 Ciba-Geigy had eighty-one thousand employees, nearly

75 percent of whom worked outside Switzerland. About a quarter of the people who work in the Swiss factories commute there every day from their homes in France and West Germany. In the United States and Canada, where Ciba-Geigy derives 35 percent of its sales, nearly fifteen thousand people are employed. Ciba-Geigy ranks fourth in worldwide drug sales behind Merck, American Home Products, and Hoechst. Its pharmacopoeia includes the prescription painkillers Voltaren (thirteenth-best-selling drug in the world) and Butazolidin; the high blood pressure pill Lopresor; the antiepileptic Tegretol; and Nitroderm, a patch that time-releases a heart medication directly into the bloodstream. The patch uses a delivery system developed by Alza, a Palo Alto, California, company which Ciba-Geigy rescued in the late 1970s and early 1980s by direct cash infusions.

Ciba-Geigy's product lineup in the United States also includes the appetite suppressant Acutrim; Vision Care and Softcolor contact lenses; Privine nasal spray; and Nucercainal ointment. But the company's forte does not seem to lie in the area of consumer products. In 1974 it bought the Airwick business for $45 million, and by 1984 it had become the 114th-largest advertiser in the United States with an expenditure of $35 million behind such products as the Airwick air fresheners, Binaca breath freshener, Chore Boy scouring pads, Drain Power drain clear, and a clutch of carpet cleaners (Carpet Fresh, Glamorene, and Spray 'N Vac). It sold off this army of cleansers in 1985 to the British company Reckitt & Colman for $200 million.

The United States remains a major focal point for Ciba-Geigy. During the 1970s, in addition to Airwick, it bought the pigments business of Hercules and one of the world's largest seeds producers, Funk Seeds of Bloomington, Illinois. In 1985 alone it made half a dozen deals in the American market, including the acquisition of the contact lens business of American Optical; the purchase of minority positions in Phytogen, a Pasadena, California, firm specializing in plant molecular biology, and Spectra-Physics, a San Jose, California, laser maker; the formation of a fifty-fifty venture with Corning Glass to operate a medical diagnostics business; and the signing of a worldwide licensing agreement to use the biotechnology products of Genentech in the animal health field. In 1987 the Swiss company became the 100 percent owner of Spectra-Physics.

Ciba-Geigy is one of those companies affected by everything that goes on in the world, enough so that it has to pause in its annual report to assure shareholders that it suffered "only insignificant disruption of our worldwide transport" as a result of "local civil disturbances, warlike action, or bad weather." It does have busy hands everywhere, operating more than 150 companies in fifty-nine countries. In 1985, an average year, it opened offices in Beijing and Shanghai (followed the next year by an announcement of a joint venture to make drugs in China); sharply increased insecticide sales to rice growers in Bangladesh; began turning out passion-fruit juice in the northern Brazilian port city of Belem; helped defeat a referendum in Switzerland that would have curtailed laboratory experiments with animals; put up new drug plants in Argentina, Colombia, and Ecuador; increased its sales in South Africa despite the "turbulent political conditions"; began the first trials of a drug developed in conjunction with the World Health Organization for the control of the tropical disease river blindness; and increased its research expenditures to 1.7 billion Swiss francs (about $700 million), more than 9 percent of sales, which constitutes one of the largest research budgets in the corporate world.

But Ciba-Geigy, like many chemical and drug companies, attracts the most attention when it gets into trouble, which, for Ciba-Geigy, is often.

In one of its worst drug scandals, a Tokyo court found in 1978 that a Ciba-Geigy drug used since 1955 to treat diarrhea caused a degenerative neurological disease, SMON, that killed one thousand people and injured thousands more. The medication, clioquinol, had to be taken in large quantities over a long period to cause the disease, and the court blamed Ciba-Geigy's "excessive propaganda" for its overuse. The court also said it was "deplorable" that Ciba-Geigy continued to stress the drug's safety for humans while warning veterinarians that it could cause epilepsy in dogs. The company settled the case, without admitting guilt, by agreeing to pay restitution to victims and their families; payments totaled $150 million by mid-1984. Ciba-Geigy stopped making all oral products containing clioquinol and contributed conscience money of 10 million Swiss francs to support a World Health Organization program to control severe diarrhea through oral rehydration therapy.

DBI, the antidiabetic drug that Charles Revson unloaded on Ciba-Geigy in 1970, was ordered off the market by the Food and Drug Administration in 1977 after reports piled up of its association with lactic acidosis, a metabolic disorder that is often fatal.

In a 1976 exercise that became infamous after disclosure of the circumstances, six Egyptian boys—volunteered by their parents for pay—stood barefoot in a cotton field as it was sprayed with a Ciba-Geigy insecticide, Galecron, that was already suspected of having carcinogenic effects. The point of this experiment, done supposedly at the behest of the Egyptian government, was to determine how much of the chemical would be absorbed in the boys' bodies. The Egyptian children who were sprayed came down with headaches and stomachaches, diarrhea, and irritated eyes. After this experiment received wide notoriety, Ciba-Geigy conceded that its employees in Egypt had used poor judgment.

Galecron was a powerful chemical, a successor to DDT, that proved to be very effective against the insects that attack cotton crops. However, it was found to be such a dangerous substance that Ciba-Geigy closed its plant at Monthey, Switzerland, for two years (1976–78), detoxified it, and brought it back into production with safety regulations so stringent that they were described as "without parallel" in the chemical industry. In the new plant Galecron was produced in a "closed system" to shield employees from direct contact. If workers did enter the sealed-off area where it was made, they had to wear protective clothing. And the plant employees were given constant health checkups. That was fine for Switzerland, where Galecron was no longer allowed to be sold, but after the Monthey plant started up again in 1978, Ciba-Geigy was soon selling Galecron for spraying on cotton fields in Colombia, Mexico, Honduras, Egypt, Nicaragua, and Guatemala, places where safety standards were not high. A Swiss-based activist organization, the Berne Group, launched a campaign against Galecron, pointing out that Third World countries do not provide the safety conditions that are necessary to protect people handling this chemical. As evidence accumulated showing that workers in cotton fields were absorbing into their bodies levels of chlordimeform (the active ingredient in Galecron) far higher than the thresholds recommended by Ciba-Geigy, the World Health Organization issued a warning about the health hazards associated with Galecron. In 1982 the Berne Group asked for "an immediate stop of Galecron production and export." The plea fell on deaf ears in Basel. In January 1987 Ciba-Geigy announced that it would halt production of Galecron because of what was called "erratic safety precautions," which is precisely what critics were saying a decade ago.

Sometimes a drug company ends up with a black eye even when it thinks it's performing a service. Ciba-Geigy developed two chemically related antiarthritic drugs, Butazolidin and Tanderil, which were marketed for more than twenty-five years before the company itself (pulling together reports from different parts of the world) found in 1983 that the painkillers had apparently been responsible for the deaths of 1,030 people and serious injuries to nearly 5,000 more. The side effects ranged from internal bleeding to leukemia. The question then becomes, What does a responsible company do with such a finding? Ciba-Geigy's solution was to advise public health authorities all over the world that the drugs should be prescribed only for acute illnesses, with use limited to one week. The internal report was not made public, but before long it was leaked, and Ciba-Geigy found itself in the middle of a raging controversy. Health-care activists charged that the cases of death and injury cited by the company were probably only the "tip of the iceberg" because of under-reporting, and they demanded the worldwide withdrawal of the drugs. Norway did ban both of them. France, Japan, and Britain took actions to curtail their use. In the United States Ciba-Geigy was able to convince the Food and Drug Administration that the drugs were safe with a package label warning doctors not to prescribe them except for severe rheumatic diseases. In 1985 Ciba-Geigy, for market not health reasons, did withdraw Tanderil from the American market. In an interview with Alan Friedman, Milan correspondent of the *Financial Times,* Ciba-Geigy chairman Louis von Planta said that the one thousand reported deaths represented "a relatively small proportion of 150 million people [the estimated number of users] over twenty to thirty years."

In 1985, as it was withdrawing Tanderil from the U.S. market, Ciba-Geigy was slapped with a $1.4 million fine by the state of New Jersey for illegally dumping hazardous wastes at three landfills near its Toms River dyestuffs plant (it's the largest producer of dyes in the United States). The company also agreed to pay $2.6 million to remove fourteen thousand drums of toxic waste and dispose of them properly.

Back in its hometown, Ciba-Geigy can be a good neighbor—even to a competitor. In 1976 the Basel drug company Hoffmann–La Roche suffered its own disaster when a chemical plant at Seveso in northern Italy dusted nearby communities with a cloud laden with the lethal chemical dioxin. After the cleanup the problem was what to do with the wastes, which had been stored in forty-one barrels. At one stage they dropped from sight in an eight-month odyssey through France before turning up

The Insurance-Prone Americans

Nowhere does insurance flourish so much as it does in the United States. According to the Swiss Reinsurance Company, which keeps track of such things, $498 billion of insurance premiums were paid in 1984 in the 55 countries which account for 99 percent of the total business. And of that total Americans paid 54 percent. Japan was second at 14.8 percent of the total. All the countries in the European Economic Community accounted for 19.7 percent of the premiums.

again behind a butcher's shop. That was in May 1983. In 1985 the dioxin-laced barrels were trucked to the Ciba-Geigy plant in Basel where they were incinerated in a furnace that heats up to 2,732 degrees Fahrenheit. Ciba-Geigy marked this signal event in its 1985 annual report, declaring it "a milestone in the disposal of toxic substances."

Access   Ch-4000 Basel, Switzerland
(41) 61-361-111

Ciba-Geigy Corp.
444 Saw Mill River Rd.
Ardsley, N.Y. 10502
(914) 478-3131

Club Méditerranée

Sales $988 million
Profits $48 million
U.S. Sales $336 million (sales of U.S. subsidiary)
Rank World's 11th-largest hotel chain
2d-largest French hotel chain
5th-largest non-American hotel chain
Founded 1950
Employees 21,600
Headquarters Paris, France

It took a French Communist to come up with an "escape from civilization" concept and parlay it into a unique chain of vacation villages around the world.

Gilbert Trigano, whose parents were Moroccan Jews, founded Club Méditerranée after World War II almost by accident. Trigano fought in the Communist resistance during the war and after France was liberated he signed on as a reporter for the Communist daily *L'Humanité*. He then drifted into the family business, selling surplus U.S. Army tents. One of his customers was a Belgian, Gerard Blitz, who ran a communal summer vacation camp on the island of Majorca off Spain. It was called Club Med. Europeans came there for an inexpensive holiday. They slept in sleeping bags, cooked their own meals, and washed the dishes. It was organized as a nonprofit sports association. Trigano converted it into a highly profitable chain of resorts that emphasized play and abolished dress codes.

The basic appeal—discard the cares and trappings of civilization—was a winner, and Trigano used it to forge a business, opening new villages in France, Italy, Greece, and Africa. The tents were replaced by thatched Polynesian-style huts. In its early days Club Med enjoyed a racy image as a place where people could throw off their clothes (and inhibitions) and have a good time. By merger, acquisition, and internal expansion, Club Méditerranée grew to the point where in 1987 it was operating more than one hundred vacation villages in thirty countries.

They weren't all beach resorts. Club Med has ski resorts in Switzerland and the Rocky Mountains (Copper Mountain, Colorado). It runs a four-star hotel in Paris. In a unique partnership with the Mexican government, it operates five inns at Mayan ruins in the Yucatan.

While Club Med has become a big business and caters more to families today, the original Trigano formula remains more or less intact: Put up specially built villages in exotic climes; run the business as a membership organization (Club Med has 893,000 members); collect all payments in advance, including air fare, housing, meals, and entertainment (in that way guests need not worry about having enough cash, and Club Med has a "float" up front on which it can earn money); provide an atmosphere uncluttered by telephones, radios, televisions, clocks, or newspapers; set sumptuous buffets; hold nightly talent shows. Club Med guests are known as GMs, *Gentils Membres.* And they are met at the villages by GOs, *Gentils Organisateurs*—professional, trained staffers who cannot always be distinguished from the guests, they are there to maintain the liberated vacation spirit.

Highly conscious of its reputation as a mecca for "swinging singles," Club Med has been introducing new features. Today members can go to some Club Meds and get training on a computer keyboard, take lessons in a foreign language, receive instruction in carpentry or underwater photography, and park their kids in a "miniclub." As Trigano told a *New York Times* reporter in 1985, "The days of senseless sunbathing are over." The new Club Meds are definitely upscale. On March 15, 1987, the company opened its first village in Florida, the Sandpiper, on the Atlantic Ocean forty-five miles north of Palm Beach. The company itself called it "the most luxurious Club Med ever." It has a forty-five-hole championship golf course, five swimming pools, a health-and-fitness center, and a "Baby Club" and a "Mini Club" for children up to the age of eleven, where "counselors supervise or entertain them daily with arts and crafts, picnics, lessons in tennis, sailing, swimming." Also, if you tire of the Sandpiper, Club Med will arrange sightseeing excursions to nearby Disney World. It's a long way from the surplus Army tents on Majorca. A new chapter in Club Med history was slated to open at the end of 1987 with the launching of the first village in Japan, on the island of Hokkaido. Some twenty thousand Japanese were already enrolled as GMs, cavorting in Club Meds outside of Japan.

Although he left the Communist party long ago, Trigano's sympathies are still with the left. "The Communists saved my life," he pointed out to a reporter in 1985. He has long been a friend of François Mitterrand, a Socialist who was elected president of France in 1981. In 1985 Mitterrand named Trigano to head a project to train thousands of jobless people to use computers.

Leftist ideas have not impaired Trigano's business abilities. He has been particularly resourceful in securing financial backers. Among the people who put money into Club Méditerranée were the Rothschilds, the Bronfmans (Seagram), the Agnellis (Fiat), and a wealthy Saudi Arabian, Gaith Pharaon. Three French financial institutions owned by the government—Crédit Lyonnais, Union des Assurances de Paris, and Caisse de Depots—have seats on the board to reflect their stockholdings. Gerard Blitz, who started it all, was serving as honorary chairman in 1986.

In 1984 Trigano set up a new company, Club Med Inc., to operate all the Club Meds in the United States, Mexico, Central America, and the Asia/Pacific region, and he raised $50 million by selling off 27 percent of its stock to American investors. So the parent company, Club Méditerranée, trades on the Paris Bourse while this 73 percent–owned subsidiary, Club Med, trades on the New York Stock Exchange. Sitting on the Club Med board with ex-Communist Gilbert Trigano are Evan G. Galbraith, a Wall Street investment banker who was formerly U.S. ambassador to France, and Richard A. Voell, president of the Rockefeller Group.

Trigano's son, Serge, forty-one in 1987, serves as vice chairman of Club Med. To help him relocate from Paris to New York City in 1984, the company loaned Serge $1.4 million, interest-free. For that sum he might have been able to find a simple Club Med–like residence in New York.

One advantage that Club Med has with the press is that everyone likes to visit a village and write about it. In 1977 Michael Wolfe visited Club Med in Martinique and wrote about it in the now defunct *New Times;* in 1979 Berkeley business school dean Earl Cheit went to the Club Med in Cancun, Mexico, and described it in his *San Francisco Examiner* column; in 1980 Robert Dallos of the *Los Angeles Times* went to the Club Med in Guadeloupe; in 1983 *Wall Street Journal* correspondent Erik Larson visited the Club Med in Punta Cana, the Dominican Republic; in 1985 Paul Lewis of *The New York Times* visited the Club Med in Cargese, Corsica; and in 1985 Eleanor Foa Dienstag visited the new Club Med in Turks and Caicos in the Caribbean to write about it in *The New York Times* travel section.

As Gilbert Trigano put it in the opening sentence of the 1985 annual report of Club Med: "Even though we live in an unpredictable world, we are confident of this: As life each year grows more pressured and complex, the true vacation will become an ever more precious commodity."

Marriott

Marriott, the world's seventh-largest hotel chain, will manage a thousand-bed hotel going up in Warsaw. The hotel, Poland's largest, is expected to open in 1989.

Access   25, rue Vivienne
Place de la Bourse
75002 Paris, France
(33) 1-42-61-8500

40 West 57th St.
New York, N.Y. 10019
(212) 977-2100

Compagnie Générale d'Électricité

Sales $21.6 billion
Profits $475 million
U.S. Sales $1.2 billion
Rank France's largest industrial company
World's 2d-largest maker of telecommunications equipment
World's largest installer of digital switches
World's largest builder of nuclear reactors
World's largest maker of alkaline batteries
World's largest builder of power stations
World's largest supplier of videotex terminals
World's 2d-largest maker of postage meters
World's 2d-largest maker of gas turbines
World's 3d-largest maker of railway engines
World's 4th-largest electrical contractor
Founded 1898
Employees 240,000
Headquarters Paris, France

You can pick up a telephone these days, in the United States and many other countries, punch in a number and be connected instantly to someone halfway around the world. The equipment that makes this possible—switches, underwater cables, transmission lines—constitutes an enormous market (well over $100 billion a year on a worldwide basis). Compagnie Générale d'Électricité (CGE) emerged in 1986 as a front-rank contender for this business. CGE was already a giant on the French industrial scene, thanks to a series of mergers and acquisitions that go back to the early years of the twentieth century. It had already established an international presence as a builder of power plants, but on the next to last day of 1986 it signed an agreement that catapulted the company, and by proxy France, onto center stage in the world telecommunications business.

The papers signed in Brussels on December 30, 1986, created a new company, Alcatel N.V., that combined the telecommunications operations of CGE (which were already named Alcatel) with those of ITT, the American conglomerate whose original name was International Telephone & Telegraph. Incorporated in the Netherlands but based in Brussels, Alcatel began life with assets of $9 billion, annual sales of $12 billion, and 164,000 employees in seventy-five countries: an instant multinational. At its birth in the telecommunications industry it ranked second in the world to American Telephone & Telegraph, whose manufacturing subsidiary, Western Electric, has long been the premier company in this field by virtue of its access to the world's largest telephone market.

The CGE-ITT venture symbolized, in dramatic fashion, the trends that were transforming telecommunications from a domestic to an international business, and from a business owned or tightly controlled by national governments into one where the players are increasingly privately owned, profit-seeking entities confronted with competitors from various parts of the world. The signs of this transformation were appearing everywhere in the mid-1980s. In the United States the Bell System was dismembered, and AT&T's monopoly on telephone equipment was shattered. In Britain, British Telecom was privatized. In Japan, Nippon Telephone & Telegraph was in the process of being privatized. Telephone users in the United States can remember when the only phone they could have was one made by AT&T. Now they can buy all kinds of phones from various suppliers. This is comparable to the changes occurring in the equipment market, where the buyers are the companies that provide telephone service. Alcatel N.V. is France's bid to become the world's preeminent supplier of telecommunications equipment.

The formation of Alcatel also signaled the retreat of ITT from the business that gave birth to it. In return for passing to Alcatel all its telecommunications operations, ITT received a cash payment of $1.1 billion, plus a 37 percent interest in the new company. But the lion's share of the new company, 63 percent, went to CGE and its European partners (CGE got 55.6 percent, the Belgian holding company Société Générale took 5.7 percent, and the French bank Crédit Lyonnais bought the remaining 1.7 percent). And it's CGE, not ITT, that will manage this new global entry in telecommunications. ITT's role in the business that was once its mainstay has been reduced to that of a minority investor.

It's a far cry from the days when ITT was out to conquer the world. International Telephone & Telegraph was formed in 1920 by two brothers, Sosthenes and Hernand Behn, to operate two small telephone companies, one in Cuba (thirty-three thousand customers) and one in Puerto Rico (five thousand customers). However, the very name they adopted gave some clue to their ambitions, which were realized in 1925 when, under pressure from the U.S. government, AT&T sold its International Western Electric business to ITT. Western Electric's international business encompassed operating companies in fifteen countries and was seven times as large as ITT. This deal put ITT on the world map: AT&T would take care of the United States, ITT would take care of the rest of the world.

It's this business, started by AT&T and developed by ITT, that has now been lodged with CGE-controlled Alcatel. Among the ITT companies in this basket are Standard Electrik Lorenz of West Germany, Bell Telephone Manufacturing of Belgium, Standard Electrica of Spain, Standard Telefon of Norway, Standard Radio and Telefon of Sweden, and Standard Telephone and Radio of Switzerland. The ITT companies, together with the Alcatel telecommunications operations of CGE, hold an estimated 45 percent of what is called the European public exchange market, meaning the equipment bought by the utilities providing telephone service.

Meanwhile, irony of ironies, AT&T, no longer permitted to operate local phone companies in the United States, has now returned to the international arena. Starting virtually from scratch AT&T forged an alliance with the Dutch electronics giant Philips toward becoming a major equipment supplier to telephone companies around the world. One of its major competitors will be the new CGE powerhouse, Alcatel, now armed with companies ITT bought from AT&T in 1925.

While the telecommunications market seems to be loosening up, with giants like AT&T, CGE, Philips, Siemens, Ericsson, Northern Telecom, and NEC jockeying for position, it would be foolhardy to expect politics to disappear as a factor. As *The Economist,* in its customary acerbic manner, put it in 1986: "The usual bad habit is for a single state-owned monopoly, with a resounding title like the Ministry for Posts, Telegraphs, and Telephones, to buy exclusively from a small cabal of domestic producers. In some countries, like France, these producers are state-owned too. In others, they are state-addicted—kept going by cost-plus contracts, scientific research ventures, and lucrative defense contracts. The result in Europe is eight different new digital systems. They serve a smaller total market than North America, which has only three. This increases costs; the telephone user foots the bill." That's why, *The Economist* added, a telephone call between Paris and London costs 50 percent more than one between New York and Washington, and why Japan's international telephone rates are twice those of Europe.

A perfect illustration of how difficult it is to keep politics out of this business surfaced in 1986 in a bizarre Paris sideshow to the CGE-ITT negotiations. Cie. Générale des Constructions Téléphoniques (CGCT) is another relic from the old ITT empire. As recently as 1960 it held 60 percent to 65 percent of the French market for telephone switches. But it was then crushed by French companies and nationalized by the French government in 1982. Its market share had dropped to 16 percent. The other 84 percent was held by CGE-controlled companies. Since CGE had also been nationalized in 1982, this meant that state-owned companies held 100 percent of the switch business. Even a Socialist French government agreed that was a bit much, and it decided to let a foreign company reassume control of CGCT.

The contender that seemed to have the inside track was an American-Dutch partnership consisting of AT&T and Philips. They were on the verge of buying 70 percent of CGCT when the CGE-ITT deal came along. (As part of its offer AT&T had even agreed to sell $200 million worth of French communications hardware in the United States.) What happened next was this: Siemens, the big German electronics firm, noted forcefully that the formation of Alcatel meant that the French, through CGE, would inherit ITT's 40 percent chunk of the German switch market. In all fairness, said the Germans, Siemens should be allowed to get a piece of the French market; and it was ready to buy CGCT for much more than AT&T was prepared to pay.

It wasn't just Siemens making this offer. No, the West German government in the person of Chancellor Helmut Kohl lobbied for Siemens. According to some reports, the Germans threatened that if CGCT were sold to AT&T, Alcatel might lose its supply contracts in Germany. The French wavered and apparently reopened the bidding for CGCT. That action infuriated the U.S. government, which went to bat for AT&T. American officials, including the U.S. ambassador to France, urged the French not to succumb to political pressure from West Germany. Mark S. Fowler, chairman of the Federal Communications Commission, went further. He wrote to the chief executives of all the major phone companies in the United States, asking for information about any equipment bought from Siemens. The FCC has the power of approval over such purchases.

It's not for nothing that the French are known for their diplomacy. Caught between this German and American crossfire, the French sought protection in a loophole. The conservative government of Jacques Chirac, which came to power in 1986, is committed to the privatization of the companies that had been nationalized by the Socialists in 1982. The laws authorizing this denationalization state that no more than 20 percent of the shares of any company can end up in foreign hands. Clearly it had been the intent of the government to exempt CGCT from this restriction—it had certainly raised no objections to the AT&T–Philips bid for 70 percent control. But now that the Germans and Americans were scrapping over the chance to buy the money-losing switch maker, the French solemnly announced in December 1986 that yes, the laws would have to be obeyed, only 20 percent of CGCT could be sold to a foreign company. If the French thought that this ruling would discourage the bidders, they were wrong. Both AT&T and Siemens, plus the Swedish telecommunications firm Ericsson, said they would be happy to take 20 percent of CGCT. In April 1987 the French navigated neatly between the American and German contenders by awarding the CGCT slice to Ericsson.

This political battleground is one that Compagnie Générale d'Électricité is accustomed to fighting on. Founded in 1898 to produce and sell electricity, CGE has been restructured so many times, frequently at the behest of governmental bodies imbued with the sense of what is good for *la patrie,* that most people in France probably don't know what it stands for anymore. In its current manifestation, CGE is a holding company whose parts are better known than the whole. These parts include Alsthom, a builder of ships, power plants, railroad equipment, and turbine generators; CGEE-Alsthom, a giant electrical contractor; Saft, the world's largest maker of alkaline batteries; and Framatome, a nuclear reactor builder that wields great power because of France's commitment to the atom (more than 60 percent of power there is nuclear-generated).

The telecommunications operations being yoked to ITT's units had, under the banner of Alcatel, introduced the world's first digital switching exchange in 1970. In 1985 the Alcatel group of companies had been merged with the telecommunications divisions of Thomson-CSF, another French electronics company which is 50 percent–owned by still another French electronics producer, Thomson S.A. Thomson S.A.'s previous names, reflecting various restructurings, were Thomson-Brandt and Compagnie Française Thomson-Houston.

A good deal of French industrial history is buried in these names. Alcatel, for example, has been in the telecommunications business since 1879, antedating CGE. Alsthom, which also goes back to the last century, merged in 1976 with France's leading shipbuilder, Les Chantiers de l'Atlantique. CGEE Alsthom was formed in 1971 by the amalgamation of three French electrical contractors, buttressed in 1980 by the acquisition of another leading contractor, Comsip. Thomson was founded in 1893 to exploit the electric power patents of the American company Thomson-Houston Electric, which became part of General Electric (Thomson and GE maintained close links until 1953). In 1966 Thomson acquired the

French appliance company Hotchkiss-Brandt and changed its name to Thomson-Brandt. In 1968 a new company, Thomson-CSF, was spun off by the merger of Thomson-Brandt's electronics division with Compagnie Générale de Télégraphie Sans Fil (CSF), a company founded in 1918. CGE itself resulted from numerous mergers and acquisitions over the years.

The structure of CGE is complicated. It holds varying blocks of shares in the companies under its flag. Alcatel, for example, is 60.4 percent–owned by CGE; CGEE-Alsthom, the electrical contractor, is 99.9 percent–owned; Framatome is 40 percent–owned; Saft is 79.3 percent–owned; Les Câbles de Lyon is 75 percent–owned; Alsthom S. A., the shipbuilder, railway equipment supplier, and power plant builder, is 66.5 percent–owned. We're talking here about an enormous number of companies. CGE has 650 subsidiaries and affiliates. One of its companies is a bank, naturally called Electro Banque. Another is an investment company, naturally called Electro-Financiere, which holds major interests in many CGE subsidiaries (it owns 10 percent of Alsthom, Alcatel, and Câbles de Lyon) as well as in Générale Occidentale, which a CGE leader, Jean Pierre Brunet, once euphemistically described as a "very diversified company run by the world-famous Anglo-French financier Sir James Goldsmith."

In any one year CGE companies mount an enormous number of imposing projects around the world. (CGE does 40 percent of its business outside France.) In 1986, for example, they were building the largest cruise ship in the world (a 2,600-passenger vessel for Norway's Royal Caribbean Cruise Line); a diesel power plant for Angola; hydroelectric and thermal power plants in Greece, Colombia, and Turkey; automated mail-processing centers for Mexico; a nuclear power plant in South Korea; telephone transmission lines in India; and underwater high-voltage cables for Greece. In 1985 the Câbles de Lyon subsidiary installed a 2,700-mile underwater telephone line linking Colombo in Sri Lanka with Djibouti on the east coast of Africa. In 1987 a new Alsthom plant in Union City, California, was assembling equipment no longer made in the United States (railway cars) for delivery to the Bay Area Rapid Transit.

Although CGE was nationalized in 1982, socialism did not cramp its style. If anything, it flourished. While CGE was nationalized, none of its subsidiaries was, and a dozen of them continued to trade on stock markets, including Alsthom, Alcatel, Electro Banque, and Lynch Communications, a Reno, Nevada–based telecommunications company whose shares traded on the American Stock Exchange. The shares of the CGE companies traded on the Paris Bourse tripled and quadrupled in price while their parent was government-owned. And the French government let CGE go its own way. It did not insist on high dividends; in fact, it once allowed CGE to plough back all its profits into the business. Under socialism CGE increased its return on equity from 6.3 percent to 10.3 percent, and its return on sales from 1.1 percent to 1.6 percent. It was also able, under socialism, to sell companies whose sales amounted to 20 billion francs a year and to buy companies whose sales totaled 30 billion francs a year.

And it was under socialism that Georges Pebereau, the chairman of CGE, was able to hatch the far-reaching agreement with ITT to launch a new global telecommunications giant. Pebereau, a highly regarded manager, was once described by *Financial Times* correspondent David Marsh as giving "the impression of having been born with an intricate flowchart of France's labyrinthine corridors of power already firmly etched into his brain." M. Pebereau was the toast of France after the ITT-CGE deal was announced. In an interview with Marsh at CGE headquarters in Paris, he said, "We are in the business of taking risks. Without risks there can be no industry. Companies which take none are moribund."

After the CGE-ITT deal most observers thought Pebereau's position was secure. But the pundits were wrong. The Chirac government replaced him with Pierre Suard, a thirteen-year veteran of CGE who had been heading up the Alcatel division.

The first French company privatized by the Chirac government was Saint-Gobain. That came at the end of 1986, and the shares had an enthusiastic reception. CGE was privatized in May 1987 in the biggest stock offering in the history of the French market: 11.4 billion francs ($1.9 billion). In 1982 the French government paid 4.5 billion francs for CGE. *Viva le socialisme française!*

Access 54, rue La Boetie
75382 Paris, France
(33) 1-45-63-1414

Crédit Suisse	**Revenues** $3.7 billion
	Profits $365 million
	Rank Switzerland's 3d-largest bank
	World's largest underwriter of stocks and bonds
	43d-largest bank outside the United States
	Europe's 22d-largest company (based on market value)
	Founded 1856
	Employees 14,000
	Headquarters Zurich, Switzerland

It was the French philosopher Voltaire who said, "If you see a Swiss banker jumping out of a window, follow him; there's bound to be money in it." The butt of endless jokes, Swiss bankers handle colossal amounts of money for wealthy people around the world who feel comfortable about parking it in Switzerland. *Fortune,* in 1983, declared that Switzerland "ranks third after New York and London as a financial center," and it estimated that foreign institutions and individuals had given Swiss bankers $350 billion to manage. For a small country (population 6.4 million), that's phenomenal. Switzerland has 593 companies engaged in banking, and they maintain more than 2,000 offices. Zurich alone, with a population of 1.1 million, has 550 bank branches.

In 1986 Ben Weberman, senior editor of *Forbes,* guessed that Crédit Suisse, the number three bank in Switzerland, had under "active management for investment clients at least $75 billion, and perhaps as much as $150 billion." That's quite a wide range but, as Weberman pointed out, even if you take the low figure, it's well ahead of the $50 billion managed by Citicorp, the leader of the U.S. banking industry. The Swiss institutions are trusted with this money not so much for their acumen as for their reputation as safe resting places. Numbered Swiss bank accounts have long been used by people who want to shelter income from prying eyes. High aides of the Reagan administration used a Crédit Suisse numbered account to launder money from covert arms sales to Iran and direct it to the contra forces fighting to overthrow the Nicaraguan government.

The reputation of the Swiss banker irritates a lot of people, especially in London. "It is entirely proper—even de rigueur—to bad-mouth the Swiss in London," reported Martin Mayer in his 1974 book *The Bankers.* A leading London merchant banker, Jocelyn Hambro, told Mayer, "The Swiss have never originated a business in their lives. They charge you a large commission for buying you the wrong stock, and the chap can't complain because he shouldn't have had the money there, anyway."

The Swiss themselves are great users of banks. If you divide Swiss bank savings by the population, it works out to $21,000 per person—the highest ratio in the world. In German-speaking Zurich, the financial center of Switzerland, the per capita savings is $26,000.

The "Big Three" of Swiss banking (they hold half the assets) are, in order of size, the Union Bank of Switzerland (UBS), Swiss Bank Corporation, and Crédit Suisse. UBS, the product of a 1912 merger, is headquartered in Zurich and is known for its close ties to the military: Senior officers tend to be high-ranking Swiss Army officers. Swiss Bank resulted from the amalgamation of six banks based in Basel, home of the Swiss chemical-pharmaceutical giants Hoffmann–La Roche, Ciba-Geigy, and Sandoz.

Zurich-based Crédit Suisse is the oldest of the Big Three and the one credited with the most adventurous spirit, especially in the international arena. The sterling example of this spirit is its partnership with the U.S. investment banking firm First Boston. Their joint London-based venture, Crédit Suisse First Boston became the leading underwriter in the steaming Eurobond market, raising more money for corporations (and governments) than any other European investment banking house. Crédit Suisse owns 60 percent of Crédit Suisse First Boston, which in turn owns 35 percent of First Boston. Ergo, Crédit Suisse of Zurich has bought into a big chunk of the investment banking action in the United States.

The Swiss are known for their reclusiveness. They have stayed aloof from the European wars that have raged about them, insisting pugnaciously on neutrality. They maintain the largest standing army in Europe, and fortifications gird all the mountain passes leading into the country. In an emergency bridges and tunnels can be quickly destroyed. Military service is compulsory for every male between the ages of twenty and fifty. The twenty-three cantons which make up the Swiss republic retain—and zealously guard—their sovereignty, leaving to the federal government as little as possible: regulation of the army, operation of the railway, telecommunications, and coining money.

Switzerland therefore resembles a loose confederation of independent states rather than a nation with a strong central government. The electorate has the last word. In 1959 a plebiscite backed by the federal government sought to extend the vote to women; it was defeated at the polls by the male voters (it finally passed in 1971). One hundred and eighty-two countries belong to the United Nations. Not Switzerland, which doesn't like the idea of a supranational authority. A referendum backed by the federal government authorizing Switzerland's admission to the UN was presented to the voters in 1986, and went down to a crushing defeat.

It's against this backdrop that Crédit Suisse has grown to become one of the twenty-five largest banking institutions in Europe. It was in effect a creature of the circumstances that created the modern Swiss state. Over the objections of cantons that wanted to maintain their independence, Switzerland adopted its first federal constitution in 1848. The country's population was 2.4 million. It was then that a single currency was introduced, customs barriers between cantons came down, and the federal government was grudgingly allowed to run a national postal service and conduct foreign relations. The constitution was a victory for the Radical party, one of whose leaders was the charismatic Alfred Escher, who was born in 1819 into a wealthy Zurich family. Escher was a multifaceted activist who made major contributions in politics, education, the arts, and business.

In 1848 Switzerland had little of the trappings of the nation-state, and it was Escher who realized that the country would have to create its own financial institutions if it wanted to escape dependence on the Rothschilds and other foreign lenders for development of railroads and industry. He therefore founded Crédit Suisse on July 16, 1856. To do it he used the financial muscle of a German bank, the Allgemeine Deutsche Kreditanstalt of Leipzig, but he was apparently able to convince the Germans to let the Swiss run their own show. And run it they did. Crédit Suisse from the start served as the financing engine of Swiss industry, especially for the railroads and later on, for the electric power industry. It also took equity positions in many companies. Crédit Suisse still owns a substantial stake in the Swiss utility holding company Electrowatt.

Crédit Suisse's role as the bankroller of Swiss industry is reflected in the composition of its board, which reads like a roll call of the movers and shakers of Swiss industry. On the board in 1986 were the chairmen of Nestlé, Lindt & Sprungli Chocolate Works, Swiss Air, Abegg Holding, Zurich Insurance, Sandoz, and top executives of Brown Boveri, Jelmoli Department Stores, Sulzer Brothers, Ciba-Geigy, and Swiss Aluminum.

Crédit Suisse was also responsible for the establishment of Zurich as a leading insurance center. It founded and financed Swiss Life Insurance and Pension Company, Swiss Reinsurance, Switzerland General, and Zurich Casualty. The Zurich lakefront street where the big insurance companies are headquartered today is named Alfred Escher Strasse.

Secrecy is a hallmark of Swiss banking. Although Crédit Suisse shares are traded on the Zurich Stock Exchange and the bank issues an annual report, it's not easy reading. In its 1982 report the bank said, "For the first time ever the disclosed net profit—which is up by 10 percent—has topped 300 million Swiss francs." Ah, to be privy to the *undisclosed* profit, that would be something. In any case, in 1985, only eight U.S. banks managed to earn as much money as Crédit Suisse said it did, and that was *after* the bank finished socking away, out of profits, an enormous amount of money into reserves. The bank said that since 1980 it had allocated to reserves a sum larger "than our entire share capital" to shield itself and its shareholders "as far as possible from the risk of today's world."

One way to look at Crédit Suisse is to consider it a Merrill Lynch. All the Swiss banks act as stockbrokers, and the three big ones handle about 70 percent of the trading on the Zurich Stock Exchange. Indeed, commissions represent the largest single source of income for Crédit Suisse. In 1986 they topped $660 million, accounting for more than a third of the bank's gross income (more than the interest on loans). Crédit Suisse was also managing twenty-three mutual funds (equity, bond, money market, and real estate) with total assets of $3.8 billion at the start of 1986. It claimed to be the only bank in the world to offer a range of money market funds covering all major currencies (dollar, Swiss franc, D-mark, yen, sterling).

Crédit Suisse owns thirteen financial institutions in Switzerland, operates 187 domestic offices, and runs an ever-expanding international network, including ten outposts in the United States, where its Wall Street–based Swiss American Securities holds a seat on the New York Stock Exchange. Swiss xenophobia notwithstanding, the bank seems to have made a strong commitment to the international arena. In 1985 it bought two German banks which now operate under the name Schweizerische Kreditanstalt; acquired control of a London stockbroker, Buckmaster & Moore; opened a trust bank in Tokyo; and established a representative office in Beijing. In early 1986 Crédit Suisse shares began trading on the Frankfurt Stock Exchange, the first time its shares have ever been listed on a foreign exchange. Among Crédit Suisse's other assorted holdings are interests ranging from 2 percent up to 12 percent in banks located in Argentina, Brazil, Tunisia, Luxembourg, Cameroon, Ivory Coast, Senegal, Morocco, and Guinea.

The hidden strength of Crédit Suisse was demonstrated in 1977 when it rode out what was probably the worst scandal in Swiss banking history: the Chiasso affair. Chiasso is a little town on the Italian border of Switzerland, and it was the scene of some funny goings-on. Italian "investors" brought bundles of cash over the border for deposit in the Chiasso branch of Crédit Suisse. The people running the branch accepted these deposits on behalf of Crédit Suisse but funneled them (perhaps as much as $1 billion) into a Liechtenstein-based conglomerate, Texon Finanzanstalt, which they, not the bank, controlled. Texon went on to buy more than one hundred companies all over Europe. In effect, the Chiasso managers were running a business on the side. And they got away with this off-the-books scam for sixteen years before the head office in Zurich got wind of it, such is the inviolability of Swiss—and Liechtenstein—bank secrecy. In the end the Chiasso people were tripped up when some of the Texon companies had financial difficulties, making it difficult for them to remit dividends, which in turn made it difficult for the Chiasso people to juggle the books artfully enough to pay interest to the people who had deposited money with them. Reports of their difficulties leaked out and a few of these rumors reached, finally, Zurich.

It was a delicious scandal, enabling people all over the world to enjoy the rare experience of having a good laugh at the expense of the Swiss. *The Economist* chortled: "Zapped in Zurich." *The Washington Post* headline read: "Crédit Suisse Scandal Casts Shadow over Swiss Banks." In fact the shadow vanished quickly. Crédit Suisse gnomes swarmed on the Chiasso branch and pledged to make good on any deposits that were misdirected. They took control of Texon and found that Crédit Suisse now owned about 140 companies, including Winefood (Italy's largest wine producer), a plastics business, a Milan restaurant, a baby carriage maker in France, a string of Italian gas stations, a salami producer, and a resort development on the island of Albarella off Venice. The Crédit Suisse bankers were not fazed. They sorted through the companies to see which ones could be sold, which ones had to be shut down, and which ones might, with a little Swiss first aid, be kept going as part of the bank's portfolio.

Ernst Kuhrmeier, the Chiasso branch manager, and four other principals in the case were convicted by a Swiss court in 1979. Kuhrmeier, sentenced to four and a half years in jail, died of a heart attack a week later. There were various estimates of Crédit Suisse's losses in the Chiasso affair: $400 million *(The Washington Post)*, $760 million in "dubious loans" *(The Economist)*, $805 million *(The Wall Street Journal)*. How much it did cost the bank has never been made clear, but there never seemed to be any doubt that the bank would survive. Crédit Suisse was able to dip into the secret reserves that all the big Swiss banks maintain to cover any embarrassing situations. Its two big competitors, UBS and Swiss Bank, offered to put up $1.5 billion in standby credit, but Crédit Suisse told them it wasn't necessary. (They do stick together, those Swiss banks.) As for the long-range effects, it was hardly a ripple. Phillipe de

Weck, president of UBS, said, "It was a demonstration that an important bank in Switzerland can have difficulties without financial consequences for clients."

One consequence of the Chiasso escapade was a change of the guard at the top. Heinz R. Wuffli resigned as Crédit Suisse's chief executive in May 1977 and was replaced by forty-five-year-old Rainer E. Gut, who had spent more time in London and Wall Street than he had in Zurich. Gut, a Swiss, opted for banking instead of college when he was nineteen. He was first posted to New York by Switzerland's largest bank, UBS, which he left to join Lazard Frères. He quit Lazard in 1970 to take over as head of Crédit Suisse's New York investment banking arm, Swiss American. Gut, who is married to an American, became chairman of Crédit Suisse in 1983.

At its annual meeting in 1978, a year after the undercover operation at Chiasso surfaced, Crédit Suisse served shareholders Melini Chianto Classico in long-stemmed goblets. It was Chianti produced by the Italian wine company the bank now owned. Seven years later the wine company still belonged to the bank, as did the Albarella Beach Holdings, the resort development.

The World's Timekeepers

Switzerland now produces only 10 percent of the world's watches but they account for 45 percent of the total value of watches sold. The Japanese are the world leaders, in terms of output. The 170 million watches made in Japan in 1985 represented 35 percent of world output. They also accounted for 35 percent of the value of watches sold. The Japanese watches are produced by four companies: Hattori Seiko, Citizen, Orient, and Casio.

Switzerland's watch exports in 1985 totaled $2.3 billion. They went (by percentage) to the following countries:

United States	18.3 percent
Hong Kong	11.6 percent
West Germany	8.4 percent
Italy	7.9 percent
France	6.5 percent
Saudi Arabia	4.7 percent
Japan	4.6 percent
Britain	4.5 percent
Singapore	3.2 percent
Rest of world	30.3 percent

The Chiasso scandal had one other consequence. The Swiss Federal Banking Commission, which supervises the banks, tripled its staff. It now has twenty-nine examiners. Summarizing the results of the Chiasso case, A. H. Hermann, legal correspondent of the *Financial Times,* said, "On the whole, the Swiss banks remain a closed book and proud of it."

Access   Paradeplatz 8
CH-8001 Zurich, Switzerland
(41) 1-215-4455

100 Wall St.
New York, N.Y. 10005
(212) 422-1450

Daewoo	Sales $8.7 billion
	Profits $60 million
	Rank 4th-largest company in Korea
	39th on the *Fortune* International 500 List
	69th on the *Forbes* International 500 List
	Founded 1967
	Employees 90,000
	Headquarters Seoul, South Korea

A demonic attachment to work has vaulted this South Korean conglomerate into the topmost ranks of industrial corporations. Daewoo has been running ads in the United States and Britain poking fun at its name and obscurity. Questions are posed under the rubric, "Who?" (as in "Who brings the world's toughest business questions down to earth?" or "Who went from minitechnology to microtechnology in just twenty years?"); and the answer given is: "Daewoo, that's who." But the question is not, "What does Daewoo do?" Rather, it's "What doesn't Daewoo do?"

It was Daewoo that built the Busta Airport in Libya, the state Guest House in the Sudan, and a seawater treatment plant in the Arctic Ocean. The largest containerships in the world were built by Daewoo for U.S. Lines. Daewoo owns the Hilton Hotel in Seoul. In a fifty-fifty partnership with General Motors, it built the LeMans subcompact car that Pontiac dealers began selling in the United States in 1987. One of the hottest personal computers of 1985 and 1986, the $1,500, IBM-compatible Model D, was supplied to Leading Edge by Daewoo. Northern Telecom has ordered digital switches and Boeing aircraft body sections from this sprawling industrial powerhouse. Daewoo also produces jogging shoes, television sets, pianos, oil tankers, stuffed animals, and heavy machinery. It has a factory in Pusan that's believed to be the largest shirt plant in the world, producing 3.6 million pieces a month. (You may be wearing one right now.) It has built forklift trucks for Caterpillar Tractor. It owns a brokerage house and a couple of banks. After some Third World countries paid for construction work with oil, Daewoo bought a refinery in Antwerp to process it.

Daewoo built all the cars for the new Seoul subway which will help get people to the 1988 Olympic Games scheduled for Korea. The Olympic Marina where the swimming events will be held is another Daewoo project.

One company doesn't turn out all these products. Daewoo is a *chaebol,* meaning a group of companies which are linked by common ownership and/or other special relationships. South Korea has thirty chaebols, including four giants: Samsung (1985 sales, $15.7 billion), Hyundai ($13.8 billion), Lucky-Goldstar ($9.7 billion), and Daewoo ($8.7 billion). Dozens of companies are grouped under these corporate banners. Daewoo alone has more than thirty, nine of which have sold some stock to the public. The three largest—Daewoo Corporation, Daewoo Heavy Industries, and Daewoo Electronics—are heavily traded on the stock exchange in Seoul where their progress is tracked by Daewoo Research Institute, the largest securities research firm in Korea. And their shares are bought and sold through Daewoo Securities, the largest Korean brokerage house (foreign brokers are barred from Korea).

The chaebols control a good chunk of what has been one of the world's fastest growing economies. As *New York Times* reporter Susan Chira said after a recent visit, "South Korea has moved from a nation of farmers to one of traders in little more than a generation. Men who repaired trucks for the American Army during the Korean War now head conglomerates that churn out exports of steel, autos, television sets, ships, semiconductors, and other high-technology products. Their most important market is the United States, where Korean industriousness has already left its mark, from Korean groceries in New York to semiconductor research laboratories in Silicon Valley."

Although Daewoo is obviously an enormous company, it's also the lengthened shadow of one man: Kim Woo-Choong, who was thirty years old when he borrowed five thousand dollars in 1967 to become a partner in a small trading company. His partner, who lent Kim the money, was To Dae Do; they combined their given names to come up with Daewoo, which means "big cosmos." Kim soon bought out his partner and proceeded to create an industrial giant, aided greatly by the Korean government, which has turned to Daewoo repeatedly to save failing companies.

One of those companies was Daewoo Motor, a successor to one of Korea's first automakers, Shinjin Motor. Japan's Toyota held a 50 percent interest in Shinjin until 1972 when General Motors bought the Toyota interest and renamed the company GM Korea. But the company couldn't make a go of it, and the government had to step in to save it. In the late 1970s South Korea's President General Park Chung Hee asked Daewoo to come to the rescue. GM retained management control until 1982 when Daewoo took over the reins completely. GM and Daewoo later established a $500 million joint venture to turn out the Pontiac LeMans at a new assembly plant in Pupyung. GM was looking to sell one hundred thousand of the Korean-built cars in the opening year. Forging partnerships with foreign companies is a Kim speciality, and he roams the world negotiating them. Daewoo has joint ventures and licensing arrangements with a host of U.S. companies. Kim doesn't mind that the products eventually get sold under names other than Daewoo—at least not yet.

Kim Woo-Choong believes passionately in working hard. He boasts of not having had a vacation in thirty years. In 1985 he delivered a speech in which he said "the destruction of family life" results from "immoral conduct, when there is too much free time." He added that too many Americans "are working only for leisure—they work so they can take time off. That is an alien concept in Asia. Here at Daewoo we work for pride, not leisure."

In 1984 the *Financial Times* reported that Daewoo's trading and construction company "held an employee rally in late September at 8:00 A.M. They adopted a resolution that for the rest of the year there would be no holidays and Sundays off to achieve its export target of $3 billion. Participation is not compulsory, but unwillingness to make sacrifices for the company is not a route to the top." According to Chairman Kim, "Daewoo people, including myself, believe that working diligently does not harm the family. Rather, it brings fulfillment. This attitude makes us different from people in the advanced countries." However, that did not stop twenty-one hundred unionized workers at the new Daewoo-GM plant from walking away from their jobs in the spring of 1985 and striking in support of a demand for a 23 percent wage hike. In 1987 workers at Daewoo Motor were making an average of $3 an hour, compared to automotive wages of $18 an hour in Japan and $24 in the United States.

In 1987 the U.S. Justice Department filed a complaint against Dae-

---

White-Collar Crime Gets More Than Slap on the Wrist in China

Two Chinese government officials, Zhang Changsheng and Ye Zhifeng, went on trial in 1986 for passing secrets and accepting bribes from foreign businessmen. According to one charge, after learning that regulations on car imports were about to be changed, they leaked this information to a Hong Kong exporter, advising him to back-date a contract to escape the consequences of the new rules. They supposedly also put pressure on a Chinese company to accept the price being offered by a foreign company. For his efforts Zhang received bribes totaling $250,000, of which he gave $5,000 to Ye.

Found guilty by a Beijing court, Zhang was executed on April 14, 1986. He was thirty-one years old. The forty-year-old Ye received a seventeen-year prison sentence.

woo charging that the company had used false invoices to hide the true price of steel exports to the United States. The scheme, said the government, was designed to get around restrictions on dumping steel at below fair market prices. Daewoo hired ex–White House aide Michael Deaver to represent it in this dispute, and in 1986, a settlement offer of $12 million was made to the U.S. Customs Service, which turned it down. The Justice Department asked for penalties of $163 million.

Access 541 5-GA
Nam Daemoon
Chung-Gu
Seoul, Korea
(82) 2-771-91

437 Madison Ave.
New York, N.Y. 10022
(212) 909-8200

Dai-Ichi Kangyo Bank	
Assets $250 billion	
Total Revenues $13 billion	
Profits $560 million	
Rank World's largest bank	
Founded Dai-Ichi: 1873	
Nippon Kangyo: 1897	
Employees 21,000 (average age: 36)	
Headquarters Tokyo, Japan	

Colossal amounts of money flow through the Japanese banking system (of the world's top ten banks, ranked by assets, nine are Japanese), and the biggest collector of them all is Dai-Ichi Kangyo, which was formed in 1971 by the merger of Dai-Ichi, the country's oldest bank, with Nippon Kangyo, an old-timer itself. Prior to their merger Dai-Ichi ranked sixth and Kangyo eighth in Japanese banking. The merger made them number one in Japan.

But that was just for starters. In the dozen years following the merger, Dai-Ichi Kangyo (DKB) multiplied its deposits and assets tenfold so that by the end of 1983 *American Banker* ranked it first in the world, ahead of the American leader, Citicorp. The gap opened much wider after the rise in the value of the Japanese yen. Dai-Ichi's assets at the end of 1986 reached $250 billion, compared to $196 billion for Citicorp.

Dai-Ichi Kangyo has more branches in Japan than any other bank—360—and prides itself on serving individuals and small companies as well as corporate giants. It has a customer base of twenty million—and 650,000 of these customers visit a DKB branch every day. One hundred thirty thousand companies bank with Dai-Ichi. Japan is a nation of savers and, aside from the savings system run by the government post office, Dai-Ichi has more individual savings accounts than any other institution. Utilizing a pink heart in a profusion of symbols and slogans that would put "I ♥ New York" to shame, DKB courts the individual depositor with the "Heart Telecom Information Service," providing up-to-the-minute economic news; the "Heart's Property-Ownership Plan"; and even the "Heart's Two-Generation Repay Loan," a quintessentially Japanese instrument that allows parent and offspring to pay off the bank loan over two lifetimes.

If such practices betray a soft heart, they may be traced to the influence of Shibusawa Eiichi, the founder of Dai-Ichi and one of the fathers of Japan's modern capitalist society. Shibusawa's life—he was born in 1840 and lived until 1931—spanned the Tokugawa shogunate, the Meiji Restoration, and the rise of Japanese industry. He is credited with being a pioneer not only in the launching of new companies but in the

168

formulation of a business ideology that has had lasting influence. The Dai-Ichi Bank that he organized in 1873 was the first bank established under the National Bank Act of 1872. It had the power to issue bank notes (what the rest of us call "money") until 1883, when the Bank of Japan assumed that function. One department of the bank dealt with insurance, the forerunner of today's Tokio Marine and Fire Insurance, the largest casualty and property insurer in Japan. Shibusawa is said by historian Rodney Clark to "have organized, directed, or advised five hundred companies."

In his 1982 book *Miracle by Design,* journalist and scholar Frank Gibney depicted Shibusawa as "the conscience of Japanese business." His mission, Gibney said, was to "bring respectability to business." He was not part of the *zaibatsu* enterprises (the Mitsuis, Mitsubishis, and Sumitomos), and as a reaction against these family-based conglomerates he introduced the joint stock company to Japan as a way to spread ownership and control across a wider spectrum of the community. According to Gibney, he also coined the modern Japanese word for businessman, *jitsugyoka,* which translates literally as "a practical man of affairs."

Shibusawa applied Confucian and Buddhist ethics of work to the business world. One of his sayings was: "To go bankrupt because of moral principle is not to fail, even though it is to go bankrupt. To become rich without moral principle is not to succeed, even though it is to become rich." Another was: "Morality and economy were meant to walk hand in hand."

Gibney summed up his influence as follows: "The importance of the people factor in Japanese business and its relationship to productivity comes direct from Shibusawa. No one had a clearer conviction than he that a Japanese business was only as good as the work ethic perpetuated among its people."

The other half of DKB, Nippon Kangyo, started in 1897 as a direct arm of the Japanese government, making long-term loans to companies and farmers. There were a number of such banks in Japan and, over a period beginning in 1921 and ending in 1944, they were enfolded into the arms of Nippon Kangyo. Nobuya Hagura, who became president of Dai-Ichi Kangyo in 1982, came up from the Nippon Kangyo side. In an interview he once described the tough job the bank had after World War II: "All our collateral had gone up in smoke. Real estate was the main form of security for Nippon Kangyo's loans, but the mortgaged buildings and factories had been destroyed in air raids. . . . With the collateral gone, we had to have the companies pay us the proceeds of their fire insurance or war insurance policies. It was a depressing job, but it had to be done."

Dai-Ichi went through a series of mergers of its own. Between 1912 and 1964 it merged with five other banks. And in 1971, when it merged with Nippon Kangyo to leap to the top of the Japanese banking heap, the leaders of the bank were still emphasizing its uniqueness as a large financial institution that existed outside the zaibatsu sphere of influence. In 1978, however, Dai-Ichi organized its own group from its corporate customers. Forty-five companies, all leaders in their respective fields, came together to launch the Sankin-kai ("third Friday group"), so named because the chairmen and presidents of these companies meet on the third Friday of every third month to exchange information. Dai-Ichi itself characterizes Sankin-kai "as the largest business group in Japan," with the members employing five hundred thousand people and having combined sales of 42 trillion yen (a mere $280 billion). Hitachi, Isuzu, and Kawasaki rotate in the Dai-Ichi orbit.

One bank product you are not likely to see in the United States was being offered in 1985 by Dai-Ichi as a way to help small- and medium-sized businesses which had developed new technologies but lacked capital. It was a loan package that lent out as much as $140,000 without collateral at 5.5 percent interest over seven years. Dai-Ichi crafted another no-collateral loan package for the thirty-four thousand owners of gasoline stations in Japan. Dai-Ichi has become a leader in the so-called "samurai"

The Biggest Banks in the World, or Yen Power

(By assets)

1. Dai-Ichi Kangyo (Japan)	$250 billion
2. Fuji (Japan)	$220 billion
3. Sumitomo (Japan)	$217 billion
4. Mitsubishi (Japan)	$210 billion
5. Sanwa (Japan)	$200 billion
6. Citicorp (United States)	$196 billion
7. Sumitomo Trust & Banking (Japan)	$176 billion
8. Industrial Bank of Japan	$164 billion
9. Tokai (Japan)	$142 billion
10. Mitsui (Japan)	$140 billion
11. Norinchukin (Japan)	$139 billion
12. Long-Term Credit Bank (Japan)	$122 billion
13. Crédit Agricole (France)	$121 billion
14. Banque Nationale de Paris (France)	$121 billion
15. National Westminster (Britain)	$120 billion

market for yen-denominated bonds issued in Japan by foreign borrowers. Among its clients are Sears, Roebuck, Dow Chemical, Proctor & Gamble, and American Express.

As big as Dai-Ichi is, its international presence has not been as strong as other Japanese banks'. In 1986 the bank had fifty-five overseas branches and was deriving 20 percent of its profits from outside of Japan. Dai-Ichi has stepped up its foreign exchange activities; they have more than tripled since 1981. To help its white-shirted, short-sleeved, intense young currency traders, Dai-Ichi installed what it called "the most modern communication system," HITS. The ITS stands for Integrated Trading System, the H stands, naturally, for Heart.

Measured by assets or deposits, Dai-Ichi Kangyo is clearly the leader of the world banking industry. But it falls behind when profits are tallied. In 1985 at least twenty banks in the world reported higher earnings than Dai-Ichi. But that's typical of Japanese banks, which were organized to help their customers. In the Japanese spectrum Dai-Ichi does all right. In 1986 the *Japan Times* ranked it nineteenth among all companies in pretax earnings.

Access 1-5 Uchisaiwaicho 1-chome, Chiyoda-ku
Tokyo 100, Japan
(81) 3-596-1111

One World Trade Center
New York, N.Y. 10048
(212) 446-5200

Daimler-Benz

Sales $30 billion
Profits $815 million
U.S. Sales $4 billion
Rank World's 13th-largest
 manufacturer
 World's largest producer of
 heavy trucks
 West Germany's largest company
 Largest bus manufacturer in
 Europe
 2d-largest defense contractor in
 West Germany
 World's 14th-largest car maker
 World's largest maker of diesel
 engine cars
Founded 1886
Employees 320,000
Headquarters Stuttgart, West Germany

Hundreds of times a day, uniformed West German workmen slam car doors, adjust them, and slam them again. And again. They're getting that characteristic Mercedes *thunk* just right. A small detail, perhaps. But getting things right is the wellspring of the Mercedes legend. It's a legend of engineering excellence that has made the cars from Daimler-Benz coveted around the world as a symbol of wealth, prestige, and power. And it's a legend that has held fast under various regimes (monarchist, fascist, and democratic) and various owners (the founders, followed by bankers, convicted Nazi war criminals, and a Middle East sheikdom).

Mercedes-Benz cars work hard for their status. Basically boxy, they have inner virtues: a tradition of a taut, firm ride, unerring handling, excellent braking, superb design. They're resolute over rough roads and better still at high speeds. Given the chance—and a lot of money—most Americans would buy a Mercedes, surveys show. In the early 1970s Mercedes passed Cadillac as the world's top-selling luxury car. The company bridles at the "luxury car" description. "For us, luxury lies in building a car that we think is right," a top Daimler executive once lectured a reporter.

Underlying the mystique is a deep-rooted philosophy of building cars that perform well and are both comfortable and safe for the occupants. Mercedes-Benz machines used to be fixtures on racing circuits, and the advances tested in that crucible were later incorporated in production vehicles. The company owns a long string of automotive firsts. It produced the first car equipped with a supercharger (1921), the first diesel passenger car (1936), the first car with gasoline fuel injection (1954), the first inline five-cylinder car (1974), the first car with ABS anti-lock brakes (1978), the first turbocharged diesel (1978), and the first car equipped with an air bag (1980). One of the car's early fans, Adolf Hitler, bought his first Mercedes in 1923 with Nazi party funds. He once explained to his colleagues why it was his favorite automobile: "My decisive experience with the Mercedes was a collision between my car and another vehicle on the Nuremberg-Munich highway. The other car was totally wrecked; on mine, only the bumpers and running board were damaged. It was then I decided to use only a Mercedes for the rest of my life."

As anyone who has ever ordered a Mercedes knows, Daimler-Benz takes the time to get things right. The company makes major model changes infrequently—every seven or eight years. American customers may have to wait months for their car, Europeans as long as two years. Not that there's anything wrong at the factory. It's just a deliberate company policy to let supply lag behind demand. The policy, like the breathtaking price (the cheapest Mercedes available in the United States in 1986 had a retail sticker price of $26,400), adds to the Mercedes cachet. One reason the factory starves its 431 dealers in the United States is that it wants to ensure the Mercedes owner a high resale value. It's an advantage the company advertises. Owner loyalty is so high that in Germany 90 percent of Mercedes owners buy another; in the United States, the figure is 75 percent.

"A Japanese manufacturer asked me once how we build quality into our cars," Daimler-Benz chairman Werner Breitschwerdt remarked once to *The New York Times*. "I told him just like the English with their lawns: cut twice a week, water regularly and be doing it for one hundred years." Breitschwerdt wasn't joking. At Daimler-Benz the nurturing of engineering talent goes back that far. The pivotal date in its corporate annals, and in automotive history, was January 29, 1886, when Karl Benz of Mannheim received a patent for his three-wheel car powered by an internal combustion engine. It was the world's first automobile patent. Later that same year another German engineer, Gottlieb Daimler, working sixty miles away in a Stuttgart suburb, built a four-wheel automobile.

It is certainly legitimate then for Daimler-Benz to lay claim to having been the company that launched an industry that changed the world. During the company's centennial celebrations in 1986, journalist Richard Reeves asked an impertinent question that only an American would ask: "Why do I think Henry Ford invented the automobile in 1902?" Bernd

Gottschalk, director of public affairs for Daimler-Benz, replied, "Yes, that is a problem for us. We try to go easy on the facts so as not to offend Americans. The American market is very important to us."

Whatever Americans may think, Daimler-Benz enjoys an exalted status at home. For many Germans it represents the quintessential German company, an incarnation of the native talents of superb engineering and exemplary workmanship. And the two men who gave their names to the enterprise are revered. The greenhouse Daimler used as his workshop has been preserved as a museum. The cities of Mannheim and Karlsruhe both have monuments to Benz. And the centerpiece of Daimler-Benz's corporate headquarters in Stuttgart is a three-story automobile museum that was opened in 1961 to mark the seventy-fifth anniversary of Karl Benz's invention and completely remodeled (and enlarged) in 1986 to mark the one hundredth anniversary. Containing models of the earliest automobiles built in the world, it's a must visit for a car buff.

Those who do visit will find themselves in the southwest corner of Germany, in the state of Baden-Württemberg, a region rich in historic, religious, and architectural vestiges. Stuttgart is the capital of a territory known as Swabia (*Schwaben* in German). Settled in the third century, it became a major European battleground in the feudal, religious, and political wars that swept the Continent from the ninth to the nineteenth centuries. Its height of power was from 1488 to 1534 when the Swabian League united more than twenty-five cities and numerous nobles, knights, and prelates in a court that had a powerful army and a formal constitution. The religious split stemming from the Reformation broke it apart. The Swabian region today is bounded on the west by France, on the south by Switzerland, and on the east by upper Bavaria. It's an area of spectacular beauty, containing a mountain range (the Swabian Jura), two of Europe's great rivers (the Rhine and the Danube), and the Black Forest. In Germany Swabians have a reputation for intelligence, diligence, and thrift. They have been called "the Scots of Germany." Karl Benz and Gottlieb Daimler were both born into Swabian families whose roots in the area go back many generations.

Until his parents' generation, Benz's forefathers were blacksmiths in the northern Black Forest town of Pfaffenrot. His father, Johann Georg, started out as a smithy too, but when the railroad came to Baden in 1840, he signed on first as a stoker and then an engineer. He died in 1846, when Karl was two years old, from pneumonia contracted after he had helped to lift a locomotive back on the tracks. Karl was brought up by his mother in the Rhine city of Karlsruhe and inherited his father's fascination with machines. In his memoirs he wrote fondly of fixing Black Forest clocks while a student at the Karlsruhe Lyzeum and "learning to feel the marvelous language that gear wheels talk when they mesh with one another." He graduated from a famous engineering school, the Karlsruhe Polytechnikum, and he eventually settled with his bride, the former Bertha Ringer, in the Rhine city of Mannheim. He had his own machine shop there by 1872, and his memoirs recount the moment on New Year's Eve 1879 when he got his first engine to run:

> After supper, my wife said, "Let's go over to the shop and try our luck once more. Something tells me to go and it will not let me go." So there we were, back again, standing in front of the engine as if it were a great mystery that was impossible to solve. My heart was pounding. I turned the crank. The engine started to go put-put-put and the music of the future sounded with regular rhythm. We both listened to it for a full hour, fascinated, never tiring of the single tone of its song. The two-cycle engine was performing as no magic flute in the world ever had. The longer it played its note, the more sorrow and anxiety it conjured away from the heart. It was the truth that if sorrow had been our companion on the way over there, joy walked beside us on the way back. For this New Year's Eve we could well dispense with the congratulations of our friends and neighbors, for we had known the heartiest kind of happiness that evening in our poor little workshop, which had now become the birthplace of a new engine. We stood around the courtyard listening for quite a while, and through the stillness of the night we could still clearly hear the put-put-put.

It was this engine that powered Benz's three-wheeler in 1886. In 1888, when it was fitted with a spark-plug ignition, the car caused a sensation on the streets of Munich. Reported one newspaper: "Seldom, if ever, have passersby in the streets of our city seen a more startling sight than on Saturday afternoon when a one-horse chaise came from the Sendlingerstrasse over Sendlingertorplatz and down Herzog Wilhelmstrasse at a good clip without any horse or thill, a gentleman sitting under a surrey top, riding on three wheels—one in front and two behind—speeding on his way towards the center of town. The amazement of everyone on the street who saw him was such that they seemed unable to grasp what they had before their eyes."

Benz's first four-wheel car, the Viktoria, made its debut in 1893. Its initial sales were mostly in France, where enthusiasm for the automobile was greater than in Germany. In 1894 the Benz factory in Mannheim, with an employee force of 250, turned out sixty-nine cars, which was greater than the total automobile population of the United States. The first

Benz "bus," looking very much like a stagecoach, appeared in 1895 and was pressed into mail service. In 1899 the Benz factory in Mannheim rolled out 572 vehicles, making it the largest automaker in the world.

Gottlieb Daimler was born ten years before Benz in 1834, in Schorndorf, a village in the Rems Valley fifteen miles east of Stuttgart. His father had a bakery and wine bar in the heart of the town, which was founded in 1250. Daimler was apprenticed to a gunsmith and worked at a locomotive factory before returning to school (the Stuttgart Polytechnical Institute) for training in engineering. He was interested early on in unlocking the secrets of power and was convinced that there was a better means than the steam engine, which was then in wide use. This was not an original idea. The possibility of an internal combustion engine, in which fuel is burned in a confined space or vacuum, thereby producing energy, had intrigued scientists for several centuries. The Dutch physicist Christian Huygens had built a gunpowder engine in 1680. During Daimler's time work on such an engine was going forward in a number of countries. A Belgian-born French engineer, Jean Joseph Etienne Lenoir, produced a gas engine in 1860, and as Daimler happened to be in Paris at that time he shared the excitement. Lenoir's work stimulated a German engineer, Nikolaus Otto, who exhibited a more efficient engine at the Paris Exposition of 1867. Meanwhile, Daimler, after inspecting state-of-the-art industrial plants in England, returned to Germany to become the manager of the Deutz engine factory, where Otto continued his experiments, scoring a notable breakthrough in 1876 when he invented the four-stroke engine that bore his name.

Daimler came to a parting of the way with the Deutz people in 1882, when he was forty-eight years old. They wanted him to go to Russia to run a branch factory in St. Petersburg. He left, taking with him a gifted, largely self-taught designer, Wilhelm Maybach, and started his own company in Cannstatt on the outskirts of Stuttgart. They set up shop at about the same time Karl Benz was launching his company in Mannheim.

The Daimler-Maybach collaboration was one of the most fruitful in automotive history. Inventions poured forth from their workshop. They devised engines that were lightweight but powerful (they revolved rapidly), and they solved the tricky problem of ignition. In 1885 came a motorcycle. In 1886 came a four-wheel coach and a motorboat. In 1888 Daimler fitted a two-horsepower engine to a balloon for air travel. And in 1889 he introduced a four-stroke engine with mushroom-shaped valves and two cylinders arranged in a V. This was the engine that won the day in the auto industry, thanks to its ability to deliver the most power per weight.

In addition to powering his own cars, the Daimler engine was licensed to companies in other countries. It powered the Panhard, Levassor, and Peugeot cars in France. In Britain the cars fitted with his engine became known as Daimlers. In the United States the Daimler engine was licensed to the Long Island City piano maker William Steinway. Gottlieb Daimler did not live to see the culmination of his life's work. He died on March 6, 1900. Incredible as it may seem, considering how close they lived to one another, Daimler and Karl Benz never met.

One of the early customers of Daimler was an international businessman, Emil Jellinek. The son of a Bohemian rabbi, Jellinek lived on the French Riviera where he sold Daimler cars, entered them in races, and served as consul for Austria-Hungary. It was his suggestions to the factory in Cannstatt that led to a 35-horsepower Daimler with a low center of gravity and large wheelbase. Jellinek ordered thirty-six of these cars and secured the rights to sell them in Austria-Hungary, France, Belgium, and the United States. He insisted, however, that they bear the nameplate Mercedes, the name of his eleven-year-old daughter. In 1901 the Mercedes cars that Jellinek entered in the "Nice Week" races swept the field. A French automotive writer said, "We are now in the era of the Mercedes." The Mercedes name was registered as a Daimler trademark in 1902. Another trademark, registered in 1911, was the three-pointed star symbolizing the three places where Mercedes engines were used: land, water, and air.

While Benz and Daimler were brilliant engineers, neither was adept at running a business. Both of them, in fact, lost control of the companies that bore their names. For one year, in the mid-1890s, Daimler and his sidekick Maybach left the Daimler company and set up shop in a defunct hotel in Cannstatt. Benz quarreled with his partners too, and in 1903 he left the company. He returned a year later as a director but was never again active in any management capacity. Instead, with his two sons he set up another automotive company, C. Benz Sohne, in Ladenburg, that did not compete directly against the original Benz firm in Mannheim. (This firm still exists, still under control of the Benz family. It makes automotive parts for Daimler-Benz.)

Karl Benz lived long enough to be honored as a cultural hero in Germany. In 1925 he was hailed by thousands of spectators at a motorcade which wound its way through the streets of Munich. And in 1929, when he was eighty-five, the automobile clubs of Baden, Württemberg, and Bavaria organized a cavalcade to Ladenburg under the banner, "Do honor to your master." The master died on April 4, 1929. Later that year Wilhelm Maybach died. He had left the Daimler firm in 1907, going on to help Ferdinand von Zeppelin design the airship that was to bear his name. Bertha Benz died in 1944 at age ninety-five.

The managers in control of the Benz and Daimler enterprises were not brilliant businessmen either. They dissipated the industry leadership that had resulted from the technical achievements of Karl Benz and Gottlieb Daimler, and the axis of the automotive world shifted to the United States, where Henry Ford brought out his Model T in 1908. It was so successful that Ford was outselling every company in the world by the start of World War I in 1914. After Germany's defeat in the war, the Benz and Daimler companies continued to slump, along with the rest of the German economy. In 1925 their combined output was 3,666 cars, fewer than the number they had turned out in 1911. The entire German auto industry was producing only fifty thousand cars, whereas in the United States more than four million were rolling off the assembly lines. The Deutsche Bank, then and now Germany's largest bank, dictated a solution in 1926: Daimler and Benz should merge into a new company, Daimler-Benz AG.

The coming to power of Adolf Hitler on January 30, 1933, gave a shot in the arm to Daimler-Benz. The Chancellor had an automotive policy. He abolished the sales tax on new cars, and he built the network of superhighways known as Autobahns, where no one gets stopped for speeding at more than 100 miles per hour. Hitler was one of the first politicians in the world to use the automobile in his campaigns, and it was always a Mercedes. His favorite models were the great Mercedes-Benz touring cars. He would ride next to the driver, and for parades or reviews he could tilt the seat back and stand on a specially raised platform. The cars were armor-plated. The windows were made of bulletproof glass. One model that he used was twenty feet long, seven feet wide, six feet high and weighed ten thousand pounds. The tank held fifty-six gallons of gas; the car got four miles per gallon. It was in these Greater Mercedes-Benz touring cars that Hitler entered Austria and Czechoslovakia in 1938, Warsaw in 1939, and Paris in 1940.

During World War II Daimler-Benz supplied more than limousines to Adolf Hitler. It built vehicles for the Nazi army, and it made the engines that powered the Messerschmitt fighters and the Panther and Tiger tanks. Daimler-Benz factories were prime targets of Allied bombers—and they were 70 percent destroyed. But the company made a remarkably quick recovery. At the end of the war in 1945 Daimler-Benz was down to a payroll of 2,860 people. By the end of 1946 employment had risen to 17,850 and a passenger car, the 170 V, was already in production. At the 1948 Hannover Fair a 3.5-ton truck and two 4-cylinder passenger cars—

the 170S and a diesel version—were introduced. In 1951 the 6-cylinder 220 and 300 were rolled out. In 1939, the last year before the war, Mercedes-Benz won three of the Grand Prix races conducted in Europe. In 1954 Mercedes racers returned to competition and won five out of seven Grand Prix events (Ferraris won the other two). However, in 1956 it dropped out of racing after a Mercedes driver, trying to avoid a pileup in France's famous Le Mans road race, plowed into a densely packed crowd of spectators, killing eighty-seven people. It was the worst accident in racing history.

From its Swabian stronghold, where managers and workers alike have intense pride in the quality of the cars coming off the line, Daimler-Benz has pushed ahead quietly but relentlessly. By 1968 it had produced two million cars since World War II; by 1977, five million. It shrugged off the quadrupling of oil prices in the 1970s. In 1981, when the German auto industry had one of the worst years in its history, Daimler-Benz had a record year. In 1982, to the derision of many automobile writers, it came out with its "baby" Mercedes, the 190 line. *Wall Street Journal* reporter Amal Nag took the diesel version for a test drive and reported that the car lacked power and performance. Daimler-Benz had the last laugh. In 1985 it sold 211,000 of its compacts, representing about 40 percent of its total passenger car sales. To make these compacts the company opened a new plant in the north German city of Bremen, where it instantly became the largest employer.

In 1985, when 32.6 million cars were produced in the world, Daimler-Benz made 541,039 or less than 2 percent of the total. All of these cars were made in its German plants and half of them were exported. In West Germany Mercedes captured 11.6 percent of the market. Its next best market is the United States, where 85,000 Mercedes-Benzes were sold in 1985. One out of every three cars made by the company is a diesel. Worldwide production of commercial vehicles (vans, trucks, buses) reached 12.1 million units in 1985, of which Daimler-Benz accounted for 220,213. The company made 70,000 of these vehicles in overseas plants located in ten countries. Daimler-Benz is the world's largest maker of heavy trucks (over six tons). Its wholly owned subsidiary, Freightliner Corporation, which it bought from Consolidated Freightways in 1981, ranks fourth among U.S. truck makers.

Daimler-Benz continues to insist that it makes the cars its engineers want to make instead of following fashion trends or polling consumers to find out what they want. In the company's 1985 annual report, the philosophy was stated as follows: "We will continue to pursue our strategy of qualitative growth. Quantitative growth will be acceptable only to the extent that the exclusivity of the Mercedes-Benz marque is maintained." Translation: "We are not going to make cars for the hoi polloi." In 1984 the Daimler-Benz board of directors selected a chairman who would appear to be the perfect implementer of that policy, the aforementioned Werner Breitschwerdt, a Swabian engineer who rose through the research and design ranks of the company. "Americans give the making of money all priority," he told Richard Reeves in 1986. "I watch Lee Iacocca. I read his book. He is saying that selling cars is all 'marketing.' There is more to it than marketing, believe me."

Breitschwerdt's selection in 1984 provided insight into the workings of a German supervisory board *(aufsichtsrat),* which is composed entirely of outsiders, including representatives of the employees. The Daimler board has twenty members, nine of them labor people. Breitschwerdt was elected by a vote of eleven-to-nine. All the employee representatives voted for Edzard Reuter, finance director of Daimler-Benz and an outspoken supporter of West Germany's Social Democratic party. Reuter, whose father was mayor of Berlin during the Berlin airlift of 1948–49, is one of the few SDP supporters sitting on a big corporate board in Germany. Voting for Breitschwerdt were the banking and business representatives on the board, including the three members from the Deutsche Bank, which is Daimler's largest stockholder, controlling 28 percent of the shares.

Unlike what might have happened in the United States, Reuter stayed on as finance director and a year later played a key role in a spate of acquisitions that turned Daimler-Benz into the largest company in West Germany. Indeed, his role in diversifying Daimler-Benz was so crucial that in mid-1987 he was named chief executive of the company, replacing Breitschwerdt, whose abiding interest was motor vehicles.

Past history indicates that Daimler-Benz has a life of its own that goes on no matter who chairs (or owns) the company. In 1959 Walter Hitzinger, an Austrian steelman, was recruited to lead the company because of his reputation as a tough manager. *Fortune* writer Robert Ball reported that Hitzinger's "taste for hierarchy and titles" (he insisted that he be addressed as *Herr Generaldirektor*) didn't mesh too well with the informal and undogmatic ways of Daimler. He had a five-year contract, but one Daimler executive described his tenure as follows: "For the first six months he did a lot of damage and thereafter had virtually no influence."

After ninety-nine years of doing nothing but making automotive products, Daimler-Benz went on a buying spree in 1985, acquiring control of three other companies: MTU, short for Motoren-und-Turbinen-Union, a manufacturer of engines for planes, ships, and tanks; Dornier, a producer of commuter planes, rockets, satellite parts, and medical equipment; and AEG, a giant electronics company that makes everything from computers to vacuum cleaners and typewriters. A *Fortune* writer, Louis S. Richman, asked, "Has someone been putting schnapps in the water coolers at Daimler-Benz?" Breitschwerdt explained the moves as an effort to add a high-tech component to the Daimler-Benz process. The company believes it bought electronics know-how that will help it to build better cars. "In the past we didn't need partners," said the Daimler chairman. "Today, we do. It is not Daimler but the world we operate in that has changed." The acquisitions added $5 billion to Daimler-Benz's sales volume and vaulted the company ahead of Volkswagen and Siemens into first place in the West German industrial hierarchy. It also resulted in the resignations of two directors, Marcus Bierich, chairman of Robert Bosch, and Heribald Naerger, a top executive at Siemens, who suddenly found themselves sitting on the board of a competitor.

The ownership structure of Daimler-Benz changed radically in recent years. In 1974 the Quandt Group, a major West German financial holding company, sold the 14 percent stake it had to the oil sheikdom of Kuwait, which was still holding it in 1986 (it had turned out to be a fabulous investment). Then in 1975 and 1976 the industrial titan Friedrich Flick, who was convicted at Nuremberg as a Nazi war criminal, sold his 29 percent stake to the Deutsche Bank. That left Flick with a 10 percent interest, which he sold to the Deutsche Bank on January 1, 1986. The value of Daimler-Benz's stock had escalated so much that the 10 percent slice Flick sold in 1986 was worth more than twice the 2 billion marks he got for his 29 percent holding ten years earlier.

Daimler-Benz shares were traded in 1987 in only one place, the Frankfurt Stock Exchange, where they are listed under two different names, Daimler-Benz AG and Mercedes-Automobil-Holding. About a third of the shares is now in the hands of the public. In 1983 Daimler-Benz had a market value of 18.1 billion marks. In 1986 its market value was 50 billion marks ($23 billion), which ranked it second in Europe to Royal Dutch Shell. Pictures of Gottlieb Daimler and Karl Benz grace the stock certificates.

Daimler-Benz celebrated its one hundredth birthday in 1986 in high style. It started out the year by increasing the dividend to shareholders from 10.5 marks ($5.25) to 12 marks ($6), on top of which it paid out a jubilee bonus of 2.5 marks ($1.25). Then, toward the end of the year, it rewarded its shareholders by offering to sell them one share for every eleven they held, at the bargain price of $73. At the time the stock was selling for $620 a share. More than one hundred thousand of Daimler-Benz's employees are stockholders, and they have bought more than six hundred thousand shares since 1973 under special plans which are partly subsidized by the company. In 1986 the company also paid a one hundredth birthday bonus to all employees. Each person on the payroll received a cash payment of $500 plus $85 for every five years of service. Finally, the company, enjoying the biggest profit year in its history, contributed $25 million to establish the Gottlieb Daimler and Karl Benz Foundation with a mandate to support research efforts "into the interrelationships between man, environment, and technology."

In the United States the one hundredth birthday was marked by the publication of a spectacular company history, *The Star and the Laurel,* written by Beverly Rae Kimes and produced by Harris Lewine. A 368-page outsized volume that is well researched, well written, and beautifully illustrated, *The Star and the Laurel* was financed by Mercedes-Benz of America, the U.S. arm of Daimler-Benz, in a press run of fifty thousand. Some fifteen thousand copies were distributed to libraries, colleges, and universities.

Of course not everyone recognizes Daimler-Benz as the founder of

Europe's Top Car Producers (1986)

		Market Share
1. Volkswagen/Audi (including SEAT of Spain)	2 million	17.9%
2. Fiat/Lancia (including Alfa Romeo)	1.6 million	14.0
3. Peugeot/Citroën	1.59 million	13.7
4. Renault	1.42 million	12.3
5. Ford	1.40 million	12.1
6. General Motors (Opel/Vauxhall)	1.3 million	11.7
7. Daimler-Benz	591,000	5.1
8. BMW	432,000	3.7
9. Volvo	413,000	3.5
10. Rover	404,000	3.2
11. Saab	126,000	1.0
12. Porsche	53,000	0.4
13. Jaguar	41,000	0.3
Others	31,000	0.2

the automobile industry. The French held their own centennial celebration in 1984. However, when Daimler-Benz invited dignitaries to its celebration in January 1986, even the French sent a few representatives who heard Lothar Spaeth, the prime minister of the state of Baden-Württemberg, praise the three-star company for having lifted southwest Germany "out of the poor house." Daimler-Benz has seventy thousand employees in and around Stuttgart. "A hundred years ago," Premier Spaeth said, "we exported people because they did not have enough to eat."

Access   P.O. Box 600202
D-7000 Stuttgart 60, West Germany
(49) 711-17-0

Mercedes-Benz of North America
One Mercedes Dr.
Montvale, N.J. 07645
(201) 573-0600

De Benedetti Group

Sales $10 billion

Profits Who knows?

U.S. Sales $900 million

Rank Italy's 3d-largest financial holding company

Europe's largest office automation company

World's 3d-largest maker of personal computers

World's 6th-largest typewriter manufacturer

Italy's 2d-largest food company

France's largest haute couture house

Founded 1908 (Olivetti)

Employees 110,000

Headquarters Ivrea, Italy

Carlo De Benedetti, the modern reincarnator of the Italian office machine company Olivetti, reigns as one of the princes of the Byzantine world of Italian finance and industry. It's not a rags-to-riches story. He started out comfortably. But his derring-do was nonetheless spectacular. He took over an ailing Olivetti in 1978 and propelled it into a global force in office automation. After managing that turnaround, he assembled, Italian-style, an international network of companies that reach into banking, publishing, food, automotive supplies, computer retailing, insurance, banking, and haute couture. The spider in this complicated web is the holding company, Compagnia Finanziaria De Benedetti (Cofide), which is 51 percent–owned by De Benedetti himself. It's no wonder that *The Economist* profiled De Benedetti under the heading: "Yesterday Italy, today Europe, tomorrow the world?"

This European saga emerged from the Piedmont region of Northwest Italy. It's a region bordered on the west by France and on the north by Switzerland, and it's one of the industrial strongholds of Italy. Its capital city, Turin, is home base for the country's largest privately owned enterprise, Fiat Motor. And it was in Turin that Carlo De Benedetti, the second of two sons, was born in 1934 into a Jewish family whose Piedmontese roots went back several generations.

De Benedetti had a turbulent childhood because of World War II. His family fled from the German occupation forces in 1943 by moving across the border to Switzerland, where they rented a room in Lucerne until the war ended. They then returned to Turin and after Carlo and his elder brother, Franco, became engineers, they both entered the family business, which was the manufacture of flexible metal tubing. Carlo proved to be adept not just at running a business but expanding it every which way. By 1972, when he was thirty-eight years old, he had brought together under the banner of Gilardini a clutch of companies with annual sales of about $40 million. Many were suppliers to Fiat, controlled by the most powerful family in Italy, the Agnellis. In 1976, impressed by De Benedetti's obvious flair for business, Giovanni Agnelli, the capo of Fiat, bought Gilardini and installed Carlo as chief executive of the giant automotive company. He was forty-one years old, in command of a work force of more than three hundred thousand. And he owned 5 percent of Fiat.

De Benedetti's reign lasted one hundred days. (His older brother, who came aboard at the same time, stayed for two years.) The circumstances of his departure are clouded. One version, widely reported in print and still being told in European business circles ten years later, had De Benedetti leaving because Agnelli decided to sell 15 percent of Fiat to Libya, whose Muslim leader, Muammar Qaddafi, would not tolerate Jews in high places at Fiat. It's a story that has been denied many times but persists. A more likely version is that De Benedetti left after finding he could not stomach the corporate bureaucracy. "I suddenly realized I had made a big mistake," he told *Fortune* writer Robert Ball three years later. In any case, the Libyans did buy a chunk of Fiat. And De Benedetti did quit after one hundred days.

It didn't take him long to resurface. After spending three months visiting the United States, De Benedetti plunged back into Italian busi-

ness, using as his vehicle a tanning company, C.I.R., which served as a shell for the collection of a clutch of other companies, one of the biggest being Sasib, a manufacturer of cigarette-making machinery that he bought from AMF at the bargain price of $14 million. In 1978 De Benedetti was offered the job of running Olivetti, which was then on the verge of collapse after seventy years as an independent Italian company. Promised carte blanche, he accepted with alacrity, buying $17 million of Olivetti stock at the same time. "If I don't show that I believe in myself, why should anyone believe in me?" he said.

If there's any company in the Piedmont that's as well known as Fiat, it's Olivetti, which was founded in 1908 as the first—and, as it turned out, the only—Italian company to make typewriters. The founder was Camillo Olivetti, a Jewish electrical engineer who was born in 1868 in Ivrea, a town in the foothills of the Alps midway between Turin and Milan; it had one of the oldest Jewish ghettos in Europe. Olivetti's wife belonged to the Waldenses, the fiercely independent Protestant sect started in the late twelfth century by Peter Waldo, a wealthy French merchant of Lyon; the Waldensies survived numerous persecutions, and one of their strongest outposts was in the Piedmont.

In the late nineteenth century electrical engineering was a newfangled field, and after getting his degree Camillo Olivetti went to the United States for two years, meeting two of the discipline's shining lights, Thomas Edison and Charles Steinmetz, and teaching briefly at a newly opened university, Stanford. Returning to Italy, he decided to manufacture typewriters in the town where he was born. From the beginning Camillo Olivetti emphasized an element that was to become a trademark of his company: good design. He once said, "A typewriter is not a gadget or a toy. Aesthetics must be considered. A machine must have dignity and elegance." Olivetti's products were elegant. In later years they ended up in the Museum of Modern Art rather than the Smithsonian.

This sensibility carried over into other areas. Olivetti's publications and advertising were hallmarks of clean-cut, modern design. And an Olivetti factory, no matter where it went up, was usually a building of architectural distinction. The plant it put up overlooking the Bay of Naples was so inviting that tourists used to stop and ask if any rooms were available. Another legacy of Camillo Olivetti was a social security program for employees that was far ahead of its time. It included housing near the Ivrea plant and free medical care. "No one," *Fortune* said in 1960, "can say that Olivetti's success in selling abroad is based on cheap labor."

Camillo died in 1943 while World War II still raged. He reportedly told a group of employees who came to see him shortly before his death,

"We are not yet free. Prepare to defend yourself and hide your arms. Be strong." His son, Adriano Olivetti, was jailed for three months as a Jew before fleeing to Switzerland (as the De Benedettis did) to sit out the rest of the war. Adriano reassumed the helm at Ivrea in 1946, and he presided over a heady expansion that saw Olivetti open plants in Britain (1947), South Africa (1949), Argentina (1951), Brazil (1957), Mexico, Canada, Colombia, and the United States (all in 1959). Doing two thirds of its business outside Italy, Olivetti was selling more than typewriters. It made adding machines, and it scored a major breakthrough with its printing calculator.

Olivetti's post–World War II growth was capped in 1959 by the acquisition of a major interest in Underwood, the company that dominated the American typewriter market in the early part of the century when Camillo Olivetti was starting his firm in Ivrea. It was a move whose consequences were dire, but Adriano did not live to see them. He died in 1960 of a heart attack while on a train to Switzerland; he was fifty-eight. Underwood proceeded to drain Olivetti of at least $100 million. It was a most unpropitious acquisition, coming just at the time that IBM was about to sweep the market with its electric typewriter, a machine Underwood was never equipped to make properly.

Bruno Visentini, an Italian lawyer and financier, put together a 1964 refinancing that saved Olivetti from collapsing and, as chairman of Olivetti, held the falling pieces together for the next fourteen years while a series of chief executive officers came and went (one was Adriano's son, Roberto, another was Adriano's nephew, Camillo). Visentini once characterized the Underwood escapade as follows: "We helped out an underdeveloped country, the United States. American banks never lost a cent on Underwood, because we bailed them out." It was Visentini who approached De Benedetti in 1978 and recruited him for Olivetti. (Five years later Visentini became finance minister in the government formed by Socialist Bettino Craxi.)

Carlo brought only one person with him to Olivetti, his brother, Franco. They worked in tandem, Carlo "Mr. Outside," Franco "Mr. Inside." And they wrought a remarkable transformation. In 1978, when the De Benedettis arrived, Olivetti had sales of 1.5 trillion lire and about one half of these revenues were derived from typewriters and calculators. In 1985 Olivetti recorded sales of 6.1 trillion lire. It was deriving 29.5 percent of those revenues from personal computers and 32.2 percent from minicomputers and terminals.

Carlo's prowess as a dealmaker put Olivetti on the world technology map. In 1983, after personally visiting with Charles Brown, chairman of

American Telephone & Telegraph, he sold 25 percent of Olivetti to AT&T for $260 million. The pact pledged AT&T to market Olivetti products in the United States while Olivetti did the same for AT&T products in Europe. In 1985 Olivetti produced four hundred thousand personal computers, of which 39 percent were sold to AT&T for sale in the United States under AT&T's name.

The AT&T linkup was just one of the many deals engineered by De Benedetti, known familiarly in the Italian popular press as *Ingegnere* ("the engineer," of course). In 1986, for example, Olivetti acquired, for $71 million, the Triumph-Adler office machine business (typewriters, computers) that had been part of Volkswagen. Aside from lifting Olivetti's share of the European typewriter market to 48 percent (IBM has 12 percent), the transaction had a typically sweet kicker for De Benedetti. Volkswagen bought 5 percent of Olivetti for $260 million, which is precisely what AT&T paid for its 25 percent slice three years earlier. Among others which have fallen to Olivetti are Hermes, the Swiss typewriter manufacturer; Logabax, the French data processing marketer; and Acorn, the British computer manufacturer. In the United States Olivetti had, in 1986, minority interests ranging from 2 percent to 20 percent in fifteen different high-tech companies, including Digital Research of Pacific Grove, California; Syntrex of Eatontown, Pennsylvania; Lee Data of Minneapolis; and Irwin Magnetic Systems of Ann Arbor, Michigan.

De Benedetti has deals going all over the globe. In 1985 he inked an agreement with one of Japan's electronic giants, Toshiba, which took a 20 percent stake in Olivetti of Japan. The accord was ballyhooed in *The New York Times* as the possible start of a "powerful new alliance in world electronics." Nothing more was ever heard of a Toshiba-Olivetti juggernaut, but at the start of 1987 Olivetti formed a joint venture with Japan's Canon to make copiers, laser printers, facsimile machines, and other office equipment in Italy for sale throughout Europe. The ink was was hardly dry on this agreement when Olivetti forged a joint venture with the Electronic Data Systems division of General Motors to offer data processing systems in the European market. And that deal was hardly concluded when Olivetti was announcing a tripartite venture with Seat, which prints the Italian telephone directories, and Microsoft, the largest computer software supplier in the United States, to make optical discs in Europe through a new, Rome-based entity, Eikon.

But Olivetti is just the tip of the iceberg of economic power that Carlo De Benedetti is forming. In 1985 and 1986 he put into play an intricate, Chinese-boxlike configuration of companies which have arms extending over numerous industries and numerous countries. It's a maze of incestuous, interlocking entities. Cofide, which many people consider the master holding company, has its shares listed on the Milan Bourse. And while De Benedetti holds more than half of Cofide's shares, the minority investors include a constellation of investment bankers and managers from four different countries: Indosuez (France), S. G. Warburg (Britain), Nomura (Japan), and Shearson, Lehman and Dreyfus (United States).

Cofide owns 34 percent of the old master holding company, C.I.R., which in turn owns 41 percent of a French holding company, Cerus. In 1987 De Benedetti was planning to float a Spanish holding company, Cofir.

Cofide also holds a 51 percent interest in Saubadia, an Italian investment company that owns 5 percent of the Pirelli tire firm, 21 percent of the Mondadori publishing house, and 19 percent of Euromobilare, an investment banker. Still another tentacle reaches into Switzerland where Cofide and Saubadia each own 13.5 percent of Société Financiere de Geneve (Sofigen), an investment firm whose playground is financial services (banking and insurance). De Benedetti also has forged an alliance with Raul Gardini, another Italian empire builder, whose vehicle is Feruzzi, an agro-business giant that in 1986 gained control of Montedison, Italy's second-largest private company.

Beneath these financial umbrellas is a slew of operating companies, firms which do things—that is, manufacture products or provide services. Roped into the De Benedetti Group are Buitoni, the Italian pasta and candy (Perugina) manufacturer; Olio Sasso, one of Italy's leading olive oil pressers; Valeo, French automotive parts maker; Credit Romangnolo, an Italian commercial bank; and Davigel, the leading French distributor of frozen fish.

For De Benedetti it has been one acquisition after another, much of it fueled by stock issues on the volatile Milan Bourse. As 1986 drew to a close he struck out again, using his French arm, Cerus, to acquire a 37 percent stake in the French fashion house Yves St. Laurent. And in May 1987 he drove a 4.9 percent stake into S. Pearson, the English conglomerate whose interests include the *Financial Times* and *The Economist*.

Figuring out the maze is not easy. In some cases the De Benedetti holdings are large; in other cases they are just a sliver. The companies in the maze tend to own pieces of one another. More than two dozen have stock market listings of their own. The estimate in early 1987 was that if the revenues of all the companies in the De Benedetti corral were added up, the total would come to more than $10 billion—and the employee total would exceed one hundred thousand. Olivetti alone (where the De Benedetti controlling stake is 15 percent) recorded 1986 sales of nearly $6 billion and it has close to fifty thousand people on its payroll.

Carlo De Benedetti is not one of those shadowy, inarticulate business titans routinely described in the press as "secretive." He's up front about what he's doing, and he has a philosophy that he's quick to elaborate. Interviewed by the British magazine *Business,* he said, "I'm a builder, not a raider." Interviewed by *The Wall Street Journal,* he said, "It doesn't make sense to be Italian and fully invested in Italy. It's obsolete." And interviewed by *Fortune,* he said, "I love the destructive power of capitalism." De Benedetti's rise has been chronicled by Alan Friedman, Milan correspondent for the *Financial Times,* who concluded that Carlo De Benedetti shares with Giovani Agnelli "an almost unnatural hunger to control huge slices of finance and industry."

Access Via Jervis 77
Ivrea, Italy
(39) 125-525

Olivetti USA
535 Madison Ave.
New York, N.Y. 10022
(212) 371-5630

Electrolux

Sales $7.4 billion
Profits $239 million
U.S. Sales $3.2 billion
Rank World's largest maker of home appliances
Sweden's 2d-largest company
World's largest vacuum cleaner maker
World's largest chainsaw manufacturer
World's largest maker of car seat belts
World's largest maker of freezers
World's 2d-largest maker of refrigerators
World's 3d-largest manufacturer of washing machines
World's 5th-largest maker of sewing machines
Founded 1919
Employees 129,000 (25,000 in the United States)
Headquarters Stockholm, Sweden

lectrolux, a brand name well known in the United States, swept into business right after World War I with a push from the fabled Swedish entrepreneur Axel Wenner-Gren. He came up with the idea of a lightweight vacuum cleaner that could be trundled from room to room, and he combined the names of two Swedish companies, Electron and Lux, to arrive at a brand name. He planned from the start to sell his vacuum cleaners door-to-door so that they could be demonstrated in the home. His salesmen rang doorbells all over Sweden, an invasion of privacy that was exported to the United States and other countries. Wenner-Gren also planned from the start to build an international business. He wanted to vacuum the entire world. By 1930 he had Electrolux subsidiaries operating in thirty countries. Wenner-Gren was a resourceful and indefatigable promoter. He persuaded Pope Pius XI to let Electrolux clean the Vatican for a year, an idea that tapped a rich vein of publicity.

Seventy years later, in the mid-1980s, the Swedish company started by Wenner-Gren swept into first place in worldwide sales of home appliances. It had outstripped General Electric, Whirlpool, Maytag, Philips, Matsushita, Hitachi, Toshiba, and anybody else you care to name. And a funny thing had happened on the way to this mountaintop: Electrolux of Sweden was no longer connected with Electrolux of the United States.

The dissociation resulted from a series of aboutfaces typical of the higher thinking that goes on in corporate boardrooms. The Electrolux operation Wenner-Gren had established in the United States evolved over the years into a business that was linked only peripherally to Stockholm. Meanwhile, Electrolux of Sweden had drifted into the orbit of Marcus Wallenberg, the godfather of Swedish business (he once served on the boards of sixty companies and chaired more than thirty). Electrolux of Sweden managed, by the 1960s, to get its hands on 38 percent of the shares of Electrolux of the United States.

At that time Wallenberg was trying to apply a charge to a somnolent Electrolux. In 1962 he nudged the company into a merger with Elektrohelios, a maker of freezers and stoves and a subsidiary of ASEA, the Swedish counterpart of General Electric. (In 1986 ASEA still held 48.8 percent of Electrolux's voting shares.) Five years later he brought in a protégé, Hans Werthen, from another of his companies, L. M. Ericcson, to see if he could get Electrolux moving. The company's sales then were $200 million a year.

One of Werthen's first moves, in 1968, was to sell the 38 percent chunk of Electrolux of the United States. For consideration of $57 million, it went to Consolidated Foods, whose corporate name is now Sara Lee. Werthen used the money the way any good corporate manager would: He bought other companies. Indeed, buying companies became a Werthen trademark. Between 1970 and 1985 he bought more than three hundred companies in forty countries, transforming Electrolux into a maker and seller of not just appliances but food service equipment, laundries, supermarket refrigerator cases, and forestry and home maintenance products (for examples, Flymo lawn mowers and Pioneer-Partner chainsaws). It also became a major producer of car seat belts and a provider of commercial cleaning and maintenance services. And it became much more than a Swedish company. In 1986 Electrolux did more than 75 percent of its sales outside its home country.

One of the companies vacuumed up in this worldwide sweep was National Union Electric of the United States, maker of Eureka vacuum cleaners. That acquisition occurred in 1974 for roughly the same amount of money it received six years earlier for its holding in Electrolux of the United States. It produced the odd situation of Electrolux of Sweden fielding another vacuum cleaner brand to battle the Electrolux brand in the American market. Not that the people in Stockholm have any loyalty to, or affection for, any particular brand name as they march across national borders. This is not a business like Coca-Cola or McDonald's. Electrolux has scooped up companies all over the map, retaining the local brand names. In addition to the Electrolux and Eureka flags, the Swedish company sells appliances ranging from sewing machines and chainsaws to refrigerators and washing machines. These products are sold under the names Husquarna (Sweden), Progress and Zanker (Germany), Tornado and Arthur Martin (France), Tappan (United States), Therma (Switzerland), Atlas and Voss (Denmark), and Pioneer (Canada).

Electrolux became the biggest home appliance maker in Europe in 1984 when it bought Italy's Zanussi company. Zanussi is a highly regarded maker of washing machines, refrigerators, dishwashers, and ranges—that is, its technology and styling were admired. However, Zanussi was languishing under family control. Prior to this takeover, the top four European appliance houses were Electrolux, Bosch-Siemens, Zanussi, and Philips. Now it's down to three, with Electrolux in the lead position.

Electrolux became the largest home appliance maker in the world in 1986 when it negotiated the $740 million takeover of Cleveland-based White Consolidated Industries. It was the biggest foreign takeover in Swedish business history, bringing into the Electrolux closet a company that had become a dustbin for discarded appliance lines: Frigidaire (dumped by General Motors), Kelvinator (dumped by American Motors), Westinghouse (dumped by Westinghouse), Gibson (dumped by Hupp).

In 1987 Electrolux solidified its leadership in the world's appliance business by acquiring the largest home appliance maker in Britain, Thorn, whose brand names include Tricity, Moffat, Bendix, and Parkinson Cowan.

These were made-to-order acquisitions for Werthen and his lieutenants, who love to take over distressed companies and try to turn them around. They are known as tough cookies, not afraid to chop payrolls and throw out companies that aren't making the grade. Facit, the Swedish calculator company, was acquired in 1972 and sold in 1983. Hugin, a Swedish cash register manufacturer, was acquired in 1980 and sold in 1983. Emerson air conditioners, acquired in 1979 as part of the Tappan acquisition, was discarded in 1983. The Husquarna motorcycle business, bought in 1978, was sold in 1985. There was considerable Italian opposition to the Zanussi acquisition, but in the end Electrolux prevailed. Werthen told *BusinessWeek,* "They saw us as the wild Viking raiders from the north. A company [Zanussi] in that much trouble had to have a lot of skeletons in the closet. Fortunately, we are in the same business and knew what doors to open."

Hans Werthen is a no-nonsense executive who was twice named the most admired businessman in Sweden in an annual poll conducted by the

Stockholm daily *Svenska Dagbladet.* He's known for swimming in the frozen Baltic Sea during the winter, warming up afterwards with a double martini. Legend has it that Wallenberg hired him to run Electrolux after testing his ability to hold aquavit. Werthen matched him glass for glass. In 1985, when he was sixty-six years old, he made his annual summer climb to the lower peaks of the Matterhorn in Switzerland. In an interview later that year with Jules Arbose of *International Management,* Werthen described himself as "an old Danish beer horse. The only thing I am good for is to pull the beer wagon." *Fortune* once showed Werthen punching a time clock "like every other Electrolux employee." In 1986 *Fortune* reported that Anders Scharp, Electrolux's president, "padlocks his telephone to make sure no one uses it when he leaves the office."

Electrolux is the first company to make a stab at operating a global appliance business. This is not a case of a company acquiring local units and letting them continue in their accustomed ways. When Electrolux buys a company, no matter where it is, the changes are swift and dramatic. It comes in like a fury. Operating from an abandoned vacuum cleaner plant in the center of Stockholm, the Electrolux managers are tigers about efficiency and cost-cutting. In the United States and Italy plants and people were promptly discarded after the new owner took over. A refrigerator is a refrigerator is a refrigerator. "We are aiming first at coordinating components," Scharp told the *Financial Times* in 1986. "Every fridge has a compressor and controls, every washing machine has a motor and pump. We are trying to organize the group from a global point of view."

To help pay for White Consolidated, Electrolux raised $300 million in June 1986 via an international sale of eight million B shares. The offering was managed by the big Swedish banking-brokerage house Enskilda, which allocated shares to underwriters all over the world: Paribas in France, Deutsche Bank in West Germany, Mediobanca in Italy, Singapore Nomura in Japan and the Far East, Swiss Bank Corporation in Switzerland and Liechtenstein, Merrill Lynch in South and Central America, and Wood Gundy in Canada. None of the shares was offered in the United States.

Electrolux's next target is Japan, where it plans to have appliance sales of $130 million by 1988—double what it had in 1985.

Access   Lilla Essingen
S-10545 Stockholm, Sweden
(46) 8-738-6000

White Consolidated
11770 Berea Rd.
Cleveland, Ohio 44111
(216) 252-3700

ENI	**Sales** $27 billion
	Profits $400 million
	Rank Italy's 2d-largest company
	World's 20th-largest industrial company
	10th-largest company outside the United States
	World's 9th-largest oil company
	Founded 1926
	Employees 130,000 (22,000 outside Italy)
	Headquarters Rome, Italy

ENI stands for Ente Nazionale Idrocarburi, which translates literally as National Hydrocarbon Agency, but this pedestrian name belies an operation that has nearly always been fraught with high drama, Italian-style. ENI is Italy's state-owned energy company. It fills 40 percent of the country's energy needs and accounts for 7 percent of Italy's gross national product. Nearly all of the natural gas used in Italy comes from ENI—about 35 percent from liftings in the Po Valley and other Italian fields, the rest from Dutch, Russian, and Algerian imports. Not much oil has been found in Italy, but ENI pumps it in thirty countries on five continents. And it's an active buyer of crude on the spot market.

ENI has refineries, gasoline stations, and engineering companies that can build pipelines, refineries, drilling rigs, and petrochemical plants. Its AGIP service stations, familiar to anyone who has motored through Italy, pump gasoline under the ENI symbol of the six-legged dog. ENI service stations dispense close to half the gasoline sold in the Italian market. ENI's engineering companies, Saipem and Snamprogetti, built a 1,500-mile pipeline that carries natural gas from the Sahara desert in Algeria to Cape Bon in Tunisia, and then under the Mediterranean (at depths up to 1,500 feet) to Sicily, across Sicily and then under the Strait of Messina to the Italian mainland, continuing 850 miles north to Rome and Minerbio, where it connects with the natural gas grid in the Po Valley. ENI engineers also helped to build pipelines through the Alps that bring natural gas to Italy from Holland and the Soviet Union.

ENI is to Italy what John D. Rockefeller's Standard Oil Trust was to the United States at the turn of the century. But it's also much more than an oil and gas supplier. While energy represents 80 percent of its activities, that still leaves a healthy $5 billion of business in other areas—chemicals, textiles, mining, heavy machinery, motels, restaurants, even a newspaper (the Milan daily *Il Giorno*). In the rich annual report that the company issues every year—it weighs in at one pound, nine ounces—eighteen pages are required to list the five hundred subsidiaries of ENI.

However, such is the volatility of this conglomerate that many of the listings carry a parenthetical note, "winding up," meaning, of course, that they are going out of business.

From its inception ENI was a maverick. It was the creation of Enrico Mattei, a Resistance leader during World War II, who navigated recklessly through the postwar minefields of Italian politics to start ENI and steer it into position as one of the largest companies in the world. We have a good record of how he did it from Dow Votaw, whose insightful study *The Six-Legged Dog* was published by the University of California Press in 1964. ENI was always controversial. As Votaw points out, it was "at once a major political issue, a matter of national pride, a thorn in the side of the international petroleum industry, and the best hope for solution of Italy's economic ills."

Perhaps it's only in Italy that an ENI could be possible. AGIP (Azienda Generale Italiana Petroli) was a relic of the Fascist government headed by Benito Mussolini, who came to power in 1922. It was founded in 1926 as a public corporation charged with finding oil for Italy, either at home or abroad—an effort which was notably unsuccessful. After World War II the Italian government decided to liquidate AGIP. And to do this job it called upon Mattei, one of the heroes of the wartime resistance. Mattei, who left school when he was fifteen to go to work, proceeded to ignore the instructions given to him. Instead of winding up AGIP, he began drilling for oil and gas in the Po Valley—and he found gas deposits there. Then he built pipelines to transport the methane. Votaw recounted how Mattei accomplished that:

> Mattei simply ignored private and public rights and the law. He boasts of having broken eight thousand ordinances and laws, and this must be a very conservative figure. Much of the work was done at night on the theory that by morning the work would be so far along there would not be very much that anybody could do about it. . . . When serious opposition arose, Mattei often appeared on the scene himself, full of apologies for line crews who had "acted in error and without instructions," but "wouldn't it be a shame to have to dig it up now?" The mayor of Cremona is reputed to have awakened one morning to find his town bisected by AGIP's nocturnal ditch digging and traffic completely paralyzed; he was so glad to get traffic restored that he agreed to rights-of-way on the spot.

Finding natural gas at home and building a pipeline to carry it fired up Mattei, who was quick to cast himself as the messiah who would lead Italy out of its resource-poor condition. He would find the oil and gas that Italy needed to become a first-rate industrial power. The Communist party, which was very strong in Italy after World War II, applauded Mattei as he fulminated tirelessly against *le sette sorelle,* the big seven international oil companies. When ENI was created on February 10, 1953, as a state-owned holding company, the law (which Mattei drafted) gave him a monopoly on the Po Valley resources, attached to ENI various other state-owned companies engaged in the oil and gas industry, and allocated $24 million of public monies. And, of course, there was no question as to who was to run this shebang.

In 1954, after a coup inspired by the Central Intelligence Agency and backed by the U.S. and British governments had succeeded in bringing down the Mossadegh government in Iran and restoring the Shah to full power, the Seven Sisters rearranged the Iranian oil split among themselves. Seeing that a new deck was going to be dealt, Mattei asked that ENI be allowed into the game. He was rebuffed in a way that he called "shameful and humiliating to Italy." It was a turndown he was not to forget.

He mounted a strategy to make common cause with oil producers in the Middle East and Africa against the Exxons, Shells, and Mobils. In 1957 he signed an agreement with the Shah of Iran to develop new oil under a seventy-five–twenty-five split—75 percent to the Iranians, 25 percent to ENI. The deal infuriated the big oil companies, used to their fifty-fifty split. In 1959, to the displeasure of the U.S. State Department, he flew to Moscow and worked out a deal to buy oil at cheap prices. He began to wage price wars against Exxon and British Petroleum. In Italy he spruced up the AGIP stations in bright, cheery colors, adding bars and restaurants to some of them. "Mattei," said British journalist Anthony Sampson, "made the Seven Sisters look not only mean and unloved, but boring and unimaginative."

Mattei played out a scenario in which he was the champion of Italy's interests against international predators. And he was virtually untouchable in his home country. As Votaw's study makes clear, he ran ENI as a one-man show. He was ENI, and ENI was him. He became the most powerful person in the country, a hero to the working class for his denunciations of foreign capitalists, and a hero to the industrial leaders for delivering to them the oil and gas they needed to make the "Italian miracle."

Although ENI's charter limited the company to activity in "hydrocarbons," Mattei was never one to bother about the legal niceties. He was soon expanding in all directions. ENI's mandate could be stretched to include petrochemical plants, pipelines, maybe even motels near gasoline stations. But electronics? Publishing? Textiles? Mattei behaved much the way his counterparts at the heads of conglomerates in the United States and Britain behaved. They all had sticky fingers. In Dow Votaw's apt phrase, Mattei resembled a "Socialist robber baron."

Governments in postwar Italy fell regularly. Only Mattei and ENI seemed permanent. "Not only was Enrico Mattei able to go his own way," Votaw pointed out, "but he also on frequent occasions took Italy along with him. Italian foreign policy in the Middle East has been largely Mattei foreign policy since 1954. . . . The same can be said for Italian policies in Africa, especially in Egypt, Libya, and Morocco. . . . Probably no Italian government of the last ten years could have stood against determined Mattei opposition."

Enrico Mattei died in a plane crash in 1962 when he was fifty-six years old. His brother insisted that Mattei was murdered, but several investigations failed to turn up evidence supporting that charge. P. H. Frankel, a British petroleum expert, wrote a biography of Mattei in which he said he had no reason to suspect foul play, but he also remembered a 1960 conversation he had with an executive of a very large American oil company who said that "he failed to understand why no one had found a way to get Mattei killed."

The ENI Mattei left is a hydraheaded monster that would seem almost impossible to administer. Indeed, Votaw, writing just after the death of Mattei, wondered whether the company might "disintegrate" without his charismatic leadership. ENI did nothing of the kind. On the contrary it has ballooned under a succession of leaders. To a great extent it was profitless growth as ENI became a "hospital" for sick companies that the government wanted it to take on just to provide jobs. ENI also found itself enmeshed in various scandals. It took on a huge load of debt ($11 billion in 1982) and began to lose colossal amounts of money ($1 billion in 1982). In one four-year period (1979–83), ENI ran through five different chairmen.

But ENI, like big companies in all parts of the world, has turned out to have staying power, with a life that went on no matter who was in power, in government, or in the chief executive's chair. And in 1983 ENI was reinvigorated with some of its old-time drive when a Socialist government led by Bettino Craxi named Franco Reviglio to run ENI. A Socialist, Reviglio is an economics professor who served as Italy's finance minister in 1979 and 1980. The "Socialist" discipline that he brought to ENI called for running the enterprise not as a ward of the government but as if it were a private business bent on—forgive the expression—making a profit.

Under Reviglio operations that couldn't cut it have been discarded, employment has been reduced, and strong, profit-making units like Saipem, Italgas, and Nuovo Pignone have been partially privatized by having pieces sold off to investors and their shares listed on the stock exchange. In October 1983, after Reviglio had been installed, *BusinessWeek* cast doubt on whether ENI could make its target of breaking even in three years. It did better than that, coming through in 1985 with record profits of $500 million, helped probably by a plunge in oil prices. For most companies in the oil business, low prices are death. But ENI remains in many ways what it was when it started out: oil-poor. It buys nearly two thirds of the oil that it uses. And in a depressed market, it's the buyer, not the producer, who wins.

Reviglio's performance was so good that in 1986 he was appointed to another three-year term. He opened 1987 by putting up for sale ENI's eleven-factory, $420 million Lanerossi textile subsidiary.

ENI makes its headquarters in a twenty-story glass building in the south part of Rome, where it's surrounded by other sterile-looking government buildings. Among its neighbors are Alitalia, the Post & Telegraph Department, the Treasury, and the Merchant Marine Department. ENI's operating companies are based elsewhere. The holding company, where the paper work is done, has fifteen hundred staff members.

The house that Enrico Mattei built has become much more than just an Italian company. It's deriving 35 percent of its annual revenues from foreign activities, and at any one time it has a host of projects in gear all over the world. In 1985, for example, ENI signed an agreement to help Argentina develop its natural gas; started to build a fertilizer plant in Jagshpur in the Indian state of Uttar Pradesh; used the semisubmersible vessel *Scarabeo* to drill a well in the Gulf of Mexico; landed an order from the Soviet Union to build a 160-mile slurry line for coal; started to lay pipe for a 550-mile pipeline that will bring oil from Iraq to Turkey; and, in a joint venture with France's Elf Aquitaine, discovered an oil and gas field in the offshore waters of the Congo.

The survival of ENI—it still has some of the problems it started out with (the big one being that it remains oil-poor)—raises the interesting question: What is the difference between a government-owned company and one that's privately owned? In 1964, after looking closely at the formation and growth of ENI under Mattei, Dow Votaw answered, in effect, "Not much." He concluded: "Just as large American corporations occasionally make the traditional bows in the direction of the shareholder, so does ENI make a traditional gesture in the direction of the Ministry of State Participations and the government, and both managements go on doing much as they please in very much the same way and, oddly enough, for very much the same reasons."

In 1986 and 1987, as Franco Reviglio was putting ENI through the same "rationalization" and "profit-maximizing" exercises being practiced by the asset restructurers in the United States, that conclusion seemed to be right on the mark.

Access   Piazzale Enrico Mattei 1
00144 Rome, Italy
(39) 6-59001

Evergreen

Sales $1.2 billion
Profits $50 million
Rank World's largest container shipper
Taiwan's 3d-largest company
Founded 1968
Employees 3,900
Headquarters Taipei, Taiwan

Here's a worldwide company that's easy to spot. If you see something green moving on an ocean waterway, the chances are good it's a vessel carrying the shipping containers of Evergreen Lines. Evergreen paints all its containers—and it had 150,000 of them in service in 1986—a bright green. Evergreen surrounds itself in a green environment. Naturally the filing cabinets are green but so are the file folders, carpets, telephones, and the new headquarters building in Taipei. The women who work in the building all wear bright green jackets.

Container shipping revolutionized international freight forwarding after World War II. Previously, cargo was shipped loose on bulk carriers. It had to be trucked or sent by rail to a port, unloaded, reloaded onto a ship, unloaded when it reached a port, and then dispatched by truck or rail to its final destination. The system was slow, labor-intensive, and highly susceptible to thievery. Containerization arose as a reaction to those deficiencies. A container can be loaded at the factory site of a shipper, placed on a chassis, trucked to a port, and loaded directly onto a ship. When it reaches its destination, it can be unloaded directly onto a chassis that's hooked to a truck, which deposits the container at the customer's doorstep. Visit any major port today and you can see flat-tops moving in and out with containers stacked on their decks. Containers range in size from twenty to forty feet in length and from four feet, three inches to nine feet, six inches in height. They can hold anywhere from 38,000 to 89,000 pounds. New ships built recently in South Korea carry 4,482 20-foot containers.

If anyone can be called the father of container shipping, it's Malcom McLean, who ran a trucking operation that bore his name out of Winston-Salem, North Carolina, and who came up with the idea of moving a cargo-laden, truck-borne container right onto a ship. He started Sea-Land, the first containership company, in 1956 and sold it in 1969 to R. J. Reynolds Tobacco for more than $100 million.

The established shipping companies either converted to containers or dropped from sight. It was, and is, a very competitive business. It's also clearly, almost by definition, an international business. In addition to the American shippers (U.S. Lines, American President Lines, Sea-Land), the major players include Denmark's Maersk Lines, Germany's Hapag Lloyd, and the C. Y. Tung Group of Hong Kong. To ensure that everyone makes a profit, shipping lines form "conferences" which set rates to which all members are supposed to adhere. However, there are always some lines that opt out and resort to price-cutting. The pressure to slash prices is intense when you are staring at an empty ship. Ships cost a lot of money, and if you guess wrong—that is, fail to find customers for the vessels you ordered—the consequences are not pleasant. Bankruptcies are common.

In 1968, out of nowhere, came Evergreen, a Taiwanese company started by Y. F. Chang, the son of a ship's carpenter. It began with bulk carriers and moved into containerships in 1975. And in a very brief time—ten years—it eclipsed everyone in the industry with a massive investment in ships, new services, and cut-rate prices. Evergreen's Taipei factory makes containers for itself and others, turning them out at the rate of one every twenty-five minutes. To sell its services, it has seventy sales offices around the world.

Evergreen has been very price competitive on the Pacific routes, which are the biggest container waterways in the world. In 1984 it introduced an around-the-world service, linking up its vessels (and the vessels of other lines if necessary) to provide customers with a through service. Evergreen has an eastbound sailing every seven days that follows a route from Singapore to Pusan to Tokyo, through the Panama Canal, to New York, across the Atlantic, through the Suez Canal, and back to Singapore. A westbound service leaving every seven days starts from Tokyo, continues through Korea, Singapore, and the Suez Canal to Europe, and on to New York, down through the Panama Canal and out to Tokyo. It takes an Evergreen ship seventy-seven days to circumnavigate the world.

To make money at it requires pinpoint timing, which Evergreen achieves by satellite communications and facsimile transmissions linking each of its ships with all of its offices. For example, an Evergreen vessel calls every Friday at the port of New Orleans. From there it heads for Kingston, Jamaica, where it transfers cargo to an around-the-world ship that calls at Kingston every week, and goes on to deliver cargo to Caribbean ports. The ship then circles back to New Orleans, via Houston. It's a three-week roundtrip, meaning that Evergreen needs three ships to operate this feeder service.

To make money at it also requires low costs, which Evergreen apparently achieves by state-of-the-art equipment that allows it to employ fewer people. Diane Ying and Chuang Su-Yu, two reporters for the *Free China Review,* said that Evergreen can employ seventeen sailors for a major-tonnage ship while a competitor will need thirty. Richard Gibney, editor of *Container Insight,* which is published in Kirkcudbrightshire, Scotland, found that Evergreen's cost of delivering a twenty-foot container was $835, compared to $1,320 for U.S. Lines. Furthermore, he estimated that Evergreen was making a profit of $80 on each container it handled while others were lucky to earn $10—and many were losing money on each shipment.

Evergreen's fleet of sixty vessels all bear names beginning with "Ever"—for example, *Ever Guard, Ever Going, Ever Glory, Ever Golden, Ever Lyric, Ever Onward, Ever Shine, Ever Orient, Ever Superb,* and *Ever Trust.* Between 1983 and 1986 it invested $1.5 billion in new ships, freight terminals, trucks, and container factories. Where did the money come from? No one is quite sure, and Chang isn't talking, although reports say that the Japanese trading house Marubeni is Evergreen's behind-the-scenes financier, while others speculate that American and Japanese banks have staked Evergreen.

Overcapacity plunged the shipping business into a depression in the mid-1980s, and carriers in all parts of the world found the going very rough. Some cut back sharply on their service. Others went out of business. Sailing through the storm, and making a major contribution to the overcapacity, was Evergreen. By 1986 it had an estimated market share of 10 percent on the mainstream east-west routes; and Gibney was predicting that it would move up to 20 percent by 1994.

Everyone agrees that the driving force behind Evergreen is Chang, who had experience as a shipping clerk, sailor, and sea captain before launching Evergreen. To begin with he set out to serve the Taiwanese exporters, who operate in one of the world's fastest growing economies. But everyone knows now that his game is more than mastering the Taiwan trade—he's out to conquer the world. His Evergreen Group is also more than a shipper. It encompasses fourteen companies. The two main ones are Evergreen Marine, a shipping company incorporated in Taipei, and Evergreen International, a shipping company registered in Panama. A third shipper, also registered in Panama, is Uniglory. The others include the container manufacturer (Evermaster), a huge container terminal at Changan in Taiwan (Eversafety), a trucking company (Everglory Transport), a Japanese trading company (Everlaurel), and a software supplier (Evergenius).

Chang wants to continue this diversification. He's thinking about hotels and inland transportation. "Shipping has its limits," he told *Journal of Commerce* reporter William Armbruster in 1986. "We have probably gone to the limit." At the start of 1987, the Evergreen Group was still privately owned—with Chang owning 75 percent of the shares and employees the remaining 25 percent—but plans were afoot to bring the largest unit, Evergreen Marine, public in the latter half of the year. This was not Chang's idea. The Taiwanese government was pressuring successful enterprises to offer their shares to the public. A Taiwan Fund, holding shares in Taiwanese companies, burst onto the American Stock Exchange in 1987 and doubled in price overnight.

There was bitter irony for Malcom McLean in Chang's climb to the top of the containership mast. In 1978, after leaving the R. J. Reynolds board, he returned to the containership business by acquiring slumping U.S. Lines. Five years later he took over another old and declining American shipping company, Moore McCormack Lines, which he blended into U.S. Lines. In 1986—whipsawed by low rates, saddled with a huge debt incurred by ordering twelve jumbo containerships from Korea's Daewoo yards, and squeezed by the seemingly endless growth of Evergreen—McLean filed for bankruptcy. It appeared to be the end of the line for what was once the largest shipping company in the United States, and for the founder of containerized shipping.

The Scotsman, Richard Gibney, asked, "Mirror, Mirror on the wall, . . . Is Chang the greatest of them all, or is he a maverick who derives pleasure from antagonizing other mainstream market carriers?"

Mary Bosrock, international editor of the publication *Foreign Trade* visited Evergreen in Taipei in 1985. She drew this picture:

> The headquarters building on Sung-Chiang Road is manned by about 430 people with an average age of thirty-four years. The office desks are arranged in Japanese style—desks paired, facing each other in a long row ending at the desk of a section chief. There are no tea cups or other such personal effects among the papers and stationery items on the desks. At work no one smokes, sips tea, reads newspapers, or uses the telephone for personal matters. The staff members follow a practice of coming early and leaving late.
>
> The atmosphere reflects youth both in movement and in appearance. The well-groomed men have neat haircuts and are dressed in white shirt and tie and shining black shoes. The women, in bright Evergreen uniforms, are equally crisp.
>
> An air of politeness and quiet efficiency prevails. In the office, the staff has learned to keep voices down in discussions, a rule, among others, taught new recruits during their orientation period. A visitor can sense a disciplined environment.

On Taiwan, an island of 19 million people, Evergreen is considered a very desirable place to work. It's among the highest payers, according to the *Journal of Commerce*'s Armbruster, who said a section chief with five years' experience could be pulling down $18,000 a year. Lunch is free to all employees in the company's cafeteria. Chang interviews every job applicant. Evergreen prefers to train its own people rather than hire from other companies.

The Evertrust building in Jersey City serves as U.S. headquarters for Evergreen. The Chang family owns the building. Heading up American operations is Chang's son, K. H. Chang.

Access   330 Minsheng East Rd.
10444 Taipei
Republic of China
(886) 2-505-7766

Evertrust Plaza
Jersey City, N.J. 07302
(201) 915-3200

Fiat	**Sales** $22.5 billion
	Profits $1.6 billion
	U.S. Sales $1 billion
	Rank Largest company in Italy's private sector
	World's 27th-largest industrial company
	15th on the *Fortune* International 500
	World's 6th-largest automaker
	Europe's 2d-largest automaker
	Italy's largest automaker
	World's largest carburetor maker
	World's largest producer of crawler and
	4-wheel-drive tractors
	Founded 1899
	Employees 230,000
	Headquarters Turin, Italy

Family control of a huge automotive enterprise is going out of style, but the message hasn't reached Italy yet. There Giovanni Agnelli, grandson of the founder of Fiat, continues to rule an automaker that has grown to become one of the world's largest industrial enterprises—and "rule" is the appropriate term. Agnelli, sixty-six in 1987, may not make the day-to-day decisions (he once said publicly, "My name is Agnelli and I can't run Fiat"), but there's no question who's in charge here.

The market value of Fiat, based on the price of its stock in mid-1986, was $10.1 billion (twelfth in Europe). And the Agnelli family was then believed to hold about 40 percent of the shares. (A year later Fiat's market value was $20 billion.) Through their family investment company, Instituto Finanziario Industriale (I.F.I.), the Agnellis hold interests in a host of other companies, including the well known Italian department store chain Rinascente; the Cinzano vermouth business; banks and insurance companies; not to speak of the Turin soccer team, the Juventus. According to the *Financial Times,* companies in which the Agnellis have major shareholdings account for one third of the total capitalization of the Milan Bourse, which is *the* Italian stock exchange. It's no wonder Agnelli has been called the "uncrowned king of Italy." References to his regal standing are common. In 1985 *The Wall Street Journal* said, "In Turin, the royal house of Savoy, which once ruled Italy, has given way to the house of Agnelli, which commands a national deference bordering on awe." In 1986 the *Financial Times* said, "Fiat is to the Italian state what the Duke of Burgundy was to the medieval kings of France—technically part of the kingdom, but barely less powerful than they were."

Giovanni Agnelli has superstar recognition in Italy. In 1975 his visage appeared on the covers of eleven national magazines (and these were not magazines he owned). He has been celebrated outside Italy too. He counted President John F. Kennedy as his friend. In 1969, during a period of labor strife in Italy, he made the covers of both *Newsweek* and *Time.* He is an international jet-setter, at home in Paris, London, and New York. His maternal grandmother was American, as was his wife's mother. He speaks French and English fluently. In 1986 the Italian daily *La Republica* conducted a poll, which showed that Giovanni Agnelli was clearly the most popular Italian male in the minds (and hearts) of Italian women, who were asked whom they could fall head-over-heels in love with. It was an easy win for Agnelli, who garnered the votes of 35.4 percent of the women polled, leading Sylvester "Rambo" Stallone (26.8 percent), English pop singer Simon Le Bon (10.7 percent), and a young politico, Claudio Martelli (7.1 percent).

This adulation might surprise Americans whose knowledge of Fiat is limited to the company's humiliating adventures in the U.S. market. While Fiat is accustomed to being a market leader in Europe, where its small cars have won a reputation for liveliness and durability, it has never been able to make much of a dent in the American market. It mounted an effort after World War II—Franklin D. Roosevelt, Jr. was one of the distributors—and its best year was 1975, when 103,000 Fiats were sold, making it the fifth best-selling import. After that, it was all downhill as

reports circulated about the mechanical, electrical, and severe rust problems associated with the Fiat. In 1982 fourteen thousand Fiats were sold in the American market. In 1983 Fiat stopped sending cars to the United States.

Fiat's dismal showing in the world's largest automobile market belies its accomplishment in teaching more countries how to build cars than any other manufacturer. General Motors and Ford have made their mark overseas by establishing subsidiaries to make cars. The Japanese and the Germans have been mainly interested in exporting cars from their home factories. Fiat, on the other hand, has embraced a variety of relationships—wholly owned subsidiaries, partially owned affiliates, licensees—to penetrate foreign markets. Thus, in 1984, Fiat produced 1.4 million cars in sixteen of its own plants in Italy, Portugal, and Brazil while another 2.1 million cars were being made by licensed or affiliated companies in eleven countries: Yugoslavia, Poland, Spain, Turkey, Indonesia, Thailand, Egypt, Morocco, South Africa, Zambia, and Argentina. Fiat has run a turnkey plant operation for countries around the world, coming in to show them how to make cars. The Seat auto company that Volkswagen bought in 1986 from the Spanish government was originally a Fiat affiliate. The Yugo, which entered the American market in 1986, comes from a Yugoslavian plant set up by Fiat. The Lada, which the Soviet Union exports, is a model derived from the old Fiat 124. Indeed, Fiat built from the ground up the Russian automobile plant on the Volga River six hundred miles east of Moscow. Completed in 1970 the plant accounts for about half of the Soviets' annual production of 1.4 million cars. Togliatti, the city that grew up around the car plant, has become the fastest-growing metropolis in the Soviet Union, with a population of 640,000 in 1986. The city was named for Palmiro Togliatti, a lawyer who was one of the founders of the Italian Communist party and who held cabinet positions in the Italian coalition governments of 1944 and 1945.

Fiat was happy to build car plants for Communist countries while fighting Communist-led labor unions at home. The faces of Italian capitalism and Italian communism confront each other in Turin, the capital of Piedmont. Fiat was born in Turin in 1899 when the first Giovanni Agnelli, a former cavalry officer who was a Socialist intellectual, began making cars two years before the Ford Motor Company was started. The company Agnelli formed was called Fabrica Italian Automobili Torino, later shortened to Fiat. Turin was also the birthplace of the Italian Communist party. The city has had a popular Communist mayor for many years, and the Communists regularly get one third of the Turin vote in national elections—more than any other party. The Fiat headquarters in the Corso Marconi is a nondescript, steel-gray building that has the ambience of a data processing center. The offices are spartan and dark, as if lights were dimmed to save money. Not far from the headquarters is a charming Piedmontese restaurant, La Smarrita, where Fiat executives repair to for lunch and dinner. It's located on the Corso Unione Sovietica.

The Fiat plants that ring and undergird (factory tunnels run under the streets) Turin are highly automated. In terms of the use of computers and robots, Fiat is on a par with the Japanese automakers. It surprises many visitors to learn that the automated technology is not bought but provided by Fiat's machine tool subsidiary, Comau, which is a world leader in the development of automated production lines. Comau robots assemble cars at Fiat's Mirafiori plant in Turin, but they also work on the assembly lines of many other companies, including Chrysler, Ford, General Motors, Volvo, Renault, BMW, and Daimler-Benz. In 1985 GM bought a 20 percent interest in Comau's Troy, Michigan–based unit, Comau Productivity Systems. In 1986 Comau robots began assembling bodies for Jaguar in a $75 million investment that will enable the British car builder to nearly double its output, reaching sixty thousand cars a year by mid-1989. Comau, on its own, has annual sales exceeding $300 million a year, more than half coming from outside Italy. Perhaps the most impressive Comau installation is a new engine plant at Termoli in southern Italy. Built at a cost of $300 million, the Termoli plant is the ultimate in automation, having five parallel assembly lines each "manned" by 148 robots and "handlers" controlled by 600 personal computers, which in turn are coordinated by 103 large computers. The Termoli plant is designed to turn out 2,600 engines a day, or 572,000 a year. The total work force: 950.

Automation enables Fiat to turn out as many cars today as it did in 1980 with 30 percent fewer workers. Between 1980 and 1984 the number of robots in use at Fiat grew from 150 to more than 1,000. Over that same period the number of employees declined from 340,000 to 240,000.

How, given the strength of the Communist-led trade union movement in Italy, did Fiat manage this drastic downsizing of the employee force? After all, as Diana Johnstone, European correspondent for the left-wing American biweekly *In These Times,* has pointed out, "Fiat, and especially the Mirafiori body shop, is historically Europe's most eventful battlefield in the class struggle. Workers are combative, management is shrewd, and the stakes are high. Fiat workers have been in the forefront of battles that have in the past two decades won Italian workers not only higher living wage standards but political power at the factory level."

Johnstone made these comments in late 1979 in the wake of a series of attacks on Fiat managers by the terrorist organization the Red Brigade. On September 21, 1979, Carlo Ghiglieno, Fiat's planning director, was assassinated. He was the third Fiat executive murdered since 1975. On October 4, 1979, Cesare Varetto, manager of union relations at the Mirafiori body shop, had his legs riddled by three young gunmen. He was the seventeenth Fiat executive wounded in attacks since 1975. In retaliation Fiat fired sixty-one workers suspected of being allied to the terrorists. That move posed a conflict for the unions; they were not Red Brigade supporters but they didn't want to appear to be tools of management. Diana Johnstone predicted: "The atmosphere created by Red Brigade terror has convinced Fiat that it can win a test of strength with the workers." Those were prophetic words.

In 1980 Fiat management, led by strongman Cesare Romiti, newly installed by Agnelli as chief executive officer, decided to have that test of strength. He served notice that the company needed to eliminate twenty-four thousand jobs. The announcement provoked a bitter five-week strike that ended on October 14, 1980, in a march that became a landmark in the modern history of the European labor movement. An army of Fiat workers estimated to number forty thousand marched through the streets of Turin to defy the pickets and demand that they be allowed to return to work. It may be that many of the marchers were foremen and white-collar workers, but their militance shocked union leaders into negotiating an immediate settlement with Fiat management. The upshot was that twenty-four thousand employees were laid off under Italy's *cassa integrazione* law, which meant they were eligible for government unemployment compensation amounting to 93 percent of their pay, and Fiat promised that it would either rehire fifteen thousand of them by 1983 or help them find comparable jobs. It was a turning point in labor relations at Fiat. The company had in effect won the right to employ as many workers as it thought it needed. Today only one out of four Fiat employees belongs to a union. And of the fifteen thousand workers placed on the "reinstatement" list, only four thousand, at the most, were ever rehired. Fiat had broken the power of the left-wing trade unions in Italy.

The crushing of the 1980 strike signaled the emergence of affluent professional classes in Italian society. It also reflected a waning of the Socialist vision, giving ground before the relentless advance of a consumerist society. That not everyone accepts this development as progress is clear from the continuing strength of the Communist party in Italy. However, Italians, like Americans, seem interested in buying the trinkets that go with a mass production economy. In the fall of 1986, when Fiat announced a contribution of $4 million to help restore a national treasure (the eighteenth-century country palace Villa Reale, outside Turin) the company's managing director, Romiti, took note of the changed mood. "The 1970s," he said, "were a period of great worry. There was an attempt to depict private enterprise as a danger to society's well-being." Today, he added, "the sad season is behind us." People's optimism was reflected in a booming stock market in Milan; as it exploded in 1986 into one of the fastest-growing bourses in the world, *L'Unita,* Italy's Communist daily, began printing the stock tables.

In the freewheeling days of the early 1980s, Fiat managers were in their element. While they were withdrawing from the American market, they bet a bundle on a new small car, the Uno, which turned out to be a smashing success. In 1983, the first year out of the starting gate, Fiat sold 325,000 Unos. Fiat was also the leader of the surging stock market in Milan. The price of its shares soared, making it easier for the company to raise money. Holders of Fiat stock made out very well. One of those stockholders was the Libyan government headed by Muammar Qaddafi. In 1976, when the Italian auto company was hard up for cash, it managed to sell 15 percent of itself to oil-rich Libya for $400 million. It was a case of a former colony coming to the aid of the country that once had colonized it (Italy succeeded Turkey as the ruler of Libya in 1912).

The Libyans proved to be ideal shareholders. They placed two representatives on the Fiat board but never interfered with the management. In 1986, however, the Libyan presence became an embarrassment to Fiat because of the growing hostility between Washington, D.C., and Tripoli, culminating in an American air attack on Libya in retaliation for alleged Libyan involvement in terrorist activities. On May 15, 1986, the wrath of Washington came down on Agnelli's head. Fiat's U.S. subsidiary, Fiatallis, had locked up a $7.9 million order to supply 178 bulldozers to the U.S. Marine Corps. But Defense Secretary Caspar Weinberger intervened to block the deal on the grounds of Fiat's tie to the Libyans. The message was not lost on Agnelli, who then persuaded the Libyans to sell out their entire Fiat position for $3 billion, which is not a bad return on a $400 million investment. Fiat's reward was quick. The Pentagon named it as a prime contractor on a $2 billion "Star Wars" project.

Defense contracting is not new to Fiat. It made tanks and planes for Mussolini, and it once had an advertising slogan, "Fiat on land, sea and in the air." Outside of the state-owned Breda group, Fiat is Italy's largest arms maker; and now it may even be first, thanks to its 1983 acquisition of a controlling interest in Snia, Italy's main producer of munitions and rocket fuel. In 1985 Fiat's defense contracts totaled more than $600 million. It makes engines for the Tornado fighter plane, and in 1986 it joined with Sikorsky of the United States in a successful bid to take a 29.9 percent share in the British helicopter maker Westland.

Most people know Fiat only as a car maker, but automobiles now represent a little under half of its total revenues. Add trucks, tractors, and construction machinery, and the percentage goes to 70 percent. But that still leaves about $7 billion of business that Fiat has in an assortment of fields, including civil engineering (it's building a hydroelectric dam in Argentina, the second bridge over the Bosphorus, a sewer in Montreal, and a hotel at Luxor in Egypt), automotive components (its Weber division makes 4.5 million carburetors a year), bioengineering (pacemakers, heart valves), tourism (Ventana travel agency), and publishing (the Turin daily *La Stampa*).

Despite this diversification the automobile is where Fiat lives and dies. It makes cars ranging from the Panda at the mini level up to the Ferrari sports car at the top. (Ferrari, which had a record year in 1986 with output of 3,300 cars, is 51 percent–owned by Fiat.) The Lancia is also part of the fleet. Fiat took it over in 1969 to save the company from extinction. It helps to be in a country where people are crazy about cars. A census taken in 1980 showed that Italy had an auto population of 310 for every one thousand inhabitants. That's higher than the ratios prevailing in Japan (203) and Britain (276), even though per capita income in those two countries is higher than it is in Italy. West Germany has 377 cars for every one thousand persons, but its per capita income is *twice* that of Italy. It's clear that the first thing Italians do when they have some money is buy a car. It helps also to have a government policy that protects the home team. Ford and General Motors were barred from building an auto plant in Italy, and the Italians have also succeeded in limiting the Japanese imports to 2,200 cars a year. Fiat thus has no trouble dominating its home market (where its share is 54 percent)—and with that head start it's a major contender in the European market (where its share is 12.7 percent).

The race for first place in Europe is always very close. At the start of the 1980s, Renault was in first place. In 1984 the finish looked like this: Ford, 12.8 percent; Fiat, 12.7 percent; Volkswagen, 12 percent; Peugeot, 11.5 percent; General Motors, 11 percent; Renault, 10.9 percent. In 1985 Volkswagen edged ahead of Ford and Fiat into first place. Giovanni Agnelli, who has an international outlook, believes the number of major players in the world automobile industry will dwindle, and he has expressed himself more than once on the desirability of mergers. Fiat tried to team up with Citroën in the late 1960s, but that combination fell apart in 1973.

In 1985 Ford and Fiat had serious talks about merging their European car operations into an entity that would then be the clear leader with 25 percent of the market. The negotiations went on for nine months before collapsing because neither side was willing to play second fiddle. Agnelli explained, "The dream of merging Ford and Fiat was very, very attractive and we had been working on it for a year. But we couldn't finalize. Why? Because Ford, rightly, is a very proud company and Fiat is a very proud company." Agnelli added that Fiat would still be interested in a marriage with another car maker if the terms could be worked out. While they couldn't get together on cars, Ford and Fiat did join forces in the truck field. In 1986 the two companies merged their heavy truck operations in Europe. The combination made Iveco, the Fiat truck division, a very strong second to Daimler-Benz in the European market.

However, the ink was hardly dry on this deal when Ford and Fiat went to the mat in Italy over Alfa Romeo, the ailing sports car manufacturer. Sometimes called "Europe's sickest car maker," Alfa Romeo had become a ward of the Italian government, kept alive for reasons of national prestige and the thirty-three thousand jobs it provided. Coming into 1986 the company had lost money for thirteen consecutive years, and its share of the Italian market had dropped to 6.5 percent, behind Peugeot, Volkswagen, Renault, and even Lancia. The Instituto per la Ricostruzione Industriale (IRI), the big state holding company, decided to put Alfa Romeo up for sale, and Ford surfaced quickly as a would-be buyer. But the Ford offer never had a chance in the emotional arena of Italian politics. In the end Fiat snatched Alfa Romeo after politicians from virtually every party came forward to insist on an "Italian solution." *The Wall Street Journal* pegged Fiat's winning offer at $700 million. Fiat said it would merge Alfa Romeo with its Lancia operations to make luxury cars that would give Germany's BMW a run for its money. Italian sources said Fiat would not sit still for a Ford takeover because that would have given the American company access to Alfa Romeo's 350 dealerships—Fiat sells half its cars through the Alfa dealers. Luciano Lama, a former Italian trade union leader, said that selling Alfa Romeo to Ford "would be like signing Fiat's death certificate."

Fiat named one of its ace managers, Vittorio Ghidella, to the presidency of its new Alfa Romeo division. He plans to double Alfa's production to 400,000 cars a year. And he is counting on Americans buying at least 60,000 of those Alfas. So Fiat will return to the United States in an Alfa Romeo.

Access   Corso Marconi 10
10125 Torino, Italy
(39) 11-650-3131

Fiat USA
375 Park Ave.
New York, N.Y. 10152
(212) 486-3300

Fujitsu	**Sales** $12.3 billion

Sales $12.3 billion
Profits $148 million
U.S. Sales $1.2 billion
Rank Japan's largest computer maker
30th-largest company in Japan
Japan's 2d-largest robot maker
58th on the *Fortune* International 500
Japan's 5th-largest semiconductor maker
Founded 1935
Employees 84,300 (Average age: 30)
Headquarters Tokyo, Japan

A strong streak of arrogance runs through this company, Japan's largest computer manufacturer. An offshoot of Fuji Electric, an electric machinery maker with strong ties to the German electronics giant Siemens, Fujitsu seems to require a lot of pumping up. And it always has its dukes up. In 1980 the company was described in *The New York Times* as "an insular enterprise, stubbornly pursuing its own ways."

That characterization by journalist Mike Tharp was prompted by Fujitsu's go-it-alone behavior when it moved into the computer field in 1954. Other Japanese companies, almost all of them bigger than Fujitsu, forged links with American computer makers. Not Fujitsu. Under the leadership of Kanjiro Okada, a computer engineer, Fujitsu made its own way, preferring not to humble itself before any foreign potentate.

Tharp also pointed out that Taiyu Kobayashi, who was then president of Fujitsu, "rarely meets foreigners and is said to have once broken off discussions with an American peripheral equipment manufacturer merely because of a perceived breach of business protocol by the United States company." However, in June 1980 Steve Galante of *The Wall Street Journal* wangled an interview with Kobayashi, who was delighted to disclose that for the first time Fujitsu's total sales (then $1.47 billion) had passed the sales of IBM Japan (then $1.46 billion). Galante's story began: "Taiyu Kobayashi speaks like a man possessed. His demon is IBM Japan Ltd." During the interview, Galante reported, "Mr. Kobayashi and other Fujitsu officials constantly drew comparisons with the American-owned rival."

Takuma Yamamoto, an engineer who was trained as a kamikaze pilot during World War II, succeeded Kobayashi as president in 1981, and he explained then why Fujitsu had become number one in Japan. "At IBM," he said, "they don't commit themselves to specific delivery dates. It seems they act superior to their customers." Two years later Yamamoto

216

was saying, "We are no longer in an IBM-dominated computer world. The growth is in small business computers, personal computers, and word processors, where IBM hasn't done too well traditionally."

Shoichi Akazawa, who worked thirty years for the powerful Japanese agency, the Ministry of International Trade and Industry (MITI), before joining Fujitsu in 1973, addressed the World Computing Services Industry Congress in San Francisco in 1980, and he took the occasion to lecture Americans. In the early days of the computer industry, he said, "many Japanese producers established technical relations with IBM, UNIVAC, GE, RCA, and others. Today, not one Japanese computer relies on foreign technology." Akazawa noted that while Japanese schools are turning out people trained in electronics, American schools are producing more and more lawyers. "Your country has 450,000 lawyers, compared with fifteen thousand in my country." To the charges that the Japanese government subsidizes the computer industry, Akazawa countered that U.S. industry is subsidized too—by the Defense Department. Finally, Akazawa pointed out that the president of Fujitsu personally awards prizes to employees submitting the best suggestions for improvements. "How many presidents of *Fortune* 500 companies make such awards in their companies?" he asked.

A little while later Norihoko Nakayama, the president of Fujitsu America, continued the lecture in an address to the Commonwealth Club in San Francisco. Nakayama explained that U.S. electronic companies cannot match the quality of Japanese-made products "because they are slaves to the quarterly reports to their stockholders. The result is that the Japanese companies are ready to make the next generation of semiconductors and computers, but it may take their American competitors considerable time to catch up."

Fujitsu's derision of IBM takes on added interest in light of a secret agreement between the two companies, details of which were disclosed for the first time in 1986. To settle a dispute over copyright violations, Fujitsu apparently agreed in 1983 to pay stiff penalties to IBM and also agreed to submit to periodic inspections of its software development. A copy of the agreement was leaked in 1986 to the Japanese newspaper *Asahi Shimbum,* which printed it. The leak occurred after IBM complained anew about what it called Fujitsu's "extensive copying of IBM programs."

Fujitsu has had a difficult time breaking into the U.S. market. Its computers, sold in Japan under the FACOM name, are virtually unknown in the United States. In 1980 it formed a joint venture with TRW to market point-of-sale terminals and small computers in the American market. But it folded the partnership after three years by acquiring TRW's

49 percent interest in the venture, declaring, "It's better to have a one-sided business decision process."

Fujitsu's main vehicle in the United States is Amdahl, a Sunnyvale, California, maker of IBM-compatible mainframe computers. Fujitsu raised its stake in Amdahl from 30 percent to 48 percent in 1984. In 1986, as the yen appreciated sharply in value against the dollar, Fujitsu moved to take advantage of that buying power. It began making magnetic disc drives for large computers in Hillsboro, Oregon; it bought the facsimile division of Burroughs; and it signed a pact with GTE to launch a joint venture in Tempe, Arizona, that will attack the office telephone market (PBX systems). Fujitsu owns 80 percent of Fujitsu GTE Business Systems.

But Fujitsu's biggest play in the American market was foiled by the Reagan administration. On October 23, 1986, the Japanese computer maker announced that it would buy 80 percent of Fairchild Semiconductor, the loss-plagued manufacturer of integrated circuits (or "chips") that was acquired in 1979 by the French oil services giant Schlumberger. The deal came unhinged in 1987 when Commerce Secretary Malcolm Baldrige, upset over Japanese trade practices, and Defense Secretary Caspar Weinberger, citing national defense reasons (Fairchild is a minor Pentagon supplier), both expressed their opposition. Fujitsu promptly withdrew its offer and then decided to build its own semiconductor plant at Gresham, a suburb of Portland, Oregon.

It wasn't the first time that Fujitsu was defeated on American turf by politics. In 1981 it had emerged as the low bidder for an AT&T contract to build a fiber-optics transmission line between Boston and Richmond. Fujitsu's bid was $56 million, but AT&T awarded the contract to its subsidiary, Western Electric, whose bid was $75 million, after intense political pressure was brought to bear. The Federal Communications Commission ruled that it would not be in the national interest to have a foreign supplier. Deputy Defense Secretary Frank Carlucci said that if the U.S. telecommunications network became dependent on foreign technology, it might be difficult to replace it after an enemy attack—an argument that Fujitsu ridiculed by pointing out that the cable would be American-made and that virtually all the work would be carried out by AT&T, which would have a detailed blueprint of the system.

During the course of the flap Joseph Fogarty, one of the FCC commissioners, told *The Wall Street Journal* that Fujitsu's bid lost because it was "illegally low." The combative Fujitsu leaders were enraged. Yamamoto, the ex-kamikaze pilot, went to the Foreign Correspondents Club in Tokyo to state, "It is very regrettable that business activities between two private companies are distorted by pressures from congressmen and government officials." (Of course this never happens in Japan.) "To add insult to injury," he added, "our reputation was soiled by totally unfounded allegations of illegal pricing. This is no way to conduct business between two nations." Fogarty apologized to Fujitsu for his remarks. The company said it was "satisfied" with the apology but regretted that "such an inaccurate statement was printed in *The Wall Street Journal.*"

Fujitsu became an independent company in 1935 to make telephone equipment, and it's still one of the largest companies in this field. It has long been a major supplier of telecommunications hardware to Nippon Telephone & Telegraph, the AT&T of Japan. However, computers and data processing systems now represent two thirds of its sales. In 1986 Fujitsu's share of the Japanese mainframe computer market was estimated at 27 percent, followed by IBM at 23 percent, Hitachi at 19 percent, and NEC at 16 percent. Fujitsu also owns 41 percent of Fanuc, which ranks as the world's largest maker of numerical controls for automated machine tools. Fanuc, the principal robot supplier to General Motors, operates from a yellow-walled industrial complex at the foot of Mount Fuji.

"Fanuc Man," the world's largest robot (it was sixteen feet tall and weighed twenty tons), was one of the hits of the Fujitsu pavilion at the 1985 international exposition held at Tsukuba, a science city thirty miles north of Tokyo. This was a humanoid robot that could move its head, eyes, legs, and hands. "Fanuc Man" was able to lift a barbell easily, but its hands were skillful enough to perform delicate tasks. Japanese fairgoers waited three hours and more to get into the $12.5 million Fujitsu pavilion, where the main attraction was a three-dimensional computer graphics

---

The Big Seven of the Japanese Drug Industry

	*Annual Sales**
Takeda	$2.8 billion
Sankyo	1.5 billion
Shionogi	1.1 billion
Fujisawa	1.0 billion
Eizai	810 million
Taisho	660 million
Daiichi Seiyaku	630 million

*Sales in year ended March 1986.

simulation projected onto and around a dome so that the audience was enveloped in—and enthralled by—a sight-and-sound show that told how the world came to be.

Fujitsu is nothing if not ambitious. The theme of its Tsukuba exhibit was: "What Mankind Can Dream, Technology Can Create." Celebrating its fiftieth anniversary in 1985, the IBM killer declared, "In its next half century Fujitsu will be helping to automate offices and factories all over the earth, and to bring the miracle of electronics and new information services into the home. It will be helping to turn the world we have always known into the kind of place we would like it to be."

Watch for Fujitsu on your block.

Access　6-1, Marunouchi 1-chome, Chiyoda-ku
Tokyo 100, Japan
(81) 3-216-3211

680 Fifth Ave.
New York, N.Y. 10019
(212) 265-5360

Générale Occidentale

Sales $3.1 billion
Profits $66 million
U.S. Sales $2.8 billion
Rank 10th-largest U.S. supermarket chain
12th-largest holder of U.S. forestlands
France's 2d-largest book publisher
Founded 1962
Employees 23,000
Headquarters Paris, France

B eing dull to begin with, business would be insufferable if not for characters like Sir James Goldsmith, who founded Générale Occidentale, the most visible of a tangle of companies that he controlled in the United States, Britain, Belgium, the Cayman Islands, Panama, Guatemala, Liechtenstein, Hong Kong, France—and who knows where else?

Goodyear Tire & Rubber, one of the dullest companies in America, caught Sir James's fancy in 1986, and he soon had the world's largest tire maker squealing over his bid to capture it for $49 a share, or roughly $5 billion. Goodyear, which never won any prizes for imagination, immediately ran up the flag of jingoism, depicting Sir James as a "foreign invader" out to rape the pride of Akron. Employees of Goodyear began circulating petitions of protest during halftimes in Ohio football games, and Goodyear Tire dealers across the country ran an ad warning against sacrificing a company "as American as baseball and apple pie" on the altar of the British pound. The dealers had this warning for Sir James (misaddressed in the ad as "Sir Goldsmith"): "You may buy this great company—but you will never buy our loyalty!"

If Goldsmith was unnerved by this assault, he didn't show it. On November 18, 1986, the very day the dealers displayed their provincialism, he appeared, cool as an English cucumber, before a hostile congressional committee to defend his bid to save Goodyear from itself. The tire maker, he said, had lost its way, doing things like building a $900 million pipeline to carry oil from California to Texas refineries—a project Sir James called "a wholly lunatic idea." Sitting on this committee was John Seiberling, an Ohio congressman whose grandfather and granduncle founded Goodyear in 1898. He was blunt: "Who the hell are you?" The fifty-three-year-old Sir James allowed that he was "an active investor" who could turn Goodyear around. Later on, when Seiberling continued his probing, Sir James retorted, "Check your facts before jumping to another prejudiced conclusion."

221

It was a vintage Goldsmith performance, as was his move two days later in accepting a buyout of his shares by Goodyear. Sir James had, with the help of his investment banker, Merrill Lynch ("We're bullish on America"), accumulated 12.5 million shares of Goodyear at a cost of $530 million. He sold the whole wad to Goodyear for $620 million, giving him a profit of $90 million. Not bad for a fortnight's work.

Goldsmith is an old hand at playing "Monopoly" in the real world. Only a year before his Goodyear foray, he had brought Crown Zellerbach to its knees in a ferocious battle that resulted in the dismemberment of the San Francisco–based forest products company, leaving Sir James in control of 1.9 million acres of prime American timberland. Sir James had put in an appearance before Congress during that fight too. Testifying on June 12, 1985, at hearings held by a Senate banking committee, Goldsmith disarmed at least the Republican senators by describing how congenial the United States is to the entrepreneurial spirit. "In a truly competitive economy," he said, "you do it right or you get eliminated." Jacob Hecht, the junior senator from Nevada, was so moved by these pieties that he said, "Sir James, I would like to invite you to become an American citizen and join the Republican party. You could be one of our top spokesmen."

Sir James may one day take him up on that. He carries British and French passports but he has not shown much loyalty to either country. In 1986, as he was stalking Goodyear, *BusinessWeek* characterized him as follows: "His lifestyle is one of studied rootlessness, inherited from a childhood spent in hotel suites across Europe as the son of a British hotelier based in Paris and a French mother. Now, with houses in Paris, London, and New York, plus vacation homes around the world, Goldsmith rarely spends more than a month at a time in a single location." (At last, the true multinational!)

In the 1960s and 1970s, as he was building a business empire based largely on foods and stores, Goldsmith shuttled between London and Paris. He had a clutch of British companies lodged in a holding company called Cavenham. He had a passel of French companies under the Générale Occidentale banner. They included France's largest producer of mustard and vinegar, a leading European ketchup maker, a famous British meat extract company (Bovril), a biscuit baker and chocolate maker, a drugstore chain, a grocery store chain. In 1973 he reached across the Atlantic to buy the Grand Union supermarket chain in the United States. And five years later he deepened that stake by acquiring Atlanta-based Colonial Stores and Houston-based Weingarten.

In 1976, on the recommendation of a Labour prime minister, Harold Wilson, he was knighted. In 1978 he became a knight of the Legion of

Honor in France. He controlled a food business that was ranked third in Europe behind Unilever and Nestlē and a supermarket business that was one of the ten largest in the United States.

But corporate empire building is not what James Goldsmith is about. He's too mercurial for that kind of patient endeavor. In 1980 he began to dismantle his conglomerate. By 1982 he had sold off all his food companies and retailing operations in France and Britain. Then, in 1987, he sold a controlling interest in Générale Occidentale for $240 million to the French telecommunications giant, Compagnie Générale d'Électicité.

Meanwhile, Sir James was logging super-profits by ambushing American timber companies, which was much more fun. In 1980 and 1981, in a two-part play, he knocked off Ohio's Diamond International, paying a total of $660 million, nearly all of which he quickly recouped by selling off the operating companies (a canner, pulp and paper mills, Diamond Match), leaving him with 1.7 million acres of trees. In 1984 he went after two other timber companies, Saint Regis Paper and Continental Corporation, forcing them to restructure (or disappear into the hands of others), making millions on the difference between what he paid for their stock and what he was paid for relinquishing it. He also took a successful flier in Colgate-Palmolive stock.

Goldsmith is known to be an habitué of casinos—in fact, he and his buddy, John Aspinall, own a couple of London's poshest gambling dens— but this interest did not deter Sir James, after acquiring Diamond, from shedding its U.S. Playing Card unit. This Cincinnati-based company is the nation's largest maker of playing cards (Diamond and Tally-Ho are among its brands), and Sir James let the managers of the division buy it.

One of the press's favorite descriptions of Sir James is "enigmatic." However, for someone who is supposed to be mysterious, he has generated a tremendous amount of ink on both sides of the Atlantic. The reason, of course, is that he is such good copy. Financial publications such as *BusinessWeek, Fortune,* and *The Wall Street Journal* love to gossip not just about his business adventures but his personal life, which tends to be as polygamous as his corporate relationships. These stories recount how he eloped, when he was twenty years old, with eighteen-year-old Isabel Patino, the Bolivian tin heiress. They had a daughter a year later, but Isabel died of a brain hemorrhage either in childbirth or shortly afterwards (the stories conflict). He then married a French lady, Ginette, who was his former secretary, and they had two children. They lived in Paris while Goldsmith openly kept a mistress in London, Lady Annabel Birley, the daughter of the Marquis of Londonderry, who bore him two children. *Fortune* reported that Goldsmith once vacationed in Sardinia, installing his wife and their children at one end of the island and his mistress and their children at the other end, commuting between the two by motorboat.

In 1978 Sir James divorced his French wife and married Lady Annabel. And they then had a third child. In 1986 *The Wall Street Journal* reported that while still married to Lady Annabel, he now had a new mistress, Laure Boulay de la Meurthe, the niece of the Count of Paris, who was installed, with their daughter, in Goldsmith's three-story town house on East 80th Street in New York City.

Goldsmith is a tall, strapping man who dresses elegantly and has, in the words of more than one reporter, "a commanding presence." James B. Stewart and Philip Revzin of *The Wall Street Journal* put it this way:

> Force of personality and physical presence have often made Sir James's message difficult to resist. He is six feet, four inches tall, solidly built, usually tanned. A former employee says that his deep-blue eyes turn deep black when he is angry, although the anger rarely gets out.
>
> He enjoys luxury, and he uses it: Sir James insisted that Goodyear's chairman, Robert Mercer, meet him for the first time at Sir James's Manhattan town house, where the home-court advantage includes silk damask wallpaper, original art, Limoges, French antiques, and a courtyard paved with marble. He also owns an English country estate, a Paris town house, and an Andalusian farmhouse in Spain. He frequently takes vacations on borrowed yachts or at rented homes in Southampton and Palm Beach.

Goldsmith has a love-hate relationship with the press. Politically, he is a conservative and he suspects that journalists are leftward leaning or worse yet, that they are agents, witting or unwitting, of the KGB. In 1986 he made inquiries to determine if a *BusinessWeek* reporter covering him was a Communist (*BusinessWeek* disclosed this tidbit). He apparently relishes combat with the press. A British television program once aired an unflattering profile of his business dealings, suggesting, among other things, that he bought companies to strip them of their assets (and employees), and that he was deserting England for France. Sir James showed up the next week and for thirty minutes excoriated the hosts, two London financial journalists, hardly letting them up for air. According to *The Wall Street Journal,* he once called up another British journalist, Barbara Conway, after she said in print that the annual reports of his companies were hard to understand, telling her, "I live for the day when people like you choke on your own vomit."

During the 1970s he became a natural target for the London satirical magazine *Eye,* which liked to call him "Goldenballs." In 1976 he sued the magazine for criminal libel and won an apology and damages. In 1981 the German newsweekly *Der Spiegel* sued Goldsmith for libel after he charged that the magazine, in its campaign to discredit Christian Democratic leader Franz Josef Strauss, had been subverted by the KGB. The suit was withdrawn in 1984 after Goldsmith said he didn't mean to imply that *Der Spiegel* was "controlled" by the KGB, and after *Der Spiegel* said it "fully" accepted Goldsmith's description of how Soviet Intelligence operates, though it was "not conscious of having been used in the manner mentioned by Sir James Goldsmith."

To get across his views, Sir James would like to be a press lord himself. He once owned an interest in Britain's Beaverbrook newspapers, and in 1979 he started his own magazine, *Now!*, which died after losing $17 million. He tried (and failed) to buy various American magazines—*Esquire, New York, U.S. News & World Report*—but he did own France's leading newsweekly, *L'Express,* and a Belgian magazine, *Lire.* Under his ownership, *L'Express* underwent a complete sex change, becoming right-wing instead of left-wing. In 1986 he beat back Carlo De Benedetti of Italy to gain control of France's second largest book publisher, Presses de la Cite.

Another reason why the press has loved to write about Goldsmith is that it provides an opportunity to construct those wonderful charts detailing the proverbial maze of companies through which he operates. At the center of the chart was usually a Liechtenstein entity, the Brunneria Foundation, the base of the Goldsmith Empire. Arrows out of Brunneria went to a Panama holding company, Compania Financiera Lido, and General Oriental, a company based in the Cayman Islands but whose shares trade on the Hong Kong stock exchange. General Oriental, in turn, owned sizeable chunks of two French companies, Trocadero Participations and Générale Occidentale. Trocadero, a private company, owns one third of Générale Occidentale, whose shares trade on the Paris Bourse—and it was his 51 percent stake in Trocadero that Sir James traded to CGE for cash. Sir James is the most important shareholder in *all* these companies. Grand Union, L'Express, and the Diamond timber operation function as subsidiaries of Générale Occidentale. The old Crown Zellerbach timberlands are lodged in a company called Cavenham Forest Industries, which is 97 percent–owned by Sir James personally. Even after the sale to CGE Sir James continued to hold 5 percent of Générale Occidentale.

When Sir James does his deals, they can be sluiced through any one of these conduits or new ones that he floats. In the hostile takeover of Crown Zellerbach, for example, Goldsmith formed a new Cayman Islands entity, Oriental & American Investments, to raise funds specifically for such takeovers. And here, according to *Fortune,* is the way the Diamond International takeover was organized:

> Sir James had Générale Occidentale . . . put up $225 million toward the purchase of Diamond in return for 37 percent of the profits. The actual buyer, which gets the other 63 percent of the profits, was a Hong Kong company owned 90 percent by Goldsmith and the foundation. In essence, Goldsmith had his 42 percent–owned French company lend money to his 90 percent–owned Hong Kong company so that the Hong Kong company could buy Diamond. The banks and outside shareholders of the French company put up the money; Goldsmith and his foundation, through their combined holdings in the French and Hong Kong companies, get 72 percent of the profits.

Welcome to the world of high finance, Goldsmith-style. Sir James usually has a network of European bankers and friends who go in on his deals with him. The French and British Rothschilds are frequent allies. They are also distantly related to Sir James.

Goldsmith's family came to England in the 1860s from Germany, where they were wealthy Jewish bankers in Frankfurt under the name Goldschmidt. Goldsmith's father, Frank Goldsmith, graduated from Oxford, served as a major in the British Army, and was a member of Parliament before going into the hotel business in France, where he operated the Lotti in Paris and the Carlton in Cannes. He married a Catholic from the province of Auvergne.

Sir James was born in Paris in 1933, the second of two sons. His father sent him to Eton but he dropped out, joining the British Army at eighteen, emerging two years later as a lieutenant. He then began his very successful career of buying and selling companies and marrying different ladies, maintaining households in at least three different countries. His elder brother, Edward Goldsmith, is an environmental activist, publisher of the bimonthly British magazine *The Ecologist.* Sir James is one of the backers of his brother's work. Harold Gilliam, a columnist for the *San Francisco Chronicle,* interviewed Edward Goldsmith in 1986, characterizing him as "an imperialist in reverse." Gilliam described the elder Goldsmith brother as "a stocky, bearded man . . . overflowing with the kind of dynamism identified with the empire builders." Goldsmith was raging against the Third World development that results in big dams, displacement of people from their homes, deforestation, and a shift to cash crops (instead of people growing food to feed themselves). Goldsmith told Gilliam that "old-fashioned colonialism may be over, but economic colonialism continues." The Gilliam interview took place in San Francisco, where Sir James had just conquered Crown Zellerbach.

Access   42, avenue de Friedland
75008 Paris, France
(33) 1-763-1213

Grand Metropolitan

Sales $9.5 billion
Profits $500 million
U.S. Sales $3.8 billion
Rank 4th-largest company in Britain
World's largest wine and spirits
company
World's 2d-largest seller of gin
World's 2d-largest seller of Scotch
whiskey
Britain's 4th-largest brewer
Largest seller of canned dog food
in the United States
Britain's 2d largest dairy company
Britain's largest yogurt seller
World's largest purveyor of vodka
World's 9th-largest hotelkeeper
World's largest retailer of eye-care
products
Founded 1934
Employees 155,000
Headquarters London, England

While some of the companies in this sinful complex can trace their histories back to seventeenth- and eighteenth-century England, Grand Metropolitan is very much a creature of modern times. It was spliced together, from many different strands, by Sir Maxwell Joseph, who died in 1982 after a quarter of a century of taking over other companies, often against their wishes, in Britain and the United States. The result was a sprawling enterprise spanning a host of human passions: beer, wine, whiskey, milk, hotels, foods, cigarettes, gambling.

Sir Maxwell's successors have continued his work, reaching an intoxicating climax in early 1987 when Grand Metropolitan acquired the U.S.-based wine and spirits group Heublein, thereby displacing Seagram as the world's largest producer of alcoholic beverages.

In the beginning, there were hotels. They formed the base of the empire built by Sir Maxwell, who went to work in 1926, when he was only sixteen years old, at a London real estate agency. When he set up his own agency in 1931, he was believed to be the youngest real estate agent in Britain. Real estate provided the insight into property values that propelled him into the hotel business after World War II. He bought a series of rundown hotels in London and the provinces, the biggest being the Mount Royal at Marble Arch in London. Looking back in 1979, he told the *Financial Times:*

> "Between 1950 and 1965 there wasn't a real estate man in the country who knew the value of hotels. I knew. I had a feel. You can't devise a formula to value a hotel. You need a feel for the combination of property value and profit. I know hotels. The last one I bought was the Hotel d'Angleterre in Copenhagen. I knew the hotel and I didn't need to visit it again. I knew £15,000 a room was right."

Sir Maxwell's hotel operations were conducted under various names—Grand Hotels (Mayfair) Ltd. and Mount Royal Ltd. were the two main ones. On July 10, 1962, the name Grand Metropolitan Hotels was adopted. In 1973 it was abbreviated to Grand Metropolitan.

From hotels Sir Maxwell had Grand Metropolitan branch out into other businesses, and he had no fear of going after companies much bigger than his own. Among those that fell to his forays were Express Dairy, the Truman brewery, the Berni Inns, the Mecca bookmaking parlors, and the Watney Mann brewery. The 1972 Watney Mann acquisition was bitterly contested and constituted the biggest takeover in British financial history up to that time. On the menu was more than beer. Watney Mann itself had just ballooned up by acquiring a venerable wine and spirits house, International Distillers and Vintners (IDV).

This imbibing has given Grand Metropolitan a formidable presence in Britain and Ireland. Some 4,700 pubs fly the Watney Mann & Truman flags. Another 1,700 pubs and steak houses are operated under the names Chef & Brewer, Open House, and Berni. Watney Mann & Truman, Britain's fourth-largest brewer, markets fifty-seven different draft and thirty-nine different bottled and canned beers, including three foreign brews—Foster's, Carlsberg, and Budweiser—made under license. Mecca operates 630 betting shops, mostly in London and southeast England, and it also runs six casinos in central London. Express Dairy delivers milk to 1 million homes a day (Britain is one of the world's last strongholds of home-delivered milk). IDV companies produce J&B Scotch whiskey, Gilbey's gin, Bombay gin, and Bailey's Original Irish Cream (Express Dairy supplies the cream from Irish dairies).

It was J&B Scotch that inspired Grand Metropolitan's entry into the United States. J&B, a Scotch for people who don't like Scotch, spurted after World War II into the best-selling Scotch in the American market (it has since been displaced by Dewar's) through the efforts of its distributor, Paddington Corporation, which merged in 1966 with cigarette maker Liggett & Myers (L&M, Lark, Chesterfield). After taking over Watney Mann in 1972, Grand Met became the proprietor of J&B, which it continued to supply to Paddington. It then occurred to Sir Maxwell: "Why shouldn't we own this U.S. importer of our whiskey?" But Paddington, the importer, couldn't be pried loose from the Liggett Group. So be it. Grand Met decided it would buy the entire Liggett operation, cigarettes and all. It wasn't that easy. Liggett's management fiercely resisted Grand Met's overtures, but in the end, Sir Maxwell, as he usually did, got his way. For $600 million he absorbed the Liggett Group in 1980. Lust for Scotch had now encumbered Grand Metropolitan with the worst-selling cigarette brands in the American market, Alpo dog food, DP 'Fit for Life' exercise equipment, and two Pepsi-Cola bottling plants (in Fresno, California, and Columbia, South Carolina).

A year after grabbing Liggett, and shortly after he was knighted, Sir Maxwell came up with another $500 million to buy the Intercontinental Hotel chain from cash-strapped Pan American World Airways. In 1986 Intercontinental was operating ninety-six hotels in forty-six countries, including the Mark Hopkins in San Francisco, the Carlton in Cannes, and the Mount Kenya Safari Club in Nairobi. It's a far cry from the seedy hotels Sir Maxwell started out with. In 1985 Grand Met it also acquired Dallas-based Pearle Health Services, which owns and franchises more than 1,300 eye care stores in forty-two states and five countries outside the United States. Pearle is the largest U.S. seller of prescription eyeglasses and contact lenses.

Grand Metropolitan is at home in the world of pubs but can do without the smoke. In a three-part play executed in 1985 and 1986, it sold off all the Liggett tobacco businesses, even the best-selling chewing tobacco in America, Red Man. It also moved to get out of the exercise equipment business by putting up for sale Opelika, Alabama-based Diversified Products Corporation. While it was giving up smoking and exercising, Grand Met was still gung ho for drinking. In March 1987 it paid RJR Nabisco $1.2 billion in cash to acquire Heublein, a Hartford, Connecticut-based marketer of nearly one hundred brands of spirits and wines, including Smirnoff vodka, Jose Cuervo tequila, and Inglenook and Lancers wines. Also part of the package was America's fifth-largest table wine maker, Almaden, which Heublein had just agreed to buy.

In the incestuous liquor business, Heublein and Grand Met were old friends. Gilbey, one of IDV's spirit arms, began marketing Smirnoff vodka outside the United States in 1953. And Heublein had been marketing

IDV's Black Velvet Canadian whiskey in the United States. In guzzling Heublein Grand Met tapped into the world's second-largest selling liquor brand. *Impact,* an industry newsletter, places Smirnoff's worldwide sales at 14 million nine-liter cases a year (half of that in the United States). Only Bacardi rum sells more.

The Heublein-Grand Met cocktail created another international colossus in the world wine and spirits field, the other giants being Seagram, Guinness (now the owner of Distillers Ltd., the great Scotch house), and an Anglo-Canadian mélange made up of Allied-Lyons and Hiram Walker. By the calculations of *Impact,* Grand Met is now first, but when Rosemary Moore, managing editor of *Impact International,* asked IDV Chairman Anthony Tennant whether he thought it was important to be on top, he replied testily:

> "I think that your statement that we are number one needs to be questioned. Number one in what sense, in volume or in profit or in what? We're making no claim about being number one about anything. It's not important to us. . . . The crystal factor from our business is to be number one, i.e., the best. That is very much our intention, to be the best wine and spirits business. Whether that happens to take us into leadership in one form or another is fine, but that isn't an end in itself. Bigness is in itself flabby and it's nothing. I mean, it's a question of how you do it, the quality of your business, that's important."

Three months later, having been passed over for the chief executive's position at Grand Metropolitan, Tennant moved to a rival company, Guinness, as chief executive. After Sir Maxwell Joseph died in 1982 leadership of Grand Met passed to his longtime deputy, Stanley Grinstead (he was later knighted), depicted in the British press as a number cruncher with a passion for horse racing. Allen Sheppard, who joined Grand Met in 1976 from the automotive industry, took over the chief executive's duties at the end of 1986.

IDV brands are historic names in the liquor trade. In 1875 Smirnoff vodka was the only brand Czar Alexander II would allow on his table. That's the year the Heublein brothers, Gilbert and Louis, set up a distilled spirits business in Hartford. Vladimir Smirnoff fled Russia after the Communist revolution of 1917, bringing with him the formula for the vodka, but his efforts to establish the brand in Europe failed. In 1939 John Martin, a grandson of Gilbert Heublein, bought the rights to Smirnoff vodka for $14,000 in a move that people called "Martin's Folly." After World War II Heublein turned it into a world megabrand.

Britain's alcoholic history can be traced through the constituent elements of Grand Metropolitan: Truman brewery, which began brewing ale in London in 1666; the Croft port house, whose cultivation of the grapes in Portugal's Douro valley resulted in the fortified wine associated with gout in eighteenth-century England; the Justerini & Brooks wine and spirits house established in London's Pall Mall in 1749, which began selling, in 1779, the forerunner of J&B—a spirit called "Usquebaugh" (the Irish and Scottish term for whiskey, or "water of life"); Twiss & Brownings, founded in 1814—they cornered the world rum market; the Gilbey brothers, Walter and Alfred, who broke the price barrier on fine wines in 1857 by importing inexpensive wines from South Africa, began distilling gin in 1872 and blending Scotch in 1887 (Glen Spey), meanwhile acquiring a French vineyard, Chateau Loudenne in the Medoc, that is still in the Grand Met wine cellar today.

In the twentieth century, all these ingredients were mixed in the following combination: Gilbey bought Croft in 1910; Twiss & Brownings, after combining with E. Price Hallowes in 1926, joined with Justerini & Brooks in 1951 to form United Wine Traders; in 1962, United Wine Traders merged with Gilbey to form International Distillers & Vintners. Ten years later IDV joined the Watney Mann stable, which in turn became part of Grand Metropolitan.

Cheers!

Access 11-12 Hanover Square
London W1A 1DP, England
(44) 1-629-7488

Grand Met USA
100 Paragon Dr.
Montvale, N.J. 07645
(201) 573-4000

Guinness

Sales $4.5 billion
Profits $330 million
U.S. Sales $500 million
Rank   World's 3d-largest alcoholic beverage
company
World's largest Scotch whiskey producer
World's largest gin producer
World's 10th-largest brewer
40th-largest company in Britain
Founded   1759
Employees   33,000
Headquarters   London, England

Every pub in Ireland serves Guinness stout, a black, bitter brew whose devotees are zealous. And it's served, from the tap, in a very special way. After being poured into a glass or mug, it's left standing for two minutes while a yeasty head forms at the top like a layer of dairy cream. The bartender removes the top of the head, retops the glass and lets the stout settle once more. The head is then leveled with a ruler or spoon—and yes, finally, the customer can drink. In 1986 Guinness fanciers in more than 120 countries downed more than seven million glasses of the stuff *every day*.

Not everyone likes Guinness stout. The beer drinkers of Europe and the United States are used to a lighter, chilled lager-type brew. As a result, even though Guinness has pushed hard to become an international brewer, exporting bottled and canned stout around the world and even opening breweries in half a dozen countries (plus licensing others, like Sapporo in Japan, to make this black "wine"), the drink has never taken hold the way it has in Ireland and Britain. An exception, for reasons unknown, is Malaysia (population: sixteen million), where Guinness is the brand leader. In the largest country in Africa, Nigeria (population: 94 million), Guinness owns 25 percent of a company that operates three breweries.

It would appear from recent studies that Ireland still accounts for more than half of Guinness stout sales. Guinness's market share in Ireland is well over 50 percent. The bulk of the remaining beer sales comes from Britain, where Guinness is at a disadvantage because it doesn't have a tied network of pubs, where most of the beer is consumed. Hundreds of beer brands are sold in Britain, and in this splintered market Guinness is the number one brand, taking down between 3 percent and 4 percent of total sales. Guinness does know how to read the bottom of beer mugs. Lager sales have exploded in Britain to the point where they account for 40 percent of the market (they had 2 percent in 1960), and Guinness has one of the leading entries in Harp, which was first brewed at its Irish brewery in Dundalk. It also fields two other lagers, Steiger and Hoffmans, and for those who have acquired a Guinness beer belly, it has an alcohol-free lager, Kaliber, that it has been trying to foist on health addicts in America, where it also distributes France's Kronenbourg beer, Germany's Fursten-berg, and Japan's Asahi.

In Britain draft Guinness accounts for more than half the total sales of the brand, which gives credence to the claims by Guinness aficionados that Guinness in cans or bottles does not compare to the product that comes out of the tap. Then again, there may be something about the pub that enhances the flavor, and that can't be exported.

The beer that's almost the official drink of Ireland was originally developed in England. It was called "porter" in honor of the fruit and vegetable porters at London's Covent Garden, who fancied the dark brew. In 1759 Arthur Guinness, using £100 left to him by the Archbishop of Castel, bought a small brewery at St. James's Gate in Dublin on the banks of the River Liffey, negotiating a nine-thousand-year lease at £45 a year. He made light and dark beers but at the turn of the century decided to concentrate on the dark beers, or porter. There were various kinds of porters—town porter, superior porter and, finally, extra stout porter, so named because it was darker than the others. This was the beer that swept Ireland. The "porter" designation disappeared, "stout" remained.

So prodigious was the Irish thirst for Guinness stout that the com-pany which brewed it grew to become the largest enterprise in the country. It employed more people than any other company, ranked as the country's largest exporter and bought half the national crop of barley. (It's roasted barley that gives Guinness its black hue.) It also grew too big for Ireland. In 1886, when stock in the company was first sold to the public, the headquarters of the company was relocated to London, where Arthur Guinness's descendants were to cut a wide—and sometimes tragic—swath in British social circles. Today Guinness is basically a British company, although it remains one of the largest employers in Ireland, with a payroll of 4,700.

For 177 years the Dublin brewery was the only source of Guinness stout. That changed in 1936 with the opening of a new Guinness brewery at Park Royal in Northwest London. Both breweries are still going strong. The St. James's Gate brewery, which has more than 8,770 years to run on its lease, was overhauled and modernized in the early 1980s, resulting in a 40 percent reduction in the work force of 2,500. Guinness sugar-coated this drastic downsizing by giving terminated workers who had spent many years at the brewery a lump sum payment of twenty thousand dollars and a pension equivalent to two thirds of salary. In 1986 the ties to Dublin were cut again when Guinness phased out a hospitality program in which it brought Irish financial journalists to London for the company's annual meeting, held at the Toucan Inn near the Park Royal brewery. The monthly business magazine *Business* reported that the Irish press was "up in arms" over this betrayal.

The man who abolished this press junket was Ernest Saunders, who became chief executive of Guinness in 1981 when he was forty-five years old. Known in British financial circles as "Deadly Ernest," Saunders was brought in to bring some order and direction to a company that was having trouble finding something useful to do with the steady profits flowing from the dark beer. Beginning in 1970 Guinness had gone on a mindless shopping spree, picking up more than two hundred companies engaged in all manner of businesses—candy making, orchid growing, car bumpers, plastics, children's clothes, animal medicines, African trading houses, mushroom farms.

To Saunders, the archetypical professional manager, this overgrown, weedy garden was made to order. He knew what to do: Cut. He got rid of companies (150 of them in two years), advertising agencies (he fired two of them in three years), and people (the payroll was chopped nearly in half). Saunders came to Guinness from the big Swiss food and beverage outfit Nestlē, where he had organized the company's defense in the infant-formula fight, but he had started his career in the London office of the J. Walter Thompson ad agency. One of his first moves on returning to London was to sack JWT as Guinness's agency. It wasn't the dismissal that was so surprising (that does happen in the agency business) as the abrupt manner in which it was done. The agency received no warning. JWT Chairman Jeremy Bullmore described it as "savage." It's an image Saunders seemed to relish. In an advertisement that Guinness paid for, the company's leader was depicted as follows: "Emotion is not the first word to spring to mind when Ernest Saunders's name is mentioned. He has had to make some tough and unemotional decisions to pull Guinness up by its bootstraps."

One division that survived the pruning is publishing. Guinness began publishing the *Guinness Book of Records* in 1955—to help settle arguments in pubs—and it's one of the great publishing success stories. In 1986 Polish and Arabic editions of the annual compilation were published, bringing to twenty-four the number of languages in which it has appeared. In addition to selling more than 3 million copies annually (more than any other book outside the Bible), it has spawned a host of spinoffs—one hundred other books, catalogs, product tie-ins, and museums (one opened in Piccadilly Circus in 1985 and attracted ten thousand visitors a week).

Ernest Saunders had his own ideas about where Guinness should be heading, and after he finished his discarding, he began accumulating. In 1984 and 1985 he had Guinness bag a bunch of British businesses: a glass bottle maker (Canning Town Glass); an operator of health spas (Champney's); forty-four convenience stores (7-Elevens); health food stores and vegetarian restaurants (Crank's); a vitamin maker (Nature's Best); three chains (Martin's, R. S. McColl, and Lewis Meeson) operating a 1,100 neighborhood stores selling newspapers, magazines, cigarettes, candy, and assorted notions; and the Arthur Bell & Sons Scotch whiskey house. The last move kicked up a fuss in Scotland.

Founded in 1825, Bell's had five distilleries in Scotland, and Bell's Extra Special was the largest selling Scotch in Britain. Among its properties were the spectacular Gleneagles Hotel at the site of the famous golf course (the only five-star hotel in Scotland) and the North British and Caledonian hotels situated at either end of Edinburgh's Princes Street. There's a good deal of Scottish history in Bell's, and the company tried to rally nationalist sentiment against the bid by an Irish company turned English. In the end Saunders prevailed, paying $500 million to take over Bell's. The argument that won was his promise that Guinness could do a lot to improve the company's performance, particularly in the United States where Bell's Scotch is almost an unknown brand. Guinness's takeover, said Saunders, would be good for "Scottish jobs and Scottish exports."

Bell's was snapped up in August 1985. In January 1986 Saunders went into the trenches again, fighting the Argyll Group for control of the largest spirits producer in the United Kingdom, the Distillers Company. Maker of 150 different Scotch whiskies, Distillers produces such bellwether brands as Johnnie Walker (the world's top-selling Scotch), Dewar's (the top-selling Scotch in the United States), White Horse (the best-selling Scotch in Japan), Vat 69, and Black & White. Among the other spirits in the Distillers lineup are Gordon's, Booth's, and Tanqueray gins. Formed in 1877 by the amalgamation of six Scottish distillers, the aptly named Distillers Company had a deadly reputation in Britain as a "sleepy" outfit. So it was a question of which contestant would do better at reviving a company in the grip of a worldwide decline in Scotch whiskey sales. The fierce battle, featuring full-page ads in British newspapers, was won by Saunders with a $3.8 billion bid. And this acquisition moved

Guinness into second place, behind Seagram, in the world spirit standings. It was Saunders's contention all along that Britain needed a giant drinks company to fight for markets across the world.

Even in victory Saunders managed to ruffle feathers, Scottish again. During the heated battle with Argyll he had pledged, in writing, that he would preserve the "Scottishness" of Distillers by naming Sir Thomas Risk, governor of the Bank of Scotland, chairman of Guinness. He made other promises too. He said he would establish the headquarters of the company in Edinburgh. And he said that Guinness would not sell the Edinburgh hotels acquired in the Bell's purchase. After he won a very close victory, getting 50.7 percent of Distillers shares, Saunders, incredibly, reneged on all the promises.

Although many people in the City of London were aghast at this flagrant breach of etiquette—the governor of the Bank of England told Saunders to his face that "you stand in danger of losing your reputation for integrity"—the Guinness leader got away with it. He had won Distillers, he had pushed Guinness to record profits, and he didn't have to answer to anyone except his cronies: among whom were Arthur Furer, his former boss at Nestlé, now with the Zurich-based Bank Leu; Thomas Ward, an American lawyer; and Olivier Roux, a flashy, thirty-six-year-old Frenchman who was Guinness's financial chief while also on the payroll of the U.S. management consulting firm Bain & Company). Saunders placed all three—none of them English—on the Guinness board. *Financial Times* writers David Lascelles and Lisa Wood depicted Roux as someone akin to Saunders, with a perspective "uncluttered by British niceties or an excessive respect for convention. Roux would scrap Britain's tied pub system or move Guinness's headquarters to Tokyo if he thought that was best for the company."

Saunders sailed through the storm of criticism. Already chief executive, he took over the post of chairman at a salary of $560,000 a year. It was the first time in the history of the company that the chairman's position had not been occupied by a member of the Guinness family. At a special shareholders meeting held on September 11, 1986, all of his proposals carried. In answer to his critics Saunders could point to the annual *Financial Times* ranking of the top five hundred companies in Europe. As of June 30, 1986, Guinness ranked thirty-ninth with a market value of $4.1 billion. A year earlier the company had ranked 176th.

The people who might have been able to stop Saunders were the Guinness family members on the board of directors. Among them they hold more than 10 percent of the company's stock. But they were supine, pleased no doubt by the rise in the value of their shareholdings. Six

Guinnesses held board seats in 1986 as Saunders was thumbing his nose at the rules of the London financial community. They were the Earl of Iveagh, whom Saunders displaced as chairman; Jonathan B. Guinness, the eldest son of Lord Moyne; Finn B. Guinness, another son of Lord Moyne; Lord Dufferin, whose mother was a Guinness and first cousin of Lord Moyne; Lord Boyd, whose mother is a daughter of the second Lord Iveagh; and Edward Guinness, a distant cousin descended from a younger brother of Arthur Guinness, the founder of the company. Jonathan Guinness's mother was Diana Mosley, one of the seven Mitford sisters. She gave birth to him during her brief marriage to Bryan Guinness (later Lord Moyne), whom she left in 1933 for the English fascist leader Oswald Mosley. In his book-length portrait of the Mitford sisters, *The House of Mitford,* which he wrote with his daughter, Catherine Guinness, Jonathan described Katharine Graham, publisher of *The Washington Post,* as the daughter of a "Jewish millionaire" and said that "she played a vital part in preparing the American public for the abandonment of Indochina to Communism as well as in exploiting the Watergate burglary to hound President Nixon out of office."

Despite all this presence on the board, the family influence on the company has waned. The younger members of the Guinness clan have been racked by mishaps reminiscent of the series of tragedies that have befallen another Irish family, the Kennedys. In May 1978 Henrietta Guinness, thirty-five-year-old sister of the company's chairman, plunged to her death from a 250-foot aqueduct in Rome. In June 1978 seventeen-year-old Natalya Citkowitz, daughter of Guinness heiress Lady Carolyn Lowell, died of a suspected heroin overdose. In July 1978 Major Dennys Guinness, an admitted alcoholic, was found dead with an empty pill bottle nearby after having been arrested for waving his ex-service pistol in a pub. In August 1978 four-year-old Peter Guinness, son of the head of the merchant banking side of the family (Guinness Mahon), died in a car crash. In June 1986 twenty-two-year-old Olivia Channon was found dead in the Oxford dormitory room of her friend German Count Gottfried von Bismarck after an end-of-term party in which champagne and drugs were freely available; she appeared to have suffocated on her own vomit. About to graduate from Oxford's elite college, Christ Church, Olivia Channon had an annual allowance of $70,000 and traveled in a fast crowd of wealthy, heroin-taking fun-seekers who called themselves "Euro-Trash" and "Aristo-sluts." Both of Olivia's parents are members of the Guinness clan. Her father, Paul Channon, was serving in 1986 as minister of trade and industry in the Thatcher cabinet. He is the grandson of a former Guinness chairman, who held the Earl of Iveagh title. Olivia's mother is

Ingrid Guinness, ex-wife of Channon's cousin, Jonathan Guinness. In December 1986 Sebastian Guinness, twenty-three-year-old cousin of Olivia Channon, was sentenced to a jail term for possession of cocaine and heroin, charges which grew out of an investigation of Olivia's death.

Just as Sebastian Guinness was pleading guilty in an Oxford courtroom, Ernest Saunders's world was beginning to unravel in London. He was undone by events three thousand miles away—the Securities and Exchange Commission's case against stock manipulator Ivan Boesky. Records in that file led British investigators to Guinness's doorstep. They found that during the Argyll-Guinness duel for Distillers, top people at Guinness (with the help of friends in New York, Zurich, Luxembourg, and London) had manipulated the stock market to drive up the price of Guinness shares. It was an illegal maneuver that worked because the Guinness offer for Distillers was partly in stock, and the higher price made its bid more valuable. On January 14, 1987, the Guinness board of directors fired Saunders and asked for the resignations of his cronies from the board. On May 7, Saunders was indicted on charges of trying "to pervert the course" of justice.

A postmortem on what was one of the worst scandals in British financial history appeared in the February 1987 issue of *Business.* Prepared by a team of seven writers and researchers, the report, which was not without a bit of the virulent strain of British superciliousness, depicted Ernest Saunders as the classic outsider who never belonged to any company, or country. "He was not, in fact, English," the article said, going on to disclose that Saunders was born in Vienna, the eldest son of a Jewish gynecologist whose name was Emanuel Schleyer. The Schleyers fled to Britain in 1937 when Ernest was two years old. The family name wasn't changed to Saunders until 1954.

"Unlike his parents," the *Business* reporters wrote, "Ernest felt no particular gratitude to England. Even as Ernest Saunders he did not entirely belong." They quote classmates of his at Cambridge who recalled, "He always seemed older than we were," and "undergraduate life seemed to pass him by."

Saunders spent four years at J. Walter Thompson; moved to a client, Beecham; then to a Swiss engineering firm, Eutectic; and then to Nestlē. According to the *Business* researchers, it was a calculated progression, part of the modern scene of headhunters, "gray men who move rising executives about the world like pieces on a chessboard."

By this analysis Saunders was a classic outsider, a loner who didn't trust people; and these were the attitudes he brought to Guinness in 1981. His downfall, concluded the article, was caused not so much by vanity as

Drink Up, Buy a Missile

Britain's Scotch Whiskey Association lodged a complaint with the European Economic Commission in 1986 about a new levy imposed by the Turkish government. It seems that every bottle of Scotch whiskey sold in Turkey must now carry a label informing the imbiber that the price includes a donation of one hundred Turkish lira (about fifteen cents) to the Turkish defense industry.

"ambition," "ruthlessness," and a "passion for secrecy." The writers said that by defying the financial establishment in Britain, Saunders ensured that "nothing he did thereafter would escape their notice. It was a risk only an outsider would have considered taking."

Two months after Saunders was sacked, his chief executive's post at Guinness was filled by Anthony Tennant, who had been chairing Grand Met's International Distillers & Vintners unit. The *Financial Times* called

WORLD'S TOP TEN LIQUOR BRANDS	1985 Case Sales
1. **Bacardi** rum (Bacardi)	18.8 million
2. **Smirnoff** vodka (Grand Met)	13.8 million
3. **Ricard** anisette (Pernod Ricard)	7.2 million
4. **Gordon's** gin (Guinness)	6.8 million
5. **Johnnie Walker Red** Scotch (Guinness)	6.5 million
6. **Seagram's 7 Crown** whiskey (Seagram)	5.3 million
7. **Suntory Old** whiskey (Suntory)	5.2 million
8. **J&B** Scotch (Grand Met)	5.0 million
9. **Jim Beam** bourbon (American Brands)	4.8 million
10. **Suntory Red** whiskey (Suntory)	4.7 million

him an "aristocrat" with an "old Etonian manner." A colleague of Tennant's said, "He is a man with a world knowledge of the alcohol business. Mind you, give him the choice between a boring meeting and the races at Cheltenham, and there is no doubt that he would choose the races."

No more outsiders for Guinness. It just needed one to lift the company out of the morass into which it had fallen.

Access Park Royal
London NW10 7RR, England
(44) 1-965-7700

Hanson Trust

Sales $6.2 billion
Profits $524 million
U.S. Sales $2.8 billion
Rank 9th-largest industrial company in Britain
Largest battery and flashlight maker in Britain
World's largest seller of portable typewriters
World's 3d-largest lighting company
World's 3d-largest producer of titanium dioxide (whitening agent)
5th-largest shoe maker in United States
Britain's largest cigarette maker
Britain's largest snuff maker
Largest maker of clay bricks in the Western world
World's leading maker of shovels
5th-largest cement maker in the United States
2d-largest maker of hot dogs in the United States
Largest U.S. maker of fireman's boots
Founded 1964
Employees 92,000 (33,000 in the United States)
Headquarters London, England

If you're the manager of, or large stockholder in, a business that has attracted the attention of Lord Hanson and Sir Gordon White, you might as well give up. These two Yorkshiremen are the takeover artists *ne plus ultra*. Since the mid-1960s, when they joined and then took over a small publicly held company that had bought their respective family businesses, they have created an Anglo-American powerhouse. They did it by acquiring company after company and then demonstrating that they knew how to run them better than their previous owners. Not the least amazing feature of this piracy is their adeptness at the hostile takeover. Over and over again they have captured companies against the wishes of management.

The result, at the start of 1987, was a variegated enterprise that owned 491 plants that turned out humdrum products like bricks, pillows, shoes, pumps, rakes, cement, office chairs, aluminum windows, yarns, and ledgers. Part of the picture was a pack of visible brand name products like

243

Smith-Corona typewriters, John Player cigarettes, Ever Ready batteries (in Britain), Lea & Perrins Worcestershire sauce, Encino shirts, and Nancy Lopez golf shoes.

The two prime movers, James Hanson and Gordon White, were born in the early 1920s into Yorkshire families who already had successful businesses. Hanson's was a trucking firm in Huddersfield, White's was a printing-publishing-advertising business in Hull. They were brought together by the death of Hanson's younger brother, Bill, of stomach cancer in 1954. Bill Hanson was, as journalist Stephen Fay pointed out in *Business,* "an extraordinary figure: youngest major in the British Army at the age of nineteen; star of Britain's show jumping team by 1953." He was twenty-nine when he died. White and Bill Hanson had served together in the British Army, and after Bill's death White became close to James.

Every story about Hanson and White (and there have been many on both sides of the Atlantic) recounts their playboy days in swinging London during the late 1950s and 1960s. Both well over six feet tall, they traveled in a fast crowd of rising young British businessmen. They gambled at Annabel's. They squired actresses and models around Mayfair. Hanson was engaged for one year to aspiring actress Audrey Hepburn. White dated Joan Collins. Little did the British establishment realize what Hanson and White had in store for them.

They began acquiring companies in the late 1960s. Not glamorous ones—brick makers, contractors, building materials, construction equipment. And they brought to this endeavor traits for which Yorkshire is known—no frills, bluntness, shrewdness about money. They looked especially for companies that were run poorly, and they didn't have a lot of trouble finding them.

In 1973 White left to do in the United States what the two were doing in Britain. "We're not interested in France, Germany, or the Third World," he said. "We'll leave them to more adventurous companies." Again, nothing glamorous. His first purchase was a fishmeal company, his third a hot dog maker (Hygrade, the Detroit supplier of Ball Park Franks). White became a virtual permanent exile although he Concorded across the Atlantic frequently; and no one was ever surprised to see him show up at Ascot, a beautiful model or actress on his arm. White has been married and divorced twice. In 1979 he was knighted for his services to British industry, a euphemism for buying up American companies.

Hanson was knighted when Labourite Harold Wilson was prime

minister, and he became a peer when Margaret Thatcher occupied 10 Downing Street. He married an American, the former Geraldine Kaelin, in 1959, and they have three grown children.

In the United States White bagged such corporate prizes as McDonough, whose major holdings were Ames, a big West Virginia tool maker, and Endicott Johnson, a leading shoe maker (nineteen million pairs a year) and shoe store operator (six hundred of them); and the sprawling conglomerate U.S. Industries. In Britain Hanson bagged Ever Ready, the battery maker, and Allders, operator of department stores and duty-free shops at airports in Britain, Canada, and Australia. Their adventures were crowned in 1985 and 1986 when both the American and British wings carried out audacious, hostile raids. In America White mounted a successful takeover of SCM despite a ferocious attempt by management—and Merrill Lynch—to defeat the bid. So into the Hanson hopper came Smith-Corona typewriters, Glidden paints, and Durkee foods. In Britain Lord Hanson went head-to-head with United Biscuit, one of Britain's biggest food companies, in a battle to take over the Imperial Group, whose many holdings included tobacco (42 percent of the British cigarette market), beer (Courage), frozen foods, pubs, hotels, and restaurants. Hanson came out on top with a $3.7 billion bid even though Imperial's management favored the United Biscuit offer.

The twin victories lifted the British parent, Hanson Trust, into the top twenty ranks in the United Kingdom and the American arm, Hanson Industries, into the top one hundred ranks in the United States, based on their sales volumes immediately after these acquisitions. But trying to draw a bead on Hanson is always tricky because it's a moving target. As active as it is on the acquisition front, it's also a prodigious discarder. After buying SCM for $930 million, White sold off six pieces of it, including Glidden paints (which went to Britain's Imperial Chemical Industries for $580 million) and Durkee's Famous Foods (which went to another British company, Reckitt & Colman for $120 million). The six disposals raised $926 million, which meant that Hanson acquired SCM's typewriter, titanium dioxide, and industrial chemicals businesses for nothing.

On the other side of the Atlantic, Lord Hanson was indulging in the same kind of arithmetic. After winning Imperial Tobacco, he sold off the Courage beer business for $2 billion, the Golden Wonder potato chip business for $130 million, and the restaurants and hotels for $280 million. He therefore recouped 65 percent of the price he paid for Imperial while retaining the tobacco business, one of Britain's largest packaged food franchises (H&P and Lea & Perrins sauces, and frozen and chilled foods sold under the Ross and Young's labels), and the Ground Round restaurant chain in the United States.

These were typical Hanson-White parlays. They pride themselves on running a no-nonsense operation. They specialize in "low-tech" businesses, and they don't believe in big overheads. The first piece of SCM business to be sold off was its corporate headquarters leasehold in New York. They never hesitate to cast overboard any unit that doesn't deliver on the bottom line. And if people have to be fired, so be it. (That's why unions representing Imperial Group employees favored the United Biscuit bid.) Sir Gordon and Lord Hanson go about this pruning with cold-blooded detachment. Sir Gordon, for example, has never visited any of the many companies he has bought in the United States. And he's proud of that record. "I don't need to see them," he says. "There are no royal visits."

Lord Hanson doesn't permit the heads of Hanson Trust companies to sit on his board, preferring that they stick to running their companies. They are showered with bonuses for good performance. British investors deciding in 1986 whether to go with Hanson or United Biscuits could not fail to be impressed by these comparisons: Hanson earned $283 million on sales of $3.3 billion in 1985, while Imperial netted $211 million on sales of $6.1 billion, and United Biscuits made $73 million on sales of $2.3 billion.

It's a Yorkshire performance that has them cheering in the City, London's counterpart to Wall Street. As of June 30, 1986, Hanson Trust was ranked tenth in Britain in terms of the market value of its stock: $4.6 billion. It was, in other words, worth more than Beecham, Grand Metropolitan, Rio Tinto-Zinc, Allied Lyons, Barclays, and Lloyds Bank—all of them bigger than Hanson by almost any other measure. In the 1980s Hanson Trust shares split six times and more than quintupled in price. They began trading on the New York Stock Exchange in November 1986. In the summer of 1987 Sir Gordon struck again, moving to acquire, for $1.8 billion, the Kiddle conglomerate, whose parts include Faberware cooking ware, Jacuzzi whirlpools, Globe security guards, and Universal gyms.

Hanson Trust's track record is so clear that the future is predictable. More companies will be acquired, on both sides of the Atlantic. White once said that he wouldn't rest until Hanson Trust was the largest corporation in Britain and the American company ranked among the top fifty in that country.

Access   180 Brompton Rd.
London SW3 1HF, England
(44) 1-589-7070

Hanson Industries
410 Park Ave.
New York, N.Y. 10022
(212) 759-7195

<table>
<tr><td>

Hard Rock Cafe

</td><td>

Sales $26 million
Profits $5 million
Rank World's largest international sitdown
restaurant chain
Founded 1971
Employees 540
Headquarters London, England

</td></tr>
</table>

The Hard Rock Cafe is one of that rare breed, a multinational restaurant chain. Fast-food outfits such as McDonald's and Kentucky Fried Chicken have exported their formulae to many areas of the world, but it's extremely unusual for a conventional restaurant, where customers are seated and served by waiters and waitresses, to expand beyond the borders of one country. The restaurant business is tough enough without putting an ocean between your establishments.

The Hard Rock has done it with a lot of show biz hype. At the start of 1987 Hard Rock cafes were operating in London (where it all started), New York, Los Angeles, Dallas, Chicago, Houston, San Francisco, Tokyo, Stockholm, Amsterdam, Bombay, Bangkok, and Manila. However, even though they all carried the Hard Rock name, they weren't all connected to each other. The ones in Amsterdam, Bombay, Bangkok, and Manila were started up by local entrepreneurs who decided to capitalize on the name (and no, they didn't bother to ask permission). On top of that, the Hard Rocks in Los Angeles, San Francisco, Houston, and Chicago didn't belong to the company that operated the Hard Rocks in New York, London, and Dallas. This is a complicated story.

Two rich American kids, Isaac Tigrett and Peter Morton, were lolling around London in 1970, and, like all American kids abroad, what they really lusted for was a juicy hamburger. Morton, who hails from an old Chicago restaurant family, got his hamburger by opening an American-style restaurant in Chelsea. He called it The Great American Disaster. It was an instant hit. Then he met Tigrett, the son of a wealthy Tennessee financier, John Burton Tigrett, who had moved his family to England when Isaac was fifteen. Isaac went to a private school in Lugano, Switzerland. One of his London gigs was buying used Rolls-Royces and reselling them to Americans.

Tigrett and Morton, each twenty-two years old at the time, hatched the idea for the Hard Rock Cafe and opened it on June 14, 1971, largely with money put up by their parents. The idea had a number of parts. It was a throwback to the old malt shops, featuring a variety of sundaes and shakes alongside any kind of hard liquor you wanted from a well-stocked bar. The menu had a decidedly American flavor: steaks, burgers, barbecued ribs, corn-on-the-cob, apple pie. It had pinball machines and raucous rock and roll music. It was purposely brash, like a highway truck stop. And it had an outrageous decor based on memorabilia from the world of rock and roll music. Among the artifacts that adorn the Hard Rocks today are Elvis Presley's motorcycle and original tour jacket, Chubby Checker's "Checkerboard Boots," Bo Diddley's box guitar, and Ringo Starr's autographed snare drum (Tigrett has been living with Maureen Starkey, Ringo's ex-wife, since 1976).

Location was important. Morton wanted a place accessible to both natives and tourists. Tigrett, a little turned off by the British class structure, wanted it to make a statement, and he was therefore delighted to put a swinging, informal cafe that served hamburgers and didn't have a dress code on Park Lane, a posh street in Mayfair. It was his way of saying, "So there, take that!" Looking back in 1986 Tigrett confessed to an interviewer, "I was a raving Marxist at the time." Three years later, in 1974, he became a Hindu convert. Pictures of his spiritual leader, Sai Baba, hang in the Hard Rocks in New York and London. A vegetarian now, Tigrett says, "I'm here to serve the Lord. I just sell burgers to finance the project."

The Hard Rock turned out to be handy to entertainers who were holed up in Mayfair's posh hotels and who wanted to escape their stiff dining rooms. Steven Spielberg had a hamburger there every day when he filmed *Raiders of the Lost Ark* in London. The place became a hangout for young people and entertainers. Restaurateurs don't make money, however, on people who just hang out. After consulting with a sound engineer at Muzak, Tigrett and Morton turned up the decibel level at the Hard Rock. This meant people had to shout to make themselves heard. It also made them eat faster so that they could escape the noise. In London turnover increased fivefold after the sound level was raised.

The Hard Rock Cafe was a smash hit, but Tigrett and Morton had a falling out and went their separate ways. However, each wanted his Hard Rocks. After various legal squabbles, they agreed on a division of the spoils. In October 1982 Morton opened a Hard Rock Cafe in Los Angeles with backing from show business investors: Spielberg, who never forgot his London hamburgers; studio mogul Barry Diller; actor Henry Winkler; and singers Willie Nelson and John Denver. That was all Morton's show. Two years later Tigrett opened his Hard Rock Cafe on 57th Street in New York City, with comedian Dan Aykroyd as his partner. Morton then opened a Hard Rock in San Francisco in a former automobile showroom. Tigrett opened a huge Hard Rock in Dallas in November 1986.

The ex-partners divided the country in half, with Morton getting the

West and Tigrett the East. But Morton got his hometown: Chicago. And while Tigrett has Dallas, Morton was assigned Houston. Outside the United States Morton has the Hard Rock rights for Australia, Brazil, Israel, Venezuela, and Vancouver, Canada. Tigrett has the rest of the world. They will have to hire a bunch of lawyers to sue people who have appropriated their idea.

Tigrett took his Hard Rocks public in 1984 by selling a small piece of the company to investors in London, where the shares trade on the over-the-counter market. Toward the end of 1986 you could have become a stockholder of Hard Rock Cafe plc by purchasing a share for $1.20, which is what the Hard Rock charges for a Coke Float (Coca-Cola topped with vanilla ice cream). In 1987 Drexel Burnham Lambert sold another small piece of the company to American investors in a $40 million offering. The shares, now traded on the over-the-counter market, came out at $16 per unit (good for five London shares) and quickly plunged to $10.

The prospectus for the U.S. offering disclosed that the Hard Rock does not live by food and drink alone. Each restaurant sells merchandise such as t-shirts, jackets, hats, and watches featuring the Hard Rock logo. These sales account for 46 percent of total revenues. The Dallas restaurant, the biggest with seating for 421, was serving 2,276 diners a day and was taking in $12,586 a day for food purchases, $8,714 for drinks, and $15,914 for merchandise.

The money raised by the U.S. offering was earmarked for new Hard Rocks in Boston and Washington, D.C., and for a separate store to sell Hard Rock merchandise near the New York restaurant on 57th Street.

Hard Rock's biggest stockholder after Tigrett, who owns a third of the shares, is a British investment manager, Terence P. Ramsden. The thirty-five-year-old Ramsden held 22 percent of the stock in early 1987. In 1986 twenty-nine-year-old Thomas J. Weaver III was recruited to serve as chief executive officer of the company. Weaver hails from Tigrett's hometown, Jackson, Tennessee, where he had been the commercial lending officer of the First American National Bank. To induce him to join the company, the Hard Rock gave him options to buy 1.5 million shares at $1.14 each. He was preparing to sell 1.2 million of these shares in the initial U.S. offering, which should have yielded him an instant profit of $2.4 million. Weaver was down for an annual salary of $65,000, plus the company contracted to pay $60,000 a year to a consulting company that he owns. In addition, the Hard Rock gave Weaver an automobile and a $75,000 annual expense account.

One mysterious entry in the ownership records is Libco No. 1, identified as a Liberian corporation which "is not affiliated with any of the

Swedes Insist on Beer Control

One company, Pripps, controls more than half of the Swedish beer market—and it became a state-owned company in 1986 after Anheuser-Busch, the American brewer of Budweiser, made a move to take it over. In Sweden, where there is a strong temperance movement, it was deemed inappropriate for a foreign company to control the nation's largest brewer.

Company's directors, officers or other Principal Shareholders." Libco No. 1 owned 18 percent of all the shares, but these were apparently vested with ML International, a company owned 100 percent by Isaac Tigrett. ML International is a Bermuda-based company that Tigrett and Morton originally established as the owner of the London restaurant. It stands for "Meat Loaf," an abbreviated version of Peter Morton's former corporate name: Don't Let Your Meat Loaf Restaurant Company.

Access   7 Old Park Lane
London W1Y 3LJ, England
(44) 1-629-0382

221 W. 57th St.
New York, N.Y. 10019
(212) 489-6565

Hattori Seiko	**Sales** $6.2 billion
	Profits $20 million
	Rank World's largest watchmaker
	World's largest clockmaker
	World's largest manufacturer of shutters for cameras
	World's largest maker of computer printers
	Founded 1881
	Employees 30,000
	Headquarters Tokyo, Japan

T he Swiss watch industry used to hold an annual chronometry competition that was the most prestigious event in the world of timepieces. Coveted awards were given to watches and clocks based on how accurately they kept time. The Swiss usually swept the boards. In 1968, however, the Japanese planned to enter their newly developed quartz watches in the production-line category. Realizing how accurate the quartz watches were, the Swiss suspended the competition—and never resumed it.

The year 1968 was a turning point in the history of watchmaking: it signaled the end of Swiss domination of the industry. The Swiss knew about electronic timepieces (in fact, the first electronic watch was produced in Switzerland), but, like many who sit on the top of a field, they were complacent, regarding the quartz watch as a fad. It wasn't. Electronic watches were to sweep the world—and the Japanese were in the vanguard. In the vanguard of the Japanese was Seiko, the brand adopted by the Hattoris (*seiko* means "precision" in Japanese).

In an engaging and insightful history of clocks and watchmaking, *Revolution in Time,* David S. Landes points out that watchmaking differs from almost all other forms of manufacturing because it's not bound to any location. "The reasons are obvious," he says. "First, the raw materials used in clock- and watchmaking represent a small fraction of total cost; hence, there is no need to be near the source of supply. Second, the manufacturing process itself uses little fuel or energy; hence no need to be near coal or waterpower. And finally, the transport of the light final product is easy and relatively inexpensive; hence no need to be near the market. In short, clocks and watches can be made anywhere—anywhere, that is, where skilled hands can be guided and supervised by ingenious technical and creative designers."

In practice, of course, they have not been made anywhere. In 1881, when the Swiss were being challenged by the American assembly of watches from machine-made parts (the early leaders were Waltham and

Elgin), Kintaro Hattori, the son of a second-hand goods merchant, opened a clock store in Tokyo. He imported clocks from abroad and sold them to high government officials. Hattori began to manufacture wall clocks in 1892, and three years later he was making pocket watches. In 1913, when Waltham was turning out one million watches and the Swiss more than fifteen million, Hattori made sixty thousand pocket watches and added wrist watches to his line. The Seiko name first appeared on a watch in 1924.

Kintaro Hattori also trained his three sons in the watch business, and Hattori family members continue to rule this company today.

During World War II, when Hattori made fuses and ammunition for the military, the main plant in Tokyo was bombed out. So the company opened its Lake Suwa works in Nagano prefecture 200 miles west of Tokyo. There's an interesting correspondence here to the Swiss experience. Swiss watchmaking was centered in the mountain villages of the Jura range that runs along the French-Swiss border. It's a remote, barren area frequently shrouded in clouds; ideal, some have said, for "theological contemplation." Landes recounts that when watchmaking was introduced into the area in the early eighteenth century, it "drew in all the members of the family except the very young and very old; and it called upon just those skills that centuries of isolation and self-reliance had fostered."

The setting was similar in Hattori's Lake Suwa plant. Marvin J. Wolf, an American journalist, described it in his book *The Japanese Conspiracy*. The Nagano region, he said, is "so isolated that it was unknown to the West until after the turn of the century, when Walter Weston, a British clergyman and mountaineer, first toured this relatively obscure area. Nagano is the heart of the Japanese Alps. . . . Watchmaking and fine instrument manufacturing tucked away in small, neat factories on the outskirts of its villages moved there for safety during World War II and remained. Throughout Japan, the people of Nagano have a reputation—in a nation of overachievers—for a special tenacity."

This analysis of conditions favorable to watchmaking has a mystical tone; but the revolution ushered in by Seiko probably had more to do with high technology than mountain air. Even before the quartz crystal watch appeared, Seiko automated its plants. "The real craftsmanship in Seiko watches," *Fortune* noted in 1965, "comes from the specially designed lathes and machines that turn out precision parts, and the electronic testing devices that insure accuracy."

When the quartz technology was developed for watchmaking, Seiko was quick to embrace it. And unlike the purely electronic houses such as Casio, Sharp, and Texas Instruments, Seiko never forgot that it was a watchmaker. It paid attention to design and fashion and to the way the face of the watch looked. Seiko eschewed the supermarket $9.95 rack. It built its business with the jewelry trade, first tackling the middle of the market ($50 to $300), and then spreadeagling the entire market with a multiple-brand strategy: Lassale and Credor for the high end, Alba and Lorus for the low end, Pulsar for the low middle range.

Seiko produced hundreds of models featuring all kinds of electronic gimmicks—calendars, calculators, world time instruments, miniature television receivers, computers. At Tokyo's 1964 Olympic Games Seiko was, of course, the official timer. It supplied 1,278 stopwatches in thirty-six different models. Since then it has regularly played the timekeeper's role at 150 major sporting events. Seiko's name is up in neon lights all over the world. It spends more than $60 million a year on advertising in the United States.

Seiko introduced its first quartz crystal watch in 1969, and before reaching its one-hundredth birthday in 1981 it had become the largest watchmaker in the world. In 1985 Seiko sold more than sixty million watches, about 15 percent of the world market.

Automation remains a key feature of Seiko's operation. Herb Brody, senior editor of *High Technology,* described in 1986 how a forty-seven-robot line produces the high-end Lassale and Credor watches at the rate of one hundred thousand a month at the Shimauchi factory in Nagano. The robots, which are also made by Seiko, "will pick up a part (such as a gear) from one side of its workspace, transport it laterally, then lower it into the partly made watch; the entire operation takes three to four seconds. About once an hour a new model of watch starts coming down the line. The robot might then have to prepare itself for a different task— say, by putting down its gripper, dipping its bare wrist into a tool pallet, and attaching itself to a screwdriver. A central computer continuously monitors each robot's actions; upon detecting a problem, the computer orders the robots upstream of the malfunction to stop, avoiding a pileup. . . .

"The watchmaking robots execute their tasks with an almost military crispness. When the hand reaches its destination, it stops with barely a shiver."

This watchmaking expertise has spilled into other areas. The Hattori Group produces half of the shutters used in Japanese-made cameras, makes eyeglass frames, and squares off against much bigger companies in the fiercely competitive computer industry. Its Epson printer (Epson stands for "son of electronic printer") is the leading dot matrix printer (the original IBM personal computer graphics printer was made by Epson), and the Epson name graces a line of computers. Seiko claimed in 1986 that the Epson PC was "the second-largest IBM plug-compatible make after Compaq."

One of the Hattori holdings is Wako, probably the poshest jewelry store in Tokyo's Ginza. It's not far from Hattori's headquarters. In Japan Hattori also does such a splendid job marketing Schick safety razors and blades that they are the market leaders in wet shaving. It's one of the few places in the world where Gillette is trounced.

Seiko sells its watches all over the world, the way the Swiss do, but Seiko watches are all made in the automated plants in Japan. However, as the yen shot up in value against the dollar, Epson began to move some of its production to other countries. In 1986 the Japanese plants were turning out 150,000 printers a month, 80 percent of which were exported to the United States and Europe. In 1987 Epson planned to turn out forty thousand printers a month in its Oregon plant and another forty thousand at a new plant in Britain. A small plant in France makes four thousand printers a month.

The organization of the Hattori Group is complicated. In fact, it's not organized. A maze of companies interlock under Hattori family ownership. Only one of them, Hattori Seiko, is publicly traded—and the Hattoris hold about a third of the stock. It has twenty-six consolidated subsidiaries, which employ ten thousand people. The two big, non-consolidated companies (meaning their results are not integrated with those of Hattori Seiko) are Seiko Instruments & Electronics, which has eight thousand employees, and Seiko Epson, which employs eleven thousand.

Heading up Hattori Seiko in 1987 was Reijiro Hattori, sixty-six, grandson of the founder. The two non-consolidated units were headed by another grandson of the founder, fifty-five-year-old Ichiro Hattori, Reijiro's cousin, who died suddenly on May 26, 1987, while playing golf at a resort near Tokyo.

Japan has four companies that make watches—the other three are Citizen, Orient, and Casio—and they have an annual output of 170 million. The Swiss have not disappeared. By units they held 10 percent of the world market in 1986—but more than 40 percent in terms of value. Eighty percent of these Swiss watches were quartz. Their big marketplace winner was the electronic, plastic-sheathed, fashion-designed Swatch. In 1985 120 to 130 assemblers, most of them women, turned out 8.3 million Swatches in Switzerland; meanwhile, two hundred to three hundred workers were producing seven hundred thousand Omegas.

To the Hattoris, electronic timepieces are the handicrafts of the twentieth century. Reijiro Hattori looks across the world and what he sees are millions of wrists unadorned by watches. He likes to make the point that while there are 5 billion people in the world, fewer than 500 million watches are being produced every year.

Access 6-21, Kyobashi 2-chome, Chuo-ku
Tokyo 104, Japan
(81) 3-563-2111

Hattori Corp. of America
640 Fifth Ave.
New York, N.Y. 10019
(212) 977-2800

Heineken	**Sales** $2.3 billion
	Profits $116 million
	U.S. Sales: $300 million
	Rank World's 3d-largest brewer of beer
	Largest brewer in the Netherlands
	No. 1 beer exporter to the United States
	10th-largest company in the Netherlands
	245th on the *Fortune* International 500
	Founded 1864
	Employees 28,400
	Headquarters Amsterdam, the Netherlands

It's risky being the head of an internationally prominent company, especially if your name matches the one on the door. That risk hit Alfred H. Heineken with full force on November 9, 1983, when, right in front of his company's Amsterdam headquarters, he and his longtime chauffeur, Ab Doderer, were kidnapped by hooded gunmen, whisked away to a waterfront hideaway, chained to a wall, and held for three weeks before being rescued by Dutch police. The rescue came two days after a ransom, said to be $10 million, had been paid. Police arrested twenty-four members of the kidnapping gang, all members of one family, and recovered most of the ransom.

The ordeal did not deprive Freddy Heineken of his sense of humor. He reportedly greeted his rescuers with a variation of a well known Dutch advertising slogan: "That's the way to do business—get two and pay for one."

The kidnapping was a worldwide story because Heineken is a worldwide beer brand. The Dutch company is the only brewer with a business that is truly global. Beer is sold under the green-and-white Heineken label in 140 countries. In some places, such as the United States, Heineken arrives from Holland in container ships. In other countries beer is brewed in plants owned wholly or partially by Heineken. And in still other countries, Heineken is brewed under license—by Whitbread, for example, in Britain, and by Kirin in Japan. The company has financial stakes in breweries operating in Canada, Haiti, Brazil, Nigeria, Ghana, Chad, Singapore, Jordan, and Lebanon, among other countries. And in a number of those markets the breweries are turning out local brews—Gulder in Nigeria and Zaire, Primus in Rwanda and Burundi, Kaiser in Brazil. A laconic note in the 1985 annual report disclosed that due to the political situation in Lebanon, "there was a sharp setback in sales of Heineken to that country."

Freddy Heineken, who was sixty years old when he was kidnapped, is the third Heineken to head the Dutch brewery. The first was his grandfather, Gerard A. Heineken, who bought a dilapidated brewery in Amsterdam in 1864 and put the family name on it. He was able to buy the brewery by convincing his mother that if she advanced him the money for the purchase (he was twenty-two at the time), he would be able to improve the product of the brewery, with the result that she might see fewer drunks in church on Sunday because he would convert them from gin to good Dutch beer. (Today Heineken distills the largest selling Dutch gin, Bokma.) The brewery he bought had a history going back to 1592. Another old brewery, De Sleutel (The Key), known as the oldest industrial establishment in the Netherlands, became part of Heineken in 1953 when Freddy Heineken's father, H. P. Heineken, headed the company. De Sleutel was founded in 1433.

Heineken tastes like Heineken wherever it's brewed. One reason is the use of a special yeast developed by Freddy's grandfather, who was a chemist. He hired a pupil of Louis Pasteur to isolate a yeast in 1879, and this original Heineken yeast has yielded trillions of clones which are used in the brewing process. Heineken ships the yeast to breweries around the world. (In 1961, in honor of Freddy's father, the H. P. Heineken Prize was established to recognize outstanding achievements in biochemistry and biophysics. Awarded every three years, it currently carries a cash award of 200,000 Dutch florins—about $75,000 at 1987 exchange rates.)

Heineken and its affiliates brewed more than one billion gallons of beer in 1985, only 15 percent of which was sold in its home country. It has a presence in every European market except West Germany, where laws against additives in beer effectively shut out foreign brews, and it's the number two selling lager in Britain behind Carling Black Label. The United States is probably Heineken's most important foreign market, one that it has cultivated over a number of years. Heineken beer first arrived in America in April 1933 on the heels of Prohibition's repeal. It was the first legal shipment of imported beer in thirteen years.

During a crossing of the Atlantic on the liner *Nieuw Amsterdam* in the mid-1930s, Freddy's father met Leo van Munching, a bartender on the ship. He was so impressed that he hired van Munching as his U.S. distributor. And it was van Munching who, after World War II, built Heineken into a major brand in the United States. It was the first foreign beer to make a serious run at the American market, and it has never been dislodged as the import leader despite a flood of new contenders from all parts of the world. Heineken, in the mid-1980s, accounted for one third of the total import market. And Heineken was the fifteenth largest selling brand in the United States, with a 2.5 percent market share, ahead of

Michelob Light, Meister Brau, Hamm's, Colt 45, and (oh, how the mighty have fallen) Schlitz.

Freddy Heineken was in on the start of this American push because his father dispatched him to the United States in 1946 when he was twenty-three years old. And there he learned about beer marketing at van Munching's side. When he returned to Holland two years later, he told incredulous people in the Heineken brewery about a phenomenon he had discovered in America: advertising. Freddy Heineken also brought home an American bride, Lucille Cummins, who comes from a Kentucky whiskey-making family.

Freddy Heineken pays a lot of attention to his name. In 1981 he told *Fortune* writer David Tinnin, "There is magic in a name, and Heineken is a good name for a beer because it sounds German. In some places, that is an advantage." But, he added, it "must be written correctly." So over the years he has tinkered with the family name. "If you print Heineken in block letters," he pointed out, "you have eleven harsh and unfriendly vertical lines. I rounded and tilted the *e*'s so that they now smile. I made the *n*'s and *k* fat and friendly. The impression is one of hospitality."

And you thought selling beer was easy?

Heineken has expanded its reach by buying other companies and going into other lines of business. In 1985 it was doing more than 10 percent of its sales in soft drinks—it bottles Pepsi-Cola and Seven-Up in the Netherlands—and 6 percent in wines and spirits. In 1968 it merged with another Dutch brewer, Amstel. In 1972 it acquired a majority interest in a French brewery, Albra, which it later parlayed into a 51 percent share of a larger group, Sogebra, the second-largest beer producer in France, holding about 25 percent of the market. In 1974 it acquired a majority interest in an Italian brewer, Dreher. In 1980 it bought a British distiller, Duncan, Gilbey and Matheson. It owns a Greek brewer, Athenian Brewery, and an Irish one, Murphy Brewery. In 1984 it bought a 37.8 percent interest in a Spanish brewery, El Aguila, which holds 20 percent of the beer market in Spain. And in 1986 it acquired a 1 percent stake in its British licensee, Whitbread.

Where beer is drunk, you'll find Heineken.

Heineken shares trade on the Amsterdam Stock Exchange, where they had a market value of $1.7 billion in mid-1986 (127th highest in Europe), but more than half is held by Freddy Heineken through a family holding company. Although it's just a beer company, Heineken tends to have a heavyweight supervisory council (the Dutch equivalent of a board of directors). Members of that council in 1986 included Dirk de Bruyne, former president of Royal Dutch Petroleum; Jonkheer J. Loudon, chief

Beer: The Top Ten U.S. Imports

*1986 sales
(millions of 2.25-gallon
cases)*

1.	Heineken	The Netherlands	35.7
2.	Corona Extra	Mexico	13.5
3.	Molson	Canada	13.0
4.	Beck's	West Germany	11.2
5.	Moosehead	Canada	5.7
6.	Labatt's	Canada	5.5
7.	St. Pauli Girl	West Germany	4.3
8.	Amstel Light	The Netherlands	3.3
9.	Tecate	Mexico	2.5
10.	Dos Equis	Mexico	2.5

Source: Impact Data Bank.

executive of the giant Dutch chemical company Akzo; and Baron H. H. Thyssen-Bornemisza, scion of the German Thyssens, who built an industrial empire of his own and whose villa at Lugano holds the finest private art collection in the world.

Access 21, 2e Weteringplantsoen
1017 ZD Amsterdam, the Netherlands
(31) 20-709111

Van Munching & Co.
1270 Ave. of the Americas
New York, N.Y. 10020
(212) 265-2685

<table>
<tr><td>

Hitachi
Ltd.

</td><td>

Sales $32 billion
Profits $690 million
Rank   World's 15th-largest industrial company
          Japan's 3d-largest company
          World's 3d-largest electronics company
          Japan's 4th-largest computer maker
          World's largest maker of memory chips
          World's 4th-largest maker of semiconductors
          World's 5th-largest color television maker
          Japan's 4th-largest color television maker
Founded   1910
Employees   165,000 (average age: 36)
Headquarters   Tokyo, Japan

</td></tr>
</table>

One of the least known of the world electronic giants, Hitachi makes more than twenty thousand different products, including refrigerators, turbines, television sets, computers, railroad cars, nuclear power plants, robots, electric wire and cables, microwave ovens, batteries, semiconductors, CRT displays, videotape recorders, and electric vibrators.

Hitachi does a third of its business outside Japan and has been moving increasingly into local manufacture. In 1986 the company employed more than four thousand people in the United States at twenty-nine sales and manufacturing subsidiaries in nine states. Hitachi makes television sets and videocassette recorders at Anaheim, California; ignition coils and other automotive components at Harrodsburg, Kentucky; magnets at Valparaiso, Indiana; and tapes at a plant in Conyers, Georgia, outside Atlanta. Hitachi was also turning out television sets and videocassette recorders in Britain and West Germany; and it was one of the first Japanese companies to enter the Chinese market, where it hoped to be producing nearly one million color television sets in 1987.

Although it's clearly a colossus, Hitachi does not have—in the United States at least—the name recognition enjoyed by other Japanese companies. That's because it does not have widely promoted brand names. Hitachi may have made the television sets that J. C. Penney and Montgomery Ward sell in their stores, the videocassette recorders marketed by RCA, and the IBM-compatible mainframe computers sold by a unit of National Semiconductor, but these products do not carry the Hitachi name. And while many Americans may buy Maxell tapes, few would know that this too is a Hitachi product.

Hitachi has developed as a powerful engineering company, adept at selling to other companies but clumsy at selling to consumers. Even in

Japan, where it's prestigious because of its size, the company has the reputation of being a bureaucratic, do-it-by-the-numbers outfit. The company was founded in 1910 by Namihei Odaira, a chain-smoking electrical engineer who was appalled to find Japan so dependent on foreign technology. Odaira managed an electrical repair shop at a copper mine near the fishing village of Hitachi, 125 miles north of Tokyo on the east coast of Japan (Hitachi means "rising sun"). Odaira's first product, which he designed himself, was a 5-horsepower electric motor. When World War I broke out and Japanese power companies found it difficult to get turbines from Germany, Hitachi was there to fill the void. And it went on to make generators, cranes, compressors, pumps, electric locomotives, and other bread-and-butter items of an industrial society.

Odaira stressed Japanese pride, and he built up a strong research capability inside Hitachi, one that has resulted in the company being awarded more than fifty thousand patents. He was also a frugal taskmaster. Norman Pearlstine, now managing editor of *The Wall Street Journal,* profiled Hitachi for *Forbes* in 1979, disclosing that at one point employees were unable to get a new pencil without turning in the nub of the old one and that the company recycled envelopes mailed to it from the outside for its interoffice correspondence. Pearlstine also interviewed two former Hitachi people who painted the company as relatively unsophisticated in overseas dealings. "They are so arrogant about doing things the Hitachi way," said one, "that they don't bother to appreciate the difference between working in Japan and working elsewhere."

This insensitivity (an analyst once called Hitachi "childish") led to one of the most embarrassing episodes in the company's history, when the company was caught red-handed in 1982 paying $612,000 to buy what it believed were IBM secrets. It was a classic "sting" operation. As jubilant Hitachi employees began removing IBM's identification from the materials delivered to them, FBI agents entered the room to announce, "This is the FBI. You're under arrest." It was an ironic twist for a company that had prided itself on developing its own technology. Hitachi pleaded guilty to the charges and was fined $10,000. It also settled out of court a civil action brought by IBM, agreeing to pay the big computer maker fees of $2 million to $3 million a month for eight years to cover use of IBM-developed software. In a statement issued after its guilty plea, Hitachi said it "will take the lessons of this case in complete sincerity and make this case a springboard for our development as a true international enterprise."

In 1985 Hitachi became embroiled in a new flap when it slashed prices on semiconductor chips to expand its share of the American market. The Justice Department investigated the company after a memorandum issued to the U.S. sales staff was leaked to the press. The memo instructed the sales staff on the "10 percent rule," which worked as follows: "Quote 10 percent below competition. If they requote, bid 10 percent under again. The bidding stops when Hitachi wins."

Hitachi executives brushed aside criticism, attributing the memo's language to the "excessive enthusiasm" of "our young American employees."

What is one to do with these difficult Americans? In 1985 Hitachi sent Tsuneo Tanaka to Tarrytown, New York, to head up Hitachi America, and he conceded, in an interview with the *Los Angeles Times,* that "in the past we were too keen to increase sales. We realize the company's behavior in the U.S. society is very, very important. We have to consider the behavior. It must be well accepted." As Americans started to groan loudly about the trade imbalance with Japan, Hitachi sent a "buy America" mission to the United States, visiting forty companies in thirteen states as part of a plan to increase its buying from American companies to $350 million a year. And then, toward the end of 1985, Hitachi set aside $20 million to start a new American entity, the Hitachi Foundation, to give grants in the United States for educational and cultural programs, with the emphasis on increasing understanding between Japanese and Americans. To head the foundation Hitachi recruited Elliott Richardson, who held four different cabinet positions and was U.S. ambassador to Britain during the Nixon and Ford administrations.

In Japan Hitachi likes to take good care of its employees. Between 1972 and 1974 it relocated three plants from maddeningly urban Tokyo to remote rural areas. One plant was moved from the Pacific Coast side of Japan to the Japan Coast side. Of the affected employees in Tokyo, 70 percent agreed to move with the plants. Hitachi ended up relocating six thousand workers and their families. To help employees with housing, workers were offered loans of up to $37,500 to buy a new home. Employees who had to leave families behind were given separate allowances. And for children who could not leave their schools in the Tokyo area, Hitachi provided an allowance for dormitory living. Fifty workers who lived beyond the reach of commuter trains were given automobiles to drive to work.

(It was a little different from the scene in Wales where Hitachi opened a plant to make television sets for the British market. The average age of the Welsh employees was forty, and Hitachi decided that the reason the plant wasn't doing well was that the workers were too old. In 1984 Hitachi sent a letter to the Welsh workers, pointing out to them that older workers are slower, more prone to sickness, have poor eyesight, and are resistant to change. Hitachi therefore invited everyone over the age of thirty-five to take early retirement and make way for more youthful workers. It offered each employee willing to leave a tax-free payment of $2,160 and the chance to nominate a sixteen-year-old school dropout to fill the vacancy.)

In Japan, as the rise in the value of the yen hurt profits severely in 1986, Hitachi slashed the salaries of all its top managers. The sixty-eight hundred people in the upper echelons saw their pay reduced by 5 percent. Board members took a 10 percent cut. Hitachi was Japan's second-largest profit maker in 1985, but it fell to eleventh place in 1986.

Hitachi shares are traded on the Tokyo and the New York stock exchanges (they doubled in price during 1986), and in Japan eight other Hitachi affiliates (Hitachi Cable, Hitachi Chemical, Hitachi Credit, Hitachi Koki, Hitachi Maxell, Hitachi Metals, Hitachi Plant Engineering & Construction, and Hitachi Sales) have their shares listed for trading. The

U.S. Patents Awarded in 1986

	Number of Patents
1. Hitachi (Japan)	730
2. General Electic (United States)	713
3. Toshiba (Japan)	691
4. IBM (United States)	597
5. Canon (Japan)	522
6. Philips (the Netherlands)	503
7. RCA (United States, now part of GE)	484
8. Fuji Photo (Japan)	446
9. Siemens (West Germany)	409
10. Westinghouse (United States)	398
11. Bayer (West Germany)	389
12. Dow (United States)	369
13. Mitsubishi Electric (Japan)	358
14. Mobil (United States)	337
15. Motorola (United States)	333
16. Du Pont (United States)	325
17. AT&T-Bell Labs (United States)	322
18. General Motors (United States)	293
19. Honda (Japan)	280
20. Nissan (Japan)	280

parent company, Hitachi Ltd., owns more than half the shares of seven of these companies and 27.6 percent of the eighth.

At the helm of Hitachi in 1987 was Katsushige Mita, a sixty-three-year-old engineer who worked his way up from the ranks. He moved from head of the computer division to president in 1981. Interviewed in 1986 by Marc Beauchamp of *Forbes,* he said, "We cannot live with tradition alone. I have to make Hitachi a more modern company."

Access   6, Kanda-Surgadi 4-chome, Chiyoda-ku
Tokyo 101, Japan
(81) 03-258-1111

Hitachi America Ltd.
50 Prospect Ave.
Tarrytown, N.Y. 10591-4698
(914) 332-5800

Hoechst	**Sales** $19.8 billion

Sales $19.8 billion
Profits $770 million
U.S. Sales $4.2 billion
Rank World's 3d-largest chemical company
World's 2d-largest prescription drug
producer
7th-largest company in West Germany
4th-largest chemical company in France
18th-largest chemical company in the
United States
World's 2d-largest synthetic fiber producer
World's largest producer of offset printing
plates
Founded 1863
Employees 180,500 (23,000 in the United States)
Headquarters Frankfurt, West Germany

I n 1980 Dr. Howard M. Goodman, a brilliant Brooklyn-born biochemist, journeyed to Frankfurt, the headquarters of this German chemical giant, and proposed a deal. As succinctly described by science writer Katherine Bouton, Goodman's proposal came down to this:

"Give me enough money to create a one-hundred-person department of molecular biology at an American university, guarantee me ten years of unrestricted basic research and, in exchange, I'll let you see what I do."

Hoechst, already the world leader in pharmaceuticals but not in the forefront of biotechnology (an estimated 80 percent of Germany's biochemists fled the country during the 1930s), jumped at the offer and agreed to fund Goodman to the tune of $70 million. It was the largest single grant ever made in biology.

Goodman, who was then at the University of California at San Francisco, had become a luminary in molecular biology in 1977 when he and William J. Rutter headed the research teams that succeeded in splicing a gene so that the "cloned" bacteria could produce human insulin. He did some consulting for Hoechst, which is why, when federal funding for basic research began to dry up, he thought of approaching the German company for support.

Goodman's Hoechst-funded genetic laboratory was established at Massachusetts General Hospital in Boston, the largest teaching facility of Harvard University. He has attracted to the venture top graduates of Ph.D. programs in biology. The arrangement with Hoechst gives Goodman carte blanche to do the kind of research he wants to do. There will

266

be no direction from the company. Any discoveries will be patented by the hospital, but Hoechst, for its $70 million, will have first claim on licenses to make products. The German company also has the right to send up to four of its own scientists to spend time in the lab every year.

Who knows whether the $70 million investment in Howard Goodman will ever pay off? But this is not an unfamiliar gamble to Hoechst. The company financed Paul Ehrlich, the German-Jewish scientist who developed in 1910 an arsenic compound, salvarsan, to cure syphilis. It was a milestone in medical history, marking the first time a man-made compound was able to cure an infectious disease. Hoechst was also the first company to make the diphtheria antitoxin developed by Emil von Behring. And according to a *Fortune* report in 1987, the German company is already benefiting from the work being done at Mass General. Hoechst developed a new weed-killing herbicide, Basta, that has such little discrimination that it also kills healthy crops. The scientists in Goodman's lab supposedly formulated a theoretical answer, based on genetic engineering, that will enable Hoechst to make desirable plants immune to its herbicide.

Hoechst (pronounced "Herkst") traces its origin to 1863 when a chemist, Eugene Lucius, joined with two relatives to form a company to make red dye from a coal tars. Founded in the village of Hoechst on the River Main, Meister, Lucius & Company produced its first artificial dyestuff in 1868, and then, according to a company history, "the firm struck fortune when its green aldehyde dye colored a new gown for the Empress Eugenie of France, wife of Napoleon III. Instead of appearing blue in the light of the Paris Opera's gas lamps, the Empress's green dress remained a vivid, true green." By 1890 the company, then known as Meister, Lucius & Bruning, had developed or reproduced more than ten thousand different dyes. It had also started to make pharmaceuticals. In the early 1900s the company changed its name to Faberwerke Hoechst Atkiengesllschaft—or the Hoechst Dyeworks Inc.

In 1925 the three big German chemical companies—Hoechst, Bayer, and BASF—were combined into the infamous I. G. Farben cartel, harnessed later on to the Nazi war machine. After World War II the three companies were reborn under their pre-1925 names, each an independent entity. Each quickly grew to be bigger than I. G. Farben and bigger than the chemical companies in the United States (Du Pont and Union Carbide) and Britain (Imperial Chemical Industries). The trio has rotated the leadership of the world chemical industry. In 1982 Hoechst was number one; in 1984, Bayer; in 1985, BASF; in 1986, by a whisker, Bayer. Who's first frequently depended on who made the last acquisition. Hoechst surged to the top in early 1987 by acquiring the tenth-largest U.S. chemical producer, Celanese.

Hoechst encompasses 475 companies operating in 140 countries. It does three quarters of its business outside West Germany and has emerged as a worldwide leader in prescription drugs, plastics, synthetic fibers, paints, fertilizers, waxes, and electronic equipment for the printing industry.

France and Germany fought three wars between the late nineteenth century and the middle of the twentieth century, but Hoechst has become one of the few German companies to establish a successful Franco-German venture. Hoechst took a minority position in Roussel Uclaf, a French pharmaceutical company, in 1968. It was the first time that two private European firms had cooperated within the framework of the European Common Market. In 1974, after the death of Jean Claude Roussel, Hoechst increased its stake to 58 percent. This holding was cut back to 54 percent after the Socialists came to power in France in 1981 and the government acquired 40 percent of Roussel Uclaf. So Hoechst is now a partner in France with the French government. Roussel Uclaf is a $1 billion company on its own, one of the leading drug producers in France. It also owns the Rochas perfume house.

Hoechst is more pharmaceutically oriented than its two former I. G. Farben partners, BASF and Bayer. Drugs are, in fact, its biggest business, accounting for 16 percent of total sales in 1985. And that accounts too for its very serious commitment to research. In 1985 it invested $709 million, or 5 percent of total sales, in research. Among its major drugs are the broad-spectrum antibiotic Claforan; the diuretic Lasix; the oral anti-diabetic DiaBeta; the topical corticosteroid Topicort; and the laxative Doxidan.

Hoechst, like Bayer and BASF, now has a major presence in the United States. Even before the Celanese acquisition, it was operating fourteen plants in eleven states. It will now rank as the seventh-largest company in the U.S. chemical industry. The American operations have not been particularly profitable, but Hoechst takes a decidedly un-American view of such matters, a clue as to why it backed Howard Goodman. In 1981 Dieter zur Lye, who was then chief operating officer of American Hoechst, said, "If your goal is to build a business for the 1990s, you are probably willing to sacrifice some of the return on investment for the near future, even for five years."

And that attitude seems to be all right with the Middle East sheikdom of Kuwait, which, through Kuwait Petroleum, bought 24 percent of

Hoechst's stock in 1982. Hoechst is one of the world's largest employers, and it reported in 1986 that its total personnel expenditures for the year was $6.5 billion, or $36,000 per employee.

Access   Postfach 80 03 20
D-6230 Frankfurt 80, West Germany
(49) 69-3051

American Hoechst
Route 202-206
North Somerville, N.J. 08876
(201) 231-2920

F. Hoffmann–La Roche

Sales $5 billion
Profits $250 million
U.S. Sales $1.7 billion
Rank World's 7th-largest drug
producer
World's largest vitamin producer
World's largest producer of
psychopharmaceuticals
World's 2d-largest maker of
flavorings and perfume
fragrances
4th-largest company in
Switzerland
2d-largest operator of medical
test labs in the United States
Founded 1896
Employees 46,500 (12,000 in the
United States)
Headquarters Basel, Switzerland

Illness knows no national borders. And few companies are as attuned to that truth as Hoffmann–La Roche, a company which, though operating from one of the world's smallest countries, became one of the world's leading pharmaceutical houses by stocking a medicine chest that doctors have drawn upon again and again.

Roche, as the company is generally called, was born a multinational shortly before the turn of the century. In 1896, when it was founded in Basel, Roche set up a plant in Germany by the simple expedient of crossing the Rhine River into the neighboring town of Grenzach; otherwise, the drugs exported from Switzerland would have enjoyed very short patent protection in Germany. In its ninetieth year Roche was manufacturing drugs in twenty-seven countries and selling them in more than fifty, and its home country accounted for only 4 percent of sales. The Grenzach plant was still important, it was Roche's second-largest production facility. The first was in Nutley, New Jersey, serving the company's largest market, the United States. Roche's global outlook is reflected in the ability of telephone operators at Basel headquarters to speak at least three languages. Secretaries must be able to write in several languages.

The key to the development of new drugs, as the pharmaceutical industry never tires of telling us, is research—and this is an area where Roche does not stint. In 1985 it was spending $2 million a day on research that it hoped would lead to new pharmaceutical remedies. On the other hand, just to show the power of a top seller in this business, it was taking in more than $1 million a day on the sale of just one drug, Valium, a tranquilizer once described as "America's psychic aspirin." Valium followed another successful Roche tranquilizer, Librium. Valium and Librium are only two of more than one hundred pharmaceutical specialties marketed by Roche. In addition to being one of the world's premier drug houses, Roche synthesizes more vitamins than any other company in the world (the vitamins you use, no matter what brand name they carry, more than likely originated at Roche); operates the second-largest clinical laboratory business in the United States (these are the labs that analyze the blood and urine samples sent by your doctor); and, through its Givaudan and Roure Bertrand Dupont subsidiaries, ranks second in the world in the production of flavorings and perfumes used by food and cosmetics companies (they are the perfumeries of the perfume makers).

Roure Bertrand Dupont, based in Grasse, the floral capital of the south of France, is the oldest company in the Roche group, dating from 1819. Nina Ricci's *Air du Temps,* Yves St. Laurent's *Opium,* Givenchy's *Ysatis,* Dior's *Poison,* and Calvin Klein's *Obsession* perfumes all originated in the Roure labs. Of the eight most successful perfumes in the world, six come from Roure Bertrand Dupont.

Givaudan has a multinational history of its own. Two brothers, Xavier and Leon Givaudan, both chemists, started their company in 1895 in Vernier, Switzerland, a town near Geneva and their hometown of Lyons, France. From the start they were interested in the chemistry of flavorings and aromatics, and they built up a business of international scope. They expanded to the United States in 1924 with the acquisition of a failing synthetic perfume maker in Delawanna, New Jersey. It became their second-biggest facility after Vernier. Xavier outlived his younger brother by thirty years, became the doyen of the French community in Geneva (he never gave up his French citizenship), and died on July 16, 1966, six months short of his one-hundredth birthday. He had stepped down from the active management of the company only three years earlier, at which point it was sold, with his approval, to Roche.

Roche pumped money into Givaudan to modernize its operations. And one untoward result was an incident in Italy that became, in Roche's own words, "a symbol for the ecological dangers inherent in the chemical industry." In 1946 Givaudan had acquired an interest in Icmesa, a small chemical company located eighteen miles north of Milan in the Lombardy community of Seveso. Six years after acquiring Givaudan, Roche bought the remaining shares of Icmesa. A year later it began revamping the Italian plant under a program that called for, among other things, the production of trichlorophenol, an intermediate chemical used to make the disinfectant hexachlorophene.

Disaster struck on July 10, 1976, when a white chemical cloud emanating from the plant dusted Seveso and three other villages (Cesano Maderno, Desio, and Meda) with traces of dioxin, a poison one hundred times more deadly than cyanide. The emissions routed 736 families from their homes, killed thousands of their pets and farm animals, contaminated their crops, triggered skin lesions in two hundred children, and raised agonizing fears that unborn babies might suffer deformities. As time passed, the effects of the contamination seemed to be less grievous than feared, though very little is known of the poison's long-term impact. Roche, in 1984, was claiming that "the only cases today where any visible scarring remains are two children with blisters caused by caustic soda."

Roche's conduct in this crisis raised a lot of eyebrows. It was hours before local authorities were told there had been an explosion. It was days before Roche officials disclosed that the blast had sprayed dioxin over the countryside. It was two weeks before families were evacuated from their homes. And it was years before the area was completely decontaminated. The sophisticated multinational operator Hoffmann–La Roche also reverted to Swiss provincialism in the days immediately following the accident. According to the periodical *Science for People,* Roche's chairman, Adolf Jann, went on Swiss television to declare, "Italians, especially the women, are always complaining. Everybody knows the Italians are highly emotional. . . . Capitalism means progress and progress may occasionally bring some inconvenience."

In 1986, ten years after the dioxin leak, which has never been fully explained, *Wall Street Journal* reporter Philip Revzin returned to Seveso to find a cleared field where a factory once stood and an oak and pine forest where homes and gardens were once located. Seveso no longer has a chemical plant but its name lives on. Revzin told why:

> It was a turning point. The heightened awareness of dioxin led to better tests for it, more widely applied. . . . The Seveso accident led to far-reaching rewriting of environmental legislation in Europe and the United States. It touched off a still-controversial $1 billion research effort into dioxin's effects on humans, and was one of the first cases where a multinational company . . . had to clean up after accidentally creating a serious public health problem.

Seveso was one of a number of controversies that swirled around Hoffmann–La Roche in the mid-1970s.

In the United States, the most pill-popping nation in the world,

Valium came under attack as over-priced and over-prescribed. One study done by the Justice Department's Drug Alert Warning Network found that over a one-year period more than twice as many people sought emergency treatment after taking too much Valium than after taking heroin. The combination of Valium and alcohol was found to be a lethal one. After Congress conducted hearings on tranquilizers, limits were imposed on how many times a prescription could be refilled without the approval of a physician.

As first Librium and then Valium became the preferred choice of doctors trying to set their patients' minds at ease, Roche came under fire on various continents for pricing policies that struck many governments as being unbridled capitalism at its worst. According to estimates made by industry insiders, in the dozen years following the introduction of Librium in 1960 (Valium came along in 1963), the two tranquilizers generated earnings of $2 billion for Roche. In 1973 Britain's Monopolies and Mergers Commission ordered Roche to reduce the prices of Librium by 60 percent and Valium by 70 percent. In West Germany the Federal Cartel Office ordered the company to cut its prices by 40 percent (Librium) and 35 percent (Valium). In Canada Roche was charged with competing unfairly by giving away massive amounts of Librium and Valium to customers such as hospital pharmacies in order to prevent them from buying competing drugs.

Roche stonewalled all inquiries into its profit structure, vigorously defended itself in the courts (the legal battle in Germany went on for six years before Roche got the Supreme Court to overturn a lower court ruling that would have forced it to cut prices by 24 percent), and even broke with the Swiss canon of secrecy to argue its case in public arenas where it insisted on the right to price its products in such a way as to yield the profits needed to conduct research for new healing aids. Along the way it also came up with some novel defenses. In 1975 Jann, Roche's chairman, told a *BusinessWeek* reporter, "How can a government say a drug is too expensive? In England, the actual price for a daily dosage of Valium costs less than a single cigarette. In Switzerland, the daily dosage costs less than a glass of beer." And in 1973 Roche's vice chairman, Alfred Hartmann, told Felix Kessler of *The Wall Street Journal*, "If all the people who take Valium can work an extra two days a year, then British industry and the government would have regained all the extra profits they say we've earned."

Roche also found itself on the losing end of an antitrust action brought by the European Economic Community, which found that the Swiss company had joined with six other companies in a cartel to fix the prices of vitamins. This case resulted in human tragedy. The evidence incriminating Roche came from its own files, which were turned over to the EEC in 1973 by Stanley Adams, a Maltese-born British citizen who had been worldwide product manager for Roche vitamins at the Basel headquarters. EEC officials blew Adams's cover by handing over to Roche the photocopied documents—and then they failed to warn Adams that he might be in trouble if he ever set foot in Switzerland again.

In 1974 Adams did cross into Switzerland from Italy, was promptly clapped into solitary confinement, and charged with selling economic information to a foreign power, which in Switzerland constitutes a criminal offense against the state. Adams's thirty-one-year-old wife was interrogated by Swiss police and told that her husband might have to spend twenty years in jail. Two days later she committed suicide. It took the police two days to inform Adams of his wife's death, and he was denied permission to attend her funeral. Adams was released on bail after three months and fled the country. In 1976 he was tried in absentia, sentenced to a year in prison, and barred from Switzerland for five years. The sentencing came three weeks after the EEC fined Hoffmann–La Roche $385,000 for its vitamin price-fixing.

The Swiss appealed the ruling to the European Court of Justice in Luxembourg, which upheld it three years later but reduced the fine by a third. Meanwhile, Stanley Adams initiated a case against the EEC, alleging that the calamities he had suffered resulted from its negligence in exposing his identity and not warning him about returning to Switzerland. The case reached the European Court of Justice in 1985, and Adams was awarded damages of $715,000.

Having lived down these scandals, Roche was confronted in the mid-1980s with a business problem resulting from the expiration of its U.S. patent on Valium, meaning that it would hence have to compete against lower-priced generic versions of the drug. In Valium's heyday, U.S. druggists dispensed sixty million prescriptions a year; in 1984, the last year without patent protection, they dispensed twenty-five million Valium prescriptions worth $240 million. In anticipation of the end of patent protection, Roche's American subsidiary laid off one thousand employees, or 9 percent of its work force. It marked the first time it had ever resorted to layoffs. Roche clearly needed a new blockbuster drug. Its search has taken it into gene-splicing technology, a new strategy of drug licensing, corporate acquisitions, and collaboration with small, innovative companies. However, it continued to bank heavily on its own research in its own laboratories. Roche maintains ten research centers around the world, and no company anywhere spends a higher percentage of its sales dollar (13 percent) on research.

If the past is any guide, Roche can be counted on to make new breakthroughs. It has a long history of pharmaceutical firsts. Vitamin C was first synthesized in Roche's Basel laboratory. The tranquilizers Librium and Valium emerged from Roche's Nutley labs. And it was the first to come up with drugs effective against nerve-muscle disease (Prostigmin), tuberculosis (Rimifon), Hodgkins disease (Matulane), Parkinson's disease (Larodopa), cystic acne (Accutane), and severe psoriasis (Tegison). Roche was working on a number of frontiers in 1987. It is, for example, one of the major producers of two gene-spliced human proteins, interferon and interleukin-2, which were being tested in humans as possible anti-cancer and anti-AIDS agents. In June 1986 the Food and Drug Administration approved one of Roche's interferon drugs, Poferon, for use against hairy-cell leukemia.

Roche's devotion to research goes beyond immediate commercial interests. It supports two basic research institutes—the Basel Institute for Immunology and the Roche Institute for Molecular Biology in Nutley—where scientists have the right to set their own agendas and where Roche, despite its sponsorship, has no proprietary rights to their discoveries. In 1984 Niels Jerne and Georges Kohler, two scientists who worked at the Basel lab (Jerne was the director for its first ten years), shared the Nobel prize for their research into the structure and regulation of the body's immune system.

The emphasis on research goes back to the company's founder, Fritz Hoffmann, the son of a well-to-do Basel silk merchant. Hoffmann went into business after demonstrating in school that he had no aptitude for science. In 1893, when he was twenty-five years old, his father bought him a partnership in an oldline Basel trading firm, Bohny, Holliger. A year later he and a German chemist, Max Carl Traub, took over a small laboratory that had belonged to Bohny, Holliger and began producing pharmaceutical extracts and tinctures. Traub departed in 1896, and Hoffmann (with his father as a silent partner) continued the business under the new name F. Hoffmann–La Roche & Company. La Roche was the maiden name of Fritz's wife, Adele, the daughter of another Basel silk family. (It's a Swiss custom for a husband to append to his surname the maiden name of his wife.)

Fritz Hoffmann had no training as a pharmacist or a chemist—he hired those people—but he had a keen sense of the shortcomings of the drug industry at the turn of the century. In those days prescription remedies were compounded from raw materials at the pharmacy. No medicine was ever quite the same twice. There were some packaged drugs, but they were patent remedies and usually hokum. Hoffmann's idea was to draw upon research to manufacture reliable drugs, produce them in quantity, and sell them under a company name that would command respect from scientists, doctors, druggists, and patients alike. In his visits to France, Hoffmann had reportedly been impressed by the habit of Frenchmen to order not just cognac but "Fine Napoleon." He proposed to do the same in the drug business and was a pioneer in the use of promotion directed at doctors as well as pharmacists and consumers.

The early years were certainly not easy. While the company expanded to a dozen countries largely on the strength of three medicines—a flavored cough syrup called Sirolin (Thiocol in the United States); Diagalen, a heart medication made of an extract of digitalis leaves; and Pantopon, a painkiller derived from alkaloids of opium—the finances were perpetually rocky. World War I brought the company to the brink of bankruptcy. The Allies looked askance at Roche because its main factory was on the German side of the Rhine. The Germans also looked askance because they suspected Roche was secretly selling its drugs to France. And it was a crushing blow when the Bolsheviks came to power in Russia and seized the Roche plant in St. Petersburg. Russia represented one fifth of Roche's total business.

In 1919 F. Hoffmann–La Roche & Company was recapitalized as a joint-stock company, with a quarter of the shares going outside the family for the first time. There was another recapitalization in 1920 when the number of shares outstanding was doubled, much of the new investment coming from the Bassler Handelsbank, which was headed by Fritz Hoffmann's brother-in-law, Rudolf Alber Koechlin-Hoffmann. (That was the last time the company ever had to raise new capital.) As these new Swiss francs were being pumped into the company, Fritz Hoffmann died of a kidney ailment on April 19, 1920. He never saw the realization of his dreams.

The mantle fell to Emil Christoph Barrell, a chemist who was hired by Fritz Hoffmann in 1896, the year the company was founded. An austere Swiss martinet, Barrell held the chief executive's reins at Roche from 1920 to 1953. Between the two world wars he presided over the widening of Roche's research horizons into biochemicals and synthetic drugs, and he supervised its international expansion. It was during the 1930s that Roche decided to establish research centers abroad, in England and the United States. At the outbreak of World War II it had fifteen factories outside of Switzerland. They usually had some architectural distinction that marked them as Roche outposts. Hans Fehr, a company historian, reported that Barrell kept "a vigilant eye on the timekeeping and work of every employee, from departmental director to factory worker. Hierarchical distinctions were strictly observed; he did not approve of fraternization between different grades and categories of staff." In a eulogy presented after his death at age eighty in 1953, Barrell was characterized as follows: "In his treatment of people he acted more like a surgeon than a physician, but how else could he do his job?"

Increasingly, the star of Roche's international constellation of companies was its American subsidiary in New Jersey. It had begun in 1905 simply as a sales outlet for Roche products, but as World War II approached it gained in importance, becoming a haven for Roche researchers who would have not fared well in a Nazi-occupied Europe. One of these refugees was Leo Sternbach, a Polish Jew who had been working in the Basel lab. After World War II he was to invent Librium and Valium at Nutley. After the fall of France in 1940, Barrell himself moved to Nutley for the remainder of the war years.

The man who had built up the Nutley subsidiary and turned America into Roche's biggest market was supersalesman Elmer Bobst. Hired as a clerk in 1911, he rose to the presidency in 1928, an impressive rise for a man who got his job through his penmanship! Handwriting analysis was then in vogue, and Bobst's written application met with approval. (What his superiors didn't know was that Bobst's wife had penned it for him.)

Bobst ended his career at Roche in 1944 after a clash with Barrell. With so much business and research power concentrated in the United States, Bobst proposed that Barrell transfer part of the shares of the subsidiary to American hands, including his own. When Barrell refused, Bobst quit and launched a second career at Warner-Lambert.

Realizing the tendency of nations to go to war with one another, a tendency that Switzerland has always resisted successfully, Roche hit upon the ingenious plan of dividing the company into two parts in 1926. The original company, Hoffmann–La Roche, has reporting to it all the units in Continental Europe, the Middle East, and North Africa. The other holding company, Sapac, encompasses the Roche companies in North and South America, Asia, Oceania, central and southern Africa, Australia, and Britain. Sapac was originally based in Liechtenstein. However, after Austria was annexed by Germany in 1938, the headquarters was moved across the Atlantic to Panama. And after World War II the registered office of Sapac was established in New Brunswick, Canada, although the head office is supposed to be in Montevideo, Uruguay.

Swiss Police Find New Use for Plastic

Police in a rural district near Basel, home base of Swiss chemical giants, are now accepting credit cards for payment of fines. Patrol cars are equipped with billing forms and printers.

Anyone with the slightest familiarity with Roche knows that all the decisions continue to be made in Basel. How did the Sapac name come about? It stands for Societe Anonyme de Produits Alimentaires et de Cellulose, which indicates that at the time of its formation (1926) there was some idea about going into the food and paper businesses. However, none of that came to pass, and the only thing left from the plan is the acronym.

Hoffmann–La Roche and Sapac are linked structurally as sister companies, that is, they are twins: Each shareholder in Roche automatically receives shares in Sapac. There aren't too many of those sharehold-

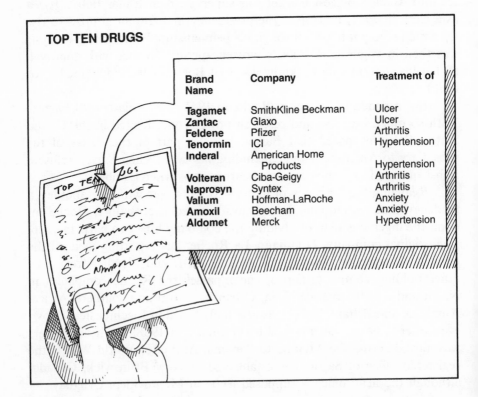

TOP TEN DRUGS

Brand Name	Company	Treatment of
Tagamet	SmithKline Beckman	Ulcer
Zantac	Glaxo	Ulcer
Feldene	Pfizer	Arthritis
Tenormin	ICI	Hypertension
Inderal	American Home Products	Hypertension
Volteran	Ciba-Geigy	Arthritis
Naprosyn	Syntex	Arthritis
Valium	Hoffman-LaRoche	Anxiety
Amoxil	Beecham	Anxiety
Aldomet	Merck	Hypertension

ers. Emanuel Hoffmann, eldest son of the founder, was accidentally killed in 1932. His widow later married Paul Sacher, the founder and conductor of the Basel Chamber Orchestra. Sacher, who was eighty years old in 1986, has long held a seat on the Roche board, along with his stepson, Lukas Hoffmann, onetime president of the World Wildlife Federation, and his stepson-in-law, Dr. Jakob Oeri, a Basel surgeon. The Hoffmann family descendants are believed to control at least half of the stock.

Is it possible to buy any Hoffmann–La Roche stock? Yes, but you need a lot of money. The company has issued only 16,000 voting shares and 61,440 non-voting shares. In 1987 the share price quoted on the Basel Stock Exchange was $100,000—that's for *one* share. It's the highest-priced stock in the world. Roche has no plans to split the stock to attract investors. The company likes to keep to itself, although as each year goes by, more and more information is disclosed in the annual report. However, because there were a lot of complaints about the high price of the shares, it's now possible to buy one tenth of a non-voting share. The price in 1986 was $10,000. Hoffmann–La Roche finds all this amusing. In its company handbook it noted that the clamor for a lower price "led to the creation of the so-called babys. (This grammatical travesty should be overlooked; that's the way they want it at the stock exchange.)"

Access   CH-4002, Basel (Roche is the only private company to have its own official government post office for employees), Switzerland
(41) 61-271122

340 Kingsland St.
Nutley, N.J. 07110
(201) 235-5000

Honda	**Sales** $20 billion
	Profits $585 million
	U.S. Sales $9 billion
	Rank World's largest maker of motorcycles
	World's 10th-largest automaker
	Japan's 3d-largest automaker
	America's 4th-largest automaker
	Founded 1948
	Employees 53,700 (average age: 31)
	Headquarters Tokyo, Japan

One of the canards of our time is that American workers can't build a good automobile. It took a Japanese company to demolish that myth. In 1982 Japan's Honda Motor began assembling four-door Accord passenger cars in a 1.7-million-square-foot plant plunked down in the middle of farm fields thirty miles northwest of Columbus, Ohio. Honda had been producing motorcycles in an adjoining plant since 1979.

Honda was the first Japanese manufacturer to build cars in the United States, and by 1986 the Marysville, Ohio, plant was up to an annual production of 230,000 automobiles. That, together with the 430,000 cars being imported from its Japanese plants, made Honda the top-selling Japanese nameplate in the American market, ahead of both Toyota and Nissan. Moreover, a survey of automobile owners found that people who had bought the American-made Accords were happier with their cars than those who had bought the Japanese-made Hondas. A Honda dealer in Detroit began offering "Made in U.S.A." stickers for Accord bumpers.

Pleased with the quality of the Ohio-built cars, Honda announced in 1987 that it would build an engine and powertrain plant in the state so that engines would no longer have to be shipped from Japan. By 1990 Honda expects its American-built cars to have a domestic content of 66 percent.

The Marysville plant has become a mecca for reporters who want to tell the story of a piece of Japan transplanted to Ohio. Between 1982 and 1986 it was visited by reporters from *BusinessWeek,* the *Christian Science Monitor,* the *Los Angeles Times, The New York Times, Newsday, The Wall Street Journal,* and *The Washington Post.* Their stories told of an immaculate plant, workers clad in white uniforms, a parking lot with no reserved places, an on-site sports complex, a cafeteria where everyone ate (no separate dining rooms for the bosses), a fruitful employee suggestion program, an average wage of $26,000, and the division of line workers into only two job classifications—production associate and maintenance associate (everyone is called an "associate").

Kitry Krause, a *Washington Monthly* writer, summed it up in 1986 by saying that Marysville worked because the workers there were trusted to build productivity themselves. The United Auto Workers targeted Marysville for organizing but never felt strong enough to put the question to a vote by the work force. It did win one small victory by gaining for workers the right to wear UAW caps and badges with their Honda smocks.

Not all the reports from Marysville were glowing. The line moves swiftly and more than one reporter felt the workers were under heavy pressure to keep up. Nearly all the visitors remarked on how young the work force looked. The average age is twenty-eight. Honda was not looking for any battle-scarred veterans of the auto industry. And one worker complained openly to a reporter that Honda "treats us like children."

That Honda would become the first Japanese company to open an auto plant in the United States (others soon followed) is in keeping with its tradition as the maverick of the Japanese car industry. Honda Motor was not part of any prewar *zaibatsu* (ruling economic cliques). It was not programmed by the bureaucrats at Japan's MITI (Ministry of International Trade and Industry). It sprung from the heads of its founder, Soichiro Honda, and his sidekick, Takeo Fujisawa, neither of whom had a college degree, which meant that in America they never would have been hired by a big company and in Japan they never would have gotten anywhere in a big company.

Soichiro Honda is the classic embodiment of the entrepreneur, someone who perceives a social need and proceeds to fill it. He did it first with motorcycles and then with automobiles. In both cases he came up with state-of-the-art products that surpassed, in one way or another, the models previously on the market. And he did it with a global sense. Honda's two-wheeled and four-wheeled vehicles were designed to conquer not only the Japanese but the world market. Honda Motor is the most multinational of all the Japanese automakers. It began exporting to Southeast Asia in the 1950s, and half its motorcycles still go to that area. It was the first Japanese company to build abroad after World War II, putting a moped plant in Belgium in 1962. In 1985 it was manufacturing at fifty-one plants in thirty-one countries. Before joint ventures between car makers of different nations became common, Honda was designing and producing cars with British Leyland. In 1985, when Honda made 1.3 million cars and 3 million motorcycles, 63 percent of its sales were outside Japan. Honda is the only Japanese auto company whose shares are listed on the New York Stock Exchange and the only one whose financial statements are audited by a "Big Eight" accounting firm (Peat, Marwick, Mitchell).

Soichiro Honda is also that rare leader who knows his own limitations. He feels most comfortable dressed in overalls with a wrench in his hand. Early on he brought in Fujisawa to run the business side of the company. Both Honda and Fujisawa also knew when to quit. In 1973, when Honda was sixty-six and Fujisawa sixty-two, they both retired from day-to-day management, leaving the company in the hands of younger people, none of whom is a relative. Nepotism is barred at Honda Motor. Honda explained to writer Mitz Noda why he stepped aside:

> "I lost my sex power. I don't say I have lost all my sex but I must admit frequency of doing and recovery have not been the same as when I was young. Great leaders love sex, and I am not a great leader anymore. I can't drink anymore. Two cups of sake is enough. For entertaining customers and employees, presidents should be able to drink more. I know what I can't do. I don't understand data processing and electronics. Today, automobiles require automation. I am too old to study computers; I have no willingness to learn new technology anymore. Without sex power, drinking habits and work desire, I should quit the life of an entrepreneur."

It was quintessential Soichiro Honda: outspoken, unsparing, racy. He has been called the "Henry Ford of Japan." Both were self-educated tinkerers from humble backgrounds. But they had different personalities. Honda was born in 1906 in a rural village that is now part of Hamamatsu, a southern coastal city on Honshu, Japan's main island. He was the eldest son of a poor blacksmith. In his biography, *Honda and His Machines,* Sol Sanders describes Soichiro's early fascination with motors and machinery. He did poorly in school because "I did not like reading and writing," he told Sanders. "I found writing things down very troublesome." But he retained vivid memories of his little town being electrified and his first views of a car and a plane. In his initial encounter with a car, he became "literally intoxicated" with the smell of the oil that dripped from it. "I put my nose down to the ground and took deep breaths of the smell. I must have looked like a dog, bent over sniffing the oil. Then I rubbed it over my hands and arms."

He was to have many opportunities to repeat that experience. At age sixteen he went off to Tokyo to work in an automobile repair shop, returning when he was twenty-two to open a branch of the Tokyo garage.

Meanwhile, he tinkered. He built a speedboat. He attended mechanical engineering classes at a local technological school. And he raced cars and caroused.

Honda's exploits on the drinking and racing circuits have been well chronicled since he seems never to have been shy about recalling incidents from his hell-raising youth. In 1936, while racing a modified Ford at 100 miles an hour in the All-Japan Speed Rally, his car collided with another vehicle and somersaulted three times. He was thrown clear, unconscious but not seriously hurt. Another time, coming back from a drinking party with geishas, he drove his car off a bridge into a river. He recalled another time when he threw a geisha out of a window; she became entangled in electrical wires, causing a blackout.

Honda always remained this feisty character, gregarious and fun-loving, but a mechanical genius, too. During World War II he made piston rings. When the war ended he was thirty-nine years old and not sure what he wanted to do. So he sold his business and settled down to a year of serious drinking and playing the *shakuhachi* (a bamboo flute). He bought a barrel of pure alcohol, watered it down, and had drinking parties. In an interview with the Japanese theatrical director Keita Asari, he described what happened next:

> "My wife was going out on her bicycle to buy black market rice. But then she couldn't find any more in the area. She got mad and said to me, 'For once, *you* try going out and buying the rice.' No way did I want to do that, so I picked up a little motor, something the army must have thrown away, and I hooked it up to the bicycle for her. I make it sound simple, but putting that motor on the bike took some doing. To make a gas tank I needed a sheet of steel. But ordinary steel would rust and get into the gasoline, so I really wanted tin plating. But with the controls on the economy, tin-plated

steel was hard to come by. So I went to this night market and bought a hot-water bottle—the kind you use as a bed warmer—and made it into a gas tank."

Everyone who saw the motorized bike wanted one, including Honda himself. "I did not want to ride the incredibly crowded trains and buses," he told Sanders. "And it became impossible for me to drive my car because of the gasoline shortage." Thus was Honda Motor Company born. He invited Fujisawa to join him because he realized that while he knew how to make things, he didn't know how "to collect money" from customers. It was Fujisawa who set up Honda's distribution system.

But it was the technology pioneered by Soichiro Honda and his engineering team that made the company a formidable contender. Honda revolutionized the worldwide motorcycle market by designing a lightweight bike propelled by a small but powerful engine. The C-100 Honda, introduced in 1958, featured a "step-through" design similar to that of the American girl's bicycle—the bar that normally ran from the handlebars under the seat to the back of the bike was removed, enabling a rider to stop and put his feet on the ground. The C-100 could also be fitted with a platform behind the seat for use as a delivery vehicle. The C-100, called the Super-Cub, became a worldwide best-seller. Honda alone has sold more than fifteen million of them. In Japan it became, as Sanders put it, "the vehicle of the masses. In the 1950s and 1960s it was a typical scene on a Japanese street to see a motorbike loaded down with father, mother, and perhaps a child or two with an infant stuck between the handlebars. It became the standard method of delivery—for everything from groceries to textiles and lumber and heavier manufactured goods."

The Honda bikes also conquered overseas markets. A U.S. subsidiary, American Honda Motor, was established in Los Angeles in 1959. By 1968 it had sold one million motorcycles in the American market. Honda changed the image of the motorcycle from an artifact of juvenile delinquency to a "cool" accessory of mobile youths, reflected in one of the famous advertising campaigns of the 1960s: "You meet the nicest people on a Honda."

The engineering smarts that pushed Honda to world leadership in motorcycles eventually scored in the automobile field too, although not before some false starts in the 1960s with under-powered cars that failed to win many fans. The N360 air-cooled minicar, introduced in 1966, was described once as a vehicle that "had a habit of turning over at high speeds." Honda redeemed itself in 1972 when it stunned Detroit by introducing the Honda Civic, a car whose midget proportions belied its irreverent zippiness and whose new engine (the CVCC or vortex-controlled combustion engine) solved the pollution problem by producing clean exhaust without the addition of a catalytic converter. Using front-wheel technology, the Civic was one of the first cars to marry the idea of comfort with small size. And it didn't hurt that the Civic delivered better than forty miles per gallon at a time when the OPEC nations were quadrupling oil prices.

Honda followed the Civic in 1976 with the Accord, which taught a new lesson. Automotive journalist Brock Yates, writing in his book *The Decline & Fall of the American Automobile Industry,* identified the Accord as a "milestone automobile" because it shook the industry from Michigan to Stuttgart. The message, Yates said, was this: "The Japanese were obviously no longer limited, either by national perceptions or commercial intentions, to the small, low-priced segment of the car market. The Accord indicated that the Japanese had not only shed their image as manufacturers of rolling tinware but proved themselves capable of mass-producing automobiles that rivaled the quality once considered to be the exclusive property of Mercedes-Benz, BMW, and Porsche."

The Civic and Accord represented team efforts. Honda Motor was not a one-man company. Indeed, Soichiro Honda was the champion inside the company of the air-cooled engine. He had been impressed by the stories that came out of World War II of how the air-cooled Volkswagens had helped the Germans put up such a good fight against the British in the Sahara campaign. It was the younger engineers at Honda Motor who eventually persuaded the company founder to give up on the air-cooled engine. "That," Honda later told an interviewer, "was when I began to feel that I couldn't keep up, that I had reached my limit. I was a beat-up old hulk. So I figured I'd better quit." It was a long way from earlier days when Honda practiced what he called his "thundering method" of education: To get the attention of his engineers, he would rap them over their heads with a wrench.

Honda Motor is the biggest company started in Japan since the end of World War II, and it received crucially important early financial backing from the Mitsubishi Bank, which was willing to take a chance on its two unconventional leaders even though Soichiro showed up for his first meeting at the bank in his regular working uniform of overalls and mechanic's cap. The Mitsubishi Bank remains an important minority shareholder. Today Honda is more than cars and motorcycles. It makes portable generators, general-purpose pumps and engines, and lawn mowers—and these power products bring in more than $1 billion a year in revenues.

Honda managed to avoid entanglements with other Japanese companies, resisting merger overtures from the Mitsubishi Group. He was receptive in 1975 to a proposal from Ford Motor that it supply engines for the Fiesta model that Ford was planning to introduce as its "world car." In his book *The Reckoning,* David Halberstam reported that Lee Iacocca, then president of Ford, flew to Japan to meet with Soichiro Honda, and they agreed on Honda delivering three hundred thousand engines to Ford at $711 apiece. Iacocca was delighted with the deal. But it was killed when it reached the desk of Henry Ford II, who reportedly said, "No Jap engine is going under the hood of a car with my name on it."

Honda had traveled to Detroit a year earlier, in 1974, to receive an honorary doctorate from Michigan Technological University. On that occasion he told the graduating students:

"No matter how much progress and development is made in science and technology or social structure, it must not be forgotten that it is men who operate them. And this cannot be done by one person alone. It takes a heart-to-heart unity of purpose of many people if they are to become 'masters' who effectively operate machines and social structures and thus contribute to mankind. It is with this thought in mind that I tell young employees of my company, 'Don't be used by the machine, use the machine.' "

Access 2-1-1, Minami-Aoyoma, Minato-ku
Tokyo 107, Japan
(81) 3-423-1111

American Honda Motor
100 W. Alonda Blvd.
Gardena, Cal. 90242
(213) 327-8280

Hongkong and Shanghai Bank

Assets $92 billion
Profits $392 million
Rank Largest bank in Hong Kong
19th-largest bank in the United States
World's 14th-largest bank
Founded 1865
Employees 46,000
Headquarters Hong Kong

n the fall of 1983, when people in Hong Kong were nervous about the outcome of the Chinese-British talks on the future of the Crown Colony, one of the city's largest banks, Hang Lung, failed. However, it was rescued by the Hong Kong government and the Hongkong and Shanghai Bank, which agreed to make available senior personnel to straighten out the mess at Hang Lung. In the middle of 1985 a small bank in New York's Chinatown, Golden Pacific National Bank, was closed after the comptroller of currency found it was seriously overextended. To the rescue came the Hongkong Shanghai Bank, which scooped up Golden Pacific for $6.5 million, changed its name, and reopened it with its own managers.

Meanwhile, banks in Hong Kong were having difficulties and Hongkong Shanghai was available once again to play its "good soldier" role. It ferried senior managers to the Overseas Trust Bank, which was taken over by the government to keep it from collapsing, and it teamed up with the Bank of China, an arm of the People's Republic of China, to provide a line of credit for another troubled bank, Ka Wah. At the end of 1985 its 61 percent–owned Hang Seng Bank, one of the largest in Hong Kong in its own right, agreed to acquire a majority stake in still another problem bank, Wing On.

In 1986 its Canadian subsidiary took over most of the assets and liabilities of the Bank of British Columbia.

So if your town has a bank failure, call up the people at Hongkong Shanghai. They don't like to see banks go down the tube, especially if it presents them with an opportunity to extend their sphere of influence. Extending that sphere is what Hongkong Shanghai is all about. It's a bank founded by Britons who conquered Hong Kong; now, using Hong Kong as their base, they're out to conquer the world.

In Hong Kong this bank is king of the hill, holding 60 percent of all the bank deposits, operating three hundred branches, issuing the local currency, and driving every kind of financial vehicle you can think of (insurance, leasing, mortgage lending, foreign exchange). It owns a big merchant bank, Wardley's, and it has an assortment of other interests, including substantial holdings in three shipping lines. In 1986 and 1987 it pocketed $350 million by selling stakes in Cathay Pacific Airways and the *South China Morning Post,* the leading English-language daily in Hong Kong.

The bank's international expansion, which began in earnest after World War II, has carried it into fifty-five countries, where it has twelve hundred offices. It is a major presence in the Middle East via the British Bank of the Middle East, which it acquired in 1959, and its 40 percent–owned Saudi British Bank in Saudi Arabia. Its 20 percent–owned Cyprus Popular Bank has ninety branches in Cyprus. It owns one of Britain's largest stockbrokers, James Capel. It opened its first full-fledged branch in Australia in 1985. It has a 30 percent stake in the Korea International Bank of South Korea.

In short, Hongkong Shanghai has joined the league of supranational bankers who move money across national borders while you are sleeping. In 1985 it launched Hexagon, an electronic banking system for corporate customers who can now punch up on their computer monitors detailed information about their bank accounts around the world and then send instant instructions to any branch hooked into the system. (Example: "Attention Bahrain, please send 80 million Eurodollars to the Channel Islands.")

The Hongkong Shanghai Bank invaded the United States in 1980 by acquiring 51 percent of Buffalo-based Marine Midland, then the twelfth-largest bank in the United States. The move was not exactly welcomed with open arms. Muriel Siebert, banking superintendent of New York State, refused to approve the foreign takeover, arguing that the strong international orientation of the Hong Kong bank might dry up Marine Midland's loan funds in the state. But they aren't Hong Kong traders for nothing. Hongkong Shanghai ran an end-run around Siebert by getting Marine Midland to convert from a state-chartered to a federally chartered institution. The feds gave the nod to the $230 million bid, dismissing one letter sent to the comptroller of the currency alleging that the Hong Kong bank "is acting as agent for the British monarchy in the management and financing of the worldwide opium trade."

The objector appeared to have been reading his history books. The Hongkong Shanghai Bank was, as *The Economist* once put it, "conceived on a slow boat to China in the nineteenth century when the British Empire was reaching its apogee." Indeed, one of its first missions was to finance the British opium trade in China. It financed other trade as well, notably silk and tea. The early leader of the bank was—as is the case with many overseas British commercial ventures—a Scot, Thomas Sutherland.

As an instrument of British imperialism, the bank grew to become a commercial powerhouse in Southeast Asia, surviving various calamaties, among them a couple of Sino-Japanese wars, two Chinese revolutions, and two world wars. During World War II, when the Japanese occupied Hong Kong, the bank moved its headquarters to London. After the war it returned to Hong Kong ready to play its role as bankroller of new businesses. The triumph of Mao Tse-tung's Communist forces in 1949 shut the bank out of mainland China, and so it turned to financing Chinese businessmen who had fled China and wanted to start factories in Hong Kong. In 1976 Guy Sayer, who had risen to the chairmanship of Hongkong Shanghai after service with the bank in Peking, Tientsin, Osaka, Kota Kinabalu (Malaysia), and Rangoon, explained to *Fortune* writer Louis Kraar how it was at that time: "We understood the risks because we knew the Chinese. No bank in New York would have done what we did." What it did was grease the financial wheels for an ascent that established Hong Kong as one of the world's major economic forces. Between 1945 and 1986 Hong Kong's population soared from 500,000 to 5.5 million.

So this is a bank tied intimately to the fortunes and misfortunes of Hong Kong, a territory making up the southernmost tip of China. It became a British colony in the nineteenth century in three steps. Hong Kong Island itself was ceded to Britain by a weak China in 1842. In those days the British were interested in pushing opium as a way to pay for tea. China wanted to stop the opium trade, but Britain had the guns to make the Chinese say uncle. In 1860, after another conflict, Britain scooped up the Kowloon Peninsula across the bay from Hong Kong Island. And in 1898 they took an even bigger slice, acquiring a ninety-nine-year lease on the New Territories, a 350-square-mile area stretching from Kowloon to the Chinese province of Guangdong. Those three pieces make up what is today called Hong Kong. The British lease is up in 1997, and the agreement worked out in 1984 between China and Britain calls for the following:

- On July 1, 1997, China will reassume sovereignty over all of Hong Kong.
- Hong Kong's current social and economic systems—its unbridled capitalism, if you will—are to remain in place for the next fifty years.
- The people in Hong Kong will become Chinese citizens but will be guaranteed freedom of speech and press. The legislature will be elected.

So Hongkong Shanghai figures it will be around well into the next century, doing what it has been doing since 1865. Hong Kong is a Chinese city, but the Hongkong Shanghai bank is a British institution. *Very* British. Few of its officers and directors are Chinese. The bank has long recruited its management cadre from Britain—half of them from elite British institutions such as Oxford and Cambridge. Once recruited, they are posted to various parts of the world and expected to remain with the bank the rest of their working careers. Retirement age is fifty-three. As recently as 1984, according to *New York Times* reporter James Sterngold, on Saturdays, a half day at the bank, a trolley was still coming around from which workers could order a pink gin. William Purves, a Scot who succeeded Michael Sandberg as chairman in 1986, told Sterngold, "One of my great regrets now, a real mistake that we have got to do something about, is bring in more senior Chinese staff. That has to be remedied at some point if we're going to be a successful bank here."

While Hongkong Shanghai has developed an international network of some significance (it's now the largest foreign bank in half a dozen countries, including the United States), it seems that it can't go home again. In 1981, just after the Marine Midland play, it made a $1 billion bid to take over the Royal Bank of Scotland—a little like the prodigal son coming home. But the Scots beat back this takeover attempt, using the same reasoning that Muriel Siebert had used in New York: Hongkong Shanghai had international interests that were not congruent with the domestic interests of Scotland. On the other hand, once a China hand, always a China hand. In 1985 Hongkong Shanghai became the first foreign bank allowed to open a full-service branch in the People's Republic.

Hongkong Shanghai is a huge financial institution, but getting a clear fix on it is not easy. The bank's reports are skimpy, so meager that *Forbes* magazine doesn't list it on its roster of the largest international companies; and *BusinessWeek,* while listing the bank, is unable to present figures on revenues and margins. In its appraisal of the bank as an investment opportunity, Merrill Lynch said, "The earnings of the Group are difficult to predict with great accuracy because of the presence of inner reserves. . . . Published net profits are stated after transfers to inner reserves whose amount in any one year can at best be a matter of conjecture." Hongkong Shanghai itself admits to being the fourteenth-largest banking group in the world (it was seventy-fifth in the late 1970s and one hundred tenth in the mid-1970s). One figure that it does report regularly—aftertax profits—is very impressive. Its 1985 profits of $349 million were topped by only nine other banks in the world; excluding U.S. banks, by only four.

If the bank's financial statements are fuzzy, there is nothing unclear about the statement it made in 1986 when it opened its new headquarters building at the same address it has had since 1865: Number One Queen's

Road Central. A forty-two-story high-tech structure that looks a little like an oil drilling platform, it was designed by the British architect Norman Foster and it came in as perhaps the most expensive building in the world: a trifle over $1 billion, counting all the professional fees and financing costs.

A shimmering structure of steel, glass, and aluminum, Foster's building is like an anatomical design with a glass skin: you can see all the innards. It features a 170-foot central atrium that rises eleven floors. The floors themselves are prefabricated elements suspended from trusses. Banking halls on either side of the atrium have built-in solar calculators for customers to use and a row of eighty-eight teller positions. A sunscoop suspended on the outside of the building directs sunlight through curved aluminum mirrors down through the atrium to a plaza. There is no central service core to the building so that lavatories, for example, are provided by modules that were built in Japan and dropped in—they are similar to bathrooms on airplanes.

The building has twenty-three high-speed elevators that stop at every five floors (Foster wanted people to move about the building a lot to meet colleagues and customers). He conceived it as a series of villages. To do that he relied heavily on escalators, sixty-two of them, more than any other building in the world, including two freely supported ones which, at eighty-one and one-fourth feet, are the longest in the world. And they too are encased in glass sheathing so that you can see the inner workings. Standing at the entrance of the building are the two bronze lions that have guarded the entrances to previous Hongkong Shanghai headquarters buildings.

The bank always has had a penchant to make a statement with its buildings. The one opened in 1886 had verandahs and a domed banking hall that smacked, as the *Financial Times* said, "of late nineteenth-century colonial pomposity." The twenty-two-story building opened in 1935 had, at its center, a huge banking hall with a barrel vault lined in mosaics. It was the tallest building between Cairo and San Francisco and fifteen years later it was still twice as tall as any building in Hong Kong.

Hongkong Shanghai's new building is once again the tallest in Hong Kong, befitting an institution that, in its hometown, is simply called "The Bank." But it won't be the tallest for long. The Bank of China, an arm of the People's Republic of China, is putting up its own headquarters building a quarter of a mile from Norman Foster's structure. To be opened in 1988, it will go up seventy-two stories. It too is expected to come in at over $1 billion. The architect is the Chinese-American I. M. Pei. Hongkong Shanghai people put it down as "just a conventional skyscraper."

Hong Kong's Biggest Business: Betting

The biggest business in Hong Kong is betting on horse races. The colony has two race courses, one the historic Happy Valley on Hong Kong Island, which held its first meeting in 1846, the other a sleek track at Sha Tin in the New Territories, which opened in 1978. Racing in Hong Kong is under the jurisdiction of the Royal Jockey Club, which also runs 128 off-track betting parlors. In 1986 the club collected betting revenues of $2.8 billion, which tops the sales of any Hong Kong–based company. The club employs twelve thousand people. Hong Kong bettors back their hunches by wagering about $40 million a day, or more than $5 million for each race run. The Happy Valley course holds about forty-two thousand people. On an average day the punters will plunk down $240 apiece in bets.

Access   1 Queens Road Central
Hong Kong
(852) 5-267111

5 World Trade Center
New York, N.Y. 10048
(212) 839-5000

Hyundai	**Sales** $14 billion
	Profits $100 million
	Rank South Korea's 2d-largest company
	South Korea's largest construction
	company (one of the world's largest)
	South Korea's largest shipbuilder (one of
	the world's largest)
	South Korea's largest automaker
	Founded 1947
	Employees 156,000
	Headquarters Seoul, South Korea

Korea, a 600-mile-long peninsula jutting out from Manchuria, is one of the oldest countries in the world, dating back to the seventh century. However, from 1905, when the Russian-Japanese war ended, until 1945, when World War II ended, Korea was forcibly occupied by Japan. The Japanese in fact formally annexed Korea in 1910. Given that history, it's no mystery why South Koreans both relish and bridle at the description of their country as the "new Japan."

The Republic of Korea, which governs the southern part of the Korean peninsula, was created in 1945 when Korea was partitioned into two zones along the 38th parallel. Five years later the two zones fought a war that ended in 1953. The appellation, "new Japan," refers to the remarkable economic development that has transformed this small country (population: forty-two million) into an industrial powerhouse. The components of that development are hard work, low wages, a repressive government and, yes, a determination to show the Japanese what the Koreans can do.

One of the principal engines of the Korean economic miracle is the Hyundai Group, a collection of thirty-two companies that makes a wide range of products—ships, bridges, buildings, cars, cement, steel, chemicals, oil drilling platforms, microchips, sneakers, pipes, furniture, locomotives. They add up to sales of more than $14 billion. The Hyundai Group constitutes the second-largest enterprise in Korea. In 1986 *Fortune* ranked it as the twenty-fifth-largest industrial company in the world outside the United States. Hyundai generates 5 percent of Korea's gross national product. Eight Hyundai companies have their shares traded on the Korean Stock Exchange.

As huge as Hyundai is, it's the lengthened shadow of one man, Chung Ju Yung, the eldest son of a poor rice farmer, who started a construction company after World War II and never stopped building.

His appetite for work is legendary. It's not unusual for him to be up at dawn, and he's liable to show up at any Hyundai installation anywhere to cheer the troops on. Chung is known as a man willing to tackle the impossible (and unwilling to accept "no" from a subordinate). The World Bank reportedly told General Park Chung Hee, the president of Korea until he was assassinated in 1979, that it would not be possible to build a Seoul-Pusan expressway at the low price Chung quoted. Hyundai Engineering and Construction proceeded to build it at the quoted price. Korea had never built huge ships until Chung put a shipyard complex into Ulsan that became the largest in the world, covering 5 million square meters (53.7 million square feet). Chung was not fazed by lack of shipbuilding experience. He sent sixty Koreans to naval architectural schools in England.

In the Middle East, where Hyundai became one of the largest construction companies, competitors used to say that the Koreans bid on a project first and learned how to build it later. Hyundai landed its first construction gig in the Middle East in 1974 when it signed on to build a $140 million drydock repair yard in Bahrain, a small island in the Persian Gulf. Hyundai sent one thousand workers there to do the job. They finished four months ahead of schedule. Saudi Arabia immediately gave Hyundai a $1 billion contract to build an industrial port in its new city of Jubail.

In 1978, by which time Hyundai had contracts all over the Middle East, *New York Times* correspondent Youssef M. Ibrahim presented this American oilman's graphic description of Hyundai construction crews at work in the Middle East:

> "These guys are something else. They go in there like a tornado. They bring their own workers from engineers on down, their own clerks, cooks, food, doctors, clothing, movies. They build their own housing. They do the job faster than anyone else, working fourteen-hour shifts, seven-day weeks. They only mix with one another, and once they are through with one job, they're moved on to another or sent back home. They're like a disciplined, paramilitary, single-minded, self-sufficient machine—simply amazing."

Chung has been called the Korean John D. Rockefeller, Henry Ford, and Henry Kaiser all rolled into one. He and his family are the largest stockholders in the Hyundai companies. How much wealth that amounts to is not known but could make Chung a candidate for the richest man in the world. In 1978 *Fortune* reported that his 1977 *income* totaled $16.4 million and that he paid $8 million in taxes. In 1983 *The Wall Street*

Journal cited estimates that he made "$2 million a year." Actually no one outside of Chairman Chung really knows what these figures are.

Hyundai companies are known as brash, bruising competitors. In 1980 the construction company was barred from doing business in Saudi Arabia after the Hyundai manager there was found guilty of trying to bribe a government official. The manager was sentenced to thirty months in jail, and Hyundai was fined $90,000. Hyundai construction crews have since returned to Saudi Arabia, and in 1985 the company built and donated to the capital city of Riyadh a Korean garden to symbolize the amity between the two countries.

Almost no business escaped Chung's attention. In the early 1980s he decided to make Hyundai a factor in the electronics industry, focusing at first on production of semiconductors. As part of that plan, Hyundai opened a $40 million plant at Santa Clara in California's Silicon Valley in 1984. It was a twin to a Hyundai plant in Inchon, South Korea. Then came the recession in the semiconductor industry. On September 30, 1985, two hundred workers arriving at the Santa Clara chip-making plant found the doors locked. The plant was closed, with workers receiving severance pay of two weeks. When *San Francisco Chronicle* reporter John Eckhouse went to Korea in 1986, J. W. Lee, Hyundai's director of strategic planning, told him that the company was not giving up on the semiconductor business, just on the American plant. "In Korea," he explained, "employees willingly work long hours, late at night, Saturday, even Sunday. But we found we could not expect that in Silicon Valley."

Hyundai is not giving up on electronics. The Blue Chip IBM-compatible personal computer that began moving into K mart, Target, and other American discount houses in 1986 was supplied by Hyundai. It undercut by $350 the successful Leading Edge computer, which was supplied by Hyundai's Korean rival, Daewoo.

The management style at Hyundai is authoritarian. When Chung comes into a room, subordinates stand up and salute. He is always referred to as "the chairman," even in his family. Karl Moskowitz (no relation to the author), president of Korea Strategy Associates, a consulting firm with offices in Cambridge, Massachusetts, and Seoul, says, "Korean companies do not have an egalitarian or consensus-oriented management style. Korean companies—and all Korean organizations—have a top-down, authoritarian style in which the 'consensus' is what the boss says it is. Period." Harry G. Kamberis, an AFL-CIO representative in Seoul, calls Hyundai "one of the most antilabor of large companies here." In reaction to these policies, Hyundai workers went out on strike in 1987, returning only after the Korean government pressured Chung into recognizing a union.

Chung's five brothers, six sons, and son-in-law have all had their shot at running different parts of the Hyundai empire. (Fortunately, there are plenty of Hyundai companies to go around.) On January 28, 1987, the seventy-one-year-old Chung announced what few people believed, that he was relinquishing control to his younger brother, fifty-eight-year-old Chung Se Yung. Reporters in Seoul believe the heir apparent to be Chung's eldest son, forty-eight-year-old Chung Mong Koo, who chairs five of the Hyundai companies.

The newest Hyundai facility in the United States is at Garden Grove in Orange County, California, where the Koreans have taken over an abandoned waterbed warehouse and turned it into a dull, gray headquarters of Hyundai Motor America, importer of the Excel automobile. With the help of Japan's Mitsubishi Motors, which has a 15 percent holding in Hyundai Motor (one of the few foreign investors Chung has allowed in), Hyundai has become the largest automobile manufacturer in Korea. And the company scored a coup when its Pony became the top-selling import in Canada in 1985. In 1986, with more than one hundred American dealers signed up, Hyundai began bringing in on its own ships the Excel, a front-wheel compact powered by the same engine that's in the Mitsubishi-built Colt. (In the United States, the "Pony" name is registered by Ford.) The Koreans didn't claim the Excel was superior mechanically. It went right to its advantage: price. Thanks to the low wages in Korea (assembly line workers at the Hyundai auto plant in Ulsan make three dollars an hour), the Excel could be sticker-priced at $5,000, well under any Japanese import. The Mitsubishi people from Japan were amazed to find that the Hyundai assembly line moved faster than their own.

To market the car in America, Hyundai raided the nearby headquarters of Toyota in Torrance, California. It came away with a couple of dozen people, topped by Max Jamiesson, who had been with Toyota for fifteen years and with Ford for ten years before that, and who was named second in command of the Hyundai invasion of the United States. One thing bothered Jamiesson and his ad agency, Backer & Spielvogel, known for its zany Miller Lite commercials. That was the name, "Hyundai," which means "modern" in Korea, and is pronounced, "hi-un-die." Jamiesson went to Korea and told Chairman Chung that he felt it would be better if the car could be called "Hunday" to rhyme with Sunday and Monday. Chung, ever the pragmatist, told Jamiesson, "Max, if you can sell one hundred thousand cars in America, you can call it anything you want." In 1986 Hyundai sold 168,882 cars, the most ever sold by an import in its first year.

As the company set this record, S. H. Park, the Korean who is president of Hyundai Motor America, announced that his company would contribute $1 million toward the construction of a memorial in Washington, D.C., to honor Americans who fought in the Korean War. In a letter to President Reagan, Park said, "As a boy of eight, I remember the outbreak of hostilities and my father going off to fight the Communist invasion. Our family were refugees moving often as the tide of the war shifted. I will never forget the personal kindness shown to us by the GIs we met."

Access   140-2 Kye-Dong, Chongro-ku
Seoul, Korea
(82) 2-741-4141/70

One Bridge Plaza N.
Fort Lee, N.J. 07024
(201) 592-7766

Imperial Chemical Industries

Sales $15 billion
Profits $880 million
U.S. Sales $3 billion
Rank World's 5th-largest chemical company
Britain's 4th-largest company
World's largest paint maker
World's largest maker of industrial explosives
World's 3d-largest agro-chemical producer (fertilizers, herbicides, pesticides)
Britain's 2d-largest drug maker
World's 19th-largest drug maker
World's 3d-largest maker of plastic acrylics
World's 2d-largest maker of polyester film
World's 2d-largest maker of polyurethane (insulation, shoe soles)
3d-largest synthetic fiber producer in Europe
Founded 1926
Employees 121,800 (20,000 in the United States)
Headquarters London, England

The chemistry may at last be right for Britain's lead-footed giant, Imperial Chemical Industries, known almost universally as ICI. In 1986 the company marked its sixtieth year by vaulting into the number one spot among the world's paint makers with the $580 million acquisition of Glidden paints of the United States. It was the flashiest move yet in a long overdue campaign to get Britain's largest industrial entity back into fighting trim. The deal underscored ICI's persistence. It had made a previous pass at Glidden, only to be rebuffed by the paint company's parent, SCM. Another British company, Hanson Industries, then succeeded in a hostile takeover of SCM. Hanson was happy to peddle Glidden to ICI. Call it British solidarity.

Glidden's decorative paints (third in the United States behind Sherwin Williams and PPG Industries) joined an ICI lineup that includes plastic bottles, synthetic silk, antacid tablets, fertilizers, nylon, explosives, heart medications, chlorine, sporting ammunition, animal feeds, pesticides, and seeds. Such is the diversity possible when you are one of the world's largest chemical producers. In fact, ICI make hundreds of products besides the ones named above, and it markets them all over the globe.

Although it's the youngest of the international chemical giants (Bayer, BASF, Du Pont, and Hoechst are the top four), ICI used to be the world leader. It dropped out of first place in the 1970s, an apparent victim of myopia and hardening of the arteries. The shocker—to British business circles—came in 1980 when the company reported the first loss in its history and cut its dividend. The directors decided then that a change was in order. And to bring it about they went to John Harvey-Jones (later Sir John), who was then one of ICI's three deputy chairmen. He was named chairman in 1981, after which the other two deputy chairmen quit.

Harvey-Jones became the delight of the British press, since he doesn't fit the mold of an uptight, conservative chief executive of a major corporation. It was rare for a story about ICI to run in *The Economist, Financial Times,* and other British publications without some mention being made of Harvey-Jones's shaggy hair and loud ties. Most top executives in Britain are Tories; Harvey-Jones is a member of the new Social Democratic party. He was nearly always eminently quotable. In 1982 he gave a press conference in Brussels where he was asked why the recession had hit Britain harder than other countries. "Well," he quipped, "we've got Thatcher" [a reference to Conservative Prime Minister Margaret Thatcher]. Two years later a *Forbes* reporter asked him how ICI was holding up in the recession. He said, "These have been bloody uncomfortable years."

His sense of humor belied his readiness to make tough decisions to get ICI moving again. He was not a newcomer to the company, although his route to the top was unorthodox. Sir John arrived at ICI in 1956 after twenty years with the Royal Navy in school (he entered a naval preparatory academy when he was twelve years old), aboard submarines (he served in World War II while a teenager), and in naval intelligence work (he spent time in the Soviet Union and was once an advisor to the British cabinet on Soviet affairs). The memory of twice being aboard sinking ships may have flashed through his mind when he took the helm at ICI.

Once in command Harvey-Jones hacked away at the layers of management (the number of senior managers was reduced from one hundred sixty to twenty), closed dozens of plants at home and abroad, and eliminated more than thirty thousand jobs, enraging the trade unions by failing to consult with them before announcing what the British call "redundancies." He was, however, more than a cost-cutter. He had a strategic plan one of whose planks was to make ICI less dependent on low-margin bulk chemicals. When low-priced imports crippled ICI's ability to make money as a volume producer of polyester, he decided to jettison bulk production of the synthetic fiber the company had introduced during World War II. He also ended production of polyethylene. The British press joked that Harvey-Jones had cut everything except his hair.

"For every step we had to make backwards," Sir John once explained, "we tried to take another forward in a new direction." For example, ICI found new high-tech uses for polyester fiber as a film base for video and cassette tapes. With renewed stress on research, ICI perfected a water-based paint that eliminated the pollution problems car makers had with popular metallic finishes. Chemists also came up with a product that can keep jet fuel from igniting in a crash and a washoff paint to replace the usually hard-to-remove protective wax coating for automobiles headed to dealers (it publicized the latter product by using it to mark the route for the 1985 London marathon).

ICI also poured money into pharmaceuticals, achieving great success with its heart drugs, Inderal and Tenormin (they were both on the top ten list of the world's best-selling prescription drugs in 1985). Another widely recognized ICI brand is the antacid Mylanta.

Sir John was never loathe to buy his way into markets. In 1985 (the year he was knighted), he had ICI ante up $750 million to acquire the chemical operations of the Beatrice Companies. This gave ICI entree to a chemical field known as "advanced materials"—composites and thermoplastic compounds used in the aerospace and defense industries. In that same year ICI acquired another U.S. company, Garst Seed, which gave it a base for biotechnology research.

These acquisitions advanced another Harvey-Jones goal: broaden ICI's international reach, especially in the American market. Under his prodding ICI has more than tripled its sales in the United States, where it has manufacturing plants in twenty states, directed from a command post in of all places Wilmington, Delaware. (Those chemical companies do stick together.) ICI's stock was listed on the New York Stock Exchange in November 1983. American investors hold 15 percent of the total.

ICI's global expansion caused some British commentators to suggest that the company swap the "imperial" in its name for "international." The company now does more than 75 percent of its business outside Britain. There were historical reasons for the imperial designation. ICI was formed in 1926 by the amalgamation of four companies: British Dyestuffs, Brunner, Mond & Company, Nobel Industries, and United Alkali. Harry McGowan, who later became a peer, engineered the four-way merger to keep the British companies from being taken over by U.S. and German firms. McGowan then joined with Du Pont of the United States and I. G. Farben of Germany in a cartel-type agreement that divided up the world. ICI got Britain and British Commonwealth countries, agreeing to stay out of the United States and Continental Europe, while Farben and Du Pont agreed not to confront ICI in the British empire.

It was that kind of legacy that Harvey-Jones had to repudiate. His effort to transform ICI into a multinational operator was reflected in the unusual composition of the board of directors. Sir John brought onto the board Walher Kiep, head of Gradmann and Holler, a big West German insurance firm; Shoichi Saba, president of the Japanese electronics giant Toshiba (he's the first Japanese executive to sit on the board of a British company); and Thomas Wyman, who, when he was named a director in the summer of 1986, was chairman of CBS. Six weeks later Wyman was fired by CBS, but he's still on ICI's board.

Harvey-Jones left the ICI chairmanship on April Fool's Day in 1987, having reached the retirement age of sixty-two. He had already picked his successor, Denys Henderson, a Scottish lawyer whose father had been a tea planter in Ceylon (now it's called Sri Lanka). At fifty-four Henderson was the youngest chief executive ICI had ever had. After his selection was announced, Henderson said he would continue Sir John's policies (what else could he say at that point?). *The Economist* said, "He is unlikely to emulate Sir John's flamboyant style, particularly in neckwear."

One policy he did emulate was expansion by acquisition. In 1987 ICI acquired Stouffer Chemical of the United States to lift it into third place in the world business of herbicides and pesticides. "We believe very strongly that the good farmers will be the most efficient ones," Henderson said, "and those will be the ones who use agrochemicals."

Access   Millbank
London SW1P 3JF, England
(44) 1-834-4444

645 Fifth Ave.
New York, N.Y. 10022
(212) 644-9274

IRI

Sales $37.6 billion

Profits $225 million

Rank Largest company in Italy

World's 11th-largest industrial company

World's largest state-owned company

Biggest non-oil company outside the United
States

World's 3d-largest steel producer

Largest banking group in Italy

3d-largest company in Europe

11th on the *Forbes* International 500

Founded 1933

Employees 440,000

Headquarters Rome, Italy

RI, which stands for Instituto per la Ricostruzione Industriale (Institute for Industrial Reconstruction), was created by Benito Mussolini to rescue failing Italian banks during the great Depression of the 1930s. It wasn't only Italian banks which were having a hard time then. Italian companies were in hock to the banks, with the result that IRI found itself in control of half of the national economy. The original idea was to return the companies to the private sector, but that proved to be impossible: Who was going to buy these companies from the government? In 1937 IRI became a permanent state institution, running not only banks but many of the biggest companies in Italy.

IRI (pronounced "eerie") survived World War II and helped to revitalize Italian industry after the war, serving as an economic lever of whatever government happened to be in power. There are a lot of jokes about IRI. *Fortune* once said it was known to most Italians as *Il Ottopode,* the Octopus. On the other hand, *The Wall Street Journal* said that even though IRI employs more people than the Italian Army, a lot of Italians have never heard of it. *The Economist* labeled it "a golden dustbin for the industrial problems and ambitions of countless Italian governments." *BusinessWeek,* a little less elegant, quoted an unnamed executive who called it a "garbage pail" for unprofitable companies.

It's said that IRI employs 3 percent of the Italian labor force. (The only industrial entity in the world to employ more people is General Motors.) It accounts for 8 percent of all Italian exports. To be accurate, one shouldn't say that IRI does anything aside from shuffling papers. It's a holding company. Only 550 people work in its headquarters on the Via Veneto in Rome. The boxcar figures—annual sales of more than $30 billion—are generated by the companies that belong to IRI, in whole or in part. No one is ever sure how many companies IRI has. One estimate said 1,200, another 1,078. It depends on which day the count is made.

The IRI companies, a number of them giants in their own right, make up a cross section of the Italian economy. They include SIP, the Italian telephone monopoly; Finsider, Europe's largest steel producer; Alitalia, the national airline; RAI, the state broadcasting company; Finmare, operator of 20 percent of Italy's merchant fleet; Fincantieri, which builds 70 percent of Italy's ships; Italstat, builder and operator of half of the highways in Italy; SME, which supplies 24 percent of Italy's ice cream, 22 percent of its processed tomatoes, and 13 percent of its frozen food; Alivar, which operates highway restaurants and owns four of the leading food brands in Italy—Pavesi, Pai, Motta, and Alemagna. IRI still plays a strong hand in banking. It owns about sixty banks, including Banca Commerciale Italiana, Credito Italiana, Banco di Roma, and—wonderful name—Banco di Santo Spirito (Bank of the Holy Ghost).

In a diabolical Italian way, IRI works. It has pumped money and energy into the Italian economy. It has backed huge schemes that private enterprise never would have on its own—steel mills and aluminum smelters, for example. And it has certainly provided jobs for tens of thousands of Italians, especially in the Mezzogiorno, the depressed southern part of Italy.

To traditional security analysts, the people who inhabit Wall Street and the City, IRI is a joke because it doesn't yield to the conventional yardsticks by which companies are measured. For example, it rarely seems to make money. It lost $1.8 billion in 1983. It cut that to $1.5 billion in 1984 and to a mere $900 million in 1985. But those were final adjustments after all the companies reported in. The losses can be attributed in large part to the Finsider steel company, which has been suffering in a fashion similar to U.S. Steel and, for that matter, steel companies all over the world. Many of the other companies in the IRI tent were making money.

IRI holds together in an anarchic way familiar to Italians. It just doesn't conform to the stereotypes. And since the accession of a forty-three-year-old economics professor, Romano Prodi, to the presidency of IRI in 1982, the Italian conglomerate has been doing much better than privately owned American conglomerates such as ITT and Litton Industries. Prodi has in fact tried to introduce capitalist tricks into the IRI repertoire. He has sold off a slew of companies, including the Alfa Romeo auto works, which went to Fiat for more than $1 billion, and a Naples bank, the Banca Centro Sud, which went to Citicorp. He has reduced the payroll of IRI companies by more than one hundred thousand. And he has sold off minority stakes in IRI companies to private investors. These sales raised more than $2 billion and resulted in the listing of the shares of these partially privatized companies on the Milan Stock Exchange. IRI thus can make a quick check on the market value of its holdings.

Eighteen IRI-controlled companies now have listings on the Milan Bourse. They account for 22 percent of the total market value of all the shares traded there and 35 percent of the dividends paid by all the companies listed on the exchange. And IRI still has majority control of these publicly traded companies. The public companies (and IRI's ownership) include STET (84 percent), Alitalia (77.8 percent), SME (64.4 percent), and Autostrade (87.1 percent). Prodi also gave notice in 1987 that he could even opt for 100 percent privatization. He said IRI was planning to sell its remaining 65 percent stake in Banca Commerciale Italiana, the second-largest bank in Italy and the owner of 20 percent of Mediobanca, the most important investment banking firm in Italy.

When is a state-owned company not a state-owned company? When it's IRI. Prodi has argued, with Jesuitical logic, that IRI companies can follow their own paths without political interference unless an important national issue is at stake (that was the case with Alfa Romeo, which Ford Motor wanted to buy—a move the Italian government would not allow). Prodi has also pointed out that unlike the situation in Britain, where the government needs the permission of Parliament to privatize a state-owned entity, IRI is under no such constraint. It doesn't need the permission of the Italian government to sell off a piece of government property. It can just charge ahead on its own.

In early 1987 Prodi went before the Italian Parliament to report that IRI had broken even in 1986. It was the first time since 1973 that the holding company was out of the red. Prodi then asked the legislators to appropriate $1.2 billion for IRI so that it could put down some high technology companies in Calabria, electronics plants in Sicily, and a compact disc plant, in cooperation with Philips of the Netherlands, east of Rome.

IRI is also pushing ahead on the international front. It owns one hundred companies whose head offices are outside Italy, and its foreign sales accounted for more than 20 percent of total revenues in 1985. IRI companies built the Karakaja Dam in Turkey and the port of Sines in Portugal; and in 1986 they were putting up a $1.5 billion iron and steel works in the Soviet Union, and expanding a thermoelectrical plant in China. Eleven percent of IRI's foreign sales come from China and the Communist countries in Eastern Europe.

In 1985 *Fortune* reported on the venture of one IRI company,

Italy Supports Culture

Arts organizations receive, by U.S. standards, lavish support from the Italian government. The state subsidizes La Scala, the famed opera house at Milan, to the tune of $22 million a year. In addition, thirteen other music and theater companies receive a total of $250 million from government grants.

Bonifica, in the United States. Bonifica, whose annual sales are in the $25 million range, planned to set up an industrial park and fill it with outposts of Italian companies (shoes, cheese, medical equipment). And the site of this industrial park? The South Bronx, which is as depressed as the Italian Mezzogiorno. Franco Bollati, president of Bonifica, told *Fortune* that IRI was not out to make a lot of money in the South Bronx. It was getting only a $1 million fee for its efforts. "For us," he said, "it's a matter of pride. We come to the South Bronx to introduce ourselves to the United States and show off the fruits of our experience. If we do well, we hope

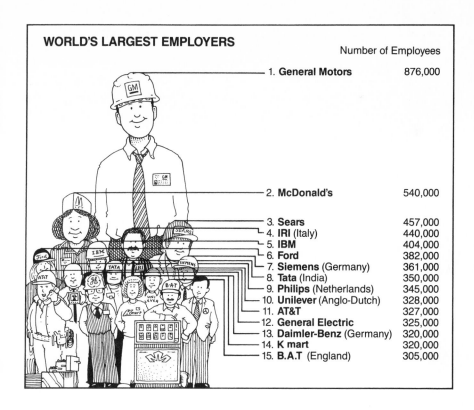

WORLD'S LARGEST EMPLOYERS

Number of Employees

1. **General Motors**	876,000
2. **McDonald's**	540,000
3. **Sears**	457,000
4. **IRI** (Italy)	440,000
5. **IBM**	404,000
6. **Ford**	382,000
7. **Siemens** (Germany)	361,000
8. **Tata** (India)	350,000
9. **Philips** (Netherlands)	345,000
10. **Unilever** (Anglo-Dutch)	328,000
11. **AT&T**	327,000
12. **General Electric**	325,000
13. **Daimler-Benz** (Germany)	320,000
14. **K mart**	320,000
15. **B.A.T** (England)	305,000

to get many jobs from other cities in the same position. If not, we go home."

So, in the end, what does IRI stand for? Is it socialism? State capitalism? No, it's just Italian business.

Access   Via Veneto 89
00187 Rome, Italy
(39) 6-47271

<table>
<tr><td>

Jardine, Matheson

</td><td>

Sales $1.3 billion
Profits $61 million
U.S. Sales $190 million
Rank Hong Kong's largest trading company
World's 8th-largest insurance broker
Founded 1832
Employees 19,400
Headquarters Hong Kong (registered office: Bermuda)

</td></tr>
</table>

Most people outside of Hong Kong have never heard of Jardine, Matheson. But millions of readers *have* enjoyed James Clavell's blockbuster novel *Noble House,* which was published in 1981 with the curse-like dedication, "I would like to offer this work as a tribute to Her Britannic Majesty, Elizabeth II, to the people of Her Crown Colony of Hong Kong—*and perdition to their enemies."* The 1,206-page novel is a steamy, multilayered story of conniving, spying, corruption, double-dealing, and wild speculation set against the backdrop of Hong Kong, a city that even tourist books describe as a place where "anything goes." The centerpiece of the novel, Noble House, is described on the book's dust jacket as "the oldest and most important trading house in Hong Kong." In real life the oldest and most important trading house in Hong Kong is Jardine, Matheson—and Clavell has had to deny many times that he modeled Noble House on Jardine.

The European trading company of the early seventeenth century was one of the earliest manifestations of corporate capitalism on a multinational scale. Organized by private investors, these enterprises received royal charters to explore and exploit various parts of the world. Thus, on December 31, 1600, Queen Elizabeth I chartered the East India Company, giving it a monopoly on markets in the Far East. The Dutch East Indies Company, the very one that bought Manhattan Island in 1626 for allegedly $24, was chartered in 1602. On May 2, 1670, Charles II granted a charter to a company headed by his cousin, Prince Rupert—an enterprise that later came to be called the Hudson's Bay Company. The crowned heads of Europe thought nothing of casually disposing of huge chunks of the world to these private, profit-seeking adventurers. East India, for example, had hunting rights in a territory that extended through the Indian subcontinent and out to China. Dutch East Indies was awarded the commercial rights for about half the earth's surface. Hudson's Bay was allotted 1.5 million square miles encompassing what is today 40 percent of Canada and big pieces of the states of Minnesota and North Dakota.

In 1662, when Charles II, a licentious monarch who enjoyed the favors of thirty-nine mistresses, married the very pious Portuguese Infanta, Catherine of Braganza, Portugal gave him a dowry of the island of Bombay off India. Six years later the king rented the island to the East India Company for the nominal sum of £10 a year. The trading company, which by then was operating a fleet of thirty ships, promptly established the island as its Far East headquarters. East India introduced tea to the British isles in 1651. And it provoked the Boston Tea Party of 1774. In his history of the world, *The Outline of History,* H. G. Wells delineated the company's role in India:

> These successes were not gained directly by the forces of the King of England; they were gained by the East India Trading Company, which had been originally . . . no more than a company of sea adventurers. Step by step they had been forced to raise troops and arm their ships. And now this trading company, with its tradition of gain, found itself dealing not merely in spices and dyes and tea and jewels, but in the revenues and territories of princes and the destinies of India. It had come to buy and sell, and found itself achieving a tremendous piracy. There was no one to challenge its proceedings. . . . The English Parliament found itself ruling over a London trading company, which in turn was dominating an empire far greater and more populous than all the domains of the British Crown. To the bulk of the English people India was a remote, fantastic, almost inaccessible land, to which adventurous poor young men went out, to return after many years very rich and very choleric old gentlemen.

One other aspect of the British trading companies was the Scottish influence. In *Company of Adventurers,* an admirable history of the Hudson's Bay Company, Canadian writer Peter C. Newman detailed this influence, noting that nearly all the great leaders of the company grew up in Scotland. Summed up Newman: "The residual Calvinism of the early Scots was the real religion of the first Hudson Bay posts: inbred obedience to authority and eagerness to bear the burden of Calvinism's earthly path to salvation—hard work."

It was from this milieu that William Jardine and James Matheson sprung.

Jardine was a Lowlander, born in 1784 on a farm near Lochmaben between the Nith and Annan rivers in the shire of Dumfries in southwest Scotland. (No fewer than thirty partners of Jardine, Matheson were to come from this same shire.) Matheson was a Highlander, born in 1796 at Lairo in the shire of Sutherland in northern Scotland; his father was a baronet. Both Jardine and Matheson originally went out to the Far East under auspices of the East India Company but didn't meet until 1820, in Bombay. Jardine was a doctor who shipped out in 1802, when he was eighteen, as a surgeon's mate aboard the *Brunswick*, a three-masted schooner operated by East India. It turned out to be commerce rather than medicine that intrigued him—and on voyages of six to eight months, he had plenty of time to contemplate that question. Matheson came from an East India family, and in 1815, at age nineteen, he went out to Calcutta to join a trading office managed by his uncle. Jardine and Matheson each drifted into partnerships with others before they joined forces. Matheson had settled in the southern Chinese city of Canton in 1820. Jardine arrived there in 1822. In 1832 they formed the company that still bears their names today. It's one of the oldest companies in the world operating continuously under the same name.

China, in 1832, was still a closed society. Although it held one third of the world's population, it didn't maintain diplomatic relations with any other country. Canton, which lies at the head of the Pearl River estuary leading into the Gulf of Canton and out to the China Sea, was then the only place in China where foreigners were allowed to live. Foreign residents had to be males (Western women were allowed only as far as Macao, the Portuguese colony near the entrance to the estuary) and they were restricted to a narrow strip of land on the north bank of the river. But 1832 was a propitious time to start a business there because two years later the monopoly held by the East India Company was broken by the liberal reform movement in Britain. East India literally disappeared from China, and in the free-for-all that followed, the trading house of Jardine, Matheson emerged as the frontrunner.

The two staples of the China trade were silk and tea. Tea had become a major item to feed a growing British appetite for the beverage. In the 1830s the Chinese would bring as many as fifty million pounds of tea a year to Canton, where they would be loaded on European-bound vessels. Jardine, Matheson was soon the biggest shipper of tea leaves. The problem that arose for Jardine was how to pay the Chinese for the tea. And that was quickly solved by running Indian-grown opium into China. Although opium had been banned in China by an imperial edict of 1729, it was freely bootlegged by private traders. The Calvinist ethics of Jardine, Matheson did not prevent it from helping to spread opium addiction in China.

In fact, Jardine brought what historian Peter Ward Fay called "a positive enthusiasm" to the opium trade, building fast clipper ships, armed to repel pirates, to carry the opium from India to China in all seasons. At the beginning of the 1830s, fewer than twenty thousand chests of opium were arriving annually in China. Near the end of the decade, forty thousand were coming in and Jardine accounted "for a considerable share," according to Fay, who noted the absence in Jardine of "much worry on the moral score," adding, "In their letters, the partners employ the word 'drug'—so many chests received, stored, sold—with a nonchalance quite startling until one remembers that the word had none of the associations it has today."

The pro-opium forces were not unanimous, however. The Mathesons had more evangelical roots than the Jardines, and dealing in opium did bother Donald Matheson, a nephew of co-founder James Matheson, who became *taipan* (a Chinese word which means "supreme boss") in 1844. After much agonizing Donald Matheson resigned from the firm in 1848. He was the last Matheson family member to be a partner. The descent was henceforth from the Jardine side. But, as Fay pointed out, "he was unusual. The general run of private merchants did not worry this way."

And indeed they didn't. Jardine, Matheson's central role in the opium trade enabled it to grow and become a major actor in developments resulting in the opening up of China. In 1839 the Chinese, alarmed by the social effects of opium smoking, decided to crack down on the trade. Chinese forces surrounded the foreign trading houses in Canton and seized twenty thousand chests of opium (seven thousand of them coming from Jardine) for flushing into the sea. Offended by this action—how *dare* the Chinese interfere with opium trading?—the British sent gunboats to the South China coast. In planning this foray the British Navy had the direct counsel of William Jardine, who had coincidentally ended his China service in 1839 and was then back in London. He went to see the British foreign secretary, Lord Palmerston, unrolled his charts of the China coast, and explained how an expedition force could navigate those waters.

The Chinese, no match for the superior firepower of the British, were forced in 1842 to sign the Treaty of Nanking, which opened up five Chinese ports, including Shanghai, to British trade and ceded the island of Hong Kong to Britain. Jardine, Matheson put its headquarters on the east point of the new British colony (it was the first company to buy land

there), returned to the full-scale running of opium and, in 1844, opened a branch office in Shanghai. The first Opium War turned out to be very good for Jardine, Matheson.

The second one, which broke out in 1856 after the Chinese seized a British ship in Canton harbor, also served Jardine interests. It resulted in the 1858 Treaty of Tientsin under which the Chinese agreed to open up eleven more ports to foreign traders, allow Christian missionaries to come to China, and legalize the importing of opium. ("Not only do you have to take our opium," the Chinese were told, "you have to take our clergy.") The treaty also called for the opening of foreign legations in Peking ("You have to take our diplomats too."), but after the Chinese reneged on this promise, hostilities resumed in 1859. British and French forces invaded Peking and burned down the Imperial Summer Palace. In 1860 the Chinese were humiliated by a new treaty which forced them to cede to Britain the tip of Kowloon Peninsula across from Hong Kong and another island in the harbor, Stonecutters. The third piece of what is now Hong Kong was acquired in 1898 when the Chinese, weak after being defeated by the Japanese in the 1894–95 war, leased to Britain the 350 square miles known as the New Territories. The lease expires in 1997.

These successive defeats also forced China to accept the principle and practice of extraterritoriality whereby foreign powers (and their business satellites) enjoyed exemption from local laws. The result was the establishment of enclaves—British, French, German, Russian—in Chinese cities. The most famous of these was the International Settlement in Shanghai, China's largest city, which was to become a bustling commercial center that looked very much like a Western metropolis—skyscrapers, billboards, stock exchanges, the works.

It was development made to order for Jardine, Matheson, part of the foreign tide. They followed the British flag to Foochow, Tientsin, Hankow, and Ichang. In the process Jardine became more than just an import-export house. It helped to build an economic infrastructure. It operated silk filatures and textile mills. It sent the first steamship up a Chinese waterway and built China's first railroad. It opened a bank and an insurance company, operated mines, published a newspaper, introduced sugar refineries, ran an extensive shipping line. By 1872 it had exited the opium business entirely. The Chinese, by then, were growing their own—and Jardine, Matheson had plenty of opportunities in lines of business that wouldn't offend the evangelical sensitivities of a Scottish Calvinist.

Jardine was also becoming expert at penetrating closed markets. In 1859, five years after Commodore Matthew Perry had succeeded in opening Japanese ports to foreign ships and nine years before the Meiji Restoration ended the Tokugawa Shogunate, the trading ship *Nora* sailed into Yokohama harbor, bringing with it William Keswick, a great-nephew of co-founder William Jardine, and a cargo of cotton goods and elastic bands, along with forty thousand Mexican dollars, a currency then in wide use on the China coast. The *Nora* was one of the first Western merchant ships to reach Japan. The next year Jardine bought Lot No. 1 on the waterfront in Yokohama's first land sale (just as it had bought Lot No. 1 on the Shanghai waterfront). By 1861 Jardine was shipping thirty thousand bales of Japanese silk to Europe, where it commanded a higher price than Chinese silk, which, of course, Jardine was also supplying.

But China was to remain Jardine's main field of endeavor, and there are many milestones to mark its progress. It made its first sizeable loan to a Chinese government in 1867. In 1881, with financing arranged in London, it formed the Indo-China Steam Navigation Company, which, by 1905, was operating a fleet of twenty ships, both oceangoing vessels and steamers plying the Yangtze River. In 1886 it organized the Hongkong & Kowloon Wharf & Godown Company, which evolved into a major real estate developer, cargo handler, and hotel operator in the colony. In 1889 it helped to form the Hongkong Land Company, which was to become the Crown Colony's number one landlord. In 1898 it joined with the Hongkong & Shanghai Bank to establish the British & Chinese Corporation, which built railroads and then served as a financial agent for the Chinese government.

By the middle of the nineteenth century Shanghai was becoming as important a place for Jardine as Hong Kong. And by the end of the century the taipan was just as likely to fly his flag in Shanghai as in Hong Kong, or there might be two taipans, one for Hong Kong and one for Shanghai. A mark of the importance of Shanghai was the opening of Jardine's new building there on November 15, 1922. Dedicated by the British consul, Sir Sidney Barton, whose son, Hugh, was later to be the taipan of Jardine, it was a massive piece of Edwardian splendor topped by a 135-foot flagpole and featuring columns of solid granite, a bronze and marble staircase, and accomodations—"including bath facilities," the firm's history notes—for the coolie staff. The building was put up on the Bund, a waterfront street that was one of the grand thoroughfares of Shanghai, which was then the most important commercial center in the Far East. By 1930 the Jardine shingle was up in thirteen Chinese cities, plus two in Japan, one on Formosa, and two in Manchuria. There was also an all-important office in London, the "mother" financial center, and a minor outpost in New York (Jardine never could figure out what to do in the United States). The staff numbered 113,000, which must have ranked as one of the largest corporate payrolls in the world at that time.

Through all these vicissitudes, Jardine remained a family-controlled enterprise, with the purse strings going back to London where redemptions were made in the only currency that really mattered: pound sterling. The typical pattern was for Scots to come out to the Far East, make their pile, and retire to baronial estates in Scotland, where they stood for Parliament and collected their knighthoods. A considerable amount of money was to be made, even in the very early days. When co-founder James Matheson retired to London in 1843, his partnership interest was worth $1.2 million. The firm used to pay off retired partners by consigning to them the proceeds of cargo shipments. Dr. Jardine still had money in the firm when he died; the entire proceeds from the tea shipped that year on two clippers, the *Passenger* (bound for Leith) and the *Walker* (bound for Hull), went to his estate.

Those early pioneers tended not to marry—or if they did, it was after they left the Far East and retired to Scotland. Many died bachelors. Young men who joined Jardine used to need the permission of the partners to marry. Some Jardine men would live with a Chinese mistress whom they would maintain with a trust fund after they returned to Britain; the firm thoughtfully took care of such matters for its people.

Co-founder James Matheson married after he retired from the firm, but he never had children. William Jardine never married. So the line of descent went mainly from Jardine's sister, Jean, who married a David Johnstone. Their only son, Andrew, born in 1798, served briefly in the Far East but retired early. According to the family chronicler, Maggie Keswick, who put together the company's one hundred and fiftieth anniversary volume, *The Thistle and the Jade,* Andrew was "much attached to horses and ladies." He also never married. However, Andrew's two sisters, Mary and Margaret, married. Their children were active in Jardine. Mary's grandson, John J. Paterson, was taipan in Hong Kong when the Crown Colony fell to the Japanese shortly after the attack on Pearl Harbor. He spent the war years in Hong Kong's Stanley Prison. Margaret married Thomas Keswick (whose mother was a Jardine, though not related to the Jardines of Lochmaben), and the Keswick name has since figured prominently in Jardine, Matheson's history, contributing five taipans. In 1905 Robert Jardine, the last nephew of the founder (he was the son of Dr. Jardine's brother, David), died, leaving his considerable interest in the firm to his thirty-seven-year-old son, Robert, who had no interest in a Jardine, Matheson career. As a result, Jardine, Matheson was restructured in 1906 from a partnership to a limited-liability company.

The firm was definitely Scottish. Scottish names—Macdonald, Stewart, MacAndrew, Macleod, Laird, Macdougall, McKie, Reid—are prominent in the roster of partners and directors of Jardine since its founding in 1832. This perusal will disclose very few Chinese names, although Jardine, in company with other foreign enterprises, used compradors, Chinese factotums who managed the Chinese staff and dealt with Chinese customers on behalf of the foreign devils. Jardine, Matheson maintained a separate comprador department until 1950. A number of Jardine's compradors left to establish their own businesses and became quite successful. It was clear they were not going to get very far at Jardine.

William Keswick, Margaret's eldest son, was the first of the Keswick taipans. He came out to China in 1855 when he was twenty-one years old, opened the Japanese office in 1860, and became taipan in 1874, just as the British were about to gain control of the Suez Canal. He later spent most of his time in London while his younger brother, James J. Keswick, ran the company in the East. Photographs of James show him with a long, overflowing beard. In 1884 he married the daughter of Sir Harry Parkes, who was then in Peking serving as British ambassador to China.

William's two grandsons, William J. ("Tony") Keswick and John Keswick, were in Shanghai as World War II approached. Tony had become taipan in 1934 when he was thirty-one years old. His younger brother, John, started with Jardine in London in 1928 and then went to New York briefly before joining the Shanghai office where one of the first questions he asked was whether he could learn Chinese. The answer: "Good idea, none of us do." When war broke out in Europe in 1939, John left (he was later to serve on Lord Mountbatten's staff in Ceylon) while his brother remained in Shanghai. In 1941, in his capacity as chairman of the Shanghai Municipal Council, Tony Keswick was addressing a meeting when the head of the Japanese community stepped up to the dais, took out a revolver, and shot at him two times. According to his brother John, who related the story in an essay in *The Thistle and the Jade,* Tony was wearing a thick, fur-lined overcoat and was not seriously injured. He did, however, leave Shanghai shortly afterwards. "His assailant, Haiyashi, was hailed as a hero in Japan," said John Keswick.

When the war ended, Jardine, Matheson returned to China. The Hong Kong office was quickly reopened by the people who had been imprisoned by the Japanese. William J. Keswick, the last taipan in Shanghai, did not return to the Far East after the war. He stayed in London where he ran Jardine's affairs there and served for many years as a director of the Bank of England. He was knighted in 1972. His two sons, Henry and Simon, both followed him into the firm—and both became taipans.

His younger brother, John, did return to China to reopen the Shanghai office. He described how in the winter of 1945, the heating systems having been dismantled by the Japanese for scrap iron, he was sitting in his office, freezing, wearing a long Chinese silk padded gown, when an American sailor popped in to say, "Hey, Chink, where's this guy Kes-wick?"

John Keswick and Jardine were prepared to pick up where they had left off in Shanghai. At that time, Jardine, Matheson owned an airline (Hong Kong Airways), textile mills, real estate, a brewery, wharves, and warehouses. They were responsible for ten thousand jobs in Shanghai. China was soon engulfed in the civil war that pitted the Communists (Mao Tse-tung) against the Kuomintang (Chiang Kai-shek), but Jardine was prepared to do business with whomever triumphed. So when the Communists triumphed in 1949, Keswick didn't flee. He placed an ad in the *North China Daily News* asking for help in clearing the garden outside his house of land mines. He knew some of the Communist leaders from the war years, and he hoped to remain in business. But it was not to be. The Communists didn't care to deal with a Jardine. In 1951 John Keswick left the country. And in 1954 the office was officially closed, and Jardine had to write off $20 million in assets left behind in China.

Still, Keswick didn't give up. He tells how, four years after leaving China, he and his wife, Clare, "found ourselves walking back over the railway bridge at the Lowu frontier post on the first of many trips to Peking and around the country. A new start was under way." It was not until 1979, however, that the Chinese government would let Jardine, Matheson return to China. A representative office was opened then in Peking. In 1986 Jardine also had offices in Shanghai and Guangzhou (Canton). But it's nothing like the prewar period. In 1986 Jardine, Matheson was doing very little of its business—the estimate was as low as 1 percent—in the country that was once its *raison d'être*.

In Hong Kong, of course, it was a different story. No company has the symbiotic relationship with Hong Kong that Jardine, Matheson has. The idea of Hong Kong as a British colony from which traders could operate was first hatched by Jardine, Matheson people. The Star Ferry, which now makes more than 400 crossings a day between Hong Kong Island and Kowloon, was organized by the company. Nine streets in Hong Kong—Bulkeley, Perceval, Irving, Anton, Landale, Matheson, Paterson, Johnstone, and Keswick—are named for Jardine taipans. The cannon that is fired every day at noon in Hong Kong is a Jardine, Matheson tradition. The story is that many years ago Jardine, Matheson shot off a gun at noon to salute one of its taipans. The colony's British governor was infuriated when he was told why the gun was shot, and he ordered Jardine to continue to do it—every day at noon. It's a custom memorialized in Noel Coward's song "Mad Dogs and Englishmen." The gun still goes off every day in Hong Kong from the East Point site where Jardine, Matheson opened its office in 1842.

The clout that Jardine has in Hong Kong resulted in pandemonium on June 15, 1961, when the firm made its first offering of stock to the public. Investors in the colony went wild trying to become Jardine, Matheson shareholders. Some nine hundred thousand shares—25 percent of the total number—were offered at a price of 16 Hong Kong dollars per share. Orders came in for fifty-six times as many shares. Allocations were made by a lottery. When the stock opened for trading on the Hong Kong Stock Exchange, the only place where it still trades, the price went to $31.25 at the close of the day. Based on that price, Jardine had a market value of 100 million Hong Kong dollars in 1961. At the end of 1985 its market value was about 6 billion Hong Kong dollars ($725 million, U.S.).

Hong Kong experienced an explosive growth after World War II, developing into an anarchic, multinational hub of commerce where the pursuit of the dollar is sacred. Refugees from the Chinese mainland poured into the colony, boosting its population from 500,000 at the end of the war to 5.5 million in 1986. Hong Kong's per capita income in 1986 was $6,500 a year, which ranked it as the most prosperous place in the Far East after Japan and Singapore. Hong Kong is a free port where twenty thousand oceangoing vessels call every year. It has 128 commercial banks. Thirty-two airlines land there.

How could the company that virtually invented Hong Kong not benefit from this expansion, especially since it had its fingers in so many pies? The answer to that question is: "Well, it could happen—times change." Jardine, Matheson no longer wields the power it once did in a Hong Kong that was a colonial satrapy. Hong Kong is a Chinese city-state energized largely by Chinese merchants and Chinese laborers who have an ill-concealed contempt for the *gweilo* (the foreigner). It's a cynical place where the denizens love to gamble (at the Happy Valley racetrack, the stock exchange, or the Macao casinos). Hong Kong has also become part of the global marketplace for currency traders and equity investors. It's an international meeting ground. In short, it's no longer the Hong Kong fashioned in the last century by Scottish traders, and Jardine, Matheson has had difficulties navigating in the new waters. Consider this sequence of events:

- In 1979 the Chinese entrepreneur, Li-Ka-shing, gained control of one of Hong Kong's big conglomerates, Hutchinson Whampoa.

- In 1980 another legendary Chinese empire builder, Y. K. Pao, took over the Jardine satellite Hongkong & Kowloon Wharf & Godown.

- Frightened that these Chinese merchants would then go after Jardine, Matheson, David Newbigging, who was then taipan in Hong Kong (his father was an earlier taipan), engineered a cute deal in which Hongkong Land acquired 40 percent of the stock of Jardine, Matheson while Jardine, Matheson acquired a like amount in Hongkong Land. (Hongkong Land, considered by some to be the world's largest property owner, was established by Jardine in 1889; it owns 70 percent of the office space in Hong Kong's central business district.) The cross-holdings were designed to stave off a possible takeover, and they did. But in 1982, when the boom in the Hong Kong property market leveled off, Jardine found itself crushed by a staggering load of debt on properties whose market values were falling (for the first time since the end of the war).

- That meant curtains for Newbigging, who, in 1983, was ousted in a well-publicized power play that saw forty-year-old Simon Keswick, great-great-great-grandnephew of William Jardine, come in from London to take over as taipan. (The Keswicks are said to hold 10 percent of Jardine's stock.)

- Simon Keswick chopped hundreds of staffers and eliminated a bunch of businesses that had been acquired, many of them during the early 1970s when his elder brother, Henry, had been taipan.

Among the Keswick discards were a majority stake in Rennies, a South African trading group (originally founded by another Scottish family); property developments in the continental United States, Hawaii, and Britain; an offshore oil servicing unit; and sugar growing in Hawaii (part of the 1973 acquisition of Theo. H. Davies & Company, one of the original five trading companies in Honolulu). Finally, showing he is no sentimentalist, Simon Keswick shed one of Jardine's oldest businesses when he sold off the firm's entire shipping fleet (thirty-five vessels). Keswick has a modern appetite. Jardine distributes Mercedes-Benz vehicles in Hong Kong, Britain, Australia, and Hawaii, and it runs a slew of Pizza Huts, Taco Bells, and 7-Eleven stores.

The Keswick move that really shook up Hong Kong occurred in 1984 when he announced that Jardine was moving its legal headquarters from Hong Kong to Bermuda. The reason cited was uncertainty over the future of Hong Kong. The chain of events that Jardine, Matheson started in 1839, leading to the British annexation of the territories now called Hong Kong, comes to an end in 1997 when sovereignty reverts to China. Virtually all the people in Hong Kong, most of them refugees from Communist China, are nervous about this changeover.

On December 19, 1984, nine months after Simon Keswick made his Bermudian escape, the Chinese and British reached an agreement under which China guaranteed that Hong Kong could stay the way it is for fifty years after 1997, that is, it will remain a free port and will continue to enjoy the liberties now in place. It will even get what it does not have now: an elected legislature. It was a ringing vote of confidence from China's Marxists in Hong Kong's role as a bastion of mindless capitalism. But Jardine was not having any of it. Two years later, in another complex restructuring of the firm, taipan Simon Keswick created a new holding company, Jardine Strategic Holdings, which was also incorporated in Bermuda. Huge pieces of the Jardine's empire—Dairy Farm supermarkets and the Mandarin hotel chain—were turned into publicly traded companies, with Jardine retaining a strong interest in both.

This restructuring was the work of an American lawyer, Brian M. Powers, who in 1987, at age thirty-seven, was named managing director of Jardine.

As Hong Kong moved to become more of a Chinese city, Jardine, Matheson was looking elsewhere. Writing from Hong Kong in early 1986, a correspondent for *The Economist* quipped that while Jardine, Matheson was once known as the "noble house," now it's known as the "faded poppy." The Keswicks remember losing everything in mainland China

---

Top Chinese Companies

It's not quite a *Fortune* or *Forbes* or *BusinessWeek* roster, but the People's Republic of China identified the following as its four largest companies (based on their "profits," a nebulous concept):

> Daqing Petroleum
> Anshan Iron & Steel
> Yanshan Petro-Chemical
> Wuhan Iron & Steel

Among the top twenty companies, only one is not an industrial heavyweight. That is the Shanghai Cigarette Factory, which ranked sixteenth. All of these companies are state-owned.

after World War II. Now they're not taking any chances. They want to be sure they are on British turf.

Access   World Trade Center
P.O. Box 30748
Causeway Bay, Hong Kong
(852) 5-228011

Theo. H. Davies & Co.
841 Bishop St.
Honolulu, Hi. 96802
(808) 531-8531

Jefferson Smurfit

Sales $1.5 billion
Profits $60 million
U.S. Sales $1 billion
Rank Ireland's largest company
World's 7th-largest paper company
3d-largest newsprint producer in the United States
Largest recycler of paper
1st in the United States in production of folding cartons
2d-largest United States producer of corrugated containers
Largest United States producer of plastic drums
2d-largest United States producer of spiral tubes
3d-largest United States maker of fiber partitions
Founded 1934
Employees 28,000
Headquarters Dublin, Ireland

I t was a signal day in 1934 when John Jefferson Smurfit, a master tailor from St. Helens in Northwest England, was married to a Belfast girl whom he had met when both were vacationing on the Isle of Man. The wedding took place in Belfast, the capital of Northern Ireland, which then as now was the scene of bitter strife between Irish nationalists and the British citizens of the 5,400-square-mile territory that geographically, if not politically, is part of Ireland. The priest who married Jefferson and Ann Smurfit had become involved, through a parishioner, in a small box-making factory in Dublin. In fact, he owned an interest in the company but didn't know anything about business. The bridegroom appeared to be familiar with business, and before the day was over, Smurfit had agreed to acquire the priest's interest in the carton plant.

Smurfit returned with his bride to St. Helens, where he had just set himself up in a shop. He was not going to abandon the tailoring business that he had spent a number of years learning. Smurfit's father, a shipyard worker and a diabetic, had died when John Jefferson was ten years old, and when he was fourteen Jefferson had to leave school to go to work. (He was to say later, "Life had made me into a little old man by fourteen.") He had a strong drive to succeed in the tailoring business but decided to look into the Dublin plant by traveling there once a week. He ferried back and forth for the next four years, expanding his tailoring business in St. Helens to four shops while trying at the same time to learn everything he could about box making.

In 1938 Smurfit acquired full control of the Dublin company and decided it was time to move there. A year later World War II broke out. Ireland remained neutral, and Smurfit kept the business going through the war, although paper was very scarce. He devised a machine that could make paper from straw. It is said that Irish schoolchildren who used Smurfit notepads during the war still remember that thick paper.

The Smurfits had eight children—four daughters (Katherine, Ann, Sheila, and Barbara) and four sons (Michael, Jefferson, Alan, and Dermot)—and in the late 1950s, the two eldest sons, Michael and Jefferson, Jr., went to work on the factory floor. According to a history distributed by the company, "managers had strict instructions to give them no preferential treatment." The company's business expanded steadily, but when shares were first sold to the public in 1964, it was not a huge enterprise. Annual sales were $2 million, and Jefferson Smurfit & Sons ranked sixty-second on the roster of sixty-four companies listed on the Irish Stock Exchange.

In 1968, when he was fifty-nine years old, Jefferson, Sr., set the company on a course that was to catapult it into the topmost ranks of the world's paper and packaging producers. The sling he used was the one in common use in America: takeovers. In three years, using combinations of cash and stock, he bought three Irish companies: Temple Press, Browne & Nolan, and the Hely Group. The capture of Hely was a coup: It was Ireland's largest packaging company and three times Smurfit's size. Jefferson Smurfit was suddenly the third-largest company in Ireland.

In 1970 Smurfit's shares were listed on the London Stock Exchange, and in 1972 the company made its first British buy: W. J. Noble, a carton maker in the North of England. Two years later it made its first foray into the United States, buying Time Industries, a Chicago paper and container manufacturer.

John Jefferson Smurfit died in 1977, and his four sons continued what he had started. They expanded the business by acquiring other companies, particularly in the United States, where Alton Box Company, Diamond International's packaging and paperboard mills, Publishers Paper, and Container Corporation of America (CCA) all gravitated into the Jefferson Smurfit orbit. As it entered 1987 this Irish-based paper company was operating on three continents and doing more than 75 percent of its business in the United States. In the United States alone it had more than ninety mills and plant facilities, not counting sixty-five

CCA mills and plants that it was managing. The U.S. properties included eighteen paper and board mills, two newsprint mills, fifty-six corrugated container plants, twenty folding carton factories, and more than twenty industrial packaging plants.

The *Los Angeles Times* and the *Denver Post* are printed on Jefferson Smurfit paper, Kellogg and General Mills pack their cereals in Jefferson Smurfit cartons, and the Miller six-pack and Wendy's french fry holders are supplied by Jefferson Smurfit plants.

Making cardboard boxes is one thing. Making effective use of money is something else. Jefferson Smurfit has always seemed to know its way around creative finance. One source of cash in the early 1970s was the U.S. packaging company Continental Can, which at one point had a 20 percent holding in Jefferson Smurfit. In the late 1970s another source was Svenska Cellulosa, Sweden's largest paper company, which bought 49 percent of Smurfit's corrugated packaging interests in Britain. In addition to cash, the Swedish connection guaranteed Smurfit supplies of kraftliner.

The $1.1 billion deal it made in 1986 to buy Chicago-based Container Corporation of America from Mobil Oil was typical. It wasn't a simple purchase. Jefferson Smurfit formed a limited partnership with the Wall Street investment banking house Morgan Stanley—and this new entity, JSC/MS Holdings, made the acquisition via bank loans and the issuance of junk bonds, high-interest-bearing notes of less than top-grade investment quality. Jefferson Smurfit really didn't have to come up with any fresh cash. It's a fifty-fifty partnership, but Morgan Stanley's role is that of a passive investor. Smurfit will manage the business and hopes to do well enough to buy out Morgan Stanley down the road, and then bring Container Corporation into the corporate house. It's a maneuver the Irish company had executed with previous acquisitions.

Jefferson Smurfit also bought paper mills, container plants, and carton factories that CCA had in Italy, Spain, and the Netherlands. And it took over one million acres of CCA timberlands.

The company that partnered with Morgan Stanley in this audacious acquisition was Jefferson Smurfit Corporation, which is a U.S.-based, 78 percent–owned subsidiary of the Irish company, the Jefferson Smurfit Group. In 1983 the Irish company sold 22 percent of its American unit to the public—and these shares trade on the United States on the over-the-counter market, where they have *quadrupled* in price. Shares of the Irish parent trade on the stock exchanges in Dublin and London. The largest individual shareholder in 1986 was Michael Smurfit with 5.2 percent of the stock. His three brothers all held board seats and had large blocks of shares.

The Irish chutzpah of the CCA acquisition is clear from the salient financial figures. In 1985 CCA had sales of $1.7 billion, nearly *triple* the 1985 sales of Jefferson Smurfit Corporation and 25 percent more than the sales of the Irish parent. How do you buy a company that's bigger than yours? Easy. Just find someone to lend you the money. Jefferson Smurfit has become a master at this kind of financial wizardry.

Once a company gets into the acquisition business, it rarely knows when to stop—and Smurfit is no exception. It now publishes three periodicals in Ireland *(Woman's Way, U,* and *Irish Business);* markets a wine cooler, Island Cooler, in Australia; and makes plastic bags in Britain. It also sees a duty to lecture the Irish government. In his message to shareholders in 1986, Michael Smurfit complained about the tax the Irish government imposes on earnings brought back from the United States. "The government should look again at its entire package of incentives with a view to bringing consistency and stability into the investment climate. On the one hand the government introduces incentives to encourage investment and job creation by industry while on the other hand it takes away the benefits of these incentives.

"We have made proposals to the government to introduce a new incentive to attract international financial centers and investment to Ireland. The benefits from this form of incentive are obvious. . . . It is to be hoped that the government will take an enlightened view of this proposal similar to that taken when export sales relief was introduced.

"We are an Irish company, proud of it and wish to be able to continue to invest a meaningful portion of our wealth in Ireland. To make this happen, however, fairness and consistency of policy must prevail."

Access   Beech Hill, Clonskeagh
Dublin 4, Ireland
(353) 1-696622

8182 Maryland Ave.
St. Louis, Mo. 63105
(314) 746-1100

Kikkoman	**Sales** $1.1 billion

Sales $1.1 billion
Profits $24 million
Rank   World's largest soy sauce producer
        Japan's 2d-largest wine producer
Founded   1661
Employees   3,500 (average age: 41; average
        number of years with company:
        21)
Headquarters   Noda, Japan

Kikkoman may well be the oldest continuously operating company in the world. Its principal product, soy sauce, is the cornerstone of the Japanese diet—"as necessary to Japanese cooking as a motor is to an automobile," Edwin O. Reischauer, Harvard historian and former U.S. ambassador to Japan, once pointed out. Another historian, W. Mark Fruin, in his book-length history *Kikkoman: Company, Clan, and Community,* has stated that Kikkoman's soy sauce is the only traditional Japanese product that has ever succeeded internationally.

Shoyu (the Japanese word for soy sauce) is brewed from soy beans, wheat, and salt (with yeast added for the fermentation). It is not unlike the brewing of beer, except that the fermentation of the soy mash takes longer (at least a year and, according to some recipes, more than two years). Soy sauce was first developed in Japan by Buddhists who, being vegetarians, needed vegetable-based seasonings and sauces. The earliest version—a liquid fermented entirely from soy beans and called *tamari*—was made by a thirteenth-century Zen priest, Kakushin.

Soy sauce as we know it (with wheat added) was first made in the seventeenth century. One of the early manufacturers was Takanashi Hyozaemon, who began brewing shoyu in 1661 in the rural village of Noda, about forty miles north of Tokyo, not far from today's Narita Airport, which was—and is—bitterly opposed by the farmers of that region.

Noda's convenient location (in the farm fields but with easy access to the rapidly growing city of Tokyo) helped establish it as a prime supplier of the soy sauce that was becoming a staple of the Japanese diet. In 1662, a year after Takanashi started to make shoyu, another Noda farmer, Mogi Shichizaemon, began brewing *miso,* a soybean paste similar to soy sauce. Over the next century the Takanashis and Mogis joined forces, launching a business-family dynasty that was cemented over and over again by intermarriages. In the two centuries following 1738, Fruin has noted, there were forty-six Mogi-Takanashi intermarriages. It was a quite conscious business strategy. In the 1870s, for example, when the

Noda shoyu brewers were having trouble with the distributors who controlled the Tokyo market, one of the Mogis married his second son into a distributor family to help him secure access.

The Mogis and Takanashis became major soy sauce brewers but they were very far from dominating the business. Other brewers operated in Noda, and there were literally hundreds of brewers in other parts of Japan. Competition was ferocious. In 1887 the eighteen brewers of soy sauce in Noda formed a cartel, the Noda Shoyu Brewers Association, to buy raw materials, coordinate shipping, and set prices and wages. The majority of the cartel members were Takanashi or Mogi family members. But at the time the combined output of all the Noda breweries accounted for only 10 percent of the soy sauce consumed in Japan. The cartel functioned until 1917 when nine Mogi-Takanashi families formed their own firm, the Noda Shoyu Company, Ltd. This was the predecessor company of Kikkoman. It ranked in 1918 as the seventieth-largest industrial company in Japan. At the time there were three thousand producers of soy sauce. Noda Shoyu held 7 percent of this fragmented market.

Kikkoman, a private brand of the Mogi Saheiji family, became the flagship brand of the new company after the organizers agreed to pay the family 300,000 yen for its use. The family had taken the unusual step of registering the brand in 1838. And shortly after the Meiji Restoration which followed the opening of Japan by Admiral Perry, the Mogi Saheiji family began entering Kikkoman in world's fairs. It won a prize at the Austrian fair in 1873, and ten years later it achieved international recognition by winning a gold medal at the World's Fair in Amsterdam. Meanwhile, in 1879, Kikkoman was registered in California as a legally protected brand name. Kikkoman, when written in Japanese, has three characters: *ki,* the symbol for tortoise, which means good luck and longevity; *ko,* which means first-rate; and *man,* which connotes ten thousand or forever. The shape of the tortoise shell resulted in the symbolic rendition of the brand name as a hexagon with the character for *man* appearing inside the hexagon. (Check your Kikkoman bottle.)

Workers at the Noda Shoyu breweries were treated like indentured servants, and the mean conditions led to labor turmoil in the 1920s. In 1927–28 the company was the target of a seven-month strike, the longest walkout recorded in prewar Japan. It resulted in the firing of one thousand workers and the virtual destruction of the trade union. Noda Shoyu came out in better shape. By the start of World War II, it had increased its market share to nearly 15 percent, and it had three thousand employees, triple the number in 1918. Following the Japanese Army, it had also opened outposts in China and Korea.

After World War II the company was reorganized as Kikkoman Corporation and began to take on the trappings of modernity. Its shares were listed on the Tokyo Stock Exchange; it diversified into foods, soft drinks (it owns a Coca-Cola bottler), liquor, wines, and restaurants (ten in Japan, six in Germany, two in the United States—at Disneyland and Disney World); and it began to export its soy sauce to the United States and other overseas markets.

In 1968, to meet a growing demand in the United States, it started to ship Kikkoman soy sauce in stainless steel tanks to Oakland, where it was bottled by Leslie Salt. Then in 1972 it opened its own soy sauce plant in Walworth, Wisconsin, close to soybean- and wheat-growing farms. Kikkoman's naturally brewed soy sauce quickly overtook the chemical soy sauces marketed by Chun King and LaChoy. By the mid-1980s Kikkoman held 50 percent of the American market. In Japan its market share had risen to 30 percent. Kikkoman now makes soy sauce in Brazil as well.

Kikkoman suffered a black eye in 1985 over adulteration of its wines, which are sold in Japan under the Manns label. While they carried the proud designation "Domestic Estate Wine," it turned out that Manns had been blending its vintage with bulk wines imported from Austria. If that wasn't bad enough, it turned out that the Austrian wines contained ethylene glycol, good old antifreeze. Manns recalled its wines from stores and then, under a court order, had to shut down its entire operations until the storm blew over.

All seven directors of Kikkoman resigned, including Katsumi Mogi, president of the company and a descendant of the founders. In its 1985 annual report, Kikkoman said, "We sincerely apologize to our stockholders for causing great concern as a result of our subsidiary Manns Wine's disgraceful affair. We intend to do our best in restoring trust and rebuilding the wine business, and we ask for your support and understanding."

Access   339, Noda, Noda City
Chiba 278, Japan
(81) 471-23-5111

Kikkoman International
50 California St.
San Francisco, Cal. 94111
(415) 956-7550

Krupp	**Sales** $8.8 billion

Sales $8.8 billion

Profits $35 million

Rank 64th on the *Fortune* International 500
12th-largest industrial enterprise in West
  Germany
West Germany's 2d-largest steel maker
World's 10th-largest engineering company
World's largest maker of specialty stainless
  steel (used in pots and pans, surgical
  instruments)
World's largest maker of permanent magnets
World's largest builder of cement plants
World's 3d-largest maker of fire-fighting
  equipment

Founded 1811

Employees 68,000

Headquarters Essen, West Germany

"**A**s Krupp goes, so goes Germany." That well-worn saying retained its validity well into the latter half of the twentieth century, even after World War II devastated the Krupp plants in the Ruhr, leveled its shipyards in Kiel, and left its leader, Alfried Krupp, imprisoned for having employed one hundred thousand slave laborers in more than one hundred factories and concentration camps sprawled across Germany, Poland, Austria, France, and Czechoslovakia.

Krupp's role as handmaiden to Adolf Hitler is documented in macabre detail in *The Arms of Krupp,* the 942-page book that took William Manchester seven years to research and write. Published in 1968, it was dedicated to "the children of Buschmannshof"—these were the children born to Ukrainian women while they worked in the Krupp plants in Essen. The newly born infants were separated from their mothers and sent to their own concentration camp, Buschmannshof, thirty-seven miles away; only one out of four survived.

The story begins with the first Krupp, Arndt Krupp, a merchant who settled in Essen in 1587 and acquired considerable property around the turn of the century when the bubonic plague hit the town. Seemingly impervious to the disease, Arndt bought land cheaply from people who wanted to go on a last binge. His son, Anton, married into a gunsmith family, and during the Thirty Years War (1618–48), he sold a thousand gun barrels a year. He was the first Krupp to make arms. Friedrich Krupp, born in 1787, inherited a fortune when his grandmother died in 1810, and in the following year he established a factory in Essen to make English cast steel. That is generally taken as the founding date of the company, whose formal name is Fried. Krupp. Success eluded Friedrich. When he died in 1826 the firm had only seven employees and was virtually bankrupt.

Krupp's great growth occurred in the nineteenth century under the reign of Friedrich's son, Alfred, who was only fourteen years old when his father died. It was Alfred who built Krupp into the world's largest industrial enterprise, an integrated company that had its own coal and ore mines, blast furnaces, and metalworking and manufacturing shops. He introduced the Bessemer and open-hearth steelmaking processes on the European continent. He became Europe's leading gun maker, saluted as the "cannon king." During the Franco-Prussian War of 1870–71, Krupp's mighty steel breech-loaders turned the tide of battle at Sedan, sealing the defeat of Napoleon III. The victory made Prussia the foremost military power in Europe.

Successful as he was as an arms manufacturer, Alfred Krupp considered his greatest accomplishment the invention of the seamless railway tire—a wheel that was not welded. He forged that product in 1852 and was soon selling fifteen thousand wheels a year, many of them to American railroads, which also used Krupp rails. In 1875 he made the wheel the symbol of the company, a design of three interlocked circles. It remains Krupp's trademark today.

Alfred Krupp did have his idiosyncrasies. He had what William Manchester called "a potpourri of phobias," and these were all reflected in Villa Hugel, a three-hundred-room castle that he began building in 1870 on the north bank of the Ruhr River as a place capable of entertaining crowned heads. Alfred was afraid of fire, and so no wooden beams could be used, only steel and stone. His personal bedroom was guarded by three barriers of triple-locked doors. And since he hated drafts, all the windows were permanently sealed. Smells also had special meanings to him. He believed, for example, that the smell of horse manure was enriching, and when he built Villa Hugel, which Manchester called the "German equivalent of the Albert Memorial," he put his study over the stables so that ducts could waft the smell to him.

Another of Alfred Krupp's legacies was a paternalism that lavished social benefits on the company's work force. The company introduced health insurance in 1836, a pension plan in 1855, employee housing in 1861, company stores in 1868, and a Krupp hospital in 1872. These innovations were the models for the social legislation adopted by the Bismarck government after 1871. Women looking for a good match used to place ads in newspapers specifying Krupp husbands.

Alfred's son, Fritz, had a lonely childhood and after he succeeded his father in 1887, he left his own mark. He continued Krupp's gun making. He also built a Navy for Kaiser Wilhelm, delivering nine battle-ships, five cruisers, and twenty-two destroyers. Fritz also liked to go to the Isle of Capri to party with young boys. According to Manchester, "Fa-vored youths were enlisted in a kind of Krupp fan club. Members received keys to the place and, as a token of their benefactor's affection, either solid gold pins shaped like artillery shells or gold medals with two crossed forks. . . . In return they submitted to sophisticated caresses from him while three violinists played. An orgasm was celebrated by skyrockets." Some of these scenes were photographed. Stories began to appear in the Italian press and were then picked up in the German press. In 1902, at age forty-eight, Fritz Krupp committed suicide at Villa Hugel.

The Krupp empire passed to his daughter, Bertha, who was sixteen when her father died. Bertha devoted herself to good works, particularly looking after the needs of Krupp workers. She was never an admirer of Hitler. The same could not be said for her husband, Gustav von Bohlen und Halbach, whom she married in 1906, supposedly at the instigation of the Kaiser himself. The Kaiser had Gustav assume the Krupp name.

It was Gustav Krupp who led the company during the first half of the twentieth century, slavishly kowtowing to anyone who was in power in Germany. He named the big 420-mm guns used against the Allied forces in World War I the "Big Berthas," after his wife. Manchester was unpityingly vitriolic about Gustav, describing him as "one of the least flamboyant men ever to emerge in public life. . . . He was the man who never does anything wrong, never misses an appointment, and never shows the faintest flicker of imagination." Gustav supposedly kept his office temperature at fifty-five degrees to keep him alert, and he believed, Manchester recounted, "in brisk meals. Several visitors can remember that when then they tried to make amiable conversation, their plates were snatched away. . . . Efficiency was his religion. One of his oddest hobbies was reading train timetables, looking for typographical errors. When he found one, he would seize his telephone and denounce the railroad."

Gustav and Bertha Krupp had nine children (Gustav allotted sixty minutes of his precious time to them every week). The eldest, Alfried, was born in 1907 and was known throughout his life for keeping his emotions bottled up. He was an early member of the Nazi party, joining the SS in 1931 when he was an engineering student. He joined the family firm as deputy director in 1936 and was therefore on hand to supply the arms Hitler needed for his blitzkrieg. Krupp turned out all kinds of guns as well as tanks, submarines, battleships, and aircraft parts. Alfried's young Oxford-educated cousin, Kurt von Wilmowsky, was interned by the British after the war broke out and then sent on a ship to Canada. He died at sea, his ship sunk by a Krupp U-boat firing a Krupp torpedo. Alfried's younger brother, Claus, flew for the Luftwaffe, and he crashed and died in 1940 on a test flight. Gustav Krupp had the first of a series of strokes in 1941, and his son, Alfried, took complete control of the Krupp arsenal in 1943, staying in command until he was arrested by American troops in April 1945.

Convicted in 1948 at the Nuremberg war trials (the prosecutors would have preferred Gustav as a defendant, but he was senile by then), Alfried was sentenced to twelve years in prison; the court also ordered his property confiscated. However, in 1951, John J. McCloy, the U.S. High Commissioner for Germany, commuted his sentence and restored to him the Krupp properties. McCloy doubted that Krupp had had personal responsibility for the use of slave labor, and he felt that Krupp was being punished as a symbol of the German armaments industry. Manchester's opinion is that Krupp was let out to rebuild his industrial empire to suit the West's needs in its escalating Cold War with the Soviet Union. Alfried Krupp was released on February 3, 1951, seven months and nine days after the outbreak of the Korean War.

Krupp did indeed rebuild the Krupp empire. It no longer made cannons but it had coal mines, steel mills, and shipyards. It became one of the world's great engineering concerns, building cement plants, nuclear power stations, and giant rail ferries. As sole proprietor of the company, Alfried was soon identified as "the richest man in Europe." Krupp helped to spark the postwar comeback of West Germany as an industrial power-house.

Much of the credit for the rebirth of Krupp went to Berthold Beitz, a super-salesman hired by Alfried as the operating head of the company. During the war Beitz had run Poland's oil industry for the Nazis. But he was known for his compassion. Stories surfacing after the war cited him for saving the lives of thousands of Poles and Jews. He was honored after the war by both the Polish and Israeli governments. For Krupp, Beitz traveled to Eastern Europe and the Middle East to find customers. One of his impressive sales was a multimillion-dollar contract to build steel mills in the Soviet Union. He worked hard to change Krupp's image, but, as he once told an interviewer, the Krupp name itself was a problem. "Krupp! Krupp! Krupp!" he exclaimed. "It sounds like a cannon going off."

The very structure of the company (it was wholly owned by one person) posed problems in the 1960s. German banks had financed the company's growth with loans on top of loans. Alfried stubbornly refused to go to the public and raise money by selling stock. The company was still his personal fief. That was all right as long as sales and profits went up and up. But coal and steel went into a slump after 1965, and the company found itself making no profits while it owed 263 banks something like $2.1 billion. As a result, Alfried Krupp was forced by his bankers into a radical restructuring of the family enterprise. On April 1, 1967, he announced his decision to convert the company into a corporation whose stock would be held by a public foundation. On July 30, 1967, Alfried Krupp, two weeks short of his sixtieth birthday, died. The cause of death was never made clear, although it was widely believed to be lung cancer. Alfried had chain-smoked Camel cigarettes for thirty years.

His death brought to an end the Krupp dynasty. Alfried had been married and divorced twice. His only child was a son, Arndt, who was born in 1938. Arndt had no interest in the business. He renounced all claims to the Krupp properties in return for an annual stipend of $600,000. He told one reporter, "I am not a man like my father, who sacrifices his whole life for something, not knowing whether it is really worth it in our time. My father worked more than he lived."

In 1974, thanks largely to the sales efforts of Beitz, the Shah of Iran bought 25 percent of Krupp's stock. After the 1979 revolution that installed the Ayatollah Khomeni as head of state, the new Moslem Republic of Iran continued to hold on to its Krupp stock. In 1981, when Krupp proposed to lay off four thousand steelworkers, the Iranians objected, asserting, "It is our ideology that the fate of ordinary people is more important than economic affairs." It was a view earlier Krupps might have supported. In the end Krupp reduced its work force by four thousand, and Iran continued to hold on to its stock. The other 75 percent is held by the Alfried Krupp von Bohlen und Halbach Foundation.

In late 1983 two *Wall Street Journal* reporters, Diane Coutu and Roger Thurow, took a long look at Krupp, concluding that while the company was attempting to move into such areas as synthetic fuels, nuclear medicine, and biotechnology, "there are many who believe that full-fledged diversification will come slowly at Krupp. Tradition dies hard in a company with over one hundred years of history in the steel business. Although group executives like to talk as if Krupp were just another faceless corporation, the presence of the colorful Krupp family is still deeply felt, inhibiting both profits and progress."

In 1966 Krupp had 102,000 employees; in 1980, eighty-five thousand. By 1986 it was down to sixty-seven thousand—and only twenty-eight thousand of them were steel makers. In 1986 Krupp owned fifty-seven companies in West Germany, sixty-eight in other countries, and it was getting only 20 percent of its revenues from steel. Krupp's trading arm, Krupp Handel, does all kinds of deals, the way a Japanese trading house does. It buys and sells crude oil, it markets fuel in Germany, it has a big printing company, a computer software house, and a shipping line with a cargo capacity of twenty million tons. Krupp is also involved in a project to build a supercomputer for Germany.

The biggest part of Krupp today is an area the company calls "machinery and plant." Krupp manufactures gigantic pieces of equipment such as bucket-wheel excavators used by surface miners and cranes with incredible lifting capacity. It has a new supercrane that is 458 feet high, can lift 550 tons, and barrel down the road at 39 miles an hour. Building plants is a Krupp specialty, and it can put up all kinds: rolling mills, cement factories, can-making lines, presses, sugar mills, edibile oil plants. Its biggest customer in 1985 was the People's Republic of China, which ordered a copper casting-rolling mill, two soya extraction plants, a magnesite sinter plant, and six containerships.

Krupp now does about half of its business outside West Germany. It's ready to do for the rest of the world what it did for its home country.

Access   Altendorfer Str. 103
Postfach 1022 52
D-4300 Essen 1, West Germany
(49) 201-188-2428

Kyocera

Sales $1.8 billion
Profits $121 million
U.S. Sales $500 million
Rank World's largest maker of semiconductor packaging
Founded 1959
Employees 17,300 (average age: 29)
Headquarters Kyoto, Japan

Some people in Japan consider Kyocera a "crazy" company, a designation that doesn't bother Kazuo Inamori, the charismatic founder of the firm. He has such a strong belief in the power of the subconscious that he considers "crazy" a compliment. Crazy or not, under his leadership, Kyocera became one of the most successful Japanese startups of the post–World War II era.

Work at Kyocera seems akin to a religious experience. You are expected to work long hours and to think about your work even when you are not on the job. Inamori advocates concentration, heavy concentration. He also places a high value on self-motivation, motivation so strong that it summons up energies from a person's subconscious to tackle problems. The company's bible, *The Kyocera Philosophy*, contains the thoughts of Inamori as he has expressed them over the years in talks and articles. It's a philosophy that's a cross between the California human potential movement and Jungian psychology. One of its planks is: "If we have a very strong wish and continue to desire it, any wish may eventually come true." Another is: "The result of our work or life is equal to the product of 'ability' multiplied by 'dedication' multiplied by 'thinking.'" Note the multipliers in this formula. They are what Inamori considers important, not ability. Kyocera also operates under an "amoeba management" system where employees work in clusters of ten to twenty, each group maintaining its own profit-and-loss accounts. The point is for each cell in the company "to be alive."

When new hirees at Kyocera are evaluated, they receive the highest marks for self-motivation, even impertinence, another quality Inamori respects. The lowest grades go to people who, even if they do their jobs well, do not appear to be self-starters.

The Kyocera leader preaches this gospel endlessly inside the company but he's not bashful about doing it on the outside too. Invited in 1985 to deliver a lecture on productivity at Case Western Reserve University in Cleveland, Inamori declared that "our society overly emphasizes scientific logic" and that it would be better to value dedication over ability. He said there are other words for dedication: "willpower, strong desire, zeal, dream, or romanticism. What is important is its essence. . . . I interpret our willpower to be a cry from the soul which has been shaken and awakened. And I believe that such a strong desire from our soul is an extremely powerful force. When we have a strong willpower, we become devoted." It's not the usual advice received by engineers.

It's all right to be crazy, but you also have to be lucky. When Kyocera was founded in 1959 as Kyoto Ceramics (the name was changed to Kyocera in 1982), who had ever heard of "the chip," the integrated circuit destined to become the building block of computers and modern electronics? Scientists at Texas Instruments and Fairchild Semiconductor were then developing the integrated circuit on a silicon chip. Kyocera was a tiny ceramics company in Japan but from the start it had antennae, a sensitivity to the applications of ceramics, their end uses. The first product it made was ceramic insulation for the cathode ray tubes used in black-and-white television sets. That role as a supplier to the electronics industry attuned Kyocera to its mission: Develop new ways to use ceramics by learning as much as you can about the business of your customers.

Kyocera's big breakthrough came in the late 1960s when Fairchild approached the company's newly opened branch office in California about the possibility of coming up with a better package to seal the new semiconductor devices (integrated circuits). A combination of glass and ceramics had been used but the defect rate was very high. Kyocera developed an all-ceramic package that worked. Here's Inamori's description of the technology involved: "We form ceramic powder into thin sheets, resembling sheets of chewing gum, but much, much thinner. We then use a paste made of refractory metal powder with a high melting point, such as tungsten or molybdenum, to print electronic circuits onto each one of these flexible, green ceramic sheets. These are laminated and sintered in a reduction atmosphere. In this way, a monolithic structure is obtained with electronic circuits formed of refractory metal powder inside."

So effective was this housing that Kyocera achieved a near monopolistic position. It has remained the dominant supplier of this component to chip manufacturers. "They gave this order to us, a new company with no established name or client referral list," Inamori has explained, "because it was not an easy task and an established company would not undertake something so new and difficult." Yoshimichi Aoyama, who supervised the project at Kyocera, put it another way: "Ceramics call for a special artisan technology. Mass-producing such an artisan technology is something else—almost an impossible task. But it can be done after painstaking redoing. Average American suppliers cannot put up with these endless rejections."

Today Kyocera makes more than semiconductor sleeves. It expanded on its own into a number of new business areas, and it bought its way into others by acquiring two companies that were failing: Cybernet Electronics (it used to produce CB radios, now it makes computers) in 1979, and Yashica (the camera maker) in 1983. In 1986 Kyocera was supplying industrial ceramic products such as thread guides, nozzles, and machine tool parts; consumer products like cutting tools, scissors, calculators, compact disc players, cameras, artificial gemstones (under the Cermet name), dental implants, artificial bones, even personal computers (it was the company that supplied the versatile lap computer which Tandy sold as the Radio Shack 100, Olivetti as the M10, and NEC as the PC-8201A).

Inamori, and by extension, Kyocera, is nothing if not ambitious. When the Japanese government announced that Nippon Telegraph & Telephone would no longer be permitted to have a monopoly on telecommunications, Kyocera became the first company in Japan to field a competitor, Daini Denden (which means "second phone company"), a consortium in which Kyocera holds the biggest stake. (Sony is a partner in this venture.) "For the first time in one hundred years, the monopoly has been demolished," said Inamori. "This is a revolutionary happening, and we don't want to lose the opportunity to take part."

Big as Kyocera has become, it still bears the personal stamp of Kazuo Inamori—and stories about Kyocera inevitably end up telling *his* story. The son of a printer, Inamori was born in 1932 in Kagoshima, which is almost as far south as you can go in Japan (it's at the southern tip of the island of Kyushu). His early life was punctuated by one setback after another. He twice failed to pass the entrance examination for the regional high school. When he was thirteen, he came down with tuberculosis. It was during his convalescence, according to one biographer, that he came across a religious organization called Seimei-no-Ie (House of Spiritual Growth), which taught that "any concentrated true desire sustained for a long period of time grows of itself like the power of a magnet attracting all the necessary factors to bring that desire into reality." Inamori credits this teaching with giving him the inner support to recover from TB and other disappointments in his life.

And there were others. He failed to pass the entrance examination to the pharmacy department at Osaka University. He had to go to Kagoshima University, which he himself describes as a "milk train school." After graduating with a degree in chemical engineering, he applied for a job with an oil company, Teikoku-Sekyu, but failed the entry test. "In those days," he told an interviewer, Sohichiro Tahara, "I couldn't stand myself because of all my unlucky happenings. Occasionally, I even got mad and felt like becoming a gangster. As a matter of fact, I was taking karate lessons and I had confidence that this skill could help me as a gangster."

In 1955, through a recommendation from a professor at Kagoshima University, Inamori joined a company in Kyoto, Shofu Industries, where he began working in ceramics. Three and a half years later, after a dispute with the management, he left to launch Kyoto Ceramics. Joining him were seven co-workers from Shofu, including his supervisor, Masaji Aoyama, who raised the initial capital of $10,000. The founders of Kyoto Ceramics, a little fearful of what they were doing (it's highly unusual for Japanese workers to quit their company and start a new one), signified their commitment in a blood-signing ceremony. Inamori married his wife, Asako, the day after he quit Shofu. Aoyama's son, Yoshimichi, joined the company in 1960, a year after it was started.

Kyocera, under the lead of Inamori, is not your everyday company, either American or Japanese. Its corporate motto is: "Respect Heaven and Love People." It has an intensity reflected in emotional two-day management meetings that are held every month. Managers are known to break down and cry at these sessions, which begin early in the morning and go on to as late as midnight. Kyocera tries to avoid rigid hierarchies in its offices and factories but employees at the San Diego plant can be recognized by what they wear: Salaried people have blue jackets, production workers yellow, quality control staffers white, and foremen pink. At one point Inamori became so taken with the title "Man of Responsibility," that he wanted to print up cards that carried this title. And he did appoint one man, Tsuneo Okumura, to be the company missionary, traveling from plant to plant to build employee morale. One sermon Inamori preaches to the Kyocera congregation is: "Do you create your product with love? If you make things with love, your products will sell without fail."

Kyocera's headquarters is in Kyoto, the capital of old Japan and the spiritual center of the country. Hardly any large companies are based there. It is a city of 1,650 temples—one for every thousand residents. At one of the Zen temples, Enfuku-ji, Kyocera installed a company tomb to hold the remains of two thousand employees. "We are all members of one family," said Inamori, "so it is natural to stay together after we die."

Inamori's unorthodox ways in a country that prizes consensus have gained him enemies. They pounced on him in 1985 for not playing by the rules. While a number of companies in Japan were making cordless phones (it wasn't against the law), the only phones that could be used legally were the ones made by Nippon Telephone & Telegraph (a neat catch-22). Kyocera began making cordless models and selling them at a lower price than the NTT phones. The government, responding to an NTT complaint, stepped in and shut down Kyocera. The company had to recall the thirty-five thousand phones it had sold, and stop making new ones.

In the same year the Japanese government prosecuted Kyocera for selling artificial bones to hospitals without getting the proper approval from the Ministry of Health. Impatient with the bureaucracy, Inamori had charged ahead and sold these implants to some 800 hospitals for $10 million, $8 million of which was paid by the government's health insurance plan. In the end, Kyocera was forced to recall its products, repay the hospitals, and shut down its bioceramic plant for thirty-five days.

In August 1985, after Inamori's humbling had been widely reported in the Japanese press, a newspaper polled Kyocera employees, asking them, "Do you understand and agree with the management thinking and policies?" One hundred percent replied "yes." And to the question, "Are you satisfied with your work?" 90 percent answered "yes."

Kazuo Inamori is a man of passion who acts out his passions. In 1984 he established the Inamori Foundation as the Japanese counterpart of the Nobel Foundation. Capitalized with an initial endowment of $50 million, virtually all of it donated by Inamori, the foundation was chartered to award the annual Kyoto prizes for "monumental accomplishments" in three fields—advanced technology, basic sciences, and creative arts and moral sciences—which are not covered by the Nobel prizes. Each prize carries a cash award of 45 million yen, which, at the exchange rates prevailing in 1986, translated to $300,000, making it a more valuable award than the Nobel.

In 1985, the first year they were awarded, Kyoto prizes went to Dr. Rudolf Emil Kalman, an American mathematician and engineer, for his development of a control theory to explain the workings of a dynamic system; Dr. Claude Elwood Shannon, a Massachusetts Institute of Technology mathematician who has made major contributions to the theory of information science; and Olivier Messiaen, a French composer and organist. The 1986 prizes went to this trio: Professor Nicole M. LeDouarin, a French scientist who invented a new technology that provided fresh insights into the immune systems of higher animals, including man; Dr. George E. Hutchinson, an American ecologist who has made comprehensive studies of lakes, leading to his theory of ecological niches; and Osamu Noguchi, an American sculptor and theatrical set designer.

In the first year there was one other award, the special Inamori prize, which went to the Nobel Foundation in Stockholm in recognition "of the historical role played by the Nobel prizes, which symbolize the dignity of the intellect."

Access 5-22 Kitainoue-cho, Higashino Yamashina-ku
Kyoto 607, Japan
(81) 75-592-3851

Inamori Foundation
87 Kankoboko-cho, Shijyodori, Muromachi
Higashi-iru, Shimogyo-ku
Kyoto 600, Japan
(81) 75-255-2688

Kyocera International
8611 Balboa Ave.
San Diego, Cal. 92123
(619) 576-2600

Lonrho	**Sales** $3.9 billion

Sales $3.9 billion
Profits $115 million
U.S. Sales $100 million
Rank 22d-largest company in Britain
Largest food company in Africa
2d-largest seller of Scotch whiskey in Britain
3d-largest Mercedes-Benz distributor in
Africa
Largest publisher of weekly newspapers in
Scotland
Largest printer of annual reports in Britain
World's 3d-largest platinum miner
Founded 1909
Employees 118,000
Headquarters London, England

The front cover of Lonrho's 1985 annual report evoked the geographical and business diversity of this British conglomerate. It depicted, side by side, the tiered balconies of the Princess Hotel in Acapulco, Mexico, a row of coffee fields in Zimbabwe, and a gold-filled quartz reef in the Ashanti region of Ghana. Yes, Lonrho-owned companies mine gold in Ghana, grow coffee in Zimbabwe, and operate the Princess Hotel chain, which has outposts in Mexico, Bermuda, and the Bahamas. And there's more—much more—to Lonrho. It encompasses eight hundred companies in eighty countries, ranging over various kinds of businesses: newspaper publishing, stamp printing, French wines, Scotch whiskey (Haig, Whyte & Mackay), agriculture, gambling, mining, freight forwarding, textiles, car and truck distribution.

Lonrho's roots are in Africa, having been formed in 1909 as the London & Rhodesian Mining & Land Company (hence Lonrho). It was not one of the British colonial giants, and little is known about its history prior to 1961, the year it acquired the Rhodesian companies (gold mines, farms, a Mercedes-Benz dealership) owned by Roland ("Tiny") Rowland. Far more significant than the property acquisitions was the acquisition of Rowland, who became chief executive of Lonrho and proceeded to transform the company through a series of brash takeovers and mergers.

According to press reports (he doesn't release any information himself), Rowland was born in India in 1917 to a British mother and a German father whose name was Furhop. His original name was Roland Walter Furhop. The Furhops moved to Germany after World War I and then to England in the 1930s after Adolf Hitler came to power. When World War I broke out in 1939, Roland changed his surname to Rowland.

340

Although the Furhops were anti-Nazis, that did not prevent the family from being interned on the Isle of Man as German aliens. Rowland's mother died in the internment camp in 1945. It was not an experience that inspired affection for British authority in Rowland's breast.

Rowland went out to Rhodesia in 1947 when he was thirty years old. First he farmed. Then he went into gold mining. He served as a consultant to Rio Tinto-Zinc, one of the world's mining giants. His 1961 sale of his Rhodesian interests to the London & Rhodesian Mining & Land Company was comparable to Robert O. Anderson's sale at about the same time of his Hondo Oil company to Atlantic Refining in the United States. Anderson took over Atlantic Refining and turned it into the company now known as ARCO (Atlantic Richfield). Anderson was ARCO. And Rowland became Lonrho. (Twenty-five years later Anderson and Rowland became business partners.)

Rowland's 1961 sale of his company was prescient, or lucky. It preceded by two years the breakup of British-controlled Rhodesia. Northern Rhodesia became Zambia and Nyasal and became Malawi, both black-controlled countries. The white settlers of Southern Rhodesia held out, declaring their independence from the British Commonwealth. With Rhodesia virtually isolated from the rest of the world (it was not until 1980 that the black majority gained control of the country now known as Zimbabwe), Rowland moved his base to London where he set in motion the aggrandizement whose figures speak for themselves: 1961 sales, $11.2 million; 1986, $3.9 billion.

An urbane, rambunctious character who relishes not being a "member of the club" in caste-bound British society, Rowland loves to rail against the aristocratic old-boy network of the City (London's Wall Street), where he maintains Lonrho's headquarters in Cheapside House, directly across from St. Paul's Cathedral. He picks fights with the Establishment. He squealed on British oil companies for delivering oil to Rhodesia, which was a violation of government sanctions. He teamed up with Sir Freddie Laker in his fight against government-owned British Airways. He conducted a fierce, seven-year campaign to take over Britain's most prestigious department store, Harrods (one of the few fights he lost). A six-footer, he himself insists on the sobriquet "Tiny." He signs his name that way.

Africa has remained Rowland's favorite stamping ground, accounting for nearly half of Lonrho's profits. There is hardly a corner of the continent that he hasn't explored. Lonrho operates in sixteen African countries. It grows tobacco, corn, and wheat in Zambia; tea in Malawi; and sugar in Swaziland. It bottles Coca-Cola in Zambia, Pepsi-Cola in

Nigeria. It operates breweries in Malawi and Zambia. It's one of the largest distributors of cars and trucks on the African continent, and it owns one of the world's more exotic resorts, the Mount Kenya Safari Club in Kenya. Tiny Rowland may be a big-time capitalist in Britain, where Lonrho runs a string of casinos, but he has gained the confidence of many African leaders, no matter what their political persuasion. Kenneth Kaunda, longtime president of Zambia, once called Rowland "one of my six good capitalist friends."

In 1978 Tanzania nationalized all the Lonrho interests, which included tea plantations, office supplies, and vehicle dealerships. Five years later Tanzania invited Lonrho to return to the country to resume the management of the tea estates it used to run. The Tanzanians also agreed to compensate Lonrho $13.7 million for the nationalization. In 1986 the Marxist government of Mozambique invited Lonrho to join with it in the management of farm lands and ranches. As a result, Lonrho now ranks as one of the world's largest cattle ranchers. Together with its interests in Zimbabwe, it's managing a herd of 120,000 head grazing on two million acres. "I have done more for Africa than Bob Geldof," Rowland boasted in 1986.

Zimbabwe, Tiny Rowland's starting point, is still a strong focal point for Lonrho. In 1981 Lonrho acquired *The Observer,* one of the two Sunday highbrow newspapers in Britain (Robert O. Anderson had previously saved the newspaper from going under by having ARCO buy it). Three years later Donald Trelford, editor of *The Observer,* wrote a piece about Zimbabwe that was less than flattering. It documented reports of widespread killing and beating of civilians by the Zimbabwe military forces. Tiny Rowland was furious. He accused Trelford of "trying to drive me out of business in Zimbabwe," and he fired off a letter to Zimbabwe Prime Minister Robert Mugabe, apologizing for the actions of his own newspaper. The journalistic fraternity in London was appalled.

Rows are nothing new to Rowland. In 1973 a faction of the Lonrho board attempted to unseat Rowland, and there was a government inquiry into self-dealing by Rowland and other executives of the company. It prompted a remark by Edward Heath, onetime prime minister, that Lonrho represented "the unacceptable face of capitalism." It's a comment that has been trotted out every time anyone has profiled Lonrho in the press. In 1983 Rowland referred to the Heath comment as follows: "It's the only notable thing he ever said."

Rowland is adept at playing both sides of a political fence. While he is good friends with the black leaders in Africa, he has important holdings in South Africa. What he seems to love to do is upset people. In 1987, when Ernest Saunders, the former head of Guinness, was brought up on charges, it was Rowland who posted bail. When the British government went on record frowning on any new investments in South Africa, Tiny Rowland deepened Lonrho's stake there by increasing its holding in Western Platinum from 50 percent to nearly 100 percent, thereby infuriating anti-apartheid activists in Britain. In 1986, after U.S. planes bombed Tripoli and President Reagan ordered U.S. oil companies out of Libya, Tiny Rowland flew to North Africa to see if he could work out a deal with Muammar Qaddafi under which Lonrho would take over the oil concessions that had been held by the American companies. It was vintage Rowlandism. And while the Libyan deal was cooking, Rowland got together with Robert O. Anderson, who had sold him *The Observer* in 1981 and who had left Atlantic Richfield to resume his original career as an oil wildcatter. The Anderson-Rowland partnership is pumping oil and gas in the Midwest and Rocky Mountain states.

Meanwhile, Tiny Rowland also had his eyes on the Far East. He has a working relationship with the big Japanese trading house Nissho Iwai, and in 1987 the Japanese brokerage house Nomura Securities was preparing to sell about $75 million of Lonrho stock in Japan, with a subsequent listing on the Tokyo Stock Exchange.

Tiny Rowland, who turned seventy in 1987, runs Lonrho as a one-man show, as befitting the largest stockholder. He owns close to 20 percent of the shares—his holding was worth more than $200 million in early 1987. Anyone contemplating a takeover of Lonrho would need to keep in mind Rowland's remarks on an earlier occasion, when he said that anyone trying to do in the company would need "a sub-machine gun, mortars, guns, all sorts of ammunition because I am going to protect it to the bitter end."

Access   Cheapside House
138 Cheapside
London EC2V 6BL, England
(44) 1-606-9898

<table>
<tr><td rowspan="9">

Marks & Spencer

</td><td>

Sales $6.3 billion

Profits $388 million

Rank Britain's largest department store chain
Britain's 8th-largest company (in market value)
Britain's largest exporter of clothing
Britain's 5th-largest food retailer

Founded 1884

Employees 63,100

Headquarters London, England

</td></tr>
</table>

The British royal family and its entourage may shop at Harrods, but nearly everyone else in the United Kingdom goes to Marks & Spencer. More than fourteen million customers—a quarter of Britain's population—visit one of M&S's 265 stores each week, making this venerable chain the country's favorite retailer. With stores on virtually every Main Street in Britain, stodgy but reliable Marks & Spencer delivers goods whose value is a byword in the ordinary gossip heard in pubs or living rooms.

The image of "Marks and Sparks," as British shoppers affectionately call it, is admittedly dull, but the volume and impact of its business is dazzling: Britons buy one third of their underwear and nightwear there, including half of all the ladies slips and a quarter of all the men's socks sold in the country. M&S sells more fish, fresh poultry, and houseplants than any other British store, and Britons buy a million chilled (not *frozen*) chickens there every week. The company's flagship store at Marble Arch in London appears in the *Guinness Book of Records* as "the department store with the fastest-moving stock in the world." That same store sold more shoes in 1985 than anyone else anywhere.

By sticking to a strict "buy British" philosophy, M&S is a great boon to domestic manufacturers. It buys one fifth of all the clothing made in Britain. Some eight hundred companies, employing 170,000 people, supply St. Michael brand merchandise to M&S. Forty-six of these have been suppliers for more than forty years, one hundred for more than twenty-five years.

M&S has judiciously built a close relationship with the ailing British textile industry, enabling the firm to enjoy the benefits of a manufacturing base while never owning so much as a single loom. Like America's Sears, Roebuck, M&S wields mighty clout with its suppliers, who must stick to rigid manufacturing and cost guidelines to keep the M&S business.

Never a fashion trend-setter—one analyst said the best M&S can offer is lagging the market by a season—it is nevertheless the most success-

344

ful new product innovator in British retailing. M&S is credited with springing the avocado on an unsuspecting British public in 1966. And more recently it has stunned the food industry by bringing into its supermarkets a variegated line of prepared, chilled foods that have won high marks for their quality and value. Would you believe cauliflower and cheese, Chicken Kiev, ratatouille, salmon mayonnaise with new potatoes, moules marineres, layered fish lasagne? English cooking was never like this.

Marks & Spencer has triumphed in the marketplace despite the fact that it ignores many rules U.S. retailers swear by. The stores have no fitting rooms (returns are easy), no brands other than St. Michael, no displays, no loss leaders, no frequent sales, no delivery, no mail or telephone orders, and very little advertising. They did relent in 1985 and, after testing in Scotland, introduced a charge card. In one year 1.2 million charge cards were issued, accounting for 10 percent of turnover.

The M&S winning formula of quality and value goes back to its Jewish founder Michael Marks, who at age twenty-one fled Poland for England and started peddling merchandise carried on his back. Marks's English was so poor that cottage doors in Yorkshire villages slammed in his face. In desperation he set up a stall in a Leeds marketplace in 1884, operating with a Spartan simplicity that still permeates the company. "Don't ask the price—it's a penny" became his business slogan, and sure enough, the pennies came rolling in. Needing capital to expand, Marks found a partner, Tom Spencer, in 1894, but the Marks family always ran the business. Marks's son Simon took over in 1917, and was soon joined by his childhood friend and double brother-in-law (each married the other's sister) Israel Sieff. The firm took off under their stewardship and went public in 1926. When Simon died in 1964, Israel succeeded him as head of the company.

Israel's son Marcus (later Lord Sieff) became chairman in 1972, continuing to emphasize the social responsibility that has been a hallmark of the firm ever since Simon Marks and Israel Sieff discovered clerks skipping lunches to send money home during the lean 1930s. M&S employees enjoy a wide range of benefits, including low-cost meals, medical services, profit sharing, savings plans, and pensions. Lord Sieff once told his counterparts at other British companies that "management must care for the people they employ in all aspects of their daily work."

Marks & Spencer contributes 1 percent of its pretax profits to charity and community causes. It also lends out executives to manage urban economic development, supports small business ventures, and funds youth and community action programs. In 1984, when it was celebrating its one-hundredth birthday, M&S kicked in an additional $5.4 million, on top of its contribution budget of $3.5 million, for projects designed to help the sick, the elderly, and the disabled. One project was a housing development for the elderly in Leeds, where the company was born.

Whatever M&S has spent on these do-good programs, it doesn't seem to have impinged on its profitability. In 1985 only a dozen companies in Britain made more money.

Is the Marks & Spencer idea exportable? The company has tried, but so far without much success. It has ten stores in France, Belgium, and Ireland, and it has two hundred stores in Canada operating under the names People's and D'Allairds. The stores followed the British model slavishly, which didn't exactly entice Canadian shoppers used to more flamboyant merchandising. A Scottish shareholder wrote to the company after visiting his daughter in Canada and reported that when he asked her why she didn't patronize Marks & Spencer, she replied that she didn't enjoy shopping in a "hospital ward." In France Marks & Spencer ran into trouble when it insisted on imposing its practice of no fitting rooms. "French women do not want to take garments home," said Lord Sieff in his autobiography, *Don't Ask the Price*. "They want to try on everything on the premises, including underwear. They started to do this in a corner of the sales floor, so we had to provide fitting rooms."

Still, Marks & Spencer has hopes of becoming an international presence. In 1987 it was planning to open two stores in Hong Kong and four in upstate New York—in Albany, Watertown, and Poughkeepsie—under the D'Allaird's name. In charge of this expansion is Lord Rayner, who became chairman in 1984, the first "outsider" (he's not descended from the Marks or Sieff families) to head the company. A bachelor who turned sixty in 1987, Lord Rayner joined M&S in 1953 after briefly considering the ministry. He was twice lent to the government to instill some efficiency in its bureaucracy. Upon succeeding Lord Sieff, he said, "My job is to manage change."

Access Michael House
36-37 Baker St.
London W1A 1DN, England
(44) 1-935-4422

Matsushita

Sales $30 billion
Profits $1.1 million
U.S. Sales $6 billion
Rank World's 15th-largest company
Japan's 2d-largest industrial manufacturer
World's largest consumer electronics producer
World's 2d-largest maker of television sets
World's largest videocassette recorder producer
World's largest maker of robots
Founded 1918
Employees 133,000
Headquarters Osaka, Japan

Of the nine hundred million television sets installed in the world by 1986, Matsushita figures that more than one hundred million came from its factories. In the videocassette recorder (VCR) market, the company's presence is even greater. In 1985, when twenty-eight million VCRs were sold in the world, Matsushita's share was estimated at 42 percent. As one wag once said about this Osaka giant, "They believe in peace, brotherhood, and market share."

Of course not all those appliances were sold under one brand, and none was sold under the Matsushita name, which stands for the founder of the company, Konosuke Matsushita. It's a Matsushita product if it carries the brand names Panasonic, National, Technics, or Quasar. Many products bearing the brand names of other companies are made by Matsushita. In Japan, for example, IBM's personal computer was manufactured by Matsushita. In the United States VCRs sold under the General Electric, J. C. Penney, Magnavox, and Sylvania names have come from Matsushita factories in Japan. Kodak's 8-mm video cameras were manufactured by Matsushita. JVC, whose corporate name is the Victor Company of Japan, invented the video home system (VHS) format that triumphed in the VCR market over Sony's Betamax and Philips's V-2000 systems—and Matsushita owns 50.8 percent of JVC.

Matsushita (pronounced "Mot-SOOSH-ta") makes a line of products that will not stop. Americans are familiar with its audio and video products, but in Japan the Panasonic, National, and Technics names appear on a multitude of appliances found in the home: toasters, vacuum cleaners, refrigerators, fans, food processors, washing machines, rice cookers, irons, air conditioners, kerosene heaters. You would be hard put to name an appliance that the company does *not* make (an electric shaver is apparently one). And beyond these household goods, Matsushita supplies an incredible number of industrial products, office machines, and basic electronic components, to wit: light bulbs, batteries, telephones, computers, semiconductors, robots (it's Japan's largest maker), electric motors, floppy discs, cathode ray tubes, optical memory discs, laser printers, facsimile machines, copiers. By its own count Matsushita makes more than fourteen thousand products. It's one of the world's industrial powerhouses, ranking first in the sale of electronic goods to consumers.

Matsushita is, in a number of ways, a corporate paradox. While it has this overflowing larder of products, it's sometimes derided in Japan as a company adept at capitalizing on what others invent. People used to call it *Maneshita,* which means copycat. On the one hand, it's regarded as a tough-minded, bottom line–oriented company that demands results from its managers, or else. And yet it promulgates a humanistic philosophy that's soft and mystical. It's a company whose size boggles the mind, but it grew out of the vision of one man: Konosuke Matsushita.

However, it's the nature of life to be paradoxical—and Konosuke Matsushita always seemed to have a sense of that. In an essay he wrote in 1977, he cautioned against religious dogmatism.

> There are many religious organizations and sects, each with doctrines and teachings enriched by the wisdom of generations. Despite their excellence, however, none of them has a monopoly on the truth in all its aspects. When we think of the unfathomable universe and of the complexity and subtlety of the human mind, we realize that what we have grasped so far is but a small part of the whole truth. Perhaps we could say that religion and science have only revealed part of the truth. If that is the case, we cannot hold one religion to be absolute and then criticize—let alone reject—other religious organizations and sects.

Such reflections might seem out of place in a business organization (one is not likely to encounter them at Exxon or General Motors), but they are very much at home in Matsushita. The company has a spiritual tone in keeping with the founder's dictum that business organizations should have "a secular mission to the world." Takashi Ota, a correspondent for the *Christian Science Monitor,* reported after a visit to Matsushita that "there is an almost religious atmosphere about the place, as if work itself were considered something sacred." Matsushita was the first company in Japan to have a company song, whose lyrics rhapsodize about "sending our goods to the people of the world, endlessly and continuously, like water gushing from a fountain." Matsushita has a creed:

> To recognize our responsibilities as industrialists, to foster progress, to promote the general welfare of society, and to devote ourselves to the further development of world culture.

And it's a company that has codified what it calls its "spiritual values," which are:

1. National service through industry
2. Fairness
3. Harmony and cooperation
4. Struggle for betterment
5. Courtesy and humility
6. Adjustment and assimilation
7. Gratitude

These are not pieces of window dressing, like the ethical codes of conduct drafted by many American companies in recent years. They play a large role in the daily life of a Matsushita worker. The day begins with a ten-minute meeting in which groups sing the song, recite the creed, or discuss a social problem presented by one of the members. The company's values are also part of ongoing training programs. Teenagers who join the company (and in Japan it's deemed an honor to work for Matsushita) are inculcated right away in the ideology. To Konosuke Matsushita, it was unthinkable that people would devote so much of their waking hours to work without vesting that time with spiritual significance—and he has tried to impart that significance.

Nothing's said about it in the credo or manifesto of spiritual values, but Matsushita's ability to generate *profits* is impressive by whatever measuring rod is applied. This otherworldliness laced with profit maximization led Louis Kraar, a *Fortune* writer, to describe the company as a "sprawling enterprise . . . held together by a peculiar combination of warm paternalism and cold finance." Kraar cynically observed that "Matsushita helps society only with products that yield at least a 10 percent return."

Those comments appeared in 1972 after Matsushita had experienced a slight downturn, causing Kraar to wonder if the old-time religion was losing its punch. He reported that "many in the work force, whose average age is twenty-five, are gradually growing skeptical about all the uplifting philosophy and ceremonies. Their doubts obviously pose a serious long-term challenge to the cherished corporate spirit." At the time, Matsushita had just finished a year (1971) in which the company earned $165 million on sales of $2.7 billion. Fifteen years later Matsushita was logging in only thirty-six days sales that it took a year to reach in 1971.

Unlike Sony, which made its mark in overseas marketing, or Hitachi and Toshiba, which were prime suppliers of heavy electrical equipment to industrial customers, Matsushita's base is the Japanese consumer. It has legendary clout in its home market. Matsushita's electrical appliances are carried by fifty thousand dealers in Japan, and twenty-six thousand of them are exclusive dealers; that is, they carry the lines of no other manufacturer. Matsushita's major Japanese brand name, National, is omnipresent in Japan.

Matsushita's extraordinary record as a profit generator does not surprise Zenith Radio of Chicago, which doggedly pursued Matsushita and other Japanese television set makers in an antitrust suit alleging that they dumped their receivers in the American market at artificially low prices (less than they were selling for in Japan) in an effort to destroy the U.S. television set manufacturing industry. Although the Japanese profess not to be fond of lawyers, in this case they hired high-priced American legal talent to defend themselves, dragging the case on for sixteen years before it was dismissed in 1986. In Japan consumer groups inspired by Zenith launched an eight-month boycott of Matsushita in the early 1970s. The prices in Japan came down 10 percent to 15 percent.

Another way of looking at Matsushita is as a chip off the Osaka block. Osaka, located three hundred miles west of Tokyo in central Japan, is the nation's second-largest city. It's also the merchant city of Japan, home to many of the country's greatest economic dynasties. And it has a rambunctious character more akin to Chicago than New York. It's a city where business gets done. How Osaka companies differ from the ones in Tokyo was explained neatly by George Fields, a Japanese-born market researcher, in his book *From Bonsai to Levi*'s. A Tokyo company, he pointed out, is likely to have the rigidity of the old samurai class, going back to the days of the Tokugawa shogunate, which ruled Japan for nearly three hundred years (1603–1867). But Osaka, with a commercial tradition reaching back to the sixteenth century, did not have a strong samurai class, and, as Fields notes, the Osaka merchants, "merrily indulged in commerce during the Tokugawa shogunate period." Even today, says Fields, people in Osaka greet each other with, "Are you making any money?" or "How's business?" The Tokyo style is more formal, which is why Fields believes that Osaka companies are closer in spirit to Western companies than are Tokyo's.

Konosuke Matsushita (his surname means "lucky man under the

pine tree") was born on November 27, 1894, in Wakayama Prefecture, a rural area thirty miles southeast of Osaka. His father was a well-to-do farmer, and Konosuke was the youngest of nine children. Matsushita's father lost the family fortune speculating in rice futures and when he was ten, Konosuke had to quit school to go to work in Osaka. For five years he was apprenticed to a bicycle maker and then, still a teenager, he joined the ranks of the Osaka Electric Company, where he rose after seven years to become the youngest inspector on the payroll, enjoying meanwhile a ringside seat on the electrification of Japan.

In 1918, at the ripe old age of twenty-three, Konosuke "retired" from Osaka Electric after the company rejected his idea for a double-ended socket. With one hundred yen (then equivalent to fifty dollars), he, his wife, and his wife's brother went into business to produce the socket themselves. After a bumpy start they did all right, employing fifty people by 1922. They went into consumer appliances in 1923 with a long-lasting bicycle lamp, followed by irons (1927), radios (1930), batteries (1931), electric motors (1934), light bulbs (1936). The National trademark was registered in 1925.

It's clear that even as he was thinking about these product fields, Matsushita was also developing his ideas about how a company should be run. On May 5, 1932, the fourteenth anniversary of the company, he gathered all his employees in a meeting to announce his 250-year plan. (There's nothing like short-term thinking.) In that exhortation, he told his troops that industrial companies should have as their mission the elimination of poverty by making products available at the lowest possible prices.

During the 1930s Matsushita devised a divisional structure similar to the one Alfred Sloan was creating at General Motors (Chevrolet, Buick, Pontiac, Oldsmobile, Cadillac). Under this system divisional managers were given a great deal of autonomy. Matsushita made sure they all stayed on the same wavelength by rotating 5 percent of employees to different divisions every year and by preaching the company gospel in all the divisions. In a long essay detailing the history and ethos of Matsushita, Jeffrey Cruikshank, editor of the *Harvard Business School Bulletin* in 1983, interviewed Hiroaki Kosaka, director of the Overseas Training Center that prepares Matsushita people for service overseas. "Spirit is important," Kosaka told Cruikshank. "Classical economists told us that three things are important to run a company: money, materials, and manpower. Later, technology and information were added to the list. But today, among business leaders, philosophy is also important, because once the philosophy is clear, it talks to every individual, and all communication in the company can be based on it. And a spirit can be developed."

World War II must have put a crimp in the 250-year plan. Consumer products were not high on the priority list. The Japanese government, short on materials and aware of Matsushita's experience in making wooden cabinets for appliances, ordered the company to build laminated wood propellors, wooden ships, and even wooden planes. It was not experience Matsushita could later put to good use. With the war's end the future of the company itself was in jeopardy because of General Douglas MacArthur's policy of dismantling the *zaibatsu,* the financial trusts (Mitsubishi, Mitsui, Sumitomo, Yasuda) that had dominated Japanese business. Matsushita had never really been part of a zaibatsu. It was, in fact, a classic entrepreneurial startup tolerated by the powers-that-be. The occupation authorities nevertheless lumped Matsushita with other Japanese industrial leaders, and he was barred from working at his company for four years. He retreated to a mansion in Kyoto where he meditated and met with people, including scholars and monks, to discuss ideas and refine his philosophy.

It was during this period that he founded the PHP Institute (PHP standing for peace, happiness, and prosperity), a "think tank" designed to bridge cultures and popularize Konosuke Matsushita's ideas. The institute publishes a monthly magazine of ideas, *PHP,* which has a Japanese circulation of 1.5 million. An English edition sells seventy thousand copies in eighty-four countries, and a Spanish version reaches forty thousand subscribers in twenty countries. The institute also publishes Konosuke Matsushita's books, of which there have been more than two dozen since the end of World War II. They are written for a popular audience, and several have been best-sellers in Japan.

While he was sitting on the sideline, the company bearing his name went downhill. The number of employees dropped from twenty thousand at the war's end to thirty-eight hundred in 1950 when he was reinstated. Reassuming his position, he moved Matsushita Electric into position to participate in the electrifying takeoff of the Japanese economy. In one year, 1953, the company began making television sets, washing machines, and refrigerators. In 1959 the first overseas subsidiary, Matsushita Electric Corporation of America, was established in New York. It was the start of a worldwide push.

A key move was the signing of a 1952 licensing agreement with the Dutch electronics giant Philips, a company Matsushita had chosen to be his key partner. A joint venture (Matsushita Electronics Corporation) was organized, with Philips holding a 30 percent share. The negotiations revealed the business acumen of Konosuke Matsushita. Philips, in return for the technology it was contributing to this venture, asked for a very high royalty rate. Their argument was that any company associated with Philips was assured of success, and it pointed to the records of successful factories in forty-eight countries. Matsushita was impressed by this argument, but the royalty rate was still inordinately high and he thought of calling off the negotiations and going to an American firm.

However, after thinking about it for a while, he came up with an ingenious solution. He told the Dutch that while they were charging a high entry fee for being a teacher, they were failing "to consider the ability of the student." He then made this proposal: "If you enter into a technical agreement with Matsushita, I give you my word that the results will be better than with any other firm you have dealt with so far. If your average level of success if one hundred, with Matsushita it will be three hundred. Now, the management expertise that we will provide to our joint venture also has a price. Under the circumstances, I propose that we pay you a royalty for technical know-how, while you pay Matsushita a royalty for management expertise."

The Philips people were stunned and protested that such an arrangement was unheard of. Matsushita replied that the fee was justified since "their 30 percent share could be wiped out if the joint venture were not managed properly." In the end Konosuke Matsushita prevailed. Philips signed the agreement that he had proposed. And the joint venture did perform better than any of the other Philips affiliates.

Matsushita's management expertise did not go unnoticed. In 1962 he made the cover of *Time* as the symbol of Japan's new consumer market. In 1981 his management techniques were saluted by Richard T. Pascale and Anthony G. Athos in their best-selling book *The Art of Japanese Management*—the "art" in this case being Matsushita's. These two business school professors (Stanford and Harvard), both consultants to big American corporations, concluded, "Perhaps it would not be too great an overstatement to suggest that in the person of Konosuke Matsushita the Japanese have a managerial genius of world caliber. In one man was combined the managerial gift of Alfred Sloan and the marketing instincts of General Robert E. Wood of Sears. Indeed, historians may one day view Matsushita as one of the greatest managers of our century."

The organization that Matsushita did create is, as *The Economist* pointed out in 1985, more of a group operation than a single company. The mother company is Matsushita Electric Industrial (MEI), but the family includes a host of others related by blood (MEI owns a chunk) or by a supply line. Seven of these companies—Matsushita Refrigeration

(Japan's largest maker of refrigerators and the world's largest producer of compressors), Matsushita Seiko (air conditioners), and Matsushita Housing, to name three—have their own stock exchange listings.

As Matsushita entered 1987 it was doing business in more than 130 countries, and it was turning increasingly to manufacturing overseas. About half its sales already came from outside Japan in 1986 but the company was manufacturing only 14 percent of its output abroad; it planned to increase that percentage to 25 percent by 1990. Matsushita made its first significant entry into U.S. manufacturing in 1974 when it acquired the television set plant outside of Chicago that Motorola was no longer interested in operating. Reporters from all over America (*The Wall Street Journal, Los Angeles Times,* and *The New York Times,* among them) have since descended on the Franklin Park, Illinois, plant to interview the workers and the management. They generally found that the Japanese were able to instill a new spirit there to make television set manufacturing viable; it's where the Quasar sets are made.

In 1986 Matsushita opened a VCR plant in Vancouver, Washington, and was planning to begin making car radios in Atlanta in 1987. It was on the move all over the globe, putting a new microwave oven facility into Wales, an audio and compact disc factory into France, a VCR plant into Barcelona. It was already turning out, together with the Bosch company, forty thousand VCRs a year in West Germany. Thanks to the escalation of the yen, Matsushita said it would no longer make in Japan any audio products priced under $100; they would be turned out in Singapore and Taiwan, where the wage rates were lower. Mainland China was looming as a major market. In 1986 Matsushita said it would join with the city of Peking to build a $100 million color television set plant that will be capable by 1989 of producing 1.8 million receivers a year. It represented the largest Japanese investment to date in China.

If there's one thing that Matsushita does have, it's money. Even by Japanese standards, when it comes to finance, this is a conservative company. For its size it has very little debt on its books. And Carla Rapoport, Tokyo correspondent of the *Financial Times,* determined in 1986 that Matsushita was sitting on a hoard of liquid assets—cash, marketable securities, bonds—that totaled an unbelievable 1.8 trillion yen, which translated to nearly $11 billion! That's ready cash. Even more unbelievable is what Matsushita does with this money. Rapoport, who waited months to get an interview with chief financial officer Masayo Sano, reported that virtually all of these billions were stashed away in low-risk, fixed-interest Japanese bonds or bank deposits. The return was 7 percent. Sano said,

"The foundation of our business is always to have this reservoir of money. Matsushita is a manufacturer, and as a manufacturer, we should not be investing just for the sake of yield." Rapoport said foreign investment bankers go "glassy-eyed" when Matsushita's name is mentioned. One of them told her, "We thought the Saudis were conservative. They were riverboat gamblers compared to the Japanese." (On the other hand, if you hear about Matsushita buying IBM, you read it here first.)

Matsushita's shares are listed on eight stock exchanges around the world, including the New York Stock Exchange, and foreign investors held 22 percent of all the stock in 1986. In Japan Osaka's Sumitomo Bank holds 4.6 percent, and the Sumitomo Life Insurance Company has another 4.5 percent. The largest individual holder in 1986 was still Konosuke Matsushita, who held 2.7 percent of the shares, worth roughly $500 million at the end of 1986.

A grade school dropout, Matsushita has been highly critical of Japanese education—in one book he suggested that half the universities in the country be shut down. In 1979 he put up $30 million to found his own school, the Matsushita School of Government and Management, whose aim is to train future leaders of Japan. The school is located at Chigasaki, a coastal town thirty miles southwest of Tokyo. It enrolls thirty students a year in an unstructured five-year postgraduate course of study. The initial prospectus for the school invited applications from men and women "who really love their country, and who have a strong desire to make Japan a better place to live in the twenty-first century." Would-be students were advised that "like the famous Thomas Edison" (one of Matsushita's heroes) they would be "expected to seek out problems by themselves, and also to resolve them by themselves." The school is tuition-free for accepted applicants. Matsushita was prepared to cover all expenses. A total of 904 completed applications were received for the first class. The final thirty made it through a three-stage examination and a half-hour interview with Matsushita.

Matsushita has also funded educational programs in the United States. In 1976 the company established a $1 million chair in mechanical engineering in medicine at the Massachusetts Institute of Technology. In 1983 the Konosuke Matsushita Professor of Leadership was established with a $1 million grant at the Harvard Business School, the initial holder being Abraham Zaleznik, a psychoanalyst who has done work on the social psychology of management. In 1984 the Matsushita Foundation was established with a grant of $10 million "as a token of gratitude to the American people." And in 1985 the Stanford Business School received $1 million for a Konosuke Matsushita Professorship of International Economy and Policy Analysis, the first holder being Gerald M. Meier, the author of numerous studies on the economies of developing countries.

In 1973, when he was seventy-eight years old, Matsushita stepped down as chairman of the company he founded, but continued on as an advisor and director. He was still an advisor in 1986 when he celebrated his ninety-second birthday, which was the occasion for the unveiling of a statue of "Japan's God of management" at the front gate of the company's museum. The statue was put up at a cost of $170,000 by the 85,000-member Matsushita Electric Workers Union. A small, frail man who looks as if he might topple in the wind, Matsushita was interviewed in 1982 by the *Harvard Business School Bulletin* editor, Jeffrey Cruikshank, who asked him about the story making the rounds that he planned to live to be 160. Matsushita replied:

> "That story arose the year before last. I had an opportunity to visit China. In China, they still have a strong tradition of respecting aged people—much more so than in Japan. While I was there, they learned that I was over

WORLD'S LARGEST COLOR TV SET MAKERS

	Annual Output in Millions
1. **Philips** (Netherlands)	
U.S. Brands: Magnavox, Sylvania, Philco	6.2 m
2. **Matsushita** (Japan) Panasonic, Quasar	4.7 m
3. **Sony** (Japan)	3.8 m
4. **Toshiba** (Japan)	3.2 m
5. **Hitachi** (Japan)	3.1 m
6. **Thomson** (France) Thorn in Britain	3 m
7. **General Electric/RCA** (U.S.)	2.8 m
8. **Samsung** (Korea)	2.5 m
9. **Sanyo** (Japan)	1.8 m
10. **Sharp** (Japan)	1.7 m

eighty years old. They told me that with all due respect, they could not honor me simply on account of my age, because I had not yet fulfilled my heavenly given life span on earth. According to Chinese tradition, the heavenly given span of life is 160 years. . . .

"Before my visit to China, my challenge to myself was to live in three centuries. I was born in 1894. I have lived through this century, and I was hoping to live some years in the next century. But since my trip to China, my challenge has become much greater: Now I shall live to be 160."

Access   3–2, Minamisemba 4-chome, Minami-ku
Osaka 542, Japan
(81) 6-282-5111

1 Panasonic Way
Seacaucus, N.J. 07904
(201) 348-7000

Michelin	**Sales** $7.7 billion
	Profits $315 million
	U.S. Sales $1.4 billion
	Rank World's 2d-largest tire maker
	Europe's largest tire maker
	France's 10th-largest industrial company
	Founded 1863
	Employees 114,000 (9,000 in the United States)
	Headquarters Clermont-Ferrand, France

Michelin's stock can be bought on the Paris Bourse—in mid-1986 a single share of the Class B stock was selling for $400, having more than doubled in the past year. But no one who knows anything about this French tire maker believes that the shareholders at large (especially the Class B holders) have much to say about the running of the company. Michelin family members, holders of the Class A stock, control this enterprise, both by their shareholdings, estimated to be at least 50 percent of the total, and by their positions at the top of the company.

Michelin is one of the last representatives of a French capitalist class that hid money under the mattress and didn't take kindly to outsiders. Today it doesn't hide money under the mattress, being awash in debt (more than $4 billion) assumed to finance its international adventures, but it still doesn't have the welcome sign out for strangers. In 1985, when the *Financial Times* wangled an interview with the leader of the company, François Michelin, it took pains to point out that this was the first interview "he had given to any newspaper in six years."

The interview took place at Michelin's headquarters in Clermont-Ferrand, a city in the cheese-and-wine province of Auvergne in central France. It was there that Michelin was organized in 1863 as a *société en commandite par actions,* a peculiarly French institution that is essentially a partnership which permits outside shareholders. The company still operates under the same charter, which runs to the year 2050.

In its early years Michelin, an outgrowth of a machine shop, produced rubber products and had no more than a dozen employees. The turning point came in the final decade of the nineteenth century. In 1891 Edouard Michelin invented the demountable pneumatic bicycle tire. And four years later he introduced the pneumatic automobile tire, thereby displacing carriage wheels. It was Michelin then that founded the tire industry, and the company has a long series of firsts to its credit. In 1906 it invented the first removable rim and the first inflatable spare tire. It also was the first, in 1930, to produce a tubeless tire.

Two Michelin brothers—Edouard and André—presided over the growth of this technologically oriented company during the first four decades of the twentieth century. Edouard headed Michelin until he died at age eighty-one in 1940. They ran it from Clermont-Ferrand, which became a company town dominated by Michelin. Employees received free medical care, subsidized housing, paid vacations, sick leaves, and cut-rate prices at company-run stores. They were also rewarded with bonuses for having babies, and they received free maternity care. No one was ever laid off. The Michelins eschewed the bright lights and social circles of Paris. They would pause occasionally to rail against socialism and the evils of big government. François Michelin, grandson of Edouard, once resigned from the *Patronat,* French equivalent of the National Association of Manufacturers, because he thought it was too leftist. When the Socialists took power in France in 1981, Michelin was one of the two French industrial giants *not* to be nationalized; the other was car maker Peugeot, in which Michelin holds a 9.2 percent stake.

The company always prided itself on its technology, and after World War II it scored another breakthrough with the introduction of the radial tire, which gradually took over the European market. It took fifteen years before another company marketed a radial. Although tire experts were virtually unanimous in pronouncing the radial a superior product (it lasted longer, cut down on fuel consumption, and was safer), the American companies, loathe to make the new plant investment that radials required, resisted the change for many years. So in the 1970s, after having conquered Europe, Michelin took the fight to them, opening plants in South Carolina and Alabama to "put America on radials." Goodyear Tire, lodestar of the American industry, soon saw the light. The first American-made Michelins began rolling out of Greenville, South Carolina, in 1975. Today radials hold 75 percent of the market in the United States.

The American push was part of a worldwide expansion by Michelin. Of its fifty-four plants, twenty-seven have been built since 1970. Between 1975 and 1982 it committed $2.2 billion to an investment program that resulted in modernization of its European plants, and the establishment of five plants in the United States, two in Brazil, and a third one in Canada. These were successful but costly invasions. Michelin moved from seventh to fourth place in the world tire industry by 1970. In 1980 it passed Firestone to become the world's second-largest tire maker. It has captured 38 percent of the European tire market. Its U.S. market share has risen to 10 percent. And its world market share is estimated at 18 percent, not far behind Goodyear's 21 percent. Every day four hundred thousand tires leave Michelin plants, to be marketed in more than 140 countries.

This advance strained a company accustomed to financing growth out of cash flow. Michelin went in hock to French bankers and piled up losses of about $1 billion from 1981 through 1984. In 1982 it stopped paying shareholder dividends, the first time in thirty years.

Michelin, which returned to the profit column in 1985, believed that the investment was necessary in a multinational age. It's now deriving 25 percent of its sales from the United States (versus 15 percent from France), and in the 1985 interview he granted the *Financial Times,* François Michelin said, "If we had not gone to the United States, we would be dying."

Everywhere Michelin has gone, it has encountered labor troubles, not surprising for a company whose leader, François Michelin, once said, "The presence of a union in a company merely reflects the inadequacy of the bosses." In Canada the labor movement boycotted Michelin from 1981 to 1985 after the company repeatedly beat back union efforts to organize its plants in Nova Scotia. In Britain the Transport and General Workers Union struck the plant at Stoke on Trent after Michelin tried to institute a seven-day work week. Michelin closed its plant in the Basque town of Vitoria, Spain, for twenty-one days in 1980 after a siege of violence culminated in the assassination of the factory manager. In the United States Michelin has opened plants in nonunion areas. For putting a factory into Greenville, South Carolina, it received a five-year exemption from city taxes. In 1979 Kenneth Luke, head of the Chamber of Commerce in Greenville, said Michelin had come to South Carolina because it was "looking for a place where people would give them a day's work for a day's pay."

Unlike other tire companies, Michelin has stuck to tires. It doesn't make tennis balls or put its name on blimps. But its name does appear on millions of maps, and travel and restaurant guides. The *Guide Michelin* was launched in 1900 by André Michelin to provide a listing of places in the French countryside where motorists could find gasoline, service shops, and restaurants. He seemed to have an idea, though, of its future. In the preface to the first edition, he wrote, "This guidebook appears with this century. It will last as long. The automobile has just been born. It will develop each year, and the tire with it." And so did the *guides.*

The *Guide Michelin* has become the arbiter of French restaurants, and Michelin has become one of the world's largest publishers of road maps and guides. It currently publishes 118 maps and seventy-eight meticulously researched guides to sightseeing, lodging, and eating in

Western Europe, Africa, Canada, New York City, and New England. Michelin sells twelve million road maps a year, and its red guide to France, updated every year, sells seven hundred thousand copies annually. How many Michelin stars a restaurant gets is of crucial importance in a country which takes its eating seriously. The top rating, three stars, is the glory of all glories for a French chef. In 1987 only 19 out of 3,854 restaurants listed in the guide earned this highest accolade. "Far more than any politician, cleric, or business leader, it is the *inspecteur de Michelin* who personifies rectitude and incorruptibility for the average Frenchman," Rudolph Chelminski, an American writer living in France, pointed out in an article for *Smithsonian* magazine.

André Michelin was also responsible, in 1898, for the roly-poly pneumatic man who has become Michelin's jolly advertising symbol. The original poster came about after the Michelins saw a stack of tires at an exhibition, and one of them remarked, "If it had arms, it would look like a man." A cartoonist did put arms on the stack, presenting him in a poster with the slogan, *"Nunc est bibendum"* (Latin for "Now is the time to drink"). Monsieur Bibendum was shortened later to Bib, and has served ever since as the mascot of Michelin. Roadsides in France are dotted with his likeness giving speed limits and other travel information.

Michelin acquired its holding in Peugeot when the French automaker Citroën was merged, at government suggestion, into Peugeot in 1976. Michelin had owned 53 percent of Citroën since the 1930s when the floundering auto company couldn't come up with $2.6 million for Michelin tires. Michelin also owns 93 percent of another French tire company, Kleber. This is a role cast by the French government, which doesn't want to see Kleber go flat.

Although the business world has changed somewhat since 1863, Michelin continues to operate under its original structure, with the managing partners, known as *gérants,* serving as virtual absolute monarchs. François Michelin, grandson of Edouard, has been at the helm since 1955, and in recent years he has shared power with another gérant, his cousin, François Rollier. They were joined in 1986 by a third managing partner, René Zingraff, a forty-nine-year-old chemist who is the first nonfamily member to reach such a lofty position in the company. With Michelin since 1963, Zingraff formerly headed up the tire maker's industrial operations in the United States. He has also worked in Britain. Michelin does 75 percent of its business outside France.

Under the strain of running a worldwide business Michelin's celebrated reclusiveness is beginning to break down. It has teamed up with Wuon Poong, a South Korean tire maker, in a fifty-fifty venture, the first time it has ever entered such a partnership. And in 1987, as it was trying to sell shares in its Swiss-based subsidiary, which oversees international operations, Michelin shocked the investment community by inviting a group of security analysts to come to Clermont-Ferrand for a financial briefing and a light champagne lunch. It was another first for Michelin, which still issues its annual report in French only and rarely goes out of its way to court security analysts. However, the invitees could not visit the plant. They met at a hotel and were given a spin around Michelin's test track. No outsiders are permitted inside the Michelin factory.

U.S. automakers are now accustomed to ordering tires from Michelin. But in 1986 the French company scored a victory of symbolic importance when it began supplying radial tires to McDonnell Douglas for use on its F-15E fighter planes. It marked the first time that a U.S. Air Force plane will be equipped with radials. Michelin is beginning to beat out Goodyear for Pentagon business.

Michelin's entry into the U.S. market in the 1970s was actually a re-entry. Most people have forgotten, or never knew, that Michelin did make tires in the United States prior to World War II. After *The New York Times* ran a story in 1978 on Michelin's invasion of the United States, Willis Klotzbach of Trenton sent in this memoir of his schoolboy days in New Jersey:

> Before the Depression, the company (Michelin) made tires in the expanded plant of the old Meyer Rubber Company on the shore of Lawrence Brook in the borough of Milltown. Workers came by trolley car from nearby towns to augment employees from Milltown. Several hundred people came from France to make tires and live in company bungalows. There was a secret process room with very limited access to employees.
>
> Community activities by Michelin were a boon. The French School contributed to elementary education in the somewhat bilingual town. Athletics loomed large; Michelin baseball and basketball teams compiled good records against semipro teams from much larger towns. In the 1920s, Michelin had a fenced ballpark with roofed grandstand. Several highlights of Michelin basketball games in Milltown were games with the Harlem Renaissance Big Five and the St. John's College "wonder team." Games were played in Michelin Community House, scene of dances, graduation exercises, and silent movies.
>
> The greatest of times were the two holidays in July. The borough and Michelin celebrated the Fourth and Fourteenth with parades—including French military veterans in uniform—contests, speeches, and fireworks.

A little Clermont-Ferrand in New Jersey.

Access 4, rue du Terrail
63000 Clermont-Ferrand, France
(33) 73-92-4195

Patewood Executive Park
P.O. Box 19001
Greenville, S.C. 29602
(803) 234-5000

Mitsubishi

Sales $81 billion
Profits $100 million
U.S. Sales $9 billion
Rank Japan's largest trading company (1985)
Japan's 5th-largest trading company (1986)
With interests in:
Japan's largest heavy machinery maker
Japan's largest shipbuilder
Japan's largest defense contractor
Japan's largest builder of power plants
Japan's largest brewer
Japan's largest chemical company
Japan's largest glassmaker
Japan's 5th-largest automaker
Japan's 4th-largest commercial bank
Japan's largest trust company
Tokyo's biggest landlord
Founded 1870
Employees 9,000 (average age: 36)
Headquarters Tokyo, Japan

t's difficult to legislate ways of life. After World War II General Douglas MacArthur, head of the U.S. occupation force in Japan, abolished the *zaibatsu* (the economic cliques that dominated prewar Japan). At least he thought he did. These conglomerates roped together in one corral a bank, a trading company, and a bunch of industrial enterprises. The Big Four of the prewar zaibatsu were Mitsubishi, Mitsui, Sumitomo, and Yasuda. The occupation of Japan ended in 1952, and almost overnight the Japanese companies regrouped themselves into configurations remarkably similar to the ones existing before the war. "In a way, they are the phoenix of postwar Japan—once destroyed by the cursing fire of the GHQ, they reemerged from its ashes with renewed youth, and are now living another cycle of years," said Yoshihara Kunio, a Japanese economist, in his book *Sogo Shosha*.

The *sogo shosha* (Japanese for a general trading company), is a powerful economic beast but it's not quite the same as the zaibatsu of pre–World War II days. The zaibatsu was a holding company, usually family-controlled, with direct ownership of companies in its orbit. The sogo shosha is an all-purpose trading company. It imports and exports. It puts together deals. It barters. It finances companies. It functions primarily as a wholesaler. But it is also generally linked to a phalanx of other companies, so that together they resemble a family or confederation of enterprises.

The companies in a group are connected to one another in various ways, including cross-stockholdings, but there is no single master corporation that owns all the other firms in the group. The sogo shosha has a very wide reach—the world is its habitat. And by acting as agents for Japanese companies that are producing goods (the sogo shosha doesn't make anything), these trading companies roll up incredible revenue figures—and with comparatively few employees. It's a paperwork business that operates on very thin margins, which is typical of wholesaling.

The six largest Japanese trading companies are Mitsui, C. Itoh, Sumitomo, Marubeni, Mitsubishi, and Nissho Iwai. (Yasuda was dissolved in 1946.) In recent years Mitsubishi has led the pack, with Mitsui a close second, but in 1986 Mitsubishi plunged to fifth place largely as a result of its role as Japan's largest importer of crude oil. As you know from the signs at your local service station, gasoline prices plummeted in 1986, and so did Mitsubishi's sales. Measured in yen, they were down 27 percent.

The figures reported at the top of this profile are for Mitsubishi Corporation, the trading company that is the centerpiece of the Mitsubishi constellation of companies. If the sales of all the Mitsubishi-related companies were combined, the total might reach $150 billion.

The Mitsubishi Group traces its origin to 1870 when Yataro Iwasaki, a rapacious samurai, founded a shipping business in Osaka. He devised the three-diamond Mitsubishi symbol by rearranging the Iwasaki family insignia. Japanese business, a rather new phenomenon at that time, took its inspiration from Ishida Baigan, an eighteenth-century Japanese philosopher. He was, in fact, the philosopher of the merchant class, preaching that business needed a social mission but there was nothing wrong with making a profit along the way. "The merchant's profit from sale," said Baigan, "is like the samurai's stipend. To take no profit from a sale would be like the samurai serving without a stipend." Thus was born Confucian capitalism: business for the good of all.

Iwasaki grasped the concept quickly. He made big profits supplying ships in 1874 when the government sent a punitive expedition to the island of Formosa and again in 1877 when the government put down the Satsuma rebellion in the province of Kyushu. From the profits made in shipping, he went into mining. From there he and his descendants built an industrial empire that was one of the largest in the world, encompassing banking, shipbuilding, coal mining, steel, chemicals, oil refining, paper, glass, beer, cement, and electronics. More than seventy-five companies belonged to the Mitsubishi Group and, while some of them sold stock to the public, the Iwasaki family retained control. The founder died in 1885, leaving this deathbed legacy: "Do not take up small projects. Engage in large enterprises. Once you begin something, see to it that it becomes a success. Do not engage in speculation. Do business with a patriotic attitude."

It's a message that has been heeded. When Japan bombed Pearl Harbor on December 7, 1941, Mitsubishi-made Zero fighter planes were in the vanguard. During the war Mitsubishi chemical plants made explosives, and its shipyards turned out the battleships that confronted the U.S. Navy. Mitsubishi delivered more than fourteen thousand Zero fighters to the Japanese air force.

The last of the Iwasaki dynasty, Baron Koyata Iwasaki, nephew of the founder, died in 1945 shortly after MacArthur's troops occupied Japan. He reportedly gave a farewell talk in which he said the company had only done its duty during the war, and he urged his executives to keep alive the Mitsubishi spirit. *Fortune* writer Robert Lubar spoke to people who heard that talk, and they said it "was the spark that kept Mitsubishi alive." So even though the Mitsubishi empire was split up into scores of firms, giant companies bearing the Mitsubishi name were back in business almost as soon as the occupation forces left. Of all the sogo shosha, Mitsubishi has been the most cohesive, commanding a loyalty that goes back far into its history.

In its rebirth, the Mitsubishi Group consists of twenty-eight companies, each a power in its own right. The flagship is the trading company, Mitsubishi Corporation, whose operations span the world. The Mitsubishi Bank is the fourth-largest commercial bank in Japan. Mitsubishi Chemical is the largest chemical company in Japan. Mitsubishi Electric is one of Japan's largest electronic companies (semiconductors, computers, television sets). Mitsubishi Heavy Industries builds ships, bridges, nuclear power plants, and jet planes; by itself it ranks as the tenth-largest industrial company in Japan. Mitsubishi Motors is Japan's fifth-largest automaker. Asahi Glass accounts for 48 percent of Japan's plate glass. Nippon Kogaku makes the Nikon camera. Kirin, with more than half the Japanese beer market, is the world's fourth-largest brewer. Tokio Marine & Fire Insurance is Japan's largest property and casualty insurer (17 percent of the market). Mitsubishi Estate is one of the world's largest owners and developers of real estate—*Forbes* estimated in 1986 that its holdings in

Tokyo's Marunouchi district, where many Mitsubishi (and other large Japanese) companies are headquartered, were worth $50 billion.

Mitsubishi Heavy Industries continues the arms tradition. In 1987 it supplied 25 percent of Japan's military equipment, including the F-15 and F-4 fighter planes and the Patriot and Sidewinder missiles, all of which it made under license from U.S. companies.

The Mitsubishi companies are linked in various ways. Most of them have separate listings on the Tokyo Stock Exchange, but they all seem to own pieces of one another. For example, the Mitsubishi Bank owns 4 percent of Kirin and 5.4 percent of Asahi Glass, while Mitsubishi Heavy Industries owns 3.4 percent of Mitsubishi Bank, and Mitsubishi Corporation owns another 2 percent of the bank. Mitsubishi Heavy Industries owns 1.9 percent of Tokio Marine & Fire, while the insurance company owns 2.6 percent of Mitsubishi Heavy, 5 percent of Asahi Glass, and 4.6 percent of Mitsubishi Bank.

Another way they're linked is by a meeting held on the second Friday of every month that brings together the heads of all the Mitsubishi companies. This is called the Kinyokai Club (Friday Club). They assemble as Mitsubishi people. What do they talk about? In 1980 Bunpei Otsuki, president of Mitsubishi Mining & Cement, put it this way to journalist Jon Woronoff of the *Oriental Economist:*

> "Actually, we never get together to discuss business in the sense of shall we do this or how about doing that? Rather, with more and more new presidents and chairmen, the companies naturally tend to lose contact with one another. So the idea is to keep on a friendly basis, to know one another better. . . . What the group does is to see that the Mitsubishi brand name is not misused and to discuss things that must be done by Mitsubishi as a whole, such as making donations to community-oriented activities or political contributions. . . . There are no discussions about business as such."

Otsuki added that the "traditional Mitsubishi spirit" continues in the group. "Through our business activities," he said, "we are serving our country and our society."

In 1972 Mitsubishi gave $1 million to Harvard University to establish a chair in Japanese legal studies. Ten years later Mitsubishi Electric and four of its employees were indicted by a federal grand jury in California on charges of trying to steal secrets from IBM. Mitsubishi eventually pleaded *nolo contendere* and was fined $10,000.

The Mitsubishi Group has established a formidable presence in the United States. Mitsubishi International, the New York–based subsidiary of Mitsubishi Corporation, ranks as one of the five leading exporters of

American products, and its annual trade transactions (importing and exporting) total an estimated $9 billion. The Mitsubishi Bank bought the First National Bank of San Diego in 1981 and followed up two years later with the acquisition of the Bank of California, the eighth-largest bank in the state. The system is now called the Mitsubishi Bank of California. Mitsubishi Electric and Mitsubishi Heavy Industries both operate plants in the United States, and Mitsubishi Diamond Vision scoreboards can be seen at major league parks.

One of the offshoots of Mitsubishi Heavy Industries is the car and truck builder Mitsubishi Motors, which is expected to have its own listing on the Tokyo Stock Exchange by the end of 1988. Mitsubishi Heavy has reduced its stake to 35 percent of the shares. Chrysler, which has imported many Mitsubishi-made vehicles for its Dodge and Plymouth lines, owns 24 percent of Mitsubishi Motors. In 1985 Chrysler and Mitsubishi announced that they had selected Bloomington-Normal in central Illinois as the site for a new $500 million automobile plant. A community of eighty-five thousand people, Bloomington-Normal began a "sister city" relationship with Asahikawa, a community of 350,000 people on the island of Hokkaido, in 1963. This has involved, among other things, an annual exchange of high school students.

After Mitsubishi decided to build a plant there, a decision that apparently had nothing to do with the "sister city" relationship, *The Washington Post*'s reporter Kevin Klose interviewed two of the exchange students. Scott Carnahan, who had spent the 1983–84 school year in Japan, said the plant was great news because the Japanese would teach "Americans how to make cars right." Hiromabu Mori, a sixteen-year-old student from Japan, said he had been impressed by the "bigness of America . . . there is more space between the houses, and there is Dairy Queen. I like Dairy Queen."

In 1986, as Japanese and American officials exchanged hot words on the trade imbalance between the two countries, Mitsubishi Electric launched an ad campaign in the United States to point out that it was making cellular phones at Braselton, Georgia; television sets at Anaheim and Santa Ana, California; semiconductors at Durham, North Carolina; and video phones at Milpitas, California. "With a name like Mitsubishi," said one of the ads, "it's a little difficult to get people to think of us as anything other than a Japanese company. But it doesn't stop us from trying." The Mitsubishi message then went on to say that it employs two thousand people in the United States, purchases parts from American suppliers, reinvests profits in its American operations, and tries to "strike a balance between imports and exports. As far as we're concerned, anything less would be un-American."

Minoru Makihari was sent from Tokyo to New York in 1987 to head up Mitsubishi International, an assignment that placed him in line to reach the top of the Mitsubishi ladder in Japan. Makahari, who was fifty-seven, comes from an all-Mitsubishi family, and he is certainly no stranger to America. He joined the trading company in 1957, following in the footsteps of his father, who had been a Mitsubishi executive. After World War II his father sent him to St. Paul's prep school in New Hampshire and then to Harvard, where he was Phi Beta Kappa. His wife, Kikuko, is the great-granddaughter of Yataro Iwasaki, the founder of Mitsubishi. Makihari told *The New York Times* that one of his priorities was to bring more Americans into the company.

Access   2-6-3 Marunouchi, Chiyoda-ku
Tokyo 100, Japan
(81) 3-210-2121

Mitsubishi International
520 Madison Ave.
New York, N.Y. 10022
(212) 605-2000

Moët-Hennessy

Sales $1.3 billion
Profits $133 million
U.S. Sales $350 million
Rank World's largest champagne
house
World's largest cognac house
Founded 1743
Employees 7,000
Headquarters Paris, France

I f you travel forty-four miles north of San Francisco to the Napa Valley, the premier wine-growing region of the United States, you will reach, at Yountville, the Domaine Chandon vineyard. You can dine there at a very elegant French restaurant. And you can taste Chandon sparkling wine. To most people it would taste like champagne. And it is indeed made just the way champagne is made in France, with the bottles being constantly rotated as the wine ferments to move the sediment down toward the cork. But this vineyard was established in California by Moët-Hennessy, France's largest champagne producer. It is, of course, the French view that champagne is not champagne unless it comes from the Champagne district of France. Call it what you will, Chandon has been a sparkling success since it opened in 1973. By 1981 it was selling 1.8 million bottles of champagne—oops, sparkling wine—a year. By 1985 it had reached its goal of 5 million bottles a year.

Chandon sparkling wine sells for $9 and up a bottle. The "real" stuff, which Moët-Hennessy exports from France under the Moët-Chandon, Mercier, and Ruinart labels, sells in the American market for $18 and up. And Moët-Hennessy is also the producer of the *ne plus ultra* of champagnes, Dom Perignon, which was marked up so much that by the time it reached retail shelves the price was well over fifty dollars a bottle. "Gray marketers" put a crimp in this game by showing that they could buy Dom Perignon in another country (say Britain or Argentina) and bring it into the United States to reach retail shelves at a price well under what Moët-Hennessy was trying to exact.

In Epernay, in the lush Marne Valley northeast of Paris, Moët ferments champagne in eighteen miles of caves, some as deep as one hundred feet and some dating back to Roman times. It was there at the Abbaye d'Hautvillers in the early eighteenth century that Dom Perignon, a Benedictine monk, developed the processes by which champagne is made. Upon first tasting it, he reportedly exclaimed, "My God, I'm drinking stars!"

Wine merchant Claude Moët founded his business in 1743, shortly after champagne was first developed. He acquired the Abbaye d'Hautvillers. In the early part of the nineteenth century the Moëts were joined by marriage with another wine family, the Chandons, and together they built the largest champagne house in France. Today they turn out twenty-five million bottles a year, 70 percent of it exported. Moët & Chandon is by far the biggest label in terms of sales.

Moët & Chandon merged in 1971 with another historic French spirits house, James Hennessy & Company, which was founded in 1765 by Richard Hennessy, third son of the Squire of Ballymacoy, County Cork. He had served in the "La Brigade Irelandaise" of the French Army, and according to the official story that Moët & Chandon gives out today, Captain Hennessy was wounded in battle and, while recuperating, was given cognac brandy for medicinal purposes. He supposedly recognized instantly the remarkable qualities of this libation and began shipping casks to family and friends in Ireland. Then he started a company to produce it, a company later headed by and renamed for his son, James. Thus was born Hennessy cognac.

Cognac was first made in the seventeenth century by the accidental double distilling of wine. And of course, like champagne, it's French. Cognac is brandy but not all brandy is cognac. The French insist that only brandy produced in the region known as Cognac can be called cognac. Hennessy cognac has always been aged in barrels made from the oak of the Limousin forests in central France. Hennessy owns the largest stock of aged cognac in France. One of its cognacs, Paradis, is blended only from brandies aged for at least fifty years. It sells for $135 a bottle.

Descendants of the Moëts and Hennessys were still active in the company in 1987 and controlled about 25 percent of the shares. Moët & Chandon sold stock to the public in 1962 and then became more than just champagne and cognac, acquiring Christian Dior perfumes and cosmetics, Delbard (French rose grower), Armstrong Nurseries (California rose grower), and Roc (another French-based maker of beauty care products). It has wine operations in Portugal, Argentina, Brazil, and Germany. And through ownership of its U.S. distributor, Schieffelin & Company, it owns the Simi winery of California and distributes the German import Blue Nun, which is produced by a company 50 percent–owned by Moët-Hennessy.

Moët does more than two thirds of its business outside France. Its most important market is the United States, which accounts for more than a quarter of the company's sales. In 1986 Evan Griffith Galbraith, an investment banker and previously U.S. ambassador to France, became chairman of the U.S. subsidiary.

Top Five Champange Brands in the United States

1986 *Case Sales*

1.	Moët & Chandon	475,000
2.	Mumm	205,000
3.	Tattinger	75,000
4.	Perrier-Jouët	65,000
5.	Piper-Heidsieck	65,000

Top Five Total: 885,000
Total U.S. Sales: 1.2 million

Source: Impact Databank

Top Five Champagne Consuming Countries

1986 *Case Sales*

1.	France	10,800,000
2.	Britain	1,300,000
3.	United States	1,200,000
4.	West Germany	780,000
5.	Switzerland	530,000

Top Five Total: 14.6 million
Other Countries: 2.4 million

Source: Impact Databank

In the middle of 1987 Moët & Chandon merged with fancy luggage maker Louis Vuitton to create "the perfect couple." In addition to its well-known leather goods (brand-conscious Japanese account for 20 percent of its sales), Vuitton brought to the marriage a champagne house of its own (the Veuve Cliquot, Canard Duchene, and Henriot labels), which it had just quaffed the year before, the Givenchy perfume and cosmetics business (to go with Moët's Christian Dior lines), and a 15 percent holding in Guerlain. Moët and Vuitton had a great deal in common, notably that they both sell goods priced far out of the reach of 95 percent of the world's population. Security analysts were quick to characterize the new company the world's largest supplier of luxury goods, or as *New York Times* reporter Steven Greenhouse put it, "a conglomerate for the carriage trade."

Alain Chevalier, Algerian-born lawyer who assumed command of

Moët & Chandon in 1982, said the Vuitton merger was "as easy and natural" as the 1971 Moët-Hennessy nuptials. "It was like one of those love affairs which lead quickly to to the altar," he told a press conference.

Henry Racamier, chairman of Vuitton, described the merger as "the second-best marriage" of his career. The first, in 1936, was to Odile Vuitton, whose great-grandfather founded the firm in 1854. However, Recamier did not join Vuitton until 1970, when squabbling members of the family asked him to take over.

Access   30, avenue Hoche
75008 Paris, France
(33) 1-45-63-0101

9 West 57th St.
New York, N.Y. 10019
(212) 888-6388

Montedison

Sales $10 billion
Profits $240 million
U.S. Sales $500 million
Rank 2d-largest private company in Italy
Largest chemical company in Italy
8th-largest chemical company in the world
Largest supermarket chain operator in Italy
Publisher of leading daily paper in Rome
Italy's largest drug producer
Italy's largest paint producer
Founded 1884
Employees 69,600
Headquarters Milan, Italy

n Italy the line between state-owned and privately owned companies is very thin. They cross into each other's territory all the time, propping one another up in combinations so convoluted that both business and Marxist analysts have a merry time constructing elaborate diagrams purporting to show who owns Italy. Montedison has played a major role in this drama. It's the biggest chemical company in Italy, with a product line ranging literally from *A* (acetates) to *Z* (zinc oxides). Its chemically concocted fibers go into acrylic and polyester fabrics. Other basic chemicals become fertilizers and pesticides. Its Fomblin, an antipollution coating, is used to restore and preserve Italy's historical monuments.

This Milan-based giant also has a number of other arms. It's an energy company, producing enough power for the 140 businesses under the Montedison umbrella, plus some electricity to spare. It has a pharmaceutical house, Erbamont, which is a world leader. (Its Adriamycin compound is the most widely prescribed anticancer drug in the world.) It's one of Italy's major retailers, with more than five hundred Standa supermarkets and department stores from Sicily to the Alps. It makes test tubes, thermometers, and glass slides for laboratories. One subsidiary makes detergents, another toilet tissue. Another makes car-finishing and household paints. Another, Compo, based in the United States, makes modular carpet systems and synthetic materials that go into shoes. It even owns the largest daily newspaper in Rome, *Il Messaggero,* and on July 13, 1986, readers of *The New York Times* were greeted with this ad:

Welcome to Rome, Italy. Those of you who have already been here know the enchantment of our ancient and great city. And to those of you who have yet to discover us . . . can't you feel it? The Roman breeze is a friendly breeze, and its freshness reaches across the Atlantic, as it has for the past five centuries. The rustling breeze that is blowing across this page of *The New York Times* comes directly from *Il Messaggero,* the most important daily newspaper in Rome, and one of Italy's largest daily newspapers: and it brings you the warm, friendly greetings of 56 million Italians.

You have to love a company like that.

Varied as its endeavors are, Montedison has had one constant in its history: upheaval in the executive suite. In its short life, the activity in the boardroom has been as volatile as an Italian opera or a chemical reaction gone haywire.

The company's name reflects its formation in 1966 by a merger of Montecatini Chemical with Societa Edison. Montecatini started out as a mining company in 1888, extracting copper from the hills of Tuscany, and evolved over the years into a full-fledged chemical producer, making fertilizers, explosives, paints, synthetic fibers, plastics, drugs, dyestuffs. In 1963, at its seventy-fifth birthday, it ranked as Italy's fifth-largest company, turning out two thousand products in 130 factories and employing seventy-three thousand people. That was also the year a Montecatini chemist, Giulio Natta, won the Nobel prize for his work in the development of polypropylene, a lightweight plastic now in wide use as packaging for food products.

Edison was also born in the late nineteenth century, having been founded in 1884 as an electric utility. After World War II it branched into chemicals and fibers, becoming second only to Montecatini in the Italian chemical industry. When the Italian government nationalized the power industry in 1962, Edison was the county's largest utility, producing one fifth of Italy's electric energy. The nationalization brought Edison $800 million (paid out over ten years), a dowry that was made-to-order for Montecatini, whose reckless, post–World War II expansion had left it in a precarious, cash-poor condition.

It was one of those corporate marriages that appeared to be eminently rational. Montecatini needed the cash. Edison needed to do something with its cash. Both were in similar lines of business, and both were anxious to do what all Italian companies are prone to do—get into other businesses. At the conclusion of the merger, the newly created Montedison ranked as Europe's eighth-largest industrial company and second-largest chemical producer after Britain's Imperial Chemical Industries. It wasn't long before this position was eroded.

Montedison's first boss, Giorgio Valerio, came from the Edison side of the family, and he acquired businesses—supermarkets and ready-to-wear clothing companies, for example—that had little to do with chemicals. For his aides he chose people from Edison, and they ran the company from Milan's Palazzo Edison, leaving the Montecatini managers to languish jealously in the Montecatini Building across town. One of Valerio's grandiose ideas was to explore for oil in Libya and become a gasoline distributor, thereby putting Montedison into direct competition with the state-owned oil monopoly. In 1968, in a palace coup staged by the government, Valerio was stripped of his powers. The following year he was ousted. The government had gained the whip hand by buying Montedison shares through the two big state holding companies, the Instituto per la Ricostruzione Industriale (IRI) and the Ente Nazionale Idrocarburi (ENI), the state oil company which had a burgeoning chemical business of its own. The Italian press labeled it "clandestine nationalization."

Montedison then went through a series of leaders. First came Cesare Merzagora, who was installed in 1970 when he was seventy-one years old. He had presided over the Italian Senate for fourteen years but was unprepared for the bitter squabbling that went on inside Montedison. The first annual meeting he chaired lasted twelve hours. It was also his last—he resigned after six months. He was replaced briefly by another designate of the then ruling Christian Democratic party, seventy-nine-year-old Pietro Campilli, a financier and elder stateman of the party. Then, in 1971, yet another party stalwart, Eugenio Cefis, moved over from ENI to take the reins. He held them for six stormy years during which time Montedison, although still a publicly traded corporation, was run as an instrument of national political policy. Money-losing entities such as antiquated mines were dumped into a state holding tank, and petrochemical plants sprung up all over Italy, especially in depressed areas in need of an economic shot in the arm. A fiber plant put up in a rural area of the island of Sardinia cost 298 billion lira to build and was losing 57 billion lira on sales of 74 billion lira in 1978. According to *The New York Times*'s Paul Hofmann, writing in 1975, Montedison operated virtually "as a public-private condominium" (whatever that means). In any case, Cefis was at the helm of an enterprise whose payroll had swelled to 150,000 people. Losses were also swelling, plunging to 163 billion lira in 1975, 172 billion in 1976, and 465 billion in 1977. That was the year the taciturn Cefis resigned, to be replaced by another septuagenarian Christian Democratic politician, Guiseppe Medici, who was best known for his sartorial elegance. He always wore a Panama hat and carried a cane.

It's tempting to poke fun at Italian business as a kind of Italian opera, but similar disasters occur regularly in the American business world. The fact is, Italy has always come up with more than its fair share of imaginative, effective business people, both entrepreneurs and corporate managers. In 1980 one surfaced at Montedison: Mario Schimberni, a onetime economics professor who had worked his way up the ranks on the fiber side of the company. A professional manager rather than a politician (his ties, if any, were to the Socialist party), he proved to be the catalyst the unwieldy chemical giant needed. Schimberni transformed Montedison from a sprawling, provincial enterprise that was losing half a billion dollars a year to a purposeful, internationally minded corporation that earned $60 million in 1985, the first profitable year since 1979. It was a turnaround on a par with Lee Iacocca's rescue of Chrysler.

Like Iacocca, Schimberni received help from the government. First the Italian government sold its 17 percent stake in Montedison to Gemina, a consortium of leading industrial patriarchs (the Agnellis of Fiat and the Pirellis of tire fame, among others). Thus Montedison was no longer a ward of the state. The government also obliged by taking into ENI commodity chemical plants that didn't fit Schimberni's streamlined strategy. Petrochemical and plastics plants at Priolo, Brindisi, Ferrara, and Porto Marghera were all transferred to state-owned ENI. Montedison exited a bunch of low-margin businesses where it didn't enjoy any edge: nylon, polyvinyl chloride (PVC), polyethylene, ABS resins, nitrile and acrylic rubbers, pigments, dyestuffs, ion-exchange resins, and medical instruments.

Telling shareholders that "Montedison refuses to be the symbol of all that is amiss with the Italian economy," Schimberni concentrated the company's attention and energies on specialty chemicals—fluoride chemicals, polystyrene plastics, and polyesters, for example—and pharmaceuticals. He also began to nudge Montedison into a more global posture. In 1983 Montedison teamed up with the U.S. chemical company Hercules to form a joint venture, Himont, for the manufacture and marketing of polypropylene. With two plants in the United States, four in Italy, two in Belgium, and one in Canada, Himont proved to be a spectacular undertaking. It's the largest maker of polypropylene, with a worldwide market share of 20 percent, and it's super-profitable, earning $53 million in 1985 on sales of $900 million. Early in 1987 Montedison and Hercules sold off 20 percent of Himont to the public, leaving each with 40 percent of a company whose stock market value soared to nearly $3 billion in its first sixty days of trading on the New York Stock Exchange. That's called having your cake and eating it too. In March 1987 Schimberni engineered the biggest foreign takeover of a Spanish firm in history, paying $450 million—in cash—for Madrid-based Antibioticos. The acquisition lifted Montedison's pharmaceutical sales over the $1 billion mark.

These moves were accompanied by a drastic downsizing. The Montedison work force was chopped from 105,000 to 70,000, and the sprawling enterprise was reorganized so that instead of being a holding company for some nine hundred assorted businesses, it emerged as a conglomerate with ten groups in which were lodged 140 businesses. "I would prefer to see Montedison become a $4-billion-a-year company that makes money than an $8-billion-a-year company that does not," Howard E. Harris, coordinator of corporate strategy, told *BusinessWeek* in 1982. Harris, formerly with Mobil Oil and Arthur D. Little, was one of a group of international managers Schimberni recruited to help in the transformation of Montedison.

Three other Americans who joined the team were John J. Sweeney and Stephen R. Smith, both from New Jersey–based Drew Chemicals, and L. B. Shore, formerly with Esso Europe. Giorgio Porta, an alumnus of Esso and Phillips Petroleum, also came aboard, becoming one of Schimberni's chief aides. In 1985, in a talk to the quadrennial International Industrial Conference in San Francisco, Schimberni himself depicted the management changes as follows: "Montedison top management with international experience was 15 percent in 1980, and is 70 percent in 1985. The average age was fifty-four years old in 1980, and is forty-five now. Those with experience in research and development was 10 percent and is now 45 percent. And, on line with worldwide business responsibility were five people in 1980 and fourteen people in 1985. At the same time there has been a drastic reduction in staff functions."

However, it wouldn't be an Italian opera if everything ended in sweetness and light. In 1986, after having been acclaimed for turning Montedison around, Schimberni, then sixty-two years old, found himself at the center of a new storm over his decision to acquire La Fondiaria, a Florence insurance company, without consulting the syndicate of financiers and industrialists who held big chunks of Montedison stock. Leading the fight against Schimberni was seventy-nine-year-old Enrico Cuccia, the leader of the Italian financial establishment through his kingpin role at Mediobanca, Italy's largest merchant bank whose control ultimately rests with the government. This is a complicated business. Mediobanca is an important shareholder in Montedison. Montedison, by gaining control of

La Fondiaria, became a shareholder in Mediobanca. It became even more complicated after another Italian industrialist, Raul Gardini, one of Italy's new breed of business leaders, ostensibly came to the rescue of Schimberni by acquiring 22 percent of Montedison's share, a stake he subsequently expanded to 37 percent. Gardini controls the Ferruzzi Group, a sugar-shipping-commodities conglomerate that ranks as Italy's third-largest enterprise. Gardini was therefore in control of both the second- and third-largest private firms in Italy. It was unclear whether Mario Schimberni would be able to continue to run his own show.

The Schimberni-Cuccia-Gardini struggle was played out on the front pages of Italian newspapers. And it provoked this piece of philosophizing by Alan Friedman, the astute Milan correspondent of the *Financial Times:*

> The simple truth may be that Italy, the world's seventh-biggest industrial economy, just is not ready for modern capitalism yet. . . . The Italians have certainly done a lot in the past three years: the corporate sector has been financially and industrially restructured. . . . The Milan Bourse has seen its total capitalization jump from $28 billion to $137 billion since the start of 1984. Corporate financing is becoming more sophisticated.
>
> It is not enough, however. As Mr. Schimberni pointed out the other day, 96.2 percent of Italian companies are still controlled by families, even if some of the families have big holding structures to mask their presence. The family of Mr. Giovanni Agnelli, the Fiat chairman and owner of 41 percent of Fiat shares, for example, has shareholdings which account for something like a third of the total capitalization of the Milan Bourse. . . .
>
> Italy's financial markets are modernizing, but the process is too slow for an economy as dynamic as this one. Three men—Giovanni Agnelli, Carlo De Benedetti, and Raul Gardini—now control Italy's four biggest companies (Fiat, Montedison, Ferruzzi, and Olivetti) with $41 billion of total turnover.
>
> Italy deserves a more pluralistic corporate sector, but there is still a long way to go.

So there's still another act to come.

Access   Foro Buonaparte 31
20121 Milan, Italy
(39) 2-6331

1114 Ave. of the Americas
New York, N.Y. 10036
(212) 764-0260

NEC	**Sales** $16.5 billion

Sales $16.5 billion
Profits $102 million
U.S. Sales $4.2 billion
Rank World's largest producer of semiconductors
World's largest builder of earth satellite
stations
Japan's 4th-largest electronics company
World's 9th-largest computer producer
Japan's leading maker of personal computers
7th in the world in telecommunications
equipment
Founded 1899
Employees 96,000 (5,000 in the United States)
Headquarters Tokyo, Japan

K oji Kobayashi, the chairman of NEC, believes that one day he'll
be able to pick up his phone, speak in his native Japanese, and
be heard at the other end in English (not to mention being seen
at the other end also). The technologies that would make this
instant translation and communication possible are in place at NEC, a
major producer of telephones and switches to route telephone calls. It's
a major producer of computers and the integrated circuits (semiconductors or chips) that drive them. (And for the visual part, it's also a television
set maker.)

NEC's role as a key world player in all these technologies did not
come about accidentally. It resulted from a conscious strategy of Kobayashi, who in the mid-1970s began to preach the gospel of "C&C," the
concept that fused 100-year-old telephone—or, communications—technology (analog, voice) with the new computer (digital, data) technology.
Today it's a commonplace idea. But when Kobayashi first articulated it
more than twenty years ago and made it NEC's rallying cry, he "had to
bear heavy financial burdens, internal dissension, and scorn," said Kenichi
Ohmae, managing director of the Tokyo office of McKinsey & Company.

NEC has been a tireless proselytizer of its C&C ideology. An ad
NEC ran in U.S. business magazines in 1986 featured a full-size portrait
of Ludwig van Beethoven, explaining: "When you listen to Beethoven,
you can hear the harmony at the heart of the concept that NEC calls C&C.
. . . Because at NEC we have always known that managing information
takes more than computers or communications alone. To orchestrate the
modern office, you need both, working together as a unified whole."

The tricornered position that Kobayashi wanted NEC to occupy was
once explained this way: "IBM is a giant in the computer field but it isn't

380

involved in telecommunications. Western Electric is in telecommunications but not computers. Texas Instruments is big in integrated circuits but it isn't engaged in either of the other two fields."

NEC, need we add, is involved in all three activities.

The best way to understand NEC is to imagine Western Electric, which used to be the sole supplier of telephones in the United States, deciding twenty-five years ago that it had the know-how and chutzpah to take on IBM—and then, as an afterthought, it went after RCA and General Electric as well. In fact, NEC was created in 1899 as the Japanese subsidiary of Western Electric, the manufacturing arm of American Telephone & Telegraph. In 1925 Western Electric retreated to the United States, and another American firm, International Telephone & Telegraph, acquired a 59 percent interest in Nippon Electric Company (the company's name was officially shortened to NEC in 1983). At first NEC imported telephone equipment. Later it made its own in Japan. ITT no longer has any shareholding in NEC, a loss it must regret.

NEC's early life was therefore devoted to the supply of telephone equipment. After World War II, when Nippon Telegraph & Telephone (NTT) was organized, NEC resumed its prewar role. It didn't enjoy, as Western Electric did in the United States with AT&T, an exclusive lock on the business. The NTT extended family consisted of four members— NEC, Hitachi, Fujitsu, and Oki—but as Ezra Vogel points out in his book *Comeback,* NEC was clearly the "favorite child." The first president of NTT (1952–60), Takeshi Katji, was a former NEC president. And NEC was quickly established as the major supplier to the Japanese phone system.

That's a strong base from which to start, but other companies— Western Electric, ITT, Siemens, and Ericsson—have started from such bases and were not able to do what NEC did. *The Economist* put it succinctly in 1986 when it said, "Japan's NEC has cut through electronics markets as easily as a samurai blade cuts apple pie. Uniquely, it is among the top ten competitors in each of the world's three fastest growing electronics markets: semiconductors, telecommunications, and computers."

In 1985 NEC displaced Texas Instruments as the world's largest maker of semiconductors. In 1986 it displaced IBM as Japan's second-largest computer maker. In personal computers it has been the market leader in Japan. It has supplied more than half of the world's satellite dishes (earth stations). As recently as 1967 NEC was still deriving 60 percent of its sales from the Japanese government (including sales to NTT). That proportion has dipped below 15 percent. Today NEC makes more than fifteen thousand products which it markets in 130 countries. It has fifty-two plants in Japan and twenty-four more overseas, including nine in the United States.

NEC has no qualms about moving production facilities out of Japan. It's already making microchips in Scotland and California, and it's looking forward to the day when 50 percent of its output will come from non-Japanese plants. To escape the high yen, NEC commissioned companies in South Korea and Taiwan to make television sets, microwave ovens, refrigerators, and computer monitors. In April 1987, when President Reagan slapped 100 percent tariffs on a bunch of Japanese imports, including laptop computers (which NEC makes), the company said no problem, it could convert four of its American plants to laptop production in thirty days.

Aside from its own hardware, NEC now has a stake in a company that's the third-largest computer company in the world: Honeywell Bull. This multinational partnership was formed at the end of 1986 by Honeywell (American), Bull (French), and NEC (Japanese). NEC owns 15 percent of the combine, which ranks behind IBM and Unisys (the combination formed by Burroughs and Sperry). Originally NEC learned its computer technology from Honeywell. In twenty years that relationship was reversed, and NEC became the teacher, Honeywell the student.

Unlike rivals Fujitsu and Hitachi, which produce IBM-compatible computers, NEC takes great pride in its distinctively proprietary, incompatible technology (like Apple). However, in 1987 NEC was being sued by Intel (a company in which IBM held a 20 percent stake) for microcode copyright infringement.

The cult of personality rarely rears its head in Japanese companies, but it's difficult to ignore in NEC's case. Koji Kobayashi, who holds a doctorate in engineering from Tokyo Imperial University, became president of NEC in 1964 when the company's total sales were $200 million. In 1985, when sales crossed the $13 billion mark, the seventy-eight-year-old Kobayashi was still at the helm. A short, chunky man, he has rarely been at a loss for words. He is therefore a delight to reporters, who also appreciate the crisp, clear language of NEC financial reports.

In 1967, as NEC was just starting its dramatic ascent, Kobayashi waxed poetic to *Fortune:* "American firms are like giant trees growing freely and unrestrained in a natural environment. In contrast, Japanese firms are like delicate bonsai, our dwarf trees. They require constant care. But with careful and selective administration of nourishment, the bonsai too bears good fruit."

One factor often cited to explain NEC's meteoric rise is its awesome commitment to research. In 1982 NEC allocated 11 percent of its sales to research and development: in 1983, 12 percent; in 1984, 12 percent; in 1985, 13 percent; in 1986, 14 percent. Those are unheard of ratios in the rest of the corporate world, where IBM is considered exemplary for devoting as much as 9 percent of sales to research. In tandem with this commitment is a tolerance for puny profits, although Japanese accounting practices may distort the picture. In any case, in 1986, when it was reporting sales of $13.1 billion for 1985, NEC posted aftertax earnings of $152 million. The management of an American company might be run out of town for that kind of return.

An estimated 20 percent of NEC's shares are now held by non-Japanese investors. The company's stock is traded in New York, London, Frankfurt, Amsterdam, Basel, Geneva, and Zurich. In Japan NEC is a member of the Sumitomo Group of companies, and Sumitomo firms bulk large on the shareholder list. Sumitomo Life Insurance holds 7.3 percent of NEC's shares; Sumitomo Bank, 5 percent; Sumitomo Trust, 4.4 percent; Sumitomo Marine & Fire Insurance, 2.8 percent; and Sumitomo Electric, 2.3 percent.

But the undisputed leader was Koji Kobayashi, who reached his eightieth birthday in 1987 and who has insisted all along that technology should be "a means for enriching life." In a 1975 interview with Gary M. Cooper of the *Japan Economic Journal,* Kobayashi said he had faith in the power of technology to improve life, but he added, "We need more statesmen. I have investigated how many wars there have been in Europe since the fifteenth century. France had seventy-five, England had over seventy. To solve their problems and contradictions, they easily went to war. Killing people. Everything comes to zero. Now it's impossible to have a war to solve these contradictions. Only wisdom and intelligence can solve them."

And in 1985, in an address to the quadrennial International Industrial Conference in San Francisco, Kobayashi said that in automating their factories, corporations should not "forget their responsibilities as members of society," adding, "People should be the subject of production activities. . . . The ideal state . . . will be for human beings to engage in production activities by communicating with machines in a natural way. However, since many technologies are still in their infancy, for the most part humans must now work with machines on the machine level. As technology advances, machines will become more intelligent and the man-machine interface will become more friendly to human beings, allowing anyone to be able to use machines easily."

In 1986 Kobayashi completed his fifty-seventh year with NEC.

Japan's Top Four Computer Makers

1986 Sales (billions)

1. Fujitsu $7.3
2. NEC   6.5
3. IBM Japan   5.9
4. Hitachi   4.7

Access   33-1, Shiba 5-chome, Minato-ku
Tokyo 108, Japan
(81) 3-454-1111

NEC America
8 Old Farm Rd.
Melville, N.Y. 11747
(516) 753-7000

Nestlē	**Sales** $25.8 billion
	Profits $1.2 billion
	U.S. Sales $6 billion
	Rank World's largest food company
	World's largest infant formula maker
	World's largest coffee roaster
	World's largest chocolate company
	Switzerland's largest company
	World's 32d-largest company
	17th-largest company outside United States
	Founded 1866
	Employees 162,000
	Headquarters Vevey, Switzerland

A t a press conference in Washington, D.C., on January 26, 1984, two men ate a Nestlē Crunch bar. It was not an unusual snack for Dr. Niels Christiansen, a Nestlē manager. But it was an historic munch for Douglas A. Johnson, executive chairman of a group called the Infant Formula Action Coalition (INFACT), which had been conducting a worldwide boycott of all Nestlē products to protest the ways in which the Swiss company marketed infant formula in Third World countries. Johnson's bite signified the end of this boycott, then in its seventh year.

INFACT's boycott was one of the most successful campaigns ever mounted against a major corporation. One reporter called it "an intense battle, the fiercest and most emotional ever waged against a multinational company." It triumphed on a number of levels:

- Millions of people were left with a picture of Nestlē as an unfeeling corporation more concerned with making money than the health of newborn babies.
- The campaign crossed national borders. Nestlē, the epitome of the multinational operator, became the target of a multinational protest. The campaign was particularly strong in Nestlē's most important market, the United States, where many church denominations and religious orders joined the boycott.
- And the most significant result of all: It succeeded in its objectives; Nestlē agreed to change its marketing practices in developing countries.

It's no wonder Johnson ate his Nestlē Crunch bar with such relish.

The dispute centered on charges that Nestlē's overpromotion of baby formula was contributing to infant mortality and malnutrition in Third

World countries. Critics argued that Nestlé's sales tactics—mass advertising, giving away free samples in hospitals, dressing salesladies in nurse's uniforms—influenced mothers to substitute the formula for breast-feeding. Since most pediatricians and health authorities favor breast-feeding, that influence is a problem in itself. But on top of that, in poor countries where literacy levels are low and water supplies may be contaminated, it could be downright dangerous for mothers to rely on formula. They have to be able to read the directions carefully and be sure that the water they add to the formula is boiled. The issue was described by Senator Edward Kennedy when he held hearings on the dispute in 1978:

"Can a product which requires clean water, good sanitation, adequate family income, and a literate parent to follow printed instructions be properly and safely used in areas where water is contaminated, sewage runs in the streets, poverty is severe, and illiteracy is high?"

The anti-Nestlé forces answered that question with a resounding "no." They cited a decline in breast-feeding in Third World countries, blaming the infant formula makers for it. They came up with a devastating, if unproved (it didn't matter what was proved in this fight) statistic: Problems associated with bottle-feeding kill one million infants annually. One public health official, Dr. Derrick B. Jelliffe, played a key role in getting this campaign rolling. In a paper he presented in 1971, he asserted that children in Third World countries were suffering from "commerciogenic malnutrition" caused by the "thoughtless promotion" of infant formula.

Nestlé was not the only seller of infant formula in Third World countries (thirty companies, including three American firms, Abbott Labs, Bristol-Myers, and American Home Products, made up the field), but the Swiss company held the lion's share of the market: 50 percent. It thus became the natural target when protests about infant formula marketing began to appear in print in 1973. The *New Internationalist,* a British publication, ran a cover photograph of an infant's grave topped by an empty feeding bottle and a crumpled package of Lactogen, a Nestlé product. It was followed by another British report called *The Baby Killer,* which, when it was translated into German by a Swiss activist group, appeared under the provocative title *Nestlé Kills Babies.*

It was here that Nestlé, even the company concedes today, made a strategic error. It decided to take a hard line against its critics, especially after learning that the Swiss group had a total of seventeen enrolled members, most of them university students. It sued them for libel in a Swiss court. The trial in Berne District Court, held in 1976, turned out to be a morality play in which Nestlé was the heavy. Although the defendants were found guilty of libel and fined, the Swiss judge ended up admonishing Nestlē: "If the company wishes to avoid the charge of immoral and unethical behavior in the future, it must change its promotional practices." Nestlē's trial was just beginning.

With backing from labor unions, church groups, and consumer activists, INFACT was organized in the United States to spearhead the fight against the infant formula makers. Nestlē was the primary focus. On July 4, 1977, a boycott of all Nestlē products was launched. And in 1978 the nationally televised Kennedy hearings were held. Nestlē proved, at most points, to be inept in dealing with the crusaders. Its U.S. arm didn't market any infant formula and didn't know much about the issues. At the Senate hearings Nestlē sent as its principal spokesman a distinguished nutritionist, Dr. Oswaldo Ballarin, chairman of the company's major operation in Brazil. But it made the misjudgment of putting words in his mouth that imputed a Marxist orientation to Nestlē's critics. As Dr. Ballarin, a short way into his remarks, declared that the campaign against his company was being waged by "a worldwide church organization with the stated purpose of undermining the free enterprise system," Senator Kennedy interrupted him to identify this "organization"—the World Council of Churches and the National Council of Churches.

The campaign against Nestlē escalated. It tugged on strong emotions as the boycotters succeeded in putting the issue on a moral plane where the facts didn't matter. One fund-raising appeal reduced hunger in the developing world to this simplicity: "Ten million Third World babies are starving because of the heartless, money-hungry actions of powerful multinational corporations."

Nestlē was ready by the late 1970s to make changes in its marketing approaches (in 1978 it did stop all mass media advertising of infant formula in the Third World), but it was never able to engage the protestors in a constructive dialogue. The struggle switched then to the World Health Organization, a United Nations body headquartered in Geneva, not far from Nestlē's headquarters in Vevey. There, in May 1981, by a vote of 118 to 1 (the United States), the WHO adopted a code to govern the marketing of breast-milk substitutes. Calling for such measures as the encouragement of breast-feeding, a ban on the distribution of free samples of infant formula, and sharp restrictions on how formula should be promoted (no direct advertising to the consumer, for example), the WHO action constituted the first international marketing code in history. And Nestlē's position? It was all for it. In fact, Nestlē announced on the day the vote was taken that it would abide by the code rejected by the Reagan administration.

Did that satisfy the boycotters? Not at all. The war against Nestlē had by then acquired a life of its own. The company did not even win points for its decision to implement the code unilaterally in all Third World countries even though most of those governments had not adopted the code. (By 1982 only 19 of the 118 nations that voted for the code had implemented any of its measures.) Nestlē was simply not trusted to live up to its promises. Nor were the activists impressed by new research casting doubt on the assumed link between malnutrition and use of infant formula, research that led *The Washington Post* to comment in a 1982 editorial:

> Upon closer inspection, the data linking formula marketing and infant mortality turn out to be sketchy at best. Links between duration of breast-feeding and subsequent infant survival, for example, probably have much more to do with the initial health status of the mother and child than with any presumed switch to formula. Nor is there any hard evidence of a major decline in breast-feeding among poor women in most underdeveloped countries. Common sense suggests that the expense of formula alone would prevent its widespread use among the very poor. Where a substantial decline in breast-feeding has been documented in Taiwan and Malaysia, there has actually been a remarkable drop in infant mortality—both factors being related to rising incomes, improved living standards, and more women working outside the home.

Considering the hullabaloo that had been raised about death to Third World babies by infant formula use, those findings were (or should have been) startling. But this fight was not about a quest for "truth." It had turned into a battle against a multinational giant, and that's much more fun. Nestlē, although it operated in 140 countries, was surprisingly unsophisticated in its early response to critics. It took a long time for the company to understand that it was engaged in a political struggle. Rafael D. Pagan, Jr., a public affairs operative who was later to orchestrate a winning strategy for Nestlē, pointed out later that the company's response was conditioned by its own history:

> Nestlē early on had decided on a passive strategy of Swiss ideological and political neutrality, Calvinist business ethics and product integrity, noncontroversial nutrition products, and a low profile. It favored stable relations with employees, customers, and host communities. It earned a solid reputation for nutrition research and for cooperating with health-care professionals in host countries. It chose not to own plantations and farms so as to avoid conflicts over land ownership, but instead worked with local farmers and entrepreneurs to help develop modern economic infrastructures.
>
> Nestlē's passive strategy worked for more than a hundred years. But

it had no strategy to combat the social guerrilla war that suddenly was waged against it.

The tactic that finally extricated Nestlē from this nightmare was the creation in 1982 of the Nestlē Infant Formula Audit Commission, an entity unique in the long history of conflict between business and society. Since whatever the company said about its adherence to the WHO code was not believed by the other side, Nestlē set up in Washington, D.C., an independent commission to monitor its compliance. Edmund Muskie, former U.S. senator from Maine and former secretary of state, was recruited to chair the commission, whose other members included Dr. Lewis A. Barness, chairman of the department of pediatrics at the University of South Florida College of Medicine; Dr. Omar John Fareed, former assistant to Dr. Albert Schweitzer at the Albert Schweitzer Hospital in Gabon and a leader in the establishment of medical clinics and nutrition programs in the developing world; Dr. J. Philip Wogaman, a Methodist minister and dean of Wesley Theological Seminary; and Dr. Robert C. Campbell, general secretary of the American Baptist Churches of the U.S.A.

The commission was empowered to investigate all complaints about Nestlē's infant formula marketing practices. At first the boycott groups rejected the commission as a Nestlē public-relations ploy, and they boycotted the commission by refusing to submit their complaints to it. After nine months, however, the commission's actions (for example, they had succeeded in getting Nestlē to strengthen its instructions to field personnel) convinced a skeptical press and a hostile bunch of activists that it was really independent despite Nestlē's funding. The audit commission enjoyed extraordinary powers. It could inspect the company books, make field trips anywhere in the world to inspect Nestlē operations, hire outside experts, and issue reports to the public without running them by Nestlē. If it found Nestlē at fault (and it did at times), it could (and it did) publicly criticize the company. Nestlē paid the bills, but the commission was free to follow its own path.

In November 1982 the International Nestlē Boycott Committee agreed to submit its complaints to the Muskie commission. They turned out, for the most part, to be minor; a year later the two sides sat down to work out an agreement to settle the boycott. On May 19, 1983, when Nestlē held its annual meeting in Lausanne, Switzerland, representatives of boycott groups traveled there with petitions, signed by 112,000 people from thirty-eight countries, decrying Nestlē's noncompliance with the WHO code. The petitions were carried in a baby carriage festooned with such messages as "Our signatures memorialize these needless deaths." Less than a year later the boycott was called off, and activist leaders were saluting Nestlē "as a model for the whole industry." From evil monster to hero in two years.

So what difference did it make? Reflecting on that question two years after the boycott was called off, Carl Angst, one of the seven general managers of Nestlē, conceded that the most positive result was a reinforcement of the superiority of breast-feeding. On the negative side, he cited the hardship on Third World hospitals that had relied heavily on free samples. He also noted that Nestlē's baby formula had lost market share to competitors who have not been so scrupulous. Nestlē's sales of infant formula have been static or on the decline since 1980. "That doesn't bother the activists," said Angst. "And that doesn't bother the countries. It just bothers Nestlē. We are glad that breast-feeding is on the increase. A friend said to me, 'But what are you in business for?' I told him, 'Nestlē doesn't need infants in their first four months to consume our products.' " One legacy of the fight was the concept of using an independent, company-funded body to settle such disputes. It's a remarkable model that has yet to be copied by any other multinational.

That Nestlē would go to Armageddon over a product that accounted for only 2.5 percent of its total business is appropriate, given its history. Infant formula was, after all, the first product made by the company in its founding year, 1866. Also, while Nestlē is busy today selling Lean Cuisine to American Yuppies, it has long been a major player in the developing world and can support its claim that company activities there have made positive contributions not just to the company but to the health of the population and the economies of the countries. The availability of milk in all its forms—fresh, condensed, powdered—in many parts of Latin America, Asia, and Africa can be traced to pioneering ventures by Nestlē. The company's anguish over the infant formula fight was well expressed by Pierre Liotard-Vogt, its chairman during the 1970s, who said, "It is difficult to imagine why a world company like ours would sacrifice what amounts to its integrity and *raison d'être* if these were to cost the lives of infants in the Third World."

A colossus today, Nestlē grew from two roots, one of them planted by Americans. Both roots had to do with milk and both began in Switzerland in the same year. Infant-mortality rates were as bad then in the advanced industrial countries as they are today in Asia and Africa. In Switzerland, for example, one out of every five children died before reaching the age of one. The idea for a "manufactured" milk that wouldn't spoil came from that quirky American inventor Gail Borden, who, according to legend, was returning in 1851 from England (where he had received a medal from Queen Victoria for inventing a dehydrated meat biscuit) and was anguished by the shipboard cries of hungry babies, four of whom died during the voyage from drinking contaminated milk. An inveterate tinkerer, Borden was impelled by this experience to develop a vacuum process to remove water from milk which, when mixed with sugar, would be safe for use over a long period. He received a patent for his condensed milk (40 percent sugar by content) in 1856, and the product made its mark during the Civil War when the U.S. government ordered huge quantities for its troops.

Following the Civil War Charles A. Page, a thirty-year-old midwesterner from a family of thirteen, was posted to Zurich as the American consul. Switzerland was a dairy farming country, and he quickly thought of making condensed milk there. His elder brother, George, joined him, bringing from America the equipment needed for a condensed milk plant. On August 6, 1866, the Page brothers formed a company, which they called the Anglo-Swiss Condensed Milk Company, so named because they saw Britain as their biggest market. They put their plant in the Lake Zug city of Cham in central Switzerland and began producing condensed milk in February 1867.

Meanwhile, 120 miles away in the picture-postcard village of Vevey, nestled between Lausanne and Montreux on the shores of Lake Geneva, fifty-four-year-old Henri Nestlé was tinkering with a new idea—a food product that could be fed to babies in addition to, or in lieu of, mother's milk. Nestlé had come to Vevey from Germany in 1843 and had worked as an artisan and merchant. He was said to be "a born inventor, with a passion for chemistry." Two months after Anglo-Swiss was founded, Nestlé began to make his milk food in Vevey. He used an air pump to concentrate fresh milk, which he then combined with sugar and cereal. He thought at first that the formula would be used mainly by infants over two months old, but in September 1867 he supplied it to a mother who was seriously ill and whose prematurely born baby, then fifteen days old, had refused her milk and was suffering convulsions. Seven months later Nestlé was able to report that the baby "[who] has taken nothing but my milk food, has never been ill and can sit up in his cot by himself."

Both of these milk-based enterprises prospered. By 1873, just after the Franco-Prussian War, Nestlé was shipping two thousand cans a day and selling in sixteen countries, including the United States, Argentina, and Australia. Anglo-Swiss, by that same year, had opened plants in Germany and England (where it was getting 75 percent of its sales), plus two more in Switzerland. Charles Page died in 1873, leaving his brother

George in command of the company. In 1875 Henri Nestlé sold his company to three well-to-do Swiss burghers for one million Swiss francs. He then retired to Montreux, never having anything more to do with the enterprise that was to make his name a worldwide household word. He died in 1890, leaving no heirs.

In 1878 these two twelve-year-old Swiss firms crossed swords. Anglo-Swiss began to make an infant formula, and Nestlé began to make condensed milk. It was war for the next twenty-six years until in 1905, when they agreed to combine forces under the name Nestlé and Anglo-Swiss Condensed Milk Company. It was a formidable enterprise to begin with, operating seven plants in Switzerland and eleven in five other countries (Britain, Germany, Norway, Spain, and the United States). Profits in 1906 came to 7.5 million Swiss francs. It was to become much bigger. Nestlé and Anglo-Swiss had been internationally minded virtually from the start, and this is a characteristic the company was never to lose. It looked upon the world as its market. Being based in Switzerland didn't hurt.

While World War I raged from 1914 to 1918, spreading to five continents and leaving nine million soldiers dead, Switzerland—and Nestlé—remained neutral. The company's business went forward in virtually all countries, so that by 1918 productive capacity was twice what it had been in 1914. During the Great Depression of the 1930s, Nestlé also advanced. By 1938 the company had in place 105 factories, including plants in Czechoslovakia and Yugoslavia in Europe, Japan in the Far East, Argentina and Chile in South America, and South Africa on the African continent. As the Spanish civil war with the victory of the Nazi-backed Franco forces, Nestlé was planning to open two new Spanish factories. And as the war clouds gathered in Europe, Nestlé was planning a string of new plants in Latin America. (It helped to make products—milk, chocolate, cheese—that people wanted or needed, no matter how bad the times.)

Switzerland is a small country, and the Nestlé people recognized early on that to grow they would have to be ready to manufacture locally rather than export to local sales agents. They didn't have the advantage of a huge home market that American and British companies enjoyed. Being Swiss, they kept a close watch on things from Vevey and Cham, but they were not averse to developing strong national Nestlé companies in all parts of the world, either by acquisition or starting from scratch. And unlike multinationals in other countries, Nestlé did not have the cover of a flag; Switzerland never had imperialistic designs. In 1906, for example, when Australia, the company's second-largest export market, boosted import duties, Nestlē bought the leading condensed milk company in that country, Cressbrook Dairy, which came with four farms and 1,443 head of cattle. (It was one of the rare times Nestlē acquired land holdings.) Nestlē modernized and expanded Cressbrook's manufacturing facilities, shipping in machinery made at Cham, and in 1920 it acquired eleven more Australian factories, while selling off its farms.

It was after World War I that Nestlē began its involvement in Third World development, taking over a small Brazilian milk condensery in Araras, 125 miles northwest of Sao Paulo, and sending in Swiss engineers to build an efficient operation. The project was not simply mindless milk processing. Nestlē people worked with the local dairy farmers to help them improve milk yields. They organized a milk collection system, which meant that roads had to be improved—a crucial factor because fresh milk must be processed quickly. Equipment had to be replaced. And workers had to be trained.

In four years the condensery, which bought 2,000 tons of milk from farmers when Nestlē arrived, was buying 3,500 tons, and Nestlē was ready to push farther into the interior of Brazil with a milk reception center at Santa Rita do Passa Quatro, sixty miles north of Araras. This remote dairy had to be equipped with cooling equipment, boilers, and emergency diesel engines to maintain the temperature of the milk at the desired level. It was the Brazilian experiment that convinced Vevey that it could build a business in Third World countries. Nestlē began making chocolate in Argentina (1931) and milk products in Cuba (1931), Chile (1933), and Mexico (1935).

After World War II it extended this know-how to countries in Asia and Africa. In countries such as Ghana and Malaysia, where there are no dairy herds, Nestlē imported powdered skim milk and butterfat which it reconstituted in its factories. India is one of Nestlē's great success stories. Nestlē had been exporting condensed milk and infant formula to India since the beginning of this century, but the Indian government, hoping to develop its own industries, called a halt to these and other imports in 1958. Nestlē then cooperated with the government by building a milk processing factory in Moga, a small town in the Punjab near the Pakistan border. The Moga milk producing district covers 3,500 square miles, encompassing some seven hundred villages where small farmers, mostly Sikhs, draw their milk from buffaloes. There are thousands of these farmers, each, on the average, having one or two buffaloes. It was this raw material base that Nestlē organized into a village-by-village collection system that could feed into its factory, which opened in 1961. Fresh milk production in the Punjab has soared, and most of it (95 percent, in fact) is consumed directly in homes in liquid form or as *ghee,* a type of yogurt.

In the Moga milk district Nestlē now buys about a quarter of the output. In its first year the Nestlē factory bought 2,000 tons of milk from 4,460 suppliers; in 1983, it bought 51,000 tons from 35,000 farmers. Originally the plant made only condensed milk. Today its output includes powdered milk, Nescafé instant coffee, infant formula, noodles, and condiments. All the raw materials are purchased in India. The plant employs a little under one thousand people. Originally Nestlē owned 90 percent of the operation but, in line with the Indian government's desire to restrict foreign ownership, has since reduced its shareholding to 40 percent. "This situation," Nestlē notes, "has not prevented the company from reinvesting, diversifying, growing and, in short, playing the role in development decided by authorities."

By 1986, sixty-five years after it entered Brazil, Nestlē's Brazilian company had become a powerhouse. The company had just completed a new frozen food plant in Araras, its nineteenth factory in the country, and Nestlē-Brazil was registering sales of $1.2 billion, making it the sixth-largest operation for the company (after the United States, France, West Germany, Japan, and England).

The move into Brazil proved to be fortuitous for Nestlē in that it eventually opened an entirely new vista. In 1930 the Brazilian coffee growers, concerned by huge coffee bean surpluses, approached Nestlē chairman Louis Dapples with the idea of developing a "coffee cube" product that would be soluble in hot water. Dapples turned over the problem to the Nestlē research laboratories in Switzerland. There a chemist, Max R. Morgenthaler, headed a group which found, by 1937, that the addition of carbohydrates would yield a soluble product that retained the flavor of coffee.

The result was Nescafé, the first instant coffee, which appeared in a powder rather than cube form. Ironically, because of the strict regulations there on what could or could not be called coffee, Nestlē at first was unable to make Nescafé in Brazil. The first batch of Nescafé for sale to consumers came from Nestlē's Swiss plant in Orbe. It went on sale in Switzerland on April 1, 1938. And in 1939 it was being made in France, Britain, and the United States. Nescafé was the first product made by Nestlē that did not have a milk base.

On September 1, 1939, Hitler invaded Poland, unleashing a war that was to endure for six years and leave more than fifty million people dead. Once again Switzerland and Nestlē were neutral. And once again Nestlē coped better than most companies. This time the Swiss had taken the precaution of setting up a new holding company, Unilac Inc., which was registered in Panama and had grouped under it all the Nestlē companies in the Western Hemisphere. And with the advent of World War II, Nestlē bifurcated its headquarters. Chairman Edouard Muller went to America to set up a Nestlē command post in Stamford, Connecticut, from where he directed the overseas operations of Nestlē (including those in Britain). Vice Chairman Carl J. Abegg remained in Vevey to oversee the Nestlē operations in continental Europe, then mostly overrun by the Nazi armies.

Nestlē came through the war in good shape. Most of its factories throughout the world were still standing and had indeed continued to produce, albeit at a slower pace, during the conflict. The company even expanded during the war by opening new plants in Venezuela, Colombia, and Peru. But the major benefit Nestlē derived from World War II was the boost it gave to instant coffee. Just as the Civil War had been a boon to Gail Borden's condensed milk, World War II spread the use of soluble coffee, which was easy to transport and needed only boiling water to brew. The U.S. Army made soluble coffee a staple beverage on front lines. GIs complained about missing "the real taste of coffee," but meanwhile they guzzled Nescafé. Toward the end of the war the military orders were so strong that the Nescafé output of two plants in Sunbury, Ohio, and Granite City, Illinois, went entirely to the government, with none left over for the domestic market.

World War II put instant coffee on the map, and by the end of the conflict Nestlē had on its hands a worldwide coffee business. For a while Nescafé became virtually a generic name for instant coffee. However, Nestlē was unable to secure any patent protection, and it soon encountered stiff competition from the American coffee roasters, particularly General Foods (Maxwell House).

Once the war was over and Nestlē's management was reunited in Vevey, the company moved quickly to strengthen its international presence. While many of the major companies of the Western world were busy rebuilding their home markets, Nestlē was rebuilding in old markets and opening new markets outside its home country. In the twenty years following the war, Nestlē opened more than fifty plants around the world and added others through acquisition. By the time it celebrated its one-hundredth birthday in 1966 (even though the Cuban operations, which dated from 1930, had been nationalized by Fidel Castro in 1960) it could boast one of the most farflung empires of any corporation in the world: 214 factories standing on five continents, employing eighty-five thousand people.

Those were not all baby food plants. Subsumed in the history of Nestlē are the histories of a number of other important food companies that were consumed along the way. To begin with, there's chocolate, the product most Americans associate with Nestlē. Vevey, Henri Nestlē's adopted home, is where the Swiss chocolate industry started. François-Louis Cailler, who came from an old Vevey family, began the machine production of chocolate there in 1819 when he was twenty-three years old. He was the first to deliver chocolate in individual blocks. Cailler's firm was followed by these Swiss chocolate makers: Suchard (1826), Kohler (1831), Sprungli (1845), Klaus (1856), Peter (1867), Tobler (1869), and Lindt (1879).

The Kohler company was founded by Amedee Kohler in Lausanne, and the Peter chocolate factory was established in Vevey by Daniel Peter, who had married the daughter of Cailler. Peter holds a secure place in the history of this industry because he invented milk chocolate. Inspired by the work of his neighbor, Henri Nestlē, who mixed milk with cereal to make an infant formula, Peter experimented for years until he found how to make a smooth mixture of cocoa, sugar, and condensed milk. He made his first milk chocolate in 1875. In 1878 Peter's chocolate bar won a silver medal at the Paris International Exhibition.

In a series of steps beginning in 1904 and ending in 1929, these three firms—Cailler, Kohler, and Peter—became part of Nestlē. First, Kohler and Peter merged to form the Swiss General Chocolate Company, which agreed to make chocolate under the Nestlē name, while Nestlē agreed to sell Kohler, Peter, and Nestlē chocolates in foreign markets. In 1911 Cailler joined the combine, and in 1929 the entire group was absorbed by Nestlē, which had already acquired holdings in chocolate makers in Australia, New Zealand, Italy, Spain, Germany, Argentina, Turkey, and the United States. Today, although Nestlē continues to sell chocolate under a variety of brand names, its dominant brand is Nestlē. In 1986 the company was making chocolate in twenty-one countries. It's believed to be the world's largest maker (and the Swiss are the largest eaters).

Three other companies with notable histories of their own that became part of the Nestlē entourage were:

■ The Alimenta foodstuffs business, started in 1884 by a remarkable Swiss inventor, Julius Maggi, whose aim was to improve the diet of working people. Maggi is credited with inventing—or marketing commercially for the first time—dehydrated soup, seasonings, and bouillon cubes. Nestlē took over Maggi in 1947. It's one of the company's principal brands.

- Crosse & Blackwell, whose history goes back to a produce business started in London in 1706 and operated under other names until 1830 when it was taken over by two employees, Edmund Crosse and Thomas Blackwell, whose names became a premier label for packaged foods. After World War I the firm absorbed two other English food packers, E. Lazenby, maker of a popular sauce that the English liked to smother their meats in, and James Keiler, producer of the famous Dundee marmalade. Crosse & Blackwell became part of Nestlē in 1960.

- Findus International, a company founded in Sweden in 1941 to can fruits and vegetables. The founder was Marabou, the biggest chocolate maker in Sweden. Findus later became one of the first companies to enter the frozen food business. It entered Nestlē's orbit in 1962 and ranks today as the largest marketer of frozen foods in Europe. (For incestuous reasons too complicated to go into here, the Findus label in Germany, Italy, and Austria belongs to Unilever, whereas in England, Unilever's home country, Nestlē markets Findus frozen foods against the Unilever brand, Birds Eye, which in the United States belongs to General Foods.)

Nestlē should be accorded the position of the largest food company in the world. Unilever's total sales are larger but include a passel of nonfood items such as detergents, toothpastes, toiletries, chemicals, packaging, and trading. About 95 percent of Nestlē's $25 billion in sales comes from food products, which makes the Swiss company bigger than Kraft or General Foods or Beatrice, the three giants of the U.S. food industry. Nestlē's climb to the top has been fueled by an aggressive policy of acquisitions in the American market, where it has always had difficulties. It made a disastrous acquisition of Libby, McNeil & Libby to prevent the canner from being captured by the masterful Sicilian manipulator Michele Sindona. The United States is the only market in the world where Nescafé failed to capture first place in instant coffee sales. In recent years Swiss francs brought into the Nestlē fold Beringer and Souverain wines, Alcon eye-care products, Beech-Nut baby foods, Stouffer (the frozen foods, restaurants, and hotels), Ward-Johnston (O Henry!, Goobers, Bit-O-Honey), Hills Brothers coffee, MJB coffee, and Carnation.

The acquisition of Carnation in 1985 for $3 billion was, up to that point, the largest nonoil merger ever made in the United States, and it put Nestlē into a new business—pet foods (Friskies and Mighty Dog). It also added a business, Carnation evaporated milk, that goes back to Nestlē's origins. Nestlē had tried on various occasions, both in the last century and in this century, to establish a toehold in the U.S. milk business, but it was beaten back every time, much to the disappointment of its American cofounder, George Page.

Carnation was started on the West Coast in 1899 at just about the time that Borden was crushing the Nestlē invasion in the rest of the country. Carnation's first advertising slogan, which it used for many years, was "Milk from contented cows." The "Carnation" name itself came from a cigar box that caught the eye of founder Elbridge Amos Stuart. The Nestlē and Carnation people never met face to face until after the Swiss company had made its offer. But when a delegation of four from Vevey visited Carnation in Los Angeles, they were delighted to find a company that seemed to be compatible with Nestlē. It seemed to have the same reclusiveness and stodginess. Nestlē's financial and administrative capo, Reto F. Domeniconi, said that when he returned to Vevey, he told his colleagues, "If you had to translate 'Carnation' into Swiss, you would say 'Nestlē.' "

Nestlē is the most multinational of all multinationals. Reto Domeniconi has a ready explanation: "Hundreds of years ago there were Swiss mercenaries because the father owned the farm and only one son could inherit it. So they went out in the world, they were traders, hotel people. It's in our blood, our mentality, our ancestry." The Nestlē numbers are certainly impressive. The company does 97 percent of its sales outside its home country. It had, at the end of 1985, 362 factories in fifty-eight countries. And it had 152 operating companies, each with sales of at least $7 million, in sixty-three countries. Nestlē is used to juggling many balls at the same time. In 1986 it was having great success in India, a rice-eating nation, with a new line of Maggi two-minute instant noodles. Meanwhile, in Japan, where Nescafé owns 70 percent of the coffee market and is credited with converting many tea drinkers to coffee, Nestlē introduced a ground coffee under the Nescafé label.

In Spain the company was marketing a new line of ready-to-eat breakfast cereals under the Nestlē name, while under the Findus label it was introducing Spaniards to corn-on-the-cob. King Kao chocolate drink was introduced in France, and the Lean Cuisine line, which did so well in the United States, was brought to Europe and Australia under the Findus label. In Australia the company was running a fast-food chain, Cahill's, while in Brazil it was operating a small hamburger-and-milkshake chain, Bob's. New Stouffer hotels were going up in Nashville, Baltimore, and Tucson. In Australia Nestlē deepened its stake in the local Life Savers company to 40 percent. In the United States Nestlē paid $56 million in 1986 to acquire Pasta & Cheese, which operated nine stores and five restaurants in Manhattan that got away with charging fantastic prices for spaghetti. Nestlē, in 1985, began making ketchup in India (at Moga); launched a white chocolate, Nestlē Alpine, in the United States; and introduced the Fix line of seasonings in the Far East. In Carthage, the Tunisian port city that Hannibal used as a springboard to invade the Roman Empire, the Nestlē ice cream plant was modernized.

Nestlē is admired in the international business community for its ability to maintain its balance in the midst of this product and geographical diversity. It seems to do so by constant attention to details—and by a lot of traveling. While Nestlē operating companies are encouraged to be independent, even adventuresome, they share a commonality that's reinforced by a steady stream of materials from Vevey and by regular conferences bringing people from different countries together under one roof. A Nestlē company is unlikely to bring out a new product without Vevey's approval. Long-term plans and budgets are submitted to Vevey. And there is a constant transfer of technology, products, and pure information from country to country.

Helmut Maucher, who became chief executive of Nestlē in 1981, is a great believer in face-to-face contact. He spends half his time visiting the troops outside Switzerland. The board of directors holds at least one meeting a year outside Switzerland. Twice a year Maucher chairs a meeting of the heads of Nestlē companies in the ten biggest markets. Nestlē also brings in managers from all over the world to participate in seminars held at Rive-Reine, a musty Victorian-style stone villa that serves as the company's international training center in Vevey. Participants reside at the center, which was built in 1851 by Frederick-William III of Prussia as a residence for his morganatic wife, Augusta.

Originally called Villa Augusta, the mansion was acquired by Nestlē in 1969. It's filled with period pieces and Nestlē memorabilia. Among the sessions held there in 1986 were a three-week marketing seminar attended by Nestlē managers from Britain, Lebanon, West Germany, Senegal, Sweden, and seven other countries; a four-week executive seminar that dealt with such topics as "The Evolution of Nestlē," "Production and Corporate Strategy," and "Promoting Company Interest in a Critical Environment," and a four-day class for secretaries who were required to have "perfect mastery" of both English and French.

One of the unique organizing institutions at Nestlē is Nestec Ltd., short for Nestlē Products Technical Assistance. It's the research and development arm of Nestlē, designed to bring to operating units the latest technology in all areas of food and nutrition. Some three thousand people work for Nestec in a wide range of scientific disciplines, conducting research into every link of the food chain, beginning with raw materials and ending with human consumption of foods, including the organoleptic properties (shape, color, aroma, texture). One of Nestec's mandates is to come up with new products. Another is to improve existing products. Yet another is to do basic research on diet to discover how complex food systems work. Nestec's largest installation is a new Research and Nutrition Center that opened in Lausanne in June 1987. Employing 350 people, it's one of the largest and most sophisticated food research laboratories in the world.

Grouped under Nestec are nineteen technological development units in ten countries. Usually suffixed with "reco" (standing for research company), they are organized around specific areas of food technology. They usually have pilot plants that can turn out actual products. For example, the laboratory at Orbe, Switzerland, researches instant coffee and decaffeination; chocolate technology is the province of the lab at Broc, Switzerland; Hispareco in Southern Spain studies how fruits and vegetables grow in southern climates; Londreco (at Hayes, outside London) looks into canning, the British are the great consumers of tinned foods; Novareco (at Robbio in North Italy) is located within the grounds of a large cheese factory and, naturally, studies cheese technology; Latinreco, based in the Andes mountains near Quito, Ecuador, is charged with studying food habits of Latin America with a view toward developing products of high nutritional value using local raw materials.

A Swiss who would look at home in a university laboratory, Brian-Ernst Suter heads up Nestec in Vevey. During an interview in early 1986, he cited the Quito center—and another one in Singapore (Eastreco)—as examples of Nestlé's concern with malnutrition in the developing world. At the same time he was just as proud of the research that he said had gone on for years and had finally succeeded in coming up with the Yes bar that was sweeping European markets in 1985 and 1986. Yes is a chocolate-covered sponge cake bar that dovetailed, Suter pointed out, with the worldwide move toward lighter eating.

Nestlé's Vevey headquarters, an eight-story, cantilevered structure whose glass façade looks out of place in this quaint Swiss town, is staffed with an international cadre of people who clearly know the world. Fifty-one different nationalities are represented in the staff of sixteen hundred. Speaking a second language in Vevey, which is in the French part of Switzerland, counts for nothing. Nearly everyone does. If you called the central switchboard and started talking in English or German or Spanish, you'd have little trouble getting through (try doing that with CPC International in Englewood Cliffs, New Jersey, a U.S. food company doing more than 60 percent of its business outside the country). Nestlé managers are likely to have been with the company all their working careers, and they more than likely have served outside Switzerland. One third of the middle managers at Vevey are non-Swiss. Georg Speidel, who supervised the company's international network of factories until his retirement in 1987, used to tell candidates, "Don't come to Nestlé if you want to stay in Vevey."

Nestlé executives come from various backgrounds, and they have a deep fund of knowledge about the food business. Walter D. Marchy, who was in his thirty-second year at Nestlé in 1986, said he doesn't feel "like an old Nestlé man" because he has worked in so many different situations. Head of what Nestlé calls "culinary" products (prepared foods), Marchy joined the research department at Vevey in 1954. He then spent, successively, six years in France, two years in Norway, three years back in Vevey, two years in Sweden, seven years in England, and seven years in Germany before returning to Vevey. From Vevey, he made frequent trips to the United States and Canada.

Camillo Pagano, Nestlé's top marketing man in 1986, was born in Rome to a Scottish mother and Italian father. Married to a Swiss, he has worked for Nestlé in four countries: Canada, the United States, Argentina, and Italy. The Paganos have a daughter who is Canadian, a son who is Italian, and another son who is Argentine. Explaining why Nestlé is expanding in the U.S. coffee industry in the face of a steady drop in coffee drinking, Pagano blames the U.S. coffee roasters for making a "bad" product, an interesting comment from the company that brought us Nescafé.

G. S. Gillett, a didactic Englishman who grew up in Africa, heads up raw materials purchasing in Vevey—and to spend forty-five minutes with him is to get a crash introduction to the world commodity scene. Gillett joined Nestlé in England in 1966, working first in milk purchasing, and spent five years in West Africa (Ghana, Nigeria, and the Ivory Coast) before coming to Vevey. At Nestlé headquarters he is in effect the world's largest buyer of coffee beans and the first- or second-largest buyer of cocoa beans, the raw material of chocolate. Nestlé is also a prodigious consumer of sugar, meat extracts, and of course tinplate (for packaging).

Gillett has seen and followed closely the major changes in the cocoa market. Thirty years ago Ghana and Nigeria grew more than 50 percent of the world's cocoa. Today, said Gillett, the Ivory Coast and Brazil account for 50 percent of world production, with the Ivory Coast number one. Nigeria has fallen to sixth place. European chocolate makers rely on West African cocoa, American companies on Brazilian. Is there a difference in quality? Gillett says yes. While U.S. producers can use West African cocoa as well as Brazilian, the European chocolate makers, on the whole, do not accept the Brazilian strain. European chocolate is not the same as American. "You wouldn't try and sell a Hershey bar in Switzerland, would you?" Gillett asked rhetorically. To a question about sugar being subsidized by countries everywhere Gillett has this ready analysis: "The sugar market is often misunderstood by many people, including people in our own organization. Basically it's fairly straightforward. We're talking about a world production of one hundred million tons a year, okay? Seventy-two million tons, or 72 percent, is consumed in the country in which it's produced. Okay? Another eight million, or another 8 percent, is traded under specific trade agreements, and I'm talking here of Comecon-Cuba. Okay? So you are left with a residue market which is only 20 percent, which is what we are talking about when we talk about the world sugar market. But it's only 20 percent, and it's surplus sugar, that sugar which hasn't really found a home. And in July 1985 that sugar was selling for pennies a pound, which, in real terms, is the lowest price of the century."

For years Nestlé was known as a production-driven company, a place where the factory managers and food technologists called the shots while marketing people languished in oblivion. To some extent that is still true, even though Nestlé now mounts a worldwide advertising assault for which the company spent $880 million through its many advertising agencies in 1985. Nestlé does not believe in a so-called global advertising approach. Campaigns are developed locally to suit local tastes, but there is a lot of interchange of ideas. Two American ad agencies, J. Walter Thompson and McCann-Erickson, are the shops Nestlé prefers, but Pagano emphasizes that if a local agency has a better office than JWT or McCann, it will get the business.

The production culture is still strong at Nestlé. The company's advertising has a reputation for being straightforward, filled with reason-why copy. It's certainly never flashy. There's an obsession at Nestlé with producing sound products and having efficient machinery that is kept spanking clean. Company publications delight in showing plant machinery that looks as if it had been polished endlessly. One senses the strength of the production culture in talking to Speidel, the technical division head, who has spent thirty years with Nestlé, working in Australia and the Netherlands as well as Vevey. He knows how to build from scratch any kind of food plant, whether it be a coffee spraying factory, a milk condensery, or a chocolate works.

Speidel speaks very rapid German (Swiss German, he stresses proudly), English, French, or Dutch and talks bluntly about the importance of high standards in production and a sense of camaraderie with the people who run Nestlē factories around the world. The average Nestlē plant employs between 290 and 300 people, he pointed out, which is good because it's just small enough for a factory manager to know all his people. "We have to know each other," he said. "It's far more important than elsewhere." Nestlē, he insisted, always takes the high road when it comes to ensuring product safety and quality. "If a local government has stricter standards than ours, we follow them," said Speidel. "If they are lax, we follow ours." It's especially important for a company as multinational as Nestlē. "If anything happens in Timbuktu to one of our products," he pointed out, "the world will know it. We are very vulnerable." Speidel is aware of the internal Nestlē perception that the production people are close-knit and stick together, living in their own engineering world. "We have to be that way," said Speidel. "You don't poison a customer by bad advertising."

For all its worldly ways Nestlē has a smugness—a Swiss smugness—that suggests it knows the true path better than others. Nestlē is a conservative company that does have a commitment to developing countries in that it views its pursuit of profits as compatible with a national interest to provide nutritious foods and build a healthy economy. Nestlē stands ready to work with any kind of government. It was proud to point out that Nestlē-Chile was the only multinational firm not nationalized by the leftist Allende government when it came to power in 1971. Nestlē's public relations director, François-Xavier Perroud, is a multilingual Swiss who delights in telling visitors, "Politically, I am to the right of Attila the Hun."

One can see the face of Nestlē in some of the public remarks made by Helmut Maucher, a native of Bavaria, who was named managing director of the company when he was fifty-four. In a 1984 address to the Swiss Chamber of Commerce in Tokyo, Maucher tried to draw some similarities between the Swiss and the Japanese, aside from the fact that they both make watches and have long-term outlooks. "We both have a patriarchal style in dealing with people," said Maucher. "We know that quality starts with being clean as people and in a factory. We like to be responsive to the needs of the people and their wishes, but we do not favor a 'permissive society.' "

A year later Maucher was in Mexico, speaking at the University of Guadalajara, where he made a plea for multinational corporations to play a greater role in the discussions held by governments, schools, churches, and other institutions on how to improve social problems. "We are prepared to contribute to this dialogue," said Maucher, adding, "We need leaders and managers more than ideologists." Maucher, a conservative politically, then went on to cite Lenin's prescription that when power is achieved, ideology has to give way to productivity, to people who can get things done. Continuing along this vein the managing director of the world's largest food company cited one of the foundation stones of Marxist philosophy, Freedom is the recognition of necessity (in German: *Freiheit ist Anerkennung und Verstehen der Notwendigkeiten*), drawing this moral: "This means finally that those who do not understand or support what is necessary in the interest of the whole society, do not deserve freedom! This, of course, is not our point of view in free democratic societies. But sometimes one should wish that a bit of this attitude and philosophy would also be respected in some of our permissive societies. In my opinion one of our present world problems comes from too many idealistic top people with too much power. They feel obliged to follow ideologically based policies, and controversial issues are put aside."

It's Swiss Calvinism brought up to date.

While Helmut Maucher heads the largest company in Switzerland and has presided over spectacular growth since taking the reins in 1981, not everyone in paranoid Helvetia appreciates the fact that he is German, not Swiss. After Maucher's selection was announced in 1981, a small but influential group of shareholders petitioned the company to amend its bylaws so that only Swiss nationals could hold the two top positions of chairman and managing director. Hubert Reymond, a member of the Swiss parliament from Vaud, the canton where Vevey is located, said at the time, "Nestlé enjoys an extraordinary and privileged position in Switzerland. It is thus inconceivable, in the long term, that Swiss nationals don't assume the chairmanship or the post of managing director."

Nestlé didn't back down but did assure the shareholders that the chairman's position would be filled by a Swiss. In 1985 the criticism erupted again after Nestlé paid $3 billion to buy Carnation. The *Neue Zuercher Zeitung,* Switzerland's most respected daily newspaper, faulted Nestlé for "turning itself into an American-style acquisition company" and asserted that as a Swiss company, Nestlé should have a Swiss managing director. Maucher was not the first non-Swiss to serve as managing director. A Frenchman, Pierre Liotard-Vogt, the son of a legendary Nestlé leader from the 1920s, headed the company during the 1970s. Maucher, whose father also worked for Nestlē as a supervisor in their hometown plant, must have taken some pleasure in pointing out that Henri Nestlē was born in Frankfurt am Main.

In view of the corporate structure, any fear that Nestlē would one day escape from Swiss control is groundless. Although 97 percent of sales come from outside the country, Swiss hegemony is guaranteed by a capital base that is divided two-thirds by registered shares, one-third by bearer shares, and by law only Swiss may hold the registered shares. Nestlē has about one hundred thousand shareholders. The stock is listed on the exchanges in Switzerland, West Germany, France, Austria, and the Netherlands. In 1987 a single share was selling for $6,000.

As Swiss as Nestlē would like to remain, the largest single shareholder is French. She is Liliane Bettencourt, the daughter of Eugene Schueller, founder of the French hair coloring and cosmetics company L'Oreal. Madame Bettencourt owns 4 percent of Nestlē by virtue of the Swiss company's 1974 acquisition of 49 percent of L'Oreal. With Nestlē's backing L'Oreal has come a long way from that point. Its U.S. arm, Cosmair, has acquired the fragrance lines Ralph Lauren, Polo, and Gloria Vanderbilt. And its U.S. product lineup includes the L'Oreal, Lancôme, and Anais lines. In 1985 L'Oreal reported that its worldwide sales, including $700 million in the United States, reached $2.9 billion, a significant

World's Biggest Chocolate Eaters

	Annual Consumption (pounds per person)
Switzerland	18.9
Britain	17.6
Norway	17.1
Austria	17.0
West Germany	15.4
Belgium	13.2
Denmark	13.0
Ireland	12.7
Sweden	12.5
Holland	10.5
United States	9.0
Australia	9.0
France	8.8
Italy	2.0

number. It meant that Nestlé now owns 49 percent of the world's largest cosmetics house.

Access   CH-1800 Vevey, Switzerland
(41) 21-51-0112

100 Bloomingdale Rd.
White Plains, N.Y. 10605
(914) 251-3000

News Corporation	**Sales** $3.3 billion **Profits** $250 million **U.S. Sales** $1.8 billion **Rank** World's largest media company 34 percent of all newspaper circulation in Britain 4th-largest broadcaster in the United States World's 5th-largest movie producer Australia's 2d-largest airline Australia's largest newspaper publisher Australia's largest record company **Founded** 1952 **Employees** 25,000 **Headquarters** Sydney, Australia

F ew rites of passage in recent years have drawn closer scrutiny than a ceremony that took place September 4, 1985, at the federal courthouse in Manhattan's Foley Square. It was then and there that the most controversial press lord in the English-speaking world, fifty-four-year-old Rupert Murdoch, became an American citizen. "Under Federal Communications Commission rules, Mr. Murdoch had to give up his Australian citizenship to buy U.S. television stations," *The Wall Street Journal* explained. "He was accompanied by his second wife and their two sons, all British citizens, and a daughter, an Australian, none of whom changed citizenship."

To some the inference was that Murdoch, already the owner of major television stations in Australia and a London-based satellite service, intended to keep his video empire under family control no matter where proof of citizenship might be required. "Isn't it true," wrote William Safire of *The New York Times,* "that his main reason for becoming a citizen is simple greed and lust for power?" Having asked that question, Safire answered it: "Largely true, but I don't have any trouble with it . . . most newcomers have been drawn by our economic promise."

An even more strident defense of Murdoch appeared in 1984 in *Forbes,* where writer Tom O'Hanlon sized up Murdoch as follows: "To a degree that few people, least of all his fellow journalists, yet understand or even want to admit, Rupert Murdoch is an authentic heir of some great publishing figures of the past, of William Randolph Hearst, of Henry Luce, of Joseph Pulitzer, of Britain's Lord Beaverbrook. While most media corporations today are run by relatively colorless, numbers-oriented businessmen, Rupert Murdoch, Australian born, British educated but now domiciled in New York, almost alone among them combines a zest and a feel for the product with a shrewd sense of the bottom line."

Murdoch's zest is apparent in the way he shakes up the media world on three continents. The concern for the bottom line shows in the financial performance of his media shebang. Rupert Murdoch arrived cold in both Britain and the United States and, starting from scratch, built up a significant presence in an industry—newspaper publishing—that was regarded as mature. He gave readers sensationalized newspapers on both sides of the Atlantic. In the United States he launched the tabloid *Star* to compete with *The National Enquirer* in the supermarket checkout lines. In London he took over a moribund leftist daily, *The Sun,* and in short order goosed its circulation from seven hundred thousand to more than four million by turning it into a screaming tabloid that printed pictures of nude women on page 3. During the Falklands War the Murdoch paper blared on the front page: THE SUN SAYS: STICK IT UP YOUR JUNTA. Murdoch turned it into the largest selling English-language daily in the world.

In 1987, after getting assurances from the British government that it would not bring any antitrust action against him, Murdoch bought another London daily, the recently launched *Today,* which was on the brink of folding after failing to achieve a circulation of more than 350,000. The acquisition gave Murdoch control of 34 percent of the circulation of the British national press.

Murdoch's base is News Corporation Ltd., an Australia-based holding company. Its sales and profits have skyrocketed. Anyone shrewd enough to have bought shares in the early 1980s would have seen the investment multiply tenfold. The News Corporation shares are traded on the stock exchange in Sydney, and the biggest gainer of all is of course Rupert Murdoch. His family company, Cruden Investments (named for the country house near Melbourne where he grew up), owns 46 percent of all the shares.

Murdoch's father, Sir Keith Murdoch, was a distinguished Australian journalist who helped build a powerful newspaper group radiating from the *Melbourne Herald.* Rupert was sent to the best private schools in Australia and on to Oxford. When he would return home from boarding school, his father, who had promoted Australia's first beauty contest, would order Rupert to camp out in the garden, sleeping in an unheated hut that had no running water. Sir Keith died in 1952 when Rupert was twenty-one years old, but his son's inheritance consisted only of a threadbare evening newspaper, the *Adelaide Sun.* His father did not end up owning much of what he built, and Rupert vowed that he would not repeat his father's mistakes.

News Corporation, the edifice that grew from the *Adelaide Sun,* is a sprawling enterprise that owns more than eighty newspapers and magazines in Australia, Britain, and the United States; television properties in two of those countries; and an assortment of other interests, such as 50 percent of Ansett, Australia's largest private airline, 35 percent of an Australian company that runs bingo games and football betting parlors, and 10 percent of the international wire service Reuters. In mid-1985 News Corporation looked, from its sales breakdown, like a tripartite affair: a third in Australia, a third in Britain, a third in the United States. But the tilt is now definitely toward the United States.

In 1985, in two swallows, Murdoch bought one of the world's largest motion picture companies, Twentieth Century Fox, whose library includes such all-time box office winners as *Star Wars, The Sound of Music,* and *Butch Cassidy and the Sundance Kid.* At the same time Murdoch muscled his way into television (this was why he had to become a citizen) by buying six major television stations: WNYW, New York (formerly WNEW); KTTV, Los Angeles; WFLD, Chicago; WTTG, Washington, D.C.; KDAF, Dallas-Fort Worth (formerly KRLD); and KRIV, Houston. In 1986 he added a seventh, WXNE, Boston.

Murdoch wasn't just buying his way into television and the movies. He parlayed these acquisitions into a fourth U.S. broadcasting network, Fox, which he launched in 1987 with more than one hundred affiliated stations—and from there he was thinking of the rest of the world.

Rupert Murdoch had once again confounded his critics. In 1984 *The Economist,* an erudite London weekly founded by Walter Bagehot, had wondered aloud whether America wasn't "a leap too far" for Rupert Murdoch. A Murdoch henchman was quoted as saying that in five years News Corporation "will be the biggest communications company in the world." *The Economist* characterized the claim as "an idle boast unless Mr. Murdoch can invade America more profitably than he has invaded it so far." It turned out there was nothing idle about that boast. By 1987, after a spate of new acquisitions in the United States and other parts of the globe, Murdoch could reasonably claim to be the ruler of the world's largest media empire—and the United States accounted for more than half of total sales.

In the United States, aside from his broadcasting properties, Murdoch had assembled a stable of twenty-one American magazines—some started from scratch, others acquired. The group included *New York, Elle,*

New Woman, European Travel & Life, Skiing, Flying, and *Travel Weekly.* Ranked as the thirtieth-largest media company in the United States in 1983, Murdoch's American arm, News America, had advanced to nineteenth place in three years. No one doubted that more acquisitions would follow. As a Murdoch lieutenant in London once said, "He's a buccaneer: when he sees a sail on the horizon, he wants to sink it."

When it comes to publishing, Murdoch's tastes are catholic, ranging from the raunchy to the respectable, from tabloid dailies to religious books, and from one end of the globe to the other. In 1986 he gained control of the leading English-language daily in Hong Kong, the *South Morning Post.* Then, early in 1987, when the venerable American book publisher Harper & Row was in play because of a tender offer by a perceptive entrepreneur, Theodore L. Cross, Murdoch scooped it up for $300 million. The buccaneer had thus added the 170-year-old house to a book publishing portfolio that already included William Collins in England, John Bartholomew (cartographer of the *Times Atlas of the World*) in Scotland, and Bay Books and Angus & Robertson in Australia.

Murdoch's interest in U.S. publishing did not blind him from exploiting opportunities in his native land. In 1987 he took over the largest newspaper publisher in Australia, the *Herald & Weekly Times.* Under the "Herald" name it published daily papers in Melbourne, Brisbane, Hobart, and Adelaide. With this acquisition Murdoch emerged as the largest newspaper publisher in Australia, controlling 50 percent of the total circulation of papers in the country's major cities. As part of this deal Murdoch agreed to relinquish all his broadcasting properties in Australia, a surrender already in the cards because of laws requiring Australian citizenship, a privilege he gave up to become an American broadcasting potentate. There were more than bottom-line considerations at work in the *Herald* acquisition. This is the newspaper group his father had built up, even though he did not have a major ownership interest. On winning the *Herald,* Murdoch allowed that "it would be wrong to deny that it is an emotional moment for me."

His Australian citizenship was not the only thing Murdoch had to give up to enter the U.S. television wars. Since it's a no-no to own a newspaper and a broadcasting station in the same city, Murdoch put on the auction block the *Chicago Sun-Times,* which he bought in 1984, and the *New York Post,* which he bought in 1976. His adventures with both of these dailies had brought down on his head fulminations highlighted by the Jeff McNelly cartoon showing him using the torch of the Statue of Liberty to light a cigar. Within a month after he took over the *Sun-Times,* sixty-seven people had left the staff, among them the publisher, the

editor, the general manager, the sales director, and the leading columnist, Mike Royko, who fled to the rival *Chicago Tribune.*

TURNCOAT ROYKO DISGUSTING CREEP cried a *Sun-Times* headline in fond farewell. RABBI HIT IN SEX SLAVERY SUIT cried another in the same issue. One veteran *Sun-Times* staffer, Nick Shuman, wrote to Marshall Field V, who had sold the paper to Murdoch for $97 million, accusing his former boss of permitting "an honorable American journalistic enterprise . . . to be sodomized by Rupert Murdoch." A handpicked Murdoch aide named Robert Page became the *Sun-Times* publisher, and eighteen months later Murdoch sold the paper, for $48 million more than he had paid for it, to an investor group headed by Page.

In New York selling the *New York Post* was the next order of business, although columnist Alexander Cockburn wrote that for Murdoch to sell this paper "would be like Dracula selling his coffin." Murdoch had boosted the *Post*'s circulation sharply after buying it by introducing circulation stunts like Wingo, a bingolike prize contest, and running lurid stories under lurid headlines. "Shoot Mom for 50 Cents" was a prototypical front-page banner. Others were: "Leper Rapes Virgin," "I Slept with a Trumpet," "Youth Gulps Gas, Explodes," "Headless Body Found in Topless Bar." *The Columbia Journalism Review* dubbed Murdoch's *Post* " a social problem—a force for evil." To British journalist Patrick Brogan, "The *Post*'s main distinction is not that it is sensational and irresponsible, but that it is corrupting. It panders to hate, fear, and to racial and ethnic divisions in New York."

The *Post*'s circulation dropped precipitously after the newsstand price was raised to thirty-five cents, but even after it hit its peak of one million, the paper failed to attract advertising. According to one story that made the rounds, coast-to-coast, a Bloomingdale's executive once explained why the store wasn't advertising in the *Post:* "Mr. Murdoch, you don't seem to understand. Your readers—they're our shoplifters."

Shortly after he bought the *Post,* Murdoch told an interviewer, "I don't give a damn what the critics say." In a subsequent speech to the American Newspaper Publishers Association, he bawled out his listeners for going over the heads of their readers. "I cannot," he said, "avoid the temptation of wondering whether there is any other industry in this country which seeks to presume so completely to give the customer what he does not want." The public, he said on another occasion, "certainly has no duty to support newspapers. It's the duty of the publishers to provide the type of newspaper the public wants to read."

While it's clear he is no friend of the establishment, Rupert Murdoch does own the epitome of an establishment newspaper, *The Times* of London. He bought this venerable daily from Lord Thomson in 1981 and proceeded to play hardball with the unions in the press room, eventually winning his point, which is that "when things are going badly," as he once said, "the proprietor has to step in or he's going to have no newspaper and the people who work for him, they're going to have no jobs." Buying *The Times* is considered a direct route to being knighted. But not for Rupert Murdoch, who has no interest in a title. He is believed to be the only owner of *The Times* to have refused to accept a peerage.

Nevertheless, when Barbara Walters interviewed him on ABC's "20/20" and asked, "Do you think you could stand being liked and respected?" Rupert Murdoch replied, "Yes, yes, I think I could take it."

Access 2 Holt St.
Sydney NSW, 2010 Australia
(61) 2-288-3000

News America
210 South St.
New York, N.Y. 10002
(212) 815-8800

<table>
<tr><td rowspan="7">

Nippon Steel

</td><td>**Sales** $15 billion</td></tr>
<tr><td>**Loss** $90 million (1986)</td></tr>
<tr><td>**Rank** World's largest steel maker
Japan's 8th-largest company
33d on the *Fortune* International 500</td></tr>
<tr><td>**Founded** 1901</td></tr>
<tr><td>**Employees** 65,000 (average age: 41)</td></tr>
<tr><td>**Headquarters** Tokyo, Japan</td></tr>
</table>

Steel, the symbol of the industrial revolution, has been a concern of the Japanese government for the entire twentieth century. No matter which group has ruled the nation, or whether it was peacetime or wartime, the steel industry has always received special consideration.

This special treatment began in 1901, the year J. P. Morgan bought out Andrew Carnegie and meshed ten steel producers into United States Steel Corporation, a company with an annual production of 10 million tons. While this Pittsburgh behemoth was being launched in the United States, the Japanese government started a steelworks at Yawata, a small fishing village on the southern island of Kyushu. It was close to the Kyushu coal fields and, as a result of Japan's victory in the Sino-Japanese War of 1894–95, it had access to iron ore from China. Yawata's initial capacity was 60,000 tons a year.

Yawata was the first large-scale integrated steelworks in the Orient, but it was preceded by fifty years of Japanese experimenting in the production of pig iron in a blast furnace, particularly at the Kamaishi Iron Works at Kamaishi far up on the northeast coast of Japan's main island, Honshu. It was there that Takato Oshima, an engineer who was born in a nearby town, did his early work.

The son of a physician, Oshima is regarded as the father of Japanese steel making. He introduced the blast furnace into Japan as a way to smelt iron ore, learning how to do it from a Dutch manual that he translated into Japanese. His son, Michitaro Oshima, became the first managing director at the Yawata works. Japan was four to five centuries behind Europe in this technology, and during the late 1890s and early 1900s, the Japanese leaned heavily on Western teachers. Among the foreigners who contributed to the development of the Japanese steel industry were Curt Netto, a German metallurgist who taught at Tokyo University from 1887 through 1895; Adolph Ledebur, a professor at the Freiberg Bergakademie in Germany, who never visited Japan but taught many aspiring Japanese steel makers; Walter Lwowski, a German engineer who provided the technical guidance for Japan's first tinplate mill; Benjamin Smith Lyman, an American geologist who produced the first geological map of the island of Hokkaido, showing the coal and iron resources there; and John Milne, an English seismologist who taught mining at Tokyo University for nineteen years.

Other steel companies were started later—Kobe Steel in 1911, Nippon Kokan in 1912—but Yawata Steel, being a government operation, had a certain edge. In 1913, a year before the start of World War I, it accounted for 85 percent of Japanese steel production. The Japanese steel industry was reorganized after World War I, at the direction of the government, which was preparing for military adventures abroad. In 1934, three years before the second Sino-Japanese war broke out, five years before the start of World War II in Europe, and seven years before the attack on Pearl Harbor, the Japanese government orchestrated the combination of the Yawata Works and six private steel makers into a trust known as the Japan Iron & Steel Company. Included in the merger was the pioneering Kamaishi Works. At its formation Japan Iron & Steel accounted for 97 percent of Japan's production of pig iron, 56 percent of steel ingot, and 52 percent of steel products. By the time World War II started, the company had doubled its production of these products.

The Japanese steel industry had been harnessed to the needs of the military. And when those needs disappeared, the industry was devastated. During World War II thirty-seven blast furnaces were operating in Japan; in 1946, only three, all at the Yawata Works, were still fired up. In rebuilding their industry, the Japanese steel makers received postwar help from the Americans. A group of engineers from U.S. Steel arrived in 1947. In 1950 a team of Japanese engineers went on a study mission to the United States, courtesy of the American Iron & Steel Institute.

But the occupation authority headed by General Douglas MacArthur was not having any of Japan Iron & Steel, which was broken up in 1950 into four private firms—the two biggest being Yawata Iron & Steel and Fuji Iron & Steel. However, according to Chalmers Johnson, author of *MITI and the Japanese Miracle,* government bureaucrats continued to have a soft spot in their hearts for Yawata. Johnson wrote that the press in Tokyo used to refer to MITI (the Ministry of International Trade & Industry) as the "Tokyo office of the Yawata Steel Company."

These suspicions were certainly not allayed when in 1970 the two largest steel producers in Japan, Yawata and Fuji, were allowed to merge to form Nippon Steel over the heated objections of many people. Japan's Fair Trade Commission, for the first time in its history, applied to the Tokyo High Court to get a restraining order, but the merger was finally sanctioned after Yawata agreed to sell one of its plants to Kobe Steel and Fuji agreed to sell one of its to Nippon Kokan.

In a sense, the merger re-created the combination the government had set up in 1934, only this time the company was private. And what it also did, instantly, was to create the world's largest steel company. The Japanese had modernized their old mills and built new ones, using the latest technology, such as the basic oxygen furnace. The result was an industry that was highly efficient. And that efficiency, combined with low labor costs, enabled the Japanese to land high-quality steel in the United States and Europe at prices so attractive that it produced cries of anguish from the same steel makers who were once their instructors.

In 1970, the year Nippon Steel was formed, the Japanese steel industry shipped six million tons of steel (about 6 percent of their total production) to the United States. American steel makers complained bitterly to Washington, D.C., about "dumping." Arms were twisted, and the Japanese agreed to limit their exports to America to a level that would not exceed 5.8 percent of the U.S. market. One of those who urged the Japanese to restrain their exports was Yoshiro Inayama, a commanding presence on the Japanese industrial scene.

Inayama was chairman of Yawata and then became the first chairman of Nippon Steel. A graduate of the University of Tokyo, the elite school for future Japanese leaders, Inayama went to work for Yawata in 1928 and stayed with the company through all its stages. Known in Japan as the "Emperor of Steel," in 1974, when he was seventy years old, he was still smoking five packs of Philip Morris cigarettes every day. Inayama made many trips to China, counting among his friends the Chinese foreign minister Chou En-lai. By 1980 China was taking almost as much Japanese steel as the United States, and Nippon Steel began helping the Chinese to build what is eventually expected to be one of the largest steel mills in the world. The first blast furnace at Shanghai's Baoshan mill was fired up in 1985. During the construction stage Nippon Steel sent 360 engineers to Shanghai to help bring the plant on stream.

Nippon Steel's and Japan's lead over their Western counterparts steadily lengthened. By 1985 Nippon Steel's output (29 million tons) was nearly twice that of U.S. Steel. When Nippon Steel was formed by the Yawata-Fuji merger, the United States was producing 133 million tons of steel to Japan's 100 million tons. In 1985 Japan turned out 105 million tons to 79 million for the United States. Nippon Steel makes thirty different types of steel, and outside of Japan, it maintains a network of twelve sales offices, including three in the United States, to sell products to customers.

The adversarial relationships between labor and management that have characterized the steel industries in other countries (United States, Britain, France, Italy) are absent at Nippon Steel, which hasn't experienced a plant shutdown since the 1950s. The company union at Nippon Steel doesn't make waves, accepting managment's position that steel is such a key industry that wages cannot be bumped up sharply because of the trigger effect that it would have on the prices of other products (automobiles, for example) that Japan needs to export. The peace is also maintained by use of a two-tier labor force: One group, on the Nippon Steel payroll, is entitled to a broad range of benefits, while another group of employees, hired by subcontractors, are not eligible for the lifetime employment guarantee and other benefits. Robert C. Wood, a correspondent for the *Christian Science Monitor,* went to a Nippon Steel plant in 1980 and reported that it was easy to spot the two different groups—the company employees wore silver helmets, the subcontractor people yellow ones. Wood also noticed that all the dirty jobs in the mill were being handled by the yellow-helmeted crews.

The harmonious labor relations stood Nippon Steel in good stead in the mid-1980s when the worldwide slump in the steel industry, coupled with a sharp rise in the value of the yen, forced the company to make draconian cutbacks. Nippon announced at the start of 1987 that it would close five of its twelve blast furnaces and reduce its 65,000-strong work force by 19,000 before March 1991. One of the mills being shut down is the historic Kaimishi Works, which had just celebrated the one-hundredth anniversary of Japan's first production of iron from a charcoal blast furnace. The Kaimishi Works, fronting on the Pacific Ocean, was designated in 1984 as the first historical landmark in Asia of the American Society for Metals.

While the payroll is being cut by almost a third, Nippon Steel said it would not lay off any employee. The company expected nine thousand workers to reach retirement age by 1991, and it planned to find new jobs for the other ten thousand, mostly inside the company.

Steel companies all over the world—in Australia, Britain, Germany, France, Italy, and the United States—were going through a wrenching time in the 1980s. But few showed the agility of Nippon Steel when confronted with adversity. In addition to reassuring its workers that they would not be thrown out of jobs, Nippon Steel moved boldly to develop new businesses. It has an engineering and construction division whose sales now top $2 billion a year (it put up the steel frames for the new seventy-story Bank of China building in Hong Kong), and it has made a series of moves signaling its interest in "high-tech" fields:

- A $2 million investment to finance development of a new vegetable oil by the California biotechnology firm Calgene.
- An $8 million investment giving it 21 percent of the shares of GTX Corporation, a Phoenix, Arizona, firm that makes advanced systems for computer-aided design.
- A 50.7 percent stake in TAU Giken, a Tokyo company that designs data processing systems for offices.
- A joint venture with Philips of the Netherlands to make ceramic chip condensers.
- A joint venture with the U.S. company Concurrent Computer to manufacture minicomputers.

Nippon Steel is clearly open to new ideas. In 1985, through Nittetsu Shoji, its captive trading company, it signed on to distribute Sebastiani wines in the Japanese market. Sebastiani, one of California's largest vintners, said it went with the Nippon Steel people, despite their lack of experience in wine distribution, because it felt the wines would get more attention than if Sebastiani were one of fifty wine lines brought into Japan by an importer. "They make great steel, we make good wine," said Randy Emch, group brand manager at Sebastiani. He added that the gift market is very important in Japan, and if Nippon Steel just got all its employees to buy a bottle of Sebastiani wine, that would give a big boost to sales. (Now why didn't U.S. Steel think of importing French wines?)

While Nippon Steel has said publicly that it hopes eventually to derive half its sales from nonsteel products, it's not easy to give up the habits of a lifetime. And the incestuous nature of Japanese industry has left it with holdings in a host of companies that are in, or closely allied to, the steel industry. Nippon Steel has the following interests: 49 percent of Daido Steel Sheet (Japan's leading maker of galvanized steel sheets); 44 percent of Kurosaki Refractories; 45.6 percent of Harima Refractories; 11.3 percent of Nisshin Steel, sixth-largest steel maker in Japan; 12.4 percent of Daido Steel, the world's largest specialty steel maker (and a major supplier to Nissan); 15.8 percent of Acihi Steel Works, a leading supplier to Toyota (which owns 21 percent of the company); 13 percent of Pacific Metals, Japan's largest producer of ferronickels and stainless steel; 8 percent of Japan Metals & Chemicals, a leading developer of geothermal power; and 5 percent of Dowa Mining, a leading smelter of nonferrous metals (it developed gallium arsenic wafers for intergrated circuits).

All of these companies have stock market listings of their own, which can come in handy. In the first six months of fiscal 1987, Nippon posted a loss of $73 million, but it would have been much greater had not the company sold off some of the securities it owns for proceeds of $218 million.

And no matter how much Sebastiani wine it sells, Nippon Steel is still a steel company. In March 1987 it announced a joint venture with Chicago's Inland Steel to build a new state-of-the-art sheet steel factory near South Bend, Indiana. Expected to be up and rolling by 1990, the Inland-Nippon mill will be using technology developed by Nippon Steel in Japan, technology that will enable the plant to process in one hour what takes twelve days at similar plants now operating in the United States. The technology will also eliminate five hundred to six hundred jobs. "This will help us to attain a superior position in the market," said Frank Luerssen, Inland's chairman.

"We are elated and gratified," said Yutaka Takeda, president of Nippon Steel.

Access   6-3, Otemachi 2-chome, Chiyoda-ku
Tokyo 100, Japan
(81) 3-242-4111

345 Park Ave.
New York, N.Y. 10154
(212) 593-3049

Nissan	**Sales** $28.4 billion
	Profits $135 million
	U.S. Sales $5 billion
	Rank World's 5th-largest automaker
	Japan's 2d-largest automaker
	Japan's 4th-largest industrial manufacturer
	Founded 1933
	Employees 106,000 (average age: 35)
	Headquarters Tokyo, Japan

I n 1960, shortly after the Japanese began trying to sell cars in the United States, Nissan Motor sent fifty-year-old Yutaka Katayama to California to head up operations in the western part of the country. As David Halberstam relates in *The Reckoning,* it was "as much banishment as reward." Katayama was *persona non grata* in Tokyo headquarters, having failed to play the game of internal politics. And if Nissan is anything, it's a highly charged *political* company, with the factional fights so fierce that at times everyone in Japan has enjoyed a ringside seat at the combat.

Katayama, in any case, was happy to be out of that pressure cooker and pleased with his American assignment even though he faced an apparently impossible task. The Datsuns being landed by Nissan were hopelessly underpowered for American roads. Sales were running at one hundred cars a month. But Katayama hung in there, building the dealer network and constantly badgering Tokyo about the styling and engineering improvements needed to sell a car in America. In Tokyo they continued to regard him with ill-concealed contempt even as sales began to creep up: twenty-seven hundred cars in 1963, sixty-seven hundred in 1964, twenty-two thousand in 1966, fifty-seven thousand in 1969.

Nineteen sixty-nine was a turning point because it marked the introduction of the Datsun 510, a plucky little car that had power and élan. In 1970 Nissan captured third place in the imported car field (behind Volkswagen and Toyota) with sales of 105,000. By 1975, in the wake of the oil shock and the tripling of fuel prices, the imported car standings looked like this: Toyota, 283,000; Volkswagen, 268,000; Nissan, 248,000. In 1977 Nissan sold 488,000 cars and trucks to Americans.

It looked like a brilliant achievement. But according to Halberstam, here's what happened to Katayama:

> In early 1977 he received a cable summoning him home, without explanation. It was as if he had suddenly disappeared. On arrival in Tokyo he was informed that he had retired a few days earlier. His friends back in Los Angeles did not know what was happening, but feared the worst. Mayfield

Marshall, who did the advertising and was probably Katayama's closest friend, cabled him in Tokyo, "Hope they give you more than a gold watch," he said. A few weeks later Katayama returned. He looked at Marshall and held up his wrist. On it was a gold watch. It was about the only thing they gave him.

Shortly after Katayama left the United States, Nissan fired the Los Angeles advertising agency, Parker Advertising, that had been the original Datsun agency and whose *raison d'être* was the Datsun account. Nissan was now moving to the big time. It assigned its $40 million account to William Esty of New York, one of the nation's largest agencies. (Nissan fired Esty in 1987.)

These stories are vintage Nissan. The author of this book once was taken to lunch in a fancy French Tokyo restaurant by a Nissan executive. The executive brought along his public relations person, who was clearly terrified of his boss—and with good reason. The executive expected the PR man translate the French menu, and when he wasn't up to that chore, he was publicly humiliated by a brutal dressing-down.

Fear runs through the halls at Nissan Motor. And turmoil is part of its heritage. Although Nissan likes to celebrate 1933 as its year of birth, its history as an automaker can be traced back to 1911 when a company called Kwaishinsha began to make a car known as the Dat, named by taking the first letters of the names of the three principal backers: Kenjiro Den, Rokuro Aoyama, and Meitaro Takeuchi. Not many Dats were sold, and the company went through various financial calamities before becoming part of the Nissan industrial empire put together by Yoshisuke Ayukawa in the 1920s. Nissan, an abbreviation of Japan Industries, was a conglomerate that the hard-driving Ayukawa had built to rival the old family conglomerates or *zaibatsu* (the Mitsuis, Sumitomos, Mitsubishis). He was eager to get into automobile production to challenge General Motors and Ford, which dominated the Japanese scene then with knock-down cars exported from American plants. Japanese auto production in 1930 totaled 458 units.

The automaker known as Nissan Motor began operating in 1933, two years before the first Toyota appeared. By that time the Dat had become the Datsun. The progression went as follows: In 1930, when a mini-Dat was introduced, the car was named Datson (son of Dat). But the soothsayers found that designation ominous because the sound of "son" in Japanese connotes "loss" or something unfavorable. After a new auto plant was opened in 1933, a typhoon caused great flooding. "It was then thought best by all concerned," says a company handout, "to change the spelling of Datson to Datsun, and thereafter to rely on the sun to protect against such 'son' as floods and other untoward happenings."

(Nissan has had trouble with names down to recent times. When cars were first exported to the United States, they were so bad that some Tokyo executives figured that it would be better not to put Nissan's name on them for fear of losing face. In 1981, after more than twenty years of promoting the Datsun name, the company decided to phase it out in favor of the corporate name. The U.S. dealer force was aghast, but Tokyo held to its decision. In 1970, when the first Japanese sports car arrived on the docks in Los Angeles, it carried the name Fair Lady. Halberstam wrote that Katayama and his men "simply pried the nametag off the car and replaced it with one using the company's internal designation for the car, 240Z.")

In 1936 Nissan and Toyota were officially licensed by the Japanese government to make cars and trucks (GM and Ford never received such authority). Nissan, more than Toyota, was a shining star of those prewar days because it was allied closely to the military leaders who were preparing to take Japan to war. Nissan became particularly associated with the Japanese occupation of Chinese Manchuria. The Nissan holding company moved its headquarters to Manchuria, and it was then that the auto division began turning out a stream of trucks, tanks, and arms for the Japanese military. During the war Nissan also made airplane engines. It was not a record that won much favor at General MacArthur's postwar occupation headquarters. Ayukawa was jailed for twenty-one months and never permitted to return to his company. Other prewar Nissan leaders were also purged. Nissan was a company that hung in the balance in 1947 when the Industrial Bank of Japan (IBJ) sent one of its own men, Katsuji Kawamata, to the automaker to watch after its interests. (IBJ was—and is—Nissan's largest shareholder, with about 6 percent of the stock.)

Kawamata knew nothing about cars (not even how to drive one) but he was ambitious. And he became the tough guy at Nissan in the days of reconstruction after World War II. He supported the firing of two thousand workers in 1949, and he played a pivotal role in the 1953 strike at Nissan that resulted in the crushing of Tetsuo Masuda, a charismatic, radical union leader who had as much power in the company as anyone in the years following the war. The Masuda union was replaced by a compliant company union whose command was taken by an arrogant young man, Ichiro Shioji. Shioji forged an alliance with Kawamata, who reached the top rung at Nissan in 1957. They ruled Nissan for the next twenty years.

The power struggles continued ("Datsun, We Are Driven"), but the changes occurring in Japanese industry did not bypass this company.

Engineers intent on designing good cars joined Nissan, borrowing ideas and techniques from other countries but also adding their own touches. In 1952 Nissan signed a licensing agreement with Britain's Austin Motor to build clones of the Austin in Japan. Nissan, along with other Japanese companies, embraced the quality control messages of the American statistician W. Edwards Deming. Virtually unknown in his own country, Deming became a demigod in Japan. So while infighting may have raged in the Nissan executive suites in Tokyo, down on the factory floor in Yokohama dedicated workers, who lived in Nissan apartment complexes, paid attention to the cars coming down the line and took pride in the rise of this company to a major auto manufacturer. A company history notes pointedly that in 1960 Nissan received the tenth annual Deming prize for excellence in industrial engineering, the most coveted prize a Japanese company can win.

Austin technology ushered the postwar Nissan into the mass production of cars. But the company quickly incubated its own engineering prowess. It was quick to grasp the importance of front-wheel drive. It embraced robots on the assembly line. It emphasized engines that were miserly gas consumers. It was a leader in the introduction of electronic components. And little by little, it happened. From production of 7,835 cars and 19,240 trucks in 1955, Nissan went to 899,008 cars and 475,014 trucks in 1970. And by 1980, when Japan passed the United States as the world's largest auto producer, Nissan was rolling out two million cars a year and had displaced Volkswagen as the fourth-largest producer in the world.

Statistics tell one story. Nissan's triumphs have been well reported on the financial pages. But they don't disclose the human costs. Nissan, perhaps more than any other Japanese company, has been the source of stories detailing alienation in the working ranks. One of the most searing accounts, written by John Junkerman after talking to employees at the Nissan's Zama plant outside Tokyo, appeared in the August 1982 issue of *Mother Jones*. It held up Nissan as "the dark side to the Japanese industrial miracle." Junkerman told of speedups, unsafe working conditions, and chafing under the strong pressure to conform. He drew this conclusion: "Harmony and diligence at Nissan are the product of union and managerial policies that reward conformity, punish even the mildest dissent with wage discrimination and ostracism from the work group, and—in extreme cases—contribute to ruthless persecution and violence."

Junkerman reached the same conclusion five years later when he visited the highly acclaimed Nissan plant at Smyrna, Tennessee, only now he found American workers subjected to speedups and harassment. Writing in the June 1987 issue of *The Progressive,* Junkerman said, "Distrust and fear pervade the plant."

Lee Iacocca and others used to ascribe the success of Japanese cars to low wages in Japan. But the sharp jump in the value of the yen during the 1980s robbed critics of this argument. Nissan Motor reported in 1986 that the average wage in its Japanese auto plants was 5.6 million yen, which translated, at current exchange rates, to $37,000 a year. Nissan also detailed publicly the following features of its labor relations program:

- Employees are required to retire at age sixty.
- Retirees are entitled to a lump-sum payment or pension. A typical example: A plant worker who has thirty years service and retires as a general foreman receives about $80,000.
- Overtime is paid at a 30 percent premium.
- Employees get twenty-two days of vacation and holidays per year. They are also allowed fifteen days of paid personal holidays (twenty days after seven years).
- Nissan maintains bachelor dormitories for employees. They hold 12,500 people. The rent ranges from $15 to $20 dollars a month. There are subsidized meals—$1.35 for breakfast, $1.65 for lunch and dinner.
- Employees are eligible for a low-interest car loan.
- Virtually all workers are required to be members of the All Nissan Motor Workers' Union.

One way to escape pressure at home is to go abroad. Nissan has led the Japanese auto industry in establishing production facilities in other countries. In fact, Nissan has identified "commitment to internationalization" as its "foremost characteristic," one that "sets [it] head and shoulders above other Japanese automakers." Nissan built its first overseas plant in Mexico in 1961. By 1983 plants wholly or partly owned by Nissan were making cars and trucks in eight countries: the United States, Mexico, Peru, Australia, Spain, Italy, Thailand, and the Philippines. In addition, Nissan had tieups in a dozen other countries where its vehicles were being assembled or made under license. Nissan bought its way into Spain by acquiring a 36 percent stake in the country's largest truck maker, Motor Iberica. In Italy it joined state-owned Alfa Romeo in a fifty-fifty partnership to build cars in a plant outside Naples. Nissan also teamed with Volkswagen in a project under which VW's Santana model is being produced in Nissan's Zama plant near Tokyo.

The overseas moves did not go forward without the usual pitched battles inside Nissan. Takashi Ishihara, an accountant by training who joined Nissan in 1937 when he was twenty-five years old and worked his way up the finance side of the company, became president in 1977. He took a dim view of a U.S. production facility, feeling that American workers are lazy. One of the strongest proponents of an American plant was Nissan's all-powerful union boss, Shioji, who had close ties to the United Auto Workers. He not only pushed for a U.S. production facility, he wanted it to be a plant where the UAW represented the workers.

David Halberstam described a 1980 meeting between Ishihara and UAW president Douglas Fraser in which the two were shouting at one another. "Your problem in America," said Ishihara, "is of your own making. . . . Nobody wants to work." Fraser retorted: "You wouldn't understand America because you're so undemocratic a man, and you come from so undemocratic a country." On the other hand, the UAW people were encouraged by indications from Masataka Okuma, an executive vice president of Nissan, that when Nissan did open a plant in the United States, it would be a unionized facility.

In 1983 Nissan took the plunge, opening a $300-million light truck plant at Smyrna under the direction of a former Ford manager, Marvin Runyon. And it was, of course, a nonunion plant. Nissan sent Okuma to attend the official ground breaking in 1981. He was greeted by more than one thousand jeering protesters who objected to the selection of a nonunion contractor to build the plant. Okuma said the demonstration didn't bother him, adding, "It's the construction peoples' problem, not ours."

Nissan encountered problems galore in 1986 and 1987 as the yen escalated in value against the dollar (thereby making every sale in the United States worth half of what it used to be when translated into Japanese currency) and as Toyota and Honda crushed Nissan in a tight vise. In the U.S. market Honda passed Nissan; in its home market Nissan saw its market share drop below 20 percent for the first time in the postwar period. Nissan piled up a huge operating loss, managing to show a profit only by financial juggling (sales of assets and securities).

In the early 1980s Nissan was also under strong pressure to open a plant in the United Kingdom. Considering the labor scene there, Ishihara was oddly enough pro-British, while Shioji and his long-time ally, Kawamata, then chairman of Nissan, were anti-British. *The Economist* reported that at the Williamsburg summit held in 1983, Prime Minister Margaret Thatcher bent the ear of Prime Minister Yasuhiro Nakasone about the wisdom of Nissan manufacturing in Britain. Nakasone returned home to lean on Nissan, which soon recognized how smart it would be to make cars in Britain. The plant at Washington in the northeast region of England opened in 1986, with the first Bluebird subcompact (called the Stanza in Japan) rolling off the line on September 8.

In 1952 Nissan people had traveled to England to negotiate the licensing agreement with Austin. The war had been over nearly seven years, but one of the Nissan executives who went on that trip recalled to Halberstam that as they walked through the Austin plant they saw "the hatred on the faces of the workers." Now it was thirty years later, and the British, their auto industry on the verge of collapse, were clamoring for the Japanese to make cars in England. Toshio Yamakazi, the Japanese ambassador to Britain, showed up for the opening day ceremonies at Washington in the fall of 1986. He pointed out to the assembled crowd that this was not the first example of successful collaboration between Japan and the northeast region of England. He noted that ninety years earlier British shipyard workers at Tyneside had built the battleships that enabled the Japanese fleet to defeat the Russians in the war of 1905. "I am convinced that this factory is the forerunner of many things to come," he predicted.

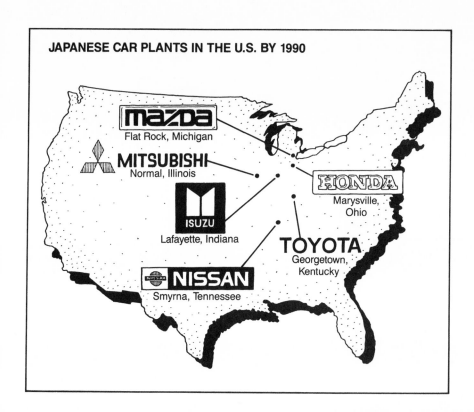

Access 17-1, Ginza 6-chome, Chuo-ku
Tokyo 104, Japan
(81) 3-543-5523

Nissan Motor Corp.
18501 South Figueroa St.
Carson, Cal. 90248
(213) 532-3111

Nobel Industries

Sales $1.8 billion
Profits $66 million
Rank Sweden's largest chemical company
Sweden's largest arms maker
343d on the *Fortune* International 500
Founded 1864
Employees 16,000
Headquarters Stockholm, Sweden

The world's most prestigious award is the Nobel prize—and at $294,000 in 1986, it's sizable, eclipsed only by the new Kyoto prize awarded by the Inamori Foundation in Japan (see Kyocera, page 334). Given for outstanding achievement in the advancement of peace and in the fields of physics, chemistry, medicine, literature, and economics, the Nobels are always presented in Oslo and Stockholm on December 10, the day Alfred B. Nobel died in 1896. The Swedish-born inventor of dynamite left virtually his entire estate to establish this awards program, and it has remained his enduring legacy, although the complex of companies that make up Nobel Industries might also be considered his offspring.

Nobel was born on October 21, 1833, into a Swedish family that traced one of its roots to Olaf Rudbeck, an intellectual giant of the seventeenth century who was depicted by some contemporaries as the "Leonardo da Vinci of Sweden." Alfred had two older brothers, Ludwig and Robert. Their father, Immanuel Nobel, great-grandson of Olaf Rudbeck, was a mercurial character. Largely self-educated, he built homes, constructed bridges, and invented all manner of things. One of his particular interests was explosives. He jumped from scheme to scheme, never quite succeeding in business. In 1832 a fire destroyed the Nobel home in Stockholm, forcing him to declare bankruptcy in the following year, when Alfred was born.

In 1837 Immanuel, who had left home at age fourteen to go to sea as a cabin boy, decided to try and change his luck by going to Russia. Off he went, leaving his family behind while he tried to build a new business in Saint Petersburg. He sent for them in 1842 after developing explosive devices that could be used to mine harbors. The Russians placed big orders for them.

Nine-year-old Alfred, his two older brothers, and their mother moved from Stockholm to Saint Petersburg. Alfred was sickly from birth, and his mother watched over him carefully. She also tutored him. He was clearly precocious, reading everything at hand, but he didn't have a very active childhood. In Saint Petersburg his education continued. His father could afford to hire private tutors. It's never clear, from the biographies of Nobel (and there have been many), how much if any formal education he had. He certainly never went to a university, and he never received a degree. However, at sixteen he knew chemistry, had read widely in literature, especially English poetry, and was fluent in German, English, and French, besides Swedish and Russian. He continued his informal education by trips abroad. He went to the United States. He lived for a while in Paris. In 1854, when he was twenty-one, he was back in Saint Petersburg, working in his father's factory and studying with a famous Russian chemist, Nikolai Zinin, who alerted him to the invention of nitroglycerine by the Italian scientist Ascanio Sobrero in 1847.

The Nobel factory was booming because the Crimean War had started in 1853, pitting England, France, and Turkey against Russia. Unfortunately Russia lost the war (and one of the lessons the new tsar, Alexander II, drew was that the Russian military equipment had been inferior). All orders for Nobel weaponry stopped, and in 1859, for the second time in his life, Immanuel was bankrupt. He returned to Sweden.

However, his three eldest sons (a fourth had been born in Saint Petersburg), did very well. Ludwig remained in Saint Petersburg and formed a partnership with a Russian to make new magazine-loading rifles. The plant they put up in the Ural Mountains became one of the leading arms suppliers to the Russian military. Needing walnut for the gunstock, Ludwig asked his brother Robert to look for a wood supply in the Caucasus. He didn't find the walnut but in Baku, on the Caspian Sea, he found oil in 1873. The Nobel brothers (Alfred came in as an investor) pioneered the petroleum industry in Russia. By 1900 it was the world's largest producer of oil.

Alfred became the most famous of the Nobel brothers. Like his father, he was an inveterate tinkerer. The explosive qualities of nitroglycerine were known, but no one before Nobel could figure out how to tame this liquid; that is, produce it without blowing up the people who handled it. Alfred eventually solved the problem but not before a nitroglycerine explosion in his laboratory outside Stockholm killed five people, including his younger brother, Oscar Emil.

In 1864 Nobel started to make a nitroglycerine product based on his detonator principle. It involved a blasting cap in which a gunpowder charge was set off, thereby detonating the surrounding nitroglycerine. This invention, using a small charge to set off a larger one, made possible the business of high explosives. Two years later, in 1866, Nobel invented a safer explosive by combining nitroglycerine with an absorbent earth substance called kiselguhr to form a paste that he called dynamite. Construction crews could now blast tunnels through mountains. Nobel went on to invent blasting gelatin and smokeless powder. Before he was finished, he had some 350 patents registered in his name.

Nobel dynamite factories went up all over the world, accompanied by the usual squabbles. Gunpowder manufacturers tried to keep dynamite off the market. The glycerin producers kept raising the price of their indispensable ingredient. In 1886 Nobel and his French associate, Paul Barbe, organized the London-based Nobel Dynamite Trust, uniting the Nobel factories in Britain with the German cartel, which included both dynamite and gunpowder plants, plus the subsidiaries of both groups on five continents. A year later the dynamite enterprises in France, Italy, Switzerland, Belgium, and South Africa became part of the trust. Russia stayed outside the cartel, as did the United States, where Du Pont successfully staved off Nobel.

Alfred Nobel, by all his biographers' accounts, was not a happy man. Michael Evlanoff and Marjorie Fluor, in their 1969 biography, called him "the loneliest millionaire." He never married, and he had few close friends. In a letter to one acquaintance, he wrote, "You refer to my many friends. Where are they? On the muddy bottom of lost illusions, or busy listening to the rattle of saved pennies? Believe me, numerous friends one gains only among dogs which one feeds with the flesh of others, or worms which one feeds with one's own." He had only one serious love affair, with Sofie Hess, a doll-like Austrian girl whom he met in a florist's shop in Vienna when she was eighteen and he was forty-three. They lived together for a while in Paris but separated after ten years. Nobel supported her for the rest of his life. Henrik Schuck, a distinguished Swedish academician, characterized Alfred Nobel as follows:

> By nature he was a melancholic, a dreamer and something of a recluse. . . . He was never a social success, though he had every quality required to be one. . . . He was a lonely man, and with his sensitive nature he suffered keenly from the misfortune of being without a home. He was born a Swede and always regarded himself as one, but at the early age of nine he had left his native country and after that returned to it only on temporary visits. . . . When he began his worldwide industrial activities, he first settled at Krummel, near Hamburg, but what he had there was more of a laboratory than a home, and most of his time was spent in railway carriages, steamship

cabins and hotels. In 1875 he acquired a house on the Avenue Malakoff in Paris, but when the laboratory there turned out to be too small, he built a new one at Sevran, on the outskirts of the French capital. But he did not take root there either, and in 1890 he moved to Italy where he bought a villa at San Remo. . . .

In 1888, two years before he moved to San Remo on the Italian Riviera, Alfred's older brother, Ludwig, ill for some time with tuberculosis, died at Cannes. A French newspaper reported the death of the wrong Nobel, and Alfred found himself reading his own obituary. It was an unsettling experience to see himself described in such terms as the "dynamite king" and "merchant of death" even though his explosives were used mostly in nonmilitary tasks. It was then, according one biographer, Nicholas Halasz, that Nobel decided to use his will "to make clear to the world the true meaning and purpose of his life."

In 1894, with a view toward spending more time in his native land, Nobel bought the Bofors steelworks and gun foundry in the western Swedish province of Varmland, near the Norwegian border. He had a laboratory built there so that he could carry on his research. In the fall of 1895 he spent two months in Paris, and it was there that he drew up his final will, the terms of which astounded the world. They were disclosed after he died at his San Remo villa the following year. He died alone, with no friends or relatives nearby.

Nobel's assets at his death was valued at 33.2 million Swedish krona or, in the exchange rates of those days, $8.3 million. The multinational character of his business was reflected in their geographical division: France, 7.2 million krona; Germany, 6.1 million; Sweden, 5.8 million; Russia, 5.2 million; Scotland (where he had put up the world's largest

nitroglycerine plant), 3.9 million; England, 3.9 million; Italy, 630,000; Austria, 229,000; Norway, 94,000.

His testament that the capital be invested in "safe securities" the interest on which would be distributed annually in prizes to those who "shall have conferred the greatest benefit on mankind" was greeted with derision in many quarters. Comments in Swedish newspapers ranged all over the place. Nobel was attacked as unpatriotic for insisting that "no consideration whatsoever" be paid to the nationality of candidates and for designating the Norwegian parliament as the body through which the peace prize was to be awarded. Others declared that the Swedish academic institutions selected to award the other prizes did not have that capability. And King Oscar of Sweden told Nobel's nephew, Emmanual Nobel, the son of Ludwig, that his uncle had "been influenced by peace fanatics." Nevertheless, the will held up, the Nobel Foundation was established, and the first prizes were awarded in 1901. A sixth leg, honoring accomplishments in economics, was added to the program in 1968 with funds provided by the Swedish national bank, Sveriges Riksbank.

Alfred Nobel's business empire was dismantled, but the pieces survived in other corporate guises. The Nobel companies in Germany became part of the Flick Group. The Nobel Trust set up in Britain was one of the main predecessor companies of Imperial Chemical Industries. And in Sweden the companies developed along two different paths. Nobel's original company, Nitroglycerin AB, continued to make explosives, changed its name to Nitro Nobel in 1965, and in 1978 became part of the Wallenberg-controlled chemical group, whose name was then changed from KemaNord to KemaNobel. Bofors, the other branch, changed its name to Bofors Nobelkrut after Alfred Nobel's death and continued to make munitions.

In 1982 Bofors came under the control of a young, aggressive stockbroker, Erik Penser, a Swedish practitioner of what Robert Reich has called "paper entrepreneurialism." Penser, who lives in London to escape the heavy income taxes of Sweden, bought into Swedish companies when their shares were low. After capturing Bofors he went after KemaNobel, and in 1984 he succeeded in acquiring the entire company from the Wallenbergs, Sweden's most powerful industrial family. Combining KemaNobel with Bofors, Penser called his new company Nobel Industries, pointing out, "Actually, it's perfectly logical. If you merge Alfred Nobel's first Swedish company with his last one, the result could only be Nobel Industries Sweden." However, Penser's attention span is short. In

1986 he sold Alfred Nobel's original company, Nitro Nobel, to a Norwegian firm, Dyno Industrier, and then lunged briefly at another Wallenberg holding, Swedish Match, before reselling his option, at a profit, to the Wallenbergs.

In 1986 the big news at Penser's Bofors unit was the signing of a five-year, $1.2-billion order with the government of India for the supply of field artillery. It was one of the biggest export orders ever won by a Swedish company. However, six months later reports surfaced that Bofors may have greased the skids for this order by making undercover payments of $4.5 million into a secret Swiss bank account.

As the Swedish and Indian governments were investigating these charges, Bofors was hit in 1987 by disclosures that it had illegally shipped arms to a number of countries around the world, including Iran and Iraq. Under Swedish law it's illegal to send weapons to any country engaged in an armed conflict. Nobel executives, three of whom were fired and faced prosecution, got around this restriction by falsifying documents and/or shipping arms to neutral countries from where they were forwarded to nations involved in some kind of fighting. Sara Webb, a reporter with the *Financial Times,* interviewed a defense consultant who told her, "Only the Swedes could think of selling weapons to people who promise not to use them. It's like selling cigarettes to nonsmokers."

There was also bad news for Nobel Industries in the United States, where its subsidiary in Muskegon, Michigan (Bofors Nobel Inc.) filed for Chapter 11 bankruptcy in 1985. Bofors bought this company in 1977 when its name was Lakeway Chemical, apparently not realizing that for fifteen years the company had been dumping its wastes into lagoons which seeped into Big Black Creek, Mona Lake, and, eventually, Lake Michigan. Lakeway's sludge had accumulated to cover twenty acres and weigh 374 million pounds. Poor Bofors. It was sued by the Michigan Natural Resources Commission and agreed to spend between $12 million to $15 million to clean up pollution it hadn't even caused. The costs came in much higher, which persuaded the Swedish company to take the Chapter 11 route. As Chairman Anders G. Carlberg told shareholders: "We have decided to leave Bofors Nobel Inc. in Muskegon, USA, which is no longer consolidated in the Group." No longer owning NitroNobel, they can't even dynamite it out.

Meanwhile, the Nobel prizes go on, seemingly destined to outlast Nobel's commercial ventures. When the prizes were first awarded, they were worth $30,000. So they have appreciated by nearly ten times in this century, in line with the growth of the endowment, which was worth $118 million in 1986.

Access Nobel Industries
Gustav Adolfs Torg 18
Box 16397
S-10327 Stockholm, Sweden
(46) 8-10 39 10

Nobel Foundation
Box 52322
S-10245 Stockholm, Sweden

<table>
<tr><td>

Nomura

</td><td>

Sales $6.2 billion
Profits $1.1 billion
Rank World's largest financial services company
      (by market value)
      World's 2d-largest stockbroker (behind
      Merrill Lynch)
      Japan's 2d-largest profit maker (1986)
Founded 1925
Employees 12,000 (average age: 32)
Headquarters Tokyo, Japan

</td></tr>
</table>

Hindsight is always better for figuring out the stock market. If investors in the middle of the 1970s had been blessed with pre-science, they would have plunked down their money on the Tokyo Stock Exchange, where over the next decade it would have tripled in value—just in yen—simply by buying the averages. That was the best return one could have gotten on any of the major stock exchanges operating in the world. (By contrast, an investment in stocks representing the Dow Jones Industrials would have only doubled.) And if the swing in currency is counted, the gain would have been much greater. In 1975–76 a U.S. dollar bought 300 Japanese yen; in 1986, only 150. In short, if your Japanese stock didn't go up by a single yen, you would still have had a 100 percent gain just by the fluctuation in the exchange rate.

In terms of where the action is, the Tokyo Stock Exchange is the second most active exchange in the world after the New York Stock Exchange. More business is done on the Tokyo exchange than on the London, Amsterdam, Paris, and Frankfurt exchanges combined. In 1985 the average number of shares traded on the Tokyo Stock Exchange each day was four hundred million. In the wild days of 1986, volume shot up to two billion shares a day.

Wouldn't it be nice to be sitting in the middle of this chaos? Well, Nomura Securities does. In Tokyo, as is the case with stock exchanges everywhere, investors must go through a broker to buy or sell. The "Big Four" of the Tokyo Stock Exchange are Nomura, Nikko, Daiwa, and Yamaichi. Nomura is by far the biggest broker of them all, racking up a volume nearly double that of any of its three main competitors. Nomura handles 18 percent of the stock trading and 25 percent of the bond trading on the Tokyo Stock Exchange. The post–World War II boom in the Japanese stock market vaulted it into second place in the world brokerage industry, topped only by Merrill Lynch of the United States. Although by several measures—market value and profits—Nomura is first, Merrill still leads in terms of total revenues.

Nomura had some special Japanese-style advantages in making its climb. Whereas it has experienced little difficulty in penetrating the financial centers of New York and London, its foreign counterparts (the New York and London stockbrokers) have not found it so easy to crack the Tokyo market. The Kabutocho, the financial district of Tokyo, is nowhere as freewheeling as Wall Street. Nomura was able to get a seat on the New York Stock Exchange in 1981 for $285,000. It wasn't until the fall of 1985 that three American investment houses—Merrill Lynch, Goldman Sachs, and Morgan Stanley—gained seats on the Tokyo Stock Exchange, and they each had to shell out more than $5 million for this access.

Nomura has also benefited from fixed commission rates which make it impossible for anyone to compete on a price basis and which translate into profit margins that might be characterized as obscene. In 1986, when the Tokyo Stock Exchange went on a tear, Nomura's revenues soared over the $6 billion mark (Merrill Lynch was taking in $9.5 billion), and its aftertax profits reached $1.1 billion (Merrill Lynch was earning $364 million). Nomura has emerged as one of the most demonic money-making machines in the world.

In 1986 Nomura jumped from fifth place to second place in the Japanese standings of companies ranked by their pretax profits. Only Toyota Motor earned more. Nomura the stockbroker made twice as much money as such industrial giants as Matsushita, Hitachi, and Toshiba. In 1987, when its profits were running 90 percent ahead of 1986, Nomura seemed to be heading for first place. *The Wall Street Journal,* in 1986, ranked the hundred largest companies in the world, based on their market value (what the stock market says all their shares are worth). Nomura ranked tenth, with a market value of $23 billion on June 30, 1986, ahead of such industrial heavyweights as Royal Dutch Shell, Daimler-Benz, Du Pont, and Ford. As *Fortune* noted, "In a takeover financed with stock, Nomura could swallow Merrill Lynch like a bit of predinner sashimi." (Merrill Lynch had a market value of $3.9 billion at the end of 1986.)

Nomura's ascendancy may yet win it some respectability in Japan, where it has never had the same standing or influence as the commercial banking houses. Nomura was founded on December 25, 1925, as the offshoot of an Osaka bank (now the Daiwa Bank). It was named for its founder, Nomura Tokushichi, who opened an office in New York in 1927 just in time to catch the 1929 crash. Japan did not have much of a public market for stocks and bonds in the pre–World War II period, and it wasn't until after the war that the brokerage houses edged into the business of underwriting, or raising money, for corporations. Yamaichi Securities used to be the leading Japanese broker, but when the Tokyo Stock Market collapsed in 1965, it almost went under. The Bank of Japan bailed out Yamaichi, and it was then that Nomura surged into the lead.

Nomura is trying to live down a reputation as a high-pressure pusher of stocks to small investors. It has a sales force of twenty-three hundred women who hold Tupperware-style parties in homes to sell stocks to Japanese housewives. It also became notorious for its "stock of the week" program in which it touted a security the way a department store advertised a sales item. Nomura has more than 120 branches in Japan to reach investors. *BusinessWeek,* in 1985, reported that the Yokohama branch had a sign on the wall exhorting: "One hundred calls a day." *The Wall Street Journal,* in 1986, noted that critics accuse Nomura of "running up share prices at the expense of the last investors to buy into the campaign." It was put this way by the research director of the Tokyo office of a major British investment firm, who was interviewed by Canadian journalist Susan Goldenberg (for her 1986 book *Trading*): "The accepted rule of thumb under this practice [of brokerage houses pushing stocks] is that investors will lose about 30 percent of their money with Yamaichi, half with Daiwa and Nikko, and end up owing Nomura money."

In 1986 Nomura gave $1.8 million to the graduate business schools of New York University and $1.5 million to the Sloan School of Management at the Massachusetts Institute of Technology to establish Nomura professors of finance. *The Financial Times* took note of these contributions: "Whether it will help eliminate the rather sharp image that Nomura has in Japan remains to be seen. Japan's patrician bankers still look down their noses at brokerage houses, which used to be popularly known as *kabu-ya,* or stock shops, having about the same prestige as a *yao-ya* or greengrocer."

Nomura people, who tend to be engaging but hard-driving salesmen, brush off these criticisms as either "sour grapes" or "inevitable" because of the firm's size. With four million customers in Japan, no one will gainsay its ability to move merchandise. In 1983 it stunned the investment community by selling its customers 2.2 million shares of IBM. But the firm's reputation was not enhanced by a Tokyo court finding in 1987 that Nomura had "churned" a customer's account (bought and sold stocks without his authorization). The court ordered the securities firm to pay back the customer $111,000.

Tokyo is located strategically between the New York and London time zones, and Nomura has signaled its determination to become a first-rank player in international finance. To that end, it has opened thirty-four offices in twenty countries, including five in the United States. Nomura sees itself as the gatekeeper into—and out of—Japan. It begins with an enormous base, since the Japanese have replaced the Middle East countries as the world's biggest lenders. So in New York Nomura is buying U.S. Treasury notes for Japanese customers. In London it's selling Japanese securities to European investors. Back in Japan it's selling American and European securities to Japanese investors. In all its offices it will help investors find—and buy—Japanese stocks. In Japan Nomura is also helping foreign companies gain a listing on the Tokyo Stock Exchange. Since 1973 it has sponsored eighteen companies for such listings, including Dow Chemical, General Motors, American Express, and Volvo.

Yoshihisa Tabuchi, who became chief executive of Nomura in 1985 (at fifty-three he was one of the youngest heads of a major Japanese company), said, "International business is becoming as important to our future health and prosperity as our domestic business." In 1986 international business, including the purchase of foreign securities by Japanese investors, accounted for a quarter of Nomura's business; it expects that ratio to go to 50 percent by the early 1990s.

Nomura gained a seat on the London Stock Exchange on March 4, 1986. In the previous five years its London staff grew from 100 to 360; of the 160 professionals in the office, 60 were Japanese. In New York Nomura increased its staff from 194 to 415 between August 1985 and January 1987; Japanese nationals in the New York office number 50.

Old-line investment bankers in New York and London showed some bitterness over the way Nomura and other Japanese houses had bought their way into underwriting deals by giving very good terms to borrowers. Flush with profits in their home market, the Japanese could afford to sacrifice profits overseas just to get the business. *Fortune* writer Gary Hector explained that the Japanese can offer below-market interest rates to borrowers because of their "stuffing" power (one $300-million General Electric Eurobond offer in 1986 carried an interest rate of only 7 percent). "With their vast retail networks in Japan," said Hector, "the securities firms can shove billions of dollars of bonds into the hands of small investors. Interest rates that look low in the highly competitive international market may look dandy in Sapporo or Osaka."

In any case, Nomura has become a powerful force in the international arena. In 1984, when British Telecom was denationalized in the biggest public stock offering in history, a Japanese syndicate headed by Nomura came away with 6 percent of the $5-billion deal. An American syndicate headed by Morgan Stanley got exactly the same slice. In 1986, among other deals, Nomura was selling $479 million of Euroyen for the Canadian government, $200 million of Eurobonds for IBM Credit Corporation, and another $200 million of Eurobonds for General Motors Acceptance Corporation. Results posted in early 1987 showed that Nomura's London office had become the largest underwriter of new Eurobond issues, passing the longtime leader, Crédit Suisse First Boston.

One of the skills required today in selling debt instruments is coming up with packages that have creative features. Nomura seems to know how to play this game. In 1985 its swaps department in London, managed by Blaine J. Tomlinson, won the "Swap of the Year" award for a "heaven and hell" bond issue that raised $100 million for IBM. The innovative configuration in this deal was a bet made by investors on what the yen/dollar ratio would be in ten years. The bond, at maturity, paid out more than the par value if the dollar increased in value (heaven) and less if the dollar declined against the yen (hell). Japanese financial institutions were the big buyers of the bonds.

When the Japanese economy was reorganized by the Americans after World War II, the U.S. model of separating commercial banking from investment banking was followed. So Nomura can do a brokerage business in Japan but it can't be a regular bank. However, General Douglas MacArthur's influence did not extend to Britain. In 1986 Nomura was issued a license to do in London what it can't do legally in Japan: operate a bank. Called Nomura International Finance, the bank went into business on November 3, with a staff of thirty (only three Japanese) headed by an American banker, Andreas Prindle, who said, "We are much more interested in profitability than in racing up the banking leagues." Time will tell.

Nomura has had an interest in research from its founding, and in 1965 it split off as a separate entity an organization called Nomura Research Institute (NRI), which qualifies for the title, "Japan's largest think tank." The Tokyo office of NRI, not far from Nomura's headquarters in Kabutocho, conducts economic and investment research. At the Kamakura headquarters in a wooded enclave south of Tokyo, NRI has an interdisciplinary staff available for hire by private companies to do studies in such areas as energy development, urban planning, pollution control, and computer software programming. NRI has a staff of more than five hundred.

Nomura also owns 3 percent of Japan's eighth-largest brokerage house, Sanyo Securities.

The Yen for Gold

Who was the biggest buyer of gold in 1986? Japan, which geared up to buy two hundred tons of bullion worth about $2.2 billion. The Japanese purchase would absorb 12 percent of total gold supplies in 1986. And what were they planning to do with all that gold? Mint commemorative coins to mark the sixtieth anniversary of Emperor Hirohito's rule.

Access 1-9-1, Nihonbashi, Chuo-ku
Tokyo 103, Japan
(81) 3-211-1811

180 Maiden Lane
New York, N.Y. 10038
(212) 208-9300

Norsk Data	
	Sales $350 million
	Profits $50 million
	U.S. Sales $10 million
	Rank Norway's 15th-largest company
	Europe's 5th-largest supplier of minicomputers
	Founded 1967
	Employees 3,600 (30 in the United States)
	Headquarters Oslo, Norway

Norway is home to one of the most adventurous startups in the computer industry: Norsk Data. Part of the adventure lies in its location, Norway, a country with a population of 4.1 million and an economy not strong enough to support a high-powered electronics industry. The three engineers who founded the company— Rolf Skar, Per Bjorge, and Lars Monrad-Krohn—knew all about that. They went ahead anyway.

In 1968, when Norsk Data was only a year old, two hard-nosed board members quit because they felt the minicomputer company was run more like a fairy tale than a serious business. They were right about the fairy tale, but dead wrong about the rest. Norsk Data is still, as Chairman Terje Mikalsen admits, "a place where the wildest of dreams can and do come through." But today it's also a company that turns a neat profit fielding a full line of general-purpose minicomputers used for business data processing and high-speed scientific applications.

American companies such as Digital Equipment, Hewlett-Packard, Data General, Wang, and Tandem are all active in this market, they all purport to do what Norsk Data says it does—"help our customers perform better and at a lower cost than with competing systems." And they are all much bigger than Norsk Data. However, this plucky Norwegian company has hung in there for twenty years, a feat in itself in this turbulent industry. In the 1980s, when sales more than quadrupled, it could lay claim to be the fastest-growing company in the industry. In some quarters it's regarded as the European alternative to the American product.

Skar, Bjorge, and Monrad-Krohn, all graduates of the Norwegian Institute of Technology at Trondheim, were working on computer technology for Norway's defense establishment when they got the notion that the commercial market was ripe for their ideas. Their first product after launching Norsk Data was a computerized ship's guidance system called NORD 1. It was delivered in 1969. In their early help-wanted ads, they asked for "good-humored and fun-loving" engineers (almost a contradiction in terms).

440

The fledgling firm turned an important corner in 1972 when it landed a contract from the European Center for Nuclear Research (CERN) in Switzerland to build a computer to analyze results from CERN's new particle accelerator. The thought of a five-year-old company from Norway producing such an advanced computer seemed farfetched at the time, but Norsk Data brazenly threw its hat into the ring with eighty-seven other bidders. Its price and technology won the day. And the order put Norsk Data on the map.

Five years later Norsk Data came out on top in another battle with bigger competitors. It was selected to build a computer that would power a flight simulator used to train pilots to fly the F-16 fighter planes built by General Dynamics. The Norsk Data "supermini" is the only European-made component in the entire F-16 program. How did a Norwegian company come away with a slice of Pentagon business normally reserved entirely for American firms? Well, Norway was one of four European countries that ordered F-16s for their defense forces, and the sale agreement specified that companies in those countries would be eligible to compete for subcontracts. When Norsk Data put in its bid, the Norwegian government went to bat for it in Washington, D.C.

Norsk Data has experienced the usual tribulations of a "high-tech" startup. It was never all smooth sailing. Of the three founders, only one, Rolf Skar, remains. He's the chief executive. The Norwegian government, at one point, put considerable pressure on Norsk Data to become part of a bigger electronics company. The Norsk Data people insisted on staying independent. Then there was the continual struggle to raise capital, exacerbated by Norwegian paranoia about foreign invaders.

Norsk Data sold stock to Norwegian investors in 1975, and the shares were listed on the Oslo Borsen. In 1981, showing the daring that has been its trademark, Norsk Data secured a listing on the London Stock Exchange. Aside from Norsk Hydro (Norway's largest company), it was the first Norwegian company to have its shares listed on a foreign exchange. In 1983 it was ready for New York, selecting Morgan Stanley as its underwriter. However, there was a problem. Norwegian law stated that foreigners could own no more than 20 percent of a Norwegian company. Such a small piece of a small company would not raise much money on Wall Street. Norsk Data succeeded in getting an exemption allowing it to have up to 49 percent of its shares owned by foreigners. However, that wasn't enough either for a U.S. underwriting. So Norsk Data, after a lot of back-and-forth negotiating with government bureaucrats, received permission to create a new class of B shares that have no voting rights but are free of restrictions on how many may be in the hands of foreign devils.

Those B shares were the ones Morgan Stanley brought out in the United States. And they are the shares traded on the American over-the-counter market. They represent 38 percent of the capitalization of Norsk Data.

From time to time, there is still a crisis. In February 1987 trading in Norsk Data had to be temporarily halted on the Oslo Stock Exchange because foreign ownership of the A shares was right up against the 49 percent limit. After authorities determined that the company was still in Norwegian hands, trading was resumed. (Oslo is one European city where Nomura Securities does *not* have an office.)

Virtually all employees of Norsk Data own stock in the company, their holdings amounting to 7.4 percent of the total, and they are encouraged to buy more. Norsk Data, in company with some "high-tech" leaders in the United States, has an egalitarian streak. It operates through a flat organization with a minimum of titles and levels. Work is carried out in groups of ten to twelve people who set their own goals. There is no central personnel function, and no rules about when you report to work. Each group does its own hiring. Employees have long been represented on the board of directors, and there is also a Corporate Assembly whose members are elected by shareholders and employees.

Rolf Skar feels strongly about this democratic corporate culture. "We go to extremes to avoid class differences," he told Norwegian journalist Per Oyvind Heradstveit. "Take a look at my office. It's not that I am thrilled to have a small office. Maybe it would be more comfortable to have a bigger one. I know, however, that I am setting standards. Therefore the size of my office is irrelevant. Nor will I fly first class when none of the other employees do. . . . We have one canteen in the building. All of us sit together. Some of these rules may sound funny to an outsider, but in reality it is the small details that matter. These details ultimately amount to a spirit, a tone, a philosophy of relationship between people of equal worth."

This evangelical tone carries over to the business side where Norsk Data now talks about achieving a high "terminal density" in offices. In most offices, the company points out, people have their own telephones—the telephone density is 100 percent. The next stage, in which Norsk Data expects to play a leading role, will bring 100 percent computer density to offices. In 1986, the company installed twenty thousand online terminals, up from six thousand in 1983. It likes to point out that in Norway it's now half the size of IBM, an indication of "our potential in other markets."

In 1986 Norsk Data increased its sales and profits for the fourteenth consecutive year. Half of its sales came from outside Norway. *Financial*

> MacGregor, the U.S. maker of golf clubs, bags, and related gear, is Finnish-owned. Amer, one of Finland's leading makers of sporting equipment, bought control of MacGregor from Jack Nicklaus for $8 million in 1986.

Times technology writer Alan Cane is so impressed that he calls Norsk Data "the shooting star of the Norwegian industrial filament."

Access P.O. Box 25, Bogerud
0621 Oslo 6, Norway
(47) 2-626000

180 West Park Dr.
Westborough, Mass. 01581
(617) 366-4662

Olympia & York	**Assets** $18 billion
	Rank World's largest real estate developer
	Canada's 5th-largest oil producer
	World's largest producer of newsprint
	Founded 1955
	Employees 20,000
	Headquarters Toronto, Canada

N ew York City's biggest landlord has its address in Toronto. That's an unlikely scenario but it's in keeping with other aspects of Olympia & York, the company that owns more commercial buildings in New York than any other firm. Olympia & York is the company started, managed, and owned by the Reichmann family—and the Reichmanns are Orthodox Jews. This means that at 4:00 P.M. every Friday all work stops in their thirty-second-floor offices on the seventy-two-story First Canadian Place building in downtown Toronto in observance of the Jewish Sabbath, which begins at sundown Friday and lasts through Saturday at sundown. No business of any kind is conducted on Saturdays. But on the other six days of the week (Sunday included), well, that's another story.

Real estate development is essentially gambling (you're betting that the property you buy will be worth more after you get through with it), and gambling might come naturally to Hungarian Jews who were raised in Vienna and Tangier. Albert, Paul, and Ralph Reichmann were born in Vienna in the 1930s (they were, respectively, fifty-seven, fifty-six, and fifty-four years old in 1987), the sons of Samuel and Renée Reichmann, who had left their native Hungary in the 1920s.

Samuel Reichmann was apparently successful wherever he alighted. According to one account, from Vienna he wholesaled eggs across various national borders. According to another, he ran a glass factory. According to still another, he had a small construction business. In the mid-1930s, in the middle of Europe, Jews with a nose for survival had to keep one step ahead of the Nazis. The Reichmanns went from Vienna to Paris and then made their way to the North African city of Tangier, which was an international zone. There, in a city celebrated for its trading (and smuggling), Samuel established a banking house that became celebrated for its probity.

The Reichmann boys were bar mitzvahed in Tangier, became fluent in a half dozen languages, and were brought up as devout Jews. None ever received a conventional college education. After World War II Paul spent five years studying at Jewish schools in England. Albert once told Canadian journalist Susan Goldenberg, "When you learn the Talmud, you learn everything."

In 1956, as Tangier was about to lose its international status and become part of Morocco, the Reichmanns pulled up stakes again, moving to Toronto, which is a little like moving from New York to Omaha. Samuel, who died in 1975 (he came to the office on a Friday and died on the weekend), lived to see his sons launch a business that was to become the world's largest real estate empire. The empire began with a tile company that the Reichmanns found in *The Wall Street Journal*'s "for sale" ads and gravitated quickly toward property development in the form of warehouses and factories ringing Toronto. Their first big project, in the early 1960s, was an office tower development in the Toronto suburb of Don Mills. Buying five hundred acres from real estate operator William Zeckendorf for the bargain price of $17.8 million, they reportedly recouped their investment in six months, proving along the way that downtown could be moved to the suburbs. The complex was called Olympia Square—Olympia supposedly because Ralph was an avid student of ancient history. Another project was called York Development—York being the county where Toronto is located. Hence the name: Olympia & York.

As any home owner knows, the name of the game in real estate is leverage, meaning: How much money can you borrow? For a small amount of money, you can own a house worth much more, providing the lender is willing. The Reichmanns turned out to be daredevil borrowers, pyramiding one deal atop another to take command of properties stretch-

ing across the entire North American continent. It's possible to be killed in this kind of game if property values collapse and you have trouble renting the buildings you bought and/or put up, but the Reichmanns seemed to have a sure sense of timing.

The deal everyone talks about is the one they did in New York in 1976, the year after their father died. At the time New York City was in the doldrums, teetering on the brink of bankruptcy, and the recipient of (in the words of a famous *New York Daily News* headline) a "drop dead" message from the White House. The Reichmanns, sitting in Toronto, didn't believe that "New York was going to be closed down," and when National Kinney came along with an offer to sell eight Manhattan office properties known as the Uris Buildings, the brothers jumped. They bought the package for $320 million, putting up only $50 million in cash. Among the properties were the Park Avenue headquarters buildings of ITT and American Brands, and the Harper & Row building on 53rd Street and Madison Avenue. In five years office rents in Manhattan tripled. And what was bought for $320 million in 1976 could be sold for $1 billion in 1981 and $2 billion in 1983. In 1982 the Reichmanns sold the two smallest Uris buildings for $160 million.

When property values escalate so sharply, it provides the owner with that much more borrowing power, and the Reichmanns used it. Since Olympia & York is not a publicly owned company, it's impossible to know all the deals they have done, but their projects are so large that most of them are very visible. In their home city, Toronto, they have reshaped the skyline with First Canadian Place, the Toronto Star Building, Foresters House, and the Exchange Tower, a thirty-six-story building that rises above the new trading floor of the Toronto Stock Exchange.

In Toronto they also built Queen's Quay Terminal, a complex of offices, residential condominiums, and stores in a renovated warehouse on Lake Ontario. They own the thirty-three-story Shell Canada Center in Calgary; the sixty-three-story office and residential complex, Olympia Center, in Chicago; and the forty-story Exchange Place tower in Boston. They're developing the twenty-two-acre Yerba Buena project in San Francisco, and they are landlords in half a dozen other American cities, including Hartford, Dallas, Miami, and Los Angeles. They control 45 million square feet of real estate in the United States and Canada.

To see the biggest of all the Reichmann developments, one has to repair to the foot of Manhattan Island. In 1980 they won a $1.5 billion contract to develop Battery City Park on fifteen acres of Hudson River landfill. When plans were announced for the construction of new skyscraper office buildings in the shadow of the recently completed World

Trade Center, many people thought the Reichmanns had finally come a cropper. They had to rent more than 8 million square feet of space. The maneuvering that ensued while construction was going on is a textbook case of real estate wizardry.

The Reichmanns got tenants to sign up by agreeing to buy their old buildings. They rented 1 million square feet of space to Home Life Insurance under a thirty-five-year lease calling for rent payments totaling $850 million, and they bought Home Life's old building for $175 million. They rented 2.3 million square feet of space to American Express under a thirty-five-year lease calling for a total of $2 billion in rental payments, and they agreed to buy the old American Express building for $240 million. The Reichmanns then persuaded Merrill Lynch to give up its Liberty Square location on Broadway and rent 3.9 million square feet of space in two buildings in which it will have a minority interest.

As a result, before the first tower opened in 1986, 90 percent of the space was spoken for. American Express, after thinking about its commitment, renegotiated the deal so that instead of renting space, it's buying one of the towers from Olympia & York for $493 million. Under those new conditions the purchase price on its old building was reduced to $160 million. Asked if he was sorry about losing "pride of ownership," Paul Reichmann noted that he and his brothers "still have pride of authorship."

That authorship is important in the Reichmann scheme. People who have worked with the brothers don't pass them off as real estate manipulators who care about nothing but the bottom line. The Reichmanns put up their developments twice as rapidly as competitors by using modern construction methods. Their buildings are usually ready when promised and they are not devoid of aesthetics. The Battery City Park, now renamed the World Financial Center, features granite-jacketed towers designed by the architect Cesare Pelli and a glass-enclosed winter garden that vaults as high as Grand Central Terminal. The development has been hailed by architectural critics as the most interesting skyscraper development in New York City since Rockefeller Center went up. In 1987 Olympia & York owned 24 million square feet of rentable property in New York City, more than twice its nearest competitor. Its annual rent collections in New York were said to be $750 million.

In 1987 the Richmanns made their first foray into Europe when they signed a contract to take over the seventy-one-acre Canary Wharf project along the Thames River in London. At $4.5 billion it's the biggest commercial property development in Europe.

The Reichmanns like to keep their money (and borrowing power) in motion, and they have expanded well beyond the confines of real estate. They have, in fact, acquired a sizable chunk of Canada. It began in 1980 with the acquisition of 50 percent of Brinco, a mining company and oil and gas explorer. And it continued with a series of other acquisitions that found them, in 1986, in control of Gulf Canada, the fifth-largest oil producer in Canada; Abitibi-Price, the world's largest producer of newsprint; and Consumers Gas, an Ontario utility. They also owned 49 percent of the Hiram Walker distilling business (Kahlua, Canadian Club, Ten High bourbon).

None of these investments has paid off the way the real estate deals did, and in 1987 the Reichmanns were planning to spin off these holdings into three separate publicly traded companies that they will continue to control. Olympia & York also had holdings in assorted other Canadian enterprises, including major real estate developers such as Cadillac Fairview and Trizec. However, it's always a changing scene.

How much it all adds up to is not known. Being a private company, Olympia & York does not have to say. We do know how big Gulf Canada and Abitibi-Price once were (they have been cut back). Abitibi-Price, prior to being acquired, had annual sales of $1.4 billion and eighteen thousand employees. Gulf Canada had sales of $3 billion and eighteen thousand employees in 1981. In 1982 *Fortune* estimated that the Reichmanns could sell off all their holdings and pay off all their debts and still be left with $5 billion.

In her book *Men of Property,* Susan Goldenburg says, "Although thousands of people work, shop, and eat in Olympia & York buildings . . . the average person would not know the Reichmanns, especially as they have not allowed newspaper pictures to be taken of them since 1965." This is a constant refrain of magazines and newspapers that write about the Reichmanns. They have been called "publicity-shy" *(Financial Times),* "secretive" *(The New York Times),* "bashful millionaires" *(Fortune),* and "reclusive" *(Financial Post).* But the files are thick with voluminous stories about them, and their pictures appeared in various newspapers and magazines in the 1980s.

In 1983 Jeffrey Robinson, a *Barron's* writer, reported: "Part of the myth that surrounds them is that when journalists were granted audiences, conditions were laid down beforehand, including the types of questions that would be permitted. But when this writer telephoned Albert Reichmann to request an interview, he answered his own phone, agreed to meet, and put forth no conditions."

The numerous articles on the Reichmanns differ on many details but agree that the brothers continue to be pious Jews, observing all the customs of their faith. They wear dark suits and yarmulkes, obey the Jewish dietary laws, and write contracts which specify that no work is to be performed on Saturdays or high holy days. They also bring up their numerous progeny—Albert has four children, Paul and Ralph each have five—in a strict Jewish environment. *BusinessWeek* reported in 1983 that the Reichmanns also enforced Jewish prudery—secretaries in Olympia & York offices had to wear sleeves down to their elbows.

The Reichmanns are not active in Toronto's social life, but it has been reported that they give away 10 percent of their incomes to charitable causes. When it comes to business, though, they are all business. Paul told Canadian writer Debra Black, "Business is profit-driven, that's the motive. I think that's the motive for every successful businessman in the world. Those who want to do business with idealism end up like in some parts of the world where there is no free enterprise."

Access First Canadian Place
Toronto M5X 1B5, Canada
(416) 862-6100

245 Park Ave.
New York, N.Y. 10017
(212) 850-9600

Pearson

Sales $1.4 billion
Profits $112 million
U.S. Sales $400 million
Rank Britain's 60th-largest company (by market value)
World's largest maker of bone china
World's largest publisher of paperback books
Largest grower of pistachio nuts in the United States
Britain's leading publisher of financial periodicals
Britain's largest publisher of free weekly newspapers
Britain's largest textbook publisher
Founded 1844
Employees 27,800
Headquarters London, England

Who would believe that the building of drainage ditches in Mexico City during the last century would lead one day to an eclectic conglomerate whose operations include publishing, pottery, oil field services, vineyards, investment banking, and tourist traps?

It may not be completely fair to attribute Pearson's ascendancy to ditch digging in Mexico City, but the Mexican adventure did turn out to be pivotal for Weetman Pearson, who inherited—and greatly expanded—a building business started by his grandfather in Yorkshire. When he was still in his early twenties (he was born in 1856), Pearson built the main drainage system for the Lancashire city of Southport. Relocated to London in 1882, Pearson's firm went on to build harbors, docks, reservoirs, dams, sewers, tunnels, and factories. Its work in Britain led to assignments abroad. By the 1890s it was the largest contractor in the world. For the Pennsylvania Railroad, Pearson built the first tunnel under the Hudson River.

In Mexico, in addition to putting in drainage systems, Pearson built railways and the harbor at Vera Cruz. Weetman Pearson also found oil in Mexico, and he established a company, Mexican Eagle, to lift it. In 1910 he became the first Lord Cowdray, and when his coat of arms was struck ("Do It With Thy Might"), it featured an underwater diver and a Mexican in a serape and sombrero.

Those stereotypical images were appropriate for Lord Cowdray, who was basking in the enormous profits flowing from Mexican Eagle, which had fought off Rockefeller's Standard Oil to become the dominant oil producer in Mexico. Cowdray's good fortune was enhanced by cozy relations with two dictators, first Porfirio Diaz and then Victoriano Huerta, who came to power in 1913 in a bloody coup. Woodrow Wilson, who sent American troops to Mexico in support of dissidents trying to overthrow the dictatorship, suspected that Lord Cowdray was financing Huerta. The U.S. ambassador to Mexico had written to Wilson: "If Taft had had another four years, Cowdray would have owned Mexico, Ecuador, Colombia . . . with such a grip on the governments as would have amounted to a mortgage." Lord Cowdray sold his company to Shell Oil in 1919. Mexican oil had made him one of the wealthiest men in England.

Once in oil, though, it's hard to get rid of the habit. Lord Cowdray plunged back into the business in the United States, forming Amerada, which found oil in Oklahoma, Kansas, Louisiana, Arkansas, and Texas, going on to become one of the leading independent producers in the country. But politics is never far from the oil business. In 1926, a year before his death, Lord Cowdray sold off more than half of his Amerada stock (although he retained effective control), a sale which Pearson's own history says was dictated by the "considerable hostility to this foreign ownership of oil in America." Then, when World War II broke out in 1939, the British Treasury, anxious about oil supplies, stepped in and bought out Cowdray's remaining petroleum interests in the United States.

Meanwhile in Britain Lord Cowdray established a holding company that has sometimes been called "a collection of rich men's toys." He bought his first newspaper, the *Westminster Gazette,* in 1908. He preferred papers that supported the Liberal party. In 1920 he acquired a major stake in the Lazard Brothers investment banking firm. When you are rich, you don't have to do market surveys to determine what to buy. The Pearson holding company went into the pottery business in the 1920s when Lord Cowdray invested in Booths, an earthenware manufacturer in Stoke-on-Trent. According to the company history, "This was not part of a corporate strategy; the business was in financial difficulties and Cowdray's sister-in-law was married to Booths's London manager! Cowdray eventually bought the company outright."

The pattern stitched by the first Lord Cowdray was continued by his descendants, although they have wandered at times into areas motivated by their own passions. Many tourists who come to London see Madame Tussaud's waxworks. Pearson owns it. Pearson also owns the London

Planetarium adjacent to Madame Tussaud's, the Chessington Zoo just outside London, and Warwick Castle, the most popular stately home to visit in Britain (more than 150,000 Americans trooped through in 1985).

Another Pearson holding is a 53.6 percent interest in the famous Chateau Latour vineyard, one of France's premier Bordeaux houses. When this stake was driven in 1963, the purchase had to be cleared with General de Gaulle, who reportedly said, "Why not, they can't take away the soil."

Mostly, though, Pearson has expanded the businesses started by the first Lord Cowdray. It publishes a string of more than fifty regional newspapers in Britain, including the *Bradford Telegraph & Argus* (in the city where Weetman Pearson grew up), and twenty-four newspapers (you should pardon the expression) in the state of Florida, these mostly consisting of real estate and shopping guides which are foisted on people. The Pearson publications litter eleven counties on Florida's West Coast and the communities of Jacksonville, Orlando, Fort Pierce, Okechobee, Sebring, Bradenton, Sarasota, and Venice. And while it's distributing these advertising-laden, free-circulation papers to benighted Americans, in London Pearson is the force behind two of the world's most prestigious periodicals: It owns the *Financial Times,* always instantly recognizable because of its pink paper, and it has a 50 percent interest in the acerbic, pun-loving weekly *The Economist.*

Pearson has become a powerhouse in book publishing. It owns one of the oldest British publishing houses, Longman, founded in 1724 and renowned as the publisher of *Gray's Anatomy* (1858), *Roget's Thesaurus* (1852), Dr. Johnson's first dictionary (1755), and the works of Robert Louis Stevenson. It bought its first interest in Longman in 1968 (it now owns all of it). And in 1970 and 1971 it acquired the British paperback house Penguin, which later acquired Viking Press and New American Library in the United States. Other British book publishing imprints that belong to Pearson include Hamish Hamilton, Michael Joseph, Pitman, Ladybird, Sphere, Rainbird, and Churchill Livingstone (Britain's largest medical publisher).

The Lazard Brothers connection continues—Pearson has a 50 percent interest in the London house and smaller stakes in the New York and Paris partnerships. The pottery business that Lord Cowdray started has grown substantially to include the tableware lines of Royal Doulton, Royal Crown Derby, Minton, Royal Albert, Paragon, Colclough, and John Beswick.

The oil business persists, although the vehicles change. After World War II Pearson built up a strong minority holding in Ashland Oil, a leading U.S. independent producer. Today Pearson's participation in the oil industry comes through a U.S.-based company, Lignum Oil, which drills in the Southwest and the Gulf of Mexico, and a British-based outfit, Whitehall Petroleum, which has concessions in the North Sea. Pearson also owns Camco, a Houston-based oil field services supplier whose shares trade on the American Stock Exchange. Still another American holding is a 39 percent interest in Blackwell Land, which owns twenty-two thousand acres of farmland in California's San Joaquin Valley. It was an original investment of the Lazard Brothers dating from the last century.

Cowdray family members—there are more than one hundred of them—continue to be active in the company as shareholders and executives. They hold 20 percent of the stock. Lord Blakenham, whose mother was a daughter of the second Lord Cowdray, became chief executive of the company in 1978. Two other Cowdray members who sit on the board are Lord Gibson, who was chairman before Lord Blakenham, and Mark W. Burrell, managing director of Lazard Brothers in London.

There was a flurry of excitement in 1986 when Hutchison Whampoa Ltd., a Hong Kong trading company controlled by property billionaire Li Ka-shing, acquired a 4.9 percent stake in Pearson. Lord Blakenham said he would prefer that Li Ka-shing not acquire any more shares, but the move led to speculation that Pearson might become a takeover target. To forestall such an attack, the New York partners of Lazard Frères bought 5 percent of Pearson's stock. Confronted with such unfriendliness, Li-Ka-shing sold his shares. The buyer appeared to be the Italian wheeler-dealer, Carlo De Benedetti, who suddenly surfaced as the owner of 5.9 percent of Pearson.

Business reporter Martin Dickson analyzed Pearson in 1987, noting

how difficult it was for the company to shed its image as a company of "gentlemen engaged in business." Dickson cited another well-worn description of the company's business as a "pedigree dog's breakfast." His analysis appeared in the Pearson-owned *Financial Times*.

Access   Millbank Tower
London SW1P 4QZ, England
(44) 1-828-9020

Lazard Frères
1 Rockefeller Plaza
New York, N.Y. 10020
(212) 489-6600

<table>
<tr><td rowspan="2">**Pemex**</td><td>**Sales** $10 billion</td></tr>
</table>

Pemex	**Sales** $10 billion
	Profits (Your guess is as good as any.)
	Rank Mexico's largest company
	Latin America's largest company
	World's 5th-largest oil producer
	9th on the *Fortune* International 500 (1985)
	40th on the *Fortune* International 500 (1986)
	Founded 1938
	Employees 175,000
	Headquarters Mexico City, Mexico

In 1980 Dan Rather, reporting for the CBS Television program "60 Minutes," went to Mexico to interview Jorge Diaz-Serrano, the director-general of Pemex, which stands for Petróleos Mexicanos, the national oil company of Mexico. Rather asked him about reports of corruption in Pemex.

"Really," Diaz-Serrano replied angrily, "you are making charges to the Mexican people that are really offensive. I wish that you withdrew that."

Six years later another "60 Minutes" reporter, Morley Safer, asked the same man the same question. "False," Diaz-Serrano responded. "Absolutely false. It's something nobody can prove. It's just a political scheme, to sink people like me."

While his answer in 1986 was the same as it had been in 1980, Diaz-Serrano's circumstances had changed. He was no longer director-general of Pemex, and this time he was speaking from Reclusorio Sur, a federal penitentiary, having been arrested on charges that he, along with other Pemex officials, pocketed $34 million in a deal involving the purchase of two tankers.

In early 1987 Diaz-Serrano, after having spent three and a half years in jail, had still not been brought to trial, nor had the government's "moral renovation" program reached very far into the ranks of the union representing more than one hundred thousand Pemex workers. And "representing," in this context, is a euphemism. SRTPRM, the union of Mexican oil workers, operated in a way no labor union in the world operates. It took a cut of 2 percent on every purchase made by Pemex. In addition, on 40 percent of the contracts let by Pemex, the union had the right to act as a subcontractor; choosing, for example, which company will drill at a certain site. The union also decided who gets to work at Pemex. It did the hiring, and it even charged for this "service." An engineer, for example, may have had to pay as much as $5,000 to land a job with Pemex. And after being hired he would pay a percentage of his salary to the union.

Pemex union leaders socked some of their gains into luxury condominiums in the United States. Others were known to be heavy gamblers at Las Vegas casinos.

It's clear that there is a lot to steal. Mexico has a tremendous amount of oil, and new fields keep being discovered. Pemex itself announced a few years ago that it was the world's fourth-largest oil producer, behind Saudi Arabia, the United States, and the Soviet Union. Result: The potential for corruption is endless. In his "60 Minutes" report Morley Safer talked to an opposition politician, Herberto Castillo, who said that he had taken a look at Pemex's books for the years 1978 and 1979 and found literally millions of barrels of oil unaccounted for—$4 billion worth, to be exact! Safer said flatly on air that "the money was stolen through direct theft and through fancy bookkeeping: padded payrolls for executives, paychecks for people who did not even work for Pemex, tanker loads of oil sold with no record of the transaction."

Those two years—1979 and 1980—were probably the greatest years in Pemex history, what with crude oil having gone up more than ten times in price thanks to the OPEC cartel of which Mexico is not a member. In late 1977 the exchange index of the Mexico City stock market (Bolsa de Valores) stood at 300. In a year and a half it went to 1,800. "Everybody wants to boogey to the bank with Mexico," one investment broker said. "Suddenly," the *Chicago Tribune* reported, "Mexico has become the new girl at the party and nations that had once spurned her are falling all over one another in an effort to get her attention."

Pemex's fifty-story headquarters, the tallest building in Latin America, rose in the center of Mexico City, in control of more than sixty-five ports, offshore facilities, tanker fleets, refineries, and drilling sites throughout the country. Pemex had indeed become a "state within a state." Even after the money siphoned off by sticky fingers, Pemex was paying nearly half the taxes the government collected and bringing in nearly 75 percent of Mexico's foreign revenues.

Pemex was also running up a quarter of Mexico's debt. By the mid-1980s Mexico owed about $100 billion to more than five hundred foreign banks, with the biggest debt lodged with the biggest banks in the United States. And the bottom had fallen out of the petroleum market. What had been going for $30 a barrel was lucky now to fetch $15. Beginning in 1983 Mexico began borrowing just to pay the interest on what it already owed. Even before that the nation's real money was in flight, stashed overseas by people who were able to get it out of the country. The police chief of Mexico City reportedly got away with $1 billion.

Adriana Quinones, columnist for the Mexico City daily *El Universal,* estimated in 1986 that $50 billion in Mexican capital—half the country's debt—had been taken out of the country and stored in U.S. and European banks. Sergio Sarmiento, an editor of *El Financiero,* drew this moral: "In the 1970s, we were exporting about $3 billion a year and we were growing. Now we're exporting close to $20 billion a year, and in fact our standard of living has tended to drop in the past few years."

Some foreign bankers have suggested that Mexico could pay off its debt by selling its oil resources. That's not likely to fall on responsive ears. Allen Pusey and Jim Landers of the *Dallas Morning News* have pointed out, "Mexico has regarded control over the nation's oil as control over the nation's destiny, a control more important than wealth itself." A Pemex public relations man put it this way in 1981: "Oil is as sacred as the Virgin of Guadalupe for many Mexicans." This nationalist sentiment dates back to 1783, when Mexico was a colonial vassal of Charles III of Spain, who declared that the "juices of the earth" were the property of the crown. After Mexico won its independence and oil began to find its place in industrial societies, President Porfirio Diaz amended Mexico's constitution to allow foreign investors to develop its oilfields.

"In reality," Jorge Diaz-Serrano told the late Joseph Kraft in 1979— this was at the height of the oil boom, when Diaz-Serrano was in command instead of in jail—"Mexico is one of the oldest oil producers. Oil has been coming out of this country commercially since 1904. During the First World War, the industry was rapidly developed by British and American companies, and some people even say that the war was won by Mexican oil. In 1921 Mexican production hit a high of 530,000 barrels a day, and, after the United States, we were the world's largest producer. But Article 27 of the Constitution of 1917 declared that subsurface resources belonged to the nation. It implicitly staked a claim for nationalization. So the companies began easing up on their work here and moving to Venezuela."

The Diaz-Serrano version may constitute a bland revision of history. It took a right-wing dictator, Porfirio Diaz, to invite the big oil companies into Mexico, and a left-wing successor—Lazaro Cardenas, who was president in 1938—to kick them out. In his book *Distant Neighbors,* Alan Riding of *The New York Times* described how Cardenas came to that decision. The SRTPRM, an amalgamation of twelve trade unions, had been formed in 1935, and during 1936 and 1937 it argued with the oil companies over wages and benefits. The dispute was referred to an arbitration board, which ordered a 27 percent wage increase plus new benefits such as sick leave and vacation pay. This ruling was upheld in early 1938 by the Mexican Supreme Court, but the oil companies continued to balk.

They met finally with President Cardenas, who, according to Riding, "reassured them that the cost of the wage hikes would not exceed $7.2 million, approximately half the companies' estimated profits." When the representatives of the companies continued to remonstrate, Cardenas told them, "You are unduly disturbed, gentlemen. The sum won't be more than $7.2 million because my experts say so. I guarantee that you won't have any problems." To that reassurance one of the oil company men responded, "Mr. President, those are your words. Who guarantees for you?" That remark, said Riding, "served to seal the companies' fate."

On March 18, 1935, Cardenas told the Mexican people in a nation-wide broadcast that the seventeen British and American companies were being expropriated for their "arrogant and rebellious attitude." The companies then said they would grant the wage increase, but it was too late. The nationalization of the Mexican oil industry created the first governmental oil monopoly in the non-Communist world, expropriating holdings of such foreign giants as Standard Oil of New Jersey and Royal Dutch Shell. And, unlike the cannier Venezuelans, who allowed foreign managers and specialists to continue in place, the Mexicans kicked out *everybody,* which meant they had to learn the petroleum business from square one. And through Pemex, they did.

Pemex was a giant at its birth, and it has never stopped growing. Just how big it is can never be easily determined. Who knows what the real figures are? In 1986 *Fortune* listed Pemex as earning $6.1 million, while *Forbes* reported Pemex's profits at $4.3 *billion*—and *BusinessWeek* pegged profits at $2.5 *billion. Fortune* said that Pemex had 183,000 employees, *Forbes* cited 149,000. The magazine *South* put the employee total at 175,000. In 1985, while *Fortune* was reporting Pemex's revenues at $19.4 billion, *South* was relaying the information that in the company's biennial report, Pemex had an income of $32 billion of which it paid the Mexican government $22 billion. But in 1983 *BusinessWeek* said that Pemex's reported earnings of $16 million on revenues of $19.2 billion "are meaningless, and details on costs and spending are something of a mystery."

One statistic is as clear for Pemex as it is for every other oil company in the world: In 1986 Pemex sold its oil at an average price of $11.84 per barrel, down from $25.83 in 1985. The price erosion, combined with the devaluation of the Mexican peso, more than halved sales.

In December 1984 the entire world reacted in horror to the lethal Union Carbide gas leak that killed two thousand people in Bhopal, India.

World Population: Up and Up

The world population passed 5 billion in 1987, up from 4 billion in 1974. It will reach 6 billion before the end of the century. Based on current population growth rates, India will become the world's most populous country, reaching 1.7 billion by the year 2010. And by that year Mexico is expected to reach 199 million (up from 82 million in 1986). Nigeria (105 million in 1986) will have a population of 532 million by the middle of the next century.

And that disaster sticks in the memory. However, few people today can recall that two weeks before Bhopal, at San Juan Ixhuatepec, a northwestern suburb of Mexico City, a Pemex liquefied gas storage plant exploded, leaving 499 dead, 1,300 injured, and 10,000 homeless. An investigation traced the explosion to a burner in the Pemex facility. "That was it," a spokesman for the attorney general of the state of Mexico said. "Pemex is guilty. What else is there to investigate?"

Two months after the blast, in a speech at Guadalajara that was reported by *Los Angeles Times* correspondent Juan Vasquez, Mario Ramon Beteta, then director-general of Pemex, said it was a form of cannibalism for Mexicans to criticize Pemex, an enterprise that through its foreign oil sales brought in $16 billion a year and kept the Mexican government afloat. Vasquez reported in early 1985 that the Mexican government had begun paying out checks of $10,400 to survivors of the people who were killed at San Juan Ixhuatepec. The payment was "calculated on the basis of a formula tied to the minimum wage of $5.05 a day."

Access   Ave. Marina Nacional 329
Mexico D.F., Mexico 11300
(90) 5-250-2611

655 Madison Ave.
New York, N.Y. 10022
(212) 759-9501

Pernod Ricard	**Sales** $1.5 billion
	Profits $74 million
	U.S. Sales $150 million
	Rank Largest spirits company in continental Europe
	World's 8th-largest spirits producer
	World's largest producer of anise-based spirits
	France's largest wine producer
	Number one soft drink seller in France
	France's largest producer of apple juice and cider
	World's largest processor of fruit fillings for yogurt
	Founded 1805 (Pernod)
	Employees 10,600
	Headquarters Paris, France

In France, as in the United States, the trend is away from hard liquor. And who should know that better than Pernod Ricard, the largest beverage company on the continent of Europe? Pernod Ricard resulted from the 1974 merger of the two companies which make the anise-based apertifs favored by the French—Pernod, Ricard, and Pastis 51. Tasting like licorice, anise drinks account for about 30 percent of French liquor consumption, and Pernod Ricard has two thirds of this business. Ricard was invented after World War I by a young Frenchman, Paul Ricard, who named the drink after himself. His son, Patrick Ricard, now runs Pernod Ricard, which since the merger has developed an insatiable appetite for other companies.

In a series of acquisitions in 1976, Pernod Ricard brought into its lineup four wine-based aperitifs: Ambassadeur, Byrrh, Cinzano, and Dubonnet. Sitting in a French cafe these days, you can see people ordering Coca-Cola as an aperitif. Pernod Ricard collects here too because it has become the principal bottler of Coke in France. It also owns, thanks to a 1984 lunge, the company that makes Orangina, a fruit-based soft drink (previously sold in the United States under the name Orelia). Coca-Cola is number one and Orangina number two in the French soft drink market.

Acquisitions have become a way of life for Pernod Ricard. It squeezed into the apple business in 1976 by buying Cidreries Distilleries Reunies. In 1982 it became the world leader in fruit preparations for dairy desserts by acquiring SIAS-MPA, a move that it buttressed in 1984 by acquiring Flavors from Florida.

As a result Pernod Ricard now has a big stable of drinks, alcoholic and nonalcoholic. It owns Bisquit, the fifth-largest cognac producer in France. It's France's largest apple processor, from which it makes apple cider, apple juice, and apple brandy. No one makes more Calvados than Pernod Ricard. It bought the House of Campbell in Scotland (House of Lords, King's Ransom, White Heather), and in the United States it scooped up Austin Nichols, a wine importer and distiller of the potent Wild Turkey bourbon. It's still selling plenty of Pernod and Ricard in France. In the world liquor standings, based on gallonage consumed, Richard ranks third behind Bacardi rum and Smirnoff vodka.

Aside from the liquids it owns, Pernod Ricard distributes spirits for others, in France and many other countries. It's the exclusive French distributor of Stolichnaya vodka, Gilbey's gin, Bacardi rum, and Cutty Sark Scotch.

Nineteen eighty-five saw the company still active on the acquisition trail as it gained full control of La Société des Vins de France, which ranks as the largest producer of table wines in the very fragmented French

WHO SENDS WINE TO THE UNITED STATES?

Country	%	Brands		
Italy	50.3%	Riunite Cella Canei Folonari Bolla		
France	23.9%	Rene Junot Partager		
W. Germany	10.8%	Blue Nun		
Spain	6.1%			
Portugal	3.5%	Lancers Mateus		
Japan	0.9%			
Yugoslavia	0.8%	Netherlands	0.3%	
Greece	0.4%	U.K.	0.3%	
Chile	0.3%	Rumania	0.3%	

market. Its major labels are Le Bien Venu, Les Maitres Vignoux, La Villageoise, and Vieux-Papes. Also acquired in 1985 was the Italian spirits company Ramazzotti. In 1987 the Dutch spirits producer Cooymans joined the fold. Cooymans owns half of the liqueur market in the Netherlands with its two brands, Cooymans and De Korenaer.

When Pernod joined hands with Ricard in 1974, their sole business was alcoholic beverages. Today spirits account for 60 percent of its volume. However, when it comes to profits, it's the alcoholic-based products that are still supreme. They bring in 80 percent of Pernod Ricard's profits. The company does about a quarter of its business outside France. It hoped to do more, but it's not easy getting people to like the taste of anise.

The victory of the right-wing parties in the March 1986 elections in France brought the appointment of Charles Pasqua as minister of the interior. Formerly sales director of Pernod Ricard, Pasqua is a Corsican businessman and a fierce enemy of the Socialists. Diana Johnstone, Paris correspondent of *In These Times,* described him as "almost a caricature of a right-wing populist." As interior minister, Pasqua launched a drive against pornography, banning five magazines and threatening *Penthouse* and others with the same fate. Pasqua considers them a corrupting influence.

Access   142, boulevard Haussmann
75008 Paris, France
(33) 1-43-59-2828

Austin Nichols
1290 Ave. of the Americas
New York, N.Y. 10020
(212) 903-9400

Perrier	**Sales** $1.5 billion
	Profits $30 million
	U.S. Sales $230 million
	Rank World's largest producer of bottled water
	Founded 1868
	Employees 12,500
	Headquarters Paris, France

It's not every product that can carry a label declaring it's being produced "in the public interest." Perrier water, which bubbles up from a natural spring at Vergeze in Southeast France, carries such a label in France. Right under the brand name is the designation, *déclarée d'intérêt public*. And a band wrapped around the lower part of the familiar green bottle notes that the product was officially sanctioned by the French government on June 23, 1863. That was the date Emperor Napoleon III authorized the commercial exploitation of this natural spring water, "for the good of France."

It wasn't an idea that occurred to him spontaneously. Mineral water had been bubbling up at Vergeze, a village outside Nîmes, for as long as anyone can remember. But it wasn't until 1841, when Alphonse Granier became the owner of the property where the "Source" was located, that thought was given to charging people for access. It kicked up a row in this small town—Granier put up a fence around the spring—and the controversy simmered for many years. Finally in 1858 Granier got a court decree affirming his right to the spring. Five years later he got Napoleon to issue his decree. In 1868 he formed a company, Société des eaux de Vergeze, to build a health spa where people would come to take the baths and sample the waters. The spring was known then as *Les Bouillens* (boiling waters).

The naturally carbonated water that bubbles up through layers of limestone at Vergeze—and is today called Perrier—goes back so far in time that Perrier may have a reasonable claim to be the oldest product in the world. Volcanic in origin, the fizzy water has been the subject of a number of geological studies. One published in 1979 traced the origin of the Source to the Cretaceous age, more than 130 million years ago. In more recent times, comparatively speaking, the Carthagenian warrior Hannibal reportedly stopped at Vergeze in 218 B.C. to quench his and his troops' thirst on their way to fight the Romans.

The Romans occupied Gaul for five hundred years, and the area around Nîmes abounds with their ruins. They built an amphitheater and an aqueduct there, and they bathed in the waters of Vergeze. From the earliest times great curative powers have been ascribed to natural spring

water. A French encyclopedia published in 1804 stated that the Vergeze waters could cure a number of ailments, especially skin disorders. This healing connotation still adheres to mineral water.

However, Granier's attempt to capitalize on this medicinal promise never worked, even with the sanction from Napoleon III, who was not in great favor after leading France into a losing war with Bismarck's Prussia in 1870. Granier's company was dissolved, and in 1888 his property was auctioned off to a local landowner and merchant, Louis Rouviere, who didn't know anything about water. But he did know whom to hire: Dr. Louis Eugene Perrier.

Perrier was born in 1835 in Domessargues, a town near Vergeze. After graduating from the medical school at the University of Montpellier, he set up a practice near his hometown, but his passion—in school and afterwards—was hydrotherapy. He did his doctoral thesis on how steam baths and consumption of mineral water help sufferers of arthritis. In 1875 he became medical director of a spa at Euzet (there is no shortage of springs in France, some twelve hundred still bubble today), and his reputation spread.

Hired first as a consultant, Dr. Perrier ended up buying Les Bouillens from Rouviere in 1898. He focused on the healing properties of the water. The Vergeze water was bottled with a label promising that it would be "sure to ward off infectious ailments." Dr. Perrier's name appeared on the label, but the names "Les Bouillens" and "Vergeze" were more prominent. Dr. Perrier pursued all manner of hydrotherapeutic devices (inhalators, vaporizers, and special showers), and he developed equipment that used water to treat the throat, larynx, nose, ears, and uterus. But commercial success eluded him, as it had his predecessor.

France's paternalistic interest in Les Bouillens did not prevent the spring from falling into British hands in 1903. But that turned out to be just what the doctor ordered. In need of financing, Dr. Perrier sold the property to A. W. St. John Harmsworth, the younger brother of two Fleet Street press barons, Lord Northcliffe and Lord Rothermere (they founded and operated the *Daily Mail* and the *Daily Mirror* in London). Dr. Perrier stayed on as medical director until his death in 1912, watching the new owner transform the company. Harmsworth shelved the spa to concentrate on selling bottled water. He put Perrier's name on the bottle, and he changed the name of the spring to La Source Perrier. He popularized the bubbly drink in Europe, peddling it to private clubs and restaurants as "the champagne of bottled waters."

Harmsworth also came up with the distinctive little green bottle, which was patterned after wooden Indian clubs that he held in his hands in an exercise routine to help keep his upper body in shape. Shortly after buying the spring and coming to Vergeze, Harmsworth was injured in an automobile accident that left him paralyzed from the waist down. He had an incline built down to the mud, and he would propel his wheelchair down this incline to soak his legs in the legendary healing dirt of Vergeze. This regimen did not alleviate his condition.

Perrier in the little green bottle was a grand success. By 1914 Harmsworth was selling two million bottles a year. By 1933, when he died, sales were up to nineteen million bottles a year. Perrier remained in English hands until after World War II, when it attracted the attention of a canny French businessman, Gustave Leven. Leven, together with some friends, bought it in 1947 and did a public stock offering of 30 percent of the shares in 1949. He was soon selling more than one hundred million bottles a year.

Leven, seventy-three years old in 1987 and still very much in command, took what was a very small mineral water company and built it into one of France's leading beverage and food suppliers. He was quick to realize that the movement away from alcoholic beverages presented Perrier with a sparkling opportunity, especially in the United States, where mineral water had never been a popular drink. He gambled in the late 1970s with a massive U.S. campaign that did what all advertising is supposed to do but rarely does: Establish your brand as the one people order when they think of the product category. More and more drinkers began ordering Perrier instead of a Martini or a Manhattan or a white wine or "mineral water." Perrier's U.S. sales went from $600,000 in 1976 to $60 million in 1979. Value is certainly in the eye of the beholder. As the premier brand in the bottled water business, Perrier is priced accordingly. In 1987 a six-pack was selling in American stores for $3.35.

The other way Leven has expanded, on both sides of the Atlantic, is by buying other companies. In France he acquired the bottled waters

Contrexeville, Vichy, Volvic, and Saint-Yorre. Contrexeville is a non-sparkling water that used to sell two hundred thousand bottles a year, mostly in French drugstores. Under Leven's wing sales went to 600 million bottles a year, and it dominates the flat water segment. In Italy Perrier acquired a 35 percent stake in the Italian mineral water company San Pellegrino. In Britain Perrier bought Buxton mineral water, which was originally discovered by the water-crazed Romans.

In the United States Leven quaffed water companies all over the country. Perrier acquired Poland Springs on the East Coast, Zephyr Hill in Florida, Oasis on the Gulf Coast, and Calistoga on the West Coast. In 1987 Perrier made its biggest buy when it bought the Arrowhead bottled water company from Beatrice, a move that will double its U.S. sales to nearly $500 million a year. Arrowhead, whose main market is California, ranks number one in U.S. bottled water sales, which exploded in the 1980s to the point where Coca-Cola, Pepsi-Cola, and Anheuser-Busch (the Budweiser brewer) were all gearing up to enter the market and put Perrier in its place.

In France Perrier bottles soft drinks. One of its brands is Pepsi-Cola. It also controls various milk and cheese companies, marketing Roqueforts under the labels Société, Rigal, and Maria Grimal and dairy products (milk and cream) under the Lactel name. Perrier's American arm distributes Lindt's Swiss chocolates and the Bonne Maman French preserves.

The source of it all remains the natural spring in Vergeze, which continues to gush water at the rate of twenty thousand gallons an hour. Perrier is still bottled at Vergeze, but Leven has moved the company's headquarters to Paris. The stone Victorian mansion that Harmsworth built to give him an English country home in France still stands at Vergeze, along with a manicured English lawn garden. It's open to the public for viewing.

Perrier is fond of telling people that its water is a natural drink to which nothing is added. "Earth's first soft drink" was the line its U.S. advertising agency came up with. However, in 1985 it brought out a citrus-flavored line (lemon, lime, and orange) after noting how many Americans ordered their Perrier "with a twist." And long ago, as far back as the turn of the century, Perrier stopped bottling the water directly from the source. Gas tended to escape during this process, making it difficult to maintain consistency. The solution was to separate the water from the gas, and this is the procedure followed today. The gas and the water travel in different channels to the plant, where they are reblended in just the right bubbly proportion "Nature put there in the first place," says the company propaganda.

One element hasn't changed: the emphasis on health. Perrier makes a major effort to associate its product with fitness and health. It sponsors marathons and conducts studies on nutrition. In the late 1970s it also helped more than two hundred communities in the United States put up an outdoor exercise path called a Parcourse. The message is the same as the one that was put forth by Dr. Perrier: Drinking the water from Vergeze is good for you. *À votre santé!*

Access   18, rue de Courcelles
75008 Paris, France
(33) 14-563-0611

Great Waters of France
777 W. Putnam Ave.
Greenwich, Conn. 06830
(203) 531-4100

Petrofina

Sales $10 billion
Profits $410 million
U.S. Sales $1.9 billion
Rank Belgium's largest company
22d-largest company in Europe
World's 15th-largest oil company
6th-largest oil company in Europe
52d-largest company in Europe (by
market value)
4th-largest producer of polypropylene
and polystyrene in the United States
Founded 1920
Employees 22,200 (3,400 in the United States)
Headquarters Brussels, Belgium

After winning a war the victors like to sit down and redraw the maps of the world: Petrofina is a company that sprung up from the spoils of World War I.

Germany lost the war and with it the interests it had in the oil fields of Rumania, Europe's largest petroleum producer after the Soviet Union. In 1914 one third of the Rumanian oil assets were in German hands. In 1921 the principal players were: Rumanian, 35.75 percent; British, 16.85 percent; French, 16.35 percent; Anglo-Dutch (Shell), 10 percent; American, 9.29 percent; and Belgian, 8.36 percent. The Germans had been expropriated.

Belgium had fought on the side of the Allies, and a group of Belgian financiers who knew nothing about oil were the ones who ended up with the Rumanian assets, which were offered to them by a Swiss group. On February 25, 1920, they organized the Compagnie Financière Belge des Pétrole (Petrofina) to take over four Rumanian companies. The lead investor was the Société Générale de Belgique, the most powerful financial institution in the country, which had behind it thirty-five years of brutal but successful exploitation of the Belgian Congo (Zaire today). The Rumanian adventure looked like a steal in terms of the assets being bought for 25 million Swiss francs, but it was not without its risks. Rumania was in turmoil after World War I, and it shared a border with Russia, which had just become the world's first Communist state.

It turned out to be another shrewd investment by the Belgians. With Rumanian crude as its base, Petrofina became an integrated oil company in the span between the two world wars, moving into shipping, refining, and the marketing of gasoline via its own service stations in Europe. Then came World War II. Belgium was invaded once again by the Germans and

Petrofina lost its two refineries, all its tankers save one, and its sole source of crude oil. After the war Joseph Stalin showed little inclination to return the Rumanian oil fields to the Belgians.

So the Belgians had to scrap. Under Baron Laurent Wolters, Petrofina regrouped after the war, buying its crude from British Petroleum, which always had more than it needed, and building up new refining and marketing facilities. It also went into petrochemicals (polyethylene, polypropylene, polystyrene), paints and coatings, coal transport and coal mining, insurance. And it never lost sight of where oil comes from, pushing ahead with exploration in Europe, Canada, the United States, and Africa.

Petrofina was either very lucky or very smart. In the early 1970s a drilling team managed by Phillips Petroleum struck oil in the Norwegian Ekofisk field of the North Sea; Petrofina was down for 30 percent of this action. In Canada, after building up an operation that included oil and gas leases in the western part of the country, coal rights in Alberta and British Columbia, a 95,000-barrel-a-day refinery near Montreal, and 1,100 Fina service stations in the eastern part of the country, Petrofina sold its 72 percent–owned Canadian subsidiary to the Canadian government for $1.2 billion in 1981.

In the United States, by dint of acquisition after acquisition, Petrofina's 82 percent–owned subsidiary, Dallas-based American Petrofina, operates refineries in Big Spring and Port Arthur, Texas; petrochemical plants in Houston, Calumet City, Illinois, and Carville, Louisiana; and a 1,600-mile network of pipelines feeding crude into its terminals. Gasoline is marketed through 4,239 Fina service stations in twenty-two states. In 1986 American Petrofina was prospecting for oil in the Gulf of Mexico and in the Bering and Beaufort seas off Alaska. It has chemical partnerships with Borg-Warner, Hercules, and Hoechst.

American Petrofina had sales of $1.9 billion in 1986, ranking it as the twenty-first-largest company in the U.S. petroleum industry. The Belgians take no chances about losing control. The American subsidiary has two classes of stock, A and B, which are identical except that the Class B holders elect a majority of the board members. The public owns 18 percent of the A stock—the Belgians own 100 percent of Class B.

Petrofina, in 1986, was taking small amounts of oil out of Angola, Zaire, and Tunisia. The North Sea accounted for two thirds of its oil production, but the company was pumping only a third of the crude that it ran through its refineries. This meant that it was still crude-poor, having to buy from others, not a bad position to be in during an oil glut and plunging prices. While the world's major petroleum companies were groaning and resorting to downsizing, Petrofina was soaring. Its sales and profits more than tripled in the decade ending in 1985, moving up steadily every year, even though employment was static through the entire ten years.

In 1986, when just about every oil company in the world was posting a decline because of low prices, Petrofina chimed in with a gain of 7.4 percent in profits. Outsiders are at a loss to explain this Belgian wizardry. *Wall Street Journal* reporter Mark M. Nelson, a Petrofina watcher from Brussels, wrote in 1987:

> Few have been able to penetrate Petrofina's inner circle to discover just how the company does so well. . . . Petrofina won't say where it makes its profits or how it buys its oil. It won't disclose how much it makes on production of crude oil and how much it makes on refining and chemical manufacturing. Some analysts think it has a special trading department that specializes in seeking out the best deals and making fast decisions on the world's crude oil markets. Others think the company bought a huge reserve of oil when the price bottomed out and will use it only after the price rises.

Just wait 'til the next world war.

Access   rue de L'Industrie 52
1040 Brussels, Belgium
(32) 2-233-92-87

American Petrofina
Fina Plaza
Dallas, Tex. 75206
(214) 750-2400

Peugeot	**Sales** $17 billion
	Profits $600 million
	U.S. Sales 15,000 cars, 100,000 bicycles
	Rank World's 7th-largest automaker
	Europe's 3d-largest automaker
	France's 4th-largest manufacturer
	World's largest diesel engine builder
	38th on the *Fortune* International 500
	Founded 1810
	Employees 165,000
	Headquarters Paris, France

Peugeot, the world's second-oldest automobile manufacturer, has been a force on the French economic scene for nearly two centuries. The Peugeots are Huguenots from the Alsace region of France, and the family has held the company together through one war after another and through political upheavals that have transformed France from a monarchy to one republic after another (it's now the Fifth). When François Mitterrand and his Socialist party swept into power in 1981, Peugeot was conspicuous by its absence from the roster of companies that were nationalized. It became the largest company in France *not* owned by the government.

The Socialists nationalized companies to revitalize them. On that count Peugeot was, in 1981, a good candidate. It was mired in a life-threatening slump and compared unfavorably to Renault, France's largest car producer, which had been nationalized after World War II. By the mid-1980s the tables had turned. After a decade of financial jolts as harrowing as the hairpin turns in car rallies, Peugeot appeared to be making a strong comeback, while Renault was in the pits for repairs. Peugeot prospered under socialism, Renault deteriorated.

Politics had really little to do with the misfortunes or resurgence of Peugeot. The company undermined itself in the 1970s by pursuing a strategy aimed at turning itself into the "General Motors of Europe." It was a strategy loudly applauded by the French government and pompous analysts with their noses buried in statistics. They argued that to succeed in the modern automobile industry—that is, to compete against the Americans and the Japanese—a car company had to be big and had to have an international reach. Peugeot embraced the argument. It would defend France—and Europe.

Already the number two automaker in France, Peugeot absorbed the third-largest producer, Citroën, in 1976. Two years later Peugeot took an even bigger bite by acquiring all the European operations of the embattled

Chrysler Corporation, which had enough problems in the United States (these were the pre-Iacocca days) without worrying about Europe. The Chrysler deal brought into the Peugeot column plants in Britain (Rootes), France (Simca), and Spain.

Peugeot had catapulted into the topmost ranks of the world automotive industry. It was the largest car company in Europe with an annual output of 2.2 million cars, well ahead of the 1.6 million that Ford and Renault each produced. Based on 1977 registrations of these companies, the new Peugeot claimed these healthy market shares: France, 45 percent; Spain, 23 percent; Italy, 12 percent; Britain, 10 percent; Germany, 6.5 percent. There was also the tantalizing prospect of penetrating the American market, a feat no French car maker had ever accomplished. Chrysler, teetering on the brink in 1978, sold its European operations for $230 million in cash and a 12.5 percent stake in the new and expanded Peugeot company. The talk at the time was that Peugeot would be able to use the Chrysler dealer network in the United States to sell its European cars to Americans.

That was the pipedream, anyway.

It turned out to be a nightmare. First of all, Peugeot more than doubled its productive capacity at a time when oil prices were going through the roof. Second, either the Peugeot people didn't know or didn't examine carefully what they were buying. The Chrysler properties in Europe were in sorry shape, featuring antiquated factories that made cars nobody wanted to buy. Peugeot woke up in 1979 to find itself strangled with too many workers, too many plants, and too many competing car models. It changed the name of the Chrysler entities to Talbot, the nameplate of a stable of famous racing cars of the 1930s. General Motors had five divisions (Chevrolet, Buick, Oldsmobile, Pontiac, Cadillac), Peugeot now had three (Peugeot, Citroën, Talbot). But the facelift was purely cosmetic and failed to frighten away the evil spirits. Peugeot couldn't make the combination work. The crash came in 1979 when Automobiles Talbot, the new name of Chrysler-Europe, lost $130 million. The next year Peugeot itself, dragged down by its new appendages, plunged into red ink.

It was the first in a string of five years of losses, clearly an embarrassment to a company as bourgeois as Peugeot. For 170 years Peugeot had been run along paternalistic lines, drawing its strength from its original base in the Jura mountains near Switzerland. There it avoided entanglements with Communist-led trade unions. The Peugeots demanded absolute loyalty from their employees. In return they catered to the needs of employees. They could boast, up to the time of their escapades in the 1970s, that they had never laid off a Peugeot worker. There was no way that policy could be maintained in the face of mounting losses and unsold cars.

The new Peugeot proved itself equal to the unpleasant tasks of closing plants and dismissing workers, and confronting militant labor unions in Britain, France, and Spain. The euphoria evoked by the 1978 annexation of Chrysler-Europe was no better illustrated than in the remarks of a Scottish worker at the Chrysler plant in Linwood, outside Glasgow. "It's a great thing," he told a British reporter. "I don't see any problems. Peugeot has not had a strike for ten years, and I think they understand our problems. They are not like Americans. They are Europeans and they know what goes on here."

In 1981 Peugeot permanently closed Linwood, the only automobile plant in Scotland, axing forty-eight hundred employees. At the start of 1979 Chrysler had twenty-eight thousand employees in Britain; by 1982, it was down to ten thousand. Similar cuts went on elsewhere. In Spain nine thousand Talbot workers lost their jobs. In France Peugeot won in a bitter face-off with workers, many of them Moroccan immigrants, at the old Simca plant at Poissy, outside Paris. One of the planks in the settlement agreement called for a stipend to workers who wanted to return to North Africa. Between 1978 and 1987 Peugeot eliminated one hundred thousand jobs.

To be able to get rid of one hundred thousand workers and still survive is a monument to twentieth-century logic. It would have strained the credulity of the Peugeot brothers, Jean-Pierre and Jean-Frederic, who started this enterprise in 1810. The brothers set up a foundry in the Alsatian village of Sous-Cratet near Herimoncourt, where their father, a weaver, had been mayor at the time of the French Revolution. La Maison Peugeot expanded steadily in the nineteenth century to make a variety of metal-based products, beginning with saws and moving to clock and watch springs, hoop skirt frames, coffee mills, umbrella ribs, corset stays, and the pince-nez part of eyeglasses.

All this growth took place in various Alsatian towns of eastern France. The Peugeots adopted as their symbol the Lion of Belfort, which also serves as the symbol of the seventeenth-century Alsatian fortress city Belfort. During the Franco-Prussian War of 1870–71, Belfort withstood a German siege of 108 days, a defense that so impressed the Germans that they left the Belfort region in French hands when they annexed the rest of Alsace after the war. To commemorate that siege, the French sculptor Frederic Bartholdi, the builder of the Statue of Liberty, carved his colossal Lion of Belfort statue out of the rock that flanks the city. The Lion of Belfort still adorns every Peugeot.

Armand Peugeot, a grandson of Jean-Pierre, studied engineering at the University of Leeds in England, where he became a cycling enthusiast. Upon his return to France he pushed the family company into manufacturing bicycles. The first Peugeot cycles were produced in 1885, using as spokes the thin metal rods that the company once used to make corset stays. A turn-of-the-century company history was thus able to boast that Peugeot products pervaded French life: "At every hour of the day, Peugeot is present. Madame gets up, puts on her corset (Peugeot stays), turns on her gramophone (Peugeot spring), opens her umbrella (Peugeot frame). Monsieur winds his watch (Peugeot spring), adjusts his spectacles (Peugeot frame), does odd jobs about the house (Peugeot hammer and saw), tidies up the garden (Peugeot pitchfork), and takes a turn around town (Peugeot bicycle)."

Bicycles led to automobiles. At the Paris Exposition of 1889, when the Eiffel Tower was unveiled, the inventive Armand introduced a three-wheel car powered by a coal-fired steam engine. "A diabolical invention" was the verdict of one French reporter. After building three more steam-driven cars, he switched to gasoline power with a Daimler-designed engine purchased from Panhard and Levassor, one of the first licensees of Gottlieb Daimler. (Panhard, whose name appeared on some of the world's first running automobiles, is part of Peugeot today.) Peugeot must then be the world's oldest surviving automobile brand name.

In 1894 Armand Peugeot's car shared first place with a Panhard in the world's first automobile race, the Paris-Rouen Trials. And a year later Armand's car won the Paris-Bordeaux-Paris race. Another Peugeot finished last in the field of ten, but it had the distinction of being the first car equipped with air-filled tires. The Michelin brothers, André and Marcel, drove the car and changed fifty flats on the 732-mile route. (Like the Panhard firm, Michelin's business dealings have been deeply entwined with Peugeot's.)

Armand Peugeot broke away from the rest of the family in 1897 to launch a company to make cars, setting up his factory at Lille in northern France near the Belgian border. But after cars had proved their staying power, his enterprise was reunited with the original family business in 1910. Automotive products soon overshadowed Peugeot's other lines. A new automobile plant was built in 1912 at Sochaux in Alsace (it's still Peugeot's main plant). On the eve of World War I the company was turning out ninety-three-hundred cars, more than half of France's output.

In its early years Peugeot built formidable racing cars. In 1912 a four-cylinder Peugeot captured the Grand Prix de France (the Le Mans race) and in the following year finished first at the Indianapolis 500.

Peugeots dominated the Indy 500 for the next five years, culminating in 1919 with the American Triple Crown: Indy, the American Grand Prix (in Santa Monica), and the Vanderbilt Cup. Peugeot also pioneered with the engine invented by Rudolf Diesel. In 1922 it built the first car powered by a diesel engine, and in 1928 it began turning out diesel engines in quantity at its Lille plant. It's an expertise that has persisted. In 1985 Peugeot jumped from third place to first place, passing Daimler-Benz and Fiat, to become the world's largest producer of diesel engines with an output of 561,000. However, Peugeots no longer burn up rubber on the race course. Instead, the cars built by the company have garnered a reputation as reliable, stolid vehicles, geared to a sedate, cautious, bourgeois clientele—much like the Peugeots themselves.

It's quite a contrast to the reputation of its partner, Citroën, known for flamboyant marketing and eccentric cars. Founded in 1915 by an engineer, André Citroën, who built his automobile assembly plant on a thirty-acre Parisian site that once held vegetable gardens, the Citroën company became the car company where engineers loved to work. Its cars were rarely uninteresting. First was the 1919 Type A, a 10-horsepower vehicle that was Europe's first mass-produced car, rolling off the assembly line in completed form. In the 1920s Citroën began supplying the cars that became the distinctive taxicabs of Paris. Citroën built cars for both the rich and the hoi polloi. Its classic, low-slung models were favorites of politicians and gangsters. (Charles de Gaulle loved them and used them as the official state limousines, but when Valery Giscard d'Estaing came to power in 1974, he replaced them with Peugeot's top-of-the-line 604.)

One of the most famous of all Citroën models is the "deux chevaux" (2CV, for short), a minicar that resembles a "sardine can on wheels" and goes sixty-five miles on a gallon of gas. It became one of the most ubiquitous cars on European roads after World War II. In 1987, after producing nearly five million of them, Citroën announced that it was closing its old factory in Paris where the 2CV had been made since 1949. The news saddened many French motorists, but only fourteen thousand 2CVs were sold in 1986. The company said, however, that it would continue to make the car in Portugal.

Citroën always had a flair for marketing. At the Paris Motor Show of 1919, the company brought fifty demonstration cars for prospective customers to try out. André Citroën was the first industrialist to run factory tours for the public. He was also the first automaker to use skywriting, with the Citroën name spelled out in smoke. From 1925 to 1934, 250,000 electric light bulbs spelled out Citroën's name in 100-foot letters around the Eiffel Tower.

It was fun but not conducive to bottom-line results. In 1934 Citroën had to be bailed out by its biggest creditor, the Michelin tire people. André Citroën died the following year. Under Michelin's control Citroën bought the historic Panhard company in 1965 and held a majority interest in the Italian auto company Maserati for seven years. But it continued to have financial problems. In 1968 Michelin arranged for Citroën to enter into a partnership with the big Italian automaker Fiat, but that venture foundered on nationalistic jealousies. The French government was delighted in 1974 when the solid French citizen, Peugeot, began buying into Citroën. The government arranged a state loan as a dowry for the Citroën-Peugeot marriage, which was consummated in 1976. Peugeot did so well turning around Citroën that it was an easy convert to polygamy when Chrysler's European facilities became available in 1978.

The Chrysler acquisition was so disastrous that Peugeot not only failed to become the largest automobile producer in Europe (a position it had seemingly reached considering the combined sales of Peugeot, Citroën, and Chrysler), but fell back to fourth place behind Volkswagen, Fiat, and Ford. Instead of the 2.2 million cars that it was programmed in 1978 to turn out, its 1985 output was 1.6 million. In the process Talbot (alias Chrysler) seemed to be pulling a disappearing act. Incredible as it may be to remember, in 1977 Chrysler-Europe produced 774,000 cars, about half of the combined Peugeot-Citroën output. Talbot's output in 1985 was 160,000.

Peugeot appeared to be emerging from its slide in 1985 under the stern guidance of a tough ex-banker, Jacques Calvet, who had become chief executive in 1984 after demonstrating that he had the stomach to sever people and plants from the corporate body. Helping him to get Peugeot back in contention were two new small cars, the Peugeot 205 supermini and the Citroën BX. They gave Peugeot a strong grip on first place in France, with 34.6 percent of the market in 1985, well ahead of Renault's 28.7 percent. Peugeot's penetration was also strong in three other markets: Spain (18.6 percent), Portugal (15.2 percent), and Belgium-Luxembourg (14.3 percent). Its European market share in 1986 was 11.4 percent.

While these shares were nowhere near the heights projected in 1978, the showing, combined with the cutbacks, was strong enough to restore Peugeot to profitability. In 1987 Calvet said he would pay stockholders the first cash dividends since 1979. The biggest beneficiaries of this largesse were the Peugeot family members, who still control a third of the stock and who are still very active in the company's affairs. Another beneficiary was Michelin, which still owned 9 percent of Peugeot's stock. Chrysler was not a beneficiary because it sold all its holdings in 1986.

Also not sharing in the revival were the one hundred thousand people who lost their jobs in the mayhem that followed Peugeot's lunge for supremacy in Europe.

Access   75, avenue de la Grand Armee
75116 Paris, France
(33) 1-502-1133

1 Peugeot Plaza
Lyndhurst, N.J. 07071
(201) 935-8400

Philips

Sales $27.5 billion
Profits $500 million
U.S. Sales $6.6 billion
Rank World's 2d-largest consumer electronics
producer
Europe's 2d-largest employer
World's largest maker of light bulbs
World's largest maker of color television sets
World's largest producer of electric shavers
World's largest producer of laser discs
World's 2d-largest producer of medical
electronics equipment
Europe's 8th-largest industrial company
World's 22th-largest manufacturing company
Holland's largest company
3d-largest television set maker in United
States
Founded 1891
Employees 344,000 (50,000 in the United States)
Headquarters Eindhoven, the Netherlands

I f it plugs into a wall socket, the chances are good that this Dutch company makes it. Philips is an industrial powerhouse and one of the world's largest employers. However, in the United States it's one of the least known of the world's electronic giants. The company aims to do something about this obscurity (shine a light on it) by the time it reaches its one-hundredth birthday in 1991.

In any European home—and many overseas too—Philips products can be found in every room. In the living room: stereo equipment, classical records, tapes and compact discs, videocassette recorders, compact disc players, musical instruments, furniture, and light bulbs. In the bathroom: electric toothbrushes, hair dryers, and electric shavers. (Philips invented the rotary shaving head and makes more shavers than any other company in the world.) In the kitchen: microwave ovens, clocks, toasters, refrigerators, coffee makers, dishwashers, food processors. In the utility closet or laundry room: washing machines, dryers, irons, vacuum cleaners.

Philips also has a major presence in offices with fluorescent lamps, word processors, personal computers, dictation machines, and telephone switches. For the car it makes radios, mobile telephones, halogen headlights, and a navigation system that stores maps and route descriptions on a compact disc and uses a "talking chip" to relay instructions to the driver.

In industry Philips is known for its semiconductors (more familiarly known as "chips," the foundation of computer technology), electronic bank terminals, medical devices (diagnostic imaging, radiation therapy), air-traffic control systems, picture tubes, television cameras, batteries, fiber-optic cable, and scientific measuring instruments (oscilloscopes). Philips supplied the television cameras that filmed the 1986 World Cup finals in Mexico City. Its floodlights illuminate the Eiffel Tower against the Parisian night. And its LaserVision discs are recording Britain's "Domesday Book" project, a modern version of the comprehensive survey made of British society after the Norman Conquest of 1066.

Philips's forte is making consumer electrical products. It does not make the heavy electrical equipment—turbines, generators, transformers—produced by such companies as General Electric and Hitachi. If there's a company whose product lineup is similar, it would be Japan's Matsushita, whose sales, slightly ahead of Philips's, rank it number one in consumer electronics. When it regrouped after World War II, Matsushita leaned heavily on technology licensed to it by Philips.

Being outmaneuvered in a field that it pioneered is not a novel experience for Philips. It's better at making a product than promoting it. Philips was the first company to develop the audio cassette, but the Japanese were the ones who cleaned up with it in the marketplace. Most engineers who looked closely at all the entries in the VCR market agreed that the classiest product, from a technical standpoint, was the Philips machine, utilizing the company's proprietary V-2000 system. It had the clearest picture, and it could record up to eight hours. But Philips priced it too high and didn't seem to know how to exploit its technical advantages.

As a result the Japanese, led by the VHS machines introduced by Matsushita and JVC, swept the field once again. Philips couldn't even get its American satellite, Magnavox, to market a V-2000 VCR in the United States. Magnavox opted for a Japanese make. And in the end, just to stay in this market, Philips itself had to get a licence to make and sell a VHS-type VCR under its own name. Another Philips invention which Japanese companies marketed well under their own names is the compact disc player, only this time the Dutch did reap some benefit. Philips (and its minority partner, Sony) get a royalty on every CD player sold. Still, who knows that Philips invented the compact disc player?

Who knows, for that matter, that Philips is behind the American brand names Norelco, Sylvania, Philco, and Magnavox? Or that it owns the Westinghouse light bulb business in the United States? Or that it owns Polygram, a German recording company whose labels include Decca, Deutsche Grammophone, and London? Or that it has 50 percent of the

Japanese electronics company Marantz and 32 percent of the German electronics outfit Grundig? Or that the British electronic brand names Pye and Mullard are Philips properties?

This proliferation of brand names testifies to a lack of cohesiveness. Philips is the most multinational of all the big electronics companies—it does 94 percent of its sales outside its home country and it has factories in more than fifty countries—but it doesn't impose the same discipline that other companies do. It has tolerated a streak of independence in its overseas subsidiaries to form what one of its leaders once called a "democratic federation of Philips establishments."

Philips had to be different because it's domiciled in one of the smallest countries in the world. Unlike the Japanese and the Americans, Philips did not have the benefit of a huge home market as a base. It had to build its business, market by market. And in Europe, which is the company's biggest market (45 percent of sales), Philips has been hampered by a myriad of local regulations and "standards" that vary from country to country despite the progress made toward a common market. *The Wall Street Journal* described what this means for the plug factory that Philips has in Belgium: "Some [cords] sprout three prongs, others two. Prongs protrude straight or angled, round or rectangular, fat, thin, and sometimes sheathed. Philips makes circular plug faces, squares, pentagons, and hexagons. It perforates some and notches others. One French plug has a niche like a keyhole. British plugs carry fuses."

Philips makes twenty-nine kinds of electrical outlets, a dozen types of cords, twelve different irons, fifteen cake mixers. Forced to make a wider range of products than it wants, economies of scale are lost. Philips estimates that its consumer products would be at least 10 percent cheaper if Europe were a single market. The bottom-line comparisons with its major international competitors have an eloquence of their own: In 1985, when Philips was earning $363 million on sales of $21.8 billion, General Electric of the United States was earning $2.3 billion on sales of $28.2 billion, and Matsushita of Japan was earning $1 billion on sales of $22 billion.

Working in his Menlo Park, New Jersey, laboratory Thomas A. Edison invented the first practical incandescent lamp, or light bulb, in 1879. Twelve years later in Holland two brothers, Gérard and Anton Philips, were bankrolled by their banker father to go into the business of making light bulbs. Gérard was an engineer who had learned about light bulbs while working for the German company AEG. Anton was a salesman who laid down the broad strategy that Philips still adheres to: Specialize in consumer products, steer clear of heavy engineering. He basically wanted to make things that could fit on his desk. The Philips brothers put their plant down in Eindhoven, a town in southern Holland near the Belgian border. They called their company Philips Gloeilampenfabrieken (Philips Light Bulb Factory), the name it still carries.

By 1895 the company was turning out five hundred light bulbs a day, not all of which could be sold in the Netherlands. So Anton began exporting to Germany. Philips was not averse to using child labor. In fact, according to one critic, Eindhoven was especially chosen "because there were plenty of workers and plenty of children, the population was poor, Roman Catholic, reliable and content with low wages, there were no social problems, and the possibilities for child labor were great."

Philips was also not averse to cooperating with competitors. According to a study done by the Transnational Institute of Amsterdam, Philips joined in the early part of the century with AEG, Siemens, and fourteen other European light bulb producers in a cartel that fixed prices and allocated market shares (Philips was given 10.5 percent). Over the years, however, as the Philips brothers expanded their business, the company gained a reputation as a caring, if paternalistic, employer. Looking back in 1982 Boudweijn Tamineau, a Dutch journalist who considers Philips to be antilabor, presented this picture:

> Philips has been known for many years as the most social of all employers in the Netherlands. The saying went that a Philips employee was cared for from cradle to grave. His family was included in this, and his children also went to work for Philips. On arrival by train in Eindhoven, one sees the workers' paradise gliding past. One sees gigantic factories, but also the beautiful Philips parks, the Philips library, the Philips Cultural Center, the Philips football stadium, the Philips medical service, the Philips travel agency, the Philips pension fund, the Philips schools, the Philips village (Philips is the largest landlord and owns a whole city district). There is still much more to be seen, ranging from the Philips postage stamp club to the Philips brass band and the Philips pigeon club. On leaving the station, you see the founder before you, the old patriarch Anton Philips, to whom Eindhoven is indebted for everything . . . on his pedestal. He surveys the city and Eindhoven lies at his feet.

During World War I, when Holland was neutral, Philips thrived. And after the war it expanded from one product to another (X rays, radios) and from one country to another (there were subsidiaries in thirty-eight countries by 1938). It put light bulb plants into Central and Eastern Europe through joint ventures with Osram, an international cartel that linked Germany's Siemens and AEG with General Electric of the United States. During World War II, when the Netherlands was occupied by the

Nazis, Philips was active on both sides of the fence. Its European plants, including the ones at Eindhoven, produced armaments for the German war machine, although afterwards the company insisted that its Dutch workers were "masters in the development of highly sophisticated equipment without ever producing anything."

Descendants of the Philips brothers are no longer active in the management of the company. The last to hold the reins was Anton's son, Frederick Philips, who elected to remain in Holland during World War II even though the top managers of the company fled to England. An engineer like his Uncle Gérard, Frederick served as president of the company from 1961 to 1971 and became a convert to—and bankroller of—Dr. Frank Buchman, an American evangelist who founded the "Moral Re-Armament" movement. A Lutheran minister, Buchman preached a gospel of spiritual reconstruction to be carried out in groups or "house parties." His organization was stridently anti-Communist, and Buchman was an open admirer of Adolf Hitler.

Wisse Dekker, a blunt Dutchman who became chief executive at Eindhoven in 1982 after heading up operations in Britain and Asia (he worked in Tokyo from 1966 to 1971), was proud of depicting Philips as the "*only* international company holding its ground against Japan in the field of consumer electronics." Philips, unlike some big American electronics companies, makes its own products, and Dekker deplored the actions of U.S. companies in abandoning the field to Japanese suppliers. It matters, said Dekker, because electronic systems (televisions, computers, phones) are interactive, linked to one another, and if a company drops out of a crucial part like consumer electronics, then it drops "out of the learning curve" and "you will never be able to get back in."

Dekker's successor, Cornelius van der Klugt, a thirty-six-year veteran of the Philips wars, also believes in standing up to the Japanese. "The Japanese are not almighty," he told *BusinessWeek*. "We're still inventing products at Philips." These inventions spring from a massive research effort at eight laboratories, including ones at Briarcliff, New York, and Sunnyvale, California. Philips invests more than $1 billion annually in research, and it participates in a host of cooperative programs with other companies. In 1986 it had in place joint ventures with more than a dozen big corporations around the world, including Matsushita (lighting), Sony (compact discs), Kyocera (home interactive systems), AT&T (telecommunications), Du Pont (magnetic tape and optical discs), Siemens (the fifth-generation chip), Bosch (television studio equipment), and Digital Equipment (diagnostic imaging).

Philips operates subsidiaries in sixty countries, but the one it has targeted for special attention is the United States. During World War II the Dutch protected their assets in North America by sheltering them in a trust company. It resulted in a a corporate freak, the North American Philips Corporation, which was indirectly controlled by Philips (through a trust holding of 58 percent), but operated independently (by its charter) under an American management that was not beholden to Eindhoven. In effect the Dutch company had no effective control over this satellite. At the end of 1986 the Dutch masters put an end to this nonsense by abolishing the trust and taking direct control of North American Philips and another American holding, Signetics, a California semiconductor manufacturer.

In North American Philips the Dutch already have a large presence on the American scene, although the performance is not one that pleases Eindhoven. In 1986 North American Philips ranked eighty-second on the *Fortune* 500 with sales of $4.5 billion, encompassing the Norelco, Magnavox, Sylvania, and Philco businesses. The company also holds other bits and pieces, including the Genie remote control products and the Elkhart, Indiana–based Selmer Company, one of the world's largest makers of musical instruments (there's hardly a marching band in the United States in which a Selmer trumpet or trombone doesn't blare).

This aggressive action on the American front meshes with a new Philips strategy of becoming more of a global player and less a federation of independent national enterprises. It's a bit of a cultural shock because Philips prides itself on its ability to adapt to local mores. "The great strength Philips has—we speak the language, we know the people and the politics—must not be lost," said van der Klugt, who speaks seven languages, in a 1987 interview with *Financial Times* reporter Laura Raun. But all the same, Philips is moving toward greater integration of its sprawling international operations. It wants its subsidiaries to be interactive, feeding one another.

American consumers are already beginning to see the signs of this "Netherlandization." In 1983 Philips bought the Westinghouse light bulb business in the United States but didn't change the brand name. In 1985 it did, and television viewers were soon seeing a series of commercials trying to familiarize them with the Philips name. It's an uphill struggle. As van der Klugt observed, "When you say Philips in the United States, people think it is spelled with two *l*s and is in oil."

In trying to put the Philips stamp on more of this farflung electronics empire, Eindhoven has also adopted a "leaner and meaner" stance, not easy for a company that has never liked to fire people. "The need for a factory in each town, each country, is no longer a basis from which to compete," van der Klugt said in his interview with Raun. In 1980 Philips had more than 500 plants in the world; it's now down to 420. In 1976 it had 392,000 employees; today it has 344,000.

"The key word," said van der Klugt, "is global."

Access   5621 BA Eindhoven, the Netherlands
(31) 4-783496

North American Philips
100 E. 42nd St.
New York, N.Y. 10017
(212) 697-3600

Renault	**Sales** $18.9 billion
	Loss $800 billion (1986)
	U.S. Sales $1 billion
	Rank World's 9th-largest auto producer
	France's 2d-largest company
	World's 3d-largest car renter
	18th on the *Fortune* International 500
	Founded 1898
	Employees 180,000
	Headquarters Boulogne-Billancourt, France

The triumphs and failures—the glories and agonies—of France in the twentieth century are bound up in the history of Renault, a pioneer of the world automobile industry. Its cars helped France win a crucial battle in World War I. The man who founded the company was jailed in 1944 for collaborating with the Nazis. His company was then nationalized by the French government. Under state ownership Renault went on to lead the revival of the French auto industry until the company ran into serious trouble in the early 1980s. It was pulling out of its slump in 1986 when its chairman, Georges Besse, was assassinated by terrorists on a Paris street near his home. Few companies stand for their country as Renault does.

The story begins toward the end of the last century when dreamers in a number of countries were tinkering with models of power-driven horseless carriages. One of the French tinkerers was Louis Renault, who was born in 1877, the fourth son of a businessman who operated a drapery and button factory. Louis showed little interest in schoolwork but at age fourteen was already playing with engines in a shed on the family garden at Billancourt, a suburb of Paris. It was in that shed in 1898 that he modified a three-quarter horsepower engine and designed a direct transmission box. The box, which had three forward speeds and reverse, replaced the noisy belts and chains that had been used as transmissions on many of the early automobile models. This engine and box were fitted to a quadricycle and *voilà*, the first Renault. Louis, the inventor, was twenty-one years old.

Renault Frères was established in 1899 to make automobiles, Louis being joined—and bankrolled—by his two older brothers, Marcel and Fernand. The company set up shop on the Seine River in Billancourt near the family homestead. In six months the Renault brothers delivered sixty of their *voiturettes*. They also introduced, in 1899, the world's first sedan.

As soon as people began making cars, they wanted not just to ride them but race them. Races have always been a testing ground for automo-

485

biles. Renault was an early entrant and frequent winner, with Louis and Marcel behind the wheel. In 1899 they came in first and second, respectively, in the Paris-Ostend and Paris-Rambouillet races, Louis winning the latter with an average speed of 22 mph.

By 1901 the Renault voiturette was powered by an eight-horsepower engine, and the Renault brothers entered the first big "capital-to-capital" race, the 745-mile Paris-to-Berlin competition. All the stars of the newly emerging auto industry were represented in the 109 entries. Louis Renault covered the distance in eighteen hours and twenty-seven minutes, capturing first place in the voiturette class (cars weighing under 880 pounds) and eighth place overall.

In 1903 the Renaults entered four of their cars in the Paris-Madrid race, which ended in tragedy. Crowds lined the route, and spectators were killed when cars swerved into them. Drivers and mechanics were also killed and injured in crashes. One of the fatalities was Marcel Renault, who, his vision obscured by dust, didn't see a sharp curve coming up just beyond Poitiers. His car went off the road and crashed. Louis, who had arrived first at the Bordeaux checkpoint, abandoned the race when he heard about the accident. The French government, appalled by the carnage, forbade the cars to return to Paris under their own power. They were pulled by horses and carried by railway. And such was the pall cast by this event that international city-to-city racing didn't resume until 1927 with the first running of the Mille Miglia.

In that same year France emerged as the world's largest automobile producer, turning out thirty thousand cars. Renault's contribution was only one thousand cars, but whereas most of the other early French companies—Panhard, Mors, Darracq—were to fall by the wayside, Renault, along with Peugeot, would be a survivor. It survived under the ruthless direction of its founder, who gave up racing and concentrated on perfecting new devices such as the removable spark plug, hydraulic shock absorber, and a compressed gas starter operated from the driver's seat.

In 1905 a two-cylinder, eight-horsepower Renault went into service on the streets of Paris as a taxi. It was equipped with a new device that automatically calculated the fare based on the mileage traveled. Orders from the cab company doubled Renault's production. In 1906 the Renault cabs began running on London streets, and in that year Renault also introduced its first bus. It weighed five tons and carried twenty-one passengers. Sixty years later similar looking buses still traversed Paris streets.

Fernand Renault dropped out of the business in 1908 because of poor health. Louis bought all his shares, and Renault Frères became La Société Louis Renault. He ran it as his personal fiefdom. He never sold shares to anyone else. Every sou that he earned, he put back in the business. He never borrowed a centime from a bank. He used to pay his suppliers immediately to qualify for a 3 percent discount.

During World War I the company built light tanks for the French Army. But Renault's most famous association with World War I was the "taxis de la Marne" event. In September 1914 German forces were approaching Paris. They were repelled in the Battle of the Marne by French soldiers who were ferried to the front in six hundred Paris taxicabs commandeered by the army. The Renault archives show that there were only four minor breakdowns during the exercise. They also record the incidental intelligence that the government tipped the cab drivers 27 percent of the fare.

After the war Louis Renault built his company into a mighty industrial powerhouse. The factory at Billancourt expanded to eighty-seven acres. The company was producing trucks and tractors, and by 1930 it was also the world's largest builder of aircraft engines. It produced many of the components needed to build cars—tires, bearings, carburetors—and it even operated foundries to supply the steel, iron, and aluminum that it needed. Louis Renault, like France, preferred to be dependent on nobody, not even his employees, whom he seemed to regard as necessary evils.

World War II was a cataclysmic turning point for Renault and France. The French, unprepared for conflict, were quickly overwhelmed. Renault's factories were bombed heavily during the war, but the workshops that escaped damage continued to produce for the German occupation force. And Louis Renault remained in charge. After the Germans were chased from France, Renault was arrested and charged with being a collaborator. While awaiting trial the sixty-seven-year-old Renault died in the Fresnes prison on October 25, 1944. On January 16, 1945, General Charles de Gaulle signed a decree nationalizing Renault but specifying that it conduct its affairs as a regular commercial enterprise, its "financial resources to be ensured by sale of its products."

Whether the company ever followed that prescription is open to debate. Critics have charged that it always had help from the state, paid hardly any taxes, and rarely made a profit. It was nevertheless held up as a model of a successful state-owned enterprise. It certainly made—and sold—a lot of cars, beginning with the sprightly rear-engine 4CV introduced in 1947 (more than one million were produced before it was discontinued in 1961), continuing with the Dauphine (the first French car to have a model run of more than two million), and the Renault 4 (more than five million sold since 1961).

In the quarter of a century after it was nationalized, Renault grew into a giant that maintained one hundred plants in twenty-one countries, held the premier position in the European car market, led all French companies in exports, and made, through some thirty divisions and subsidiaries, cars, trucks, buses, trolleys, tractors, marine engines, bicycles, motorcycles, machine tools, and robots. It even showed the socialist flair of entering the car rental business, becoming, after its 1981 acquisition of Britain's Godfrey Davis, the world's third-largest car renter, behind Hertz and Avis (the Renault unit is EuropCar).

Meanwhile, prodded by Communist-led unions representing the Renault workers, the company pioneered in social benefits. It established a three-week annual vacation in 1955, extending it to four weeks in 1962 and to five weeks in 1982. Retirement at 75 percent of pay was set for men at age sixty-two, women at sixty-one. Wages at Renault were 15 percent higher than the Peugeot scale.

It looked so good that the state-owned enterprise received a rave review in *Fortune* in May 1981. Writer Robert Ball found that "Renault got to the top in Europe by building practical, economical cars, not dreams. The guts of its cars have always been paramount. Renault was a pioneer of front-wheel drive and of the hatchback, concepts now so widely copied that there is some justice in Hanon's [Bernard Hanon, president of Renault then] assertion: 'Everyone makes Renaults today.' " And Ball added this clincher: "The most remarkable achievement of Renault's managers, however, has been to keep a nationalized enterprise from putting on flab."

Then it all fell apart. Renault's car sales plunged 12 percent in 1981, and the company posted its first postwar loss, remaining in the red for the next five years as it sustained the biggest deficits ever registered by a French company—$1.8 billion in 1984, $1.1 billion in 1985. Yesterday's hero became today's goat. It was suddenly discovered that instead of having no flab, Renault required eight thousand workers to make twelve hundred cars a day, while Fiat needed only six thousand and Japanese automakers, four thousand.

Central to Renault's downfall was a miserable showing in the world's largest car market: the United States. In France Renault was insulated from Japanese competition because the government, its owner, restricted Japanese imports to 3 percent of the market. Besides, French customs inspectors always know what to do with unwanted imports. One could always find some Japanese beetles in the carburetor. However, in the United States Japanese cars were big sellers, while Renault had to beat an ignominious retreat after its Dauphine fell apart on American roads. In 1978 Renault tackled the United States with a new strategy: It bought a controlling interest in the fourth-largest U.S. automaker, American Motors Corporation. AMC would sell Renaults in the United States, Renault would sell AMC's Jeeps in Europe, and together they would become one of the survivors in a world market capable of supporting fewer and fewer players. Renault, a major truck producer, also took a 40 percent interest in Mack Trucks.

The AMC investment coincided with an erosion of Renault's market position in France (it lost leadership to Peugeot) and Europe (Fiat, Ford, General Motors, and Volkswagen passed it). The French trade unions complained that the money being invested in America could be better spent at home. And there was no way Renault could point to any benefits accruing from its AMC tieup. AMC car sales declined from 163,000 in 1979 to 123,000 in 1985. A new Honda plant in Ohio was soon outselling American Motors. In 1985, on sales of $4 billion, AMC rolled to a loss of $125 million. Renault was looking at red ink on both sides of the Atlantic, and its name still meant nothing to most Americans.

Under socialism or capitalism the solution is the same: Fire the man at the top. Columbia University–trained Bernard Hanon, who became chairman of Renault when the Socialists came to power in 1982, was dismissed in 1985. In his place the Mitterrand government installed George Besse, the first outsider ever to head the auto company. Besse came from another nationalized outfit, the Pechiney metals company, which he had pulled out of the red by the capitalist tricks of cutting the work force and discarding unprofitable operations. He immediately began to apply the same remedy to Renault. At its peak Renault had 225,000 employees in all its 225 divisions, at home and abroad. By 1986 this payroll had been pared to 195,000, and the biggest cuts were still to come in the French automobile plants.

Renault's losses were reduced in both 1985 and 1986, and the fifty-eight-year-old Besse was promising a return to profitability in 1987 when he was gunned down on November 17, 1986. The killing, committed by a man and a woman on a motorcycle, was believed to be the work of the French terrorist organization Direct Action.

Besse was replaced by another outsider, Raymond Levy, who also had a reputation as a fearless cost cutter and job eliminator. In his first message to employees, in January 1987, Levy vowed to turn Renault into "the most prosperous auto company in Europe." Two months later he announced that Renault was selling its 46.6 percent interest in American Motors to Chrysler. Renault, he said, would concentrate on rebuilding its market shares in France and Europe. First things first. Globalization could wait.

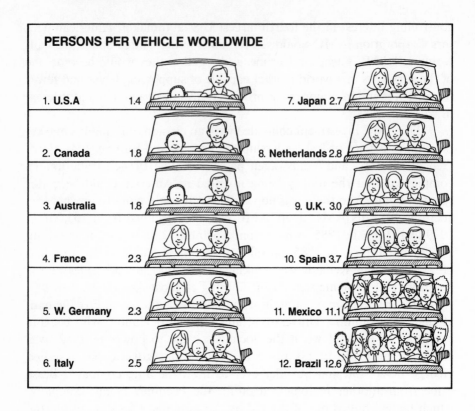

PERSONS PER VEHICLE WORLDWIDE

1. U.S.A — 1.4
2. Canada — 1.8
3. Australia — 1.8
4. France — 2.3
5. W. Germany — 2.3
6. Italy — 2.5
7. Japan — 2.7
8. Netherlands — 2.8
9. U.K. — 3.0
10. Spain — 3.7
11. Mexico — 11.1
12. Brazil — 12.6

It was clear, from various interviews with top French officials, what the Chirac government, which came to power in 1986, would like to do with Renault: Return it to private hands. One report said the government was considering a plan to give away shares in the company to every French citizen. However, before that could be done, Renault's finances would have to be improved. The state-owned company was staggering in 1987 under a debt load of $10 billion.

Access   34, quai du Point-du-Jour
B.P. 103, 92109 Boulogne Billancourt Cedex, France
(33) 1-46-09-1530

Reuters	
Sales	$930 million
Profits	$121 million
U.S. Sales	$150 million
Rank	World's largest financial information network
	World's 2d-largest news service
Founded	1851
Employees	6,850
Headquartered	London, England

Too late to catch the sailing of the English mail ship from New York the morning of April 15, 1865, James McClean, the U.S. correspondent for a youthful news service named Reuters, hired a tug, caught up with the mail ship, and threw aboard a canister containing a written news dispatch. The story told of the assassination of Abraham Lincoln, and in England Reuters was two days ahead of everyone with the news. Reuters likes to celebrate this event, which was depicted in the 1940 motion picture *Dispatch from Reuters,* starring Edward G. Robinson as Baron Reuter.

But if the truth were told, news scoops at Reuters have been few and far between. The news service, which allegedly competes with the Associated Press and United Press International, has rarely been the first choice of editors. And Reuters at times seemed to function as a ward of the British foreign service. During international conferences held in Geneva during the 1950s, Reuters-London used to Teletype the cricket scores daily to keep the British diplomats there *au courant* with the important matters in life. However, very few people realize that delivering the news has become a sideline of this outfit, and a not-too-profitable sideline to boot. From the very beginning of its existence in Germany, Reuters has had its eyes fixed firmly on the pursuit of money, and it has now come full circle.

The story begins on July 21, 1816, with the birth of Israel Ben Josaphat Beer in Kassel, capital of the German state of Hesse. His father was a rabbi, and not only did the son *not* follow in his father's footsteps, but he changed his name to Paul Julius Reuter and converted to Christianity. Reuter's first job was with a bank owned by a relative. There he learned the importance of timely news. Bankers needed to have the latest stock market quotations from Paris, but the newly launched telegraph system didn't reach everywhere. Reuter bridged the gap between Brussels and Aachen by organizing a fleet of carrier pigeons that could bring the news in two hours (as against nine hours by stagecoach). It was a coup (also celebrated in the 1940 movie) that marked him as a man destined for the news business.

London was the money center of the world, and Paul Julius Reuter headed straight for it, with a brief stopover in Paris to see Charles Louis Havas (a French Jew who was to establish the Havas news agency that eventually was taken over by the French government and became one of France's largest advertising agencies). Reaching London in 1851 Reuter set up shop in the City (the financial district) where he fed bankers and stockbrokers financial news from correspondents he recruited on the Continent. Soon he was relaying political and general news, conceiving the idea of selling this service to the British newspapers. In 1857 Reuter became a British citizen. And a year later he made his biggest sale, getting *The Times* to subscribe to his news service at the rate of two pounds, six shillings per twenty words, *if* Reuters was credited, and five pounds per twenty words if Reuters was not credited. He was always a canny businessman.

Reuters soon had offices throughout the world, especially in the British colonies (and ex-colonies), and Paul Reuter became a man-about-town in Victorian London. "He had a disconcerting habit," journalist Don Dallas once recounted, "of hiring a hansom cab in the middle of the night—sometimes clad only in pajamas and dressing gown—and descending upon the office, there to demand the latest news and issue directives." In 1871 the Duke of Saxe-Coburg-Gotha in Germany made Reuter a baron "in acknowledgement of his extraordinary qualities." And twenty years later Queen Victoria allowed Baron Reuter to have the same rank in Britain so that the title was passed on to his son.

On February 25, 1899, the Reuters news agency released a seventeen-word story: "Baron de Reuter, the founder of Reuters' Agency, died at Nice this morning in his eighty-third year." That was all he wanted. *The Times*, which had snubbed him at first, ran a long obituary hailing him as "one of the most intelligent men of his day."

Reuter's son, Herbert de Reuter, was very British. Educated at Harrow and Oxford, he married a Scottish lady, Edith Campbell, and was known for his bookishness. He presided over Reuters from offices at 24 Old Jewry in the City. Like his father he was fascinated by financial information, but in his case it led to a near disastrous diversion when he decided to have the company enter the banking business. In 1913 Reuters Bank was established with a capital base of £1 million. In less than two years the bank was losing so much money that it swallowed all of the reserves carefully husbanded over many years by the news service. In

1915, three days after the death of his invalid wife, Baron Herbert de Reuter shot and killed himself. A year later his only son, Hubert, died in Flanders, fighting in the ranks of the famous 42nd Highlanders. He chose a Scottish regiment because his mother had been a Campbell.

Roderick Jones, who had headed up Reuters in South Africa, took the helm in London in 1915 when he was only thirty-seven years old. Backed by the Union Bank of Scotland, he bought out all the Reuter family shares. In 1917, when he sold the Reuters Bank, he was able to repay the loan from the Scottish bank. Jones (later Sir Roderick) remained in command of Reuters until 1941, and it was his idea, taken from his experience in South Africa, to forge an alliance with the British newspaper publishers. Thus, they came to own the Reuters news service the way American newspaper publishers own the Associated Press.

A combine was formed that by 1946 included not just the British newspaper publishers but the publishers in Ireland, Australia, and New Zealand. The agreement bound Reuters to be impartial and free from propaganda in the handling of the news. A key clause pledged the press barons to treat their shares "as a trust rather than an investment." Since the shares were practically worthless when this agreement was struck, the admonition was easily observed. However, in 1984, when Reuters sold stock to the public, the lucky publishers realized a windfall of $280 million. They also retained the majority of the shares. To preserve the integrity of the news service, the public was allowed to buy only Class B shares, which carry one vote, while the publishers held on to all the Class A shares, which carry four votes each.

How Reuters came to be worth $1.2 billion in an initial stock offering had nothing to do with delivering the news to newspapers and broadcasting stations. That part of its business now accounts for only 9 percent of total revenues. In a throwback to its founder, Reuters rediscovered that business people will pay good money for timely information.

The transformation began in 1964 when Reuters began selling stockbrokers in Europe a terminal on which they could summon up instant price quotations from the New York Stock Exchange. That was a winner. The next leap came in 1973 when Gerald Long, then managing director, decided to gamble the agency's financial future on a cockney clerk's idea for an electronic tote board for money. It was perfect timing. The system, called Monitor, came into play just after the world's currencies were set afloat. It was a tool made to order for the frenetic currency traders. In 1981 Reuters refined this service so that it can be used as a marketplace. *BusinessWeek,* in 1985, described how:

Foreign-exchange trader Tim Broome is hunched over his desk, enveloped in the din of Barclays Bank's vast trading room in London. Currency rates blink on one of his three Reuters monitors. On another screen, a code flashes—an outside dealer is calling via Reuters's financial communications network. It's Banca Toscana in Florence, asking for the spot rate for West German marks. Broome types in the price, and, two seconds later, the anonymous trader buys $1 million worth. The traders arrange to transfer the money and sign off. Elapsed time: seven seconds.

What Reuters does then is collect financial information from all corners of the world and feed it into electronic data bases not simply for the edification of its subscribers but for use in their businesses. And for *immediate* use because this is "real time" information reflecting transactions just made somewhere in the world. The Reuters information belt covers currency and money market instruments, stocks and bonds, commodities, shipping, spot oil trading. And Reuters increasingly wants to be not just an information source but a dealing arena. It wants its computers to connect buyers and sellers, thereby replacing exchanges.

Reuters derives its information from three sources: its own reporters; 113 securities and commodities exchanges and over-the-counter markets around the world; and twenty-seven hundred subscribers who supply information about the markets in which they deal.

The people who subscribe to these services—and Reuters had forty-two thousand subscribers at the start of 1987—are people who *need* the information. They can be stockbrokers, banks, institutions that are large buyers of securities and financial instruments, governments, traders, and companies such as the ones profiled in this book—they do business in a variety of currencies and it's essential for them to know what's going on. A developing country that's heavily dependent on commodity sales (coffee, cocoa) needs this kind of information quickly too. At stake is a lot of money—real money, even though those quotes look like just blips on a Reuters screen.

Reuters sells its hardware and software at hefty prices, but when the information is so vital, a buyer is not going to quibble too much. The name of the game is to get your terminals into a customer's office. In 1987 Reuters had 108,000 terminals in place in 158 countries. In the global marketplace for financial instruments that was evolving in the 1980s, Reuters was sitting pretty as the seller of this information. It has competition, but as an early starter, it built up a long lead. "Reuters was way ahead of its time," said an admiring Keith Fuller, president of the rival Associated Press. "They did for business what the telephone did for the traveling salesman."

It doesn't take much elaboration to show that Reuters is on the right electronic track. In 1979 the company had revenues of $169 million; in 1987 it was a cinch to do more than $1 billion.

The Reuters financial news service does rely on the attribute that has always been the *sine qua non* of a news service: speed. "It's becoming increasingly difficult to divorce the concept of information from the concept of telecommunications," says Glen McG. Renfrew, a former reporter who succeeded Long as managing director in 1981. "The faster and further you move information, the more valuable it becomes."

In 1983 *Fortune* writer Shawn Tully drew this moral: "Reuters's managers stopped to ask themselves in a fundamental way what business they were in. The answer was information. The step from news dispatches to computerized quotes seemed natural after that." It's a moral Baron Reuter would undoubtedly have approved of. His bust stands today on the ground floor of the Fleet Street headquarters of Reuters, smiling benignly.

There's an old adage that journalism leads to everything—as long as

WORLD'S BIGGEST DAILY NEWSPAPERS	Circulation
1. **Pravda** (Moscow,Soviet Union)	10.7 million
2. **Yomiuri Shimbun** (Tokyo, Japan)	8.9 million
3. **Asahi Shimbun** (Tokyo, Japan)	7.5 million
4. **Izvestia** (Moscow, Soviet Union)	7 million
5. **Renmin Ribao** (Beijing, China)	7 million
6. **Bild** (Hamburg, West Germany)	6.3 million
7. **Mainichi Shimbun** (Tokyo)	4.1 million
8. **The Sun** (London, England)	4 million
9. **The Mirror** (London, England)	3.1 million
10. **Nikon Keizai Shimbun** (Tokyo)	2.2 million
11. **The Wall Street Journal** (New York)	2.1 million

you get out of it. Reuters has always known that. Of its 6,850 employees in early 1987, only 1,037 were journalists.

Access   85 Fleet St.
London EC4P 4AJ, England
(44) 1-250-1122

1700 Broadway
New York, N.Y. 10019
(212) 603-3500

Rhône-Poulenc

Sales $8.7 million
Profits $333 million
U.S. Sales $400 million
Rank France's largest chemical company
World's 10th-largest chemical producer
Largest chemical company in Brazil
World's largest producer of rare earth
oxides
Europe's largest maker of cigarette filters
World's 4th-largest producer of herbicides
and pesticides
World's 2d-largest producer of sodium
silicates
World's 3d-largest serum and vaccine
producer
Founded 1858
Employees 80,000 (48,000 in France)
Headquarters Paris, France

There's nothing like a dose of socialism to get a company moving again. That's the remedy the newly elected Socialist government of France prescribed in 1982 when it nationalized six industrial giants and thirty-nine private banks. In their number was Rhône-Poulenc, France's ninth-largest company and one of the major players in the world chemical industry.

State intervention in French industry is nothing new. It goes back to the seventeenth century and Jean-Baptiste Colbert, the father of mercantilism. French governments, no matter what their political orientation, have always kept a watchful eye over business enterprises, making sure they were doing well by *la patrie.*

In a major restructuring of the French chemical industry in 1968, a revamping orchestrated by the French government, Rhône-Poulenc emerged as Europe's third-largest chemical producer, ahead of the German trio of BASF, Bayer, and Hoechst. A dozen years later Rhône-Poulenc had slipped to seventh place—far behind its German rivals. Poulenc was simply not performing well, by capitalist standards. The company reported a horrendous loss of 1.9 billion francs in 1980, followed by a loss of 335 million francs in 1981. *Alors,* the Mitterrand government decided to give Rhône-Poulenc an injection that its capitalist owners didn't seem capable of administering.

It worked. By 1986 Rhône-Poulenc was reporting aftertax profits of a quarter of a billion dollars. The state-owned enterprise closed unprofitable factories, reduced employment, tied executive compensation to performance, and instituted profit-sharing plans for all employees. In 1985 Roger Ricklefs, staff reporter of *The Wall Street Journal,* visited an aging Rhône-Poulenc plant at Saint-Fons, near Lyon, to find that it had been transformed from a money loser into a profit maker. He reported that after Rhône-Poulenc was nationalized, Communist labor leaders told plant manager Jacques Cornilliat: "This is a nationalized company. We represent the workers. Now we'll decide what's going to be." Cornilliat's response, according to Ricklefs, was: "You represent workers, but I represent 50 million Frenchmen, and my job is to run a modern factory."

The nationalization law of 1982 decreed that six of Rhône-Poulenc's eighteen directors must be elected by the employees and seven appointed by the government. However, that representation did not mean the preservation of jobs at all costs. Rhône-Poulenc, under government ownership, chopped more than ten thousand people from the payroll.

Rhône-Poulenc is the embattled successor of a host of businesses, the two most important of which were a pharmaceutical company started in Paris in 1858 by a young pharmacist, Etienne Poulenc, and a chemical company, Société Chimique des Usine de Rhône, founded in Lyon in 1895. The two branches were united in 1928 as Rhône-Poulenc, which became France's standard-bearer in the chemical industry. Rhône-Poulenc was the first company in the world to develop cellophane. It also invented the chemical compound that SmithKline marketed in the United States as Thorazine, a tranquilizer that emptied beds in mental hospitals. As befitting a company with strong roots in Lyon, the textile capital of France, Rhône-Poulenc has long been an important producer of chemical fibers (nylon and polyester). It ranks among the world leaders in production of agricultural chemicals (fertilizers, herbicides), silicones, magnetic tapes, and floppy discs. And it is the world's number one supplier of rare earths (oxides), which are used in the glass, optical instrument, and ceramics industries.

Rhône-Poulenc's 50 percent–owned subsidiary, Institut Merieux, joined forces in 1984 with the famed Institut Pasteur of Paris in a joint venture that will produce serums and vaccines and conduct biotechnology research. The two groups had already worked together to develop the HPA23 vaccine, the treatment AIDS victim Rock Hudson had sought when he came to Paris before his death in 1986. Institut Merieux, based outside Lyon, has the distinction of being the world's largest user of placentas, which it employs in the production of disease-fighting blood derivatives. Marcel Merieux, who founded the laboratory in 1897, was a former pupil of Louis Pasteur.

Rhône-Poulenc has a mighty international presence, deriving 70 percent of its sales outside France. It went to Brazil in 1919 to make perfume sprays for the annual carnival. It stayed to become the Rhodia Group, the largest chemical producer in the country, with sales of about $1 billion a year. The French chemical company also does a substantial business in Communist bloc countries. In 1980 it signed a ten-year trade agreement with the Soviet Union to provide the Russians with chemical plants, fertilizers, and animal feedstuffs in return for raw materials such as naphtha, methanol, and crude oil. As a result Rhône-Poulenc sold $300 million worth of products to Eastern Europe in 1984. Rhône-Poulenc's sales to China are on a par with its sales to Canada or Algeria. The company is also the only Western outfit to have survived the Vietnam War in Vietnam: It kept its office in Ho Chi Minh City (formerly Saigon), where it has a fifty-fifty venture with the Vietnam health ministry, producing Vitamin C, aspirin, and cough syrup.

The United States has been a minor market for Rhône-Poulenc, accounting for about 5 percent of its sales. In 1978 it drove what appeared to be an opening wedge when it acquired 20 percent of MortonNorwich, a Chicago-based company whose products included Morton salt, Pepto-Bismol, Unguentine, and Fantastik spray cleaner. Four years later it sold off its holding at a profit. In 1986, however, flush with Socialist-induced profits, Rhône-Poulenc forked over $575 million to Union Carbide to take

---

World's Largest Sellers of Agrochemicals (euphemism for pesticides and herbicides)

1. Bayer (West Germany)	$2.3 billion
2. Ciba-Geigy (Switzerland)	1.8 billion
3. Imperial Chemical Industries[1] (United Kingdom)	1.4 billion
4. Rhône-Poulenc (France)[2]	1.4 billion
5. Monsanto (United States)	1.0 billion
6. Du Pont (United States)[3]	1.0 billion

World market: $17.4 billion

[1]Including 1987 acquisition of Stauffer Chemical's agrochemicals business.
[2]Including 1985 acquisition of Union Carbide's agrochemicals business.
[3]Including 1985 acquisition of Shell's agrochemicals business.

over the American company's worldwide agricultural chemicals business. It was said to be a good match because the French company had been traditionally strong in herbicides and fungicides, while Carbide's strength was in insecticides.

The Carbide business swung into the Rhône-Poulenc column with annual sales of $450 million, 3,600 employees, and U.S. facilities at Institute, West Virginia; Research Triangle Park, North Carolina; Woodbine, Georgia; Clinton, Iowa; Saint Louis and Saint Joseph, Missouri; and Ambler, Pennsylvania. Outside of the United States, the Carbide name was replaced by Rhône-Poulenc at plants in Calgary, Canada; Beziers, France; and Cubatao, Brazil. Not included in the sale was the Union Carbide pesticide plant at Bhopal, India. Whew!

Access   25, quai Paul Doumer
92408 Courbevoie Cedex, France
(33) 1-47-68-1234

Black Horse Lane
Monmouth Junction, N.J. 08852
(201) 297-0100

Rover	**Sales** $5.1 billion
	Profits Nil ($1.3 billion loss in 1986)
	Rank Britain's largest automaker
	Britain's 2d-largest seller of cars
	World's 16th-largest automaker
	Britain's 5th-largest employer
	Founded 1906
	Employees 73,000
	Headquarters London, England

Imagine a multiple-car collision, with a dozen or so vehicles smashing into one another, and you have arrived at a fair approximation of what has happened in the British automobile industry. Rover, the mangled result of nearly a century of incompetent management, is a state-owned enterprise formerly called BL Ltd., and before that, British Leyland. Under whatever name, it's a disaster.

Britain was on the winning side in World War II, but afterwards the Japanese and German auto industries outstripped their British counterparts. Newspaper and magazine headlines tell an unremitting tale of woe: "Saving Leyland Is a Job for Hercules," "British Leyland Hovers on the Edge of Extinction," "Can Britain's Nationalized Carmaker Stay on the Road?" It has been a well-ventilated struggle for survival.

When BL Ltd. held its annual meeting on July 8, 1986, a proposal to change the company's name to the Rover Group failed on a show of hands to get the required 75 percent majority. And just before that vote, a motion to censure the board of directors *passed* by a vote of 849,000 shares to 611,000. However, in the final tally, one person voting the government's shares easily overturned those results. Her Majesty's Government happens to own 99.7 percent of all the shares. Most of the other shares are held by diehards who refused to sell them when a Labour government nationalized the company in 1975.

During the 1986 meeting the company's new chairman, Graham Day, a Canadian who was recruited from the shipping industry, argued for the corporate name change by pointing out that Rover was about to introduce two new cars in the American market—the Rover Sterling and the Range Rover. He thought it wise "not to remind people of the problems" associated with the Leyland and BL names, as if anymore than .2 percent of the U.S. population had ever heard of Leyland. When one shareholder commented that BL "was a ridiculous name in the first place," Day replied, "May I say amen to that."

The Leyland name as the corporate monicker preceded the government takeover. Leyland Motors was a profitable builder of trucks and buses in the post–World War II years. It grew by taking over Standard-Triumph in 1961 and Rover in 1967; the former it saved from collapse, the latter it saved from being a small company in a world increasingly dominated by giants. At the time Leyland was the largest truck builder in Europe. It then used the profits from trucks to subsidize the passenger car business. It was a double-fault strategy. The cars flopped in the marketplace, and under-investment in the truck side eroded what had been a dominant position. Between 1968 and 1980 Leyland didn't introduce any new truck models. In addition, Leyland's engines developed a tendency to "blow up," making them difficult to sell. In the 1970s Leyland's share of the British truck market was halved.

Meanwhile, the two pioneers of the British auto industry, Austin Motors (founded in 1906) and Morris Motors (founded in 1910) merged in 1952 to form British Motor Corporation, and subsequently—after acquiring Pressed Steel Company, a builder of automobile bodies, and Jaguar—it became British Motor Holdings. The merger of British Motor Holdings with Leyland Motors yielded British Leyland in 1968. Seven years later, on the verge of bankruptcy, British Leyland was rescued by the government.

Grouped in British Leyland were just about all the British-owned vehicle manufacturers, save some small producers like Rolls-Royce and Lotus. Outside the pale were the foreign-owned operations of Ford, General Motors (Vauxhall), and Talbot (Peugeot). Building cars in Britain was always an idiosyncratic affair. They certainly produced vehicles that caught the imagination of car fanciers: the Rolls-Royces, the Morgans, the Morris Minis, the Austin-Healeys, the MGs, the Jaguars, the Land Rovers, not to mention the ill-fated Woolseley. Woolseley came out in 1925 with its Silent Six model—it had as its radiator ornament six Ku Klux Klansmen in a circle. Woolseley advertised its car as being utterly silent; as a result, owners returned their cars to the factory at the slightest noise. Woolseley, under water by 1927, was acquired by Morris at a bargain price. It was the first of the acquisitions leading to the quagmire of BL Ltd.

More than one observer has noted that the British have never put together a disciplined automobile industry to match the Americans, Germans, Japanese, French, and Italians. The leaders of the British auto industry—Lord Nuffield (Morris) and Lord Austin—didn't build strong companies. There's a famous picture that appears in many automotive histories showing Morris cars being assembled in 1925 at the Cowley plant near Oxford by workmen standing at stationary places; Morris didn't put in a moving production line until the 1930s. G. Turner, a British historian of the motor industry, described Austin and Morris in the 1930s as "essentially one-man operations which had outgrown their founders, who failed to provide them with either management in depth or organization geared to the growth of the industry." Even after the 1952 merger of Austin and Morris, the two companies maintained separate boards of directors and separate books until 1966. And according to one study, the "cars assembled partly in one company's plants and partly in the other's were sold from one company to another, and sometimes back again." Leyland Motors was not much better. One analyst described it as a "loose collection of lorry companies, often competing with one another."

That was the legacy of British Leyland. In 1978, three years after the nationalization, *Fortune* summed up the situation as follows: "British Leyland seemed to be driven by a death wish, under a management that was at once lavish in spending, slow in reacting, and lacking in circumspection. . . . Leyland's plight sprang from its ineffective management, unworkable organization, outdated models, and reputation for poor quality. Its labor-relations record has been so bad that 250,000 cars—a quarter of potential output—were lost in work stoppages last year."

In 1977 Sir Michael Edwardes arrived on the Leyland scene. He was like a British Iacocca. A diminutive, South African–born dynamo, he was ready to play hardball with truculent labor leaders and ineffectual managers. In his five years at the helm, he eliminated eighty-two thousand jobs, closed four car plants, two truck plants, and a bus factory. He fired a militant shop steward, Derek Robinson, and made it stick. And despite many anguished cries from sentimentalists, he closed down the MG line. Did it work? Not really. When Sir Michael left in 1982 BL was still losing money, its market share had fallen from 28 percent to 18 percent, and its payroll had fallen from 198,000 to 105,000. Still, not too many people were ready to fault him. They blamed history.

Sir Michael did initiate a new venture that some people see as the salvation of the company. The Austin Rover division is working with Japan's Honda Motor to produce Honda-designed cars at the old Morris plant in Cowley. The first of those cars was the Triumph Acclaim, introduced in 1981 at a price of $7,500. Another product of this Japanese-British combo is the $19,000 Sterling, introduced in the United States in 1987. (The same Honda design is sold as the Acura Legend.)

John Koten and Lawrence Ingrassia, two *Wall Street Journal* reporters, visited the Cowley plant at the end of 1983 and reported that the "single biggest plus of the new BL model was its high quality. As production began on the assembly line, workers were astonished at how well pieces went together. . . . BL believes the car reflects well on all its models and has helped repair its reputation for shoddy quality." The Honda engineers also brought an egalitarian style to the workplace. They ate in the cafeteria with factory workers rather than with BL managers. David Buckle, a union official at Cowley, said, "After a while, the lads were saying they wished Honda would take over the whole company."

That may one day come to pass. In 1984 the Jaguar division of BL was privatized, with shares sold to management, employees, and the public. The stock became one of the most heavily traded issues on the American over-the-counter market. In 1986 talks were initiated with General Motors and Ford about buying different pieces of Leyland. Ford was interested in Austin Rover, and GM was interested in the truck factories if it could also have the Land Rover, one of the icons of British colonialism. News of these negotiations kicked up a ferocious political storm. Prime Minister Margaret Thatcher said that the government could not continue to throw money at BL. Labour opponents rose in Parliament to declare that it would not be in the interest of Britain to have decisions about its automobile industry made in the boardrooms of North America. A public opinion poll showed that 77 percent of the British public wanted the company kept in British hands.

In the face of these protests, plans to sell or privatize BL were put on a back burner. However, big chunks of the company were sold off, including bus manufacturing, a spare-parts unit, the Australian subsidiary, a computer systems division, and the once-powerful truck operations. Leyland Trucks was spun off into a new Anglo-Dutch company controlled 60 percent by Daf of the Netherlands. It signaled the virtual end of truck manufacturing in Britain.

These divestitures raised cash and enabled Graham Day to concentrate on the two remaining parts of the company, Land Rover and Austin Rover. Land Rover makes the four-wheel-drive vehicles known for their ability to traverse rough terrains; its production in 1986 fell to twenty-one thousand, the lowest in thirty years. The Austin Rover division makes a series of cars ranging from a mini up to the Rover 800 luxury sedan sold in the United States as the Sterling.

Day, because of his previous jobs, has a reputation as a tough manager, a cost cutter. A lawyer who graduated in 1956 from Dalhousie University in Halifax, Nova Scotia, Day got his first job with Canadian Pacific. "To work for Canadian Pacific," he told Hazel Duffy of the *Financial Times,* "you were working for the country, not just earning a living. I want to feel that I'm doing more than earning a living."

America's Top Ten Exporters

1985 Exports (billions)

1.	General Motors	$8.8
2.	Ford Motor	6.7
3.	Boeing	5.8
4.	General Electric	4.0
5.	IBM	3.4
6.	Chrysler	2.9
7.	McDonnell Douglas	2.6
8.	Du Pont	2.5
9.	United Technologies	2.1
10.	Caterpillar Tractor	1.9

Britain's Top Ten Exporters

1985 Exports (billions)

1.	British Petroleum	$8.5
2.	Imperial Chemical Industries	4.5
3.	Shell	3.5
4.	Esso	3.4
5.	British Aerospace	2.4
6.	IBM	2.2
7.	General Electric Co.	2.1
8.	Ford	1.5
9.	British Steel	1.4
10.	Conoco	1.3

He is. His job is to salvage the largest British-owned automaker. In 1986 Rover's share of the British auto market fell below 16 percent, the lowest in thirty-five years. Britain's top seller is Ford, which runs a close second to Rover in British car production and also brings in more than one hundred thousand cars from its factories in continental Europe. Imports hold more than half of the British automobile market.

When British Leyland was nationalized in 1975, it had close to two hundred thousand employees. In 1987 seventy-three thousand were left.

Access Canly Rd.
Coventry CV5 6QX, England
(44) 203-70111

Austin Rover
8325 N.W. 53rd St.
Miami, Fl. 33166
(305) 593-1878

RTZ	**Sales** $6.4 billion
	Profits $360 million
	U.S. Sales $1.5 billion
	Rank World's largest mining company
	World's largest uranium producer
	World's largest producer of borates
	Produces 6 percent of the Western world's copper
	World's 3d-largest lead producer
	World's 3d-largest zinc producer
	Mines 5 percent of the West's iron ore
	Britain's 7th-largest industrial company
	Britain's 2d-largest cement company
	Largest producer of silica sand in the United States
	Britain's 25th-largest company (by market value)
	47th on the *Fortune* International 500
	Founded 1873
	Employees 82,550
	Headquarters London, England

Rio Tinto-Zinc, one of the more romantic names in the corporate firmament, was rubbed out at the annual meeting in 1987 when the shareholders of the company approved a proposal by management to adopt the name RTZ Corporation, thereby joining the long list of bloodless corporate acronyms (CPC, Primerica, Unisys, PPG, NYNEX). Rio Tinto had been a fixture on the British financial scene for more than one hundred years.

Over the course of that time it's difficult to think of something Rio Tinto-Zinc has *not* been accused of. Raping the land. Polluting the environment. Desecrating sites sacred to the native populations of Australia and Papua New Guinea. Helping to support the apartheid policies of South Africa. Exploiting Third World countries. Putting mineral rights above human rights. These—and other charges—have been regularly deposited on RTZ's elegant doorstep in London's St. James's Square, from which vantage point it oversees the digging, drilling, and extraction of natural resources on five continents. It has an interest in virtually every metal and fuel used in the world.

It all began in 1873 when Hugh Matheson, a Scotsman, leading figure in London financial circles, and an elder of the Presbyterian Church (he was known for his work in reclaiming London prostitutes), founded the Rio Tinto company for the sole purpose of reopening a 5,000-year-old copper mine in Spain. One activist group put it in more crass terms when it described the founding as follows:

> With vast profits from his uncle's opium trade [Matheson was a nephew of James Matheson, cofounder of the famed Far East trading company, Jardine, Matheson. See profile on page 307.], plus two million pounds raised from London speculators by understating risks and overrating capital returns, taking time off from endowing churches and reclaiming prostitutes, he bought the Rio Tinto Mine, named after the adjacent, heavily polluted river. Spain survived the major damage inflicted upon its economy, and the Rio Tinto Company flourished, becoming within five years the biggest mining company in the world. . . . Suppression of wages, exploitation of women workers and minimizing revenues to the Spanish government kept profits flowing—sulphur emissions blowing and many miners dying—until the late 1920s when Auckland Geddes took over.

Sir Auckland Geddes, the second in a series of Scotsmen to lead Rio Tinto in the erosion of the earth's surface, was a former anatomy professor at a Canadian university, a onetime British ambassador to the United States (Rio Tinto people have had a habit of going back and forth between the company and the government), and a clandestine playwright. *Through the Veil,* a psychic drama that he wrote under a pseudonym, was performed on the London stage in 1931 while he was running Rio Tinto. At the 1937 annual meeting, when civil war was raging in Spain, Geddes told the shareholders, "Since the mining region was occupied by General Franco's forces, there have been no further labor problems. . . . Miners found guilty of troublemaking are court-martialed and shot."

Geddes changed Rio Tinto from a one-mine company into a multinational operator. He teamed up with Sir Ernest Oppenheimer's mining company, Anglo American Corporation, to invade, in somewhat ruthless fashion, the Northern Rhodesian copper belt. After World War II Sir Val Duncan turned Rio Tinto into a world mining giant, extending its shafts into Canada, Australia, and South Africa. The key move was a 1962 merger uniting Rio Tinto with Consolidated Zinc, itself the result of a merger in the late 1940s combining Imperial Smelting with the Zinc Corporation.

It was through Consolidated Zinc that Rio Tinto acquired its fancy digs in St. James's Square. More important, the two companies meshed their mining operations in Australia, where Consolidated had started out in 1905 mining lead, zinc, and silver at Broken Hill, site of one of the world's richest ore bodies. Their Australian company was called, unimaginatively, Conzinc Riotinto, which later was shortened to CRA. It was Consolidated Zinc which made possible the Australian aluminum industry through its 1955 discovery of the Weipa bauxite deposits in Queensland. Bauxite is the raw material from which aluminum is formed, and the Australian lode is the richest in the world.

CRA was therefore a mining colossus on its own, and from its beginnings the Australian government looked askance at the Scotsmen in London pulling the strings. There has been constant pressure to Australianize the company, and Rio Tinto's share, 90 percent in 1962, was brought down to 49 percent in 1986. CRA ranks as the third-largest company in Australia. One of CRA's holdings is a 57 percent interest in the Argyle mine in Western Australia; it's now the world's largest producer of diamonds.

Being a partial owner is neither a new nor uncomfortable situation for RTZ. The mining business is so capital intensive that companies, more often than not, welcome partners to share the risk. Rio Tinto has a number of these partnerships going all over the world. Its Canadian arm, Rio Algom (uranium, stainless steel), is 52.8 percent–owned. Its Bougainville copper and gold mining unit in Papua New Guinea is 28 percent–owned. Many of these partnerships are with governments (Portugal, Panama, and Papua New Guinea). It has partnered with Kaiser Aluminum in a number of places.

If there's something to mine anywhere in the world, Rio Tinto will do it. So extensive is the company's worldwide mining operation that wags in London say that if there's a serious shortage of any natural resource, a government minister simply calls up RTZ and asks the company to take care of it. After the discovery of nuclear energy during World War II, the company started to mine uranium in Canada and Australia. It then spent twelve years putting in what is now the world's largest uranium mine in Namibia, the South-West African territory that South Africa continues to control in defiance of United Nations resolutions calling for its independence. The Rossing uranium mine began producing in 1976. It's 46 percent–owned by RTZ, which ranks as one of the largest foreign investors in South Africa and stands, as Anthony Sampson pointed out in his 1987 book *Black and Gold,* on the right wing of the political spectrum over the issue of apartheid.

Sampson recalls that in 1973 when Adam Raphael wrote a series of articles for the *Guardian* on wages paid by British companies in South Africa, Rio Tinto-Zinc was found to be paying more than half the workers at its Palabora copper mine below the poverty line. After the *Guardian* stories RTZ hiked its wages 50 percent, although Sir Val Duncan, when asked about reinvestment, said, "Palabora is in the position of being so profitable that the question of African wages is, in that context, irrelevant."

A 1968 move brought RTZ into California's Mojave Desert in still another mining escapade when it acquired a British company whose main holding is United States Borax & Chemical. That company mines the sodium borate known as borax that ends up as the cleanser 20 Mule Team, serves as an agent to control the rate of nuclear reactions, and has a variety of other uses (it's an ingredient of glass, glass-fiber insulation, and enamel). The Mojave mine and refinery near the town of Boron produces more than half of the Western world's borax. Six years after the acquisition, it was the scene of a violent labor confrontation between the company and striking members of the longshoremen's union. In the mid-1980s RTZ assumed a commanding position in the U.S. silica sands industry (silica is used to make glass, concrete, and many other materials) by acquiring first Pennsylvania Glass Sands and then Ottawa Glass.

RTZ's interest in nuclear energy brought Alistair Frame to the company in 1968. Once described as a "phlegmatic Scottish engineer," Frame had spent the previous thirteen years with the United Kingdom Atomic Energy Authority, where he rose to become director of the reactor and research groups. At RTZ he helped bring in the Rossing mine in Namibia and two years later in 1978 he became chief executive officer. Frame was responsible for changing the shape of RTZ, lessening its dependence on the cyclical metals business by moving the company into oil, chemicals, engineering, construction, and metal fabrication. As a result, by 1986 RTZ was doing only 35 percent of its sales in metals. And it no longer had to live and die by the rise and fall in the prices of copper and other commodity metals that it mines. Frame was knighted in 1981.

By now it's a tradition. People come to the annual meeting of RTZ and complain bitterly about the company's operations. Antinuclear activists come to protest RTZ's uranium mining. Opponents of South African apartheid come to denounce the company for its involvement in South Africa. And for years now representatives of the Australian aborigines have journeyed to London to hurl insults at RTZ, claiming its mines are ripping up their sacred sites. Australian mining executives are cynical about these claims. One of them once told a reporter, "The aborigines have an apparent capacity to find sacred sites wherever minerals are found, and they can usually set a price on that sacred site." At the 1985 annual meeting dissidents called for a one-minute silence honoring the victims of RTZ worldwide—and after the regular meeting was over, they held an alternative one. During the meeting Sir Alistair Frame accused a minister, the Reverend David Haslam, of being "un-Christian" for wanting the uranium mine in Namibia closed, thereby throwing people out of work.

Protests against RTZ have also found their way into a torrent of books, pamphlets, magazine articles, and films. Among them are: *River of Tears,* by Richard West; *Black Death, White Hands,* by Paul R. Wilson; *Massacres to Mining,* by Jan Roberts; *Ground for Concern,* by Mary Elliott. Britain's Granada TV produced the 1979 documentary *Strangers in Our Land* describing RTZ's mining operations in Australia and featuring interviews with leaders of the aborigines. After the film was shown on Australian television, RTZ's Australian unit, CRA, sued for defamation—and won. An Australian court ordered ABC Television of Australia to pay $295,000 to CRA. It was the biggest defamation award ever given an Australian company.

Through it all RTZ has kept a stiff upper lip. By now it is accustomed to the criticism. It remains the most profitable mining company in the world. In one of its recent ads, the company had this answer for its critics:

Multinationals have been subjected to a great deal of criticism, much of it ideological in origin and much of it ill-informed. Corporations should make certain that their policies are correct and in tune with current thinking. It is not enough for international companies to shelter behind the laws of the country in which they invest; their responsibilities go beyond that.

Any foreign investor has a clear responsibility to its employees and their families and, in the case of a mining company, to the local community, especially the indigenous population. The question both we as investors and the people who will be affected by a new operation must ask is, whether the benefits of major investment outweigh the disadvantages change may bring.

We do believe that the advantages overwhelmingly outweigh the disadvantages as we see the rising standards of living in the areas where we operate.

Of course when an investment becomes unprofitable, RTZ is not likely to maintain it for the benefit of the local community. Copper prices were so low in the 1980s that companies mining the red metal found it difficult to make money or even survive. The situation provoked an agonizing decision for RTZ, which owned 49 percent of Rio Tinta Minera in southern Spain, the very mine that gave the company its start—and name. *Financial Times* reporter Tom Burns visited Minas de Rio Tinto in 1986 and found the community up in arms over RTZ's plans to shut down the mine, which is located in a village with "prim little villas built for British engineers in the last century." Pickets had blockaded the open pit mine, hanging scarecrow dummies symbolizing the *capitalismo Ingles* and *ladrones* (robbers).

Jose Recio, minister of development in the Andalusian regional government, told Burns, "Rio Tinto Minera is more than a company. We're talking about five villages, about three hundred thousand people, who have lived off copper for more than one hundred years." The company's viewpoint was: "It is costing us 350,000 pesetas ($2,800) to produce one metric ton of copper, which we are presently able to sell for 185,000 pesetas—and that's simply operating costs without including financial charges."

By the end of the year, Rio Tinto-Zinc had closed down the mine that was the company's birthplace. At the same time the managers decided it was silly for one of the world's major corporations to carry the name of a small river in Spain.

Access   6 St. James's Square
London SW 1Y 4LD, England
(44) 1-930-2399

U.S. Borax
3075 Wilshire Blvd.
Los Angeles, Cal. 90010
(213) 381-5311

<table>
<tr><td rowspan="6">

Saatchi
&
Saatchi

</td><td>

Billings $8.2 billion (advertising placed on behalf of clients)

</td></tr>
</table>

Saatchi & Saatchi	**Billings** $8.2 billion (advertising placed on behalf of clients) **Revenues** $1.2 billion (commissions and fees) **Profits** $110 million **Rank** World's largest advertising agency group **Founded** 1970 **Employees** 13,000 **Headquarters** London, England

They did the advertising that helped the Conservative party defeat Labour and bring Margaret Thatcher to power. Their futuristic advertising for British Airways runs in fifty-one countries. They're handling Procter & Gamble advertising in thirty-four countries, M&Ms in twenty-five, IBM in six. They're advertising Ritz crackers in Italy, Pepsi-Cola in Korea, and the scenic splendor of Puerto Rico in West Germany. They changed the name of United States Steel to USX. They're Saatchi & Saatchi, the whirling dervish of the ad agency business.

Two brothers, Charles and Maurice Saatchi, started this agency in London in 1970 when they were twenty-seven and twenty-four years old, respectively. They did provocative advertising. An ad for the Health Education Council showed a man with a bloated stomach, the headline asking: "Would You Be More Careful If It Was You That Got Pregnant?" A 1983 poster for the Conservative party left the impression that the Labour party platform was identical to that of the Communist party. Television viewers will recall the British Airways commercial showing the entire island of Manhattan moving across the Atlantic Ocean.

Such is the capricious nature of this business (clients think nothing of sacking an agency if they believe they can get better work elsewhere) that Saatchi & Saatchi soared straight to the top in London, the most vigorous and sophisticated advertising market in the world outside of New York. Saatchi eclipsed agencies that had been around for more than five decades, including the former leader in the United Kingdom, the London arm of J. Walter Thompson.

Meteoric rises in the ad agency business are not new. It doesn't take a lot of capital to start an agency. All one needs is a client. But it's clear by now that Saatchi & Saatchi is a phenomenon of an entirely different order.

First: Their view of the world was global, and they sought to position themselves as the agents of globally minded advertisers. They used as their rallying cry the thesis mounted by the Harvard Business School guru Theodore Levitt: "The global corporation operates as if the world (or major regions of it) were a single entity. . . . Corporations geared to this new reality can decimate competitors that still live in the disabling grip of old assumptions about how the world works."

Second: They were very businesslike. They won a lot of advertising awards and made a lot of money. That was a plus for an agency that early in its life—in 1977—sold stock to the public. There's nothing investors appreciate more.

Third: They saw that the shortest route to the top was by doing what their clients do—acquire other companies. It helped to have a public stock listing, since it enabled them to scoop up other agencies by offering shares that had a ready market value.

Fourth: They not only thought—but acted—globally. They began by acquiring agencies in Britain and soon extended this shopping spree to other countries, especially the United States, the world's advertising capital.

Fifth: They aimed high. They wanted to become the biggest force in the worldwide advertising business. They put it this way: "We have long been believers that it was good to be big, better to be good, but best to be both." In 1986 they reached their goal. They become the world's largest advertising agency group.

Subsumed in Saatchi & Saatchi are at least fifty other companies. Most of them still operate under their own names, with their own clients. The size of the acquisitions have been stunning. In London the third-ranking ad agency, Dorland, is owned by the Saatchis, as is the tenth, KMP Humphreys Bull & Barker. In the United States Saatchi & Saatchi owns advertising agencies which rank second (Saatchi & Saatchi Compton), third (Ted Bates), sixteenth (Dancer Fitzgerald Sample, or DFS), twenty-second (William Esty), twenty-fourth (Backer & Spielvogel), and twenty-seventh (Campbell-Mithun).

Agencies are anonymous characters, and so those names don't mean much to people outside the business. What it does mean though is that Saatchi & Saatchi is the creative force behind the advertising for Miller Lite and Hyundai (Backer & Spielvogel), Tide and Comet (Saatchi & Saatchi Compton), Toyota cars and True cigarettes (DFS), Nature Valley granola bars and Betty Crocker potatoes (Campbell-Mithun), Xerox and Panasonic (Ted Bates), as well as many, many other products.

The common wisdom in the advertising business had been that an agency couldn't grow in this manner because of account conflicts. It's a no-no for an agency to do the advertising for a product that competes with the product of another client. Saatchi & Saatchi wasn't the first to try to get around this unwritten rule by having a group of agencies whose only ties were common ownership. The Interpublic Group (McCann-Erickson, SSC&B Lintas, Campbell-Ewald, Dailey & Associates, Lowe Marschalk) was operating on this concept when Saatchi & Saatchi was born. But no one, before the Saatchis, had put the concept to work on such a grand scale.

Not that there weren't strains in 1986 when the DFS, Backer & Spielvogel, and Ted Bates deals were done. General Foods removed Ted Bates from its agency lineup. Colgate-Palmolive pulled $100 million of advertising billings out of Bates, which had aligned itself with agencies handling the archenemy, Procter & Gamble. Procter & Gamble, Saatchi & Saatchi's largest client, wasn't happy either. It yanked $85 million of billings from two Saatchi agencies because of perceived conflicts with Johnson & Johnson and CPC International products.

Robert Goldstein, the late advertising director at P&G, explained the client's position: "It's not clear to me why two or three agencies operating with one ownership as parallel networks will contribute anything either to the clients or to the public, which those same agencies operating separately would not contribute. . . . They are basically saying that the companies we own are bigger, but the parts aren't going to work together. If the parts aren't going to work together, how can the clients be served?"

It's virtually impossible for a group of advertising agencies to avoid conflicts if the constituent members are to be of any size. At the start of 1987, for example, Saatchi & Saatchi agencies in the United States were handling the advertising for these automobile makes: American Motors and Renault (Compton), Toyota (Dancer Fitzgerald Sample), Nissan (William Esty), and Hyundai (Backer & Spielvogel). And overseas Saatchi & Saatchi agencies were handling Renault in Italy (Compton), Rover (Compton) and Honda in West Germany (Ted Bates), and Subaru (Compton) and Daihatsu (Ted Bates) in the Netherlands. Four months into 1987 Nissan announced that it would replace Esty as its American agency after ten years.

The Saatchis naturally don't agree that these are conflicts. They feel that parallel networks of agencies each can provide good service to their respective clients. And they have been successful in persuading clients that this is possible. In 1986, for example, Saatchi & Saatchi agencies were handling each of the following clients in three or more countries: Exxon and British Petroleum, Bayer and American Home Products, American Express and Citicorp. And each of these clients was being handled in five or more countries: Nabisco and Mars, IBM and Xerox, Panasonic and Philips, Heinz and Reckitt & Colman.

The way the Saatchis see it, "we live in an era of global communications," and the commercial victories will go to those who adopt "a global approach." The Saatchis in 1987 were able to offer advertisers two different international networks: Saatchi & Saatchi DFS Compton and Ted Bates Worldwide. In addition they were fielding a bunch of other agencies that had lives of their own. In the United States, for example, they owned twenty different advertising agencies.

The Saatchis look at their business the way a client looks at its marketplace: "How can we increase our market share?" In 1987 the Saatchis looked around the world and saw this picture: (1) They were the leading ad agency in the United States, Britain, and seven other countries; (2) they were among the top five in twelve other countries; (3) they had 150 offices around the world; (4) they were servicing sixty of the world's one hundred largest advertisers; (5) when one added up all the advertising done in the world, the Saatchi & Saatchi share came to 5 percent. The moral—to Saatchi & Saatchi—was clear. There is plenty of room to grow. The Saatchis undoubtedly have a shopping list of agencies to buy. In 1986, after the spate of Saatchi & Saatchi acquisitions, a small New York agency ran an ad identifying itself as a "non–Saatchi & Saatchi agency."

In the advertising agency business, a small number of people—copywriters and artists, buttressed by researchers and lorded over by account supervisors who deal with the clients—produce work (print ads and broadcast commercials) on which an enormous amount of money is spent according to decisions made by the agency's media department. The money goes, of course, to buy space in publications and time on radio and television. It's a peculiar business in that the agency is compensated for its services by a 15 percent commission granted to it by the media (newspapers, magazines, radio and television stations). In 1986 the Saatchi & Saatchi units handled a total of $8.2 billion of work for its clients. That money came in from clients and went right out. The gross revenues—the commissions from the media—came to $1.2 billion or 15 percent of client billings. An agency's biggest expense is people. Saatchi & Saatchi pays out about half of its income to its staffers in salaries.

Business, the Saatchis have also deduced, does not live by advertising alone. They built a company that does more than advertising by buying their way into a a variety of allied service businesses—management consulting, market research, public relations. Among the firms in the tent are the Philadelphia-based Hay Group (a leader in the design of compensation-and-benefit programs for companies); Rowland, a New York–based public relations outfit (one of the ten largest in the United States); Kingsway, a London public relations firm (one of the ten largest in the United Kingdom); Siegel & Gale, a New York design firm specializing in corporate identity programs; and the New York–based research organization Yankelovich, Skelly & White (the three principals of whom left in 1986 to start a new firm that doesn't bear their names). The Saatchis figure that in this area, which they call "consulting," their market share is even lower than it is in the advertising field. So they undoubtedly have a shopping list here too. Watch out, McKinsey, Arthur D. Little, and Booz, Allen & Hamilton!

The Saatchis themselves are remote characters. Operating in a flamboyant business, they stay on the sidelines, rarely giving interviews. That may account for the conflicting stories of their origins. According to a 1982 profile in *Advertising Age,* the Saatchis are first-generation Britons whose parents came from the Middle East ("the name is reportedly of Iraqi Jewish origin"). According to a 1984 profile in *Fortune,* the Saatchis are sons of a North London textile manufacturer "whose Sephardic Jewish forebears arrived in England generations ago."

The Saatchis themselves don't bother to correct the discrepancies. Their company speaks for itself. Since shares were first sold to the British public, they have appreciated in value by 100 times. In 1983 they became available on the American over-the-counter market through a Morgan Stanley underwriting at $16.50 a share. In the next three years they tripled in price, which is understandable in view of the profit performance: $7.8 million in 1983, $42 million in 1986. Saatchi & Saatchi was expected to earn more than $100 million in 1987.

The Saatchis are committed to achieving "for ourselves the very goal we are helping our clients to achieve—a sustainable competitive edge." They characterize their company as one that "enjoys an irresistible appetite for growth."

Access   15 Regent St.
London SW1 4LR, England
(44) 1-930-2161

767 Fifth Ave.
New York, N.Y. 10022
(212) 755-0060

Saint-Gobain

Sales $12.7 billion

Profits $237 million

U.S. Sales $2.2 billion

Rank France's 6th-largest industrial company

54th on the *Fortune* International 500

World's largest maker of cast-iron pipes

World's 2d-largest flat glass manufacturer

World's largest maker of "bricks" used in glass-making furnaces

World's 2d-largest maker of fiber cement for roofing and pipes

World's 2d-largest maker of insulation materials

Europe's largest maker of cardboard boxes and paper bags

World's 2d-largest maker of bottles

World's largest manufacturer of small bottles (for perfumes and drugs)

Founded 1665

Employees 142,400 (7,300 in the United States)

Headquarters Paris, France

One of the world's oldest companies, Saint-Gobain is a child of mercantilism, the virulent "each-country-for-itself" economic philosophy put into practice in the seventeenth century by Jean-Baptiste Colbert, finance minister for Louis XIV. It's a philosophy that says a nation should be as self-sufficient as possible. Therefore: Keep out foreign goods or tax them heavily, grow and make as much as you can yourself, export more than you import, and collect all the gold and silver you can lay your hands on. It's a philosophy that has endured in France.

Colbert started the Royal Glass Factory of Saint-Gobain (the name comes from a town fifty miles northeast of Paris) because he didn't see why the French had to import mirrors from Venice. Glass is made from sand

and the French could learn to make their own mirrors, he reasoned. And so they did, although it took about fifty years for the French to capture their home market from the Venetians. What made it possible was an invention by Bernard Perrot, a glassmaker from Orleans. In the 1680s Perrot developed a method of casting glass on a table. The molten glass was removed from the oven and tipped onto a copper table equipped with a laminating roller that worked the glass into a flat sheet of even thickness. The sheets were then cooled for eight days. This new technology displaced the glass blowers of Venice.

Perrot perfected his invention at Saint-Gobain, which built the long series of gilt mirrors that line the Hall of Mirrors at Louis XIV's Palace of Versailles. Protected by a government-sanctioned monopoly, Saint-Gobain went on from there to become Europe's largest glassmaker. Three centuries after its founding, Saint-Gobain was making glass in plants all over Europe, including three in Italy (at Caserta, Pisa, and Savigliano). The company supplies about one third of Europe's flat glass. On a world-wide basis it holds 15 percent of the market, second only to Pilkington of Britain.

Saint-Gobain has been international for a long time. It went into Germany in 1840, Italy and Spain in 1885. In 1986 it was operating 108 companies—fifty in France, fifty-eight in other countries—and deriving 63 percent of its sales outside France. Seventy percent of its employees worked outside France. And they do more than make glass. Saint-Gobain produces jars, bottles, insulation materials, refractory bricks (used to line furnaces), fiberglass, paper, plywood, and pipes (both plastic and iron). It also has a contracting and services division whose units build roads, construct buildings, airports, dams and power stations, distribute water, and pick up garbage. Saint-Gobain makes seven billion bottles a year. Its pipes carry water in more than one thousand cities in one hundred countries.

For a couple of centuries Saint-Gobain was managed for the benefit of rentiers, and it did little to innovate. It was, for example, one of the last glass companies in the world to convert its production facilities to the more efficient float-glass process developed by Pilkington. Saint-Gobain was so lethargic that in 1968 it became the target of a takeover attempt by BSN, a French glass container manufacturer one-third its size. The bid failed, thanks to the help Saint-Gobain received from the powerful Suez Group, investment banking descendant of the old Suez Canal Company. But two years later the Suez people forced Saint-Gobain to merge with Pont-à-Mousson, another old-line French company that had started out processing iron ore and became the world's largest maker of cast-iron pipes. The merger created a company with a long name, Saint-Gobain-Pont-à-Mousson (the Pont-à-Mousson was later dropped), and provided a lot of jokes, since Pont-à-Mousson was considered no more forward-looking than Saint-Gobain. *Forbes* called it a "shotgun wedding." One analyst called the combine "an over-muscled giant with no ideas." Another referred to it as "a Gallic tortoise."

Toward the end of the 1970s Saint-Gobain astounded European business circles by making a dramatic entry into high technology. It partnered with National Semiconductor of the United States to build a microchip plant in France, acquired a strong minority interest in France's largest computer maker, CII-Honeywell-Bull, and took a 30 percent interest in Italy's Olivetti. These moves were all made with the blessing of the French government, anxious to have France develop a strong high-tech industry. In 1981, however, the Mitterrand-led Socialist party was swept into power. Saint-Gobain feared the worst and ran a series of ads hoping to stave off nationalization. One pleaded:

> If we have succeeded in maintaining a considerable position abroad, and if we have become 50 percent international while retaining our French identity, it is because we have succeeded in becoming Brazilians in Sao Paulo, Germans in Aix-la-Chapelle, and Italians in Milan. Saint-Gobain and Pont-à-Mousson have been members of a partnership almost unique in the world because of its diversity and the balance of its international components. If one is willing to admit that this group has served France well, let us not take the risk of weakening it.

The appeal fell on deaf ears. Saint-Gobain was nationalized by the government. On top of that, the Socialists decided that Saint-Gobain was not the appropriate vehicle for French involvement in computers, and they forced the company to abandon its activities in this area.

Saint-Gobain's outpost in the United States is Certain-Teed Corporation, a Valley Forge, Pennsylvania, manufacturer of insulation and building materials (roofing, siding, windows). Over a period of years ending in 1976, Saint-Gobain accumulated 57 percent of the shares of Certain-Teed (whose annual sales exceed $1 billion), and it dispatched a Frenchman, Michel L. Besson, to head the company. In 1981 Besson was asked by *The New York Times* whether the nationalization of Saint-Gobain might result in the company concentrating its energies in France and forgetting the rest of the world. Besson replied, "These people, they are Socialists, but they are not stupid." And he added, "Whatever system you are working in, you need to make a profit."

Saint-Gobain did in fact fare well under state ownership. Its top management went unchanged, it trimmed its work force and in 1986, when a Conservative government bent on privatization came to power, it was making much more money than it did when it had a stock exchange listing. The Socialists may have ruled computers out of bounds for Saint-Gobain but they did permit the company to take a major stake in a large construction company (Société Générale d'Enterprise-Sainrapt et Brice) and a 20 percent participation in Compagnie Générale des Eaux. This huge, cash-rich company ($4 billion in sales) happens to be the world's largest distributor of drinking water and is busy across the world in a bewildering range of activities including the operation of three cable television networks in France; the cleanup of India's Ganges River; the building of a hydroelectric power plant at Montgomery Creek, California; and the supply of heating/incineration management services to the cities of Miami and Glen Cove, New York. Saint-Gobain wanted to have more than 20 percent of the water company, but the Socialist government said, "No, 20 percent is enough."

Saint-Gobain did become the first French company to be privatized by the Chirac government. The offering in November 1986 was a spectacular success. The stock was offered to the public at $50 a share, shot up immediately to $60 on the Paris Bourse, and went to $70 in 1987. Employees of the company and small investors were given preference by the government. Ten percent of the shares were reserved for the employees, who could buy them at 5 percent discount. Investors who wanted ten shares or less had their orders filled in full before any large blocks were allocated. And as an incentive for people to hold on to their stock, the government said it would issue one free share for every ten bought if the purchaser held the shares for eighteen months (up to a total of five free shares).

Prior to being nationalized Saint-Gobain had 250,000 shareholders. Now it has 1.5 million. Four thousand of them showed up on February 27, 1987, at the Zenith rock music concert hall in Paris to attend the first "free again, free again" annual meeting. To greet the new shareholders Saint-Gobain had more than one hundred attractive hostesses. The affair set the company back $400,000. On the other hand, it was reporting record profits. Socialism had been a tonic to Saint-Gobain. As the French daily *Le Monde* commented in 1985: "There is hardly any difference in France between state capitalism and private capitalism."

Access   18, avenue d'Alsace
92096 Paris-La Defense, France
(33) 1-47-62-3000

Certain Teed Corp.
750 Swedesford Rd.
Valley Forge, Pa. 19482
(215) 341-7000

Schlumberger	**Sales** $4.5 billion
	Profits Nil ($2 billion loss in 1986)
	U.S. Sales $1.7 billion
	Rank World's largest oil well tester
	Founded 1919
	Employees 49,660
	Headquarters New York, Paris, and Tokyo

Did you ever wonder how oil companies know where to drill? Wonder no more. The answer lies in Schlumberger, a worldwide engineering giant founded by two brothers, Conrad and Marcel Schlumberger, who were born in the Alsace region of France in 1878 and 1884, respectively. The brothers were financed by their father, Paul Schlumberger, who made them swear to put research ahead of profit—and they went on to prove Henry Higgins wrong. It is Professor Higgins, in *My Fair Lady,* who insists, "The French never care what they do, actually, as long as they pronounce it properly." In real life the folks at Schlumberger Ltd. are used to hearing their name mispronounced every whichway, from "Shlum-burger" to "Slumber-jay" (correct is "Shloom-bear-zhay"), but when it comes to what they do, they care very much.

At stake is domination of the petroleum landscape in 115 countries to the point where 70 percent of the measuring and logging of oil and gas reserves throughout the world—more than 90 percent in some places—is the work of Schlumberger crews. Indeed, it bespeaks not just faithfulness to the original fatherly fiat but the sheer size of the company that Schlumberger spends more each year on research than its closest competitor earns in profits.

Much of the research aims at refining and improving the "wireline" techniques that Schlumberger developed to divine not only whether oil or gas is present, but what kind, what quality, and the best way to get at it. Schlumberger sells this service for a hefty price (the company's profit margin—how much it earns on its sales—has been among the highest in the world), but the buyers, oil prospectors, are happy to pay it. They have a lot riding on Schlumberger's predictions. And what they pay for those predictions is only a fraction of what they will have to spend on drilling a field. So they consider it money well spent.

For Schlumberger it has translated into a bonanza the likes of which the founders could never have imagined. In 1979 *Forbes* found that Wall Street investors were willing to pay so much for Schlumberger shares that the company had the fifth-highest market value of any company listed on the New York Stock Exchange—after IBM, AT&T, Exxon, and General

Motors. In 1982 the company earned $1.3 billion *after* taxes, a profit exceeded by only fourteen other companies in the world. And even in 1987, when its stock was selling at less than half of what it sold for six years earlier, *BusinessWeek* found that in terms of market value Schlumberger ranked fortieth in the United States—ahead of such biggies as Boeing, Citicorp, Weyerhauser, and Xerox.

In 1981 *New Yorker* writer Ken Auletta bounced around Wall Street asking two questions: "What's the best company in the world?" and "What's the best company with an extraordinary chief executive officer?" The answer to both questions turned out to be the same: Schlumberger, a company most people outside the oil patch had never heard of.

The extraordinary chief executive was an articulate, elegant Frenchman named Jean Riboud. (Auletta described him as "a fiercely competitive capitalist who nevertheless calls himself a Socialist.") In many ways the antithesis of the establishment image, Riboud included artists, poets, journalists, and President François Mitterrand among his closest friends. He would come to be called, in the words of investment banker Felix Rohatyn, "a unique person—a true Renaissance man."

Born in Lyon in 1919, Riboud joined the French Resistance in World War II, was captured by the Germans and sent to Buchenwald, emerging at war's end ridden with tuberculosis and weighing ninety-eight pounds. The Communists imprisoned at Buchenwald had saved his life so that, as he later told interviewers, nobody "could make me believe that the French Communists were bad."

Auletta recounted that Riboud's first job after the war was to open a New York office for French investment banker André Istel. "You're out of your mind, Monsieur Istel," he said. "I've never worked and I can't speak a word of English. What can I do for you?" Istel shrugged. "If I had Napoleon at my disposal, I wouldn't be asking you," he said. "But I don't have Napoleon, so it's my problem, not yours."

In due course Riboud's work as an investment banker came to the attention of an aging Marcel Schlumberger, one of Istel's principal clients, and a similar conversation ensued. "I don't like banking," Riboud confessed. "Why not come to work for me?" Schlumberger suggested. "Doing what?" Riboud asked. "I haven't the foggiest idea," Schlumberger said. Nonetheless, in 1965, a dozen years after the death of Marcel Schlumberger, his son Pierre stepped down as president, and the family named Riboud to succeed him. Within two decades, throughout a reign that ended only a month short of his own death from cancer in 1985, Riboud was instrumental in forcing four more Schlumbergers to leave the company. "If you want to be Saint Francis of Assisi," he once said, "you should not head a public company."

But in those same two decades the value of a share of Schlumberger grew to be thirty-five times what it was when Riboud took over. And his philosophy that one must "shake the tree" to guard against inbred complacency has prevailed to the point where today, while ownership of 25 percent of the stock has made them one of the world's wealthiest families, not a single Schlumberger descendant remains an officer of the company. However, in 1986 three Schlumbergers—Pierre Marcel Schlumberger (a lawyer in Houston), Nicholas Seydoux (chairman of the French film company, Gaumont), and Georges de Menil (an economics professor at the prestigious École des Hautes Etudes en Sciences Sociales in Paris)— held seats on the board, along with Felix Rohatyn of Lazard Frères and Jerome Weisner, former science advisor to President Kennedy.

It's a far cry from the November day in 1919 when Paul Schlumberger, his own scientific dreams frustrated by the demands of an ultrasuccessful textile machinery business, formed a partnership with his two sons—Conrad the scientist and Marcel the engineer—to find the best way to probe the earth's subsurface. The breakthrough came in 1927 with the successful use of a "sonde," a measuring device lowered by cable into a hole drilled in the earth. The sonde confirmed Conrad's theory that if the electrical resistivity of various rock formations could be measured, it would be possible to make an accurate prediction of whether oil was present. The Schlumbergers produced in effect the first X ray of an oil well. The designer of the sonde was a young engineer, Henri Doll, who was married to Conrad's daughter.

Ten years after this discovery Schlumberger was testing a thousand wells a month around the world. Its success did not go unnoticed. In 1940, with the German armies advancing on Paris, Halliburton, the U.S. oil field service company that was Schlumberger's chief rival, offered Marcel $10 million for the company. According to the account related by Riboud to Auletta, "Marcel made no reply but slowly rose from his chair, and beckoned (Erle P.) Halliburton to follow him. They walked silently to the elevator, where Marcel thanked his visitor and said goodbye." Why did he refuse? Riboud explained, "Because there are some things you never discuss. If somebody were to come and ask you to sell your wife, you wouldn't hesitate to say no, would you?"

Schlumberger evolved into the quintessential multinational: Incorporated in a Caribbean tax haven, the Netherland Antilles; it has executive offices in New York, Paris, and Tokyo; its shares are listed on the stock exchanges in New York, Paris, London, Amsterdam, Frankfurt, and Zurich; its board of directors in 1986 included citizens of France, Japan, and the United States; it had a worldwide employee force of fifty thousand but fewer than two hundred people at its corporate command post in New York. Riboud was proud that Schlumberger had no single national identity and that a third of its employees were coming from the Third World. "If I have one purpose today," he told Auletta, "it is to expand the concept of merging together into one enterprise Europeans, Americans, and citizens of the Third World."

The cash gusher uncorked by its ability to detect the presence or absence of oil enabled Schlumberger to acquire a number of other businesses. It paid $1 billion in 1984 to buy the giant offshore driller, SEDCO. Now it's one of the world's leading suppliers of oil drilling rigs, on land and offshore. It is also the world's largest producer of electric meters and maybe water and gas meters as well. And its Paymatec subsidiary is France's largest producer of "smart cards," which herald the brave new world where consumers will not need cash or checks to make purchases.

However, Riboud's most fateful purchase, for $425 million in 1979, was California-based Fairchild Camera & Instrument, erstwhile leader of the semiconductor industry—the manufacture of the tiny chips, or integrated circuits, that power computers. Riboud rhapsodized about the synergy. "We are collectors and interpreters of data," he told the New York Society of Security Analysts in 1980. "Fairchild is the keystone to Schlumberger measurement technology. Coal and oil have made the Industrial Revolution because they brought abundant and cheap physical power. Microprocessors and memory will make another revolution because they bring abundant and cheap intellectual power."

The reality was something else. Despite an infusion of more than $500 million into new plants and research facilities, Schlumberger was no more able to turn Fairchild around than any of its previous leaders. Fairchild was a drag on profits from the time it was bought through 1985, when Schlumberger took a massive writeoff of $511 million, resulting in the lowest profits for the company in more than a decade. During that 1979–85 period Fairchild's work force was reduced from twenty-five thousand to eleven thousand.

Michel Vaillaud, an engineer whose father had worked in the French postal system, succeeded Jean Riboud as Schlumberger's chief executive in September 1985. Just before taking the helm, he told the *Financial Times* that Schlumberger had the patience to wait out its Fairchild commitment. "We could go on forever," he said. "We are peasants. It could take one hundred years. If it takes one hundred years, it doesn't matter."

A year later, Vaillaud was out—replaced by Dr. Euan Baird, the first American to head the company—and Schlumberger announced that it was giving up on Fairchild. The company said it had agreed to sell 80 percent of the chip maker to the big Japanese computer company Fujitsu. However, the United States government then stepped in and blocked the deal, declaring that national security would be threatened by Japanese control of Fairchild. Schlumberger was finally able to sell Fairchild in August 1987 to National Semiconductor at a huge loss.

For Schlumberger it was a trying time. With the world awash in oil and prices depressed, no one was rushing to put up oil rigs. The erosion of its oil field business, together with the end of its Fairchild experiment, led to writeoffs resulting in a $2 billion loss reported for 1986. On top of that, Schlumberger found itself in a fight with the Internal Revenue Service, which was seeking back taxes for logging operations in the outer continental shelf. Down through the years Schlumberger's tax rate has been about 25 percent. In the Netherland Antilles, where the company is incorporated, the tax rate is 3 percent. Schlumberger pays taxes in more than one hundred countries around the world.

No matter what happens, Schlumberger can handle it. The company is virtually debt-free and had liquid assets of about $2.8 billion at the start of 1987.

Access   277 Park Ave.
New York, N.Y. 10172
(212) 350-9400

42, rue Saint-Dominique
75007 Paris, France
(33) 1-40-62-1000

7-1, Nishi-Shinjuku 2-chome, Shinjuku-ku
Tokyo 160, Japan
(81) 3-342-1551

Shell

Sales $64.7 billion
Profits $3.7 billion
U.S. Sales $16.9 billion
Rank World's largest manufacturing company
  (ranked by assets)
  World's largest oil company (ranked by
  reserves)
  World's 2d-largest oil company (ranked by
  sales)
  World's 3d-largest manufacturing company
  (ranked by sales)
  World's 3d-largest company (ranked by
  profits)
  World's largest company outside United
  States
  World's largest seller of gasoline
  Largest seller of gasoline in the United States
  World's 9th-largest chemical company
Founded 1907
Employees 138,000 (34,000 in the United States)
Headquarters London, England and The Hague,
  the Netherlands

When you pull up at a Shell service station in the United States, you have reached the end of a long and complicated supply line. It's most unlikely that the gasoline you pump into your car was refined in Port Sudan from oil piped up in Gabon—but with Shell, it's possible. Shell does bring up oil from the fields offshore of the East African nation Gabon, and it does operate a refinery in the North African city of Port Sudan. However, those facilities are undoubtedly serving markets closer at hand than the United States, where Houston-based Shell Oil is big enough to stand on its own feet, without much help from its sister Shell companies.

In fact, the Shell gasoline you put in your car may be derived from crude oil pumped by another oil company. Shell happens to be a company that buys more than half the crude oil it needs on the open market. After running the crude through its refineries, Shell sells it as Shell gasoline. Or, depending on the supply and price situations, a Shell company will buy gasoline from another company's refinery, and sell it as Shell gasoline. This is a company whose trademark is flexibility.

Shell has a mystique that sets it apart from the other giants of the petroleum industry. It is first of all the most international of all the oil companies, with operations that literally span the globe. Shell has companies operating in 103 countries of the world, deriving 46 percent of its sales from Europe, 24 percent from the United States, 18 percent from other countries in the Eastern Hemisphere, and the remaining 12 percent from other countries in the Western Hemisphere. You can travel from one end of the world to the other and, with the exception of the Communist bloc countries in Europe, everywhere you go, you will see that bright yellow scallop shell on a red field. It means gasoline in, among other places, Brunei, Turkey, Zimbabwe, Italy, Argentina, New Zealand, the Fiji Islands, Japan, Iceland, Ethiopia, South Korea, and the Ivory Coast.

Shell has somehow managed to keep that ubiquitous flag from carrying any particularly strong national connotation—that is, the company appears British or Dutch or American, as the case may be. Shell Française maintains a strong French character, and Deutsche Shell strives to be German. Most Americans probably believe Shell is an American company. And around the world, while Esso and Caltex and Total and British Petroleum are quickly identified with their home countries, that is not so much the case with Shell.

Gerrit A. Wagner, a Dutchman who spoke five languages fluently and who headed Shell from 1972 to 1977, once called the company "one of the three most truly international institutions in the world." The other two he was thinking of were the Catholic Church and the United Nations. His predecessor, David Barran, a monocled Englishman who spoke three languages fluently and who graduated from Cambridge, declared, "More than any other company, we are so international that nothing can happen in any part of the world without it affecting our interests." (Shell has the scars to prove it. When the Communists took over Russia in 1917, Shell was quickly expropriated. And when Mexico nationalized its oil industry in 1938, Shell lost another of its outposts.)

Of course one reason it's so difficult to pin down Shell to any one country is that it does have dual nationality: Dutch and British. Shell has two parent companies, the Royal Dutch Petroleum Company, headquartered in The Hague, and the "Shell" Transport and Trading Company, headquartered in London. The accent is slightly on the Dutch side, since Royal Dutch owns 60 percent of the pot to "Shell" Transport's 40.

However, both Royal Dutch and "Shell" Transport are publicly traded companies. Their shares sell on the stock exchanges of nine countries, and they are among the most widely held securities in world equity markets. Royal Dutch has 500,000 shareholders, "Shell" Transport 320,-000. Each is separately listed on the New York Stock Exchange. At the end of 1986 the geographical breakdown of all shareholders showed Britain in the lead with 38 percent of the total, followed by the United States, 23 percent; the Netherlands, 21 percent; Switzerland, 11 percent; France, 4 percent. Since 1983 American ownership has increased by 50 percent.

Shell is therefore an enterprise headquartered in two different countries with nearly a quarter of its shareholders located in a third country. The answer-defying question always is: How the devil does it work? And no one ever seems to have a good explanation.

In 1985 Ian Hargreaves of the *Financial Times* opened a commentary with these remarks: "Royal Dutch/Shell has always been the oil company which should not work. Governed by a tangled matrix of committees divided between the sleepy Hague and London's concrete South Bank, even Shell veterans have difficulty in explaining how the company functions. Genetically, a hybrid of Dutch dourness and English class-consciousness, Shell has a slightly musty image; reliable, but a bit dull." Later on in this commentary Peter Holmes, who had just been installed as chairman of "Shell" Transport, imparted this wisdom: "We are foreign. We are complicated."

Holmes, who has never worked for another company, was in line to succeed L. C. van Wachem in the very top job at Shell, chairman of the committee of managing directors, but he might miss out because of his age. The inflexible rule at Shell is that the top post alternates between the head of the Dutch company and the head of the British company. The other inflexible rule is that at age sixty, you must retire. Van Wachem, an Indonesian-born mechanical engineer who worked all over the world for Shell, became president of Royal Dutch Petroleum in 1982 and succeeded Sir Peter Baxendell as chairman of the whole shebang in 1985. He was then fifty-three years old. At the same time Holmes moved up to become chairman of the British parent. He was then fifty-two years old.

In his incisive book *The Seven Sisters,* British journalist Anthony Sampson managed, with more success than most, to get at the essence of Shell. "Shell men regard Exxon as a provincial company," wrote Sampson. This is a view rooted in the histories of these companies. Exxon began life as a domestic producer of oil and then went overseas; Shell was *born* in international waters. "We've been in politics all our lives," a Shell director told Sampson, who added this postscript:

> Shell's executives have become recognized as a kind of junior diplomatic service. In Britain, their traditional nurseries have been Oxford and Cambridge, their children are educated free at public schools, and many of the directors become commanders or knights of the British Empire. Shell men like to cultivate almost the opposite style to Exxon's; while the men in Sixth

Avenue prefer not to talk about diplomacy, Shell men prefer not to talk about anything as squalid as profits.

Exxon is the perfect counterpoint to Shell. The two largest oil companies in the world (which one is first depends on what's being measured), they have battled each other for nearly one hundred years, beginning in the closing decade of the last century. Not content with having established his Standard Oil Trust as the dominant petroleum company in the United States, John D. Rockefeller, convinced he was doing God's work, set out to soak the world in oil. By 1885 two thirds of his sales came from abroad. He brought to overseas markets the same ruthlessness that he had employed at home to drive competitors to the wall.

However, two companies survived his onslaught. One was a Dutch outfit formed in 1890 to develop an oil field in Sumatra in the East Indies—it had a royal charter and called itself Royal Dutch. The other was an English trading company which grew out of a shop that had been started in the East End of London in 1833 by Marcus Samuel, a Jewish merchant.

Samuel dealt in antiques and bric-a-brac such as Oriental shells, which were popular during the Victorian era. The shells were imported from the Far East, and Samuel expanded his business into a general import-export house. After Samuel's death in 1870, his two sons, Marcus Samuel and Samuel Samuel, took over the business and expanded it further into a trading house with a network of agents in the Far East and a coal-exporting subsidiary in Japan.

The eldest son, Marcus Samuel, went head-to-head with Rockefeller for the first time when he bought kerosene made from Russian crude and sold it in the Far East under his "Shell" name. The Russian oil was controlled by a syndicate headed by the French Rothschilds. John D. Rockefeller's "secret weapon" in the United States had been his insight that victory would go not to the people who controlled the production of oil but to those who controlled its distribution. Marcus Samuel had the same insight about kerosene. Rockefeller's ships were carrying it to the Far East in cans. Samuel knew he could undercut John D. by shipping it in tankers. The problem was that kerosene-loaded tankers had a habit of blowing up and were banned from the locks of the Suez Canal. So Samuel had a British naval architect, Fortescue Flannery, design a new tanker in which oil compartments were separated by water-filled bulkheads.

Despite a heated campaign by the Standard Oil forces, including charges that it was all a "Hebrew" plot, the Suez Canal directors approved the new tanker (after Lloyd's agreed to insure it). On July 26, 1892, the tanker *Murex,* named of course for a shell, sailed from England to pick up kerosene at the Black Sea port of Batum, sailed through Suez and headed for Singapore and Bankgkok, where Samuel had thoughtfully put in place deep-water jetties and storage tanks to receive the cargo. Samuel made a profit on the kerosene, selling it at half of Standard's price.

The next year more tankers, all named after shells (the *Conch,* the *Clam,* and so on), sailed out from the Black Sea. (After the tankers were steam-cleaned in the Far East, Samuel made sure they were reloaded with spices and other products he could sell in Europe.) It was Marcus Samuel who established the tanker as the most efficient way to ship oil. In 1897, rejecting a buyout bid by Standard, he formed his new London-based company, "Shell" Transport and Trading. The following year his name appeared on the Queen's honors list: Sir Marcus, the first oil knight.

At the turn of the century Rockefeller's Standard Oil Trust was still by far the largest factor in the world oil business. "Shell" Transport, by comparison, was a pygmy, but it was also a different kind of animal. Standard worked off a huge petroleum base in the United States. It owned producing oil wells. Although Samuel had gained access to oil fields in Dutch Borneo, he was functioning primarily as he always had—as a trader (a skill and predilection that survives in today's Shell).

Meanwhile, in the Far East, Royal Dutch, a company smaller than "Shell," was a rising and obstreperous force in the business under the lash of Henri Deterding, the son of a Dutch sea captain. Deterding, who had the financial intricacies of oil implanted in his head, had no trouble matching the ruthlessness of Rockefeller. Only thirty-two years old in 1900, he was ready to take on both Standard and Shell. In 1903 he formed an alliance with "Shell"—and the Rothschilds. They organized Asiatic Petroleum as their marketing arm in the Far East, continuing to compete against each other—and Standard—in other parts of the world. That led to the great merger of 1907, on terms largely favorable to Deterding. Royal Dutch and "Shell" Transport combined, on the sixty-forty basis that remains in place today, to form the Royal Dutch/Shell Group. It was Deterding's company to run, a role he relished. He now had an organization of some size to pit against mighty Standard. The British were miffed that control of the company had passed to Dutch hands (it was one reason the government bought 50 percent of Anglo-Persian, predecessor of British Petroleum, in 1914), but Deterding was a rootless character. He moved to England and bought a big spread in Norfolk. During World War I Shell became a major supplier to the Royal Navy. And in 1921 Deterding was knighted.

Deterding put in place the producing interests that Shell lacked so that it could properly fight Standard. He found new sources of crude in Russia (1910), Egypt (1911), Venezuela (1913), and Trinidad (1914). In 1919 he bought Lord Cowdray's Mexican oil company, Eagle. In 1912, a year after the Supreme Court broke up the Standard Oil Trust, Deterding moved Shell into the United States to battle John D. on his home turf. His first base was a depot in Tacoma, Washington, which received Shell oil shipped from Sumatra. To refine it into gasoline, Shell built its first U.S. refinery at Martinez on the northern end of San Francisco Bay in 1915. Shell quickly tapped into U.S. oil, making important discoveries in California and acquiring producing companies in other parts of the country. By 1920 Shell had in its arsenal wells that were producing 100,000 barrels a day, or more than 5 percent of the world total of 1.92 million. By 1929 Shell gasoline was sold in all forty-eight states.

A year earlier, at a castle in Scotland, a summit meeting of petroleum industry leaders, including Deterding, Walter Teagle of Jersey Standard, Sir John Cadman of British Petroleum, and William Mellon of Gulf, was held to initiate discussions that resulted in the "as is" agreement under which the major oil powers carved up the world markets among themselves, agreeing to set prices and allocate supplies. It was a pact that was to stand until 1942. Deterding and his colleagues had anticipated OPEC by forty-five years.

The United States served as a port of entry for Shell into the chemical business. Shell Chemical was formed in 1929 to develop fertilizers from natural gas and synthetic solvents from refinery gases. A similar company, Mekog, was started at about the same time in the Netherlands. Chemicals became a major business for Shell. In 1986 its chemical sales came to $8.5 billion, a volume which exceeded the sales of such chemical majors as Monsanto and Union Carbide.

The big oil finds in the Middle East were made by producers other than Shell—perhaps because they had the backing of their governments, while it was never clear to which government Shell belonged. Shell was as elusive as ever in terms of national identity. Not that it seemed to suffer much. As the world's second-largest oil power, it was strong enough to compete against anyone anywhere. In 1938, on the eve of World War II, Shell was producing 580,000 barrels of oil a day, which was a little more than 10 percent of the world total of 5.72 million. The company that virtually invented the tanker business was also operating a seagoing tanker fleet of 180 vessels. And what happened to the founders? Sir Marcus Samuel retired as chairman of "Shell" Transport in 1921 to become the first Lord Bearsted. Sir Henri Deterding remained with the company until

1936, but his erratic behavior became increasingly embarrassing to his fellow directors. His second wife was a White Russian, and he became a virulent anti-Communist. His German secretary became his third wife, and he then became a Nazi zealot, moving to Germany to be close to his idol Adolf Hitler. He died in 1939, six months before the outbreak of World War II.

Shell marched on without the Samuels and the Deterdings. In the years following World War II Shell companies supplied 7 percent of the world's oil. They also pioneered the discovery of natural gas fields and the delivery of liquefied natural gas (LNG). In the 1970s, when natural gas filled 15 percent of Europe's energy needs, Shell and its partners were responsible for about half of that supply. In 1972 Shell began delivering LNG to Japan from Brunei.

Shell remained true to its heritage as an adept trader, a scrambler in the world oil markets. That was not always the best position to be in, for it precluded Shell from making the kind of profits available to Exxon, BP, Texaco, and Chevron through their access to incredibly cheap crude in the Middle East. But after the Middle East and North African nations asserted themselves and took control of the oil in their lands, Shell's position was enhanced. Its competitors could no longer reap those superprofits at the wellhead, and Shell, always a better performer in downstream markets, enjoyed an edge that has enabled it to come close to achieving Deterding's goal: eclipse Exxon as the world's largest oil company.

Shell's success in the American market is certainly a good example of its prowess as a marketer. It has consistently ranked at or near the top as a gasoline seller even though it ranks fourth or fifth as an oil producer. It has just been able to outmarket its stodgy, slow-footed competitors, buying oil on the open market to meet its downstream needs. Since 1978 the number of Shell service stations in the United States has declined from 17,000 to 11,200. But they are much bigger stations pumping much more oil. In 1985 the average Shell station pumped 96,000 gallons of gas a month, up from 63,000 in 1978. And in 1986 Shell moved into first place in the American market in sales of gasoline to motorists.

The company's success has frequently been attributed to decentralization, letting subsidiary companies carve out their own identities. That's true—up to a point. In 1984 the Hague-London axis decided that it wanted to be the one 100 percent owner of Shell Oil of the United States. Royal Dutch/Shell had for many years owned 69.5 percent of the shares in its American subsidiary—the remainder traded on the New York Stock Exchange. The parent offered to buy out the U.S. stockholders for $55 a share or 25 percent more than the shares were selling for on the New York

Stock Exchange. The outside directors of Shell Oil, who held a majority of the board seats, deemed that to be an inadequate offer.

In the end Royal Dutch/Shell paid $60 a share, or $5.7 billion, to acquire the 30.5 percent of Shell Oil that it did not already own. The Shell people in Europe assured the American managers that they would continue to have their independence; they would even be permitted to have their own board of directors. Royal Dutch/Shell just thought that buying Shell Oil of the United States was the best use of their spare cash—and if there is anything Royal Dutch/Shell has, it's ready money, because the oil business is like a perpetual cash machine. At the end of 1983, just before making the bid for the American company's shares, Shell had about $8 billion in its coffers to put on the table. To buy the shares from American investors, Shell had to borrow only $1.2 billion of the $5.7 billion purchase price; it came up with the bulk of it from its petty cash box.

Having too much money can be a problem. In January 1984 Shell

---

"We Just Want to Pump the Oil"

A coalition of political conservatives distributed this appeal in 1986 asking American motorists to boycott Chevron and Gulf (now part of Chevron) because they continue to produce oil in Angola, whose Marxist government was opposed by the Reagan administration. Angola might be the only place in the world where Cuban troops guard an American industrial facility against possible attacks by rebel forces (supported by the Reagan administration). Angola, on the west coast of Africa, was previously a Portuguese colony, and left-wing activists used to urge a boycott of Gulf for supporting a colonial regime. Chevron's position was stated as follows:

"Our presence in any country does not necessarily imply an endorsement of its particular form of government. . . .

"We cannot afford to take sides or become involved in domestic politics. . . .

"Chevron's aim is to seek profitable opportunities for the benefit of our stockholders. . . .

"Both as Chevron and as Gulf, the Company has been operating in Angola for thirty years. Despite civil strife and several government changes in Angola during those years, Chevron/Gulf has been successful in maintaining continuous operations.

"This long record is, in large part, the result of a consistent policy of avoiding domestic politics in the more than eighty countries in which Chevron operates."

discovered new oil in the Beaufort Sea off Alaska. However, Edward V. Newland, a veteran Shell man, seemed to be distressed that the find was so close to the already built Alaskan pipeline—in fact, just twelve miles away. As a result he moaned to a *BusinessWeek* reporter, "It's not going to absorb another $2 or $3 billion. It's going to be another cash cow."

The Royal Dutch/Shell Group is so huge that the annual reports issued by Royal Dutch Petroleum and "Shell" Transport and Trading have to telegraph news in a kind of shorthand language. Here are some snippets from the 1985 annual report:

> Interesting discoveries of oil or gas were made in more than twenty countries.
> A 50 percent interest was acquired in Occidental's operations in Colombia.
> In Syria, an oil discovery at Thayem is being developed.
> The Thai government purchased a 25 percent interest in the Sirikit field.
> Additional reserves of oil and gas were confirmed offshore in Brunei.

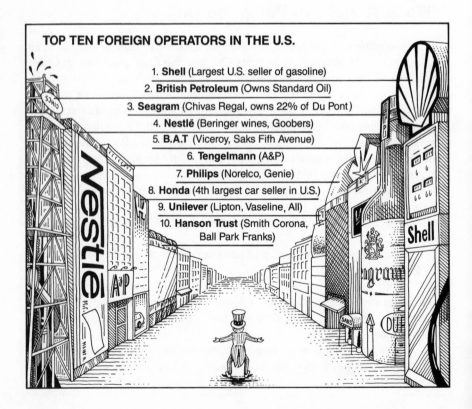

TOP TEN FOREIGN OPERATORS IN THE U.S.

1. **Shell** (Largest U.S. seller of gasoline)
2. **British Petroleum** (Owns Standard Oil)
3. **Seagram** (Chivas Regal, owns 22% of Du Pont)
4. **Nestlé** (Beringer wines, Goobers)
5. **B.A.T** (Viceroy, Saks Fifh Avenue)
6. **Tengelmann** (A&P)
7. **Philips** (Norelco, Genie)
8. **Honda** (4th largest car seller in U.S.)
9. **Unilever** (Lipton, Vaseline, All)
10. **Hanson Trust** (Smith Corona, Ball Park Franks)

Acquisition of the Hoechst polystyrene plant at Breda, in the Netherlands, adding to Shell strength in expandable polystyrene.

Commissioning of the 250,000 barrels daily refinery at Al Jubail, Saudi Arabia, operated by a joint venture between the state company Petromin and Shell.

In Saudi Arabia, commissioning of the chemical manufacturing complex operated by a joint venture between Saudi Basic Industries and a Shell Oil subsidiary.

It's just laconic Anglo-Dutch understatement.

Access   Royal Dutch Petroleum
30 Carel Van Bylandtlaan
2596 HR The Hague, the Netherlands
(31) 70-779-111

"Shell" Transport and Trading
Shell Centre
London SE 17NA, England
(44) 1-934-1234

Shell Oil
One Shell Plaza
P.O. Box 2463
Houston, Tex. 77001
(713) 241-6161

Siemens

Sales $26 billion
Profits $800 million
U.S. Sales $2.6 billion
Rank World's 6th-largest electrical equipment
      company
      West Germany's 3rd-largest company
      Europe's 5th-largest company (by market
      value)
      13th on the *Fortune* International 500
      4th-largest nuclear plant builder
      World's 6th-largest maker of
      telecommunications equipment
      World's 2nd-largest factory automation
      company
      World's 4th-largest light bulb
      manufacturer
      World's largest maker of medical
      equipment
      World's largest supplier of capital
      equipment to the graphics industry
      Europe's 2d-largest employer
Founded 1847
Employees 362,000 (18,000 in the United
      States)
Headquarters Munich, West Germany

When the Russian nuclear power plant at Chernobyl blew up in 1986, it wasn't good news for Siemens, a giant of the electronics industry and the world's fourth-largest builder of nuclear power reactors through its wholly owned subsidiary Kraftwerk Union (KWU). It's not that Chernobyl was a KWU installation. It had nothing to do with the Soviet plant—and KWU's safety record is good. But accidents of this kind cast a pall over the entire nuclear power industry and inject adrenaline into antinuclear activists. Chernobyl, it turned out, was also not so far away. Radioactive fallout drifted over West Germany. Sensitive detectors in KWU facilities were set off by employees who had collected radioactive dust on their shoes. Soon demonstrators led by the Greens, Germany's environmentalist party, were picketing outside KWU's gates. Klaus Barthelt, chairman of KWU, said, "We Germans have a tendency to be emotionally excitable."

Chernobyl heated up an already smoldering dispute between Austria and West Germany over a nuclear reprocessing plant that a consortium headed by Siemens was getting ready to build at Wackersdorf in Bavaria, seventy-five miles from the Austrian border and one hundred miles north of Siemens headquarters in Munich. The Austrians had been trying to persuade the Germans not to build this plant, but in the summer of 1986, after a meeting with Austrian Chancellor Franz Vranitzky, West German Chancellor Helmut Kohl refused to back down. Kohl attributed the Austrian fears to "superstition," adding, "Wackersdorf will be built. There will be no period for rethinking."

The antinuclear forces in Austria have been so strong that the only nuclear power plant ever built in the country, at Zwentendorf, was never used after being completed in 1978. After Chernobyl the Austrian government moved to dismantle it. West Germany in 1986 had eighteen nuclear power stations working, with another five under construction. Nearly all of these—and the one at Zwentendorf—were built by Siemens.

The profound effect that nuclear orders, or the lack thereof, can have on Siemens was clear in 1986 when its sales fell nearly 20 percent below the previous year's level. In its 1984–85 fiscal year, Siemens logged revenues from three new nuclear power stations in West Germany; in 1985–86, it had no such sales to record. In fact KWU hadn't booked a nuclear order since 1982, and after Chernobyl its salesmen found it difficult to close orders with customers in the Netherlands, Switzerland, and Finland. Still, there might be a silver lining in this nuclear cloud. The Soviet Union decided that after Chernobyl, it would upgrade its other nuclear plants, and it was considering giving the job to Siemens. Russia, it so happens, is an old stamping ground of Siemens.

Nineteen eighty-six was a trying year for Siemens on another count. On July 19, Karl Heinz Beckurts, its highly regarded head of research, and his driver, Eckart Groppler, were murdered when a twenty-two-pound, remote-controlled bomb blew up their car, a BMW that had been armor-plated to foil such an attack. The left-wing terrorist group Red Army Faction claimed responsibility for the bombing, the latest in a series of executions of German corporate executives. In a letter left at the scene of the blast, a Munich suburb where Beckhurts lived, the terrorist group identified the Siemens executive "as a representative of international capitalism" and said that he had been targeted for execution because of his role in "Western Europe's biggest high-tech concern and the world's third biggest atomic concern."

The loss of the fifty-six-year-old Beckhurts was a blow to Siemens, which had recruited him in 1980 to breathe new life into research labs that had been characterized as "lethargic." Beckhurts, a physicist, had previously directed the German nuclear research center at Julich. At Siemens he came to preside over a research and development effort that is one of the largest of any company in the world. In 1987 Siemens had a worldwide research staff of forty thousand people backed by a $3.3 billion budget. A big chunk of that expenditure supported the Mega Project to develop memory chips with capacities of one and four megabits, which would usher in the "Fifth Generation" of computers.

Siemens has a research legacy that goes back to its founder, Werner von Siemens, an engineer, inventor, and zealous Prussian patriot. Born in 1816 on a farm outside Hanover, he was one of thirteen children and the eldest surviving son. He went to Berlin when he was seventeen years old to enroll in the Prussian artillery, spending the years 1835 to 1838 at the Berlin Artillery and Engineering School. Looking back when he was seventy-five years old, he remembered those three years "to be the happiest of my life."

If there was ever a child of the nineteenth century, it was Werner von Siemens. He grew up at a time when the Age of Science was dawning. In 1831 when Werner was fifteen years old, England's Michael Faraday discovered electromagnetic induction and built the first dynamo, forerunner of the generators that were to produce electric power. It was also a time of political upheavals characterized by nationalist movements that sought to undo the gerrymandering of the Congress of Vienna, which had divided Central Europe into territories that made no sense except to the monarchs who ruled them. Werner chafed growing up in the Kingdom of Hanover, then under English rule. He described the English princes as caring little about the country, "which they regarded chiefly as a hunting ground. The game laws were in consequence very strict, so that it was a common remark that in Hanover to kill a stag was more criminal than to kill a man!"

While serving in the Prussian Army, Werner continued his engineering studies and started, on his own, to experiment in the laboratory. He had an aptitude for science, and he was interested always in a practical application of theory. In 1842 he invented an electroplating process. He tried to produce a gun-cotton that would replace gunpowder. And then he started to work on an electric telegraph system, trying to improve on the earlier models that had been developed. The firm, Siemens & Halske, was formed in Berlin in 1847 to manufacture needle or dial telegraphs. His partner was a skilled craftsman, Johann George Halske, who built what Siemens invented.

Siemens & Halske was to grow into one of the premier electrical engineering firms of the world, in the forefront of many of the technological breakthroughs of the past 140 years. If they didn't invent it at Siemens, they quickly picked up on the inventions of others and turned them into practical products. In the beginning their mandate was to cover the world with telegraph poles. It's difficult today, when instant communication across the world is commonplace, to realize how revolutionary the telegraph was.

In 1848, using bell-shaped porcelain insulators, Siemens & Halske built Europe's first long-distance telegraph line connecting Berlin with Frankfurt three hundred miles away. The purpose was to relay to Berlin as soon as possible the actions taken by the National Assembly meeting in Frankfurt. In 1852 Siemens went to Russia, returning with an order to build a telegraph system that by 1855 linked Warsaw with St. Petersburg and extended to Moscow and Sebastopol on the Black Sea. It also included a submarine cable between Oranienbaum and Kronstadt in the Gulf of Finland. One of the firm's major triumphs was the stringing of the India Line, which ran from London across Prussia and into Russia to Teheran, where it interconnected with a line through the Persian Gulf to Karachi and then down to Calcutta. Completed in 1870 it covered 6,600 miles and remained in service until 1931.

Johann Halske was a craftsman of the old school who had no enthusiasm for mass production techniques and the bureaucracy of a big firm. He left the firm in 1867, just as the India Line project was going forward. The parting was friendly. (His son and grandson later worked for Siemens & Halske, which remained the corporate name until 1966.)

Werner Siemens's passion for scientific invention did not prevent him from participating in politics. He was elected to the Prussian Chamber of Deputies in 1862, and he fervently supported the Prussian military in the wars waged against the Austrians, Danes, and French. He was delighted in 1848 to place submarine mines of his own making in the harbor of Kiel to blow up any Danish warships that might venture there. He longed for the unification of German-speaking areas into one nation. In his memoirs he described his feelings in 1866 when Prussia declared war against Austria:

> It was brought strongly home to me, what a power lies in the glorious past of a people. In perilous times it enhances self-confidence, allows no pusillanimity to spring up, and awakens in everybody the resolve to contribute his part to overcoming the danger, as his fathers had done before him. . . . All political disputes were forgotten or at least postponed. Every man had but one thought: To do his duty.

Werner married twice (his first wife died), both times to daughters of cousins several times removed. His second marriage, in 1869, was to

Antonie Siemens, the daughter of Professor Carl Siemens of Hohenheim, a town near Stuttgart, capital city of the Swabian region. Werner used to joke that this marriage could be "looked upon as a political act," foreshadowing the unification of the North and South of what is now Germany. A year after this marriage Prussia went to war against France—and Werner was his old gung ho self. His daughter, born as the war started, was named Hertha after a German warship of that name. His sixteen-year-old son, imbued with his father's patriotism, telegraphed: "I MUST JOIN TOO"—even though the Prussian Army wouldn't accept volunteers until they were seventeen. Werner said his son's feelings were emblematic of "the deep emotion and courage that had taken possession of all Germany."

Werner's younger brothers followed in his path. He was their mentor. William, five years younger than Werner, emigrated to England where he established a branch of Siemens & Halske and became one of the most distinguished members of the British scientific community. An inventor in his own right, he developed the water meter and was one of the first to apply electric power to railways. With his younger brother, Friedrich, he invented a regenerative furnace that led to the open hearth furnace later used in the German, British, and U.S. steel mills. William married a Scottish lady, Anne Gordon, and in 1883 Queen Victoria knighted him. In that same year, at age sixty-one, he died, eulogized at Westminister Abbey and in a *Times* of London obituary, which said: "His name recurs upon every page of iron manufacture since he came among us."

Friedrich built up a furnace-building business in Germany and then ran a glassworks at Dresden. On the eve of the electrical age, he used the regenerative principle of heating to increase the illuminating power of gas, an action which Werner noted had "retarded the victory of the electric light over gas" but hadn't "produced any friction in our fraternal harmony."

The Siemens clan was close. Carl, thirteen years younger than Werner, was dispatched to St. Petersburg in 1853 to manage the Russian telegraph network. He later moved to London to work with William in running the British company, returning to St. Petersburg in 1880 because his two daughters, who had been born in Russia, were homesick. The Siemens Russian company became a major supplier of lighting and electric power, and Tsar Nicholas II raised Carl to Russian nobility in 1895.

The two youngest Siemens brothers, Walter and Otto (they were seventeen and twenty years junior to Werner), also ended up in Russia. Siemens & Halske put up telegraph lines in the Caucasus and opened a branch office in Tiflis to operate this business. Walter was sent to manage this office, and he came across a copper mine at Kedabeg in the shadow of Mount Ararat. It's one of the oldest copper mines in the world. In 1864, with money put up by Werner and Carl, the Siemens family bought the mine. Four years later Walter died in Tiflis after falling from a horse. In 1871 Otto, who always suffered from poor health, also died in Tiflis, only thirty-five years old. He had been married for two years to the widow of General Prince Mirsky, a brother of the governor of the Caucasus.

Werner von Siemens collected his thoughts about his family and his life in a memoir that he began in 1889. It was published in 1892, the year he died. One of his last thoughts was: "A main reason of the rapid growth of our factories is, in my opinion, that the products of our manufactures were in large part results of our own inventions. Though these were in most cases not protected by patents, yet they always gave us a start on our competitors."

There's no gainsaying the long line of inventions that flowed from the House of Siemens. Many stemmed from the dynamo that Werner built in 1866, incorporating his discovery that mechanical power could be converted to electric currents without the use of permanent magnets. Called the "dynamo-electric" principle, it ranked among the foremost scientific discoveries of the period, paving the way to electric power transmission. Its first use, in 1867, was as a mine exploder. The "siemens" is now the international unit of electrical conductivity.

Because research in new applications of electrical engineering was going on simultaneously in a number of countries, it's not always easy to determine who was first with what. But Siemens was certainly among the first with many products. It built an electric railway in 1879, an elevator in 1880, and a trolleybus in 1882. It received a patent in 1896 for an X-ray tube, and in that same year it built Europe's first subway in Budapest. The breakthroughs continued in the twentieth century: tantalum, which led to the metal filament incandescent lamp (1905); an automatic telephone exchange (1909); a high-speed telegraph that transmitted one thousand characters a minute (1912); radios (1923); traffic lights (1926); autopilots (1934); and the electron microscope (1939).

In 1897 Siemens & Halske began its expansion to the outskirts of Berlin, starting construction of a complex of factories that by 1913 was already being called *Siemensstadt* (Siemens City). It was to serve as the focal point of Siemens activities for fifty years. By 1914, when World War I broke out, Siemens was a formidable enterprise, one of the largest in the world. It had an employee force of eighty thousand, factories in ten countries, and business operations in forty-nine. As a result of the war, it lost 40 percent of its assets, mostly the installations outside Germany.

It regrouped in 1919 under the leadership of the founder's youngest son, Carl Friedrich von Siemens (the two eldest sons, Arnold and Wilhelm, died in 1918 and 1919, respectively).

The period between the two world wars, marked by the rise of Adolf Hitler and the Nazi party in Germany, saw Siemens growing. By the time World War II broke out, it had 183,000 people on its worldwide payroll. Carl Friedrich had democratic sympathies which brought him into politics during the days of the Weimar Republic. He was elected to the Reichstag in 1920 as a member of the left-liberal German Democratic party. He was not a bankroller of Hitler.

Siemens always had its sights fixed beyond the borders of Germany. After World War I the company returned to a country it knew well: Russia, now the world's first Communist state. The Soviets needed power and turned to Siemens to build the world's largest storage-dam station on the Dnieper River at Zaporozhye. A Siemens company also helped the Russians build the Moscow Metro. Vladimir Lenin, the leader of the Russian Revolution, was fond of saying, "Communism is Bolshevism plus electricity."

Politics brought Siemens to Ireland. The Irish revolted against British rule in 1916 and established their own republic in 1919. Not wanting to be dependent on the English, they invited Siemens to build a large power station on the Shannon.

Cartels, a way of dividing up markets, were common in the electrical equipment industry, and they functioned on national and international levels. In 1919, to get into the international game, Siemens joined forces with two other German electrical equipment companies, AEG and Auer, to mount a combined German entry in the light bulb business. The name they adopted was OSRAM, a compound of Osmium and Wolfram, the chemical elements from which the threads of bulbs are made. It became one of the most well known brands in Europe. A Siemens subsidiary today, OSRAM ranks as the world's fourth-largest bulb maker. The Cadillac Seville and Lincoln Mark VII are among the cars using OSRAM headlights.

World War II was devastating to Germany and Siemens. This time the company lost 80 percent of its assets. During the war Allied bombers raked Siemensstadt, and the company moved many of its operations to other locations. Siemens was one of the firms tapped by the Nazi war machine to operate a plant near the Polish concentration camp, Auschwitz. Employing 250 slave laborers from the camp, it turned out electrical apparatus for aircraft and submarines. Siemens later claimed that the foreign workers, prisoners of war, and Jews who were pressed into work in its plants "were treated far more humanely and worked under better conditions than those outside." Siemens also said that during the Nazi persecution of Jews in the 1930s, it tried to transfer Jewish employees to overseas subsidiaries of the company.

Carl Friedrich von Siemens, the last son of the founder, died in July 1941 and was succeeded by his nephew Hermann von Siemens, who remained in command through the war years. After the war he was briefly jailed by American occupation forces but no Siemens manager was ever formally charged with war crimes. Hermann was released from prison in 1948 and reassumed the helm of the company. He faced an awesome rebuilding task. Siemens not only had lost most of its plant capacity but, as a result of Germany losing the war, it had forfeited all its patents and trademarks without compensation. So it was a little like starting from scratch.

Siemensstadt, which had been reduced to rubble, was rebuilt and is today once again the largest manufacturing center of Siemens, with eight plants and 26,500 employees, representing 16 percent of total employment in Berlin. However, since Berlin is located in East Germany, Siemens moved its headquarters to Munich, where it took over a classically styled building on Wittelsbacher Platz that was once owned by the Bavarian court architect Leo Klenze.

Rising like a phoenix, Siemens helped to spark the postwar German economic miracle, becoming Europe's second-largest electronics firm (behind Philips) by dint of what *The Economist* once called "all those virtues that have driven West German industry since the Second World War: tight organization, loyal employees, financial conservatism, devotion to systems, and management led by engineers." In Germany Siemens is a household word. To get a fix on it, one has to imagine General Electric, IBM, and Western Electric combined into one company. Siemens operates 155 manufacturing plants in thirty-eight countries, fielding a product lineup that runs into the thousands, including computers, telephone switching systems, turbines, cables, fire alarms, floodlights, factory control systems, meters of all kinds, motors, fans, pumps, and the world's most extensive line of medical engineering equipment (X-ray systems, pacemakers, ultrasonic therapy equipment, tomography systems, sonographs, cardiovascular diagnostic aids, artificial respirators, hearing aids, dental chairs, ultrasonic descalers, dental burr drives).

Siemens has close ties to the West German government, where it's called "Auntie Siemens." It is, as *The Wall Street Journal* pointed out, "a very important relative," representing Germany's foremost contender in the world of high technology. Siemens gets nearly 10 percent of its sales from the West German government, most of it from the Post Ministry, which operates the country's telephone system. Siemens would like to supply the Bell companies in the United States the way it does the Post Ministry in Germany. To that end, in 1986 Siemens bought its way into a small piece of the American market by acquiring control of the transmission equipment business formerly operated by GTE, the largest independent telephone company in the United States. And in early 1987 Siemens scored a breakthrough by securing a $12-million contract to install a public exchange switch for Ameritech, the Chicago-based holding company for the Bell systems in Illinois, Indiana, Ohio, Michigan, and Wisconsin. The Siemens-GTE alliance parallels the AT&T-Philips and ITT-Alcatel combinations in the fight for market share in the world telecommunications field.

Through all those sea changes, the Siemens family hung in there until 1981 when Peter von Siemens, then seventy years old, retired. His successor, sixty-six-year-old Bernhard Plettner, became the first non-Siemens family member to hold the chairman's post. Hermann von Siemens, the wartime head, died in 1986. He was 101 years old.

Siemens, like many electronic companies, partners with counterparts all over the world. The Mega Project is a joint venture with Philips of Eindhoven, backed by funding from the Dutch and West German governments. Among the other companies Siemens has forged alliances with are Westinghouse (the world's largest nuclear reactor builder), Toshiba, Bull (a French computer manufacturer), ICL (a British computer manufacturer), and GTE (a telecommunications giant). Siemens also has a long mentor relationship with Fuji Electric, a major supplier of power equipment in Japan and the owner of 16 percent of Fujitsu, Japan's largest computer maker (Fujitsu came out of Fuji). In 1987 Siemens still held 8.4 percent of Fuji's shares. In Germany Siemens has a fifty-fifty partnership with Stuttgart's Robert Bosch. That venture, Bosch-Siemens Hausgerate, ranks as West Germany's largest—and Europe's third largest—maker of electrical home appliances.

Nearly half of Siemens's sales now come from outside Germany. The United States accounts for only 10 percent of the company's revenues, but that's because Siemens didn't begin to focus on the American market until 1976. It has since acquired more than a dozen U.S. companies and turned one joint venture, Siemens-Allis, into a wholly owned subsidiary now renamed Siemens Energy & Automation. It helps companies automate their production lines, throwing thousands out of work. Siemens has thirty manufacturing locations in the United States. One of its holdings is a 15 percent interest in Advanced Micro Devices, a leading semiconductor manufacturer in California's Silicon Valley.

More American companies are expected to fall into the Siemens net, which is no surprise considering the weak dollar and the hoard of cash that this German company sits on. Its balance sheet at the end of 1986 showed liquid assets amounting to something like $10 billion. They joke in Germany that Siemens is really a bank that dabbles in electronics.

The American putsch is also no surprise considering the views of Karlheinz Kaske, a physicist who received his Ph.D. at age twenty-two and became chief executive at Siemens in 1981 after a thirty-one-year association with the company (he left for seven years to teach at a mining school in Aachen). Kaske believes Americans have frittered away their manufacturing edge. Talking in 1987 with *Financial Times* reporter Terry Dodsworth, he said: "It is a trend which started about twenty-five years ago when the U.S. gave away consumer electronics manufacturing to the Far East. Consumer electronics is that part of the business which uses a high volume of semiconductor products. So the Japanese got two things at the same time—first they took control of the consumer products and then they moved into the manufacturing of the microelectronics which go into them.

"Five years ago the same mistake was made when IBM and others went and gave away their designs of personal computers to be made in Taiwan, Korea, and Singapore."

The view from the Siemens bridge is similar to the one taken by its Dutch neighbor, Philips. They're both moving into the United States to teach Americans to keep their technology to themselves.

Leaders of the Nuclear Club

(Nuclear Power Capacity in Kilowatts)

United States	77,840,000
France	37,530,000
Soviet Union	27,760,000
Japan	24,520,000

Note: Japan's nuclear power is generated by thirty-two nuclear power stations. They deliver 26 percent of Japan's electricity.

Access Wittelsbacherplatz 2
D-8000 Munich 2,
Federal Republic of Germany
(49) 8923-40

767 Fifth Ave.
New York, N.Y. 10153
(212) 832-6601

Singapore Airlines

Sales $1.6 billion
Profits $207 million
Rank World's 7th-largest international airline
World's 11th-largest airline (passenger miles)
World's 11th-largest airline (cargo miles)
Singapore's 2d-largest company
Founded 1937
Employees 15,800
Headquarters Singapore

I t would seem, on the face of it, to be ridiculous. Here's a country, Singapore, with a population of 2.5 million living on an island that's twenty-six miles long and fourteen miles wide. An airplane can fly over it in a couple of minutes—and yet it's fielding one of the largest airlines in the world.

For patriotic reasons every country likes to have its own flag carrier, which is why virtually every country in the world has one, whether it makes money or not. But Singapore is a Third World country with an airline that never loses money and keeps expanding, year after year. It carried nearly five million passengers in 1985, and it filled 71.8 percent of its seats, a load factor U.S. airlines would kill for. Singapore Airlines is an entrepreneurial triumph, a vivid demonstration of what can be accomplished when people set their minds to a task. It helps, too, to have geography on your side—and a supportive government that harnesses people to social goals. (In Singapore families are made to feel like pariahs if they have more than two children.)

The roots of Singapore Airlines go back to 1937 with the formation of Malayan Airways. However, while the airline was organized then, it didn't get off the ground until ten years later, after World War II, when a five-seat Airspeed Consul began service from Singapore to the Malayan cities of Kuala Lumpur, Ipoh, and Penang. The fledgling carrier proceeded to undergo a series of transformations dictated by political upheavals. It fell under the control of British Overseas Airways Corporation and Qantas when the Federation of Malaya became an independent state (1957). It changed its name to Malaysian Airways when the new government of Malaysia was formed (1963). It became jointly owned by Malaysia and Singapore when Singapore decided to secede from Malaysia (1965), changing its name to Malaysian-Singapore Airlines (MSA). That arrangement lasted until 1972 when the airline was split in two—Singapore taking the international routes under the name Singapore Airlines, Malaysia getting the domestic Malayan routes under the name Malaysian Airline System.

Singapore Airlines set its cap on becoming one of the giants of international travel by emphasizing service, modern equipment, and competitive pricing. Its Singapore "girls," dressed in Pierre Balmain–designed Malay sarongs, ply passengers—even those in economy class—with one of the most lavish food and beverage services in the air. Singapore Airlines did not join the airline cartel, the International Air Transport Association, leaving it free to go its own way and thumb its nose at more established competitors. Irritated by the aggressive "free market" stance of Singapore Airlines, Pan American World Airways once asked the U.S. government to repeal its aviation agreement with Singapore. The Singaporean airline retorted that Pan Am was trying to create "a monopolistic regime" because it couldn't "thrive in open competition." When Lufthansa objected to deep discounting by Singapore, the airline suggested that some Europeans had lost their "old flair and drive."

In 1979, in a talk that's still remembered in airline circles, Lim Chin Beng, then managing director and later deputy chairman of Singapore Airlines, addressed a convention of Australian travel agents and delivered a blistering indictment of the Australian government and Qantas, accusing them of trying to drive the airlines of developing countries to the wall with a new International Civil Aviation Policy (ICAP), which he characterized as "a new four-letter word" and "a dangerous, self-serving form of protectionism." Lim told the travel agents: "We have a right to compete for your business. It is in your interests that we should do so. We don't believe Qantas or any other European airline owns a specific market. And in return for fair access to your market, we trade your access to ours. Our national airlines have been set up to serve our countries. Singapore Airlines is there to serve Singapore's interests. Qantas is there to serve Australia's. What is wrong with ICAP is the belief that Australia is there to serve Qantas rather than the other way around."

In a world where businessmen rarely get beyond platitudes, it was a remarkable talk and an example of how Singapore Airlines is always ready to fight for its share of the air travel market. Singapore's big bargaining chip in this fight is its location at the hub of the Orient. Situated at the southern tip of the Malay Peninsula, equidistant from Calcutta to the northwest and Hong Kong to the northeast, Singapore has long been a major stopping point for traders. It's a gateway to Southeast Asia, Australia, and Europe. In the post–World War II years, Singapore, whose population is 75 percent ethnic Chinese, turned into one of the great success stories of Southeast Asia under the puritanical, benevolent leadership of Prime Minister Lee Kuan Yew. The island republic has become a financial and high-tech center symbolized by its skyline of skyscrapers and a port that's the fourth busiest in the world. Those are all reasons why airlines want to fly to Singapore.

In 1986 more than forty carriers were touching down at Singapore's gleaming Changi Airport. The international airline business has an old rule: "If we let you land in our country, you must let us land in yours." Singapore invoked that rule to get into the airports of the world and then used its exotic charm to capture customers. By 1986 it was carrying 26 percent of the passengers on international flights.

The history of Singapore Airlines is one of constant expansion. In 1985, for example, it inaugurated new routes to Vienna, Karachi, Malta, Beijing, Shanghai, and Mauritius. In April 1986 it began serving three new cities, Manchester, New Delhi, and Bali, bringing its total number of destinations to fifty-one cities in thirty-four countries. Singapore, one of the best friends Boeing ever had, closed out 1985 with a fleet of twenty-one Boeing 747s, four 757s, and six 310 Airbuses. It claims to have the youngest fleet in the airline industry—its planes are, on average, two and a half years old. In 1986 it placed an order with Boeing for twenty of its new B747-400 jumbo jets. At $3.3 billion it was the biggest order ever made for a single aircraft model.

Singapore Airlines accounts for 3.6 percent of the gross national product of Singapore. It employs one out of every eighty-nine workers in the country, and in 1985 it contributed $140 million to the government's coffers.

A major development in 1985 was the first sale of shares to the public. The airline sold 100 million shares to investors located primarily in Singapore, Britain, and the United States. The shares were priced at five Singapore dollars apiece ($2.40), and the offering left the government holding 63 percent of the shares, the employees 20 percent, and the public the remaining 17 percent. J. Y. Pillay, chairman of Singapore Airlines from its inception, noted the significance of this sale in the annual report:

> "Public listing imposes a measure of discipline on the Company and its employees. Employees recognize that with the flotation, their responsibilities take on an additional dimension: meeting the aspirations of a global and critical shareholdership. They realise that to justify the issue price of five dollars, annual profit cannot be allowed to fall below $300 million [$140 million in U.S. dollars]. They will not fail the test, even if it means belt-tightening. After all, they own a sizeable chunk of the Company."

The World's Oldest Airline

The oldest airline in the world is KLM Royal Dutch Airlines. It was founded on October 7, 1919.

In the year ended March 31, 1986, Singapore Airlines earned, in Singaporean dollars, $311 million before—and $250 million after—taxes. In the next year it made even more money, and the government, in the middle of 1987, unloaded another batch of shares, bringing its holdings down to 53.5 percent. Whereas it collected $5 a share in 1985, the government was now getting $13 ($6.20 U.S.). Terms of the original offering restricted foreign ownership to 20 percent, but the government moved in 1987 to move that limit up to 25 percent. (Attention, Singaporeans, watch out for Frank Lorenzo and Carl Icahn!)

Access   Airline House
25 Airline Rd.
Singapore 1781
(65) 542-3333

8350 Wilshire Blvd.
Los Angeles, Calif. 90211-2381
(213) 655-8830

Société Générale de Belgique

Value of Holdings	$1.8 billion (tip of the iceberg)
Remittances	+$200 million
Rank	Economic tsar of Belgium
Founded	1822
Employees	147 (commanding a multitude)
Headquarters	Brussels, Belgium

Meet the outfit identified by *The Wall Street Journal* as "the company that runs Belgium." Société Générale de Belgique is one of six holding companies, or trusts, that control major chunks of the Belgian economy—and Société Générale is the biggest one of them all. It's believed to control companies which mine 40 percent of the coal, produce 50 percent of the steel, process 65 percent of the nonferrous metals, and generate 35 percent of the electricity produced by this northern European country of 10 million people. (The other five Belgian trusts are Brufina-Confinindus, with companies active in the steel, coal, electricity, and engineering sectors; Groupe Solvay, chemicals; Groupe Copee, steel and coal; Empain, electrical equipment and transportation lines; and Banque Lambert, oil.)

Société Générale has spun an intricate web of corporate entities that cross various fields (industrial, financial, agricultural, shipping, real estate) and various national borders (at one time it owned a sizable piece of Africa). Its labyrinthine structure defies penetration. Even determining how many companies are tied to it is not easy. The companies in the maze own pieces of each other, and many of them have subsidiaries of their own. Some are publicly traded companies. Others are completely private. Société Générale may be the only company that issues a supplement to its annual report that has an index of the companies mentioned. In the 1985 edition 364 companies were indexed, but that doesn't begin to exhaust the number of enterprises connected to Société Générale. One estimate put the total at twelve hundred.

The best way to define Société Générale might be as a development bank. Its mission is to serve Belgium by promoting industry and trade. The holdings it does have in companies, while influential if not controlling, are usually minority interests. And the sales and profits of these companies are not consolidated in Société Générale's balance sheet. That's why, powerful as it is, Société Générale never makes the international ranking lists compiled by *BusinessWeek, Forbes,* and *Fortune.* Société Générale works its financial wizardry behind the scenes.

Fewer than 150 people work in its rue Royale offices in the heart of Brussels, not far from the headquarters of the European Common Market. However, the number working in companies partially or wholly owned by Société Générale may exceed a quarter of a million. And if the sales of all the companies it started, backed, acquired, or sheltered were combined, the revenues would be in the billions of dollars. In 1970, in a rare moment of disclosure during a visit to New York, Max Nokin, an engineer who then headed this Belgian holding tank, revealed that Société Générale had controlling interests in companies whose assets totaled $5.5 billion and whose employees totaled 150,000. Two years later, in the euphoria of its one-hundred-fiftieth anniversary, the company owned up to being "the driving force of a whole collection of companies" which provided jobs for "nearly 260,000 workers, of whom 200,000 were in Belgium." Since then: silence.

The people at Société Générale get irritated at outsiders poking around its vaults, depicting the company as a mysterious, rapacious conglomerate. In a moment of exasperation in 1979, the two top officials at Société Générale—Governor Paul Emile Corbiau and Director-Secretary Baron de Fauconval—wrote to the *Financial Times* to lecture the paper about trying to apply English accounting standards to their company, which they described as "a special structure, virtually unknown in the English-speaking world, and fundamentally different from specialized industrial holding companies, who generally own 100 percent of their subsidiaries." At Société Générale, they explained, the "subsidiaries are, in fact, divisions constituted as separate legal entities."

Some of these "separate legal entities" are big enough in their own right to make the tables that rank the biggest companies in the world. One of the stars of this constellation is Générale de Banque, Belgium's largest bank, and the fifty-ninth-largest bank outside the United States, which is 17.2 percent–owned by Société Générale. Belgium may be a small country but Générale de Banque maintains 1,176 branch offices, far more than the number of Bank of America offices in California or Dai-Ichi Kangyo offices in Japan. Only nine U.S. banks have greater assets than Générale de Banque ($52 billion). Other major satellites of Société Générale include:

- Union Minière, a 100 percent–owned subsidiary active in nonferrous and precious metals (copper, zinc, cobalt, germanium, platinum). Union Minière, in turn, has a 56.5 percent stake in another Belgian company, Métallurgie Hoboken-Overpelt, a processor of nonferrous metals whose 1985 sales were $1.4 billion; and a 93.8

percent holding in Union Mines of the United States, which operates a zinc mine in Tennessee.

- ARBED, based in Luxembourg, is one of Europe's leading steel producers. Société Générale holds 25 percent of the stock. The other major holder (30 percent) is the Luxembourg government.
- Tanks, a 100 percent–owned investment company that itself owns 8.7 percent of Ashton Mining, an Australian company that, in turn, has a 38.2 percent stake in the Argyle Diamond Mine in Western Australia. Tanks also owns the Benguela Railway in Angola (where service has been spotty in recent years because of a civil war), and 50 percent of Dillon, Read Ltd., the London investment banking arm of the Wall Street firm of the same name.
- Petrofina, the sixth-largest oil company in Europe. Société Générale has an indirect holding of 10.4 percent.

That short list doesn't do justice to the breadth of Société Générale. Its holdings are so diverse that the people in its Brussels headquarters may not be aware of all the pieces in the puzzle. You can see the hand of Société Générale in an abandoned coal mine in Bicknell, Indiana; the mothballed Oracle Ridge copper mine in Arizona; zinc foundries at Viviez and Auby, France; distribution of Ford vehicles and tractors in Britain; a leading French advertising agency; a hydroelectric power station at Lubilanji in Zaire (the former Belgian Congo); diamond mines in Zaire; a new brewery at Zhuhai in the People's Republic of China; manufacture of railway cars and escalators; laser instruments; residential development in Florida and Belgium; a shipping line; life and casualty insurance; paper making in Belgium; Valencia orange groves in Spain.

Just sorting out the complex relationships is an exercise in accounting legerdemain. In 1985, for example, Société Générale owned directly 14.86 percent—and indirectly another 21.7 percent—of Tractionel, itself a holding company in the fields of energy, engineering, and telecommunications. And Société Générale also owned directly 10 percent—and indirectly another 15.84 percent—of Electrobel, still another holding company active in generation of electricity, distribution of gas, engineering, and telecommunications. Tractionel, on its own hook, owned 5 percent of Petrofina, the big Belgian oil company, and 100 percent of a French company, INEC, which in 1985 bought 10 percent of a German company, Geiger. Then there was still another holding company, Electrafina, 26 percent–owned by Société Générale, which owned 9 percent of Electrobel and 11 percent of Tractionel. And on top of that Tractionel and Electrobel had a joint venture, Telfin, which had joined with the giant French electronics company Compagnie Générale d'Électricité (CGE) in a pan-European telecommunications consortium.

This was too complicated even for Société Générale, which announced at the end of 1985 that it planned to merge Electrobel and Tractionel.

In the closing days of 1986, Société Générale emerged as a minority player in Alcatel, a worldwide telecommunications giant spliced together by CGE of France and ITT of the United States. The Belgians are down for 5.7 percent of a company that ranks second only to American Telephone & Telegraph in the business of making telephone systems work.

Société Générale is so busy buying, selling, and rearranging assets that it's never easy to keep up with it. One of its major dispositions in 1986 was the sale of an 18 percent interest in Genstar, a Canadian conglomerate that had extensive interests in real estate, cement, building materials, and financial services. After pocketing an $85-million capital gain on this sale, Société Générale had another one of its satellites, CBR Cementbedrijven, buy the cement part of Genstar from Imasco, the Canadian company that had bought all of Genstar. CBR is Belgium's largest cement maker, and Société Générale owns 25 percent of it.

The origins of Société Générale predate the establishment of Belgium as an independent nation. The Belgian territory was traded back and forth among a number of nations (Spain, France, Austria) before the 1815 Congress of Vienna attached it to the new Royal Kingdom of the Netherlands. The region was already known as the home of craftsmen, and in 1822, to stimulate industrial development there, King William I established the *"Société Générale de Pays-Bas pour favoriser l'Industrie nationale."* It had an open-ended mandate "to participate in any undertaking which is generally useful."

In 1830, when the Belgians revolted against Dutch rule and declared their independence, Société Générale survived the transformation even though its biggest shareholder was King William I. The new Belgian government needed money, and Société Générale provided it and became the banker for the newborn state. In those days, it was simply called "The Bank."

Serving as the development arm of the state, Société Générale helped Belgium to become the most industrialized country on the continent of Europe, a leader in railways, coal mines, and engineering. And after Leopold II came to power in 1865, that development was extended beyond Belgium. Belgian enterprises sparked industrial development in many parts of the world. The Belgians built railways in Italy, South America, and China. After the advent of electricity, Belgian-built trams, hooked to overhead lines, lurched through Florence, Cairo, Damascus, Istanbul, and Tientsin. Shortly after the turn of the century, Belgian firms were active all over Russia, accounting for 75 percent of coke by-products, 50 percent of the plate glass production, 40 percent of the sulphuric acid, and important shares of coal and oil output. Belgium had an economic weight that belied its size. And Société Générale could claim major credit for nurturing that industrial sinew.

Of course the overseas venture that Belgium was most associated with is the Belgian Congo, a huge territory in Central Africa about one third the size of the United States and eighty times the size of Belgium. Now the independent country of Zaire, the territory was colonized by King Leopold II, beginning in 1885 when the "Free State of the Congo" was established. This was not at first a Belgian colony. Leopold ran it as his personal fiefdom. His representatives, notably the Anglo-American journalist and explorer Henry Stanley (of the "Dr. Livingstone, I presume" fame) negotiated treaties with tribes that left the Belgian monarch free to exploit all the natural resources of the territory in return for such gifts as red handkerchiefs and cases of gin.

The Congo turned out to be rich in mineral wealth—copper, cobalt, industrial diamonds, tin, uranium—and for the next seventy-five years the Belgians mined those resources. No colony in Africa produced more bloodcurdling reports of cruelty toward the native population than the Belgian Congo, and these stories were factors in ending Leopold's personal hegemony over the Congo in 1908, when it officially became a Belgian colony.

To listen to the Belgians, they brought civilization to a backward jungle area. They built roads, railways, schools, hospitals. And they claimed to have "trained workers to the highest degrees of technical skills attained in Central Africa." To listen to their critics, the Belgians ruthlessly exploited the Congolese, sucking out the wealth and failing to develop native professional expertise, as the British and French did in their colonies. In 1952 Herbert Solow, a *Fortune* writer, toured the Belgian Congo and found it to be working well, with a growing economy benefiting both Belgians and natives, dispelling "the notion that all colonialism is one evil thing."

In 1960, when the Congolese were about to throw out the Belgians, a *BusinessWeek* reporter rendered a different verdict:

> One thing is sure: There will be no sympathy in the Congo for Belgian businessmen. In all the Congo's years as a colony, Belgium took out far more than it put in. Whatever investment was made in the Congo to develop

resources came almost entirely from the profits of companies already there. In the past five years alone, the net outflow from the Congo amounted to around $1.3 billion.

No matter who visited the Belgian Congo at any point between 1885 and 1960, there was no dispute as to the identity of the dominant commercial power—it was Société Générale and its associated companies. *They* operated the mines, *they* refined and processed the ores, *they* operated the shipping lines that served the colony, *they* imported the goods that were sold there, and *they* controlled the banking institutions. In the years after World War II, the Belgian Congo contributed more than half the profits of Société Générale.

The 1960 transition from a Belgian colony to an independent state was anything but peaceful. It was followed by civil war, the assassination of the most popular native political leader, Patrice Lumumba, and the installation, supported by the United States and Belgium, of Joseph Mobutu as the head of a regime widely depicted as repressive and corrupt. Société Générale's Union Minière du Haut Katanga was nationalized by Zaire, but the Mobutu government then invited the Belgians back to operate the mines. Trying to find out more about this arrangement, *Wall Street Journal* reporter Jonathan Kwitny told in his book *Endless Enemies* what he discovered:

> How much did Société Générale get when it sold its mining interest in Zaire to the Zairian government? "It wasn't for nothing, but that I cannot tell you," said Jean Dachy, director general of the company's main mineral subsidiary. How much does Société Générale make now by supplying Zaire with expertise, customers, shipping, smelting, insurance, and who knows what else? "It's an agreement between two countries and I don't think I can give you any information about that."
>
> Is the price Zaire gets for its minerals at least fair? "A lot of people have very loose opinions about that, but they don't know anything," said Dachy. "It's very dangerous to discuss this without understanding the whole arrangement. But I'm certainly not allowed to disclose that. We get something, they get something."

Attempting to understand what goes on in Société Générale has long been an exercise in futility. Just getting a fix on the ownership seems to be impossible. Société Générale stock trades on the stock exchange in Brussels (it was selling for about $100 a share in mid-1987), but it's not clear where control lies. In 1969 *Fortune* reported that two insurance companies owned the majority of shares. And who controlled the insurance companies? Société Générale, of course. Kwitny, writing as recently as 1984, repeated a version that goes back to the founding of the company when he said, "Société Générale is in large part owned by the King of Belgium as a personal business venture."

The same problems arise in assessing the influence of Société Générale. According to many versions, it's an octopus with tentacles grasping all the major economic institutions in Belgium—and many overseas. According to others, it's more like a trust which collects dividends but doesn't exert much management influence over the subsidiaries. In 1986 Roger Medart, a former Belgian government official, told *Wall Street Journal* reporter Mark M. Nelson that Société Générale never could control the big companies that were part of its portfolio. The managers of the steel and coal companies "were kings," said Medart, and Société Générale "never had the power to influence them. So they just kept making more and more steel, and acquiring more and more production facilities. There was no vision. It was an idiotic situation."

Société Générale itself once said: "It is very difficult to define the limits of the position which Société Générale occupies in the Belgian economy." It went on to point out that its influence on companies in its family varies all over the lot, depending on the number of shares it holds, its representation on the board of directors, financial structures, management organization, and "all manner of regulations and official requirements." It's not, in other words, a simple parent-subsidiary relationship. And the result? Here it is, in Société Générale's own words:

Japanese versus U.S. Investment in Europe (billions)

	Japan	United States
United Kingdom	$3.14	33.96
the Netherlands	1.69	7.06
West Germany	1.34	16.75
Luxembourg	1.22	0.46
France	0.82	7.83
Belgium	0.74	5.10
Switzerland	0.66	16.23
Spain	0.51	2.60
Ireland	0.26	3.75
Italy	0.18	5.64
Total all Europe	$11.00	$106.80

"This results in the policy of Société Générale, in the form in which it finds expression through the companies concerned, being characterized by its great flexibility. The fact that its connections are manifold gives wide repercussion to anything it does; but there are other influences by which the effect is molded into a more intricate pattern, so that its unilateral character disappears."

Access   rue Royale 30
1000 Brussels, Belgium
(32) 2-517-1672

Generale Bank
12 E. 49th St.
New York, N.Y. 10017
(212) 418-8705

Sony	**Sales** $8.2 billion
	Profits $258 million
	U.S. Sales $2.7 billion
	Rank World's 3d-largest color television manufacturer
	World's largest maker of personal stereo players
	World's largest supplier of broadcasting equipment
	Japan's 3d-largest consumer electronics company
	World's largest maker of compact disc players
	World's 2d-largest maker of compact discs
	Founded 1946
	Employees 48,700 (7,000 in the United States)
	Headquarters Tokyo, Japan

Akio Morita, cofounder of Sony Corporation, was born on January 26, 1921, in a village near Nagoya, Japan's third-largest city. He was the eldest son of a well-to-do sake brewer. His family had been making sake for three hundred years under the name Nenohimatsu. "But from the time I was a small boy," Morita once recalled, "I was interested in music—not playing it, but listening to it. That led to an interest in audio equipment. When I was a schoolboy, I made an electric phonograph."

Morita therefore broke with the family tradition of sake brewing. (A younger brother, Kazuaki, took over the family business.) He majored in physics at Osaka Imperial University and after graduating in 1944, when World War II still raged, he joined the Japanese Navy, working in a technical research laboratory. It was there that he met and befriended an engineer, Masaru Ibuka, who had a company that did electronics research for the Japanese military. After the war Ibuka and Morita teamed up with Ibuka's father-in-law, Tamon Maeda, to form Tokyo Tsushin Kogyo (Tokyo Telecommunications Engineering). Morita received permission from his father to abandon the sake trade. In fact, his father helped to finance the venture.

From the start Ibuka and Morita decided that they wanted to make innovative products. Ibuka had fooled around for a while with an electric rice cooker (now a staple in Japanese homes) but couldn't perfect it. He then made a device that could convert a standard radio receiver into a shortwave set—and it had a big response from Japanese consumers who were, as researcher George Fields put it, "starved for sounds from the outside world."

The fledgling company could have gone into the production of radios, but Morita and Ibuka rejected that "me-too" path. They were interested in products no one else was making—at least in Japan. In 1950 then, Tokyo Tsushin became the first Japanese company to produce a tape recorder. It was so new that no one in Japan knew how to use it, and Morita and Ibuka, after their technological triumph, had to educate prospective customers such as schools on how a tape recorder could be useful. It fell to Morita to handle this promotional job.

"I then realized," he recounted in his autobiography, "that having unique technology and being able to make unique products are not enough to keep a business going. You have to sell the products, and to do that you have to show the potential buyer the real value of what you are selling. I was struck with the realization that I was going to have to be the merchandiser of our small company. We were fortunate in having a genius like Ibuka who could concentrate totally on innovative product design and production while I learned the merchandising end."

It was a lesson he learned well. Morita became the company's star salesman—and he still is.

Their search for the innovative product led Morita to travel to New York in 1953. There he signed an agreement to pay Western Electric $25,000 for the use of the transistor technology that had been developed at Bell Labs. From New York he went on to tour Europe, and he remembers visiting the Philips electronics works at Eindhoven in rural Holland. He wrote to Ibuka from there, saying, "If Philips can do it, maybe we can, too."

Armed with this new technology, Ibuka and Morita worked so rapidly that they were almost the first in the world to make a transistorized radio. They were the first in Japan, but a small American company, Regency, using a Texas Instruments transistor, beat them to the punch by several months. Regency never did capitalize on its breakthrough, which occurred in 1955. In Japan, Ibuka and Morita did. They set out to make the world's smallest radio.

"Miniaturization and compactness have always appealed to the Japanese," Morita has explained. "Our boxes have been made to nest; our fans fold; our art rolls into neat scrolls; screens that can artistically depict an entire city can be folded and tucked neatly away, or set up to delight, entertain, and educate, or merely to divide a room."

Their pocket-sized radio was introduced in 1957. It was actually a little bigger than the pocket on most men's shirts, which was disappointing because they had wanted their salesmen to pitch the radio that way. They solved that problem by having special shirts made with outsized pockets for the sales force.

The small transistorized radio was the first to carry the brand name Sony. Morita, in a 1973 interview, told how the name came about: "We had decided that we wanted a short name for our products, an international name that would sound the same all over the world. So Mr. Ibuka and I worked together, checking many, many dictionaries, and we found two terms, *sonus,* a Latin word meaning sound, and *sonny boy.* So we thought: We are a group of sonny boys in the sonus business. So we combined *sonus* and *sonny* and came up with Sony."

In June 1957 Sony put up the first billboard featuring its brand name opposite the entrance to Tokyo's Haneda International Airport. By the end of the year, it had one up in lights in Tokyo's Ginza district. The company officially changed its name to Sony Corporation in January 1958, and by the end of that year the Sony name was up in lights on the Tokyo Stock Exchange.

Not many Japanese companies behave in this freewheeling fashion. And indeed the comment has frequently been made that Sony is more American than Japanese. Morita has done little to dispel that notion. If any Japanese company has a cult of personality, it's Sony. Akio Morita *is* Sony. Who outside of Japan has heard of Konosuke Matsushita? Morita is so identified with Sony that American Express used him in its series of "Do you know me?" commercials featuring prominent people who carry the American Express card.

Stories written about the company and its products inevitably end up describing and quoting Morita. In 1987, forty-one years after the founding of the company, he was featured on the cover of *BusinessWeek,* and shown skiing, a sport he didn't try until he was sixty years old. Hardly anything is ever heard about his wartime buddy Ibuka, the co-founder of Sony, whose title in 1987 was honorary chairman. While Morita roams the world hobnobbing with celebrities, Sony is run by Norio Ohga, a former opera singer who was recruited by Morita in 1959 after he criticized Sony as a company "run by engineers." Morita delights in reporting in his autobiography that in Ohga's first year with the company he did the un-Japanese act of "hiring almost forty people away from other companies."

The typical way for a Japanese company to enter an overseas market is to turn the assignment over to a big trading company that is experienced in selling all kinds of products outside Japan. Not Sony. In 1958 Sony opened its own branch office in New York, and two years later it established a full-fledged marketing subsidiary in the United States, Sony Corporation of America. To handle its advertising, Sony selected not just any advertising agency but Doyle Dane Bernbach, the leader of the creative revolution on Madison Avenue.

Morita himself moved to New York to oversee Sony's push into the American market. "From the very beginning I tried to learn the American way of doing things," he told reporter Lally Weymouth. "I was convinced America would be a very important market for us, so I wanted to know America itself. I lived at 1010 Fifth Avenue. I insisted on living in the best place because we like to be associated with good society, good families. No Japanese families lived on Fifth Avenue in 1963."

Morita had a clear idea of what he wanted to do: Establish the Sony name as a symbol of innovation and high quality. When Bulova Watch approached him with a proposal that Sony produce transistor radios under the U.S. company's brand name, Morita rejected the order even though it was for a whopping one hundred thousand units. According to Morita, the Bulova people said to him, "Our company name is a famous brand name that has taken over fifty years to establish. Nobody has ever heard of your brand name. Why not take advantage of ours?"

Morita replied, "Fifty years ago, your brand name must have been just as unknown as our name is today. I am here with a new product, and I am now taking the first step for the next fifty years of my company. Fifty years from now I promise you that our name will be just as famous as your company is today."

To a large extent Morita succeeded in establishing Sony as a worldwide brand name associated with quality. Among Japanese companies Sony's profile is distinctive. It does only a quarter of its business in its home country. Its biggest market is the United States, where it does a third of its sales. Europe accounts for another 20 percent of sales.

Sony has been readier than most Japanese companies to manufacture its products outside Japan. It began making television sets in San Diego in 1971, the first Japanese company to produce receivers in America, and Morita boasts that the Sony name was so well known by then that it didn't have to advertise for employees; word-of-mouth brought them in. Sony manufactures in England, France, West Germany, Spain, and Austria. It was planning to become in 1988 the first Japanese company to manufacture in Italy. In 1986 overseas production accounted for 22 percent of the company's sales. Sony's goal is to raise that proportion to 40 percent by 1990. To underline its commitment to a global strategy, in 1987 Sony dispatched Morita's younger brother, Masaaki, to the United States to chair the American unit while also serving as deputy president responsible for worldwide manufacturing. Name any other Japanese company that would place its head of worldwide manufacturing in New York.

Morita also pioneered on Wall Street. In 1961, only a year after Morita took up residence on Fifth Avenue, Sony became the first Japanese company in history to sell stock to American investors, raising $4 million in a public offering. Nine years later, pioneering again, Sony became the first Japanese company to gain a listing on the New York Stock Exchange. Morita, who jets across oceans the way some people take buses, was there for the execution of the first trade. Today Sony stock can be bought on twenty-three stock exchanges around the world, including all the major ones. One third of its shares are in non-Japanese hands. It has, in short, an international presence, and Morita has served as the company's good-will ambassador. He's unquestionably the most well known Japanese businessman.

Sony still tries to follow its original prescription: Come up with unique products. It was the first to make transistorized television sets. It invented the portable stereo player called Walkman (and sold more than twenty million of them), and it followed with a hand-held, flat television set, the Watchman. It pioneered the compact disc player with Philips. It revolutionized television news gathering with its hand-held video cameras. In 1985 it introduced its paperback-sized, 8-mm video camera/recorder.

Not everything has worked for Sony. A major disappointment was its Betamax VCR, which lost out to the VHS system fielded by JVC and Matsushita. As a result Sony had the unpleasant experience of being scooped on a product that it invented.

In the 1980s, as other giants of the electronics world began to creep up and compete effectively against Sony, the company reversed its long-standing practice of not making components for others. Sony plants in Japan now make video monitors for IBM and disc drives for Apple and Hewlett-Packard. For years Sony made semiconductors only for its own use. Now it makes them for others. It looks to get 50 percent of its business from industrial sources in the future. That may mean millions of dollars of products made by Sony but no longer carrying its name. Its Japanese competitors are getting their revenge. It remains to be seen, however, whether they will be able to take the measure of Sony, whose strategy has always been not to duke it out in the mass marketplace but to come up with the innovative product that commands a premium price. Beating competitors to the punch is Sony's trademark.

Sony also owns 53 percent of a smaller electronics company, Aiwa. And Aiwa apparently doesn't qualify for the "no layoff, lifetime employment" standard that Morita upholds for Sony. In 1986 Aiwa eliminated twelve hundred factory jobs, closed one of its two Japanese plants, and shifted most of its production to Singapore. Two former Sony men were in charge of this dismantling of Japanese production, which left only 470 factory employees in Japan, as against more than one thousand in Singapore. Hetaro Nakajima, president of Aiwa, said his board opposed these moves at first as being "un-Japanese," but he persuaded them. "You cannot row a boat for a long time against the stream," Nakajima told the *Financial Times* in words reminiscent of what American companies say when they move production offshore. "Management must find the direction of the stream and put the boat in that direction."

Meanwhile, Akio Morita remained his confident self, running Sony with a distinctive style. In his autobiography, *Made in Japan*, which was published in the United States and Japan in 1986, the Sony chief said that some Japanese companies are ready to resort to espionage to steal secrets, and he noted, without naming them, that several were caught in an FBI sting operation in 1982. "I have laid down strict rules against this kind of practice," solemnized Morita.

To prevent Sony people from going out after work and socializing in bars ("Tongues oiled by beer, sake, and whiskey do tend to wag."), he established the Sony Club in an unmarked building near the company's Tokyo headquarters. This is a company-owned nonprofit bar where managers can come "to entertain their subordinates." The place is for the exclusive use of Sony employees. "Nobody else, no matter how important, is ever admitted," said Morita. "Executives from section chief up get a credit card for the club, and their bar bills can be automatically deducted from their paychecks."

Anyone who reads *Made in Japan* will learn quickly enough that Morita has strong opinions on everything, and is not bashful about presenting them. One of his views is that Americans have a soft spot in their hearts for the underdog. One result, said Morita, was this: "American sympathy for China's Chiang Kai-shek as the underdog in the war with Japan (dramatized by his charming American-educated, English-speaking wife), turned into a national consensus that eventually helped to drive the United States and Japan to war."

While Morita did not enter the family's sake business, his eldest son, Hideo, did. In 1987 thirty-five-year-old Hideo Morita was second in command to his uncle Kazuaki at Morita & Company, which was still in the traditional business of making sake, shoyu, and miso but had also branched out into supermarkets and a service component, Raykay, offering language and cooking courses to the growing horde of foreign business executives in Tokyo. Hideo was apparently content to be with the original business, pointing out to *BusinessWeek* that Sony was a venture of the Morita company. Instead of repaying the loans from his father, Akio gave him stock in Sony. In 1987 Morita & Company was the largest shareholder in Sony, holding 9.4 percent of the stock, worth about $400 million. Not bad for an initial investment of five hundred dollars.

Access 7-35, Kitashinagawa 6-chome, Shinagawa-ku
Tokyo 141, Japan
(81) 3-448-2111

Sony Corp. of America
9 West 57th St.
New York, N.Y. 10019
(212) 371-5800

<table>
<tr><td rowspan="11" valign="top">

Swedish Match

</td><td>

Sales $1.6 billion

Profits $117 million

U.S. Sales $250 million

Rank World's largest match manufacturer
World's 2d-largest disposable lighter maker
World's 2d-largest maker of flooring
Sweden's largest maker of doors
Sweden's 12th-largest manufacturing company

Founded 1917

Employees 25,600 (1,770 in the United States)

Headquarters Stockholm, Sweden

</td></tr>
</table>

The world's largest maker of matches was created by Ivar Kreuger, an authentic genius and, as it turned out, a swindler on a scale never before—or since—attempted. Kreuger was a man far ahead of his time, a multinational operator who would have thrived in today's global marketplace. In the dozen years after World War I, he reached a pinnacle of wealth, power, and influence through a commercial empire that stretched to virtually all corners of the world—and on top of that, he enjoyed a reputation as a socially conscious business leader. John Kenneth Galbraith dubbed him the "Leonardo" of larcenists. John Maynard Keynes said that Kreuger had "maybe the greatest financial intelligence of his time."

The foundation of Kreuger's empire was a prosaic product, the wooden match. Man's promethean efforts to produce fire go back a long way, but it wasn't until the early part of the nineteenth century that matches were commercially made. They were needed to light kerosene lamps and gas stoves. After electricity arrived on the scene at the end of the nineteenth century, the match industry found a new market in the growing number of cigarette smokers. The first matches made were dangerous—to the makers and the users—because they contained (and sometimes released) a toxic substance, yellow phosphorus. In 1844 Gustaf Eric Pasch, a professor at the Swedish Royal Academy of Science, invented the safety match by using red phosphorus instead of yellow and transferring it from the match head to a striking surface. An oxidizing agent in the match head then ignited when (and only when) it was struck against this surface. In France, toward the end of the nineteenth century, the so-called *sesqui* matches were invented; they were the "strike anywhere" matches.

Sweden became a leader of this industry, not only because the safety match was invented there. So was one of the earliest machines to make matches. Alexander Lagerman developed that piece of equipment in 1872. Eight years later Ivar Kreuger was born in Kalmar, a city in the south of Sweden. He was born into a match making family. His father operated a match factory that had been started by *his* father. As described in Robert Shaplen's biography *Kreuger,* published in 1960, Ivar Kreuger was an amoral kid in short pants, apparently lacking any sense of right or wrong. "Once," related Shaplen, "he used a set of false keys to enter the school principal's office and obtain final term papers before they were announced—he sold them for the equivalent of a nickel to his fellow students."

Kreuger showed no early interest in the match business. He became an engineer and while his younger brother, Torsten, took over the family match factory, Ivar roamed the world, taking jobs in South Africa, Germany, Canada and, particularly, the United States, a country he repaired to for three different stretches. He loved hanging out at the New York Stock Exchange. In 1908, at age twenty-eight, he returned to Sweden, forming a partnership with another engineer, Paul Toll. Kreuger & Toll became a successful construction and real estate firm.

However, it wasn't long before he was drawn into the family match business. The Kreugers were then very small players in this industry. The dominant force in Swedish matches was Jonkoping & Vulcan, the result of a 1903 merger of three big companies—it held 75 percent of the market. Kreuger in 1913 roped together all the other match companies in Sweden into a new entity called United Match Factories. He seemed to know, even at that early stage, why he was leaving the engineering business to sell penny matches. "With typical cold logic," Shaplen wrote, "he realized that, in matches, he was dealing with something that everyone used everywhere, and that, because Swedish know-how was superior, he might become the match tycoon of Europe." What he actually had in mind was becoming the match king of the world. And—for a brief, heady period—he did just that. He wasn't the only one with this idea. Ohio Columbus Barber, the founder of the Diamond Match Company of the United States, also harbored such aspirations but was never able to pull it off. Another unsuccessful aspirant was the British company Bright & May, which put up match factories in Australia, New Zealand, and South Africa.

What the others didn't have was a ruthless Ivar Kreuger at the helm. His first target was Jonkoping & Vulcan, which he took over in 1917 by artificially inflating the value of his own company so that his smaller firm could swallow the larger one. That was the birth of Swedish Match—and a foretaste of what was to come. As soon as World War I ended in 1918, Ivar Kreuger set out to conquer the world.

Kreuger bought up match factories wherever he could, striking deals with state governments to give him a monopoly position. Where he couldn't buy out a local company, he tried to take a minority stake (sometimes secretly). One of his tactics was to send secret agents to make ridiculously low bids for factories, and after they were rejected, he would come in with a much higher bid, which the owners were glad to see. In Austria he secretly bought a major interest in the leading match company, which had satellite factories in Hungary, Czechoslovakia, and Yugoslavia. He gained complete control of the match industries in Norway, Finland, Denmark, Holland, and Switzerland. He negotiated an import agreement with Bright & May in Britain, meanwhile acquiring control of the number two British producer, Masters & Company and secretly buying up shares in Diamond Match of the United States. In some countries—India, for example—he put up his own match factories.

With these bold strokes, Ivar Kreuger put Sweden into the front ranks of international finance. The economic instability that followed World War I was made to order for Kreuger—with nations jealous of one another and wild speculation the order of the day on stock exchanges around the world. He flourished, shifting from capital to capital to make his moves, and he emerged in 1927 as not just a maker of matches but as a lender of money to national governments. These loans were usually tied to the match business—that is, Kreuger agreed to lend money to a country in return for a monopoly of the match business—although some loans, $75 million to France notably, had to be made without the *quid pro quo* of a monopoly.

By 1930 Kreuger had outstanding loans of some $360 million to more than a dozen countries, including Hungary, Poland, Rumania, Greece, Ecuador, Estonia, Bolivia, and Turkey. The loans financed some worthwhile projects. In Greece, for example, the loan repatriated Greek refugees from Turkey and Bulgaria. Hungary, Latvia, and Estonia launched land reform programs with the Kreuger loans. In 1930, when banks and governments of Europe and the United States were putting together a $200-million loan package—the so-called Young Loan—that would enable Germany to pay its war reparations, Kreuger went to the conference at The Hague and agreed to take $30 million of the loan, an action that won him praise from politicians and economists as the "savior of Europe."

Kreuger appeared to be at the zenith of his powers when he made that offer. According to Karl-Gustaf Hildebrand, an economic historian at Sweden's Upsala University and the author of a Swedish Match history, Kreuger in 1930 controlled match companies in thirty-three countries, with an annual output of 2.8 million cases or 20.16 million boxes, representing 40 percent of the world's match production. Nor were matches his only interest. Kreuger had also acquired control of three major Swedish companies: L. M. Ericsson, a telecommunications pioneer; Svenska Cellulosa, a timber, pulp, and paper producer; and Boliden, a mining company in North Sweden reputed to be sitting on the third-largest gold deposit in the world. He had built this empire in ten years!

How he built it was a story known only to himself even though a number of his companies had stock exchange listings and securities which were among the most widely distributed in the world. "Throughout his bizarre career," Shaplen said, "Kreuger alone supplied the figures for the books of his various companies, and he mostly kept them in his head." Kreuger's four main companies were Swedish Match and Kreuger & Toll in Sweden, International Match in New York, and Continental Investment in Liechtenstein. He kept money moving back and forth among them, instructing docile lieutenants what to record.

Kreuger never had trouble raising money in America. Lee, Higginson, one of Wall Street's blueblood houses, was mesmerized by Kreuger and sold $148 million of securities for him to American investors. Nearly all of that was transferred out of the country to various Kreuger affiliates. "You Swedes are blockheads," he once told a friend. "You haggle about giving me money, but when I get off the boat in New York, I find men on the pier begging me to take money off their hands."

Kreuger's view of financial accounting was recalled vividly by Bjorn Prytz, a Swedish businessman and diplomat, who told Shaplen about a conversation he had with Kreuger while they were riding across Germany in a train. Kreuger said:

> "You know, it's a curious thing how every period in history has its own gods, its own high priests, and holy days. It's been true of politics and religion and war, and now it's true of economics. We've created something new. Instead of being fighting men, as in days of old, we're all in business, and we've chosen some new high priests and called them accountants. They too have a holy day—the thirty-first of December—on which we're supposed to confess. In olden times, the princes and everyone would go to confession because it was the thing to do, whether they believed it or not. Today the world demands balance sheets, profit-and-loss statements once a year. But if you're really working on great ideas, you can't supply these on schedule and expose yourself to view. Yet you've got to tell the public something, and so long as it's satisfied and continues to have faith in you, it's really not important what you confess. The December ceremony isn't really a law of the gods—it's just something we've invented. All right, let's

conform, but don't let's do it in a way that will spoil our plans. And someday people will realize that every balance sheet is wrong because it doesn't contain anything but figures. The real strengths and weaknesses of an enterprise lie in the plans."

It was a remarkable exposition of Kreuger's views, and it foreshadowed what was to come. After the stock market crash of 1929 and a worldwide liquidity crisis, Kreuger, artful juggler that he was, had difficulty holding the center together. The shares of his companies plummeted, and French enemies out to ruin him drove his shares down by short sales. He himself gambled massively on the stock market, losing as much as $100 million. In early 1932 Kreuger's personal liabilities ran to about $260 million. The real assets of his companies, an audit later showed, were one half of what he said they were. Between February and March 1932 Swedish Match had to repay a $2-million loan, a $4-million International Match debt was coming due, Kreuger & Toll had to pay out $1.2 million in scheduled dividends, and Kreuger owed $2 million to Turkey and more than $1 million to Lithuania as installments on match loans.

Kreuger was so desperate for cash that he ordered the Stockholm firm that prepared his stock certificates to lithograph forty-two Italian government bonds and five promissory notes with a total face value of $142 million. Kreuger then forged on the certificates the signatures of G. Boselli and A. Mosconi, the director of the Italian match monopoly and the Italian finance minister, respectively. He was working from signatures he had on other documents but still managed to spell "Boselli" three different ways on the forty-seven certificates. This was shortly after Kreuger's picture appeared on the cover of *Time*.

Kreuger had reached the end of his masterful, international balancing act. On March 12, 1932, in his bachelor apartment in Paris, he shot and killed himself. He was fifty-two years old. The world was full of praise for him. Keynes, in London, declared that Kreuger "had deemed it his task amid postwar chaos to create a canal between the countries of abundance of capital and those in bitter need of it [until he] was crushed between the icebergs of this frozen world." A Swedish newspaper said, "This is the hardest blow ever suffered by Sweden's economy. Even in its general impact, it can only be compared to loss of a war." The Riksdag, the Swedish parliament, immediately declared a day of national mourning.

It took four years and an army of lawyers, bankers, and accountants to straighten out Kreuger's affairs and decide who would get what. Among the participants in these negotiations were Wall Street lawyers

Bainbridge Colby, a former secretary of state, and John Foster Dulles, a future secretary of state. The Price, Waterhouse accounting firm eventually found that Kreuger had inflated the earnings of his companies by more than $250 million between 1917 and 1932. Many millions of dollars were never accounted for. In his book *The Incredible Ivar Kreuger* Allen Churchill related the testimony of Greta Gluydes, a secretary in one of the Kreuger companies, who said that Kreuger came in one afternoon and in the course of an hour dictated the annual reports of all his companies. She was then questioned as follows:

Q. Did Mr. Kreuger consult any books or memoranda when preparing these statements of the financial position of his companies?

A. No, he seemed to get most of the information out of his mind.

Q. Did you think this strange?

A. Yes, but I accounted for it by the fact that I had often been told that Mr. Kreuger was a genius.

Just as his derring-do had reflected well on his native country, the unveiling of his financial house of matches sent tremors through Sweden, even toppling the prime minister. Faced with a crisis, the Swedish establishment rose to the occasion. Led by Jacob Wallenberg, from the family that was (and is) the most powerful family in Swedish business, the Swedes negotiated a settlement that saw some $15 million move from Stockholm to New York in return for which Swedish Match retained most of the match concessions. In short, Swedish Match was back in business, shorn of the Kreugers (Ivar's brother, Torsten, who served a year and a half in jail, spent much of the rest of his life trying to prove that his brother had been murdered).

Swedish Match, under control of the Wallenbergs, is still very much alive. In 1986 it remained the largest match producer in the world, operating thirty-four factories in twenty-two countries, including the plants of Universal Match, the largest maker of matches in the United States. Universal was acquired in 1980, and in 1987 (true to its Kreuger heritage) Swedish Match scooped up the world's second-largest match maker, Britain's Wilkinson Sword. This deal lifted its share of the world market from 18 percent to 25 percent and gave it an entry into a new business: razors and razor blades.

Even before the Wilkinson acquisition, Swedish Match had bought its way into other fields (just as Ivar Kreuger had). Today it's a major manufacturer of flooring (Tarkett), cabinets (Marbodal and HTH), doors (Sweedor), and packaging materials. Matches accounted for only 22 per-

Finland: More Saunas Than Cars

Finland is the only country in the world where saunas outnumber automobiles. Finland has about 1.2 million saunas, one for every four persons. A sauna is a small, dark room where Finns sweat in temperatures as high as 212 degrees Fahrenheit.

cent of sales in 1986. It's still very much an international company. More than two thirds of its employees work outside Sweden.

Having learned to play with fire, Swedish Match has also entered the disposable lighter business. Its brands—Feudor, Poppell, and Cricket—hold 15 percent of the world market. The Cricket line was acquired from Gillette in 1984. That's quite a switch from the old days when travelers in certain parts of the world—the Azores, for example—would be asked by customs officials to declare any lighters they were carrying and were warned that if they used them in public, they would be breaking the law and subject to a fine. The law flowed from the terms of an agreement setting up a Kreuger match monopoly. When Ivar Kreuger asked for a monopoly, he meant monopoly.

Access   Vastra Tradgardsgatan 15
Box 16100
S-10322 Stockholm, Sweden
(46) 8-22-0620

Tata Group	**Sales** $3.3 billion
	Profits $200 million (pretax)
	Rank India's largest private enterprise group
	Founded 1868
	Employees 350,000
	Headquarters Bombay, India

"**T**here is a difference between making money for oneself and creating wealth for others."

This inscription appears in the front of *The Creation of Wealth,* a 1981 book by the Indian journalist R. M. Lala. Lala relates the remarkable story of the House of Tata, India's largest industrial enterprise. As it's a book that seems to have been sponsored by Tata, one would expect it to be fawning. What one does not expect is the comment by J.R.D. Tata, patriarch of the Tata empire, in the foreword of the book's second edition. Tata congratulated the author but also said, "Where Russi Lala has perhaps failed in completing or rounding off his task was in neglecting to seek out and criticize, where due, any weaknesses or failures of the firm." Critiquing a sponsored book for not being critical enough sets a new tone for business histories. However, one finds after dipping into the story of the Tatas that it's not surprising to encounter such humility.

The Tatas are emblematic of India's small but influential Parsee community. The Parsees are Zoroastrians, a sect named for Zoroaster, a Persian prophet of the sixth century B.C., who taught that life was a struggle between the forces of lightness (Mazdah) and darkness. After Persia fell to the Muslims in the middle of the seventh century, the Zoroastrians went into hiding or fled the country. Those who came to India settled mostly in and around Bombay. They were known as the Parsees or Parsis, identifying them as having come from Persia. Hardly any Zoroastrians are left in Iran (the new name for Persia), and the Indian Parsee community numbers a little over one hundred thousand.

Although they represent only .02 percent of the population, the Parsees have left their mark in India. Well educated, sophisticated, and open to Western ideas, they were doers—but not mindlessly so. In India they became successful merchants, traders, and industrialists, with many of them building into their businesses a strong ethical component.

Jamsetji Tata, who was born in 1839, came from a family of Parsee priests. Educated at Bombay's Elphinstone College, he engaged in trading ventures in the Far East and Europe before starting his own company in 1868 when he was twenty-nine. He had been to Manchester and came away with the idea of one day making cotton goods in India. He wasn't the only one with this idea. Bombay then had about a dozen textile mills. Tata elected to put up a new mill in the central Indian city of Nagpur in the heart of a cotton-growing region. With money supplied by himself and his friends, he launched the Central India Spinning, Weaving, and Manufacturing Company in 1874. The mill opened on January 1, 1877, the day Queen Victoria was formally proclaimed the Empress of India. Tata promptly renamed the works the Empress Mills.

But Jamsetji Tata was no lackey of British imperialism. He was present at the founding of the Indian National Congress in Bombay in 1885, and he contributed generously to the Congress, which spearheaded the Indian movement for independence. However, his greatest contribution was to try to bring the Industrial Revolution to an economically backward India so that the country could stand on its own feet in the modern world. He had three specific goals: Introduce hydroelectric power as a cheap source of energy, start a steel industry, and establish a technical school. All three goals were to be reached—after his death—by his pioneering steps. Jawaharlal Nehru, the first prime minister of the independent state of India, said of him, "When you have to give the lead in action, in ideas—a lead which does not fit in with the very climate of opinion, that is true courage, physical or mental or spiritual, call it what you like, and it is this type of courage and vision that Jamsetji Tata showed."

Jamsetji Tata was a Renaissance man with an interest in virtually everything, a passion for improving life in his native land, and a concern for the people who worked for him. His plants had the first humidifiers and fire sprinklers in India. He set up a pension plan for employees in 1886. In 1895 he began to compensate workers for accidents. The eight-hour day, which was not established by law in India until 1948, was in force at Tata in 1912. In 1902, when he was thinking about the kind of steel city India should have, he wrote his son, Dorab, from abroad: "Be sure to lay wide streets planted with shady trees, every other of a quick-growing variety. Be sure there is plenty of space for lawns and gardens. Reserve large areas for football, hockey, and parks. Earmark areas for Hindu temples, Mohammedan mosques, and Christian churches."

Tata toured the world looking for ideas to bring home to India. And he was interested in more than just factories. He introduced foreign trees and plants, imported exotic animals such as greyhounds and white peacocks, and invited Japanese silkworm cultivators to India to revive that industry in Mysore. Tata built the magnificent Taj Mahal Hotel in Bombay harbor; when it opened in 1903, it was the first building in Bombay to be lit by electricity and was deemed the finest watering place between Shepherd's Hotel in Cairo and Raffles in Singapore.

In 1892 Tata endowed a fund to send deserving students abroad for higher education, helping to train many of India's early engineers, doctors, lawyers, and government officials. In 1924 a survey of the Indian Civil Service (ICS) indicated that one out of every five Indian officials had been a Tata scholar. But Jamsetji Tata really wanted India to have its own schools for higher education. In 1898 he offered to donate the income from fourteen of his buildings and four large properties in Bombay to establish a science university. It took thirteen years for the idea to come to fruition in the form of the Indian Institute of Science at Bangalore, which has since played a central role in the development of scientific research in India.

Jamsetji Tata died in Bad Nauheim, Germany, in 1904. But the work he began was continued by the Tata family. The first of three Tata power companies began supplying hydroelectric power to the city of Bombay in 1910 after a huge dam was built to capture water running off the mountain range of the Western Ghats. The steel mill was built in the jungle village of Jamshedpur in western India—it rolled its first ingot on February 16, 1912. The mill was financed entirely by Indians because the money people in London raised their eyebrows when Tata talked about making steel in India. John L. Keenan, an American steel man who was to spend twenty-five years at the Jamshedpur mill, the last eight as general manager, wrote a memoir of his days there, *A Steel Man in India,* in which he set down the London view.

> Most English money barons of the time were still circumscribed by the tradition of the East India Company; none of them was especially interested in putting anything *into* India. Particularly did they look askance at any Indian project to be run by Indians. They had furnished money for South Sea speculations, for the Hudson's Bay Company, for opium trade with China, pearl fisheries in uncharted seas, but why, they reasoned, should they finance an Indian steel plant which would eventually shut off Indian steel markets from Sheffield and the Teeside?

One British financier approached by Tata in 1903 was so amused by the idea of a steel mill in the wilds of India that he said he would eat every pound of steel rails produced there. In 1937 Keenan met this Englishman when he came out for a last tiger shoot. The Jamshedpur mill was then the largest steel plant in the British Empire—and the twelfth-largest in the world. The Londoner said to Keenan, "I can see now that my appetite in the old days must have been enormous."

Numerous enterprises followed the steel company: Tata Oil Mills, New India Assurance, Tata Airlines, Tata Press, Tata Chemicals, National Radio & Electronics, Tata Engineering & Locomotive, Indian Tube. As the Tatas were assembling their complex of companies in India, others—the Rockefellers in the United States, the Krupps and Thyssens in Germany, the Pearsons in England, the *zaibatsu* in Japan—were doing likewise.

However, the contrast between the Tata Group and the other industrial empire builders was striking. The major difference was the social dimension always present in Tata enterprises. The Tatas never inspired the resentment that was directed at the captains of industry in other countries. It was widely recognized in colonial India that the Tatas acted in the *national* self-interest. Corruption was absent in their operations. India is strewn with institutions—cultural, educational, sports—established by charitable grants of the Tatas. In a country notorious for its virulent caste system, Tata early on had an employee handbook which stated: "Our apprentices are taught the dignity of labour. If they have to carry anything, they carry it themselves; if they have to clean anything, they clean it themselves. They have none of the helper mentality which has been such a drag on India's industrial progress."

In 1904, the year Jamsetji Tata died in Germany, Jehangir Tata was born in Paris to a French mother and Jamsetji's cousin. Jehangir went to a French *lycée* and was a childhood chum of the son of Louis Bleriot, the first man to fly the English Channel (in 1909) and the first to Loop-the-Loop in a plane. J.R.D., as Jehangir came to be known, decided when he was a teenager that he would become a pilot. At age twenty-two, when he was about to go off to a university in England, he was called back to India to take his place in the family enterprises (the Tatas were short on male heirs). J.R.D. was issued India's first pilot's license. In 1930 he flew solo from Karachi to London. And two years later, flying a Puss Moth, he inaugurated India's first mail service, zipping 100 miles an hour from Karachi to Bombay. That was the start of Tata Airlines, which evolved into Air India. J.R.D. became chairman of the Tata enterprises in 1938. In 1986, at age eighty-two, he was still at the helm of a far less cohesive group.

Tata's standing in India is reflected in numerous ways. India achieved its independence after World War II under a Labour government headed by Clement Attlee, who had once lectured at the London School of Economics, a beneficiary of Tata grants. The Tatas then proposed that Air India International be established as a joint public-private venture, with the government owning 49 percent, the Tatas 20 percent, and the public the rest. The Nehru government agreed. In 1953 all the airlines in India were nationalized, but the government installed J.R.D. Tata as the chairman of Air India, a post he was to hold for the next twenty-five years.

Meanwhile, J.R.D. continued to serve as head of the Tata Group, India's largest private sector conglomerate. In a government dedicated to socialism, it was a remarkable vote of confidence. In 1978, when the government was considering a move to nationalize the steel industry, the labor unions representing employees at Tata Steel cabled a strong letter of protest to the prime minister. In 1962, in an interview with John Frazer, a reporter for *Far East Trade,* J.R.D. Tata spelled out the company—and family—philosophy: "Every man has an innate desire to be useful to others, and in India the cause of lifting our people is such a crying one that service is easier than in a completely industrialized country. We here at Tata are so obsessed with our people's poverty that we don't deserve special credit for having public service on our minds."

The Tata Group was held together in 1986 more by force of personality and history than common ownership. The group comprised thirty-three companies, but they were not linked the way divisions or subsidiaries of a conglomerate or umbrella corporation are. Public trusts in fact controlled 80 percent of the shares in these companies, with the government voting the controlling share. Also in 1987, another family industrial house, the Birla Group, was challenging Tata for leadership in the private sector. The Birlas have holdings in textiles, cement, engineering, petrochemicals, shipping, and other industries. Figures released by the Indian Ministry of Industry indicated that the combined sales of all the Birla companies may have edged ahead of the Tata Group, although Tata retained its lead in profits.

Tata family members—and there were only four active in the group in 1986—have less than 2 percent of the holdings. The heir apparent in 1986 was Ratan Tata, whose father was adopted by the Tatas when he was in a Parsee orphanage. Trained as an architect, Ratan lived in the United States between the ages of fourteen and twenty-four. He has been pushing the group into new high-tech areas: computers and telecommunications, among other fields. After being named chairman of Tata Industries in 1982, he said, "I was, in effect, handed a shell company which had an aura about it, but nothing in it."

India presents an industrial scene quite different from those obtaining elsewhere. Privately owned companies have to adhere to bizarre sets of rules. For example, take the annual report of Tata Oil Mills, the country's leading maker of soaps and detergents. It seems that by government regulation, the company must list in its annual report the name of

Tea for Russia

India exported 500 million pounds of tea in 1985—and nearly half of those exports went to one country: the Soviet Union.

every employee who earns more than 36,000 rupees ($2,800) a year. This required in the 1984–85 annual report an alphabetical listing of 1,021 persons, reporting for each one the following information: nature of duties, gross pay, net pay after deductions, qualifications, years' experience, date started with the company, age, and previous employer.

So we learn that the director of research is Dr. B. P. Baliga, who is fifty-seven years old, took his Ph.D. at the University of Texas, has thirty-three years' experience, joined the company on October 1, 1960, previously worked for the Commission for the Prevention of Alcoholism in the United States, received gross pay of 120,000 rupees ($9,600), reduced to 67,952 rupees ($5,400) after deductions. And we also learn that H. P. Saxena is a chemist, Grade II, at the Ghazabad factory, holds a bachelor of science in chemical technology, has ten years' experience, joined the company on May 17, 1979, previously worked as a shift chemist at Rajasthan Vanaspati Products, and earned 37,962 rupees ($3,090) in gross pay, 31,728 rupees ($2,500) after deductions.

Tata's American hotel arm, Taj International Hotels, operates five establishments in the United States—the Lexington Hotel in New York, and the Canterbury House, Hampshire Hotel, Quality Inn (on 16th Street) and Ramada Inn (on Rhode Island Avenue) in Washington, D.C.

Access   Tata Sons
Bombay House
24, Homi Mody St.
Bombay-400 023, India
(91) 22-25-9131

Tata International
Gotthardstrasse 3
CH-6300 Zug, Switzerland
(41) 42-23-4141

Thomson	**Sales** $8 billion
	Profits $400 million

Sales $8 billion
Profits $400 million
U.S. Sales $1.2 billion
Rank 10th-largest publisher in the United States (newspapers and magazines)
Publisher of largest number of daily papers in the United States
Publisher of largest number of daily papers in Canada
9th-largest newspaper publisher in the United States (by circulation)
2d-largest newspaper publisher in Canada (by circulation)
Largest publisher of trade and professional magazines in the United States
Largest publisher of regional newspapers in Britain
Largest department store operator in Canada
Largest holiday tour packager in Britain
Founded 1930
Employees 60,000
Headquarters Toronto, Canada

The corporate holdings of Lord Thomson of Fleet represent one of the biggest chunks of family wealth in the world—and it all started with the launching of a small Canadian radio station. In 1987 the Thomson family owned:

- Seventy-three percent of International Thomson Organization, which published sixty-one newspapers in Britain and hundreds of magazines, journals, newsletters, and directories in the United States and Britain; lifted oil from the North Sea; sold travel packages; and operated a small British airline (Britannia Airways).
- Sixty-one percent of Thomson Newspapers, publisher of the largest chain of newspapers in both Canada (thirty-nine dailies and thirteen weeklies) and the United States (102 dailies and four weeklies).
- Seventy-three percent of Hudson's Bay, the oldest company in Canada and the country's largest department store group, operat-

ing nearly six hundred stores under the names Hudson's Bay, Simpsons, and Zeller's.

- Fifty-two percent of Scottish & York, a Canadian insurance company.
- Ninety-four percent of Dominion-Consolidated, Canada's fifth-largest trucking firm.

Shares of four of these companies (all but Dominion) trade on the Toronto Stock Exchange and, based on their market values at the end of 1986, the Thomson family stakes were worth more than $5 billion.

It was a pennypinching publisher, Roy Thomson, who laid the groundwork for this empire. He started it in Canada and, in a bit of reverse colonialism, built it into a major force in Britain. Then his son Kenneth, the second Lord Thomson, extended its reach dramatically in North America.

Roy Herbert Thomson, the son of a Toronto barber, was born on June 5, 1894 and dropped out of school when he was fourteen to look for ways to make money. He was willing to try anything. His son once described him this way: "He had one thing on his mind. He wanted to be the biggest success ever. He worked like a horse, and he never gave up."

Thomson worked first in a Toronto office, then bought a farm in Saskatchewan, and then became a distributor of auto parts. They all failed to make him rich. In fact, they left him broke, nearing forty with a family of five dependent on him. But he was still ready to try anything. In 1930 he set out for North Bay, which is five hundred miles north of Toronto, to sell radios. It was a tough sell. The local transmitter worked so poorly that it was almost impossible to hear anything on the sets he was selling.

Thomson solved that problem by starting his own North Bay radio station, CFCH, equipping it with a secondhand transmitter whose signals could be heard. Through that small station he realized that money could be made by selling to advertisers something as intangible as air time. It was a revelation. He borrowed money and bought two more stations in Kirkland Lake and Timmins, gold-mining towns north of North Bay. At Timmins in 1934, when he was forty years old, he bought his first newspaper.

The *Timmins Press* was a rundown weekly that Thomson acquired by putting up $200 and agreeing to pay off the remaining $5,800 in twenty-nine monthly installments. A year later he converted it to a daily, the first of Thomson's eleven conversions of weeklies to daily newspapers. Nine years later, after buying papers in the small towns of Galt, Woodstock, Sarnia, and Welland, Roy Thomson was publishing more newspapers in the province of Ontario than anyone else.

People who buy newspapers can be motivated by various impulses—a burning desire to influence public opinion, a quest for power, or a vision of creating an important information source. None of these was a lodestar for Thomson. From the start he looked upon newspapers (and radio stations) as a way to make money by selling advertising space (and time). The editorial product held little interest for him. "Editorial content is the stuff you separate the ads with," he once said. Even as he accumulated newspapers and radio stations, he had his eye out for other money-making schemes. He went into trucking, insurance, furniture, shoe polish, and Toni home-permanent kits. Susan Goldenberg, a biographer (*The Thomson Empire*), said Thomson "could not shake the tendency to acquire anything just so long as it increased the size of his business."

Most of these side ventures flopped, but the media properties yielded a steady flow of income and Thomson steadily expanded them. In 1949 he made his first newspaper purchase outside Ontario, the *Moose Jaw Times Herald* in Saskatchewan. In 1952 he bought his first newspaper in the United States, the Saint Petersburg (Florida) *Independent.* Goldenberg said he bought the Florida paper to get a tax writeoff on a boat that he berthed there. One of the reasons for going into insurance was to save the premiums being paid by the newspapers on their policies.

Roy Thomson was a restless character. His wife died of cancer in 1951, and two years later when he was presented with an opportunity to buy *The Scotsman,* the venerable daily newspaper founded in Edinburgh in 1817, he jumped at it. He was fifty-seven years old and comfortably well off, but he was ready once again to try something new, especially since it was a newspaper, a business he now understood. Thomson's father had emigrated to Canada from Scotland, and Roy portrayed himself as a family traditionalist. "I look upon myself as a Scot," he proclaimed. "I am going to live in Scotland and I am going to die in Scotland." There was a lot of blarney in Roy Thomson. However, no one ever accused him of being sentimental. In fact, he set out to do in the United Kingdom precisely what he had done in Canada: Make a lot of money by selling advertising space. The media lords of Fleet Street were taken completely unawares. Roy Thomson, when he came to Edinburgh, owned only twelve newspapers in Canada, all of them in small cities.

Shortly after he emigrated to Scotland, the government-owned, commercial-free British Broadcasting Corporation monopoly was broken up. Thomson, who once said that "the most beautiful music to me is a spot commercial at ten dollars a whack," was one of the first applicants for a license to operate a commercial channel. He called it "a license to make money."

Thomson began selling commercials on Scottish television in 1957, and the profits were so hefty (every $100 invested in Thomson's Scottish television channel in 1957 was worth $22,000 by 1965) that within two years he was able to buy the Kemsley newspaper chain, which made him a power not only in Edinburgh but in London's Fleet Street. With the Kemsley acquisition Thomson owned a string of provincial newspapers plus three Sunday papers—the *Sunday Times, Empire News,* and *Sunday Graphic.* He continued to watch the pennies carefully. The scandal sheets *Empire News* and *Sunday Graphic* eventually disappeared because they couldn't compete against a lurid paper like the *News of the World.* Thomson built the *Sunday Times* into a major opinion leader newspaper.

While he had a reputation for being slavishly devoted to the bottom line ("I'd rather read a balance sheet than a book," he used to say), Roy Thomson's next move could not be attributed to that base motive. In 1967 he acquired one of the world's most prestigious newspapers, *The Times* of London, established in 1785. There are after all other considerations beyond profits in life. Three years later the Queen inducted him into the ranks of the nobility, dubbing him Lord Thomson of Fleet, quite a climb for the son of a Toronto barber.

Lord Thomson proved as adept at making money as was hustling *Roy* Thomson. His friend John Paul Getty invited him to join a consortium looking for oil in the North Sea. The truth is, the all-American consortium, whose members were Getty Oil, Allied Chemical, and Occidental Petroleum, needed a British partner to make their bid; Lord Thomson, who had had to give up his Canadian citizenship to accept a peerage, fit the bill. In 1971, knowing nothing about the oil business, he invested $10 million for a 20 percent stake in the drilling venture. Finding oil was a ten-to-one shot, but Lord Thomson beat the odds, as he had all his life. The consortium hit an 800-million-barrel field in 1973 and later discovered another field with 400 million barrels of recoverable oil. By the mid-1970s, petroleum was accounting for 75 percent of Thomson's profits. Lord Thomson died in 1976 at the zenith of his career.

Under Kenneth Thomson, the new Lord Thomson of Fleet, those petroleum profits were converted into publishing properties. International Thomson Organization went on an incredible shopping spree in the United States, buying up companies that publish business and professional periodicals and directories for lawyers, accountants, bankers, doctors, engineers, real estate agents, and data processing executives. The list runs into the hundreds. They include such successful publications as *Medical Economics, American Banker,* the *Journal of Taxation, Ward's Auto World, Pacific Shipper, Who's Who in Railroading.*

In 1986, after paying $618 million to buy twenty-five different publishing properties, Thomson emerged as the largest U.S. publisher of trade and professional journals. Pausing to catch its breath and count up what it did have, International Thomson Organization disclosed that in its inventory, on both sides of the Atlantic, were thirteen thousand individual products, including "106 magazines, 70 newspapers, over 10,500 books and directories, 50 electronic services, and over 2,000 other products, mainly journals and abstracts, looseleaf services and microfiche." Feeling that it was still missing something, in June 1987 Thomson outbid Simon & Schuster and Pearson to acquire Associated Book Publishers, one of Britain's leading legal publishers, for $340 million. Thank heaven, those North Sea oil rigs are still pumping.

Profits from North Sea oil also enabled the Thomson family to outbid George Weston Ltd. in 1979 and acquire 73 percent of Hudson's Bay for $650 million. Founded in 1660 as a fur trader, Hudson's Bay accounts for a significant part of department store sales in Canada.

Nor has Thomson Newspapers Ltd. stopped acquiring newspapers— in Canada or the United States. In Canada the Thomson papers have 25 percent of all newspaper circulation, including the country's largest daily, the *Toronto Globe & Mail* (circulation: 315,000). In the United States Thomson's 102 daily newspapers (that was the count in mid-1987, eleven more than Gannett) have a total circulation of 1.9 million, an average of 18,500 per paper. Thomson was still concentrating on being the only rag in a small town. Its papers include the *Mitchell Daily Republic* in South Dakota, the *Fond du Lac Reporter* in Wisconsin, the *Whittier Daily News* in California, the *Laurel Leader-Call* in Mississippi, and the *Oelwein Daily Register* in Iowa.

The fixation on the bottom line remains as strong under Kenneth Thomson as it did under his father. In 1987, when *Advertising Age* ranked media companies based on how much profit they squeezed out of sales, Thomson Newspapers ranked second among all companies and first among newspaper publishers with an aftertax return of 19.4 percent on sales. The company doesn't hesitate to shuck money losers. In 1981, after years of labor troubles and losses, Kenneth Thomson, who prefers Toronto to London, sold *The Times* of London to Rupert Murdoch. In 1985 Thomson abandoned consumer book publishing on both sides of the Atlantic because it didn't generate enough profits. Hudson's Bay is getting the same nonsentimental scrutiny. In 1987 Lord Thomson sold off the 178 stores in the remote northern wilds of Canada—these are the descendants of the original fur-trading posts established pursuant to a 1670 charter granted by King Charles II that gave Hudson's Bay control over one twelfth of the earth's surface.

An example of what happens after Thomson buys a newspaper was given by Bruce V. VanDusen, who had been editor of the *Kokomo Tribune* in Kokomo, Indiana, for two years before it was sold in 1981 to Thomson. In an article in the monthly journalism review *The Quill,* VanDusen said that in the first year of the Thomson ownership, the news staff was reduced from twenty-nine to twenty-three. Any purchase that exceeded one hundred dollars had to be approved by Thomson divisional headquarters in Canton, Ohio. No mention of Thomson was ever to appear in the paper (to maintain the aura of its being a local paper). There could be no communication with any other Thomson paper except through the publisher. Coverage of television, considered the enemy, was taboo. The paper's two-way radio communication system was stopped with the explanation that since Thomson was a Canadian company, it could not, being foreign, legally operate a radio transmitter in the United States. The incredulous VanDusen checked with the Federal Communications Commission and "learned the claim was baseless, that only agents of a foreign power are prohibited from operating radios." He reported this finding to the general manager, "who then admitted the falsehood. He said Thomson simply wanted to save the expense of insuring and maintaining the equipment."

VanDusen said that Thomson also instituted efficiency measures such as counting the number of stories and photographs per staffer that appeared in the paper. The idea was to squeeze as many stories and photographs as possible into the paper. It didn't matter what was being covered. The initial count showed that the *Kokomo Tribune* was running 2 stories and .49 photographs per staffer, which was way out of whack with the efficiency ratios on similar Thomson newspapers, where the average was 7.7 stories and 1.2 photos per staffer.

Surveying it all from his Toronto headquarters is Lord Thomson, who is much more reticent than his father. He shares with his father the same parsimony—he always flies coach and he has been known to eat cheese sandwiches for lunch at his desk—but unlike his father, who was earthy and always sounding off to the press, Kenneth Thomson is rarely accessible to reporters. Since he inherited the Lord Thomson of Fleet title, he does not have to relinquish his Canadian citizenship to hold it.

Kenneth Thomson also seems to share with his father a knack for surrounding himself with people who have keen business heads. Thomson newspapers may win very few awards for editorial excellence, but their ability to turn a buck is exemplary. One of Roy's early partners was Jack Kent Cooke, who went on to build a media-sports empire of his own in the United States. Another was Sidney Chaapman, who initiated the diversification into insurance and trucking. John Tory, a distinguished Toronto attorney, is Kenneth's chief aide at the Toronto command post. Gordon Brunton, who was hired away from another British publisher, served as Thomson's chief operating officer during the heady expansion in Britain and the reinvasion of North America. When he retired in 1984, his place at the head of International Thomson Organization was taken by Michael Brown, who moved his headquarters to New York.

Brown is very much in the Thomson mold. Prior to coming aboard in 1969, he worked for a company that made cables. He is known as a razor-sharp analyst who could be running any business—he just happens to be in publishing. His first great coup at Thomson was working out a deal with bankers to finance the North Sea drilling. He got them to advance the money in return for a royalty tied to the extraction of the offshore oil. The lenders, in other words, took a chance on the oil coming in—and the Thomson companies were not in hock to the bankers.

Brown's attention has been focused on the expansion of Thomson's business magazine properties in the United States, and at a 1983 internal meeting he spelled out to managers what their marching orders were: "The starting point should be that we adhere to our time-honored principles—what's wrong with them? To me they are *religious* commandments. Does, for example, the product have high utility value and is it well differentiated? Is it 'have to have' or is it 'for fun' and thus not essential? Will it have long life, properly updated? Will a business or employer pay the bill—or perish the thought—is it a consumer product?"

In short, don't look for Thomson to acquire *Playboy* or any entertainment publication or for that matter any magazine that a person can't get his employer to pay the subscription for. This is business, Thomson-style. The kind of bedtime reading Thomson likes to publish can be gleaned from some of its titles: *Computer Law Forms Handbook, Journal of Taxation, Law of Defamation, Practical Accountant, Law of Distressed Real Estate,* and *Practical Cardiology.*

When Roy Thomson died, *The Times* of London, which he then still owned, saluted him as having built one of the "most extraordinary business careers of modern times . . . [a] business achievement [that] cannot quite be paralleled and is unlikely ever to be paralleled." In the ten years following his death, his son more than tripled the size of the Thomson holdings—but *he* didn't start off from scratch. The bulk of Roy Thomson's estate went to trusts whose beneficiaries are his seven grandchildren. They gain access to it when they reach the age of thirty. The aim was to keep the Thomson holdings in family hands. As Roy Thomson explained in his autobiography: "These Thomson boys that come after Ken are not going to be able, even if they want to, to shrug off these responsibilities. The conditions of the trusts ensure that control of the business will remain in Thomson hands for eighty years."

Access   International Thomson Organization
20 Queen St. West
Toronto, Ontario,
Canada M5H 3R3

245 Park Ave.
New York, N.Y. 10167
(212) 557-9333

Thomson Newspapers
65 Queen St. West
Toronto, Ontario,
Canada M5H 2M8
(416) 864-1710

Hudson's Bay Co.
401 Bay St.
Toronto, Ontario,
Canada M5H 2Y4
(416) 861-6112

<table>
<tr><td rowspan="9">

Thyssen

</td></tr>
</table>

Thyssen	**Sales** $13.8 billion
	Profits $150 million
	Rank Europe's largest steel maker
	World's 3d-largest steel maker
	West Germany's 8th-largest company
	Founded 1871
	Employees 120,000
	Headquarters Duisburg, West Germany

I f any industry symbolizes the Industrial Revolution, it's steel making. And if anything symbolizes the industrial might of Germany, it's the "steel city" of Duisburg at the junction of the Rhine and Ruhr rivers. The world's largest inland port, Duisburg gleams in the night from manufacturing complexes that never shut down. In the north of the city are the steelworks of Thyssen. Covering 4.6 square miles, they include blast furnaces, three oxygen steel making shops, rolling mills, a coking plant, power plants, and 370 miles of railway track. It's the heart of the German steel industry.

Duisburg—and Thyssen—made a remarkable recovery from the massive bombing of World War II, only to find itself traumatized in the 1980s by the same problems that crippled steel makers in the United States. The world was awash in steel, much of it priced lower than the bars and sheets coming out of American and German mills. In 1977 Thyssen, the largest steel maker on the European continent, ranked twentieth on the *Fortune* roster of companies based outside the United States. By 1986 it had fallen to thirty-seventh place.

There are various ways out of this quandry and Thyssen has taken most of them. It drastically reduced its work force from 160,000 in 1978 to 120,000 in 1987. As recently as 1980 it had seventy thousand people working in its steel plants; in 1985, it had under fifty thousand. Thyssen faced the same protests that confronted U.S. Steel over the closing of mills that had been the lifeblood of communities for many years. At Hattingen, a small town on the Rhine between Essen and Wuppertal, Thyssen gave notice in 1986 that it was closing its mill there—rendering twenty-nine hundred people jobless—and immediately posters featuring pictures of Thyssen executives went up on walls under the headline: "WANTED FOR JOB MURDER."

Diversification is another escape route. Thyssen has spread its wings, evolving into a conglomerate that owns more than two hundred companies which build, among many other products, ships, bridges, locomotives, machine tools, and elevators. It also spawned a trading company, Thyssen Handelsunion, whose low-margin sales (it's basically a wholesaler, like the

Japanese trading companies) now account for more than 40 percent of Thyssen's revenues. The U.S. arm of the trading company, Thyssen Inc., does an annual business of $1 billion. Among its nefarious activities are the export of U.S. coal and the sale of Korean steel to U.S. automakers.

One American acquisition was almost the undoing of Thyssen. In 1978 it came up with $275 million to buy the Budd Company, a leading supplier of components to the automobile industry (doors, hoods, fenders, grilles), with an even longer history as a railway car builder based outside Philadelphia. In the late 1970s the American car industry was slumping, and so the decision was made to concentrate on the railway car business. Along came a chance to bid for the building of three hundred cars for the Chicago transit system. Budd won, hands down, with a bid of $133 million. No one else was even close—and for good reason. It was a ridiculously low bid, and Budd lost money on every car it delivered.

Between 1979 and 1982 Budd received orders for 552 cars from New York, Baltimore, and Miami. It was easy to bid, not so easy to fulfill the orders. It lost out on one bid to supply 825 cars to the New York City transit system, an order worth $650 million, because the U.S. government would not match a low-interest loan that the Canadian government gave to the Bombardier company. Explaining why the government wouldn't come to the aid of Budd, Treasury Secretary Donald T. Regan said the German-owned American company made an inferior product.

The disaster at Budd produced $300 million of pretax losses over the 1981–83 stretch, threw the whole Thyssen company into the red, caused it to miss paying a dividend for the first time since 1956, and prompted a move to oust Dieter Spethmann, the chief executive who had made the decision to buy the U.S. company. However, in a five-hour shareholder meeting in 1984, he survived the challenge. In 1980 he told *Fortune* writer David B. Tinnin how he had made the Budd decision: "When I look at a deal, I do not look at the company. I look at the men. I did not have to visit Budd's plants before we bought them, because I got to know the men, and I knew we could make the merger work."

In 1985, after Budd had lost out in the bidding for the last thirteen rail car contracts awarded in the United States, Thyssen split off the railway car business into a separate unit, Transit America, and sent one of its German honchos, Hans U. Wolf, to run it. (Transit America is the sole surviving rail car builder in the United States, the world's largest market for rail cars.) At the same time Thyssen's European-based locomotive company came up with something that should mesh neatly with Budd's automotive business. It developed a new industrial shredder, capable of scrapping whole automobiles.

It's not the kind of product August Thyssen was contemplating when he founded a puddling and rolling mill in 1871 near the Ruhr town of Mulheim. He expanded into coal mining, built a huge mill at Bruckhausen, and by World War I ranked as Germany's biggest iron and steel maker. August Thyssen died in 1926, and the empire he had assembled was divided between his two sons. Fritz, the eldest, got the steel mills. Heinrich got the leftovers—shipbuilding companies and some engineering outfits. In 1927 the Thyssen steel company became the centerpiece of Vereinigte Stahlwerke, a trust into which all the German steel producers were grouped. It paralleled the I. G. Farben trust in chemicals.

Fritz Thyssen was at first an ardent supporter of Adolf Hitler and helped to rally industrial support for the Nazis. But in the 1930s he became disillusioned, broke with the party, and fled with his wife to France. After the Nazis conquered France, they placed the Thyssens in an insane asylum and then in a concentration camp. After being freed by the Allies, Fritz Thyssen was arrested as a war criminal. He was acquitted of these charges in 1948, and the Thyssens then settled in Argentina to join their daughter, Anita, who had married a Hungarian count, Gabor Zichy.

The post–World War II Thyssen company was rebuilt by a tough-minded steel man, Hans-Gunther Sohl, who retired in 1973 after he had hand-picked Dieter Spethmann, a lawyer, as his successor. Thyssen family members, those descended from Fritz, continue to hold about 20 percent of the company's stock, but the Thyssen family is not active anymore in the business. A meeting of the Thyssen supervisory board (the German equivalent of board of directors) constitutes a meeting of the West German Establishment. In 1986 the board members included the heads of the two largest German banks (Deutsche Bank and Dresdner Bank), the head of the German steelworkers union, the chairmen of Volkswagen and Siemens, and the former president of the country (Walter Scheel).

The Thyssen branch descended from Fritz's younger brother, Heinrich, has a history of its own. Heinrich had married a Hungarian baroness, Margarethe Bornemisza de Kaszon, and he added the Bornemisza name to his. The Thyssen-Bornemiszas went to live in the Netherlands after World War I, and their son, Hans Heinrich, was born in The Hague in 1921. After his father died, Heinrich added other businesses to what he had been left in Germany—Dutch shipping companies and subsidiaries in Brazil. While his brother Fritz fled to France to escape Hitler, Heinrich and his family fled to Switzerland, settling in Lugano. After Heinrich died in 1947, his twenty-six-year-old son Hans Heinrich took command of what was left of the family enterprises scattered across the globe.

Baron Hans Heinrich Thyssen-Bornemisza proceeded to assemble a multinational conglomerate of his own, including inland shipping companies in Holland and Germany, a small German shipbuilder, a Dutch bank, a company that makes automatic egg-handling equipment. He also owns an American conglomerate, Indian Head, whose various divisions make glass containers, school buses, pumps, sewer pipes, and other industrial products; lease container ships; and generate data base information in microfilm and microfiche forms. Baron Thyssen, who also has a minority interest in the Heineken brewery, is now a Swiss citizen, but his umbrella company, TBG Holdings, is based in Amsterdam. *The Wall Street Journal* estimated its 1984 sales at $1.7 billion.

However, the baron, who has been married five times, is more well known for his art collection, which was started by his father and greatly expanded by him. It's the largest private art collection in the world, holding more than one thousand works—among them Picassos, Rembrandts, and Monets. They are housed in a museum on his Lugano estate, although the baron likes to take them on tour. His collection has been valued at $1 billion, which is more than the industrial holdings left by August Thyssen were worth in 1926.

Access Kaiser Wilhlem Strasse 100
P.O. Box 110561
D-4100 Duisburg 11, West Germany
(49) 203-52-1

Budd Company
3155 W. Bay Beaver Rd.
Troy, Mich. 48084
(313) 643-3520

Toshiba	Sales $23 billion
	Profits $237 million
	U.S. Sales $3.4 billion
	Rank Japan's 3d-largest electronics company
	World's 6th-largest electronics company
	Japan's 9th-largest company
	24th on the *Fortune* International 500
	World's 4th-largest color television maker
	World's 5th-largest semiconductor maker
	Japan's largest maker of electronic medical equipment
	Japan's largest lighting company
	Largest maker of Japanese-language word processors
	Japan's largest builder of nuclear power plants
	World's leading supplier of geothermal power
	Founded 1875
	Employees 120,000
	Headquarters Tokyo, Japan

Treading international waters can be hazardous. Toshiba, a Japanese electronics giant, found that out in 1987 when it became the target of American wrath. Toshiba Machine, a 50.8 percent–owned subsidiary, illegally shipped to the Soviet Union milling tools enabling the Russians to deaden the sound of submarine propellers and thus make them more difficult to track. The American reaction was swift. Congressmen gathered on the White House lawn to smash Toshiba products with a sledgehammer, and the United States Senate, in an unprecedented act, voted 92-to-5 to ban all Toshiba products from the American market for five years.

In Tokyo Toshiba was stunned. While pointing out that it did not have direct control over Toshiba Machine, the company accepted responsibility for the violation. And the two top officers of Toshiba—Shoichi Saba, chairman, and Sugichiro Watari, president—both resigned in an act that a top Japanese business leader called "hara-kiri" (samurai suicide).

These wrenching moves took place just as Toshiba had been making progress in erasing the image of sluggishness that has long clung to it.

Toshiba has been frequently described as "the GE of Japan"—and with good reason. It shares with General Electric of the United States a lineup that includes such products as nuclear reactors, turbines, light bulbs, electric locomotives, television sets, refrigerators, microwave ovens, washing machines, and generators. It has had an association with General Electric that goes back to 1895, and at one point GE owned 50 percent of a predecessor company. (GE's stake in Toshiba was down to 2 percent in 1986, but it's a sliver of a much bigger company.) Finally, GE and Toshiba have been equated because of their stuffy images.

Toshiba was depicted so often as a "sleepy giant" that its leaders were acutely aware of this reputation and had been trying to breathe fire into the organization by positioning it as a forward-looking "electronics and energy" outfit. Energy has always been a cornerstone of Toshiba. Using GE's "boiling water" technology, it's the leading supplier of nuclear reactors in Japan. It holds 40 percent of the Japanese thermal power market and 30 percent of the hydroelectric plant market. Toshiba claims more than 50 percent of the worldwide market in geothermal power. Its power plants fill 30 percent and 50 percent, respectively, of the electricity requirements of Australia and Kuwait.

Electronics is where the company would like to improve its standing. Toshiba developed Japan's first light bulb and washing machine, and before World War II it was the leader in most electrical equipment fields. But it has since been outstripped by Matsushita and Hitachi. In 1983 a Toshiba employee told *BusinessWeek,* "We have become famous for being second-best in everything."

Toshiba still has awesome technical ability. Unlike GE, which dropped out of the computer race, Toshiba is going full bore. It fields a full line of products—personal computers, disc drives, floppy discs, printers—and it's one of the Japanese companies engaged in crash research on the "Fifth Generation" of computers. In 1985 it introduced a translation system utilizing its thirty-two-bit minicomputer. This system automatically translates English-language texts into Japanese with "more than 90 percent accuracy." Just enter the English version—and out comes the Japanese.

Toshiba's technical prowess was demonstrated again in 1986 when its new laptop computer, the T3100, knocked the socks off competitors in Europe and the United States because of its power, speed, and orange gas-plasma screen. For the first time users of a portable computer found it easy to read the monitor—even in the daylight. A $100-million Pentagon order for 90,000 Toshiba minicomputers was put on hold after disclosure of the sale to the Soviets.

Toshiba is pursuing its high technology dreams under the aegis of a company-wide program called "Project I," which stands for Information, Integration, and Intelligence. It is by no means a go-it-alone strategy.

Toshiba has forged partnerships with companies all over the globe. GE is no longer its sole coconspirator. In fact Toshiba partners with GE's competitor, Westinghouse, to build color picture tubes at a plant in Horseheads, New York (Toshiba's sixth manufacturing facility in the United States). It's working with LSI Logic of Milpitas, California, to develop complex microchips to power the next generation of computers. It has an engineering exchange program with Hewlett-Packard; a research project with the German electronics giant Siemens; and a joint venture with United Technologies to develop fuel cell power plants. Toshiba also allied itself with Olivetti by acquiring 20 percent of the Italian company's Japanese unit, while at the same time it was signing with American Telephone & Telegraph (the owner of 25 percent of Olivetti) to market in Japan the American company's circuit switches and digital private branch exchanges (PBXs)—thereby positioning Toshiba directly against the Japanese telecommunications leader, NEC. One of the first U.S. companies to object to the proposed Toshiba ban was Apple Computer, which gets its desktop printers from Tokyo Electric, another Toshiba offshoot.

Even more far-reaching was the joint venture Toshiba announced with Motorola at the end of 1986. Motorola and Toshiba are, respectively, the third- and fifth-largest semiconductor manufacturers in the world. The two agreed to license each other in their respective technologies (Toshiba is stronger in memory chips, and the American company is stronger in logic chips, which process information) and to establish a joint manufacturing plant in Japan. It was another signal to NEC and Hitachi that Toshiba intends to stay in the computer ballgame.

In fielding these joint ventures, Toshiba was trying to wipe out another dated image of itself as a reclusive loner. Peter Drucker, the American management guru who has been a consultant to Japanese gov-

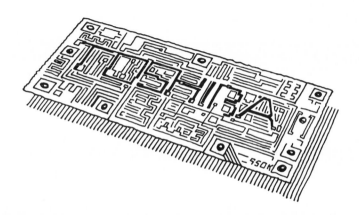

ernment agencies, once pointed out that Toshiba has had a poor record in joint ventures, compared to, say, Sumitomo. George Fields, an Australian who was born in Tokyo and who operates a leading market research firm there, suggested in his book *From Bonsai to Levi's* why this is so. Sumitomo, he pointed out, has its roots in Osaka, a city where merchants have thrived for three centuries, even during the time the samurais were entrenched everywhere else. On the other hand, he said, Toshiba "is a true-blue Tokyo company and may have all the rigidity of a samurai."

Toshiba's determination to be a major factor in the computer busi-

---

In Japan the Buck Stops at the Top

The heads of two prominent Japanese companies resigned within months of each other because of tragedies associated with the use of their products.

Sanyo Electric, a leading electrical appliance maker, also makes kerosene fan heaters, and in 1985 four people in Japan died of carbon monoxide poisoning due to a defect in one model. Sanyo quickly recalled the sixty-nine thousand heaters it had made, and on February 27, 1986, the company's president, Kaoru Iue, resigned, accepting responsibility for the disaster. Iue had been president of Osaka-based Sanyo for fifteen years, during which time its sales had skyrocketed. It was one of the first Japanese electronics companies to begin manufacturing in the United States, where it makes television sets, VCRs, microwave ovens, audio speakers, electric fans, and refrigerators at plants in San Diego, Chatsworth, California, and Forrest City, Arkansas. It's a major supplier of Sears, Roebuck. With 1985 sales of $6.2 billion, Sanyo is roughly the size of Johnson & Johnson or Hewlett-Packard (depending on which day you translate the yen figures).

Iue was succeeded by his nephew, Satoshi Iue, who was formerly executive vice president.

Two months earlier seventy-three-year-old Yasumoto Takagi resigned as president of Japan Air Lines as a consequence of the August 1985 crash of a JAL jumbo jet that killed 520 persons. Takagi was succeeded by sixty-year-old Susumu Yamaji, who had only joined JAL in July 1985. He had previously been with the Japanese government, which owns 34 percent of the airline's stock.

According to *The Wall Street Journal,* the prime minister of Japan, Yasuhiro Nakasone, had given Takagi a "dressing-down" after the fatal crash of the plane, which was flying from Tokyo to Osaka. Before stepping down Takagi spent much of his time attending funeral services for the victims and visiting their relatives. In October, at a memorial service in Osaka sponsored

ness was underlined by the company in 1984 when it moved seven thousand of its employees who had been scattered in eleven offices into a new forty-story headquarters building in central Tokyo that is a showcase of state-of-the-art office automation. The building is equipped with a fiber-optic computer network that has changed the way people work in the office.

Each employee, for example, is given a plastic identity card to use when he or she arrives in the morning and leaves at the end of the day—the computer automatically records the hours worked. In reaching the cashier at the end of the cafeteria line, an employee simply presents

---

by the airline and attended by 3,270 people, Takagi, flanked by JAL employees, accepted responsibility and asked to be forgiven.

It was not a new experience for the JAL president. In 1982, after a JAL jet plunged into Tokyo Bay, killing twenty-four people, Takagi visited families of the crash victims, apologizing and paying homage on his knees. The first president of Japan Air Lines, Seijiro Yanagida, had a similar experience in 1952 when thirty-seven people were killed in the airline's first major accident. The story told in Japan is that for many years after the crash, Yanagida would stay up late in the night copying out in gold ink a long Buddhist sutra for each family.

Reporting from Japan, *New York Times* correspondent Susan Chira detailed some of the steps JAL took after the August 1985 crash, the world's worst single-aircraft disaster:

> In the days after the accident, when family members had to travel to a small mountain village to identify the bodies, airline staff stayed with them, paying all expenses, bringing them food, drink, and clean clothes. Even after most of the bodies were identified, the airline assigned two staff members to each family to attend to needs as varied as arranging for funerals or blocking instrusive reporters.
>
> JAL set up a scholarship fund to pay for the education of children who lost parents in the crash. It spent $1.5 million on the two elaborate memorial services. The airline dispatched executives to every victim's funeral. . . .
>
> The airline could not have failed to perform acts of conciliation. To do so would have left it open to charges of inhumanity and irresponsibility. And that failure would have left families intractable in the difficult negotiations over compensation. . . . Compensation payments, which JAL will split with the Boeing Company, are expected to be substantial, perhaps exceeding $100 million.

For its fiscal year ending March 31, 1986, JAL reported a deficit of $40 million versus a profit of $35 million in the previous year.

the card, and the lunch tab is entered into a terminal and automatically charged. If a staffer wants to send a one-page document to someone on another floor, it can be transmitted in less than fifteen seconds. Top executives of Toshiba, including the chairman and president, have terminals at their desks giving them an instant reading of performance in any part of the company in any part of the world. The building is so up to date that it serves Toshiba as a sales tool.

Shoichi Saba, who resigned in 1987, is an electrical engineer whose father was a Presbyterian minister. He became chief executive at Toshiba in 1983 after forty-one years with the company. Early in his career he spent one year with General Electric in the United States. Long service is a tradition at Toshiba. The man he succeeded, Kazuo Iwata, spent nearly fifty years with the company, mostly on the finance side. He was famous for saying, "We must make more money." Interviewed in 1976 by Gary M. Cooper of the *Japan Economic Journal,* Iwata said, "I have worked more than forty years for Toshiba. A very, very long career. Too long. I'm sixty-six years old. But the former chairman of General Electric is the same age and he retired about three years ago. I'm envious."

Joichi Aoi, another long-term Toshiba stalwart, moved into the hot seat after the 1987 hara-kiri. The sixty-one-year-old Aoi is known as a demon worker. According to *Fortune,* Aoi "astounded colleagues by coming to work the day after his father died."

Access   1-1 Shibaura, Minato-ku
Tokyo 105, Japan
(81) 3-457-2104

Toshiba America
82 Totowa Rd.
Wayne, N.J. 07470
(201) 628-8000

<table>
<tr><td rowspan="11">**Toyota**</td><td>**Sales** $42 billion</td></tr>
</table>

Toyota	**Sales** $42 billion
	Profits $1.7 billion
	U.S. Sales $7 billion
	Rank World's 3d-largest automaker
	Japan's largest auto builder
	World's largest builder of forklift trucks
	Japan's largest industrial enterprise
	Founded 1937
	Employees 82,000 (average age: 33)
	Headquarters Toyota City, Japan

The ability to make small cars that hold up on roads everywhere enabled Toyota to emerge from the ashes of Japan's defeat in World War II to become the world's third-largest auto producer behind General Motors and Ford. It was a sensational climb that culminated in 1980 with Japan displacing the United States as the world's largest producer of motor vehicles (cars, vans, trucks). Toyota's success propelled the company to the top of the industrial pyramid in Japan. No other Japanese manufacturer takes in as much money as Toyota. The nearest is Matsushita, whose sales lag Toyota's by more than $10 billion.

More than fifteen million Toyotas were rolling down roads outside Japan in 1986, nearly seven million of them in the United States. Toyota owns impressive market shares. In 1986 it captured 45 percent of the Japanese passenger car market, 5.6 percent of the American market, and 8 percent of the world market. Toyota thinks in global terms. It has a 1990 goal of reaching a world market share of 10 percent. And if it reaches that, it will probably shoot for 20 percent by the end of the century. In 1986 the two industry leaders, General Motors and Ford, held world market shares of 19 percent and 12.5 percent respectively.

Toyota likes to go its own way. Unlike other Japanese auto producers, it has been reluctant to link up with foreign car makers, preferring to develop its own technology. It has a reputation for being stubborn and conservative. Six times since 1938 Toyota representatives negotiated with Ford Motor about a possible tieup. Each time negotiations broke up without an agreement. When Toyota finally did team up with General Motors in 1983 to coproduce cars in Fremont, California, it was more a case of Toyota being the teacher than anything else. GM virtually admitted that it was going to get a lesson in how to produce small cars. Toyota, meanwhile, was finding out how to deal with American workers, which was to stand it in good stead three years later when it began to build its own U.S. plant—*sans* American partners.

For all its size Toyota likes to play the country bumpkin. Shoichiro

Toyoda, president of the company, joked in a 1985 interview about how Toyota's rural headquarters leads outsiders to regard the company as "not refined, unsophisticated, too straight, not clever." Toyota City, just south of Nagoya, lies 150 miles west of Tokyo in central Japan, and it has all the trappings of the "company town"—company housing (dormitories, apartments, and houses), a huge Toyota Sports Center (Olympic-size pool, two football fields, four baseball diamonds, two gymnasiums), a Toyota Hospital (medical care is free), and clubs of all kinds.

However, there is nothing provincial about the automaking that goes on there. In 1986 some 350,000 visitors, including Japanese schoolchildren and twenty thousand people from outside Japan, made the pilgrimage to Toyota City to see what is acknowledged to be the most efficient car-manufacturing plant in the world. Today, when it's turning out 3.7 million cars and trucks a year, Toyota has the same number of production workers that it had in 1966 when the annual output was one million vehicles. In 1985 Toyota turned out four cars for every ten produced by General Motors, but its work force was only a little more than one-tenth the size of GM's. (Part—but only *part*—of that discrepancy stems from Toyota's greater use of subcontractors.)

Self-sufficient Toyota even stays aloof from bankers, who are the legendary bankrollers of Japanese companies. Toyota has virtually no bank debt, and in the middle of 1986 it had something like $6 billion in ready cash. It's no wonder that some people in Japan refer to it as the "Bank of Toyota." And just like a bank, it earns money on its money. For its 1986 fiscal year, the company reported income of $800 million from interest and dividends alone. It's a nice cushion to have. In 1986, when the yen appreciated significantly against the dollar, eroding Toyota's profits, the company assured its workers that none would be laid off.

Ever since a wrenching strike in 1950 Toyota has enjoyed harmonious relations with its employees. Visitors can feel that harmony at work in a tour through a Toyota plant. This is an enthusiastic work force, happy at what they're doing and conscientious. They shower management with suggestions on improvement in work methods. In 1985 Toyota logged 45.6 suggestions per employee, and 96 percent of them (2.4 million) were adopted. Even if you don't believe those figures, they're mind boggling.

Toyota's plants are clean and resound with music. Anyone on the line can stop the moving cars with a flick of a button. And Toyota workers are well paid—the average wage in 1986 was $18,000 a year (and that was before the 40 percent escalation in the value of the yen).

Toyota's roots go back to the last century, to a famous Japanese inventor, Sakichi Toyoda. His exploits, reminiscent of Thomas A. Edison's, were such that his life is used as a model in elementary school textbooks. The son of a poor carpenter, Toyoda was born in 1867, a year before the Meiji Restoration ushered in Japan's modern era. He was tinkering—inventing things—by the time he was eighteen. He applied for his first patent in 1890, and in 1897 he invented the first Japanese power-driven loom. He eventually received eighty-four patents for his inventions.

Things were not going well in 1910 when he was working on the development of an automatic loom, among other projects. So he took himself off to the United States where he spent six months touring the country and inspecting factories. Years later Sakichi Toyoda, who didn't have any formal training, told about that experience to a group of Japanese engineers: "To tell you the truth, I felt that my eyes had been opened. As I viewed the plants in cities all across the United States, and felt the tremendous energy of the Americans, I got angry at myself for being so blind. I was ashamed for having been ready to throw everything away after only a few failures."

In 1926, four years before his death, Sakichi developed an automatic loom and set up a company, the Toyoda Automatic Loom Works, to make this machine. The plant was established in Nagoya, a port city midway between Tokyo and Osaka that was established in the seventeenth century as one of the garrison towns of the Tokugawan Shogunate. (The Tokugawas, who ruled Japan for 265 years, came from Matsudaira, a remote, mountainous area that is part of Toyota City.) Sakichi Toyoda had grown up in Nagoya.

Toyoda's son, Kiichiro, who was born in 1894, followed in his father's footsteps. He too was an inventor, but instead of looms, he became interested in automobiles. In 1929 Sakichi Toyoda made a deal with Britain's Platt Brothers, then the world's largest manufacturer of spinning and weaving machinery, to sell them the rights to his loom patents for £100,000. (then worth $500,000). These funds were put at Kiichiro's disposal for research and development in automobiles.

In the United States Ford and General Motors were already going full tilt in the automobile business, and they were both quick to explore overseas markets. Ford organized a Japanese company in 1925 and two years later built a plant in Yokohama to assemble cars from parts shipped out of Dearborn. General Motors followed suit, building an assembly plant in Osaka in 1926. It was not until 1928, when Ford brought in 8,850 vehicles and GM 15,490, that the number of passenger cars in Japan exceeded the number of rickshaws. Both Ford and GM set up finance companies so that their cars could be bought on credit. Together they dominated the Japanese automotive scene.

Meanwhile, Kiichiro Toyoda was tinkering. In 1930 he began working on a prototype for a small passenger vehicle. And in 1933 he had come far enough along to set up an automotive department inside the Toyoda Automatic Loom Works. His plans called for a Japanese car to be built with Japanese components. It was an idea that appealed, not surprisingly, to the nationalistic and increasingly militaristic Japanese government, which began to subsidize Japanese automakers.

In May 1935 Toyoda wheeled out a prototype called the Model A-1. Only three models were made, however, as the Japanese government, preparing to go to war with China, suggested rather strongly that it wanted trucks, not passenger cars. So Toyoda turned to trucks, producing eighteen by the end of 1935. In 1936 the Japanese government officially designated the Toyoda Automatic Loom Works as a company eligible to make motor vehicles (GM and Ford were never granted such a license)—and in 1937 Toyoda began building a plant with a production capacity of 1,500 vehicles a month. It went up in Koromo (today's Toyota City), not far from the loom works in Nagoya. To finance this expansion, the automotive department was separated out as a new company. Toyota Motor Company was formed in August 1937. How it came to be *Toyota* instead of *Toyoda* is one of those mysteries that will probably never be cleared up.

There are at least four different versions of the "truth." According to one appearing in the book *My Life with Toyota,* by Shotaro Kamiya, company officials decided that *Toyota* sounded clearer than *Toyoda* and "also seemed better in terms of advertising psychology" (whatever that means). The official history issued by Toyota states that Kiichiro chose *Toyota* to lift the new company beyond its family connection and emphasize its "contribution to Japanese society." But Larry Armstrong, Tokyo bureau chief of *BusinessWeek* in 1986, derided that account, asserting that "everyone else believes . . . that he [Kiichiro] was superstitious; *Toyota* has eight calligraphic strokes to *Toyoda*'s ten, and 8 has always been a lucky number in Japan." A variation of Armstrong's explanation was given by William S. Rukeyser in a 1969 profile of Toyota in *Fortune.* He said that one of the Toyota executives "took a traditional Japanese precaution by consulting a numerologist, who advised using the modified spelling of the family name. When written in Japanese characters, *Toyoda* requires ten strokes of the pen, *Toyota* only eight. As of 1937, the number 8 was believed to be more auspicious for the Toyoda family."

Take your pick.

Shotaro Kamiya was one of Toyota's first recruits. He had grown up as an adopted child in Nagoya, where his foster father had a flour- and noodle-making business, and he went to a commercial high school whose entrance was graced with a wooden plaque emblazoned, "The world is our market." It was a message that registered. In 1917, when Kamiya was nineteen, he went to work for the giant trading company Mitsui. Asked where he wanted to work, Kamiya said, without hesitation, "New York." Instead, in 1918 he was posted to Mitsui's office in Seattle, where he stayed for a year before being transferred to London.

Ambitious and optimistic, Kamiya left Mitsui after five years to open his own trading company in London, exporting iron to Japan and brass to India, but chaotic economic conditions around the world caused the firm to fold. In 1927 Kamiya headed back to Japan, still optimistic; he was only twenty-nine and still single. In Japan Kamiya was the right man at the right time for the U.S. automakers intent on opening the Japanese market. He had business experience, he knew English. General Motors hired him in 1928 as its sales manager.

As Japan moved closer to war with China, Kamiya felt trapped in a conflict of interest. The Japanese government tapped him for information on the automobile industry, and he willingly cooperated. Meanwhile, GM headquarters in Detroit wanted Kamiya to keep them informed about the Japanese government's plan for the automobile industry—and even though the information was not secret, he felt uncomfortable doing this. Kamiya was clearly a Japanese nationalist. In his autobiography Kamiya also recalled that he was repelled by GM's harshness in dealing with the Japanese. "Their policy toward dealers was especially merciless," he wrote. "Almost daily they cut ties with dealers in financial trouble. I remember thinking that while such action might be accepted in the United States, where companies rely on written contracts, customs are different in Japan. . . . I often complained to the American staff and tried to persuade them to help dealers instead of dropping them. . . . But GM ignored my complaints." (Kamiya was later to build a very successful dealer network for Toyota in Japan, and his policy was to never rescind a dealer franchise; if a dealer got into trouble, Kamiya dispatched people—and resources—to help him.)

In 1935, after meeting with Kiichiro Toyoda, Kamiya quit GM and joined Toyota. GM had been paying him 600 yen a month; Toyota paid him 120 yen a month. "I did not care so much about the personal cost," said Kamiya, "if I could contribute to my country's development." Kamiya told his two subordinates at GM—Kanosuke Hanasaki and Seisi Kato—about his decision, and they also took pay cuts to desert GM and join Toyota (where both rose to become top executives). They weren't the only ones to follow Kamiya. Hinode Motors in Nagoya turned in its Buick dealership and became Toyota's first dealer. Other GM dealers in Japan also switched. *Banzai!*

During World War II Japanese automakers became virtual wards of the government. Toyota was converted to a military facility, turning out trucks for the Japanese troops. After the war Toyota began the long road back. At the helm were the same people who had been active in Toyota management before the war: Kiichiro Toyoda, Kamiya, Kato, Hanasaki. It was a stormy time. Toyota began making cars and trucks again, but in very small runs (between 1947 and 1952 a total of 215 passenger cars). Financial troubles coupled with a two-month strike protesting layoffs brought the company to the brink of collapse in 1950. A reorganization split the company in two—a manufacturing entity and a sales arm (they were remerged in 1982)—and labor peace was achieved with the resignations of Kiichiro Toyoda and his entire management staff. Kiichiro died two years later, at age fifty-six, no longer head of the automobile company he founded. His cousin, Eiji Toyoda, took his place as the main family representative in the company.

Under the direction of Kamiya, the sales company built up a superb dealer network patterned after the franchise system in the United States. It also shrewdly paved the way for the motorization of Japan by providing two essential ingredients: mechanics and drivers. In 1961 Toyota started a Mechanics Junior College to train people in the repair and servicing of cars. At the same time it launched two driving schools to teach Japanese how to drive. Toyota thus helped to lay in the infrastructure that turned Japan into a nation on wheels. (Japan had thirty million passenger cars on the road in 1987.)

Japan lives by exports and by 1957 Toyota was ready to invade the United States, where the Volkswagen Beetle reigned as the import leader. To do battle it sent its Crown Toyopet, described by one reporter as a "truckline sedan." It was so underpowered that the car couldn't make it up a California hill to the dealer showroom where it was to be unveiled. Kiichiro Toyoda's son, Shoichiro, had firsthand experience with this failure. He was posted to the United States. He tells of driving the Toyopet from Boston to Niagara Falls to Cleveland and to Washington, D.C., finally realizing that as far as American roads were concerned, it was a "junk" car. Toyota now makes a special point of mentioning in all its official company histories how the Toyopet flopped in the U.S. market, causing the company to rethink its strategy and return in 1965 with a more appropriate small vehicle, the Corona, followed three years later by the Corolla. Toyota's sales of passenger cars in the United States went from

5,440 in 1965 to 196,750 in 1970, 283,900 in 1975, 582,200 in 1980, and 631,000 in 1986. Toyota cars, trucks, and forklifts are all import leaders. However, the real revolution was taking place in Japan. A multinational study team organized by the Massachusetts Institute of Technology has divided the first century of the automobile into three transformational periods. The first was Henry Ford's Model T (1908) and assembly line (1914), changing a cottage industry into a mass production affair. The second was the development of a strong European automobile industry after World War II, showing there was a market for many different kinds of cars. And the third was the post–World War II surge of the Japanese auto industry, which was marked by two startling developments: the Japanese could produce cars faster than companies in other countries and with fewer workers. On top of that, the quality of the Japanese cars was so high that they didn't break down as frequently as others, resulting in a high degree of customer satisfaction. These were the qualities that enabled Japan to send its cars to all parts of the world—and win commanding market shares.

Behind the Japanese success are new methods of working—the *kanban,* or "just in time," system whereby parts are sent to the factories as needed, not far in advance; a heavy use of robots to do jobs like spot welding (the robots never tire and are never absent or on strike); and employee involvement programs such as quality circles and suggestion campaigns that give the work force a feeling that they are contributing significantly to the car being fashioned on the production line. In all these facets, Toyota is a leader.

In Japan Toyota also has a fiercesome reputation for being concerned with its people, for requiring its suppliers to produce quality parts at low prices, and for frugality. *BusinessWeek* in 1986 told the story of Shoichiro Toyoda's daughter going to school for the first time with a five-cent pencil instead of the fifty-cent ones carried by her schoolmates, her father allegedly explaining that cheap pencils write just as well as expensive ones.

So Toyota was at the heart of the revolution in automaking wrought by the Japanese industry. In 1969 Toyota overtook Italy's Fiat to become the world's fifth-largest automaker. In 1970 they passed Chrysler to advance to fourth place. And in 1971 they slipped by Volkswagen to become number three in the world. As long ago as 1969 Bill Rukeyser asked Taizo Ishida, then eighty-one and chairman of Toyota, whether Toyota would one day be the world's largest automaker. "I have that ambition," he replied.

A dramatic step toward fulfillment of that ambition came at the end of 1985 when Toyota followed the lead of other Japanese automakers and announced that it would open a production facility to serve what was still the world's largest automobile market: the United States. Toyota selected a rural site near Georgetown, Kentucky, twelve miles north of Lexington, for its American assembly and stamping plant. It's in the heart of the famed bluegrass country of Kentucky, whose governor, Martha Layne Collins, had visited Toyota headquarters in Toyota City earlier that year. (The author knows the date well—March 12—because he was there on the same day.)

Kentucky, one of thirty states to bid for the plant, made what Toyota described as "the strongest" proposal. The $125-million package called for the state to pay training costs equivalent to the first six months' salaries of the three thousand employees hired by Toyota. It also pledged to pay for trips to Japan by selected employees who will be inculcated in the Toyota way. The typical U.S. assembly plant employs between four thousand and six thousand workers to produce a quarter million cars a year. Toyota plans to produce two hundred thousand cars in Kentucky with three thousand people.

Toyota Motor Corporation (TMC) is the largest entity in a labyrinth of fourteen interlocking companies known as the Toyota Group. For example, the original company, Toyoda Automatic Loom Works, owned 4.3 percent of TMC in 1986 and in turn was 23 percent–owned by TMC. In addition to textile machinery, Toyoda Loom now assembles cars for Toyota and makes the forklifts bearing the Toyota name. Nippondenso is a major manufacturer of electrical equipment—TMC owns 21.8 percent of its stock. Aichi Steel Works, 21 percent–owned by TMC, supplies Toyota with steel. Also part of the Group are a trading company; car body manufacturers; machine tool builders; a real estate development company; and two other motor vehicle producers, Hino Motors, Japan's biggest maker of heavy trucks (11.3 percent–owned by TMC), and Daihatsu, Japan's eighth-largest automaker (15 percent–owned by TMC).

Many of these companies have stock market listings of their own. If they were all amalgamated into one company, the combined sales would come to well over $50 billion. Toyoda family members were at the helm of eleven of these companies in 1985. According to *BusinessWeek,* the Toyodas controlled companies that accounted for 3 percent of Japan's gross national product.

Even before opening its Kentucky plant, Toyota had built up a strong presence in the United States. On the basis of its U.S. sales alone, it would rank fiftieth on the *Fortune* 500 roster. And through its sales and marketing activities, including the 1,080 Toyota dealers, the Japanese company claimed to give employment to fifty thousand Americans. In

1986, for the first time, it sold more than one million cars and trucks in the American market.

Toyota may be best known to Americans for its ad campaigns. It has apparently had little difficulty adjusting to American ways, steadily beefing up its advertising to the point where it was spending $172 million in 1985, which ranked it as the nation's forty-fifth-largest advertiser. And Toyota learned quickly about the importance of hoopla in revving up the dealer ranks. Toyota is as rah-rah as any American company by now. In 1985 it flew, at the company's expense, all the U.S. dealers (and their wives) to Japan for a nine-day jaunt during which they were wined and dined everywhere they went. Yuki Togo, president of Toyota USA, explained, "Our dealers are vital to us and we want to increase the confidence they have in Toyota. We want them to feel Toyota's excitement for the future and realize Toyota's commitment to helping them succeed."

In the fall of 1986, to introduce its new models to dealers, Toyota staged a glitzy, song-and-dance extravaganza in Las Vegas, bringing in the Beach Boys and *Saturday Night Live* star Billy Crystal, who hailed the 1987 Toyota Tercel: "Look at that body, daahling, tell me, where did you get it, Dr. Aero Dynamic of Beverly Hills? But I really must tell you, and I say this from the bottom of my heart, you look maaahvelous!"

For more than ten years Toyota has supported the student exchange program of Youth for Understanding, under which American high school students get to spend eight weeks in Japan living with Japanese families while Japanese high school students do the same in the United States. The company has backed the program with more than $2 million in contributions, which is why in 1986 fifteen sons and daughters of Toyota personnel in the United States got to spend the summer in Japan. In that group were Karyn Ligorner, daughter of Martin Ligorner, owner of B&L Toyota in the Bronx, New York; Lori Rogers, daughter of Mark Rogers, sales manager of Stevinson Toyota in Golden, Colorado; and Sean Weber, son of Gilbert Weber, business manager of Down East Toyota in Brewster, Maine.

Toyota has become so established in America that it made a literary appearance in John Updike's *Rabbit Is Rich,* the third in the series of Updike's *Rabbit* novels. The protagonist, Harry Angstrom, has finally found success in his Pennsylvania hometown, where he was a high school basketball star. His vehicle is a Toyota dealership. Harry pitches a prospective customer:

"Here we're supposed to be Automobile Heaven and the foreigners come up with all the ideas. If you ask me, Detroit's let us all down. Two hundred million of us. I'd much rather handle native American cars, but

World's Car Rental Markets

United States	$ 4 billion
West Germany	$ 703 million
Japan	$ 467 million
Britain	$ 455 million
France	$ 412 million

between the three of us, they're junk. They're cardboard. They're pretend."

Access 1, Toyota-cho
Toyota City
Aichi Prefecture 471, Japan
(81) 565-28-2121

Toyota Motor Sales
19001 S. Western Ave.
Torrance, Cal. 90509
(213) 618-4701

<table>
<tr><td>

Trusthouse Forte

</td><td>

Sales $2.2 billion
Profits $145 million
U.S. Sales $190 million
Rank Largest hotel operator in Britain
World's 8th-largest hotel company
Britain's largest caterer
Founded 1935
Employees 60,800
Headquarters London, England

</td></tr>
</table>

For snobbery, it's not easy to beat the London hotel manager. One must therefore have a certain measure of sympathy and admiration for Lord Forte, formerly Sir Charles Forte and before that just plain Charles Forte, who battled his way through haughty condescension to beat the London hotel crowd at their own game. In the process he built one of the world's largest lodging and catering outfits. It encompasses more than eight hundred hotels ranging from economy (Travel-Lodge) to luxury (Plaza Athenee) in forty-four countries, and more than three thousand catering outlets, including the supply of fifteen million meals a year to passengers on 125 airlines.

This is a story of true Italian grit. Charles Forte's father, Rocco Forte, emigrated to the United States in the early part of this century from Mortale, a tiny mountain village midway between Rome and Naples. He worked in Pittsburgh as a manual laborer, becoming a foreman. But he was homesick and soon returned to Mortale, whose name has since been changed to Monforte in recognition of the fact that just about everyone who lived there was a member of the Forte clan. In 1905 he married a distant cousin, whose name was also Forte, and Charles, their eldest son, was born in November 1908.

Rocco Forte was soon off again, this time emigrating to Scotland in the footsteps of a brother, Alfonso, and a cousin, Pacifico Forte, who were operating various retail establishments there—a grocery in Kincardine-on-Forth, an ice cream shop in Dundee, for example. The Fortes in Scotland kept sending news back to Mortale and urging relatives to come out to help in these enterprises. As a result, some six hundred Fortes, all related, are living today in England, Wales, Scotland, and Ireland. Only a handful are left in Monforte, although much of the land in the Italian town is still owned by the Fortes.

After making sure that there was a viable living to be made in Scotland, Rocco Forte sent for his family in 1912. They settled in Alloa, a town of about twelve thousand people on the River Forth thirty miles upstream from Edinburgh. There Rocco ran the Savoy Cafe on the main street. The family lived in a three-bedroom flat across the street from the cafe. They spoke Italian at home, and Charles grew up speaking English with a Scottish accent.

Charles was sent to Catholic boarding schools in Scotland and Rome, but he was not a great student. He knew already when he was seventeen that he wanted to enter his father's business. His father sent him to Uncle Dominic, who ran a cafe called The Ice Cream Parlour on the beach in Weston-super-Mare on the west coast of England. Then he went to Bournemouth on the south coast, where his father had opened a large cafe, and later to Brighton, where the Fortes had two other cafes. He was learning the business.

In 1935 Charles struck out on his own, opening a milk bar on Upper Regent Street in London. A milk bar was basically an American-style soda fountain serving soups, sandwiches, and cakes in addition to milk shakes and ice cream. It was a success from the start, and the Fortes added another one on Charing Cross Road before World War II broke out. Although he had lived in Britain for twenty-six years, Charles had neglected to become a naturalized citizen, and in 1940 he was interned for three months on the Isle of Man. It left a bitter taste in his mouth, but he was soon back in the thick of the restaurant business in London. At the war's end he had five milk bars and was married to the former Irene Chierico, whose mother ran a Soho delicatessen.

After the war he built up his restaurant business, and Forte soon joined Lyons, ABC, and Express Dairy as one of the major mass feeders in London's West End. In 1958 he bought his first hotel, the Waldorf in London's Aldwych, one of the seedy hotels for which the United Kingdom is famous. At the same time he won a government concession to operate rest stop eateries along the new expressways being built in Britain, a move that never won him any Michelin stars. Charles brought his company public in 1962, offering 40 percent of the shares. They were snapped up. The company's initial market value was $28 million. (In mid-1986 the market value was $2 billion.)

A pivotal turning point came in 1970. That was the year Charles merged his company with Trust Houses, which operated a group of upscale hotels, including Grosvenor House and Brown's in London. It was also the year Charles was knighted. There was trouble right away with Lord Crowther, the chairman of Trust Houses, who had promised that Forte would succeed him as chairman. Lord Crowther came up with other candidates for the chairman's post and also encouraged a takeover bid by Allied Breweries. He underestimated the tenacity of Charles Forte, who borrowed heavily to buy nearly 30 percent of the company's shares—enough to foil the hostile takeover *and* Lord Crowther.

Eleven years later, after he had greatly expanded the company by acquisitions such as the TraveLodge chain and Knott Hotels in the United States and the George V in Paris and the Ritz in Madrid, Sir Charles tangled again with British bluebloods when he made a bid for the Savoy Group, whose London hotels include the Savoy itself (original home of the D'Oyly Carte Opera Company), Claridge's, and the Connaught, three very posh watering holes. The Group had been losing money, and Sir Charles said he could turn the hotels around. Well, it was as if a tramp had invaded the drawing room.

Giles Shepard, managing director of the Savoy, said acidly that a group which "runs service stations on the main arterial roads" is really not "suitable or qualified" to run hotels ranked "among the most renowned in the world." Sir Charles managed to buy shares equivalent to 61.9 percent of the equity of the Savoy Group, but because of the structure of the company (some shares have more votes than others), he controlled only 38.6 percent of the votes. Armed with its shares, Trusthouse Forte came back in 1982 and demanded a seat on the board for Eric Hartwell, vice chairman of Trusthouse (Hartwell had started his career in one of the Forte lunchrooms). The Savoy people opposed the nomination.

An attorney representing Trusthouse said the Savoy treated the move as if it were "an attempt to place an Argentine admiral on the decks of the Royal Navy." Sir Hugh Wontner, chairman of the Savoy, called for a vote on the motion and suggested that shareholders might want to take a glass of sherry while the votes were being counted. After the count, Trusthouse Forte, the biggest shareholder in the Savoy Group, found it had lost by six hundred thousand votes. Trusthouse Forte continued to hold on to its Savoy shares. At the end of 1985 they were worth about $135 million.

The sniping continued into 1986. Trusthouse Forte has one of the highest profit returns in the hotel industry, and its finance director, Donald Main, claimed that if it had control of the Savoy, it would be able to double the earnings. This claim drew a typically haughty riposte from Shepard, who wrote to the *Financial Times* to say that the only way that might be possible would be to "raise prices inordinately or lower levels of service to an unacceptable standard, or a combination of both. As the Savoy has been in business for nearly one hundred years, and Claridge's and the Berkeley for even longer, and each has maintained a reputation for quality throughout the world, it would be a disastrous policy to abandon such high standards." And he added, "A third way would be to pray that, with divine intervention, the number of days in a year could be doubled. But I am sure that this would be beyond the capabilities even of Mr. Main."

Lord Forte, in his autobiography, published in 1986, said that his company would not give up its fight and that he believes "one day we will own these hotels."

Lord Forte, who became a life peer in 1982, was seventy-six years old in 1986, and continued to serve as chairman, although the chief executive's baton passed to his only son, Rocco, an Oxford graduate. Olga Polizzi, his eldest daughter, holds a seat on the board and is in charge of design for the company.

Trusthouse Forte runs restaurants and hotels all over the world but none has a casino, nor do the newsstands in his establishments carry "girlie" magazines. He once explained why to *The Wall Street Journal:* "I sent five daughters to a good convent school. How could I meet their teachers, the nuns, as a man who's made his money off gambling and sex books?"

Lord Forte always went out of his way to praise employees. In 1979 he spent thirty thousand dollars on a three-minute television commercial in which he thanked his workers for helping the company to set new profit records. In 1985 the company announced a new benefit: a gift of one hundred shares of stock to all employees who had worked twenty years for the company. Trusthouse Forte shares were then selling for about $2.25 a share. Nearly one thousand employees were eligible for the award.

While the people who run the Savoy don't approve of Lord Forte,

---

World's Tallest Hotel

The world's tallest hotel is not in New York or Chicago or London or Tokyo but Singapore, where the seventy-three-story Westin Stamford, which opened on July 1, 1986. It's part of a new Raffles City complex—and it faces the hotel with a fabled Asian history, the old Raffles Hotel. The Westin Stamford has 1,235 rooms. The Raffles has 122 rooms. Westin, a subsidiary of United Airlines, has another hotel in the Raffles City complex, the Plaza, which has 796 rooms. So many new hotels have been built in Singapore that the opening room rates at the Westin Stamford ranged from thirty-eight dollars to a top of fifty-five dollars.

the Middle East kingdom of Kuwait does. Aside from Lord Forte, it holds the largest single block of shares (5.6 percent of the total).

Access 86 Park Lane
London W1A 3AA, England
(44) 1-493-4090

Unilever	**Sales** $25.3 billion
	Profits $982 million
	U.S. Sales $4.5 billion
	Rank World's largest consumer products company
	World's largest margarine producer
	World's largest soap and detergent maker
	World's largest maker of packaged tea
	World's largest ice cream maker
	World's 3d-largest advertiser
	World's 16th-largest industrial company
	3d-largest company in Britain
	Founded 1930
	Employees 350,000
	Headquarters London, England and Rotterdam, the Netherlands

Down through the years Unilever's press clippings have been depressingly consistent. In 1979 *BusinessWeek* characterized the Anglo-Dutch company as "a rather fuddy-duddy relic of the age of empire." In 1983 *The New York Times* called it "big, plodding, safe." In 1984 the *Financial Times* said Unilever was "so big that it ploughs on remorselessly like a super-tanker, scarcely able to change course." And *Forbes* in 1985 labeled Unilever "a sleeping giant."

Interspersed among these comments is the Rip Van Winkle theme, hence these headlines: "Unilever Cleans Up Its Act" *(Forbes);* "After Years of Decline, Lever Brothers Has Plans for a Comeback" *(The Wall Street Journal);* "Why Unilever Is Taking the Gloves Off" *(Financial Times);* "Unilever Alters Its Game Plan" *(The New York Times);* "Unilever Fights Back in the U.S." *(Fortune);* "Unilever Lets in a Shaft of Sunlight" *(Financial Times).*

Much of this feeling was inspired by the dismal performance of Unilever's American subsidiary, Lever Brothers, cast in the thankless role of competing against mighty Procter & Gamble. Before World War II, with its Lux, Rinso, Lifebuoy, and Spry brands, Lever held its own. However, after the war, when P&G ushered in the detergent age with Tide, Lever was overwhelmed—and the dividends remitted home from New York slowed to a trickle, at times even stopped. But it's more than the American experience that critics have reacted to. These commentators hail for the most part from the business world where Unilever is seen as a gargantuan corporation with no great facility for squeezing profits out of revenues. In 1984, for example, while Unilever was earning $583 million on sales of $18.7 billion, Procter & Gamble was earning $880 million on sales of $12.9 billion, and Nestlē was earning $632 million on sales of $13.2 billion. Unilever never actually loses money, but the suspicion is that it may not have the bottom-line zeal that other companies have.

This is not to say that Unilever is an eleemosynary institution. Marxist critics have not been shy about depicting it as a ruthless exploiter of resources and people on a global scale. So Unilever is unloved on both the right, where it's perceived as a puny profit producer, and the left, where it's perceived as a stalwart arm of imperialism.

On one point everyone can agree: Unilever is big. It's the largest consumer products company in the world. It's the world's third-largest advertiser. And it's the most multinational of all the multinational corporations. More than five hundred companies belong to the Unilever Group, and they operate in seventy-eight countries, manufacturing in most of them. A unadmiring writer once lamented that "something approaching two thirds of mankind buy from or sell to Unilever, and most people use its products every single day of their lives." The company's own literature says rather matter-of-factly: "Unilever does business in or with nearly every country in the world." No other company can claim that ubiquity. The British and Dutch empires might be down, but the Unilever Empire remains in place.

It's an empire built on fats and oils, and its binational roots go back to the latter half of the nineteenth century when the Industrial Age spawned working-class households with money to spend. Entrepreneurs began to package products under brand names and promote them to millions of the new consumers. It was the dawn of modern advertising and merchandising.

William Hesketh Lever was a child of that age. Born in 1851 in the industrial North of England, he was introduced early on to selling through the wholesale grocery business his father operated in Bolton, a city fifteen miles northwest of Manchester. William and his brother, James D'Arcy Lever, worked in the family business before starting their own company, Lever Brothers, in 1885, to sell soap packaged under the Sunlight name.

It's such a mundane product today that it's hard to realize what an innovation it was then to sell a bar of soap that was wrapped in imitation parchment and packed in a carton bearing an identifying name. Previously, most soap was sold in long, anonymous bars that the grocer sliced up to the customer's order. Lever's Sunlight soap was also softer than the soaps then in common use (which meant it dissolved more quickly), and it lathered more generously. At first Lever sold soap made by others, but in 1885 he began making his own, using this formula: A mixture of copra or palm kernel oil, cottonseed oil, resin, and tallow.

He embarked immediately on a high-powered advertising campaign for Sunlight, establishing it as one of the early national brands in Britain. "Why does a woman look older sooner than a man?" was one of his first thrusts on behalf of Sunlight. (Lever bought this idea from an American soap maker, Frank Siddall for $2,500.) Lever was not the first to discover the efficacy of mass advertising. He followed in the footsteps of a rival, Thomas J. Barratt, who took over the Pears soap company in 1875. Pears may have been the most heavily advertised brand of the nineteenth century, responsible for a host of memorable slogans ("How do you spell soap? Why *P-E-A-R-S,* of course." "Good morning! Have you used Pears Soap?") Barratt once said, "Any fool can make soap. It takes a clever man to sell it."

William Hesketh Lever was a child of his age in other ways as well. He enthusiastically supported the Liberal party, which was the agent of the new industrialists and business class, aligned against the Tories and the old landed aristocracy. The Liberals championed democratic electoral reforms, free trade, and religious liberty. They took many of their ideas from the father of utilitarianism, Jeremy Bentham, whose doctrine that the greatest happiness for the greatest number of people represents the foundation of morality seemed to be an appropriate philosophy for the capitalist revolutionaries of the late nineteenth century.

Thus it was that Lever not only began to advertise and sell soap to the masses but tried, inevitably, to imbue his venture with social significance. In 1887 he began building a new plant in Lancashire on the Wirral peninsula that juts out between the Mersey and Dee rivers into the Irish Sea in northwest England. Completed in 1889 it became the biggest soap-works in the world. It also became the center of a new town, Port Sunlight, where workers lived in company houses bordered by gardens and designed in a variety of styles—some, for example, were reproductions of Ann Hathaway's cottage. It was paternalism fired by the Liberal imagination of William Lever.

Port Sunlight had its own theater, concert hall, gymnasium, and outdoor swimming pool. In return for these amenities, the residents were expected to toe a puritanical line laid down by Lever, who felt that he knew what was best for his workers. He introduced a "prosperity-sharing" scheme in which he, rather than the employee, decided how the money was to be spent. He told his employees that if they were given a year-end bonus, "it will not do you much good if you send it down your throat in the form of bottles of whisky, bags of sweets, or fat geese for Christmas. On the other hand, if you leave this money with me, I shall use it to provide for you everything which makes life pleasant—nice houses, comfortable homes, and healthy recreation."

William Gladstone, the leader of the Liberal party in the last half of the nineteenth century, serving four times as prime minister, came to Port Sunlight in 1891 to open a new dining hall and recreation room. He told the assembled soap millers, "In this hall I have found a living proof that cash payment is not the only nexus between man and man."

Lever was an indefatigable proselytizer and accumulator. Although anti-imperialism was one of the planks of the Liberal party, Lever quickly expanded his soap business beyond the United Kingdom, moving into Europe, Australia, South Africa, and the United States before the turn of the century. He also moved to assure his own supply of raw materials (vegetable oils) by going into the plantation business. In 1905 he bought 51,000 acres in the Solomon Islands and planted them with coconut seed. By 1913 Lever's holdings there extended over 300,000 acres. He did the same in the Belgian Congo and West Africa, through concessions and acquisition of trading companies that he thought would bring him a steady supply of palm oil to feed his soap plants. World War I helped. A British blockade cut off German mills from their vegetable oil resources in West Africa—and many of these supplies were diverted to Lever Brothers, helping the company move into the production of margarine.

One by-product of soap making is glycerine, and Lever delivered this chemical to British arms makers to help them make explosives. In 1917, in recognition of his contribution to the war effort, William Hesketh Lever became a life peer: Lord Leverhulme. In 1921 Lever Brothers moved its headquarters from Port Sunlight to London, occupying an ornate, colonnaded building on the Thames Embankment near Blackfriars Station. The curved, colonnaded stone Unilever House that today stands on the same site went up in 1931, an art deco version of the earlier structure, which originally housed De Keyser's Royal Hotel, a German enterprise. In a six-year rehabilitation that ended in 1983, Unilever House was renovated and expanded by the addition of an eight-story wing—the new wing was low enough so that it did not violate the long-standing edict of London planning authorities that no building can go up to a height that would block the view of Saint Paul's cathedral from Waterloo Bridge.

An ebullient salesman who backed his products with more advertising than the world had ever seen, William Hesketh Lever also proved to be adept at acquiring other companies, for which he developed a ravenous appetite. In 1906 he bought the Vinolia toilet soap company; in 1910

Hudson's, Britain's leading maker of soap powder. He scooped up three other British soap companies between 1910 and 1915, bought out his largest competitors in Australia and South Africa, and eventually had the satisfaction of absorbing his old rival, Pears transparent soap.

In his life outside of Lever Brothers, Lord Leverhulme was also active as a builder and acquirer. In 1918 and 1919 he bought the islands of Lewis and Harris in the Hebrides off Scotland, planning, according to one British muckraker, "to create for himself a feudal estate." Local opposition defeated these plans but not before Lord Leverhulme had put together a little private empire that included trawling vessels, canneries, and a nationwide chain of fish-and-chip shops, Mac Fisheries. To supply these outlets with meat products, Sir Leverhulme also thoughtfully bought the sausage pie firm of Thomas Walls, which later turned to ice cream making to relieve the summer doldrums. It was an interesting assemblage, but in 1922 he abandoned his separate empire and sold all these businesses to—surprise—Lever Brothers. Lord Leverhulme died in 1925, four years before a titanic merger that was to catapult his company into even greater prominence on the world industrial scene. (He left a substantial part of his estate to the Leverhulme Trust, whose 6 percent holding today makes it the largest single stockholder.)

Margarine was invented in 1869 in, of all places, France. It came about as a result of a contest sponsored by Napoleon III for a tasty butter substitute. Hippolyte Mege-Mouries, a French chemist, came up with the winning spread, combining beef fat with milk. Two major butter marketers in the Netherlands—Jurgens and Van den Berghs—were immediately interested in this imitation. Both companies were based in Oss, an industrial town in south central Holland, in the heart of a dairy region. In the late 1860s they had already emerged as major butter traders, not just in their home country but throughout Europe. Jurgens was, in fact, established as the largest seller of butter in Europe. The Dutch butter merchants, whose two main markets were Germany and Britain, saw immediately the potential of margarine, which then, as now, sold for less than butter. The target consumers were working-class people who couldn't afford butter.

Initially, the margarine made by the Dutch companies used animal fats—and there was, in the closing decades of the nineteenth century, an ample supply from the American meatpacking companies in Chicago. But in the early part of the twentieth century the U.S. meatpackers formed a cartel (that was later broken up) and jacked up the price of their waste fats. The margarine makers then turned to a new raw material, vegetable oils—an alternative discovered by Wilhelm Normann, a German scientist who found in 1902 how to "harden" these oils by hydrogenation. Margarine began to be made from sesame, coconut, peanut, and palm oils. And it became important then to have efficient mills to crush the seeds and extract the oil. Nineteen hundred was the takeoff point for margarine; consumption quadrupled in the next forty years.

It's no accident that Armour, a meat company, made Dial soap, or that Procter & Gamble, a soap company, made Crisco shortening. Or that any margarine company would make a soap or any soap company a margarine. These products—soaps, shortenings, margarines—share a common raw material base: oils and fats. It wasn't long then before the two Dutch fat producers, Jurgens and Van den Berghs, began to make soaps. And Unilever began to make margarine during World War I at the behest of the British government, which was worried about being so dependent on foreign sources for edible fats. (A modern nation can't do without its fats.)

A strong characteristic of industry in the early part of the twentieth century was a yearning for monopoly. It was a desire that transcended national borders. In the United States trusts were formed to dominate the oil, tobacco, and meatpacking industries. In Germany all the major chemical companies were amalgamated in 1925 into the I. G. Farben cartel. In Britain four large chemical producers joined in 1927 to form Imperial Chemical Industries. And an audacious Swede, Ivar Kreuger, was busy buying up all the match companies of the world.

The Dutch margarine companies had been trying from as early as 1908 to eliminate competition among themselves through various profit-pooling arrangements, which didn't work too well because someone could always be counted on to cheat. They solved this dilemma in 1927 by merging their forces into the Margarine Union. The charter members were Jurgens and Van den Berghs. Together they had a lock on the European margarine business. They then had discussions with Lever Brothers about the possibility of setting up a soap trust, in which all the soap operations of the three companies would be combined, and a margarine trust, in which all their margarine activities would be merged. They couldn't get these cartels organized, and so they decided instead to merge all their operations into one big company.

The Margarine Union and Lever Brothers combined to form Unilever, which began functioning as an Anglo-Dutch enterprise on January 1, 1930. The corporate structure has never changed. To avoid double taxation, two companies were established—Unilever PLC, which is incorporated in Britain, and Unilever NV, incorporated in the Netherlands. While some subsidiaries are owned by the Dutch company and others by the British company, Unilever in practice operates as one group. It has twin headquarters—one in London, one in Rotterdam. The two parent companies have identical boards of directors. They pay dividends to shareholders that are equal in value. They report results on a consolidated basis as if they were one company. It's a unique international partnership that has survived more than fifty years.

A company midwifed by merger rarely gives up that heritage. Unilever has grown by swallowing other companies—dozens of them—all over the globe, including Lipton's (United States and Canada), Brooke Bond (Britain), Harriet Hubbard Ayer (France), Pepsodent (United States), Batchelors (Britain), Vita (Netherlands), Rondi (South Africa), Perlina (Peru), Gessy (Brazil), McNiven (Australia), National Starch & Chemical (United States). It's a practice that continues in full force today. In the three-year period from 1984 through 1986, Unilever sold more than fifty units with total sales of $3 billion a year while buying about fifty companies with combined sales of $6 billion. The biggest catch was Chesebrough-Pond's, an American company whose roots also go back to the last century. Unilever paid $3.1 billion for Chesebrough.

Unilever is not so much a collection of companies as an armada of brand names, more than a thousand of them. You are not likely to encounter the Unilever name unless you're an investor (Unilever shares are traded on the New York Stock Exchange). But who in the United States has not heard of All, Surf, Wisk, Breeze, Lux, Dove, Close-Up, Wish-Bone, and Imperial? And who in Britain has not heard of Stork and Blue Band margarines, Birds Eye frozen foods, Persil and Drive detergents, Vim cleanser, Wall's sausage and ice cream, Sunsilk shampoo, Oxo cubes, John West canned fruits and vegetables, Fray Bentos canned meats, and Haywards pickles? Who in Italy has not heard of Timotei shampoo, and who in Europe has not heard of the deodorants Rexona and Impulse? Who in West Africa has not heard of the detergent Omo? The Chesebrough-Pond's acquisition swung into the Unilever column the familiar brand names Vaseline, Pond's, Q-tips, Ragu, and Prince Matchabelli.

To make sure these brands do not go unnoticed, Unilever spent more than $1 billion on advertising in 1985: $450 million in Europe, $400 million in the United States, and $250 million in the rest of the world. From the earliest days of this enterprise, whether it's traced to Britain or Holland, advertising was a keystone of the business. It was such an important element in company affairs that Unilever developed its own house agency, Lintas (Lever International Advertising Service), which for many years ranked as one of the world's largest advertising agencies. (No longer part of Unilever, it survives today as a founding partner of SSC&B: Lintas Worldwide, the fifteenth-largest advertising agency in the world.)

In a notable defense of this means of communication, Lord Heyworth, Unilever's chairman from 1941 to 1960, devoted his 1958 address to shareholders to an explanation of why the company, then the largest advertiser in the world, spent $234 million in 1957 to promote its hundreds of brands in more than one hundred countries. Lord Heyworth said that after having spent large sums of money, time, and thought in coming up with products "we believe the consumer wants, it would be foolish indeed to stop short at that point and not take steps to tell them what we have to sell and try to persuade them to buy." As to the criticism that advertising tempts people to spend money on goods they cannot afford, thereby reducing them to a state of financial misery while tantalizing them with things they cannot buy, Lord Heyworth had this rejoinder: "This particular attack, I may say, leaves Unilever's withers reasonably unwrung, for we have yet to hear of a housewife driven to bankruptcy through lavish expenditure on soap, margarine, sausages, or toothpaste. But all such criticism leads, in the end, to protect the weak-willing and weak-witted minority against the need to leave the robust and shrewd majority with the right to pick and choose for themselves. Let us by all means continue to improve the ethics of advertising, which indeed in many countries is already subject to codes of conduct far stricter than some critics realize. But if this process of improvement results in the advertiser being deprived of the basic right to persuade the consumer to exercise his or her choice in his favor, the consumer, too, will find that she has lost something. She will have lost her freedom of choice."

That's the philosophical backdrop for the long-running Lever campaign showing people eating Imperial margarine suddenly being crowned.

This enduring faith in advertising and the sanctity of brand names is a trait Unilever shares with Procter & Gamble, General Foods, Nestlé, and other package goods producers. But it would be a mistake to identify Unilever as nothing more than the Anglo-Dutch counterpart of these companies. Unilever has idiosyncrasies rooted strongly in its history. It has always been more holistic in the sense of being involved in the entire process that results in a consumer product, beginning with the raw materials, wherever they might be located. Even today, when colonial powers have been routed all over the world, Unilever farms ninety-two thousand hectares of plantations in eight countries: Cameroon, Colombia, Ghana, Malaysia, Nigeria, the Solomon Islands, Thailand, and Zaire. Some thirty-four thousand people are employed on these plantations, producing palm oil, rubber, coconut, cocoa, and tea. And in 1984 Unilever added another thirty thousand people to this plantation work force by paying $480 million to acquire Brooke Bond, which has tea estates in Africa and India.

In Unilever one activity has frequently led to another—and the company always seemed ready to let this happen. The oil seeds crushed for use in margarine and soap yielded a by-product known as "cattle cake," which prompted a move into animal feeds. Processing the oil for use in margarine and soap yields other by-products, glycerine and fatty acids, which led Unilever into chemicals, a $2-billion business in 1986. Those millions of consumer products need to be packaged, which resulted in Unilever operating twenty-four packaging plants in six European countries. Consumer goods must also be transported, which turned Unilever into one of the largest truckers in Britain—and for fifty years, before it was sold in 1985, the Unilever-owned Palm Line was one of the biggest shipping companies out of West Africa. Unilever farms for salmon in Scotland, has prawn farms in several Asian countries, and is the major owner of a vertically integrated fishing business out of West Germany that includes catching the fish in deep-sea trawlers, processing the catch, and then selling the fish in company-owned shops and restaurants that carry the Nordsee name.

The Unilever companies originally moved into overseas territories for two reasons: They wanted to sell their products everywhere and they wanted to secure raw material bases. However, once a unit was established somewhere, it tended to be interested in all manner of businesses. Having a narrow focus is not a charge that can be brought against Unilever. For example, after planting coconut seeds in the Solomon Islands in 1905, Lever had to wait until the trees reached maturity. While waiting, the Lever outpost there began trading in pearl and tortoiseshell.

The prime exhibit in Unilever's predilection for spreading itself over many areas is the fabled United Africa Company (UAC), which William Hesketh Lever began putting together in 1910 when he bought W. B. MacIver, a Liverpool trading company operating in Nigeria. In the next nineteen years trading company after trading company in West Africa fell into the hands of Lever Brothers, culminating on March 3, 1929, nine months before the merger with the Margarine Union, in the amalgamation of the Lever-controlled Niger Company with the African and Eastern Trade Corporation. The formation of the new Lever subsidiary, United Africa Company, was announced, fittingly enough, from the Savoy Hotel in London.

Subsumed in UAC were activities of more than a dozen trading companies, most of them of British origin, one of whose histories went back three hundred years to its days as a slave trader. The trading company is a form of commercial activity unfamiliar to most Americans. It's basically a merchant business that can do virtually anything, act as a wholesaler, retailer, manufacturer, exporter, importer, banker—you name it—and UAC did it. The company's basic role was to export the crops of African farmers and import manufactured goods from Europe.

When UAC was formed, it controlled 60 percent of the exports of palm oil, 45 percent of palm kernel, 60 percent of peanuts, and 50 percent of cocoa from the four British colonies of West Africa—Nigeria, Gold Coast (now Ghana), Gambia, and Sierra Leone. In addition, UAC had extensive operations in other African countries, including the Belgian Congo, Cameroon, and the Ivory Coast. In all, it had one thousand locations on the African continent.

For the next twenty years, from 1929 to 1949, Unilever's UAC was unquestionably the largest and most important company operating on the African continent. Nor was its contribution to Unilever insignificant. In the years immediately following World War II, UAC accounted for one fifth of Unilever's turnover and, if the contribution of the plantations was added, between one third to one half of the profits. Independence movements swept Britain, France, Belgium, and Portugal out of Africa in the post–World War II years but not Unilever. To be sure, its role changed. It no longer controls the marketing of West African crops. And it has been forced to sell manufacturing units to governments, including a majority interest in its biggest subsidiary, United Africa Company of Nigeria.

In 1973, to adjust to these changing political conditions, Unilever changed the name of United Africa Company to UAC International and changed its charter as well. Based now in London, UAC consists of a group of companies whose spheres of influence extend to more than thirty countries and whose operations span a wide range of activities outside the traditional ones of Unilever (soap, detergents, margarine, foods). UAC companies brew beer in Nigeria, Chad, Ghana, and Sierra Leone (in conjunction with Guinness and Heineken), distribute Caterpillar tractors in Britain, harvest timber in Nigeria and the Solomon Islands, distribute wine in France, weave textiles in the Ivory Coast, assemble passenger cars in Nigeria, wholesale electrical equipment in France, and operate department stores in Ghana. The Lagos-based United Africa Company, now 40 percent–owned by Unilever, continues to be Nigeria's largest company (outside of the state-owned oil company). And the 60 percent–owned United Africa Company of Ghana is the largest company in that nation. Unilever is more than Lux soap.

If it had its druthers, Unilever would own 100 percent of its overseas subsidiaries. But as a seasoned sailor in international waters, it knows how and when to tack to the winds of change. The result is a crazy-quilt pattern that shows Unilever owning 100 percent of all its subsidiaries in the United States, which include Lawry's and Shedd's; 51 of percent of Hindustan Lever, the third-largest company in India; 40 percent of Lever Brothers Nigeria; 50 percent of Margarinefabrikken in Denmark; 66 percent of Lever Brothers Pakistan; and 95 percent of Nippon Lever in Japan. Unilever has found its companies nationalized in more than a dozen countries. "This nationalization," the company once noted, "may be with full compensation, as in Iraq; with deferred compensation, as in Burma; or with partial, differed compensation, as in Egypt; or anything in between."

Unilever's fine art of survival in a politically unstable world is nowhere better demonstrated than in Indonesia, the world's fifth-largest country (by population). Covering some 13,700 islands (Sumatra, Java, and Bali are three of the largest) which stretch over 3,200 miles from east to west in the South Pacific, Indonesia was ruled as a Dutch colony for more than three hundred years before it was occupied by the Japanese in 1942. Lever, after exporting to Indonesia for more than twenty-five years, had put up a soap plant in Batavia (now Jakarta) in 1935, when Indonesia's population was 60 million. Margarine production began in 1936, and during the Japanese occupation the Unilever plant was run by Mitsubishi.

After the war Unilever people returned and began to rebuild the business even in the midst of a struggle for independence that resulted in the final ejection of the Dutch troops in 1949. A new Indonesian government was established under the presidency of Sukarno, a radical nationalist leader who had been jailed many times by the Dutch before the war and who had cooperated with the Japanese invaders. Although Unilever was half-Dutch and most of its managers in Indonesia were Dutch, the company did not side with the hard-line colonialists in The Hague, and, in fact, welcomed Indonesian independence. However, in the political turmoil that followed independence, Unilever was fortunate to have dual nationality.

In 1958 the Indonesian government decided to nationalize all the Dutch companies. Unilever escaped unscathed. It transferred all the shares of the Indonesian company from Rotterdam (Unilever NV) to London (Unilever PLC) and evacuated all the Dutch employees, replacing them with Britons, Germans, and Scandinavians. ("Look, folks, we're British.") However, five years later, Sukarno got into a screaming match with the British over the creation of the new state of Malaysia out of what was once Malaya, Singapore, and two parts of the large island of Borneo—Sarawak and North Borneo (now Sabah). Most of Borneo belongs to Indonesia, hence the violent objections of Sukarno, who carried on this confrontation for three years, including the mounting of guerrilla raids into the Malaysian territory of Borneo.

Unilever, responding to the anti-British feeling, now reversed its field. In 1964 all the shares of the Indonesian company were transferred back to Rotterdam, and all the British managers were replaced by Dutch nationals. ("Look, folks, we're Dutch.") Because of the violent political strife that erupted in the country the tactic didn't work this time. In 1965 a Communist coup resulted in the assassination of eight top military officers, followed quickly by a counter-coup led by General Suharto. From 1965 to 1967, when Suharto formed a new government, Unilever lost effective control of its Indonesian operations. The subsidiary was never formally nationalized, but a combination of leftist union leaders, military leaders, and government bureaucrats called all the shots, and the business was virtually run into the ground.

Meanwhile, Indonesia was the scene of mayhem. Suspected Communists were hunted down, political groups and vandals took the law into their own hands, and some 750,000 people may have been massacred. Reports told of entire villages being wiped out in Bali and East and Central Java. Order was restored to the country by the Suharto government in 1967. The Communist party was outlawed. And on April 1, 1967, Unilever regained control of its Indonesian company, agreeing to invest $3 million to rehabilitate and expand its operations.

D. K. Fieldhouse, a British historian whose book *Unilever Overseas* was published in 1978, drew this moral: "Unilever survived as long as it did only because it was generally trusted by successive Indonesian governments and ministers; and even when its commercial death seemed imminent, Unilever was ready to die quietly. To say this is not to imply any particular virtue . . . Unilever recognized that its well-being depended entirely on the benevolence of a host government and that this could be solicited but not extorted by threat or force."

The *Financial Times* once quipped that Unilever is "the nearest thing British commerce has to civil service." It does resemble a government bureaucracy in its ponderousness and stolidity. But its ability, tested again and again, to make all these diverse parts hang together is a feat of legerdemain that would make a magician proud. Especially impressive is the almost inbred sense that this is a business with no national boundaries. Nearly all U.S. companies, even those with extensive sales outside the country, issue annual reports that are centered on domestic markets, with the international operations discussed in a separate section. Unilever organizes its annual report along both geographical and product lines. First, there is a report on Europe (64 percent of sales in 1985), then North America (17 percent), and then the "rest of the world" (19 percent). And then follow reports on the main product areas—margarine, detergents, frozen foods and ice cream, other food and drinks, chemicals—in which the fortunes (or misfortunes) of Unilever brands are reported against a worldwide landscape.

This division parallels Unilever's organizational structure in which lines of command flow from the board of directors into three channels: regional managements (geographical), product groups (detergents, frozen foods), and central staff functions (research, accounting, engineering, finance). An operating company in a particular country interacts with all these channels. In other words, if you are a Unilever manager involved in marketing a new detergent in Venezuela, your company would be reporting to a regional manager, but you would also be clued in to detergent activities in other parts of the world through the product group, and might also have recourse to one of the staff functions such as research or taxation.

The board of directors of Unilever ranges in size from twenty to twenty-five members, all of them full-time executives of the group. Three of these directors serve as the ruling troika of the company. This is Unilever's Special Committee, consisting of the chairman of the Dutch company (Unilever NV), the chairman of the British company (Unilever PLC), and the heir apparent at one of the two parents. Unilever is therefore unique in being run by a plural executive. There is no one CEO (chief executive officer). They "sit together"—in Rotterdam or London (but more often the latter)—to set top policy. They pay particular attention to management appointments. No one can be named to the chairmanship of a Unilever company, no matter how small, without the approval of the Special Committee.

Unilever counts about twenty thousand of its people as managers, ranks two hundred of them as top managers, and "stars" about twenty-five of these two hundred as the elite cadre, capable of making it all the way to the Special Committee. These are managers heading up product groups, operating companies, or staff function departments. In the mid-1980s about one thousand managers, three hundred of them British, were serving outside their native countries.

The route to the top usually includes a foreign assignment. In 1986 the ruling troika consisted of Floris Maljers, chairman of the Dutch company; Michael Angus, chairman of the British company; and Johan Erbe, vice chairman of the Dutch company. All three have had overseas experience. Maljers worked for the company in Indonesia, Colombia, and Turkey before returning to Rotterdam. Erbe, who started as a trainee in 1951 and who holds an MBA degree from the University of Wisconsin, served in Britain, Turkey, and Germany before returning to Rotterdam. Angus was a mathematics major (Bristol University) who flew for the RAF and promoted Sunsilk shampoo in France before being posted to New York in 1979 to breathe new life into the ailing Lever Brothers subsidiary on Park Avenue.

When Angus arrived in the United States, the Unilever companies were spending $160 million on advertising. He pumped it up to more than $400 million, going on the offensive with Surf, Wisk, and a new dishwashing detergent bearing the original Lever brand name, Sunlight. Previously, Lever had been looking for product niches where P&G brands were not strong. "There is no way of outflanking them," Angus told the *Financial Times*. "The only solution is to meet them head on." In 1983 Lever Brothers was profitable for the first time in seven years— and Angus returned to London to take the third seat on the Special Committee.

Unilever has strong ties to the Third World thanks to the operation of its plantations and the agricultural experiments it has carried on at the behest of, or in cooperation with, national governments. It's cultivating sunflowers in Kenya at the request of the government. It's running an Integrated Rural Development Program in the impoverished farming district of Etah in North India. It developed a technique for cloning oil palms that has resulted in new fruit-bearing trees in Malaysia. If you work for Unilever, you're reminded all the time about the importance of merging the company's interests with those of the host countries. And even when strong nationalist governments have taken control of Unilever companies, they frequently ask Unilever to stay on as a partner or at least as a manager of the enterprise. Unilever has partnership arrangements of this kind throughout the Third World.

Sir Kenneth Durham, a physicist who stepped down in 1986 as chairman of the British parent company, once explained to a reporter why Unilever thinks the Third World countries are important: "If you double the discretionary income of a German, he's not going to spend it on soap. But an Indonesian might—and there are 120 million people out there." (Actually, when he said that in 1985, Indonesia's population was nudging 150 million.)

Access Postbus 760, 3000 DK
Rotterdam, the Netherlands
(31) 10-645-911

Unilever House
London EC4P 4BQ, England
(44) 1-822-5252

10 East 53rd St.
New York, N.Y. 10022
(212) 688-6000

Universal Matchbox Group

Sales $257 million
Profits $16.5 million
U.S. Sales $161 million
Rank Hong Kong's largest toy maker
World's 7th-largest toy maker
Founded 1964
Employees 6,000
Headquarters Hong Kong

The toy business is not for the fainthearted. It's a mercurial business closely tied to fads, and it has a short time line—from Christmas to Christmas. Hong Kong is also not for the fainthearted. It has a rapid drumbeat, a dubious sovereignty, and a population composed largely of refugees from a country about to reassume control over it. David C. W. Yeh, one of those refugees, appears to thrive in this environment. He left his native Shanghai in 1949 when he was nineteen years old, learned the toy business as a representative for an American firm, and founded a company that became in two decades one of the industry leaders.

Hong Kong has 2,195 toy factories and, according to one estimate, they supply one out of every two toys sold in the world. For the most part they are making toys for companies that put their own names on them or for stores like K mart and Toys-R-Us, which order them directly from the factories. It was into this maelstrom that Yeh stepped when he launched his own company, Universal Doll Dress, in 1964 with $10,000. His little factory made dresses for dolls.

Yeh had spent the previous eight years as Louis Marx's man in Hong Kong. At one time Marx was the leading toy manufacturer in the United States—its name has virtually disappeared now—and it pioneered in sourcing products from the low-wage plants in Hong Kong. Yeh joined that army of subcontractors when he set up his own business.

The reason subcontractors supply others instead of selling their own products under their own names is that they do not have access to marketing and distribution channels. David Yeh was determined to break out of this trap. In 1977 he formed Kidco Inc. in Chicago to distribute and market his products, and in the following year he acquired 80 percent of LJN Toys, a New York–based importer and distributor of toys (it was sold off to MCA in 1985). As he once explained in an interview with *Asia Week*, "Being a subcontractor is no way to control your own destiny. Even if you're good, there are another ten like you; and if your price isn't competitive, the buyer can go to the next one and the next one."

Yeh clearly knows what he is about. He symbolizes the triumph of the colonial servant over the colonial master, the victory of the Asian subcontractor over the Western contractor.

One of the major toy companies of the post–World War II period was the Lesney Group of Britain. It introduced, beginning in 1954, the Matchbox collection of miniature vehicles, die-cast models which can be seen in airport shops around the world, selling for a dollar apiece. These miniatures were manufactured in Britain. At its height Lesney kept thirteen factories busy. Yeh, who had opened Hong Kong's second die-casting plant in 1966, remembers approaching Lesney to see if he could get some of its business. Nothing doing. Lesney was not going to move any of its production to the Far East.

In 1978 Mattel began to murder Matchbox with its Hong Kong–sourced "Hot Wheels," and by 1982 Lesney had closed down eleven factories and was bankrupt, with debts of more than $60 million. To the surprise of the British receivers handling the bankruptcy, David Yeh surfaced from Hong Kong with a check for $27 million, beating Mattel and Fisher-Price to the punch.

Yeh did what the previous Lesney owners refused to do—move the Matchbox production to the Far East. He kept one factory in England at Rochford, where large plastic toys are made (it's still the largest toy manufacturing facility in Britain). But the Matchbox die-cast miniatures now come out of Macao, the Portuguese enclave on the south coast of China, sometimes called, for good reason, the "Las Vegas of the East." Universal Matchbox, the name Yeh adopted after his English shopping trip, is the largest private employer in Macao.

Universal Matchbox continues to serve as a subcontractor for large toy companies—it has the manufacturing capacity to do it—while Yeh tries to build up his own line of products, not an easy task in an industry where yesterday's blockbuster seller is today's discarded toy. In 1985, for example, one third of the company's sales came from its Voltron toys, which were inspired by a children's television series. In 1986 Voltron was obliterated. Another television-inspired line, Robotech, was also savaged in 1986. So no matter how much Yeh would like to be master of his own destiny, contract manufacturing remains an important activity for Universal Matchbox, bringing in more than half the company's profits.

Helping to take up the slack in 1986 was Rubik's Magic, a new puzzle from the Hungarian architecture professor Erno Rubik, whose earlier toy, Rubik's Cube, sold more than 100 million units, ringing cash registers to the tune of more than $1 billion. Universal Matchbox's Hong Kongian ability to turn on a dime helped it to land Rubik's new toy.

Rubik's Magic involves the intertwining of three rings with plastic squares that turn on hinges to make possible millions of configurations. When it was previewed in February 1986 at the Nuremberg Toy Fair, a number of companies were interested in taking it on but only Yeh was confident that it could be produced in time for the Christmas selling season. Production was assigned to a Chinese factory in southern China—and six months later, in August, Rubik's Magic was being shipped to the United States.

It doesn't seem likely that Rubik's Magic, which retailed for ten dollars, will match the sales of Rubik's Cube, but Universal Matchbox said it sold 8 million puzzles in the final quarter of 1986. It professed to be pleased with those results.

David Yeh's strategy is to be a worldwide player in the toy industry. Universal Matchbox, whose sales tripled between 1981 and 1985, is about one-fifth the size of Hasbro, the largest toy maker in the United States and roughly the same size as Minnesota-based Tonka. But Yeh believes he has in place the structure that will catapult his company into the topmost ranks of the industry. He starts from a low-cost manufacturing base in the Far East—plants in Hong Kong, Macao, Taiwan, and mainland China. And to that he has grafted a network of seventy sales agents which enable him to market toys in 120 countries.

Flexibility is Yeh's long suit. In the quest for new toys, he now has research and development units functioning in the United States (Carson, California, and Moonachie, New Jersey) and England (Enfield). However, if they can't come up with hot new products, Universal Matchbox can always use its apparatus to make and sell products for others. In 1987, for example, it signed on as a worldwide distributor of the soft and cuddly toys "Mad Balls" and "My Pet Monster" made by Amtoy, a subsidiary of American Greetings. It will move that line into Europe, Asia, Australia, Africa, and the Middle East. Universal Matchbox is one of only two companies that market toys in Eastern Europe.

In 1986 Universal Matchbox was getting one third of its product from factories in mainland China, but Yeh regards his native country as more than just a low-cost manufacturing site. Looking down the road, he sees it as a market. Peter K. Yau, vice president of corporate finance, notes that China has "more than two hundred million children."

Yeh, in other words, will play any tune. And, befitting a toy maker, he does have pizzazz. He did something in 1986 that no Hong Kong company has ever done—he had a public stock offering in the United States, followed by a listing of Universal Matchbox shares on the New York Stock Exchange. It was, and is, the only Hong Kong company listed on the Big Board. In the offering Yeh sold 816,000 shares, netting him $13.7 million, and he still owns 58.8 percent of the stock.

China is slated to reassume sovereignty over Hong Kong in 1997 and while Yeh is optimistic about Hong Kong continuing in its freewheeling ways and about doing business in China itself, he's also not taking any chances. Universal Matchbox was incorporated in Bermuda in 1985, prior to the U.S. public offering. The company's first annual meeting, in April 1987, was held at the Grand Hyatt Hotel in New York City.

Universal Matchbox's international stripe is reflected in the diversity of its top managers and directors. Of the top twenty-three executives and directors, two (including Yeh) have Hong Kong nationality, three are Chinese, six are British citizens, one is Australian, one is Canadian, and ten are American. Among the board members are Gerald Tsai, Jr., one-time Wall Street wunderkind who now heads up Primerica (formerly American Can) and Carl D. Gustavson, president of San Francisco–based Hibernia Bank, which was owned by another Chinese family, the Liems out of Indonesia and Hong Kong, who put the bank up for sale in 1987.

Yeh's ambition may be gauged by his recruitment in 1987 of Thomas J. Kalinske to serve as president and chief operating officer of Universal Matchbox. Kalinske was previously president of Mattel, where he helped to build the Barbie doll into a best-seller.

Access   Tung Ying Building
100 Nathan Rd.
Kowloon, Hong Kong
(852) 3-678191

Matchbox International
41 Madison Ave.
New York, N.Y. 10010
(212) 696-5400

Volkswagen	**Sales** $29.5 billion
	Profits $324 million
	U.S. Sales $4 billion
	Rank World's 4th-largest automaker
	Largest European automaker
	Largest automaker in Latin America
	Largest European exporter of cars to the United States
	Europe's 15th-largest industrial company
	West Germany's 2d-largest company
	Founded 1937
	Employees 281,000
	Headquarters Wolfsburg, West Germany

Translated into English, the corporate name of this company would be "People's Car Inc." It sounds as if it were a company from East Germany or some other Communist state. But that's not the case. Volkswagen was conceived by a temperamental Austrian engineer whose name now graces another automobile, it became a reality at the behest of Adolf Hitler, and it survived World War II to become a bulwark of the West German free enterprise economy and an anti-Establishment symbol in the United States. A good way to look at this company is as a social phenomenon: It's an indicator of what's going on.

The man responsible for the Volkswagen Beetle—and the company that made it—was Ferdinand Porsche. He was born in 1875 in Maffersdorf, a rural Bohemian town that was then part of the Austro-Hungarian Empire (after World War I it became part of the new nation of Czechoslovakia). Porsche showed an early aptitude for figuring out how things work. Electricity came to his town when he was fifteen—and he was fascinated. In two years he was able to wire his father's house and install lights, electric chimes, and an intercom. At nineteen he was off to Vienna to work as a sweeper for an electrical company and surreptitiously attend night classes at the technical university.

It was a time of great ferment in the virgin automobile industry. Carl Benz and Gottlieb Daimler were working in Germany. Louis Renault and Armand Peugeot were working in France. The Duryea brothers, Henry Ford, and Ransom Olds were working in America. And in Vienna Porsche was working. Before the turn of the century he produced an electric motor that would power an automobile from the wheel's rim, thus eliminating the need for belts or chain drives. It was the first of 380 industrial designs that would occupy Porsche's life.

Porsche's first motorized car was made by Ludwig Lohner, who built carriages for the Hapsburg court. Lohner sent his young designer to Paris to exhibit the electric car at the World's Fair of 1900 (the very one where Henry Adams wandered through the hall of dynamos to discover that "the education he had received bore little relation to the education he needed for the new century"). In *Small Wonder*, a 1965 history of Volkswagen, Walter Henry Nelson described the exposition and Porsche's reception: "No grander fair had ever been organized than the 1900 Universal Exposition. It was attended by 51 million visitors and was described by a contemporary as seeming 'as fairy-like as a stage setting . . . creating in the heart of Paris a veritable city of dreams and illusions.

"In the midst of all this, Porsche explained his car without a transmission system, powered by hubcap motors, and exhibited it in a nine-mile-per-hour run to Versailles and back. When the awards were announced, Porsche won a grand prize. It made him famous."

Back in Vienna Porsche became chief engineer in 1906 for Austro-Daimler, a company that had strong links to the Daimler company of Germany but was locally owned. (Porsche's predecessor as chief engineer was Gottlieb Daimler's son, Paul, who returned to the mother company.) He remained there until 1923, designing a series of cars, racing them, building military hardware for Austria-Hungary during World War I, and picking up an honorary degree from the University of Vienna, which allowed him to be called "Herr Doktor Porsche," a title he reveled in. One of his first cars was the Maja, named for a daughter of Emil Jellinek, a racy character who served as Austro-Hungarian consul on the French Riviera and whose other daughter, Mercedes, saw her name become the standard bearer of the cars turned out by Daimler in Germany.

Largely self-taught, Porsche was a taskmaster and not the easiest person to work with. Beverly Rae Kimes, who wrote the admirable history of Daimler-Benz, *The Star and the Laurel*, characterized him as follows: "To Porsche, engineering was life itself. He could watch a worker turn out hundreds of examples of some small part and then suddenly pick up one of the components, measure it with a micrometer and find it below standard, by a few thousandths of an inch. The hundreds of other components would have to be measured and would invariably be found perfect; somehow Dr. Porsche had spotted the single infinitesimally errant piece."

Porsche could fly into towering rages. He had a habit, when confronting error, of throwing his hat on the floor and stomping on it. His parting of the ways with Austro-Daimler came in 1923 after he flung a table lighter at one of the directors during a stormy board meeting. Porsche by that time had been running the company but was frustrated because the bankers who controlled Austro-Daimler were unwilling to back his idea to make a small, lightweight car for the masses.

Porsche took himself off to Stuttgart where he was hired as chief engineer at Daimler, once again succeeding Paul Daimler. He became a hero there for designing cars that won races (Mercedes won twenty-one out of twenty-seven starts between 1925 and 1927). He also designed the S series, a powerful beast of a car with long, sleek lines that became, as Beverly Kimes put it, "the apotheosis of a sports car, a metaphor for the Roaring Twenties." In Stuttgart Porsche picked up another honorary degree (from the University of Stuttgart), which was useful to someone who insisted on being addressed as "Herr Doktor" since the Germans hardly recognized the Viennese degree. In 1925 Daimler merged with Benz—and Dr. Porsche once again pressed his idea for a small, inexpensive car. Once again he was rebuffed. Daimler-Benz people were happy making luxurious cars for the rich. In 1928, at another stormy board meeting, Porsche lost his temper and quit.

Now fifty-three, he returned to Vienna to work for another automaker, Steyr, which went belly up in 1930. Porsche then decided to return to Stuttgart, the center of the German automobile industry, where he set himself up as an independent consultant, continuing to work on his idea for a "people's car."

In Stuttgart, working on his own, Porsche developed the torsion-bar suspension system that became a standard feature of the Volkswagen and many other cars. The Soviet Union offered him a villa in the Crimea and a blank check to develop his small car there, but he rejected the offer. Then, under commission from a motorcycle manufacturer, Zundapp, Porsche sketched out the details of his people's car from the chassis up. It included a rear-mounted, air-cooled engine, unit body, independent four-wheel suspension, and other design features that went ultimately into the legendary Beetle. But it wasn't until Adolf Hitler took an interest in Porsche's work that the Volkswagen got its real chance.

Hitler was named chancellor of Germany in 1933, and at the 1934 Berlin Auto Show he appeared in a Nazi party uniform to deliver his call for a people's car: "So long as the automobile remains only a means of transportation for especially privileged circles, it is with bitter feelings that we see millions of honest, hardworking and capable fellow men whose opportunities in life are already limited, cut off from the use of a vehicle which would be a special source of yet-unknown happiness to them, particularly on Sundays and holidays." In May 1934 Hitler summoned Porsche to a meeting in Berlin. They met in the Kaiserhof Hotel to talk about making a people's car. Nelson, the biographer, re-created the scene:

> The two men saw eye-to-eye for several reasons. Both came from small towns in the old Austro-Hungarian Empire and, in a very real way, spoke each other's language; both were always to feel more comfortable among backwoods Austrians than among the polished members of Germany's industrial society. Both mistrusted the wealthy industrialists: Porsche because they had always frustrated his plans, Hitler for less clear-cut reasons rooted in his arsenal of hatreds. They were linked on that day in the Kaiserhof Hotel by a common boyhood, by a sense of jousting against the giants of capitalism, and by their love of cars.

Porsche came away with a contract to build three prototypes (in his garage, as it turned out). The German automobile makers, through their trade association RDA (Reichsversband der Deutschen Automobilindustrie), were instructed to develop and build the car. But having no love for the concept, they dragged their feet, causing Hitler to scream at the 1937 Auto Show, "Either automobile makers produce the cheap car or they go out of business. I will not tolerate the plea 'It can't be done.' "

In the end Hitler decided that the state would produce the car. The Gesellschaft zur Vorbereitung des Volkswagens (Company for the Development of the People's Cars) was formed, and Porsche went to the United States to recruit engineers and production managers. In Detroit he met with Henry Ford (one of Adolf Hitler's heroes, since they shared a love of cars and a hatred of Jews). Nelson recalled what happened: "They conversed through interpreters and Porsche poured out his plans for the Volkswagen. Did they worry the elder Ford? Not in the least. 'If anyone can build a car better or cheaper than I can, that serves me right.' he said." The Porsche team bought a Ford V-8 which they drove to visit various manufacturers and buy machinery for the German plant.

One of the men involved in creating the several prototypes during 1937–38 was Francis Xavier Reimspiess, an engine designer. He merits commemoration for having devised the VW logo, letters one above the other enclosed in a circle. Porsche gave Reimspiess a 100-mark bonus (forty dollars) for his contribution.

To ensure the success of the new car, Hitler designated a sponsoring agency: the KdF—the Kraft durch Freude (Strength-through-Joy)—branch of the German Labor Front. KdF, which functioned as the promoter of recreation, travel, and sports activities for German workers, organized a layaway plan. Workers were encouraged to set aside five marks ($2.50) a week toward the purchase of a VW. At that rate, it would have taken a "saver" a little over three years to pay in the full price of 990 marks ($396). No interest was to be paid on these savings. The plan began before a single car had been produced. Under this scheme, characterized by William Shirer as a "pay-before-you-get-it" plan, 336,668 Germans put away a total of $67 million. (The money, lodged in the Bank of German Labor, was confiscated by the Russians after they marched into Berlin.)

For reasons that remain obscure, the German government chose to locate the Volkswagen plant (along with what amounted to a new city to house the workers and their families) near Fallersleben in Lower Saxony, the site of Schloss Wolfsburg, a fourteenth-century castle belonging to Count Werner von der Schulenberg, who owned 7,500 acres there that had been in his family since 1135. The count was asked to accept compensation for two thirds of his land "for an important national project." He pulled every string he could to counter the threat to his ancient domain but succumbed in the end.

Albert Speer, Hitler's thirty-three-year-old minister for armament and war production, appointed a young Austrian architect, Peter Koller, to plan the people's car factory and Autostadt to house twenty-four thousand workers and their families. On Ascension Thursday, May 26, 1938, between the annexation of Austria and the dismemberment of Czechoslovakia, Hitler laid the cornerstone of the Volkswagen factory amid trumpet blasts, sixty-foot-high swatstika banners, and legions of marchers. Speaking to an assembled crowd of seventy thousand people, the Fuhrer declared that the car to be produced there would carry the name of the KdF—that is, it would be called the KdF-Wagen or "Strength-through-Joy" car. For some unfathomable reason, it was a brand name that never caught on.

Only 210 of the KdF-Wagens were ever produced (none of them at the new factory) and all were consigned to Nazi officials. As Nelson notes, "Not one was sold to a KdF-saver or any other 'little German.' " From 1940 to 1945 the plant assembled for the military fifty thousand Kubelwagens or "bucket cars," a squarish, all-purpose vehicle adapted by Porsche from his original design; fifteen thousand Schwimmwagens, an amphibious version of the VW; parts for the Ju-88 bomber; V-1 flying bombs; and 1.5 million stoves to keep the German troops from freezing on the Russian front.

Koller, the architect, may have needed one of these stoves. He joined the Wehrmacht and fought in Russia before he was captured in 1944, spending the rest of the war in a prison camp. After being released he returned to Lower Saxony to resume the building of the city. The Auto-stadt officially became Wolfsburg, after the castle, in June 1945. Today Wolfsburg, with a population of 125,000, ranks as the sixth-largest city in Lower Saxony and is, as *Fortune* writer Robert Ball said, "a company town to end all company towns."

The war had left the plant in shambles and in custody of the British, who, Nelson recounts, "soon found themselves with a mile-long white elephant on their hands and with thousands of people who expected help from them. . . . They decided to start the plant operating again, at least temporarily." By the end of 1945, six thousand workers had produced 1,785 Volkswagens. Half the workers were cleaning up the rubble, the other half virtually handtooling the cars, many of which were being bartered for scarce raw materials. The British tried to deal the plant off to various automakers—with no luck. A British commission headed by car manufacturer Sir William Rootes visited Wolfsburg and decided that the VW "is quite unattractive to the average motorcar buyer. It is too ugly and too noisy." At a meeting in 1948 to consider the offer, Henry Ford II asked Ernest Breech for his judgment. "Mr. Ford," Breech said, "I don't think what we are being offered here is worth a damn."

Having found no takers, the British caretakers turned the VW opera-tion over to the German government on October 8, 1949. By that time, though, they had already found a German, Heinz Nordhoff, to run Volks-wagen. Nordhoff, who took command of the plant in 1948, was an inspired choice. He put Volkswagen on the world map.

Nordhoff was no stranger to automobiles. Born in 1899 in the Lower Saxony city of Hildsheim, seventy miles southwest of the Wolfsburg cas-tle, Nordhoff fought and was wounded in World War I, graduated from engineering school in 1927, and began working at Adam Opel (freshly acquired by General Motors) in 1929. He spent time in Detroit learning how GM produced and marketed cars, and in 1936 he became a member of the Opel board. After the war, when GM showed no enthusiasm about welcoming him back into the fold, the British gave him a free hand to see what he could do with the VW plant. Nordhoff had the right mixture of toughness and vision for those times. He has been described by numerous writers as "autocratic," but he forged a strong partnership with the work force. He reported regularly and fully to them on the progress of the enterprise, and he made it clear that they would share in the rewards (through profit-sharing and stock ownership plans).

And what about Ferdinand Porsche? He had spent the war years performing a myriad of tasks for his Nazi overlords. He looked after the KdF-Wagen plant, which used thousands of slave laborers; he went to

Paris to oversee the Peugeot works; his office in Stuttgart designed tanks for the Third Reich. From all that's known about him, he was an apolitical person—he just wanted to be an engineer. But he was not to escape the reprisals of the postwar period. What did him in, according to Nelson, were the French automakers, who had heard about a plan by the French government to hire Porsche to design a people's car for France.

The French government had already nationalized the Renault works, after charging Louis Renault with being a Nazi collaborator, and the remaining French auto companies were fearful of a government-backed effort to build a Porsche-designed car. And so, says Nelson, "Jean Pierre Peugeot charged Porsche with war crimes." The allegations never stuck, and a French court eventually cleared Porsche of all the charges, but that was after he had been held for nearly two years, the last three months in an old, unheated dungeon in Dijon. His health broken, he was released on August 1, 1947, a month before his seventy-second birthday.

Porsche visited the Wolfsburg plant in 1950 when three hundred VWs were rolling off the production lines every day. "Yes, Herr Nordhoff," said Porsche, "that's how I always imagined it." Porsche died on January 30, 1951, at age seventy-five. (His son, Ferry Porsche, a talented designer in his own right, later established his own company in Stuttgart to make the Porsche sport cars. Until 1984, they were distributed in the United States by Volkswagen.)

Heinz Nordhoff ran VW for two decades—and his accomplishments were the stuff of which dreams are made. By 1968 twelve million Beetles had been produced, making it the biggest-selling automobile model in the world. In 1950, to cries of "ridiculous," VW introduced a commercial vehicle that was called a Microbus in Europe and a Volkswagen station wagon in the United States; whatever it was called, it revolutionized the delivery business, and by 1968 more than two million had been sold. Volkswagen became the largest company in Germany and the fourth-largest auto producer in the world. The work force grew from 7,000 to 104,000. New plants were opened in Kassel, Hanover, Brunswick, and Emden. A VW plant in Brazil became the largest automobile factory in Latin America. Auto-Union, maker of the Audi, was bought from Daimler-Benz. Volkswagen was "Exhibit A" in the postwar German economic miracle.

It was during Nordhoff's reign that shares in Volkswagen were sold to the employees and the general public. In the first offering by the government in 1960, more than 1.5 million West Germans applied for shares. The offering was rigged in favor of the small investor, being limited to low- and middle-income families. Two thirds of these initial stockholders received only two shares. Of the sixty-five thousand people then on the VW payroll, only one thousand failed to buy shares—and most of them were ineligible because of their high incomes. In a later offering in 1966, public shareholders emerged with 60 percent of the stock; the state of Lower Saxony and the federal government each retained 20 percent.

At the same time that Volkswagen became a publicly owned company, an old issue was resolved. Remember Hitler's KdF "savers"? They went to court after the war asking for their money. In 1961 Volkswagen honored the debt, agreeing to compensate all the people who had completed their payments of 990 reichmarks. Each was given this option: 100 marks ($30) in cash or 600 marks ($180) credit toward the purchase of a new Volkswagen. More than eighty-seven thousand claims were eventually approved. Half elected to buy the car they had begun saving for nearly thirty years ago.

Nordhoff died on April 12, 1968, at Wolfsburg's city hospital. Forty-five thousand workers filed past his coffin in a factory hall.

For roughly a decade after the end of the World War II, the United States saw few Beetles on its roads. However, in 1968, at the end of the Nordhoff era, Americans owned more than two million bugs—and their ranks were growing at a rate governed only by the number that VW's plants could supply (more than five hundred thousand a year). With its low—under $2,000—price and stingy consumption of gasoline, the Beetle became to many Americans an emblem of rebellion against Detroit and the big-car culture. VW took better advantage of the rebellion than did other foreign car makers (several of whom preceded the German company into the American market) by building up a strong dealer organization that stressed service and consumer satisfaction. The Beetle's unchanging appearance also appealed to Americans fed up with the annual hoopla over cosmetic design changes.

In 1959, only fourteen years after the end of the war, VW was also venturesome enough to hire an advertising agency which worked for the Israel Tourist Office, El Al Israel Airlines, and Levy's Real Jewish Rye Bread. This was Doyle Dane Bernbach, then a small New York shop that was destined to spearhead a creative revolution on Madison Avenue. Doyle Dane's ads for VW—self-deprecating (as befitting an "ugly" car), humorous, and factual—hollowed out the Beetle's niche. They became as well known as the car itself. "Think small," said one. Another, appearing during a drought, said, "Save water." Another showed a big blank space with the line: "We don't have anything new to show you in our new models." Another: "After we paint the car we paint the paint." (In 1987, twenty-eight years later, Doyle Dane was still the Volkswagen agency.)

Volkswagen peaked in the United States in 1970 when 570,000 vehicles were sold (not counting 13,650 Porsches and 7,700 Audis). The great majority of those vehicles were Beetles. VW was pulling down an astounding 7.2 percent of the new-car market in the United States. In Brazil the Beetle's influence was even more profound. Dr. F. W. Schultz-Wenck, a German who later became a Brazilian citizen, opened the VW plant at Sao Bernardo do Campo outside Sao Paulo in 1953. For the first four years the cars were assembled from imported parts, but then the plant began making Beetles from scratch. Known in Brazil as the Fusca, the Beetle dominated passenger car sales. It was in a Fusca that many Brazilians first learned to drive. On February 15, 1972, the 15,007,034th Beetle came off the assembly line in Wolfsburg—and by doing so it eclipsed the production record held up to that time by Henry Ford's Model T.

The Beetle was such a successful car and Heinz Nordhoff was such a successful manager that both proved difficult to replace, complicating Volkswagen's life through the 1970s and early 1980s.

Since Nordhoff, Volkswagen has had four chief executives:

- Six-foot, five-inch Kurt Lotz, who came from a farm background, had no academic degree, and became Nordhoff's successor in 1968 only a year after he joined VW from Brown, Boveri, the Swiss electrical engineering giant. He was fired in 1971.
- Rudolf Leiding, a dour, hard-bitten engineer who replaced Lotz and proceeded to revamp the entire VW line (out went the rear-mounted, air-cooled engines in favor of front-mounted, water-cooled engines and front-wheel drive). It was under Leiding that VW learned how to make other cars: the Audi 80 (the Fox), the Passat (called the Dasher in the United States), the Golf, and the Scirroco. Leiding clashed repeatedly with the unions at Volkswagen, not a good idea, since they hold half the board seats under West Germany's codetermination system. One bone of contention was a plan to make cars in the United States. Leiding was forced to resign in 1975.
- Next at bat was Toni Schmucker, a high school graduate who worked his way up the white-collar ranks at Ford of Germany (where his father had been a foundry worker), and who then turned around a big steel maker (Rheinstahl), which prompted the VW board to recruit him to effect a turnaround at Wolfsburg. Schmucker gained approval for a VW plant in Westmoreland, Pennsylvania, where Rabbits began limping out in 1978. A year later he diversified the automaker by paying $440 million for the

Triumph-Adler office machine business formerly owned by Litton Industries. The U.S. plant and the Triumph-Adler acquisition both turned out to be disasters, Schmucker had a heart attack, Volkswagen lost $124 million in 1982, and it needed a new chief.

- Carl Hahn, an economist who was hired by Heinz Nordhoff in 1954, returned to VW to succeed Schmucker. He had left in 1972 because he couldn't get along with Leiding, and he spent the next ten years reviving Continental Gummi-Werke, Germany's largest tire producer. Hahn headed up VW's operation in the United States during the glory years, 1959 to 1964. He came back to Wolfsburg with an Italian-born American wife. Their four children carry American passports.

Hahn was still in the driver's seat in 1987 and was doing well until the company was rocked by that most modern of calamaties, a currency exchange fraud. Like other multinationals Volkswagen collects revenues in a variety of currencies and needs to maintain a careful watch on those positions because their exchange values fluctuate. It appeared that outsiders tapped into the VW currency operations, hoping to make a killing for themselves by betting that the dollar would rebound against the German mark—and they made their bets with Volkswagen's hefty cash flow. Hahn and other top VW executives were floored to discover that this illegal venture cost the company $260 million in currency exchange losses (almost equal to 1986 net profit). The disclosure put a damper on what was to be a grand celebration of the fifty-millionth car produced by Volkswagen. Nevertheless, the event was not ignored. On March 21 Hahn drove a white Golf off the assembly line and made a short speech in which he said, "We can all feel pride and joy about the fifty-millionth car. But on this day we can also not ignore the events that have struck our firm." On July 2, the day after his sixty-first birthday, Hahn faced the stockholders at VW's annual meeting and—aside from a few hisses—received a ringing vote of confidence. Volkswagen was back on top of the heap in Europe, and neither currency scams nor the sudden acceleration of Audi models in the United States was able to dislodge the halo from Hahn's head.

Of the fifty million cars that had been produced, nearly twenty-one million were Beetles. Wolfsburg stopped making the bug in 1978, by which time nineteen million had been produced. Brazil stopped making the Beetle in 1986. That left only Mexico, where production was slated to end in 1987. More than five million Beetles were sold in the United States.

The demise of the Beetle fit the company's plan to erase its reputation as a builder of small, inexpensive cars. Hahn characterized VW's marketing strategy as one of selling "classless vehicles." It's a strategy that was working in Europe but not in the United States. In 1985 Volkswagen skipped from third place to first place in the fifteen-nation European market, capturing 12.9 percent of passenger car sales, just ahead of Ford and Fiat. But the Golf, the best-selling car in Europe, did not win many fans in the United States, where motorists may have had a bad taste left in their mouths from the Rabbit, a subcompact which they emphatically rejected (they didn't like the quality or the price). Volkswagen of America lost the import leadership to the Japanese in 1975, and it has never been able to stage a comeback, either with imports or models assembled in Pennsylvania. In 1986 VW's share of the U.S. market was 2.5 percent.

However, Volkswagen is tenacious. It has emerged as the most multinational of the European car manufacturers, with a global strategy. Daimler-Benz, the other big German auto company, makes *all* its cars in Germany. Fiat has completely pulled out of the U.S. auto market. Neither Renault nor Peugeot has achieved much penetration beyond Europe. Volkswagen on the other hand intends to make cars for everyone in the world, and it's prepared to do so under a variety of guises: local manufacture, exports, joint ventures. It will travel any route—and it doesn't mind picking up hitchhikers as partners.

In Japan Nissan Motor makes VW's Santana under license. In Germany, Volkswagen will team up with Toyota to make pickup trucks. In the People's Republic of China VW will partner with a Chinese company to produce the Santana in Shanghai. VW's Brazilian subsidiary has been exporting cars to Africa and the Middle East (particularly Iraq) for many years. In 1986 it began shipping a low-priced compact, the Fox, to the United States. And while the Golf hatchback has failed to capture the imagination of American motorists the way it has European drivers', VW's more luxurious Jetta sedan, priced ten thousand dollars and up, did so well that it outsold the Golf in the United States—and so VW now assembles Jettas in Pennsylvania.

Two landmark deals announced in 1986 speak to VW's global commitment. In Spain it acquired control of the state-owned auto company SEAT (Sociedad Española de Automóviles de Turismo), a move that will vault its annual output over three million for the first time. And in Latin America Volkswagen and Ford Motor agreed to merge their automotive operations in Argentina and Brazil into a new company called Autolatina, which will have fifteen plants with an annual capacity of 900,000 vehicles a year, 1,500 dealers, 75,000 employees, and sales of $4 billion. It will take its place instantly as the world's eleventh-largest automobile producer. Volkswagen will own 51 percent of the new venture.

By 1987 Volkswagen already had more than 60 percent of its sales outside West Germany. The evolution of Volkswagen into a world power was reflected by changes in its ownership base. In 1986 foreign stockholders owned 20 percent of VW, up sharply from 7 percent in 1977. VW was once proud of its legion of small investors. But the number of individual stockholders in West Germany declined from 521,000 in 1977 to 317,000 in 1985. The big new holders are banks, insurance companies, and investment funds. The German federal government was planning in 1987 to sell its 20 percent stake. IG Metall, West Germany's largest and most powerful labor union, denounced the selloff, its leader, Hans Mayr, calling it "the squandering of the state's assets." Mayr holds a seat on Volkswagen's board.

Access   P.O. Box 3180
Wolfsburg 1, West Germany
(49) 5361-90

Volkswagen of America
P.O. Box 3951
888 W. Big Beaver
Troy, Mich. 48007-3951
(313) 362-6000

Volvo	Sales $12.3 billion
	Profits $520 million

Sales $12.3 billion
Profits $520 million
U.S. Sales $3 billion
Rank Sweden's largest company
World's 15th-largest automaker
World's 7th-largest heavy truck maker
World's largest maker of dump trucks
Sweden's 2d-largest food supplier
Founded 1926
Employees 73,140
Headquarters Gothenburg, Sweden

In an advertisement it placed in 1985, Volvo stated:

Only 8 million people live in Sweden, less than .2 percent of the world's population. And yet Volvo produces 8 percent of the world's heavy duty trucks, 7 percent of the world's heavy bus chassis, 1 percent of the world's cars, 26 percent of the world's inboard pleasure craft engines, 18 percent of the world's off-highway dump trucks, and a very high percentage of the world's good ideas.

It was vintage Gyllenhammar. Pehr Gyllenhammar (pronounced Pare YULE-en-hommer) took command of Volvo in 1971 when he was thirty-six years old. Under his spectacular direction Volvo has more than quintupled in size. Gyllenhammar bears no resemblance to the stereotypical view of the dour and colorless Swedes. A man of forceful ideas, he's debonair, athletic (he races sailboats), not afraid of speaking his mind, at home in capitals around the world, and ready always for new adventures.

One of his first good ideas after taking charge at Volvo was to propose to the workers that they elect two deputy members of the company's board of directors. They did—one representing salaried employees, the other unionized plant workers. Another was to build a new kind of car plant at Kalmar in southern Sweden. At Kalmar the conventional assembly line was modified. Carriers propelled by underground lines trundle parts and sections of cars to light, airy work stations where small teams of workers organize their own tasks. They switch job functions frequently to combat boredom. It's one of the quietest auto plants in the world. At both old and new plants, Gyllenhammar has tried to involve workers in decision making. Kalmar became Volvo's most efficient plant, and Gyllenhammar drew this moral: "We have to change the organization so that the job itself provides more for the individual. We will never build another production line as long as I am in command at Volvo."

Volvo plans to follow that prescription in a new plant scheduled to open in late 1988 at Uddevalla on Sweden's west coast. This factory will try to do away with the assembly line completely, with workers organized into teams each of which will assemble the entire car. "I want the people in a team to be able to go home at night and really say, 'I built that car,' " said Gyllenhammar. "That is my dream."

Volvo produces an English-language annual report that is a model of clarity. The salient figures appear on the cover. For 1985 they showed that the company took in 86 billion krona on which it earned 7.6 billion krona before taxes, paid a total of 11.3 billion krona in salaries, wages, and social benefits to 67,857 employees (that worked out to about $24,000 per worker), and contributed 180 million krona (about $25 million) to an employee bonus fund. The bonus fund is a profit-sharing plan set up in 1982, with the maximum company contribution set then at 180 million krona (it was increased to 260 million in 1986). In mid-1986 each Volvo employee had an average of $2,500 in the fund.

Pehr Gyllenhammar grew up in very comfortable circumstances, and there's no secret about how he came to head Volvo: He married the boss's daughter, Christina Engellau, whom he had met when he was going through law school at the University of Lund. After graduation he practiced law for a while before joining a maritime insurance company that was then taken over by Skandia, Sweden's largest insurance company. Pehr's father happened to be running Skandia, and Pehr soon succeeded him before getting the call from his father-in-law, Gunnar Engellau, to come to Volvo and become its third chief executive officer. The first, before Engellau, was the founder, Assar Gabrielsson.

The company Gyllenhammar joined was organized in 1915 as a subsidiary of SKF, the giant Swedish company that is the world's largest producer of ball and roller bearings. But Volvo dates its real start from 1926 when it began making automobiles in Gothenburg, Sweden's largest city after Stockholm and the place where Gyllenhammar grew up. The first Volvo came off the production line on April 14, 1927, the first truck in 1928. The company, which gained its independence from SKF in 1935, likes to point out that from the very start it designed its cars "to withstand the rigors of Sweden's rough roads and cold temperatures." (Today Volvo cars have an eight-year anti-corrosion guarantee for body parts and chassis.)

Volvo moved into the international arena after World War II, and by 1986 it was deriving 84 percent of its sales from outside Sweden. The Volvo has long had a cult following in the United States, particularly, *Fortune* once noted, among "intellectuals, engineers, and anti-Establishment types as a symbol of revolt against Detroit's dinosaurs." These were the types who in 1986 didn't mind shelling out $20,000 for a Volvo. Jim Hightower, the populist commissioner of agriculture in Texas, was fond of referring sarcastically to "Volvo-driving liberals." In 1985 Volvo sold 102,300 cars to Americans. That was the first time it went over the 100,000 mark in the United States—and it represented more than a quarter of the 392,000 cars Volvo sold during the year. The next best market was Britain, where 59,500 Volvos were sold.

Durability is certainly one of the Volvo's attributes. Results of a European survey released in 1986 showed that Volvo had a higher survival rate than any other car, with 57 percent of them still on the road after fifteen years; low car on this totem pole was the Alfa Romeo—only 3 percent of them survived to their fifteenth year.

Volvo has a more powerful position in heavy-duty trucks (vehicles weighing sixteen tons or more), a market where companies all over the world have trouble making any money. In 1981 Volvo acquired the ailing truck division of Cleveland-based White Motor. And in 1986 it gave General Motors a face-saving out by forming with GM a joint venture (in which Volvo has a 65 percent interest) to make and sell heavy-duty trucks in North America. The Volvo-GM-White operation will vie with Freightliner (a subsidiary of Daimler-Benz) for third place in the North American market behind Navistar (the old International Harvester) and Mack Truck (42 percent–owned by Renault of France). On a worldwide basis Volvo ranks third behind Daimler-Benz and Renault.

A restless executive who believes in stirring up the juices inside and outside the company ("An organization without conflict is dying," he once said), Gyllenhammar has certainly not been content to stick exclusively to the automotive business. Through a series of acquisitions and mergers, he has transformed Volvo Car into the Volvo Group, with interests in oil trading, oil and gas exploration (Volvo owns 49 percent of Denver-based Hamilton Oil), drugs, insurance, and food, among other businesses. Indeed, Volvo, through its subsidiaries, ranks as Sweden's second-largest food supplier. It makes the french fries for McDonald's, and in Sweden it holds 60 percent of the processed herring market, 75 percent of the pickle business and, through its Ramlosa brand, the lion's share of the mineral water market. Cars and trucks now account for less than half of Volvo's total sales.

Volvo is also a giant in construction equipment as a result of joining in 1984 with Clark Equipment of the United States to form a fifty-fifty venture which ranks third in the world behind Caterpillar Tractor and Komatsu of Japan.

Gyllenhammar is almost as famous for the deals that got away from him. He once almost pulled off a merger with Sweden's other car company, Scandia-Saab. He once had Renault buy 9 percent of the shares of Volvo Car—but bought back this holding in 1985. The deal that would have topped all the other deals was his 1980 plan to turn Volvo into a binational corporation. He proposed to sell 40 percent of Volvo to the Norwegian government in return for getting the Norwegian oil and gas rights in the North Sea. It was a daring—and typically Gyllenhammar—move. The Volvo stockholders turned it down.

The fact is, Gyllenhammar enjoys being an *enfant terrible.* During the early 1980s he tilted with the Wallenbergs, the most powerful family in Swedish industry. He acquired chunks of stock in Wallenberg-controlled companies, and the Wallenbergs began accumulating Volvo stock. They reached a standstill agreement in 1984, and then each sold off the shares in the other's enterprises. The deal gave Volvo profits of about $200 million, which Gyllenhammar then levered into a 47 percent stake in an interesting Swedish smorgasbord called Investment AB Cardo.

Companies grouped under the Cardo banner rank among the world leaders in industrial overhead doors (Crawford), nickel-cadmium batteries for industrial use (McGraw-Edison's business in the United States was acquired in 1986), and brake systems and wheels for railway cars. Its Scanpump unit is the largest supplier of industrial pumps in the Nordic countries.

But Cardo also has a finance arm which manages a portfolio of stocks worth about a half a billion dollars. At the end of 1986 it had positions in fifteen Swedish companies, including a 4.5 percent stake in Volvo itself and interests of 7.5 percent, 11 percent, 6 percent, and 2.3 percent in Custos, Oresund, Aritmos, and Esselte, respectively. During 1986 Cardo bought 10,000 shares of International Paper of the United States and 100,000 shares of Britain's Associated Newspapers; meanwhile, it discarded 141,000 shares of Britain's Allied-Lyons and 550 shares of Switzerland's Ciba-Geigy. What fun for Gyllenhammar!

Another Gyllenhammar crusade is to get more people, inside and outside of Sweden, to hold Volvo stock. In 1985 he introduced the idea of selling Volvo shares through the Swedish Post Office. Outside of Sweden Volvo shares are now traded on the stock exchanges in Frankfurt, Hamburg, Dusseldorf, Oslo, Paris, Brussels, and Antwerp. In the United States they are traded on the over-the-counter market. More than 15 percent of Volvo's shares are now held outside Sweden. A big holder is Boston-based Fidelity Investments, the largest mutual fund manager in the United States. In 1986 Fidelity was, through its various funds, the owner of 5 percent of Volvo's stock—and that holding contributed significantly to the sterling performances of Fidelity's Magellan and Overseas funds.

This international overtone suits the cosmopolite, Pehr Gyllenhammar. He gets around a lot, carrying his tennis racket, simply from his directorships. In 1986 he was filling seats on the boards of eight other companies; four of them Swedish (Atlas Copco, Skandinavska Enskilda

Volvo Automotive Innovations

1944 Laminated windshield	1971 Inertia reel belts rear
1944 Safety cage	1972 Child-proof door locks
1954 Windshield defroster	1973 Headlight wiper/washers
1956 Windshield washers	1973 Side impact members in doors
1956 Safety steering column with shear coupling	1973 Crumple zone in steering wheel
1957 Front 2-point saftey belt anchorages	1974 Shock-absorbing bumpers
1958 Rear safety belt anchorages	1974 Multistage impact-absorbing steering column
1959 Front 3-point safety belts fitted	1974 Fuel-tank isolated and protected from rear impact
1960 Padded instrument panel	1974 Bulb integrity sensors
1965 Brake servo and rear pressure limiting value	1974 Audio-visual belt reminder
1966 Rear window defroster	1975 Stepped-bore brake master cylinder
1966 Triangle split braking system	1975 Day running lights
1966 Anti-burst door locks	1975 Anti-corrosion brake pipes of special alloy
1966 Roll-over bar in roof	1979 Wide-angle rear view mirror, eliminating "dead zone"
1966 Impact-absorbing body sections front and rear	1982 Anti-submarining guards in seats
1966 Multi-adjustable saftey seat	1982 Fuel tank forward of rear axle
1966 Impact-absorbing steering column	1984 Non-locking brakes (ABS)
1967 Seat anchorage of safety design	1985 Electronic traction control (ETC)
1967 Rear safety belts fitted	1986 Safety belt pre-tensioner
1968 Head restraints front	
1968 Heated rear screen	
1969 Inertia reel belts front	
1971 "Fasten safety belts" warning light	

Europe's Business Roundtable

If there's an elite business force in Europe, it's the Roundtable of European Industrialists, organized by Pehr Gyllenhammar, chairman of Volvo.

The group's mission is to speed up the economic unification of Europe so that its big companies can compete effectively against their Japanese and American counterparts. Gyllenhammar patterned the roundtable after the Business Roundtable of the United States. Companies must be represented by their chairman, president, or managing director.

As of mid-1987, the European Roundtable had twenty-nine members.

The Roundtable

Chairman
Pehr Gyllenhammar, *Volvo, Sweden.*

Vice chairmen
Umberto Agnelli, *Fiat, Italy.*
Wisse Dekker, *Philips, Holland.*

Carlo De Benedetti, *Olivetti, Italy.*
Jean-Louis Beffa, *Saint-Gobain, France.*
Werner Breitschwerdt, *Daimler-Benz, West Germany.*
John Clark, *Plessey, Britain.*
Etienne Davignon, *Sibeka, Belgium.*
Raul Gardini, *Ferruzzi, Italy.*
Alain Gomez, *Thomson, France.*
Patrick Hayes, *Waterford Glass, Ireland.*
Kari Kairamo, *Nokia, Finland.*
Karlheinz Kaske, *Siemens, West Germany.*
Olivier Lecerf, *Lafarge Coppee, France.*
Luis Magana, *Furnas Electricas de Cataluna, Spain.*
Helmut Maucher, *Nestlé, Switzerland.*
Hans Merkle, *Robert Bosch, West Germany.*
Jerome Monod, *Lyonnaise des Eaux, France.*
Curt Nicolin, *Asea, Sweden.*
Antony Pilkington, *Pilkington Bros., Britain.*
Stefan Schmidheiny, *Anova, Switzerland.*
Patrick Sheehy, *B.A.T Industries, Britain.*
Luis Solana, *Telefonica, Spain.*
Dieter Spethmann, *Thyssen, West Germany.*
Poul Svanholm, *De Forenede Bryggerier, Denmark.*
Josef Taus, *Constantia Industrieverwaltung, Austria.*
Pierre de Tillesse, *Petrofina, Belgium.*
Jacopo Vittorelli, *Pirelli, Italy.*
Torvild Aakvaag, *Norsk Hydro, Norway.*

Banken, SILA, and Saga Petroleum), two of them British (Pearson and Reuters), and two of them American (United Technologies and Hamilton Oil). In addition, he was serving as a member of the international advisory committee of the Chase Manhattan Bank. One other: When Henry Kissinger left Washington, D.C., and set up his own consulting firm, he recruited Pehr Gyllenhammar for his board.

Gyllenhammar can handle it.

Access S-405 08 Gothenburg, Sweden
(46) 31-590000

Volvo of America
P.O. Box 915
Rockleigh, N.J. 07647-0913
(201) 768-7300

Yamaha

Sales $5.8 billion

Profits $80 million

U.S. Sales $1.5 billion

Rank World's largest maker of musical instruments

World's largest piano manufacturer

World's largest organ maker

World's largest maker of acoustic guitars

World's largest maker of electronic keyboards

World's largest maker of electronic synthesizers

World's largest maker of fiberglass boats

World's largest operator of music schools

World's largest maker of snowmobiles

World's 2d-largest maker of motorcycles

Founded 1887

Employees 25,000 (average age: 36)

Headquarters Hamamatsu and Iwata, Japan

Which products come to mind when you hear the name, Yamaha? Motorcycles, of course. But do you think of pianos, organs, guitars, basses, electronic keyboards, synthesizers, recorders, CD players, tuners, speakers, accordions, harmonicas, and all kinds of band instruments, both wind and percussion, including trumpets, trombones, flutes, drums, timpani, vibraphones, glockenspiels, marimbas, tubas, and xylophones? When the All-American High School Marching Band sponsored by McDonald's marches in the annual Macy's Thanksgiving Day parade, all the brass and percussion instruments are supplied by Yamaha.

So much for music. The Yamaha name is also stamped on sail and power boats, scooters, golf carts, snowmobiles, skis, tennis and badminton rackets, golf clubs, archery bows, furniture, bathroom sinks, electronic metal components, and personal computers.

How did one company come to make all those products? Well, this is a classic case of one thing leading to another. To begin with, there are two companies: Nippon Gakki (which means Japan Musical Instruments) and Yamaha Motor. They're closely related—and the closeness will become more obvious in the future, since Nippon Gakki was getting ready in 1987 to change its name to the Yamaha Company.

Nippon Gakki is the original company. It was founded in 1887 when Torakusu Yamaha built Japan's first reed organ. Torakusu was a remarkable study in tenacity. Born in 1851, the third son of a samurai, he showed from a very early age a mechanical aptitude that led him first into watch repair and then the operation and repair of medical equipment. In 1885 he was asked to repair a thirty-nine-key Mason organ that had been brought from the United States and installed in an elementary school in Hamamatsu, a south coastal town 150 miles west of Tokyo.

Yamaha was able to repair the organ, which fascinated him so much that he decided to build one from scratch, with no special tools or materials. He made it up as he went along. Using a stone-cutting chisel, he shaped the reeds from brass plates. He made valves out of alloys. The keys were made from cow bones. Not having any celluloid, he substituted highly polished wood.

Yamaha's organ worked but he wanted to get it appraised by experts in Tokyo. That was easier said than done because there was no train service. He and a friend made the journey on foot, carrying the organ on a pole. In Tokyo the experts proclaimed it a "nice try" but said it didn't tune accurately. Torakusu stayed on in Tokyo for a while, taking courses at the Music Research Institute, and he then returned to Hamamatsu to build a second organ. This one, transported again to Tokyo on a pole, won the approval of the experts—and the Yamaha company was in business. One hundred years later, the largest musical instrument maker in the world, the company was still based in Hamamatsu—and Yamaha Motor was headquartered in the neighboring town of Iwata.

Yamaha's diversification began in 1921 with airplane propellers. It built propellers for the Zero fighter planes used by Japan in World War II. After the war it was back to music (guitar building started in 1946). But in 1954 Yamaha began to make motorcycles. And the following year it spun off Yamaha Motor as a separate company. Both companies are listed today on the Tokyo Stock Exchange, although Nippon Gakki (the Yamaha Company) continues to hold 39 percent of the shares of Yamaha Motor.

Nippon Gakki, in addition to the musical instruments, makes the sporting goods and electronic equipment. Yamaha Motor makes everything that's power-driven. Gen'ichi Kawakami, who succeeded his father as head of the company in 1950, was the architect of the company's ear-splitting post–World War II expansion. In 1986 he still served as chairman of both companies. His son, Hiroshi Kawakami, became president of Nippon Gakki in 1983.

The Yamaha people believe in the synergy of their technologies. They claim that this motley collection of products is not haphazard but stems directly from their expertise in five areas: woodcraft, electronics, metallurgy, chemistry, and machine engineering. Thus, they got into metallurgy from making the metals used in piano frames. They got into furniture from the woodcrafting of pianos. They made their own computer chips for their electronic musical instruments—and from there it was an easy jump to computers. (Yamaha ranks as Japan's fourteenth-largest chip maker.) Their composite, FRP (fiberglass-reinforced plastic), is stronger than steel but lighter than aluminum and finds its way into a wide variety of Yamaha products.

Nippon Gakki now outproduces every piano maker in the world (it made 177,546 pianos in 1986), but it's still not the instrument of choice for most of the leading concert pianists. When Vladimir Horowitz performed in Tokyo in 1986, he wasn't playing on a Yamaha. It grates a bit on Hiroshi Kawakami. In 1985 he related how a New York newspaper reporter who once interviewed him said that while Yamaha is the leader, volume-wise, "I don't think it's number one in the world in quality." Kawakami said he thought "this was a joke," but the reporter then continued by asserting, "The piano is a Western musical instrument. Fine pianos can't be built in Japan, which has only a short history in piano making." Kawakami gave his reaction: "I couldn't let his statement pass unchallenged. I let it be known that even in Japan, Western music is popular and I personally was raised on such music. In fact, I believe I appreciate the beauty of Western music as much as people in the West. I have confidence that I can build the world's top pianos. I never found that interview in print."

Yamaha has conquered the rock world with its electronic instruments (when Michael Jackson and his brothers went on their 1984 "Victory Tour," they were engulfed in Yamaha equipment), and it's making some progress in the classical world. Sviatoslav Richter, the Russian-born piano virtuoso, uses a Yamaha; the Yamaha concert grand was selected as the official piano of the 1985 Chopin International Competition in Warsaw; and in 1986 Yamaha was designated as the official piano of the Tchaikovsky International Competition in Moscow.

Yamaha does bring to the manufacture of musical instruments the same zeal Japanese automakers have in their business. When the Philadelphia Orchestra toured Japan some years ago, a Yamaha representative asked to borrow a rare seventy-year-old French trumpet belonging to one of the orchestra members. The Yamaha people, who weren't making trumpets yet, took the Besson apart to analyze how it was built. They then began making their own trumpets and in 1982 they asked the Philadelphia Orchestra to test them. Frank Kaderabek, the orchestra's principal trumpet player, pronounced them "first-rate."

A similar zeal to win backfired on Nippon Gakki's sister company, Yamaha Motor. In 1980 Yamaha decided the time was ripe to overtake Honda in the Japanese motorcycle market. So it revved up its production, emphasizing a fleet of new lightweight 50-cc bikes. As Yamaha's market share moved up to 37 percent in 1981, just a point shy of Honda's, Hisao Koike, president of Yamaha Motor, boasted to stockholders that "in one year, we will be the domestic leader. And in two years we will be number one in the world." As related by James Abegglen and George Stalk, Jr., in their book *Kaisha: The Japanese Corporation,* that was like waving a red flag before Honda, whose president, Kiyoshi Kawashima, responded with a vow of his own, *"Yamaha wo tsubusu!"*—"We will slaughter Yamaha." In the next eighteen months Honda introduced eighty-one new models to Yamaha's thirty-four and cut prices so drastically it was possible to buy a 50-cc motorcycle for less than the cost of a ten-speed bike. Yamaha's sales plunged, the company went into the red to the tune of $44 million, and Koike resigned in disgrace.

Koike was replaced as president by Hideto Eguchi, who moved over from the Yamaha Music Foundation, a nonprofit organization whose activities undergird Yamaha's success in musical instruments. The foundation has as one of its mandates the promotion and development of the famous Yamaha music schools started in 1954 by Gen'ichi Kawakami, who realized the crucial importance of teaching young people how to play instruments and appreciate music.

Yamaha takes children when they are four years old and teaches them in groups, usually on the electronic organ. The Yamaha method of instruction has spread throughout the world. Since they were started, more than four million students have graduated. In 1986, 680,000 Japanese children were enrolled in 9,500 Yamaha schools. Outside of Japan 170,000 children were enrolled in 1,600 schools in 33 countries, including 250 Yamaha schools teaching 15,000 children in the United States. The U.S. schools are operated by Yamaha dealers.

This emphasis on musical education has turned Japan into a nation of piano players—and buyers. One out of every six Japanese homes has a piano. And the Japanese market for musical instruments, at $3.3 billion a year, is now larger than the entire American market. In Japan Yamaha owns 60 percent of the piano market. In the United States its market share has been estimated at 25 percent. The company is believed to hold 30 percent of the world market for wind instruments, 40 percent for organs.

Yamaha manufactures pianos, Electone keyboards, and speaker components at Thomaston, Georgia; it assembles musical instruments at a plant in Grand Rapids, Michigan. Yamaha also owns the Everett piano

line, which dates from 1883, four years before Yamaha was born. In Britain Yamaha owns 40 percent of that country's leading piano maker, Kemble, which also builds uprights for Jorgenson of Denmark and Dietmann of Germany.

Hiroshi Kawakami, forty-four years old in 1986, brings a new style of leadership to Yamaha. He appears to be much more hot-tempered than his predecessors—and also more like a business school graduate. In fact, he is an engineering graduate from Nihon University and worked six years at Sony before coming to Nippon Gakki to take over from his father in 1983. In a candid interview in 1986, he revealed some of his philosophy: "My grandfather propounded three major principles: think creatively, ruffle no one's feathers, and make a contribution to society. My father, Gen'ichi Kawakami, is very individualistic and it could be said that he built Yamaha into a world-class company single-handedly. . . . I don't dare try to rule the company in a top-down fashion the way he did. . . .

"Both those men had strong ideologies, but I believe my mission lies in the internationalization of the company. It is my strongest desire to make Yamaha products known around the world for their high quality and to make the company known as a global concern."

Yamaha Motor announced at the end of 1986 that it had acquired a site near Atlanta for its first manufacturing facility outside Japan. Yamaha expects the plant to turn out forty thousand golf carts a year, ten thousand of which will be exported to Japan.

Access Nippon Gakki
10-1, Nakazawa-cho
Hamamatsu 430, Japan
(81) 534-60-2141

Yamaha International
P.O. Box 6600
Buena Park, Cal. 90622
(714) 522-9011

Yamaha Motor
2500 Shingai
Iwata 438, Japan
(81) 538-32-1111

Yamaha Motor
P.O. Box 6555
Katella Ave.
Cypress, Cal. 90630
(714) 761-7300

Author's Note

During the course of researching this book it just wasn't possible to personally visit each and every company. However, I have at one point or another made my way to thirty-one of the companies and I have certainly been in touch with all of them (as witnessed by the conversion of a hall-length closet in my home to a filing cabinet). I once even worked for one of them (Reuters). It was during that stint in London in 1953 that the seed for this book was planted. London, much more so than New York (even today), is an international arena, a place where information and ideas about the world's business come together. It was there that I first encountered companies whose horizons are global, and it was there, as a freelance correspondent for an American candy magazine (the publisher proudly listed Finsbury Park as the site of its London bureau), that I saw how Hershey's almond bar was directly related to the cocoa crop in Ghana and British colonialism in West Africa.

Gathering information about these companies, especially information that emanates from outside the companies themselves, properly requires an army of researchers. I had an army of two. One was Harry Strharsky, who assembled dossiers on all the companies and then served as the chief fact-checker. Harry has a feel for the human stories and social issues that lurk beyond the figures. He was for me the perfect scout and critic. The other indispensable contributor was my sidekick Carol Townsend (we are, in her words, "rarely out of each other's line of vision"). She chased the missing annual report, cleared up discrepancies, sorted out historical ambiguities, and conceptualized tables. She also, more than anyone, had to bear the brunt of my frustrating moments.

A book of this magnitude required help from many directions. I asked five writer friends to turn out first drafts of twenty-nine company profiles. The idea was to give me a leg up into the companies. The drafts helped to provide that access. Some of their words even survived the countless rewriting stages. The five (in order of the number of profiles they tackled) were: C. W. Miranker (eleven), Charles Einstein (eight), Frederick Borden (five), Edward Engberg (three), and Nita Whaley (two). I'm grateful for their insights.

Whenever I was stumped by a Japanese expression or needed additional information on a Japanese company, I turned to Haruko Smith, who unfailingly supplied the answers. Her contributions were major.

I had good counsel from journalists in various parts of the world: Alan Friedman in Milan, Lee Hagberg Persson in London, Michael Berger, Susumu Ohara, and Masahiko Ishizuka in Tokyo, Gordon Martin in San Francisco, and Lee Townsend and Ted Cross in New York. Thanks to the efforts of Kinji Kawamura and Seiichi Soeda of the Foreign Press Center in Tokyo, I was able to spend fruitful time at a dozen Japanese companies. I was given a similar entree to Hong Kong companies by Ernie Beyl of San Francisco.

Americans, wrapped in their monolingual isolation, need all the help they can get from knowledgeable people on the ground. My friends Lowell and Phyllis Chang opened my eyes to the real Hong Kong. My understanding of Japan was enhanced considerably by conversations with Masanobu Ishikawa and Ken Ishizu. Egon Zehnder, busy replacing chief executive officers all over the globe, interrupted his schedule to spend several hours with me in Zurich. Nora McKeon was my guide to Rome. I never got to Norway but was fortunate to meet Arild Lillebo, who enlightened me about Norsk Data and other leading Norwegian companies.

Dire warnings were posted in advance about how difficult it would be to obtain information from the companies. That proved not to be the case. With some few exceptions, the responses were good. The American concept of public relations has swept the world. For their special courtesies and extra help, I particularly remember James C. E. Fuller, Akzo Chemie America; Tadao Kashio, Casio Computer; Eijiro Sakurai and Yasuharu Tamiya, Dentsu Advertising; Mario Nola and Paola Roselli, ENI; Odoardo Scaletti, Fiat; Katsuhiko Yazaki, Hi-Sense; Yancy Y. Fukagawa, Matsushita; Leo Levine and Fred Chapman of Mercedes-Benz of North America; François-Xavier Perroud, Nestlé; Tadashi Sakuda, Suntory; Yasuo Sasaki and Dr. Shoichiro Toyoda, Toyota; Richard Power, Trust House Forte; and Michael Haines, Unilever.

My two erstwhile collaborators, Robert Levering and Michael Katz, read substantial chunks of this work as it was in progress, and their suggestions were useful and important. James R. Glenn always had a sympathetic ear for my problems (technical and editorial), as did my daughter, Abigail. Herman Hong supplied me with the no-fault word processing program. Blaine Townsend helped put together the bibliography. Laird Townsend hunted for picture possibilities. Lee Townsend, Jr., deciphered a (for me) complicated financial deal. And Eben Moskowitz explained to me (once again) how containers are used to ship goods around the world.

I relied on a variety of research banks. Anyone who tries to understand multinational corporations must be indebted to S. Prakash Sethi for his prolific writings in this field. (Prakash is always on a cutting edge.) The Data Center in Oakland was, as usual, a mine of golden information. Ron Lanstein, chief executive of **BARRA**, an investment counseling firm in Berkeley, came through with the stock market performances of the publicly traded companies on my roster (a task that the largest securities firm in the world failed to accomplish). In the day-to-day writing of this book, my three favorite backstops were the *Japan Company Handbook, The Statesman's Year-Book,* and the pink-colored *Financial Times,* surely one of the best newspapers in the world because it does far more than just print stock tables.

We all need exemplars, and I want to mention two of mine—British journalist Anthony Sampson and Canadian journalist Peter C. Newman—for the work they have done in placing corporations against a larger scaffold than the balance sheet, which is the way I also have tried to look at them.

Appendix

World's Most Valuable Company: NTT

Nippon Telegraph & Telephone (Nippon Denshin Denwa), the Bell System of Japan, became the most valuable company in the world in 1987 when the Japanese government sold 12.5 percent of its holdings at the astronomical price of 1.197 million yen per share. At exchange rates prevailing at the start of 1987 that was equivalent to $7,480. Such was the demand for the issue that a lottery was held. The winners (nearly all of them individuals) were then eligible to plunk down $7,480 for a single share of NTT.

Once the stock started to trade on the Tokyo Stock Exchange on February 9, the stampede for the shares continued. What with the price escalation and the continuing rise in the value of the yen, NTT was soon trading at $21,500 a share, which meant that the company was worth $320 billion, or more than three times the market value of the old leader, IBM.

The Japanese government expects to sell off a total of two thirds of NTT stock to the public by 1989.

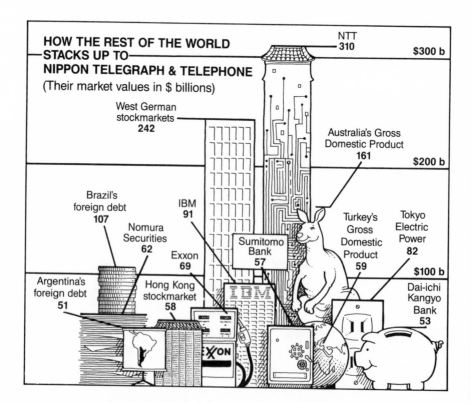

HOW THE REST OF THE WORLD STACKS UP TO NIPPON TELEGRAPH & TELEPHONE
(Their market values in $ billions)

- NTT 310 — $300 b
- West German stockmarkets 242
- Australia's Gross Domestic Product 161 — $200 b
- Brazil's foreign debt 107
- IBM 91
- Nomura Securities 62
- Exxon 69
- Turkey's Gross Domestic Product 59
- Tokyo Electric Power 82
- $100 b
- Argentina's foreign debt 51
- Hong Kong stockmarket 58
- Sumitomo Bank 57
- Dai-ichi Kangyo Bank 53

Geographic Breakdown of Companies (By country)

Australia
Broken Hill
News Corporation

Belgium
Petrofina
Société Générale de Belgique

Brazil
Bradesco

Canada
Canadian Pacific
Olympia & York
Thomson

France
Bic
BSN
Club Méditerranée
Compagnie Générale d'Électricité
Générale Occidentale
Michelin
Moët-Hennessy
Pernod Ricard
Perrier
Peugeot
Renault
Rhône-Poulenc
Saint-Gobain
Schlumberger

Hong Kong
Hongkong and Shanghai Bank
Jardine, Matheson
Universal Matchbox

India
Tata

Ireland
Jefferson Smurfit

Italy
Benetton
Beretta
De Benedetti
ENI
Fiat
IRI
Montedison

Japan
Bridgestone
Casio
Dai-Ichi Kangyo Bank
Fujitsu
Hattori Seiko
Hitachi
Honda
Kikkoman
Kyocera
Matsushita
Mitsubishi
NEC
Nippon Steel
Nissan
Nomura
Sony
Toshiba
Toyota
Yamaha

Geographic Breakdown of Companies *(Continued)*

Mexico
Pemex

the Netherlands
Akzo
Heineken
Philips
Shell
Unilever

Norway
Norsk Data

Singapore
Singapore Airlines

South Africa
Anglo America

South Korea
Daewoo
Hyundai

Sweden
Electrolux
Nobel Industries
Swedish Match
Volvo

Switzerland
Ciba-Geigy
Crédit Suisse
F. Hoffmann–La Roche
Nestlē

Taiwan
Evergreen

United Kingdom (Britain)
B.A.T
Beecham
Booker
British Petroleum
Britoil
Cadbury Schweppes
Grand Metropolitan
Guinness
Hanson Trust
Hard Rock Cafe
Imperial Chemical
Lonrho
Marks & Spencer
Pearson
Reuters
Rover
RTZ
Saatchi & Saatchi
Shell
Trusthouse Forte
Unilever

West Germany
BASF
Bayer
Bertelsmann
Bosch
Daimler-Benz
Hoechst
Krupp
Siemens
Thyssen
Volkswagen

Atlas of World's Leading Companies (Largest company in ninety-six countries)

Country	Largest Company	Sales
Argentina	Yacimento Petrofileros (Oil, state-owned)	$4.2 billion
Australia	Broken Hill Proprietary (Steel, mining, oil)	6 billion
Austria	Voest-Alpine (Iron and steel, state-owned)	7 billion
Bahrain	Bahrain National Oil Company (Oil, state-owned)	1.6 billion
Bangladesh	Bangladesh Jute Mills (State-owned)	480 million
Belgium	Petrofina (Oil)	10 billion
Benin	Sonocap (Oil, state-owned)	90 million
Bermuda	Bank of N. T. Butterfield & Son (Banking)	182 million
Bolivia	Comibol (Mining)	80 million
Botswana	Botswana Meat Commission (Cattle farming, state-owned)	109 million
Brazil	Petrobas (Oil, state-owned)	14.7 billion
Britain	Shell (Anglo-Dutch, oil)	65 billion
	British Petroleum (Oil)	40 billion
Burkina Faso	Sofitex (Textiles, agribusiness, 65 percent state–owned)	54 million
Burundi	Burundi Coffee (Coffee grower, state-owned)	100 million
Cameroon	S.A. des Brasseries (Brewery, 75 percent foreign–owned)	260 million
Canada	Canadian Pacific (Railway, steel, oil and gas, paper, real estate)	11 billion
Central African Republic	Centrafricaine des Petroles (Oil, 75 percent state–owned)	58 million

Atlas of World's Leading Companies *(Continued)*

Country	Largest Company	Sales
Chad	Cotonchad (Cotton, 75 percent state–owned)	$111 million
Chile	CODELCO-Chile (Mining, state-owned)	1.6 billion
Colombia	Empresa Colombiana de Petrol (Oil, state-owned)	1.5 billion
Congo	Hydro Congo (Oil)	180 million
Cyprus	Joannou & Paroskvaides (Engineering and construction)	627 million
Denmark	FDB/Brugsen (Retailer and food processor, a cooperative)	2.6 billion
Domincan Republic	Compania Domincan de Aviacion (State-owned airline)	65 million
Ecuador	C.E.P.E. (Oil, state-owned)	1.5 billion
Egypt	Suez Canal Company (Canal operator)	950 million
El Salvador	Banco de Comercio (State-owned bank)	19.3 million
Ethiopia	National Textiles (Textiles, state-owned)	162 million
Finland	Neste (Oil and chemicals, state-owned)	5 billion
France	Compagnie Générale d'Électricité (Telecommunications)	21.6 billion
Ghana	United African Company & Lever Brothers (Unilever)	109 million
Greece	Motor Oil (Hellas) Corinth Refineries (Oil)	693 million
Guatemala	Instituto Nacional de Electricite (Utility)	86 million
Honduras	Commercial e Inversiones Glaxia (Food, personal-care products)	62 million
Hong Kong	Jardine, Matheson (Trading company)	1.3 billion
Iceland	Samband Is. Samvinnufelaga (Food processor, retailer, cooperative)	377 million
India	Indian Oil (Oil, state-owned)	8 billion
Indonesia	Pertamina (Oil, state-owned)	11.8 billion
Iran	National Iranian Oil (Oil, state-owned)	15 billion

Atlas of World's Leading Companies *(Continued)*

Country	Largest Company	Sales
Iraq	Iraq National Oil Company (Oil, state-owned)	$10 billion
Ireland	Jefferson Smurfit (Paper)	1.5 billion
Israel	Koor Industries (Metals, electrical equipment)	2.1 billion
Italy	Instituto per la Ricostruzione Industriale (Holding company, state-owned)	37.6 billion
Japan	Toyota (Automobiles)	42 billion
Jordan	Jordan Petroleum Refinery (Oil, state-owned)	683 million
Kenya	East Africa Breweries	279 million
Korea	Samsung (Conglomerate)	16 billion
Kuwait	Kuwait Petroleum (Oil, state-owned)	14 billion
Liberia	Bong Mining	126 million
Libya	Libyan National Oil (Oil, state-owned)	8 billion
Luxembourg	ARBED (Steel, 25 percent–owned by Belgium's Société Générale)	1.3 billion
Malaysia	Petronas (Oil, state-owned)	4.4 billion
Mali	Sidi Boubacar Bally (Export-import house)	22 million
Mauritius	B.A.T Industries (Tobacco)	18 million
Mexico	PEMEX (Oil, state-owned)	10 billion
Morocco	Marocaine de l'Industrie du Raffinage (Oil, state-owned)	930 million
Mozambique	E.E. Medimoc (Drugs, state-owned)	18 million
Nepal	Royal Nepal Airlines (State-owned)	32 million
Netherlands	Shell (Anglo-Dutch, oil)	65 billion
	Philips (Electronics)	27 billion
Netherland Antilles	Schlumberger (Oil field services)	4.5 billion
New Zealand	Fletcher Challenge (Agribusiness, building materials)	2.1 billion
Niger	Cominak (Mining)	157 million

Atlas of World's Leading Companies *(Continued)*

Country	Largest Company	Sales
Nigeria	Nigerian National Petroleum (Oil, state-owned)	$11 billion
Norway	Norsk Hydro (Oil, state-owned)	7.3 billion
Oman	Petroleum Development Oman (Oil, state-owned)	4.1 billion
Pakistan	Pakistan State Oil (Oil, state-owned)	1 billion
Panama	Syntex (Drugs)	1 billion
Peru	Electralima (Utility, state-owned)	203 million
Philippines	Philippine National Oil (Oil, state-owned)	1 billion
Portugal	Petroleos de Portugal (Oil, state-owned)	1.5 billion
Qatar	Mannai (Trading, construction)	200 million
Rwanda	Rwandex (Trading company)	91 million
Saudi Arabia	Aramco (Oil, state-owned)	42 billion
Senegal	Ste. Africaine de Raffinage (Oil)	345 million
Singapore	Singapore Airlines (Airline, state-owned)	1.6 billion
South Africa	Anglo-American (Mining)	13 billion (assets)
Spain	EMPETROL (Oil company, state-owned)	3 billion
Sri Lanka	Ceylon Petroleum (State-owned)	540 million
Sweden	Volvo (Cars)	12.3 billion
Switzerland	Nestlē (Food)	25 billion
Syria	General Consumption Organization (Food)	509 million
Taiwan	Chinese Petroleum (State-owned)	5.2 billion
Tanzania	National Textile Corp. (State-owned)	620 million
Thailand	Esso Standard (Exxon)	1 billion
Togo	Sonacom (Trading company, state-owned)	53 million
Tunisia	Tunisia Electric & Gas (Utility)	252 million
Turkey	Koc (Conglomerate)	3.6 billion
Uganda	Uganda Electricity Board (Utility)	39 million

Atlas of World's Leading Companies *(Continued)*

Country	Largest Company	Sales
United States	General Motors	$102 billion
Uruguay	ANCAP (Oil, state-owned)	356 million
Venezuela	Petroleos de Venezuela (Oil, state-owned)	9.2 billion
West Germany	Daimler-Benz (Automobiles)	30 billion
Yugoslavia	Energoinvest (Conglomerate)	3.8 billion
Zaire	GECAMINES (Mining, state-owned)	872 million
Zambia	Zambia Industrial & Mining (State-owned)	2.1 billion
Zimbabwe	Zimbabwe Mineral Marketing Corporation (Minerals)	379 million

Sources: Company reports, *BusinessWeek, Forbes, Fortune, South.*

One of the World's Biggest Markets: Telecommunications Equipment

(Lines, switches, and other gear needed to make a telephone system work)

Annual Spending: $108 Billion

United States	$24.3 billion
Soviet Union	9.8 billion
Japan	7.1 billion
West Germany	6.1 billion
France	4.9 billion
Italy	4.5 billion
Britain	3.4 billion
Canada	1.9 billion
China	1.7 billion
Spain	1.6 billion

Ten Biggest Suppliers of Telecommunications Equipment
(1986 Sales)

American Telephone & Telegraph (United States)	$19.9 billion
Alcatel (Franco-American)	8.7 billion
International Business Machines (United States)	5.3 billion
Northern Telecom (Canada)	4.7 billion
NEC (Japan)	4.1 billion
Siemens (West Germany)	3.6 billion
Ericsson (Sweden)	3.2 billion
GTE (United States)	2.9 billion
Fujitsu (Japan)	900 million
Hitachi (Japan)	800 million

Who Has Telephones?

- Of a world total of 600 million telephones, more than 590 million are in the hands of less than 50 percent of the world's population.
- Two thirds of the world's population has no telephone service.
- Tokyo has more telephones than the entire continent of Africa.

Number of Telephones in Forty-four Countries		*Number of Telephones for Every One Hundred Persons*	
United States	182 million	Sweden	89
Japan	66.6 million	Switzerland	83
West Germany	37.9 million	Denmark	78
France	34.3 million	United States	77
Soviet Union	29.5 million	New Zealand	67
Britain	29 million	Canada	63
Italy	25.6 million	Norway	63
Canada	16.5 million	West Germany	62
Spain	14.2 million	Finland	61
Brazil	11.4 million	France	60
Australia	8.7 million	Australia	56
South Korea	7.5 million	Japan	55
Sweden	7.4 million	Britain	52
Mexico	6.7 million	Austria	49
China	6.2 million	Belgium	44
Netherlands	5.6 million	Hong Kong	42
Switzerland	5.4 million	Israel	41
Taiwan	5.2 million	Netherlands	39
Belgium	4.3 million	Netherlands	39
Poland	4.2 million	Spain	36
Denmark	4.0 million	Greece	35
South Africa	3.8 million	Taiwan	27
Austria	3.7 million	Czechoslovakia	23
India	3.7 million	East Germany	22
East Germany	3.6 million	South Korea	19
Czechoslovakia	3.6 million	Portugal	18
Greece	3.5 million	South Africa	14
Turkey	3.4 million	Hungary	14
Argentina	3.2 million	Yugoslavia	13
Yugoslavia	3.0 million	Saudia Arabia	12
Finland	3.0 million	Soviet Union	11
Norway	2.6 million	Argentina	11
Columbia	2.5 million	Poland	10

Who Has Telephones? *(Continued)*

New Zealand	2.2 million	Columbia	9
Iran	2.1 million	Mexico	9
Hong Kong	2.0 million	Brazil	8
Portugal	1.8 million	Venezuela	8
Israel	1.7 million	Turkey	7
Venezuela	1.4 million	Iran	5
Saudia Arabia	1.3 million	Nigeria	0.7
Nigeria	708,000	China	0.6
Hungary	705,000	India	0.5
Indonesia	670,000	Indonesia	0.4
Ethiopia	122,000	Ethiopia	0.28

(The way to read the above table: The United States has the highest telephone population in the world, 182 million. Sweden has the highest telephone density (relative to its population), 89 phones for every 100 persons, while Ethiopa has the lowest: 1 phone for every 400 persons.)

Source: Telecommunications Industry Research (Barnham, Britian); the Maitland Commission; "The World's Telephones" (a statistical compilation by AT&T); and *The Statesman's Year-Book.*

The 100 Largest U.S. Multinationals (American companies ranked by their foreign sales)

1986 rank	Company	Foreign revenue (millions)	Total revenue (millions)	Foreign revenue as % of total
1	Exxon	$50,337	$ 69,888	72.0%
2	Mobil	27,388	46,025	59.5
3	IBM	25,888	51,250	50.5
4	Ford Motor	19,926	62,716	31.8
5	General Motors	19,837	102,814	19.3
6	Texaco	15,494	31,613	49.0
7	Citicorp	10,940	23,496	46.6
8	E. I. du Pont de Nemours	9,955	26,907	37.0
9	Dow Chemical	5,948	11,113	53.5
10	Chevron	5,605	24,352	23.0
11	BankAmerica	4,659	12,483	37.3
12	Philip Morris	4,573	20,681	22.1
13	Procter & Gamble	4,490	15,439	29.1
14	R.J.R. Nabisco	4,488	15,978	28.1
15	Chase Manhattan	4,356	9,460	46.0
16	ITT	4,180	17,437	24.0
17	Eastman Kodak	4,152	11,550	35.9
18	Coca-Cola	4,019	8,669	46.4
19	Xerox	3,996	13,046	30.6
20	Amoco	3,931	18,478	21.3
21	General Electric	3,821	36,725	10.4
22	United Technologies	3,810	15,669	24.3
23	J. P. Morgan	3,654	6,672	54.8
24	Goodyear	3,450	9,103	37.9
25	Hewlett-Packard	3,290	7,102	46.3
26	American Express	3,234	14,652	22.1
27	Minn. Mining & Mfg.	3,219	8,602	37.4
28	Unisys	3,188	7,432	42.9

The 100 Largest U.S. Multinationals *(Continued)*

1986 rank	Company	Foreign revenue (millions)	Total revenue (millions)	Foreign revenue as % of total
29	Tenneco	$ 3,128	$ 14,529	21.5%
30	Digital Equipment	3,118	7,590	41.1
31	Johnson & Johnson	3,031	7,003	43.3
32	American Intl. Group	2,998	8,876	33.8
33	Sears, Roebuck	2,914	44,281	6.6
34	CPC International	2,869	4,549	63.1
35	Colgate-Palmolive	2,699	4,985	54.1
36	F. W. Woolworth	2,696	6,501	41.5
37	Manufacturers Hanover	2,610	7,794	33.5
38	NCR	2,486	4,882	50.9
39	Allied-Signal	2,470	11,794	20.9
40	Kraft	2,464	8,742	28.2
41	Bankers Trust New York	2,447	4,923	49.7
42	American Brands	2,384	6,221	38.3
43	K mart	2,365	25,350	9.3
44	Motorola	2,250	7,508	30.0
45	Monsanto	2,241	6,879	32.6
46	Atlantic Richfield	2,226	14,487	15.4
47	GTE	2,135	15,112	14.1
48	Chrysler	2,097	22,586	9.3
49	Pan Am Corp.	2,050	3,039	67.5
50	Merck	2,024	4,129	49.0
51	Pfizer	1,993	4,476	44.5
52	Sara Lee	1,913	7,938	24.1
53	Caterpillar	1,866	7,321	25.5
54	Cigna	1,859	17,064	10.9
55	Phillips Petroleum	1,833	9,786	18.7
56	Union Carbide	1,788	6,343	28.2
57	Gillette	1,717	2,818	60.9
58	Chemical New York	1,611	5,488	29.4
59	H. J. Heinz	1,601	4,366	36.7
60	Sun Co.	1,588	9,376	16.9
61	TRW	1,529	6,036	25.3
62	Occidental Petroleum	1,516	16,029	9.5

The 100 Largest U.S. Multinationals *(Continued)*

1986 rank	Company	Foreign revenue (millions)	Total revenue (millions)	Foreign revenue as % of total
63	Unocal	$ 1,506	$ 7,744	19.4%
64	Texas Instruments	1,486	4,974	29.9
65	W. R. Grace	1,472	3,726	39.5
66	Allegis	1,410	9,196	15.3
67	Warner-Lambert	1,356	3,103	43.7
68	Bristol-Myers	1,337	4,836	27.6
69	SmithKline Beckman	1,306	3,745	34.9
70	Eli Lilly	1,292	3,720	34.7
71	Dresser Industries	1,287	3,661	35.2
72	American Cyanamid	1,280	3,816	33.5
73	Deere	1,247	3,516	35.5
74	American Home Products	1,245	4,927	25.3
75	Security Pacific	1,237	5,977	20.7
76	PepsiCo	1,226	9,291	13.2
77	Kimberly-Clark	1,209	4,303	28.1
78	PPG Industries	1,195	4,687	25.5
79	Hercules	1,182	3,245	36.4
80	Rockwell International	1,181	12,296	9.6
81	Abbott Laboratories	1,175	3,808	30.9
82	American Standard	1,173	3,075	38.1
83	Honeywell	1,165	5,378	21.7
84	McDonald's	1,164	4,240	27.5
85	Aluminum Co. of America	1,146	5,315	21.6
86	First Chicago	1,131	4,001	28.3
87	Scott Paper	1,107	3,890	28.5
88	Baxter Travenol	1,091	5,543	19.7
89	Trans World Airlines	1,082	3,145	34.4
90	Continental Corp.	1,078	6,002	18.0
91	Quaker Oats	1,075	3,671	29.3
92	Kellogg	1,072	3,341	32.1
93	Bank of Boston	1,065	3,540	30.1
94	Firestone	1,048	3,501	29.9
95	Halliburton	1,045	3,527	29.6

The 100 Largest U.S. Multinationals *(Continued)*

1986 rank	Company	Foreign revenue (millions)	Total revenue (millions)	Foreign revenue as % of total
96	Avon Products	$ 1,028	$ 2,883	35.7%
97	Merrill Lynch	1,017	9,475	10.7
98	Control Data	1,013	3,347	30.3
99	Henley Group	988	3,172	31.1
100	Schering-Plough	983	2,399	41.0

Source: Excerpted by permission of *Forbes* magazine, July 27, 1987. Copyright © 1987 by Forbes, Inc. All rights reserved.

World Stock Market Performances in 1986

		Percentage Gains	
		Local Currency	*U.S. Dollars*
1.	Mexico	250	72
2.	Spain	75	100
3.	Italy	56	90
4.	Japan	55	93
5.	France	55	80
6.	Singapore	47	40
7.	Sweden	44	58
8.	Hong Kong	40	40
9.	Australia	37	33
10.	United States	18	—

World's Fifty Biggest
Industrial Corporations

Rank	Company	Headquarters	Sales (in billions of dollars)
1	General Motors	Detroit	$102.8
2	Exxon	New York	69.8
3	Royal Dutch/Shell Group	The Hague/London	64.8
4	Ford Motor	Dearborn, Mich.	62.7
5	International Business Machines	Armonk, N.Y.	51.2
6	Mobil	New York	44.8
7	British Petroleum	London	39.8
8	General Electric	Fairfield, Conn.	35.2
9	American Tel. & Tel.	New York	34.1
10	Texaco	White Plains, N.Y.	31.6
11	IRI	Rome	31.5
12	Toyota Motor	Toyota City (Japan)	31.5
13	Daimler-Benz	Stuttgart	30.1
14	E. I. du Pont de Nemours	Wilmington, Del.	27.1
15	Matsushita Electric Industrial	Osaka	26.4
16	Unilever	Rotterdam/London	25.1
17	Chevron	San Francisco	24.3
18	Volkswagen	Wolfsburg (W. Germany)	24.3
19	Hitachi	Tokyo	22.6
20	ENI	Rome	22.5
21	Chrysler	Highland Park, Mich.	22.5
22	Philips Gloeilampenfabrieken	Eindhoven (Netherlands)	22.4
23	Nestlē	Vevey (Switzerland)	21.1
24	Philip Morris	New York	20.6
25	Siemens	Munich	20.3
26	Nissan Motor	Yokohama	20.1
27	Fiat	Turin	19.6
28	Bayer	Leverkusen (W. Germany)	18.7

World's Fifty Biggest Industrial Corporations (Continued)

Rank	Company	Headquarters	Sales (in billions of dollars)
29	BASF	Ludwigshafen (W. Germany)	$ 18.6
30	Amoco	Chicago	18.2
31	Renault	Paris	17.6
32	Hoechst	Frankfurt	17.5
33	Elf Aquitaine	Paris	17.2
34	RJR Nabisco	Atlanta	16.9
35	Samsung	Seoul	16.5
36	Boeing	Seattle	16.3
37	Mitsubishi Heavy Industries	Tokyo	15.9
38	United Technologies	Hartford, Conn.	15.6
39	Procter & Gamble	Cincinnati, Ohio	15.4
40	Occidental Petroleum	Los Angeles	15.3
41	Peugeot	Paris	15.1
42	Toshiba	Tokyo	15.0
43	Imperial Chemical Industries	London	14.8
44	Petrobrás (Petróleo Brasileiro)	Rio de Janeiro	14.7
45	Atlantic Richfield	Los Angeles	14.5
46	Tenneco	Houston	14.5
47	USX	Pittsburgh	14.0
48	Kuwait Petroleum	Safat (Kuwait)	13.9
49	Total Cie Française des Pétroles	Paris	13.8
50	Thyssen	Duisberg (W. Germany)	13.8

Largest Steel Making Countries

	1985 Production (metric tons, million)
Soviet Union	154
Japan	105
United States	79
China	46
West Germany	40
Italy	24
Brazil	20
France	19
Poland	16
Britain	16
Czechoslovakia	15
South Korea	13

World Robot Population

Japan	14,500
United States	6,600
France	2,750
Britain	2,620
Italy	2,585
Sweden	2,400

Fifty Largest Banks
Outside the United States
(Twenty-one are Japanese)

1986	1985		Country	$ Thousands	Assets Percent change in U.S. dollars	Percent change in local currency	Employees
1	1	Dai-Ichi Kangyo Bank	Japan	251,533,301	51.84	8.25	20,024
2	2	Fuji Bank	Japan	219,924,600	50.88	7.57	15,403
3	3	Sumitomo Bank	Japan	214,399,190	52.58	8.78	13,989
4	4	Mitsubishi Bank	Japan	209,304,645	54.85	10.40	14,680
5	5	Sanwa Bank	Japan	200,339,313	54.65	10.25	15,341
6	10	Industrial Bank of Japan	Japan	167,147,204	69.65	20.95	5,447
7	7	Caisse Nationale de Crédit Agricole	France	156,295,970	26.28	7.27	73,228
8	6	Banque Nationale de Paris	France	143,606,020	15.85	(1.60)	58,625
9	14	Tokai Bank	Japan	142,485,151	51.53	8.03	13,296
10	15	Mitsui Bank	Japan	140,147,716	52.33	8.60	10,787
11	17	Norinchukin Bank	Japan	139,375,130	61.39	14.19	3,147
12	12	Deutsche Bank	W. Germany	133,726,588	37.94	8.43	50,590
13	8	Crédit Lyonnais	France	133,691,709	19.10	1.17	54,557
14	19	Mitsubishi Trust & Banking	Japan	132,478,581	59.19	13.49	6,229
15	16	Long-Term Credit Bank of Japan	Japan	125,773,294	44.22	2.82	3,357
16	20	Sumitomo Trust & Banking	Japan	124,548,591	51.98	8.35	5,998
17	9	National Westminster Bank	Britain	123,529,312	17.97	14.98	94,000
18	22	Taiyo Kobe Bank	Japan	120,949,666	54.44	10.11	14,130
19	11	Société Générale	France	117,431,577	19.43	1.45	43,655
20	13	Barclays Bank	Britain	117,046,340	24.25	21.11	110,000
21	21	Bank of Tokyo	Japan	115,879,206	41.46	0.09	13,569
22	25	Mitsui Trust & Banking	Japan	115,491,681	58.01	12.65	5,859
23	28	Daiwa Bank	Japan	105,450,398	52.39	8.64	9,478
24	30	Yasuda Trust & Banking	Japan	103,851,655	60.31	14.29	5,108
25	23	Dresdner Bank	W. Germany	102,323,666	32.72	4.32	36,769
26	24	Cie Financière de Paris et des Pays-Bas	France	94,380,586	28.55	9.19	28,000

Fifty Largest Banks Outside the United States *(Continued)*

1986	1985		Country	$ Thousands	Assets Percent change in U.S. dollars	Percent change in local currency	Employees
27	29	Union Bank of Switzerland	Switzerland	94,279,726	39.27	9.12	19,990
28	27	Hongkong and Shanghai Bank	Hong Kong	91,803,119	31.37	31.10	49,669
29	31	Swiss Bank Corp.	Switzerland	85,395,161	37.50	7.73	15,775
30	43	Toyo Trust & Banking	Japan	83,123,511	68.51	20.14	4,944
31	40	Nippon Credit Bank	Japan	81,547,800	56.13	11.31	2,173
32	18	Midland Bank	Britain	78,823,042	(6.07)	(8.45)	67,534
33	35	Westdeutsche Landesbank Girozentrale	W. Germany	77,056,715	32.69	4.30	7,291
34	37	Commerzbank	W. Germany	77,021,164	37.34	7.96	25,653
35	34	Banca Nazionale del Lavoro	Italy	75,881,461	28.01	2.76	26,154
36	42	Kyowa Bank	Japan	74,652,653	50.62	7.38	9,431
37	39	Bayerische Vereinsbank	W. Germany	72,825,512	34.60	5.80	13,475
38	26	Royal Bank of Canada	Canada	71,633,632	1.97	3.74	38,186
39	32	Lloyds Bank	Britain	70,906,492	12.01	9.18	71,297
40	41	Algemene Bank Nederland	Netherlands	67,508,861	30.63	3.05	29,043
41	36	Banco do Brasil	Brazil	67,192,574	19.68	(99.83)	118,281
42	45	Rabobank	Netherlands	64,298,594	34.41	6.03	31,967
43	51	Crédit Suisse	Switzerland	64,275,957	49.34	17.01	14,060
44	44	Amsterdam-Rotterdam Bank	Netherlands	64,007,825	31.69	3.89	23,489
45	49	Saitama Bank	Japan	62,941,283	41.94	1.19	8,520
46	33	Bank of Montreal	Canada	62,696,524	3.97	5.78	32,988
47	47	Bayerische Hypotheken- und Wechsel-Bank	W. Germany	62,576,409	35.94	6.86	12,490
48	52	Istituto Bancario San Paolo di Torino	Italy	60,085,138	41.55	13.63	17,845
49	50	Bayerische Landesbank Girozentrale	W. Germany	60,029,332	35.67	6.65	4,196
50	53	Deutsche Genossenschaftsbank	W. Germany	58,201,736	37.28	7.91	4,859

Source: Fortune, August 3, 1987. Copyright © 1987 by Time, Inc. All rights reserved.

World's Ten Largest Coal Producers

		Production in Tons (million)
1.	National Coal Board (Britain)	104
2.	Ruhrkohle (West Germany)	58
3.	Peabody Coal (United States)	56
4.	Broken Hill Proprietary (Australia)	45
5.	Consolidation Coal (United States)	38
6.	Amcoal (South Africa)	38
7.	Sasol (South Africa)	35
8.	Amax Coal (United States)	34
9.	Royal Dutch Shell (Anglo-Dutch)	33
10.	Trans-Natal (South Africa)	28

Who Builds the World's Ships?

	Percentage Share of World Market
Japan	55
South Korea	20
Western Europe	12
China	3
Rest of World	10

The Hundred Largest
Industrial Corporations
Outside the United States

Rank				Sales		
				($		
1986	*1985*	*Company*	*Country*	*Thousands)*	*Employees*	*Rank*
1	1	Royal Dutch/ Shell Group	Neth./Britain	64,843,217	138,000	26
2	2	British Petroleum	Britain	39,855,564	126,700	34
3	5	IRI	Italy	31,561,709	471,366	2
4	3	Toyota Motor	Japan	31,553,827	82,620	52
5	16	Daimler-Benz	W. Germany	30,168,550	319,965	5
6	7	Matsushita Electric Industrial	Japan	26,459,539	135,881	28
7	6	Unilever	Neth./Britain	25,141,672	302,000	6
8	15	Volkswagen	W. Germany	24,317,154	281,718	7
9	8	Hitachi	Japan	22,668,085	164,117	16
10	4	ENI	Italy	22,549,921	129,903	32
11	13	Philips Gloeilampen- fabrieken	Netherlands	22,471,263	344,200	4
12	17	Nestlē	Switzerland	21,153,285	162,078	18
13	14	Siemens	W. Germany	20,307,037	363,000	3
14	12	Nissan Motor	Japan	20,141,237	106,282	40
15	22	Fiat	Italy	19,669,581	230,293	8
16	19	Bayer	W. Germany	18,768,914	170,000	13
17	20	BASF	W. Germany	18,640,985	131,468	31
18	30	Renault	France	17,661,021	182,448	11
19	21	Hoechst	W. Germany	17,509,344	181,176	12
20	10	Elf Aquitaine	France	17,287,058	71,350	63
21	23	Samsung	South Korea	16,522,664	147,154	23
22	24	Mitsubishi Heavy Industries	Japan	15,932,973	88,600	47

The Hundred Largest Industrial Corporations Outside the U.S. *(Continued)*

Rank				Sales ($		
1986	1985	Company	Country	Thousands)	Employees	Rank
23	38	Peugeot	France	15,152,869	165,042	14
24	31	Toshiba	Japan	15,036,390	120,000	36
25	27	Imperial Chemical Industries	Britain	14,867,911	121,800	35
26	18	Petrobrás (Petróleo Brasileiro)	Brazil	14,701,534	64,319	76
27	28	Kuwait Petroleum	Kuwait	13,911,716	15,402	289
28	11	Total Cie Française des Pétroles	France	13,821,041	40,253	119
29	37	Thyssen	W. Germany	13,818,174	127,683	33
30	32	Nippon Oil	Japan	13,690,884	10,599	368
31	26	General Motors of Canada	Canada	13,335,100	45,994	100
32	36	B.A.T Industries	Britain	13,210,379	162,580	17
33	33	Nippon Steel	Japan	13,034,715	70,492	65
34	41	Honda Motor	Japan	12,481,447	53,730	87
35	42	Volvo	Sweden	11,795,263	73,147	60
36	48	CGE (Cie Générale d'Électricité)	France	11,681,337	149,010	20
37	43	Lucky Goldstar	S. Korea	11,433,748	64,750	74
38	54	Saint-Gobain	France	11,222,417	147,579	22
39	49	Daewoo	S. Korea	11,204,191	91,944	46
40	9	Pemex (Petróleos Mexicanos)	Mexico	11,032,902	155,907	19
41	40	Canadian Pacific	Canada	10,807,709	93,800	44
42	47	NEC	Japan	10,562,396	95,796	43
43	45	Ford Motor of Canada	Canada	10,308,776	27,512	172

The Hundred Largest Industrial Corporations Outside the U.S. *(Continued)*

Rank 1986	1985	Company	Country	Sales ($ Thousands)	Employees	Rank
44	46	Idemitsu Kosan	Japan	10,255,663	5,858	443
45	58	Robert Bosch	W. Germany	10,003,662	148,888	21
46	62	Mazda Motor	Japan	9,678,888	30,603	155
47	53	Ruhrkohle	W. Germany	9,637,210	132,570	29
48	52	Mitsubishi Electric	Japan	9,401,584	71,479	62
49	34	Petróleos de Venezuela	Venezuela	9,249,726	44,674	105
50	61	Thomson	France	9,045,864	105,000	41
51	55	Ciba-Geigy	Switzerland	8,869,925	82,231	54
52	56	Montedison	Italy	8,604,813	66,649	72
53	51	Indian Oil	India	8,076,784	31,998	148
54	74	Mannesmann	W. Germany	7,938,097	108,556	39
55	44	Petrofina	Belgium	7,847,250	22,200	220
56	83	Brown Boveri	Switzerland	7,686,342	97,500	42
57	100	Ford-Werke	W. Germany	7,683,589	46,311	98
58	68	Fujitsu	Japan	7,654,080	84,277	51
59	72	Rhône-Poulenc	France	7,608,344	84,600	50
60	108	Electrolux	Sweden	7,446,908	141,753	25
61	80	Sony	Japan	7,432,628	48,671	95
62	193	British Coal	Britain	7,352,956	199,600	10
63	101	Norsk Hydro	Norway	7,331,609	43,122	108
64	71	Fried. Krupp	W. Germany	7,299,059	68,043	68
65	64	General Electric	Britain	7,233,160	164,536	15
66	57	DSM	Netherlands	7,231,699	27,315	177
67	97	BMW (Bayerische Motoren Werke)	W. Germany	7,166,269	50,719	89
68	29	VÖEST-Alpine	Austria	7,079,471	65,100	73
69	110	Dalgety	Britain	7,072,281	20,098	234
70	73	Sanyo Electric	Japan	6,916,814	25,599	193
71	96	Adam Opel	W. Germany	6,834,236	55,438	86
72	76	Grand Metropolitan	Britain	6,757,909	131,493	30

The Hundred Largest Industrial Corporations Outside the U.S. *(Continued)*

Rank				Sales ($ Thousands)	Employees	Rank
1986	1985	Company	Country			
73	91	Michelin	France	6,689,030	119,300	37
74	78	Statoil	Norway	6,647,776	8,471	393
75	107	ASEA	Sweden	6,456,746	63,124	78
76	90	Ford Motor	Britain	6,415,967	49,000	93
77	86	Akzo Group	Netherlands	6,375,425	68,400	67
78	109	Isuzu Motors	Japan	6,325,777	25,608	191
79	60	Showa Shell Sekiyu	Japan	6,168,625	2,832	487
80	87	Sacilor	France	6,154,075	55,573	85
81	70	Nippon Kokan	Japan	6,086,493	38,106	124
82	67	Sunkyong	S. Korea	6,005,876	19,540	238
83	79	Barlow Rand	S. Africa	5,944,771	143,959	24
84	84	Broken Hill Proprietary	Australia	5,937,725	61,000	80
85	95	BTR	Britain	5,895,531	79,400	55
86	128	Nippondenso	Japan	5,879,785	42,967	109
87	81	Alcan Aluminium	Canada	5,756,000	64,500	75
88	65	Veba Oel	W. Germany	5,711,567	16,782	273
89	98	Kawasaki Steel	Japan	5,585,393	33,212	136
90	88	Kobe Steel	Japan	5,583,004	31,486	150
91	111	IBM Deutschland	W. Germany	5,537,978	28,546	165
92	89	Sumitomo Metal Industries	Japan	5,459,793	33,670	133
93	106	Sharp	Japan	5,370,672	28,873	161
94	154	Hanson Trust	Britain	5,339,905	92,000	45
95	93	Mitsubishi Chemical Industries	Japan	5,306,188	18,400	252
96	92	Chrysler Canada	Canada	5,295,095	12,093	346
97	118	IBM France	France	5,288,329	22,225	218
98	125	Canon	Japan	5,277,304	35,498	128
99	66	Esso (Germany)	W. Germany	5,233,831	3,231	484
100	130	IBM Japan	Japan	5,213,933	18,822	245

What a $1,000 Investment
Made in Each of These Companies on
January 1, 1981
Was Worth on January 1, 1987

	1987		
Akzo	$10,016	Honda	4,071
Anglo-American	1,779	Hongkong and Shanghai Bank	1,768
BASF	3,279	Imperial Chemical	3,018
B.A.T	5,702	Jardine, Matheson	1,729
Bayer	4,053	Jefferson Smurfit	3,309
Beecham	2,533	Kikkoman	3,320
Bic	3,947	Kyocera	1,937
Booker	4,840	Lonrho	2,760
Bridgestone	2,734	Marks & Spencer	2,888
British Petroleum	2,080	Matsushita	2,498
Broken Hill	2,046	Michelin	4,049
BSN	4,234	Mitsubishi	2,516
Cadbury Schweppes	2,637	Moët-Hennessy	5,583
Canadian Pacific	920	NEC	4,837
Casio	2,011	News Corporation	13,821
Ciba-Geigy	4,531	Nippon Steel	2,479
Club Méditerranée	4,058	Nissan	1,926
Crédit Suisse	1,694	Nobel Industries	4,056
Dai-Ichi Kangyo	5,638	Nomura	9,223
Daimler-Benz	8,106	Norsk Data	11,476
Electrolux	6,268	Olivetti	3,512
Fiat	14,283	Pearson	4,768
Fujitsu	2,749	Pernod Ricard	5,538
Générale Occidentale	3,097	Perrier	3,254
Grand Metropolitan	3,476	Petrofina	2,786
Guinness	3,230	Peugeot	7,667
Hanson Trust	6,107	Philips	4,145
Hattori Seiko	2,482	RTZ	2,097
Heineken	6,869	Schlumberger	408
Hitachi	5,240	Shell	1,286
Hoechst	3,507	Siemens	4,150
F. Hoffmann–La Roche	3,047	Société Générale de Belgique	3,338

What a $1,000 Investment Made *(Continued)*

Sony	2,385	Toyota	3,906
Swedish Match	3,875	Trusthouse Forte	2,718
Thomson	3,651	Unilever	3,937
Thyssen	2,969	Volkswagen	3,716
Toshiba	4,510	Yamaha	3,060

What a $1,000 Investment in These Companies (made on the date shown) Would Have Been Worth on January 1, 1987

Benetton (August 1986)	$820
Britoil (May 1983)	1,801
Nestlé (March 1985)	3,763
Reuters (August 1984)	3,717
Saatchi & Saatchi (June 1982)	3,923
Singapore Airlines (January 1986)	1,681
Universal Matchbox (March 1986)	850
Volvo (September 1983)	2,849

Note: Results include currency adjustments; i.e., if a currency appreciated against the dollar, that gain is reflected along with the change in market price. Dividend payments are excluded.
Source: BARRA, Berkeley, Calif.

Bibliography

Altshuler, Alan, Martin Anderson, Daniel Jones, Daniel Roos, and James Womack. *The Future of the Automobile.* Cambridge, Mass.: MIT Press, 1984.

Anderson, Jervis. *Guns in American Life.* New York: Random House, 1984.

Auletta, Ken. *The Art of Corporate Success.* New York: Putnam, 1984.

Barnet, Richard J., and Ronald E. Muller. *Global Reach: The Power of the Multinational Corporations.* New York: Simon & Schuster, 1974.

Borkin, Joseph. *The Crime and Punishment of I. G. Farben.* New York: Free Press, 1978.

Christopher, Robert C. *The Japanese Mind: The Goliath Explained.* New York: Linden Press/Simon & Schuster, 1983.

Churchill, Allen. *The Invisible Ivar Kreuger.* New York: Rinehart, 1957.

Chutkow, Paul. *Perrier.* Greenwich, Conn.: Great Waters of France, 1984.

Clavell, James. *Noble House.* New York: Delacorte, 1981.

Coates, Austin. *China Races.* Hong Kong: Oxford University Press, 1983.

Cochran, Sherman. *Big Business in China: Sino-Foreign Rivalry in the Cigarette Industry, 1890–1930.* Cambridge, Mass.: Harvard University Press, 1980.

Cooper, Gary M. "Would You Like to Comment on That, Sir?" Tokyo: *Japan Economic Journal,* 1976.

Crain, Keith E., Robert M. Lienert, and Albert E. Fleming. "Automotive News Centennial Celebration of the Car." Detroit, Mich.: Crain Communications, 1985.

Erni, Paul. *The Basel Marriage: History of the Ciba-Geigy Merger.* Zurich: Neue Zurcher Zeitung, 1979.

Evlanoff, Michael, and Marjorie Fluor. *Alfred Nobel: The Loneliest Millionaire.* Los Angeles: Ward Ritichie Press, 1969.

Fieldhouse, D. K. *Unilever Overseas: The Anatomy of a Multinational.* London: Croom Helm, 1978; Stanford, Calif.: Hoover Institution Press, 1979.

Fields, George. *From Bonsai to Levi's.* New York: Macmillan, 1983.

Forte, Charles. *The Autobiography of Charles Forte.* London: Sidgwick & Jackson, 1986.

Fruin, Mark W. *Kikkoman: Company, Clan, and Community.* Cambridge, Mass.: Harvard University Press, 1983.

Gibney, Frank. *Miracle by Design: The Real Reasons Behind Japan's Economic Success.* New York: Times Books, 1982.

Goldenberg, Susan. *Trading: Inside the World's Leading Stock Exchanges.* San Diego: Harcourt Brace Jovanovich, 1986.

———. *The Thomson Story.* New York: Beaufort Books, 1984.

Halasz, Nicholas. *Nobel.* New York: Orion Press, 1959.

Halberstam, David. *The Reckoning.* New York: Morrow, 1986.

Heer, Jean. *World Events 1866–1966: The First Hundred Years of Nestlé.* Vevey: Nestlé, 1966.

Heller, Robert. *The Naked Market: Marketing Methods for the 80's.* London: Sidgwick & Jackson, 1985.

Heradstveit, Per Oyvind. *Norsk Data—A Success Story.* Oslo: J. M. Stenersens Forlag, 1985.

Higham, Charles. *Trading with the Enemy: An Expose of the Nazi-American Money Plot 1933–1949.* New York: Delacorte, 1983.

Hildebrand, Karl Gustaf. *The Swedish Match Company, 1917–1939,* vol. 5, "Expansion, Crisis, Reconstruction." Liber Tryck, 1985.

Ives, Jane H. *The Export of Hazard.* Boston: Routledge & Kegan Paul, 1985.

Johnson, Chalmers. *MITI and the Japanese Miracle: The Growth of Industrial Policy, 1925–1975.* Stanford, Calif.: Stanford University Press, 1982.

Jones, Sir Roderick. *A Life in Reuters.* London: Hodder & Stoughton, 1952.

Kamata, Satoshi. *Japan in the Passing Lane: An Insider's Account of Life in a Japanese Auto Factory.* New York: Pantheon, 1982.

Kamiya, Shotaro. *My Life with Toyota.* Toyota City: Toyota Motor Sales, 1976.

Keenan, John L. *A Steel Man in India.* New York: Duell, Sloan & Pearce, 1943.

Keswick, Maggie. *The Thistle and the Jade.* London: Octopus, 1982.

Kimes, Beverly Rae. *The Star and the Laurel: The Centennial History of Daimler, Mercedes and Benz.* Montvale, N.J.: Mercedes-Benz of North America, 1986.

Kindleberger, Charles P. *Multinational Excursions.* Cambridge, Mass.: MIT Press, 1984.

Kunio, Yoshihara. *Sogo Shosha: The Vanguard of the Japanese Economy.* Tokyo: Oxford University Press, 1982.

Kwitny, Jonathan. *Endless Enemies.* New York: Congdon & Weed, 1984.

Lala, R. M. *The Creation of Wealth: The Tata Story.* Bombay: IBH Publishing, 1981.

Landes, Davis S. *Revolution In Time.* Cambridge, Mass.: Harvard University Press, 1983.

Longhurst, Henry. *Adventure in Oil: The Story of British Petroleum.* London: Sidgwick & Jackson, 1959.

Madsen, Axel. *Private Power.* New York: Morrow, 1980.

Manchester, William. *The Arms of Krupp.* Boston: Little, Brown, 1964.

Matsushita, Konosuke. *Not for Bread Alone.* Kyoto: PHP Institute, 1984.

Mead, Walter Russell. *Mortal Splendor.* Boston: Houghton-Mifflin, 1987.

Meier, Gerald M. *Emerging from Poverty: The Economics That Really Matters.* New York: Oxford University Press, 1984.

Morita, Akio. *Made in Japan: Akio Morita and Sony.* New York: E. P. Dutton, 1986.

Nelson, Walter Henry. *Small Wonder: The Amazing Story of the Volkswagen.* Boston: Little, Brown, 1985.

Newman, Peter C. *Company of Adventurers: The Story of the Hudson Bay Company.* New York: Viking, 1985.

Nobel Foundation. *Nobel: The Man and His Prizes.* Amsterdam: Elsevier Publishing, 1962.

Ohmae, Kenichi. *The Mind of the Strategist: The Art of Japanese Business.* New York: McGraw-Hill, 1982.

Olins, Wally. *The Corporate Personality: An Inquiry Into the Nature of Corporate Identity.* New York: Mayflower Books, 1978.

Pascale, Richard Tanner, and Anthony G. Athos. *The Art of Japanese Management.* New York: Simon & Schuster, 1981.

Rae, John B. *Nissan Datsun: A History of Nissan Motor Corporation in U.S.A., 1960–1980.* New York: McGraw-Hill, 1982.

Reader, W. J. *Fifty Years of Unilever.* London: Heinemann, 1980.

Riding, Alan. *Distant Neighbors.* New York: Knopf, 1985.

Sampson, Anthony. *The Seven Sisters.* New York: Viking, 1975.

———. *Empires of the Sky.* New York: Random House, 1984.

———. *Black and Gold.* London: Hodder & Stoughton, 1987.

Sanders, Sol. *Honda: The Man and His Machines.* Boston: Little, Brown, 1975.

Servan-Schreiber, J. J. *The American Challenge.* New York: Atheneum, 1969.

Sethi, Prakash S., Hamid Etemad, and K.A.N. Luther. "The Many Faces of the Infant Formula Controversy." New York: Baruch College (Center for the Study of Business and Government), 1985.

Sethi, Prakash S., Nobuaki Namiki, and Carl L. Swanson. *The False Promise of the Japanese Miracle.* Boston: Pitman, 1984.

Shaplen, Robert. *Kreuger: Genius and Swindler.* New York: Knopf, 1960.

Sibley, Brian. *The Book of Guinness Advertising.* London: Guinness Books, 1985.

Sieff, Marcus. *Don't Ask the Price: The Memoirs of the President of Marks & Spencer.* London: Weidenfeld & Nicholson, 1986.

Siemens, Werner von. *Inventor and Entrepreneur: Recollections of Werner von Siemens.* London: Lund Humphries; Munich: Prestal-Verlag, 1966.

Société Générale. *Société Générale de Belgique 1822–1972.* Brussels: Société Générale, 1972.

Stopford, John M., and Louis Turner. *Britain and the Multinationals.* Chichester: John Wiley, 1985.

Tugendhat, Christopher. *The Multinationals.* New York: Random House, 1972.

Turner, E. S. *The Shocking History of Advertising.* New York: Ballantine Books, 1953.

Turner, Henry Ashby, Jr. *German Big Business and the Rise of Hitler.* New York: Oxford University Press, 1985.

Turner, Louis. *Multinational Companies and the World.* New York: Hill & Wang, 1973.

Votaw, Dow. *The Six-Legged Dog: Mattei and Eni—A Study in Power.* Berkeley, Calif.: University of California Press, 1964.

Weiher, Sigfrid von, and Herbert Goetzeler. *The Siemens Company: Its Historical Role in the Progress of Electrical Engineering.* Berlin and Munich: Siemens, 1977.

Wheatcroft, Geoffrey. *The Randlords.* New York: Atheneum, 1986.

Wolf, Marvin J. *The Japanese Conspiracy.* New York: Empire Books, 1983.

Yates, Brock. *The Decline and Fall of the American Automobile Industry.* New York: Vintage Books, 1983.

Index

695